Off The Wall: Death In Yosemite

Books by Michael P. Ghiglieri

The Chimpanzees of Kibale Forest

East of the Mountains of the Moon: Chimpanzee Society in the African Rainforest

Canyon

The Dark Side of Man: Tracing the Origin of Male Violence

Over the Edge: Death in Grand Canyon (with coauthor Thomas M. Myers)

First through Grand Canyon: The Secret Journals and Letters of the 1869 Crew Who Explored the Green and Colorado Rivers

Off the Wall: Death in Yosemite (with coauthor Charles R. "Butch" Farabee, Jr.)

Into the Unknown: High Adventure and Hard Lessons during the Golden Age of Exploring the World's Great, Lost Wilderness Rivers

Through the Great Unknown (fiction, forthcoming)

Books by Charles R. "Butch" Farabee, Jr.

Death, Daring, and Disaster: Search and Rescue in the National Parks

National Park Ranger: An American Icon

Off the Wall: Death in Yosemite (with coauthor Michael P. Ghiglieri)

Big Walls, Swift Waters: Epic Stories from Yosemite Search and Rescue

Diving in the National Park Service: An Administrative History (with coauthor Daniel J. Lenihan)

Southern Arizona Search & Rescue and First Responder History, 1901-2000

Off The Wall: Death In Yosemite

Michael P. Ghiglieri

and

Charles R. "Butch" Farabee, Jr.

Off The Wall: Death In Yosemite

Gripping accounts of all known fatal mishaps in America's first protected land of scenic wonders

Michael P. Ghiglieri

and

Charles R. "Butch" Farabee, Jr.

PUMA PRESS
Flagstaff

The paper in this book meets the guidelines for permanence and durability of the Committee on Production Guidelines for Book Longevity of the Council on Library Resources.

FIRST EDITION, Ninth Printing, Eighth revision, April 2026, (4,000 copies)

Printing history: 52,917 copies

ISBN-13: 978-0-9700973-7-8 (Hardcover)
ISBN-10: 0-9700973-7-9
ISBN-13: 978-0-9847858-8-9 (Trade Paperback)
LCCN: 2006940914

Maps by Jack and Gay Reineck
Book jacket and cover design by Bronze Black
Cover concept by Michael P. Ghiglieri and Thomas M. Myers
Front cover photographs by Daniel K. Horner and (inset of Carl Bantel [a.k.a. Otto Miller]) by Ralph Anderson (1935), Yosemite National Park Research Library
Rear cover photograph by John Smedden, courtesy of Yosemite NP Search and Rescue photo files
Author photographs by Bill Schumell and an NPS ranger at Lower Merced Pass Lake in 1977
Interior art by Jim Myers
Book production by Mary Williams
Printed on recycled paper
Printed in USA

DEDICATION

For the millions who come to Yosemite National Park in the future, that they each may walk away enriched—and in one piece.

And also in recognition of each member of every search and rescue team—voluntary or paid—and of every companion, guide, and Good Samaritan who has risked his or her life to save those of us who otherwise never would have walked away at all. Your self-sacrifice represents what is noblest in the human spirit.

"It is a good thing to learn caution from the misfortunes of others."
—Pubilius Syrus, 85-43 B.C.

"Those who cannot remember the past are condemned to repeat it."
—Jorge Agustín Nicolás Ruiz de Santayana, 1863-1952 A.D.

For want of a nail, the shoe was lost.
For want of a shoe, the horse was lost.
For want of a horse, the general was lost.
For want of a general, the battle was lost.
For loss of the battle, the war was lost.
—13th century German proverb

TABLE OF CONTENTS

FOREWORD

Our National Parks have been described as the best idea America ever had and also as a gift we gave to ourselves. We are indeed fortunate as a nation that our forebears invested the political capital, personal energy, and funds to establish and protect our National Park System. Our parks are special places for inspiration, education, and recreation. Yosemite represents the pinnacle of opportunity to be inspired, to be challenged, and to be tempted into courting danger. It is a place of family reunions, weddings, organized outdoor adventures, solo recreational challenges, educational seminars, of birth—and also death. The Park itself hosts a community that ranges from the governmental and the commercial guest services to the various constituencies of climbing, horseback riding, hiking, fishing, skiing, photography, and art. All those groups and individuals have a stake in Yosemite. Most of these stakeholders hold great affection for the Park. They know the place and they value it. These groups—along with the millions more who come to see, sense, and enjoy Yosemite for the first time—weave the rich tapestry of human activities upon which *Off the Wall: Death in Yosemite* is fashioned.

Some Yosemite lovers are fortunate enough to live and work there. I was one of them. During my 32-year career with the National Park Service I lived and worked in Yosemite twice; first, as a protection ranger for two years beginning in 1974, then later, from 1989 to 1994, as Park Superintendent. As a result of my working in Yosemite in absolutely different roles, thirteen years apart, I developed a strong appreciation for the value that this scenic wonder represents to its visitors; I also developed a deep and abiding respect for the men and women who on a daily basis risk their lives there in order to save a life or recover a loved one who died.

Reading *Off the Wall: Death in Yosemite* reminded me of the many searches, rescues, and recoveries in which I personally participated. These events, which had been stored in some remote part of my brain, were suddenly brought to light through the presentation in this book. As a protection ranger I had spent many hours in cold, wet, windy, slippery, exposed, and dangerous circumstances, either participating in a rescue or recovering a body. The times when we saved a life created great satisfaction. The other times proved to be a source of great sorrow, especially when the facts or circumstances indicated that the premature death was due to negligence, inattention, or inadequate knowledge or skill. I remember well the sense of loss I felt as a member of the team retrieving the bodies of 22-year-old John Schwab and 21-year-old Ronald Baum from Selaginella (see Chapter 9) near Lower Yosemite Fall. I was in my late twenties then and looking forward to a full and interesting life. I looked at the bodies tangled in ropes then could not help but reflect on who these two young men had once been. What had *their* aspirations been? As a rescuer, you soon learn not to dwell on these events but, even so, you are never removed from the sense of loss they spur. This sense of tragedy is magnified when your duties include notifying the victim's next of kin and when later you meet with their relatives. This was particularly acute in the death of 21-year-old Air Force nurse Jacklyn Donahoe. A pleasant day of scrambling with friends ended due to a careless mistake that resulted in a 70-foot fall to her death (Chapter 6). I was the deputy coroner. I conducted the death investigation and I notified Donahoe's next of kin. I remember her face to this day; peaceful in death, yet now devoid of hopes, dreams, and a future. Again the sense of waste and loss always accompanies the response to death and tragedy in Yosemite. These images, these lessons, and these thoughts were still with me when, in the summer of 1989, I returned to Yosemite as Superintendent.

The pattern of accidents and incidents, many of which are well chronicled in this book by Farabee and Ghiglieri, continued unabated. My role as Superintendent removed me from the excitement and challenges of day to day search and rescue operations, but I remained all too aware of the risks to life and limb to NPS personnel and other rescue partners. These risks are more than physical. Real emotional damage can occur to those participating in these missions. I strove to make certain that the training, equipment, and cooperative agreements were in place to ensure the safest rescues and most professional and expedient care for victims. Moreover, the Park maintained and supported critical incident stress debriefing—psychological counseling for rescue personnel. Unknown in my days as a field ranger, it was now a welcome program addition. No day went by when I did not worry about the health and welfare of the NPS employees. Risks loomed everywhere: from traffic stops, to emergency medical response and the threat of blood borne diseases, to high angle rescue and body recovery.

My years in management demonstrated to me the truth of the dilemma that watching and waiting for the conclusion of a rescue operation is sometimes more difficult than physically participating in the actual event. I remember being informed on May 28, 1993, of the death of British climber Derek Hersey, age 36, during a free-solo climb on Sentinel Rock (Chapter 9). I remember watching from my home in Yosemite Valley as the helicopter maneuvered to recover him. My thoughts now were not of the tragedy of a life taken so young, but rather of the risks to the rangers engaged in the dangerous helicopter recovery of the body. Quite frankly, I resented the risk that free-solo climbing (without ropes or means of arresting a fall) presented to Park staff. I resented placing search and rescue (SAR) personnel at risk to life and limb. Notwithstanding my concern for their safety, I watched with pride and admiration as rangers, medical personnel, volunteers, and military pilots and crews worked together with a sense of purpose despite risk to their own lives. I know the deep dedication and commitment held by our rangers and other SAR personnel to ensure the health and well being of Yosemite's visitors. We are indeed fortunate as a Nation to have such dedicated and professional people.

Thus, to me this book is more about life than death. True enough, it is well researched and it chronicles investigations into the causes and circumstances surrounding death in Yosemite. However, it is much, much more than a simple accounting of tragedy. This book is rich in historical context and develops the setting and background for the deaths that are chronicled. It provides valuable lessons to be learned and lessons to be relearned and reinforced. Through the investigative reports, it puts you into the minds of some of the people involved and even into the minds of the victims. It provides insight into the world of the rangers who live and work in Yosemite. It helps answer the question: Ever wonder what rangers do when they take off their flat hats? Moreover, this book provides insight into the thinking of involved individuals through its oral history references. It shares the challenges, strategies, and personal commitment of the individual rescuers or of the people in charge of the overall incident. The reader will glean from the text, the physical demands, the misery, the pain, the injuries, sometimes even the death of NPS personnel. The authors do not artificially frame the events to highlight the self-sacrifice and heroism of the responders; nevertheless, they provide insight well beyond a mere chronicling of fatal incidents.

Farabee and Ghiglieri have taken the rather small number of deaths in Yosemite (compared to the millions of people who have visited, lived, or worked in the Park) and organized and framed them in a very instructive manner. Each chapter and its accompanying analysis establishes patterns that otherwise would not have been revealed or noted without their analysis. The authors highlight differences in sex, in age, and in activity preceding fatal incidents, yet they also demonstrate that a visit to a national park is still a very safe activity, providing you pay attention. The authors also reveal important patterns of behavior within certain gender and age groups. These patterns, while being somewhat intuitive, are supported by sound investigation and research. In terms of prevention and education, the messages of safety can now be better targeted and can lower the number of fatalities in the future.

I can think of no two better authors for this work than Butch Farabee and Michael Ghiglieri. Their insight into the subject of death is sensitive and non-judgmental. This is because both men possess extensive outdoor adventure experience. Both have made their own mistakes and lived to amend their behavior. Both men have been challenged by adversity and understand the human emotions of fear and anxiety. Both know the dangers inherent in weather, temperature, and altitude. This breadth of experience provides a lens through which the authors frame their presentation with sensitivity and credibility. They have provided a real service in an interesting and compelling piece of work.

—MICHAEL FINLEY, Superintendent of Everglades National Park 1986-1989, Superintendent of Yosemite National Park 1989-1994, Superintendent of Yellowstone National Park 1994-2001; currently President of the Turner Foundation.

ACKNOWLEDGMENTS

The number of people who helped us to make *Off the Wall: Death in Yosemite* a reality is impressive. We are very much indebted to all of them. Mary Atkinson and Barbara Wilson in the Mariposa County Hall of Records repeatedly went out of their way for hours on end to help Farabee pull one after another obscure death certificate. Paul Gallez, one of the Park's outstanding computer specialists, designed the original database from which this book then cataloged Yosemite's deaths. Whenever Farabee could not figure out how to perform some task with the Access Computer Program, Paul always seemed to know the solution.

Trail Crew Supervisor and later Park Historian Jim B. Snyder (retired) went far out of his way to provide us invaluable lessons in the history of Yosemite. Without his in-depth review and perspective and his help with the histories of local Native Americans, of the building of O'Shaughnessy Dam; as well as of several fatal events—including those of Stephen Lyman and Barry Hance—we would have gotten it wrong.

We owe much the same debt to Hank Johnston, regional historian and author of numerous well written books and articles on Yosemite. Hank seemed consistently interested in our goals and our unsolved (temporarily or otherwise) mysteries. He always made himself available to help on this project. If we wanted to know something that happened in the Park before 1900, we went to Hank for assistance. If Hank said it was so, we found, it indeed *was*.

John T. Dill, Search and Rescue Ranger nonpareil and the "Corporate Memory" of Yosemite Search and Rescue, proved crucial to our understanding of how people get into trouble in the Park, particularly while climbing, hiking, or tempting fate around moving water—he also proved helpful to our understanding of how YOSAR (Yosemite Search and Rescue) pulled them out of it. His patience and predilection for meticulously probing an incident for the true and specific causes of why things went wrong have proven a figurative lifesaver for several parts of this book and a literal lifesaver for the thousands of people that John has helped rescue since 1971. We all owe him a great debt of gratitude.

We originally suspected that the institutional knowledge of Yosemite's Chief Law Enforcement Officer Lee Shackelton (retired after several decades of service to the Park) would be extremely important to our getting things right. It turns out that we underestimated his importance. His memory and concern for processes in the past were mind-boggling. He never failed to provide us with in-depth insights (and occasional humor) into the great number of major criminal cases he helped investigate. He also provided us with key background nuances on various laws and legal stumbling blocks and on their impacts on cases. Without him we might never have made it far enough away from shore to enter the deep water.

Special Agent Daniel Horner, a long-time ranger in the Park, made himself available without fail; he reviewed the draft book in its entirety, not once but twice, and he gently corrected our far-too-many errors. His level of interest in getting the facts right in this book matched our own highest standards. All too often he went out of his way to oblige us by digging for obscure and deeply buried (literally) facts on past incidents that no one else seemed to care about any more. And when we made yet new errors with his new information he patiently corrected those as well. If the literary world had saints in it, Daniel Horner would be among them. Dan, thank you too for the beautiful photo of Half Dome that now graces the cover of *Off the Wall.*

Don Coelho, the National Park Service's Chief of Law Enforcement and previously the Law Enforcement Specialist for Yosemite, invested a great deal of time in providing input to us on many of the incidents in which he was involved during his two decades in the Park. His clarifications and facts considerably improved this book.

District Ranger Jim Tucker (retired) was born in Yosemite and has been accused of being a "walking memory bank" about places and events of the Park. He provided to us invaluable input gained from his thirty-five years on the job. Ranger-Investigator Kim Tucker possesses an even better memory that her husband Jim. She too gave us many hours of valuable personal interviews, particularly about the homicides she helped investigate.

Park Librarian Linda Eade seemed always to be there to provide Farabee assistance and access to the Park's research facilities. We used the disk containing the *Superintendent's Monthly Reports* that she provided us so often that it threatened to melt down.

Genealogists Carolyn Feroben and Ellen Croll knew where to go to fill in a multitude of details we could not find in public records and various databases.

Yosemite's Superintendent Mike Tollefson and Chief Ranger Steve Shackelton were always supportive, encouraging, and ready to provide us ideas. Knowing their interest in our producing a high quality product constituted an added incentive to get things right.

Author Rick Schloss, currently writing *Lodestar Lightning*, generously added key information about the airplane loaded with marijuana that went down in "Dope Lake." Speaking of Dope Lake, Tim Setnicka, Superintendent of Channel Islands National Park (retired) and more importantly, the Yosemite Search and Rescue Officer in Yosemite during the 1970s, not only read our manuscript critically but added yet more interesting and pivotal information about this infamous incident. We owe both men a debt of gratitude for helping to make our version of the story so engrossing.

District Ranger Dave Lattimore did yeoman's duty in fact checking and answering the many questions we had for him about the numerous events in which he was personally involved. His help improved things. Thank you, Dave.

Another major dose of our thanks goes to Jack Morehead, not only for his fine legacy in the Park Service, but also for his historical input on this project. In addition to Jack serving as a "buck ranger" in Yosemite in the mid-1950s, he then returned twice, once as the Park's Chief Ranger and then again as the Yosemite National Park Superintendent. Ranger Morehead then went on to serve as the National Park Service's Associate Director, retiring as Regional Director in Alaska. Despite his varied and demanding career, his memory for events in Yosemite many decades ago has proven as sharp as freshly knapped obsidian.

We wrote at least five drafts of this manuscript. All or parts of these were reviewed by Paula Andress, Linda K. Campbell, Chief Ranger Stu Croll, John T. Dill, Park Librarian Linda Eade, Susan Kelly Ash-Ghiglieri, Dr. Roger Hendrickson, Special Agent Daniel Horner, Historian Hank Johnston, Acting Chief of Interpretation Mary Kline, Search and Rescue Manager Keith Lober, Backcountry District Ranger Ron Mackie, Becky Myers, Dr. Thomas M. Myers, Special Agent Mike Osborne, Park Historian Jim Snyder, Special Agent-in-Charge Jeff Sullivan, Dr. Jim Wurgler, and Special Agent Steve Yu. In addition to correcting numerous errors of fact, questioning what we were trying to say where we had become confusing, catching a regiment of typos, and pointing out phrases or words we overused, these helpful "victims" of our early drafts took personal interest in making the manuscript into a better book. We owe many heartfelt thanks to each of them.

In addition to those mentioned above, the following people were gracious with their time, quick with their input or in finding arcane data, and/or helped this project in other ways: Everett Allen, Mariposa County Sheriff Jim Allen, Paul Austin, Chris Becker, Frank Betts, Dr. Bill Bowie, D.W. Burnett, Colin Campbell, Kevin Cann, Jan Cauthorn-Page, Jerry B. Chilton, Bill Coate, Mary Coelho, Gary Colliver, M. Scott Connelly, Paul Cowan, Tim Dallas, Pete Dalton, Dick DeRusha, Mike Durr, Jan Eagle, Joseph R. Evans, Peter Fitzmaurice, Mark Forbes, Mary Liz Gale, Lynn Gamma, Scott Gediman, Cliff Hance Ghiglieri, Fern Patricia Ghiglieri, Jodi Gover, Daniel Graber, David Hagee, John Henneberger, William J. Klingenberg, Nate Knight, Fred Koegler, Christopher Libby, Gary Patrick Macha (www.aircraftwrecks.com) Mark Maciha, Mike Mayer, Peter Mayfield, Glenn McConkey, Ann Means, Steve Medley (sadly deceased before publication), Barry E. Menefee, Wayne Merry, Ralph Mihan, Kerrian Neu, Dorothy O'Brien, Deb Ohlfs, Jeff Ohlfs, Mike Pass, Billie Jean Patrick, Craig Patterson, Cynthia Lee Perry, Nancy Pimentel, Megan Polk, Donnie Priest, Majid Sabet, Cindy Sage, Matthew Scholtz, Gail Sgambellone, Dean Shenk, John Smedden, Rick Smith, Carolyn Sweetwater, Pete Thompson, Steve Thompson, and Jan Van Wagtendonk. We hope we have not forgotten anyone.

Introduction

Why A Book On Death?

Although it may seem paradoxical at first glance, our intent with *Off the Wall: Death in Yosemite* is not to belabor death but to save lives. This book explores the sorts of decision making that has led to tragic outcomes for people in Yosemite National Park. More than 1,070 visitors, concession employees, and government personnel have in one way or another made fatal errors here in a wide variety of circumstances. Knowing exactly what they did wrong and why they decided to do it that way helps prevent history from repeating itself.

The complexity of the Park's terrain—canyons, cliffs, mountains, ravines, rivers, streams, ice, snow, waterfalls, polished granite, dense forests, abrupt shifts in weather—can and do challenge outdoor experts. For the less experienced, Yosemite's outback has, at times, shown no mercy. As pointed out by the editors of the Yosemite Fund's *Approach* magazine, "Walk 50 yards from any parkway curb and you are standing in Yosemite's wilderness—all 704,624 acres of it—92.4 percent of the entire Park." In fact, all too many people *have* trekked beyond those fifty yards and not lived to tell of it. Hence this book.

Blended with accounts of this unfortunate mayhem *Off the Wall* also offers a hefty portion of Park history. It chronicles the exploits of explorers and pioneers from the Gold Rush days and touches upon the lives—and sometimes deaths—of some of the area's first Native Americans. We examine challenges faced by the State of California, the United States Army, and the National Park Service as each managed this very complicated landscape. We review early travel and subsequent advent of roads. And we look at the beginnings of local wildlife management. In a somewhat voyeuristic way, *Off the Wall* highlights some of the amazing triumphs and tragedies that unfolded as mountaineering and rock climbing matured and extreme sports such as BASE jumping pushed the envelope. We also found ourselves in the unfortunate position of needing to chronicle the dark side of man as people killed themselves and each other.

We are convinced the vast majority of those who meet traumatic ends in Yosemite do not die due to an "accident" as defined by *Webster's Dictionary* as an "unforeseeable incident." Instead, someone—either the victim or a buddy or some other responsible party—generally makes a series of decisions that lead to what statisticians refer to as the "rare outcome" *one would expect to happen* given a specific set of circumstances (such as deliberately unroping from a big wall to cope with some annoying chore and then falling "accidentally").

Learning what decisions increase one's odds of being killed while camping, scrambling, hiking, climbing, rafting, skiing, vacationing, fishing, swimming, flying over, or merely driving in Yosemite cannot help but boost the likelihood of living longer for the rest of us.

We are aware, though, that when we look at decisions which contributed to someone's death—or to a harrowing near miss—we also may be treading on the toes of the victim or his companions or family. Therefore we are saying up front: The intent of this book is not to assign *blame*. Our objective instead is to *understand*. Often, however, the quest to pinpoint precisely how and why an incident occurred can be misconstrued by some as an attempt to fix blame. We take this risk and walk this fine line because it is only when we possess the knowledge of why things went wrong that we can combine common sense to this information and help to save lives.

Dr. Thomas M. Myers (a physician at Grand Canyon after more than a dozen years) and this book's coauthor Michael Ghiglieri researched and wrote a similar type of book, *Over the Edge: Death in Grand Canyon*. These days, several years after its publication, some personnel there suggest that the Park's Search and Rescue missions are decreasing in number and severity from pre-publication days. While it is impossible to zero in with precision on all the causes for this improvement, Ghiglieri and Farabee hope to help foster similar results with *Off the Wall*.

As might be imagined, a task of this scope—covering *every* traumatic fatality occurring within the current boundaries of Yosemite—was not easy. No list of deaths within the Park existed to encompass its entire historical era beginning in October of 1849 when William Penn Abrams and U. N. Reamer tracked an elusive grizzly from near Savage's Trading Post on the South Fork of the Merced to Inspiration Point and thus gained the first undisputed view of Yosemite Valley by outsiders.

In late 1999, while nearing retirement, Butch Farabee asked the Park's then Chief Ranger Bob Andrew if he saw significant value in a list of *all* deaths, natural and traumatic, within Yosemite. He jumped at this prospect, convinced that a comprehensive inventory with names, locations, ages, causes, and other relevant details would greatly aid in managing the Park, particularly from a perspective of safety. So as a volunteer, Butch, a former Yosemite Ranger and Deputy Coroner but now working on his own time and money, began compiling the first such list. Paul Gallez, one of the Park's whiz-bang computer specialists, aided this process by graciously designing a program to capture and analyze these data. After two years of research, the idea for *Off the Wall* emerged.

Merely learning of a pre-1950s death—not to mention pinpointing the incident's far more recondite details—proved highly challenging despite improved access to information due to the Freedom of Information Act. How difficult (or occasionally easy) was Farabee's task?

To identify those who died within Yosemite's current boundaries, even if he or she was taken elsewhere and subsequently expired, it was natural to start compiling data from within the Park. Housed in Yosemite National Park's Law Enforcement Office are relatively complete Coroner Files from about 1970 onward. Before that time, relevant records quickly become sketchy. An often parallel but separate set of search and rescue reports also exist, again going back to the early 1970s. A scattered few of these even covered events in the 1960s.

For earlier incidents an excellent resource turned out to be the *Superintendent's Monthly Report* (*MR*). From about 1926 until at least 1963, each park area was required to submit a monthly report to agency superiors. An important element of these *MR*s were serious accidents and deaths. These sections often elaborated upon such events in enough detail to provide clues for seeking additional information elsewhere. In contrast, if deaths were natural, the *MR* might not even mention a name or date ("three people died this month in the hospital"). This vagueness made research harder. For incidents occurring prior to the advent of the *MR*, Farabee perused the *Superintendent's Annual Report* for every year available.

Luckily, other official sources also exist beyond Park files. The Mariposa County Sheriff's Office keeps relatively complete reports for people who died in the County. These date from the mid-1950s. The Mariposa Museum and History Center retains many similar files or related records prior to this. A few extend back into the late 1800s. One stumbling block here is that until June of 1905, the State of California did not mandate Death Certificates. Thus records remain hit and miss up to this point (and even after). Fortunately, the Mariposa County Hall of Records routinely files Death Certificates and maintains a large, alphabetically-listed "Book of Deaths." This is easy to access. Better yet, the clerks are very helpful. Unfortunately, the Book of Deaths also is riddled by gaps in information on the roughly 954 traumatic fatalities and about 750 natural deaths (55 fatal events as of 2014 resulted from causes still unknown) within Yosemite's boundaries. Farabee spent many hours in the Hall of Records trying to identify deaths sketchily alluded to or chanced upon elsewhere. Often he could not find them.

Admittedly, dangers lurk in taking newspaper accounts as total fact. Even so, the only details available for many Yosemite deaths came from the local *Mariposa Gazette*. Because this small paper was published weekly, its stories, especially from the first seventy years of Yosemite history, were often only a sentence or two long or hidden deep among other text. And many were weeks old before being printed. Spellings of names and other details sometimes differed from those in other sources—if luck even provided us a second source.

This research is further complicated because Yosemite National Park includes parts of three counties: Mariposa, Tuolumne, and Madera. Each is responsible for maintaining records for deaths within its borders. This system seems clearcut until one sees how it can go wrong. Regardless of what remote section of the Park—and what county—in which a death took place, the victim and rescuers often would be funneled through Yosemite Valley in Mariposa County. This may be because the Park's hospitals were (or are) there or because the victim would be declared dead there by a physician or ranger deputized as a Deputy Coroner (several rangers are coroners for these counties).

This "switch" of counties might otherwise happen simply because the helicopter or the incident's manpower originated from the Valley. Muddying the picture even more, some victims have been transported directly from the Park's eastern edge to a town farther east in Inyo County or even in Nevada. For example, when Mathilde T. Nutting was severely burned in a plane wreck in Tuolumne Meadows she ended up dying in Reno, Nevada eighteen days later. Reno happened to be the best location for her responding helicopter—dispatched out of Fallon Naval Air Station, not far from Reno. During other incidents, due to the many isolated areas of the Park, victims reported to "outside" agencies (by calling 911) were evacuated to a distant locale without the Park even knowing anything had gone amiss. With the increased use of personal locator beacons and cell and satellite phones, this complication will continue. In yet another example, 76-year-old George Herbert Dekay died in his sleep in early September while camping at remote Royal Arch Lake in the southern part of the Park. The following day a wrangler packed out his corpse on a mule. A coroner in Madera County processed this case. Somehow Dekay's demise remained unknown to Park officials until 2006, when finally revealed only during research for this book. How long had the aged horseman been a non-statistic? He died in 1967!

The northern part of the Park, including Hetch Hetchy and O'Shaughnessy Dam, are in Tuolumne County. Sonora is its county seat. Sonora's *The Union Democrat* generally recounted deaths during construction of the dam, but its coverage often lacked details or, worse, included ones that were incorrect.

Many of these news articles might omit the victim's complete name, age, and maybe even cause of death. Wherever possible we tried to cross-reference these, but inconsistencies and/or a lack of facts often remained. In short, the farther back in time, the murkier the incident.

Further compounding an already tangled information trail is the ever-increasing sophistication of medevacs manned by paramedics and flight nurses. These now often whisk a victim from the Park and proceed directly to a trauma center in Fresno or Modesto and to the best possible care. If the person dies anyway, Park officials might not be told. In much the same way, if a death happens months after the initial accident, it easily can go unnoticed by the Park (and to nearby newspapers and county governments) due to the attending out-of-park medical facility, doctor, or coroner unknowingly overlooking the "formality" of notifying Yosemite.

Despite how patchy and conflicting our many sources were (or are), we did primarily use those from the Park and local counties. And although we often interwove details from several sources, we gave weight to that resource providing the most information or which seemed the most reliable. We also used, and noted in the text, several books by local historians. The bottom line? Our educated guess is that the database supporting *Off the Wall* is roughly 97 percent complete for traumatic fatalities in Yosemite since 1851.

Clearly, we also know gaps in our information exist. Hence, we would like to say to any person out there who can fill one: We welcome your help (via *pumapress1@gmail.com*).

The obstacles identified above illustrate why creating an accurate and relatively complete list took years. Farabee spent many hours in little rooms to find those needles in a haystack and often had no ability to photocopy the key documents uncovered. Often he had to merely scribble down the basic data. Once we decided to write this book, this bare bones set of data posed problems because we lacked the original full reference, as we also did with many of the newspaper articles used. So, despite our original plan to list all of the thousands of references used to compile the hundreds of accounts in this book, we had to face reality. We were missing too many original citations and frankly, we could not face the prospect of retracing the many lengthy steps to recover them. In the end we decided to dispense with the fifty or so pages of this book that would have listed references. Instead, we are offering you the stories themselves.

These stories—and even the skeletal facts on several incidents in this book—also serve one more function: They preserve history, especially *oral* history about events in Yosemite that otherwise might be lost, possibly forever.

We also are aware of an additional danger that exists in our writing *Off the Wall*. This is the possible hubris accompanying our approach. We identify what we believe are some of the reasons why many hundreds of people died as they did. Inherent in our doing this is the assumption we know what we are talking about. We think we do. But we definitely know we are not omniscient. Indeed, we both at times have decided to take risks of the sort that might be characterized as "There but for the grace of God...." We are not perfect. We are simply trying to give you our best interpretations based upon the data available, common sense, oral statements by participants, and our own experience in the field.

As hopefully may be clear by now, to us this book is more about life than death. We remain committed to preventing accidents. Thus we believe our analysis in *Off the Wall: Death in Yosemite* is not just a leap forward in the quest to prevent future fatalities. To us it is far more. We think it would have been dangerous to *not* have written this book—as many search and rescue veterans can attest, there are few new accidents, just new people hurting themselves in the same old ways. Identifying and graphically highlighting the unfamiliar dangers people face in Yosemite cannot help but work to prevent at least some of this repetition. If in our quest to identify exactly where that preventability might reside we step on some emotional toes, we ask that the owners of those toes also embrace this objective and sincerely examine their own values and concerns before taking umbrage.

Preventability is an often underrated consideration. *Most* of the several thousand accidents—far too many of which resulted in serious injury or death—that Farabee investigated during his more than thirty-five years in visitor safety and law enforcement were totally preventable. The needless misery, despair, and waste from these mishaps were caused by negligence, haste, inattention, imprudence, bravado, and/or just plain ignorance. In writing *Off the Wall,* we hope to educate the reader and, in our own little way, help reduce the future loss and pain these tragedies always generate.

Having now explained our goals to give you as best we could, it's time to see how some of these episodes in Yosemite indeed have been truly… off the wall.

WARNING! Some incidents in this book contain graphic descriptions of traumatic fatal events.

Photo by Daniel K. Horner

Yosemite National Park (north)

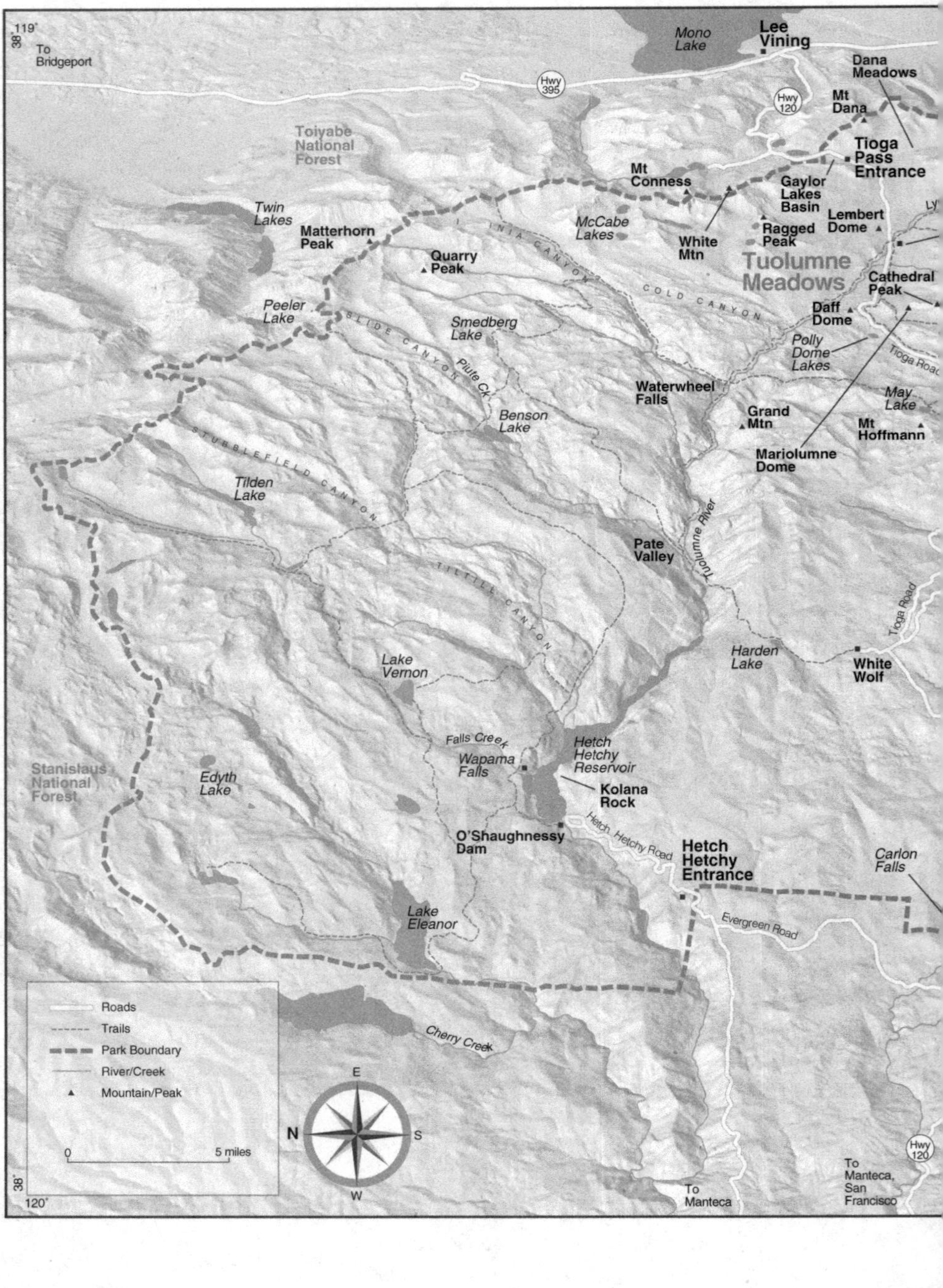

Yosemite National Park (south)

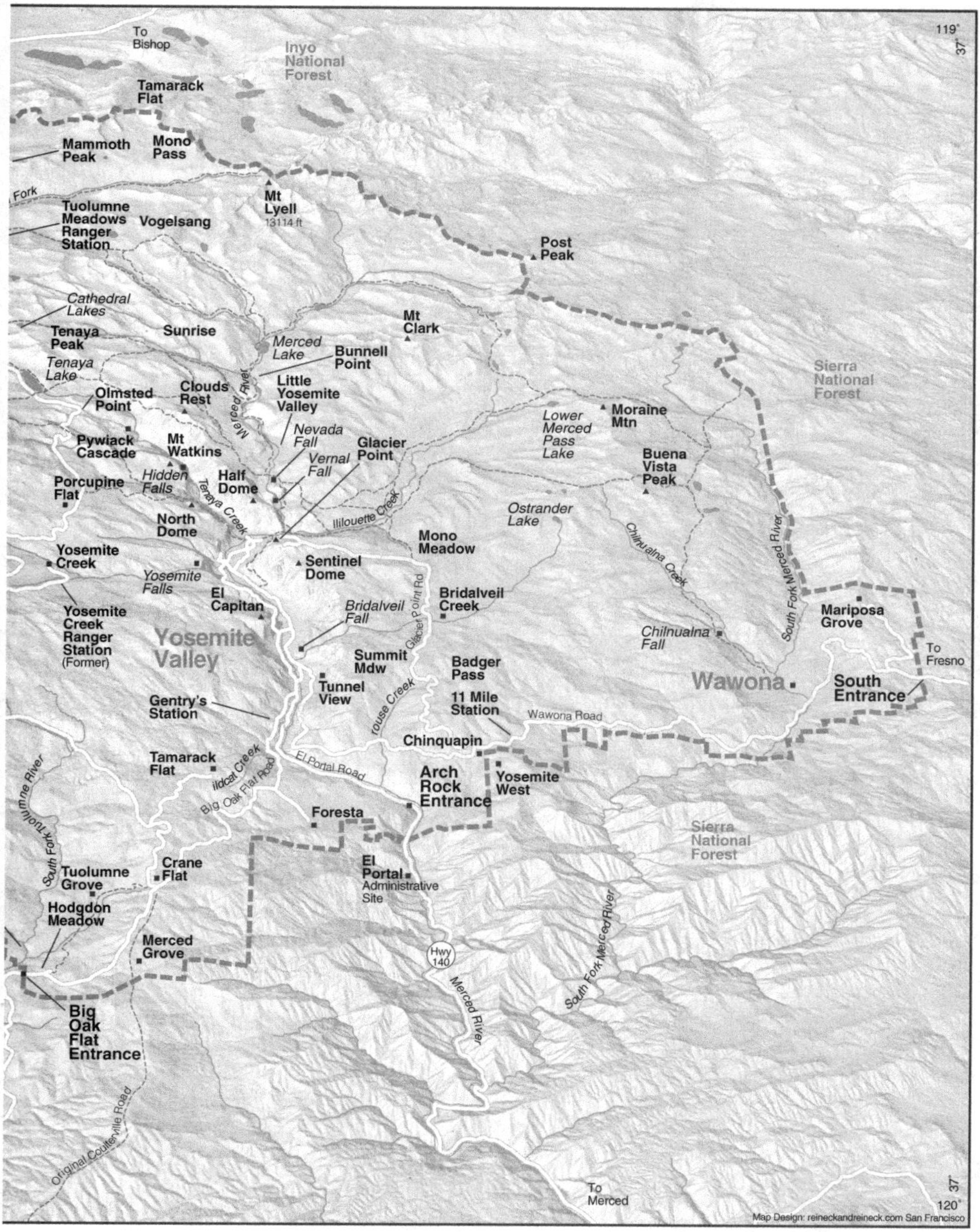

Area west of Yosemite Valley

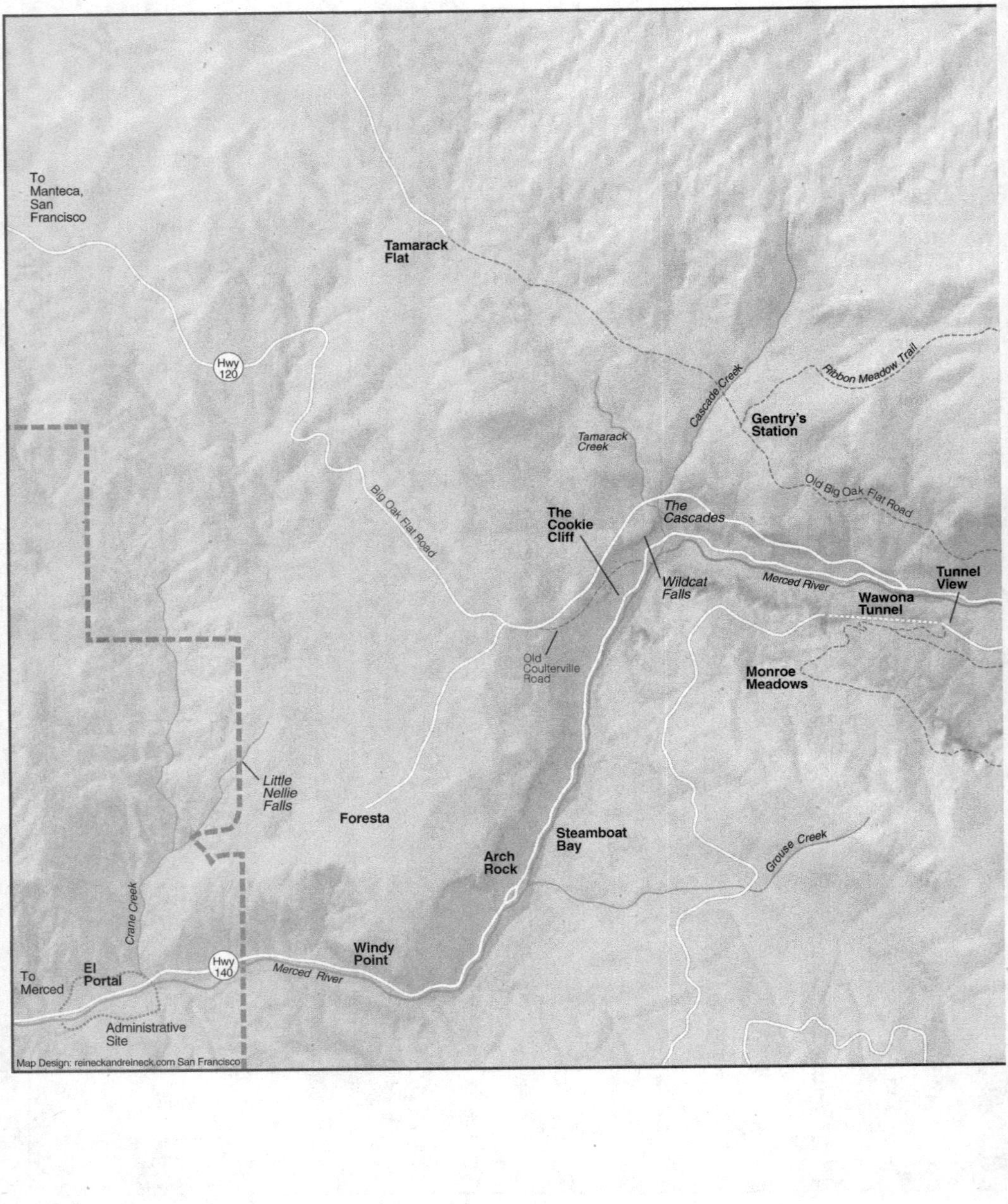

Yosemite Valley

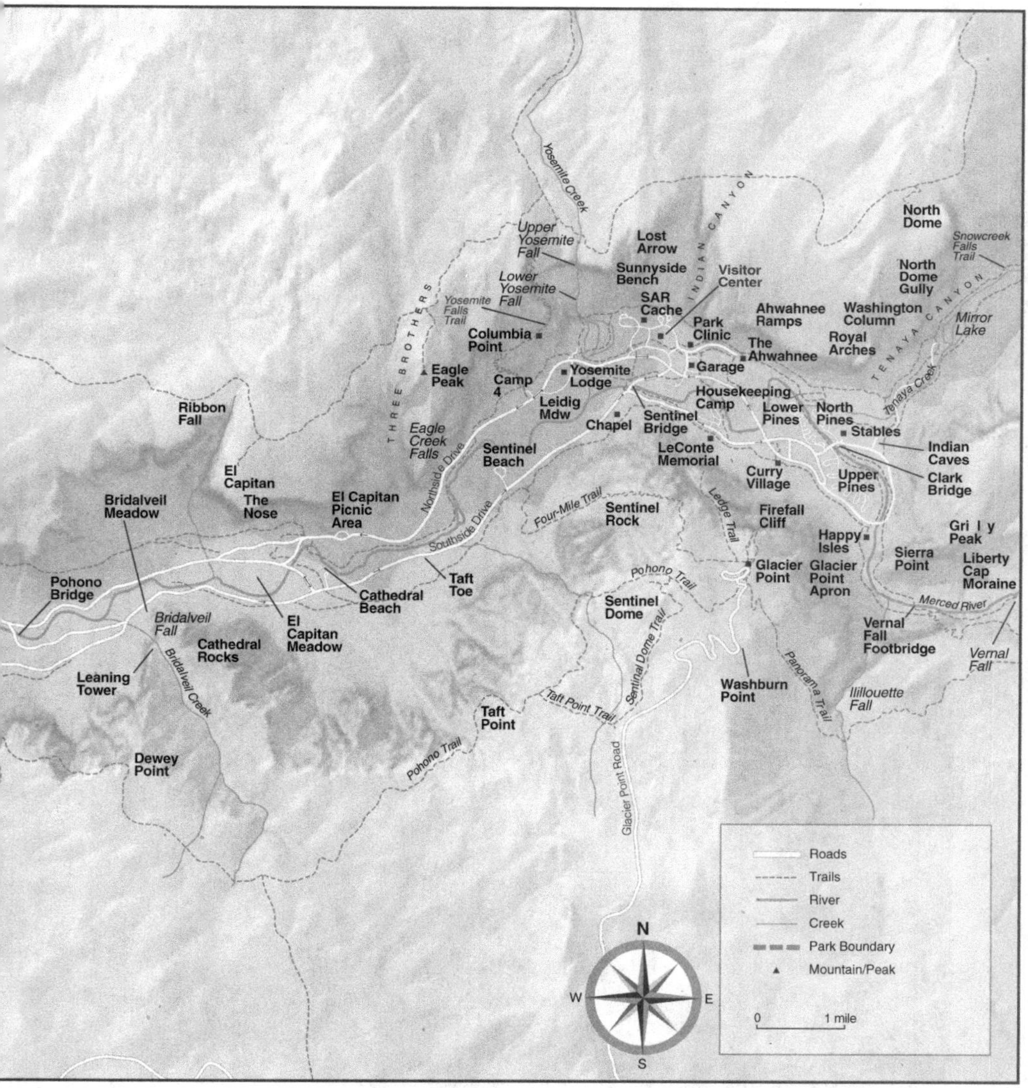

Chapter One

WATERFALLS

Each on a separate trajectory, Eric and Norma Yeoman funneled helplessly into the first drop of Waterwheel Falls. Then into the second fall. Then the third, the fourth, and the fifth. The two desperate young swimmers tumbled and plummeted though every hydraulic hammer and anvil of these impressive waterfalls on the upper Tuolumne River. No one had ever survived doing this.

"If there is magic on this planet," wrote anthropologist Loren Eiseley in his *The Immense Journey*, "It is contained in water." Indeed the fascination engendered by water, especially dramatically moving water, can act on us humans much the way a flame attracts a moth. And at times with similar finality. On July 21, 1951, 25-year-old Eric Burdette Yeoman of Alameda, California camped near the top of Waterwheel Falls in the Grand Canyon of the Tuolumne River. During a scenic hike at the brink of the falls with his wife, Eric leaned over to slurp up a drink. In this precarious location, he lost his balance and toppled into the chilly torrent. The current began racing him downstream like a greyhound out of the gate.

Eric's wife Norma Wagner Yeoman saw him take his plunge. She rushed to the riverbank to act as a lifeline. She reached out to grab him. She reached too far. She fell in.

The flow of this steep stretch of the Tuolumne now gripped both husband and wife and sped them into a series of waterfalls spanning a lethal 340-foot vertical drop. The cascades immediately ahead of the pair consist of a succession of scooped out bedrock holes into which the river plunges then erupts backward in huge explosions of spray and whitewater to form the illusion of waterwheels in the stream—thus the name.

Knowing how the falls had received their picturesque name, however, did nothing to help the two soggy lovebirds from becoming one with this natural phenomenon. Struggle as they might against the terrific pull, the pair was shot anyway over the brink to an almost certain death. Hoping for a last minute miracle or the outstretched arm of some agile Good Samaritan did not help either. Neither materialized.

While no miracle intervened to save the Yeomans from their horrendous plunge, at least they benefited from amazed witnesses at the foot of the falls. Lloyd Seasholtz, the electrical engineer for the Park, and his daughter Joyce, a student nurse, saw the two bodies careening down toward them. So did Charles Davis, a Dartmouth premed student.

To the further astonishment of all of these people, Eric somehow managed to crawl unassisted and uninjured from the turbulent Tuolumne. He was thoroughly rattled but he had miraculously survived the 340-foot high cascades. Holy #$%&, he must have thought, I made it…

His wife's luck proved far lousier. Seasholtz and Davis now scrambled into the river to drag Norma to shore. Unlike Eric, she was not at all in good shape. Perhaps the fact that she was still alive should have been cause for celebration, but it would be brief. Among her other injuries she had suffered a fractured skull, a broken back, and a cracked pelvis—each potentially life-threatening. Additionally, sharp rocks had riddled her body. Worse yet, Norma was now a long way from any road. Moreover, the routine use of rescue helicopters, so common now, still lay years in the future.

Joyce Seasholtz administered first aid to Mrs. Yeoman while the two men rounded up an evacuation crew using everyone they could find in the area. Soon a dozen men, working in shifts and fighting rough terrain along steep trails, carried the seriously battered woman on a litter for eight miles to a waiting emergency vehicle. This grueling trip encompassed nine hours of hard work by Norma's stretcher bearers—and sheer torture for her. Thanks to the prompt and selfless help of these Good Samaritans at the base of the falls, this tragedy proved not to be fatal, as it otherwise certainly would have been.

Aside from puzzling over how Eric Yeoman allowed himself to fall into the Tuolumne in such a dangerous place, one also has to feel curious as to what Norma Wagner Yeoman had to say to her husband once the hospital finally released her.

This incident occurred in Yosemite National Park but at a location many miles from the Valley, America's most incomparable and monumental glacial sculpture. It is this latter feature, a mere seven of the Park's 1,169 square miles, that has anchored the rapt gazes of millions of visitors. Why? Because, in much the same way as Grand Canyon does, at first glance this U-shaped valley appears so unique and huge as to defy belief. It demands of those seeing it for that first time that they reorganize their sense of proportion about the real world and perhaps even revise their sense of what is possible for that world to contain. John Muir, in his *The Yosemite,* agonized over how to do justice to this Sierra Nevada wonder using mere words. Ultimately he decided it required an entire book full of them. But, he wondered, how should he start such a book? Of Yosemite's many wonders, those touted earliest and most grandly are the waterfalls plunging down the sheer cliffs of its glacially-carved hanging valleys. No surprise, Muir decided his first chapter should extol these waterfalls. Even so, his brief introduction to the book captured the entire essence of Yosemite:

> But no temple made with hands can compare with Yosemite. Every rock in its walls seems to glow with life. Some lean back in majestic repose; others, absolutely sheer or nearly so for thousands of feet, advance beyond their companions in thoughtful attitudes, giving welcome to storms and calm alike, seemingly aware, yet heedless, of everything going on around them. Awful in stern, immovable majesty, how softly these rocks are adorned, and how fine and reassuring the company they keep: their feet among beautiful groves and meadows, their brows in the sky, a thousand flowers leaning comfortably against their feet, bathed in floods of water, floods of light, while the snow and waterfalls, the winds and avalanches and clouds shine and sing and wreathe about them as the years go by, and myriads of small winged creatures—birds, bees, butterflies—give glad animation and help to make all the air into music. Down through the middle of the Valley flows the crystal Merced, River of Mercy, peacefully quiet, reflecting lilies and trees and the onlooking rocks; things frail and fleeting and types of endurance meeting here and blending in countless forms, as if into this one mountain mansion Nature had gathered her choicest treasures, to draw her lovers into close and confiding communion with her.

More to the point of our chapter here, it is immediately above the Valley's profligate array of gigantic waterfalls that all too many of Nature's lovers have communed *too* closely. Even today these scenic wonders still seem deceptive in size. So much so that some visitors who make the arduous effort to hike to the tops of these falls arrive there only to fail to comprehend their power. A few of their tragic stories defy belief. Unfortunately, all too many are real. So real that at least about fifty-seven people have been accidentally swept to their deaths over one of a dozen waterfalls in the Park.

The earliest known fatal misstep occurred on May 20, 1913, when 21-year-old Austin Ramon Pohil hiked up to Snow Creek with three companions from the San Francisco Bay Area. Late May, of course, is about as close as one can get to the statistical peak of Yosemite's spring melt. On this day Snow Creek, tumbling down the Valley's north wall toward Mirror Lake, was roaring.

Pohil was a "popular" student at the University of California. With social success often comes confidence, perhaps even over-confidence. Whether any connection exists between this and his next decision remains conjecture. Either way, Pohil tried to cross the swollen stream at the top of the waterfall. He scrambled over a spray-drenched boulder and lost his footing on the slippery rock. Desperate, he struggled to regain his balance. He failed and fell more than 100 feet. Pohil became Yosemite's first known waterfall fatality.

Pohil's comrades tried in vain for hours to locate him through the clouds of mist. Two days later, the Park's Acting Superintendent Major T. L. Littlebrand ordered First Sergeant Louis Dorn, Troop A, First Cavalry, to find Pohil. Why Dorn? Because this incident occurred three years before Congress created the National Park Service, when Yosemite was still managed by the United States Army.

Dorn now instructed his troopers and Native American guides to lower him by rope to the pool below the falls. Courageously, the sergeant dived into the roiling water at the base of the hammering hundred-foot waterfall and somehow located the young man's body.

Sergeant Dorn had just upheld a tradition. The Army had usually done well as America's early park custodians—especially in light of their limited training for the job and also given that Congress had never formalized how national parks should be managed. Well before Sergeant Dorn went this extra mile to recover Austin Pohil, John Muir had praised the Cavalry in Yosemite: "Blessings on Uncle Sam's soldiers. They have done the job well, and every pine tree is waving its arms for joy." While Muir's sentiment is well taken, no amount of heroism could reverse Austin Pohil's fatal mistake.

For more than a decade afterward, Yosemite's waterfalls proved safe. Then an almost cliché error unfolded. On August 22, 1924, 16-year-old Lucille Duling from Hollywood, California hiked to the head of Vernal Fall before noon with her parents and her friend Riva Straub. There the two teenagers posed for a dramatic photo at the guardrail. Lucille's father clicked the shutter release.

The girls looked around and decided that this photo was too tame. A shot of them on the opposite side of the Merced, Lucille informed her father, would be more impressive.

This being late summer, the Merced—"the River of Our Lady of Mercy"—was now fairly low. Flows over Vernal and Nevada Falls can vary tremendously from a record low of only four cubic feet per second in late, dry summers, to several thousand cubic feet per second during major floods. Both girls crossed the river without incident. Lucille's father snapped the shutter release a few more times, until he ran out of film. Photos now taken, the girls decided to return to the trail side of the river. Riva crossed back easily.

As her father changed the film in his camera, Lucille chose to cross via a new route: by jumping from rock to rock "just above the fall." The Park's incident report succinctly explained what went wrong: "She stumbled and was instantly engulfed in the swift current. She rose to the surface, screaming, just as the avalanche of water carried her over the crest of the fall."

Lucille fell 317 feet.

Horror stricken, her father hurried down the steep slippery trail to the base of Vernal Fall. He stripped down, entered the pool, and tried to recover his daughter. The roiling current and pounding winds prevented Mr. Duling from reaching her. Riva meanwhile had sprinted back down to the Valley for rangers. When they appeared they assisted Mr. Duling by swimming out with a rope and hauling the girl's broken body to shore. Lucille Duling had become the first waterfall fatality in Yosemite as the result of a perceived photo opportunity. Ten more people would eventually die in much the same way while posing for or shooting such photos at waterfalls; these victims would constitute one-quarter of all known fatal plunges over the Park's falls. Moreover, a dozen more people yet would be swept for various errors over Vernal Fall in the future.

Again, the lure of pointing the camera from just the right place to capture a dazzling snapshot would continue to fatally seduce people. We have to jump forward from the 1920s to visit 27-year-old Mark F. Trifiro's classic example. On April 20, 1981, Trifiro of Hartford, Connecticut had hiked solo to beyond Vernal Fall. He stopped on the footbridge crossing above Silver Apron feeding Emerald Pool. Here the view intrigued him. As well it should have. In *The Yosemite*, John Muir writes of this place where Trifiro now stared around in awe:

> All the features of the view correspond with the waters in grandeur and wildness. The glacier sculpted walls of the cañon on either hand, with the sublime mass of Glacier Point Ridge in front, form a huge triangular pit-like basin, which, filled with the roaring of the falling river, seems as if it might be the hopper of one of the mills of the gods in which the mountains were being ground.

Tempted by the grandeur of the vista before him, Trifiro left the bridge and abandoned the trail to scramble along the shore. Unwitnessed, he slipped on the wet, mossy, water-polished granite and plunged into the snow-fed Merced.

The river swept him 250 yards downstream; he tumbled down the Silver Apron then drifted across Emerald Pool. Luckily he was able to haul himself free of the water before being sucked into more serious rapids again and possibly shooting over Vernal Fall. Once out, Trifiro flopped over a large boulder.

It being April, he already had become hypothermic. Witnesses quickly rushed to assist. Some built a fire to warm him. Despite this first aid, Trifiro's ability to breathe and his level of consciousness continued to plummet. One bystander hurried downhill for National Park Service (NPS) assistance. A critical helper here was visitor Jeff Beeler, an EMT-II. While performing his medical survey, Beeler discovered the victim was bleeding from the rectum. This finding announced to Beeler that Trifiro had sustained serious internal injuries during his wild ride down the water-worn rock, ricocheting off boulders scattered along the way. (Strictly speaking this was not a vertical waterfall event.) Indeed, not long after Trifiro's condition became apparent, he died due to internal bleeding despite CPR performed by arriving rangers.

Why had Trifiro decided to abandon the trail onto such dangerous terrain to begin with? One of the last things he had been able to say to Jeff Beeler before dying due to having been pounded by the river against boulders was that he had been trying to take a photo when he fell in.

The "photo-op-gone-fatal" cliché episode exemplified by Lucille Duling and Mark Trifero was reenacted by 24-year-old Louis Kitzes on June 16, 1934, and then again by 31-year-old Albert Alan Muff on June 17, 1944. Kitzes of San Francisco had waded into the Merced with four friends then jumped onto a rock at the brink of Nevada Fall to pose for a photo. He slipped off the boulder and fell into the river. It instantly swept him over the 594-foot waterfall. His body was found nine days later. After Kitzes' demise the next fatal photo episode occurred when Albert Muff left Los Angeles and went scrambling off-trail at the head of Snow Creek Falls. Here the 31-year-old man scuttled about seeking a position from which to take the perfect picture. Muff slipped on the wet, algae-covered rocks into the turbulent waters of Snow Creek and shot 100 feet over the fall. He disappeared for two months. His remains were finally located by accident, trapped under a rock in a deep pool at the bottom.

The very next victim after Lucille Duling to make a bad decision at Vernal Fall did so only three years later, on June 29, 1929, but it had nothing to do with photography. Twelve-year-old Forest Case of Burlingame, California had just hiked with Edward Shoemaker to the top of the waterfall. It being a hot day, Case leaned over the river's edge to get a drink of water. It tasted great. The boy next waded out into the river about twenty feet.

As have so many other visitors to Vernal Fall, Case seemed mesmerized by his surroundings. Muir writes of this spot:

> The Vernal, about a mile below the Nevada, is 400 feet high [actually 317 feet], a staid, orderly, graceful, easy-going fall, proper and exact in every movement and gesture, with scarce a hint of the passionate enthusiasm of the Yosemite or of the impetuous Nevada, whose chafed and twisted waters hurrying over the cliff seem glad to escape into the open air, while its deep booming thunder-tones reverberate over the listening landscape. Nevertheless it is a favorite with most visitors, doubtless because it is more accessible than any other, more closely approached and better seen and heard.

Still enthralled by the view but feeling no jitters about Muir's "staid, orderly, graceful, easy-going" fall, young Forest Case stopped in midriver. There he simply stood in the current and admired the scenery. He yelled over to his buddy Shoemaker on shore, "Look at those mountains up there, with the white clouds floating around them!"

At the instant these words left his mouth, Case lost his footing and fell. The flow instantly pushed the struggling lad toward the brink of Vernal Fall.

Shoemaker rushed into the shallows to grab the runaway boy. For an instant this would-be rescuer succeeded in gripping his friend's fingers as the water swept him along. Maddeningly, the flow tore Case away from Shoemaker's grip. Mere seconds later, it swept Case "shrieking" over the 317-foot drop. Several witnesses watched Case fly into space. Three women fainted. The boy's body was never found.

The 1940s saw five deaths (including Muff, above) by waterfalls. On July 20, 1945, 20-year-old Mary Majdick from Oakland had been trying to fill her canteen but had dropped it in the river. While trying to grab it, she lost her footing and slipped into the Merced. The flow quickly swept her screaming over Nevada Fall. As the future unfolded, four other people would repeat hapless Majdick's fatal error. On July 20, 1971, 16-year-old Randy Friedman from Hartsdale, New York hiked as part of a tour group to Vernal Fall. Once on top, he climbed over the guardrail to fill his canteen. He too slipped on the rocks and fell into the river, which carried him over the fall. Mind-bogglingly, young Friedman had become the fifth person to die going over a Yosemite waterfall during a mere twenty days (most of these are discussed later in this chapter; all are listed in Table 1)—albeit during significant high water. Despite immediate efforts and subsequent SCUBA searches during low water, Friedman's body was never found.

One year after Mary Majdick's fatal bid for her dropped canteen, on July 9, 1946, history repeated itself. Only this time it became far more complicated. Eleven-year-old Keen Freeman of Washington, D.C. had been walking along the Merced above Vernal Fall with his father, Walter Freeman, M.D. While Dr. Freeman had turned away to attend to something, Keen stopped to fill his canteen from the river. The boy fumbled and dropped it. The swift current now carried Keen's bottle toward the brink of the fall, a mere twenty yards downstream. Reluctant to lose his canteen, Keen lunged to retrieve it. He lost his balance and slipped into the river.

Meanwhile, 21-year-old Orville Dale Loos, a U.S. Navy veteran of World War II from Dayton, Ohio happened to be walking nearby in the overlook area with two other sailors. The three men saw Keen being swept toward the brink. They also could see that less than ten seconds separated the 11 year-old from a 317-foot death plunge.

All three vaulted the guardrail and jumped into the river to rescue young Keen. Orville Loos forged ahead of his companions and managed to grab the boy a mere fifteen feet from the brink of the fall. Loos valiantly fought his way back to the rocky shoreline with Keen as the other two seamen groped their way back to shore to save themselves.

Onlookers now stared spellbound. Loos wildly stroked back to safety while towing Freeman with one arm. Yes! Loos had gained a good grip on the slippery shoreline boulder. Amazingly, it looked like he and Keen were going to make it back onto the bank at the very last second before shooting over the edge…

But no. The powerful current now tore Loos' hand away from the slimy, polished granite that was his lifeline. With his grip lost, the Merced now sucked the would-be rescuer to the brink with the terrified boy still locked tightly in his other arm. In the blink of an eye, both disappeared over the 317-foot drop. Freeman's body was recovered a week later; Loos' body twelve days later, one hundred yards below the base of the fall.

The valiant but doomed attempt by Orville Dale Loos to rescue Keen Freeman, a total stranger, in the face of certain death represents what is most noble in the human spirit. What is not immediately obvious to a lot of us is just how risky such rescues are. On June 18, 1970, for example, 9-year-old Christine Fuentes of La Puente, California hiked the Mist Trail to the top of Vernal Fall with her mother, 30-year-old Yolanda Fuentes. Now at the overlook, the two metamorphosed into classic triumphant tourists.

With a family party of six, the mother-daughter pair climbed over the guardrail and past the signs posted to warn visitors of the hazards beyond. They scrambled closer to the water's edge. Amazingly, the seven people now waded *into* the river to sit on various "island" rocks or to cool off in the water during June's high run-off—and to pose for photos. Again, they did all of these things while *in* the Merced, a mere sixty or so feet upstream of the brink of Vernal Fall.

Of several nearby onlookers, Michael A. Fernandez yelled from shore "Do you know what the railing is for? It's so kids don't go over the falls!"

A woman in the wading party stared at Fernandez, but she did not otherwise respond to him. A moment later another of the women who had been standing in midriver tried to shoot a photo. Her hat fell off. The current instantly propelled it downstream. Little Christine scrambled across the flow to retrieve the dropped hat. Instantly, the river gripped her and carried her toward the waterfall. Within seconds, Yolanda, Christine's mother, began stumbling down the river to chase down Christine. She too lost her footing and was swept helplessly toward the brink.

As witnesses behind the guardrail and others safely dotting the shoreline watched in horror, the Merced swept the lost hat over Vernal Fall. Next it carried Christine—as she frantically tried to clamber back toward shore—into a death plunge. A mere second or two later Yolanda too vanished over the edge. Her decomposed body was discovered fifty-six days later, on August 13. Young Christine Fuentes' body was never found.

Only a year later, on July 10, 1971, the urge to rescue backfired yet again. On that day 21-year-old Victor Vega and his girlfriend, 16-year-old Kathleen Ann Alvarez from Torrance, California had hiked the five miles to the top of Nevada Fall. This huge waterfall drops almost twice the distance of its downstream neighbor, Vernal Fall.

Nevada Fall held a special place in John Muir's heart.

> —already chafed and dashed to foam, overfolded and twisted, it [the Merced] plunges over the brink of the precipice as if glad to escape into open air. But before it reaches bottom it is pulverized yet finer by impinging upon a sloping portion of the cliff about halfway down, thus making it the whitest of all the falls of the Valley, and altogether one of the most wonderful in the world.

July 10 was a hot day. The hike up had been sweltering. Now, facing a cool oasis surrounded by stupendous scenery, young Alvarez sallied past the four-foot-high guardrail and waded out into the middle of the Merced. There she planned to stand on a rock to have her photo taken with Vega, who followed her. The spot the girl had chosen for this scenic snapshot was fifty yards upstream of the violent brink that Muir had so eloquently described. To the two lovers, half the length of a football field must have seemed an adequate margin of safety.

Vega tried to follow her. He lost his footing. He fell forward. He instantly became one with the flow and began floating downriver. Alvarez reached out from her rock to grab Vega. In so doing she too lost her footing and slipped off. The current now swept both young people downstream. Witnesses raced and rock-hopped along the shoreline in hopes of saving the couple. Sadly, the "River of Mercy" showed none. It quickly carried Vega then Alvarez along those mere fifty yards toward the fall, then over it into a nearly 600-foot plunge. Alvarez's body was found below. Eight days later a visitor found Victor Vega's body.

At least one lesson resides in all of this. Five would-be rescuers entering the river above Yosemite's high waterfalls have not only died while trying to save an accidental swimmer, the person they intended to help also died, despite the martyred would-be rescuer. True, this statistical sample consists of only four episodes at waterfalls. And on the other side of the scale a few successful rescues have been accomplished. Even so, when we add in ten other similar such drowning-rescue attempts by Good Samaritans in Yosemite's streams and rivers it turns out that nine more men and one more woman have also died while trying to save someone in distress in the water. This grand total of fifteen would-be rescuers who died (accounting for another 7 percent of the total of all drownings and another 10 percent of all waterfall fatalities) racked up only one rescue—that of a woman who was merely standing only waist deep in slowly flowing water (see Chapter 10. Drowning).

Again this is not to belittle the last doomed efforts of these martyrs, nor is it intended to discourage well-planned rescue attempts in the future. Instead, our pointing out that many rescues having resulted in double fatalities with no one being saved is a neon warning sign to those who would attempt such efforts in cold fast-flowing water, especially above a lethal waterfall. Indeed we might just simplify this lesson by using the standard terminology, "scene safety." Clearly these big waterfalls—and moving water in general—constitute what all professional rescuers categorize as unsafe scenes. In short, would-be rescuers in such circumstances need to understand precisely what they need to do to make any rescue attempt safe before diving into a stream in hopes of simply pulling it off through good intentions. Entering the river to do this has rarely proved survivable.

On New Year's Day of 1975, during an extreme cold spell, Chris Becker, a lab X-ray technician in the Park's hospital, hiked up to Vernal Fall and witnessed yet another rescue attempt. What better way could there be to ring in the New Year? We can leave this question unanswered, but it turned out that Becker was not the only one who thought an arctic weather waterfall hike was the cat's meow. As Becker tells it:

> —the Mist Trail had a bizillion icicles draped across it. At the top of the falls, with the exception of the last twenty feet from the lip, the Merced River was frozen. There was a troop of Boy Scouts playing on the frozen river top. We had stopped for a breather.

So far this was simply an exceptionally chilly winter scene at a world-class waterfall in a World Heritage Site at a moment when Yosemite seemed to be hibernating, holding its breath as it were, in somnolent waiting for the spring thaw to bring everything roaring back into life. Well, somnolent except for that troop of Boy Scouts cavorting like idiot clowns on the frozen surface of the Merced only yards away from the lip of the falls...

What the heck could they be thinking, anyway? And what about their leaders? After all, Becker thought, Vernal Fall dumped the entire river flowing under that ice into thin air only a few yards away. What if one of those goofy adolescents slipped off the end of it? What if the ice broke?

Then it happened:

> I heard a crack like a dish breaking. I looked up and saw one of the kids fall through the ice.

The incautious boy instantly flowed under the frozen surface as the Merced carried him downstream. He was wearing an orange parka. He now appeared as an orange blob gliding along under the semitransparent ice. He now shot faster, it seemed, than one might expect. No air existed under there—just river capped with ice from bank to bank. But not being able to breathe was the least of this kid's problems. At this speed of flow he would have barely more than one second of air time after clearing the ice to escape the river before it plunged him over Vernal Fall. No one had ever managed to escape the river here under such circumstances. And no one had ever survived the drop off this waterfall.

When Becker had stopped with his hiking companions, they had stayed on the safe side of the guardrail. He and those with him now stood too far from the speeding orange blob even to make a hopeless effort at rescuing the boy. Meanwhile, seconds passed quickly as the day-glo torpedo glided submerged toward infinity.

One of the adults with the troop had been standing downstream of the breakthrough point and a lot closer to the waterfall edge of the ice. Whether or not he had purposely positioned himself there in the naïve belief that he could act as some sort of safety for his reckless charges, Becker would never learn. But what the man did next amazed him.

The would-be rescuer now scrambled downstream across the slippery ice to its perilous lip. Becker, still too far away to help, had long seconds to wonder whether he was about to witness another double fatality at Vernal Fall.

Becker watched the slipping, sliding Boy Scout guardian as he:

> —knelt down and grabbed his [the Boy Scout's] hood as he shot out and pulled him onto the ice.

Becker stood there both dumbfounded and relieved:

> In retrospect, I'm amazed that they both did not go over. The kid was waterlogged but not injured. They pulled off his pants to dry him off, and his pants froze upright in about thirty seconds. The whole incident [under the ice] lasted about ten seconds in total, and everyone acted like it was no big deal. Over the years I have thought about this incident a lot, and have always wondered how many near misses there were, and how close to the edge being in the backcountry is.

Indeed…

Consider next the experience of 40-year-old William C. Hansch of Sacramento. He intended to hike alone up to Nevada Fall. On June 3, 1947, he vanished before ever reaching this goal. Other hikers found Hansch's knapsack and personal gear set at the top of Vernal Fall about sixty-five feet from the brink. But no owner was in evidence.

Had Hansch stopped here during the June heat for water? Had he fumbled his canteen or otherwise slipped into the roaring high water of early June (more than

90 percent of all Yosemite waterfall fatalities occur between May and August) and then shot over the edge to his death? All searches for him failed. Nearly two months passed during which Hansch's fate remained a mystery. Finally, on July 27, fifty-four days after the solo hiker vanished, Assistant Chief Ranger Duane Jacobs found the missing man's body splayed among the boulders at the base of Vernal Fall. Nothing emerged from this grisly discovery to hint at what Hansch's mistake might have been.

Even so, Hansch had inadvertently set a record. At the time he became the oldest person—at age 40—ever to be accidentally (if it was an accident) swept over a waterfall fatally in Yosemite. Indeed, Hansch was also the only one over age 35 ever to have done this until June 4, 1992. Two older victims yet, 59-year-old Kenneth D. Fawcett and 73-year-old Kenneth Norman Stensby, both tumbled off next to the lips of waterfalls while apparently trying to get better views of them. Neither man actually entered the current. The average age of all victims of accidental plunges off waterfalls is roughly 23. Revealingly, more than 80 percent of victims were males. Seventy-one percent were between the ages of 11 and 29. Hansch was definitely old to have made this otherwise young person's mistake. What, though, had he done that is so common? Unfortunately, by the time the millennium ended, being swept over Vernal Fall or Nevada Fall had become, as far as lethal errors go, all too common.

Clearly both Vernal and Nevada Falls have been the scenes of an inordinate number of fatal events. Despite the absolutely terrifying and unsurvivable 594-foot plunge off Nevada Fall, 14 visitors to Yosemite (10 males and 4 females) have managed to go screaming over it, thus nominating it—after 18 deaths over Vernal Fall (12 males and 6 females killed as of 2024)—as the fifth most lethal fatal attraction in Yosemite. Vernal Fall, again, is number four. At least twenty-three people have died on Half Dome, making it number three. El Capitan is number two; as of January 2025, 34 climbers have died while "on" El Capitan; another 3 BASE jumpers have died diving off it). Other hikers yet have fallen from it. The Merced River within the Park, however, remains the uncontested top contender for tragedies with about 160 drownings, a dozen more of which occurred during Yosemite's 183 motor vehicle fatalities.

An important point here is the solo aspect of Hansch's demise and the mysterious disappearance of people hiking, trekking, or climbing alone. One in five of all such plunges off waterfalls were men who were by themselves at the time. On May 27, 1978, 23-year-old Dennison Taylor from San Carlos, California had been camping in the Valley with five friends. Alone, Taylor wandered about a mile and a half upstream of the footbridge east of Mirror Lake. He never returned. His body was found the next day, submerged in the second pool below Hidden Falls in Tenaya Creek. What led Taylor to being swept over this waterfall remains unknown.

The same uncertainty surrounds the fate of 26-year-old Richard E. Dix. On July 30, 1978, Dix had left San Mateo, California to go solo backpacking in the

Hetch Hetchy region north of the Valley. Dix left his backpack, along with drug paraphernalia, on the trail between Tueeulala and Wapama Falls on the north side of the reservoir. Evidence next revealed that he detoured off the path and sat above the cascades at the base of the 1,400-foot Wapama Falls. After a brief ground search discovered his gear but failed to locate him, the Park launched a helicopter. This SAR (search and rescue) team discovered Dix's partially nude body sprawled in the rocks below the base of the waterfall and above the reservoir.

Yet another mystery was born on July 5, 1968. On that day 19-year-old James William Gibson, Jr., from Whittier, California and his friend Luis Ortega had hiked together all the way to the top of Upper Yosemite Fall, climbing about 3,000 vertical feet. It is part of a system of three consecutive waterfalls which together drop an impressive 2,425 feet. From the Valley they can appear to flow and fall as one gigantic waterfall—the tallest in North America. In *The Yosemite*, John Muir wrote of them:

> This noble fall has far the richest, as well as the most powerful, voice of all the falls in the Valley, its tones varying from the sharp hiss and rustle of the wind in the glossy leaves of the live-oaks and the soft, sifting, hushing tones of the pines, to the loudest rush and roar of storm winds and thunder among the crags of the summit peaks. The low bass, booming, reverberating tones, heard under favorable circumstances five or six miles away, are formed by the dashing and exploding of heavy masses mixed with air upon two projecting ledges on the face of the cliff…

More to the point of luring hikers, Muir wrote, "So grandly does this magnificent fall display itself from the floor of the Valley, few visitors take the trouble to climb the walls to gain nearer views, unable to realize how vastly more impressive it is near than at a distance of one or two miles."

Atop the upper waterfall, Gibson and Ortega had splayed themselves on the granite to sunbathe. Several minutes later, Ortega, who was still bushed from the effort of the ascent and who felt pretty comfortable lying there on the warm rock, saw his friend get up. Gibson walked off alone toward the waterfall.

He never returned. Worried, Ortega searched the small area atop the fall for him. To no avail. Gibson's mangled body was located at the base of the 1,430-foot fall the next day. How Gibson fell remains a mystery.

Scrambling around the lip of a fall in search of a more "perfect" spot from which to see the water falling has been lethal at least six times. On July 27, 1970, 19-year-old Nicholas Michael Cordil from Los Angeles hiked with Donald Echenberg to the top of Upper Yosemite Fall. They arrived together but Cordil soon separated from his buddy to hike toward the world-famous scene. Over his shoulder he told Echenberg he was "going to look at the fall."

Cordil too never came back. Echenberg searched but could not find him. Three days later a hiker found parts of Cordil's badly damaged body in the deep pools below the base of the waterfall.

How easily these fatal slips occur is often hard to believe. On August 13, 1989, 20-year-old John Eric Ofner from Santa Barbara, California hiked with Gretchen Rose and Celia Denig to the top of Upper Yosemite Fall. The weather was hot. All three hikers went swimming in Yosemite Creek. Now cooled off, Ofner walked to the edge of the waterfall for a better look. He tried to peer downward. He edged a little closer, looked again, and then realized that this was the best view he was going to get. He turned around to head back upstream to Rose and Denig.

Abruptly he lost his footing on the sloping rock and fell facedown into the creek. Even though the water was flowing fairly low, it instantly swept him over the brink. Ofner fell more than 1,400 feet onto granite and was decapitated upon impact.

On August 2, 1979, another hiker was witnessed making his critical false move. Twenty-year-old Greg D. Taylor from Orange, California was solo hiking up Tenaya Creek. When he reached the brink of Hidden Falls, noted another hiker nearby, Taylor edged up to the 100-foot drop for a better view. Taylor, the witness said, traversed around the waterfall, whose lip was patchy with slick mud. As James Gibson and John Eric Ofner (above) likely had done, he too was trying to edge up closer for a vertical view. Then it happened. He slipped. Taylor slid right over the lip and became the third young man to die by falling off Hidden Falls.

In a bizarre coincidence, on this very same day two buddies from San Ramon, California were cruising along Big Oak Flat Road inside Yosemite. Eighteen-year-old Kenneth J. Mendonca was driving his blue GMC pickup with Terry Whelan riding shotgun. Mendonca pulled his truck off on a shoulder. Here the two decided to scramble off-trail, ultimately dropping down into the gorge above The Cascades.

Once the two teenagers had worked their way down the steep slopes of Cascade Creek they felt almost magnetically pulled to clamber downstream farther to the brink of the next precipice in hopes of peering directly down the 500-foot-high series of waterfalls they knew existed there.

Inconveniently, Mother Nature had configured Cascade Creek so that a person could not simply walk up to the level edge of the next fall and be able to stare straight down and watch the creek dissociate into thin air in a series of waterfalls more than twice as high as Niagara. Instead, the streambed's constrained, contorted and polished bedrock sloped dangerously before reaching a place from which one might see the water fly off the brink into the air.

Because the two had hiked all the way here from their truck and because they knew the waterfall was only a few yards farther downstream, the young men were loathe to abandon their quest. But because the rock now seemed terrifyingly treacherous to a person merely walking, they resorted to taking off their shoes and "crawling." Actually they were not so much crawling as they were "crab-walking" on their palms and feet with their butts down. Their technique worked like this:

Sit on your butt then move your hands and feet a foot or so to your side, then support your weight on your hands and feet and lift your butt up and swing your body over sideways along that one foot of distance to catch up with them, then sit down again and repeat the whole process. Mendonca and Whelan skooched like sideways inchworms along the polished sloping rock. Inch by careful inch the two crept closer to that enticing view. The roar from The Cascades grew louder.

Whelan would later explain that his friend abruptly lost the friction under his hands, feet, and butt. He began slipping and sliding down the sloping, smooth granite edge toward the falls. At first Mendonca slid slowly on his rear end—slowly enough that stopping still seemed possible. Even so, try as he might, he could not arrest his slide. When he hit the margin of moist algae—*often a thin, nearly invisible slime as slick as grease*—he accelerated. Now hopelessly unable to stop, the 18 year-old slid off the brink of the waterfall and plunged 200 vertical feet into the next rocky amphitheater.

Whelan, to his credit as a buddy, continued inching closer to the edge in hopes of helping Mendonca. But after spending ten terrifying minutes cautiously scanning from above, Whelan never got so much as a glimpse of his vanished friend.

The SAR team found that Mendonca had died upon impact. He then had sunk three feet into a water-filled hole in the bedrock. Although the two young men's misadventure may seem highly unusual, it really was not. The decisions this pair made and the risks they were willing to take just to gain a glimpse from immediately above the waterfall where it shot into space (a particular type of perspective normally difficult to both see and then to live to tell of it) epitomize the naïve mentality of several victims of waterfall plunges who seemed all too much like moths drawn to the flame.

It is hard to decide which decision is more self-destructive: Trying to peer directly over the lip of a waterfall or entering in the stream close to where it feeds that waterfall. If pressed, we would have to admit the second decision is probably worse. The latter decision has led to more waterfall fatalities (fourteen victims had entered the river deliberately, one-third of the total) than any other behavior. Sure, accidents do happen, however avoidable. Indeed one of the earliest such avoidable mishaps was that of 7-year-old Roberta Mary Hurd. On June 21, 1968, Hurd of Jackson, California had hiked with her parents to Vernal Fall. For some reason the girl was left unattended to play alone *at the water's edge* upstream of the brink. She slipped into the stream unwitnessed. Someone spotted her in the river twenty feet short of the lip—far too late. The current swept her over the 317-foot plunge. Roberta's body turned up two weeks later, on the Fourth of July.

The fourteen episodes of deliberate swimming or dunking above a falls far outnumber accidents like Roberta Hurd's. At least thirteen young men have died this way, often in spite of both signs posted and warnings by friends with whom they were hiking. On July 11, 1971, 22-year-old William Ramirez of Gardena, California hiked to Vernal Fall. He and his brother John climbed over the guardrail. Then, despite John saying he thought it was too dangerous, William continued on his own to swim in the river about 175 feet upstream of the fall.

Abruptly gripped by the current, William now sped downstream. To onlookers he seemed as if he was "in shock." Witnesses said he "made no frantic effort to save himself." His brother entered the river to rescue him but could not manage it. William shot over the brink. A visitor found his body ten days later.

More than two years afterward, on October 13, 1973, 21-year-old Patrick J. Rose of Cleveland Heights, Ohio hiked with Thomas Stropki to the top of Nevada Fall. Rose told Stropki that he was hot and was going swimming. Both men saw the posted warning signs. Stropki protested, "It's too dangerous."

Rose climbed over the barrier anyway and entered the Merced River alone. The current instantly swept him downstream. He managed to grab a shoreline rock and stop himself. Stropki yelled, "Stay put; I'll help you."

Rose ignored this—or maybe he never heard it—and tried to climb out of the river on his own. He lost his grip. The current tumbled him over Nevada Fall's 594-foot drop. Rangers recovered his body after five days.

This sort of mistake would continue to repeat itself. Almost two years later yet, on May 19, 1975, 22-year-old Gregory Edward Brazil, a Yosemite Park and Curry Company employee from Clovis, California, along with Deborah R. Morgodo, scrambled a quarter mile up Eagle Creek from Northside Drive. There Brazil, who, his partner would allege, was apparently under the influence of drugs, took off his clothes and stood in the stream above a twenty-five-foot waterfall. As Morgodo sat to remove her shoes, she heard Brazil scream. She looked up to see him sliding on his back and feet first off the edge. CPR by rescuers failed to resuscitate him.

On July 17, 1977, another Curry Company employee from Irvine, California repeated Brazil's error. Nineteen-year-old Harold A. Corwin hiked with friends to Hidden Falls on Tenaya Creek. Despite their warning him, Corwin sat in a water-carved chute which slopes and curves for forty-five feet in one part of this series of falls. Unable to stop at the end of the natural slide, Corwin shot off its end and dropped twenty more feet into shallow water. When rescuers recovered him, he was dead. They tried CPR, but in vain.

About a month later, on August 18, 1977, 21-year-old David Kingseng Chu from Fresno, California managed to drop into space from atop Vernal Fall. Uniquely, however, he never made it to the boulder-laden plunge pool at its bottom.

The young man had hiked up the Mist Trail that hot afternoon with his family. Once there, in full view of a dozen visitors plus several of his relatives, he scrambled over the guardrail—yes, the one holding the large metal signs unmistakably and graphically portraying human stick figurines going over the fall. Ignoring these blatant warnings and, more importantly, ignoring the increasing push of the current against his calves, Chu waded into the cool shallow stream. Moreover, he did this only a dozen feet from the lip of the world-famous waterfall.

Yosemite, like the rest of California, was now desiccating in the midst of one of the very driest of years of its recorded history; 1977 was *the* drought year of the century. This deceptively low flow of the Merced here now undoubtedly seduced Chu into venturing downstream those last few feet. He shuffled ever closer to where the river quietly vanished over the horizon into nothing but air.

Incredibly, given how many people had died here already (and given the hindsight of this book), his goal was to take a photo of Vernal Fall not only while looking absolutely straight down as it dramatically plunged 317 feet to the pool below but also *while he stood in the middle of the stream exactly where the water began to cascade vertically*. Chu's brother watched him on his quest. He would later report that as the force of the current hit him, Chu belatedly and suddenly recognized the peril.

He now tried to scramble back to safety. Unfortunately, rather than try to shuffle backwards, he instead made a quick, almost sideways hop toward the nearby dry rock. This was the wrong sort of move. The footing here consisted of slick algae-covered, polished granite. As he now twisted and lunged, his feet instantly slipped and flew out from under him. He fell. In the blink of an eye the river sucked the terrified, would-be photographer over the brink.

Shocked and disbelieving, Chu's relatives and other bystanders hustled down the trail's rock steps to the base of the fall. Yet stare into the pounding water and billows of mist as they might, no one could discern any sign of the ill-fated young man. Finally one of them hurried down the trail to seek help.

A Park SAR team arrived. It too searched the boulder-studded pool. The team also examined the Merced downriver from the pool. No dice in either place.

Witnesses who had been near the bottom at the moment when Chu fell felt fairly certain because of the low, mid-summer flow that the young man "never got here."

Scanning the cliff above the pool with binoculars proved of little help. Spray and the moving water obscured the gray granite face. Maybe the plummeting, would-be photographer had disappeared into one of the large crevices up on the wall behind the falls! Maybe… To test this new hypothesis, someone would have to climb up there and search those nooks and crannies up close and personal.

This process began the next morning. The most suspicious-looking location in the crevice system up there was a foot-wide, almost hidden crack 250 feet below the lip. Ranger Tom Griffiths carefully worked his way up and across the spray-drenched talus below. To reach the suspected crevice, Griffiths had to ascend about seventy-five feet above the pool at the bottom. The team watched him in his black wetsuit and an orange climbing helmet as he tailed a blue safety rope and moved laterally into and behind the falling water of the falls.

The polished, super slippery, and down-sloping narrow ledge at this point quickly proved inhospitable.

The spray and shifting winds created by the falling water soon chilled

Griffiths despite his neoprene insulation. This section of the cliff face, after all, was the waterfall zone. And drought or not, the falls now smashed down on Tom and his foot-wide ledge in quickly shifting, incessant cycles. As Ranger Griffiths, tethered to a lateral safety line, now stood on this ledge above the most likely crevice, his ability to see and search it clearly in the shade would last for only a moment before he was again engulfed by yet another shifting deluge. These downpours often proved so intense he had to hold his breath. This was no picnic at the falls. And despite an hour of searching under these conditions of disabling chill and intermittent horrible visibility, Griffiths still spotted no sign of Chu. Was the missing photographer truly up here?

At noon, (I) Farabee was next. I made my way out onto Griffiths' same ledge via a Tyrolean traverse (a clothesline-like system rigged horizontally from point A to point B). One improvement on Tom, I was more color coordinated—orange from top to bottom. More importantly, I carried a fireman's pike pole, a seven-foot long wooden "spear" with a large hook at the end of it. We had toted it up from the Park's firehouse. Despite my more colorful outfit, I now experienced precisely what Griffiths had, lousy "weather" and marginal visibility. So I probed the water-filled cracks in the cliff face for yet another hour with that pole. And I found nothing.

The conclusion that Chu somehow must have lodged somewhere else kept bugging me.

But as time passed and the sun traveled across the sky, the shifting angle of sunlight improved visibility onto the cliff face (as well as warmed things up). At the end of my hour of searching—in between bouts of "Surf's up!"—I finally caught a glimpse of a small splotch of pink. It sat wedged at least four feet deep in a shadowy, eighteen-inch-wide crevice. Our luck had just turned. With the hook on the long pike, I finally was able to snare David Chu and tug him out by hand.

Confused by the heightened emotions of this terrible experience, Chu's relatives felt that the Park should have had a rescue team on hand in the area and ready to go *when* their boy went over the waterfall. They felt that had this sort of instant response been available, David might have been saved. They made inquiries into pursuing a lawsuit to this effect. But as reason and a sense of reality soon prevailed, these efforts went no further.

At any rate, with Chu now lowered by rope from the cliff then placed in a body bag for his two-hour journey off the steep, rocky slope on the north side of Vernal Fall, Tom Griffiths and I turned our attention to drying off and getting back into our clothes. This meant first wriggling out of our wetsuits. One complication: while we had been working on this body recovery the afternoon had warmed the gorge. Four young women, probably in their late teens and definitely in their bikinis, had taken up sunbathing on a flat rock in the middle of the pool—a safe one below the waterfall—a hundred feet below us.

We now looked for a tree or rock to hide behind while we got into our hiking shorts. We found nary a bush. So we did the next best thing. We both turned around and pulled off the bottoms of our wetsuits. Of course, the wet neoprene refused to slide down as quickly as we would have liked. I guess we wiggled in our haste. Even so, we silently congratulated ourselves on getting clothed pretty quickly. We next turned around again to enjoy the view as we finished dressing. As we sat on a bench-like rock to tug our boots on the four young ladies stood up in unison. They next turned their backs toward us, and like a rehearsed chorus line, they each dropped their bikini bottoms and "mooned" us.

Rangers may not get paid big bucks but the outstanding views in Yosemite can be compensatory.

After Chu's bizarre fall and challenging recovery, twenty-six more people would fly off waterfalls in Yosemite through 2024, nearly all of them while deliberately swimming or bathing in harm's way. Seven of these would shoot off the lip of Nevada Fall. On July 1, 1984, 15-year-old Omar Antonio Morales had hiked up the Nevada Fall's trail during a family outing from San Francisco. After his hot trek, he jumped off a slab of granite into the Merced about 120 yards upstream of the brink of the huge fall. Despite more than a football field's length from the edge of the waterfall—what some people might consider a safe margin—the current quickly swept Morales toward that lip.

The young swimmer's brother-in-law saw him racing toward the drop off, so he leaped into the river to aid Morales. But the flow instantly gripped him just as implacably. Luckily the brother-in-law was able to arrest his own momentum by grabbing a midriver boulder. Several other visitors would be needed to rescue this would-be rescuer from this perilous perch. Meanwhile, despite everyone's efforts, Morales shot over the brink into a drop of 594 feet.

A year later, on June 14, 1985, 27-year-old Sonia Del Carmen Caceres from Lynwood, California made a far more stunning error. Sonia and her husband, Javier, plus their infant son and two sisters accompanied a Seventh Day Adventist Church hiking trip to the top of Nevada Fall. By the time they reached the top they felt hot.

The pair did not heed the NPS "danger" signs. The problem here is that for signs to be placed where they can be most effective they must be near the river. But when an unusual flood hits, the signs themselves sometimes become casualties of the very dangers they warn about. Replacing them is never instantaneous. One solution has been to place them farther away from the shoreline. But such placement, while fine for most visitors, can be ignored by those in a big hurry to get closer to the river and waterfall.

At any rate, Javier briefly dunked in the river while his wife watched their 8-month-old son.

After Javier climbed back onto shore, Sonia next waded into the stream. Instead of dunking or even swimming and then climbing right back out, she now began drifting on her back as if she were bobbing safely in a backyard swimming pool. In fact she was floating in an eddy immediately adjacent to powerful current flowing a mere forty yards from the brink of the 594-foot waterfall. As dicey as this might sound, Sonia did seem to her husband to be managing to stay in her small pool and out of that main stream.

Her success at remaining "safely" in that eddy lulled Javier into shifting his attention to their son. About ten minutes after Sonia began floating on the River of Mercy, Javier looked up to check on her again. To his shock she was no longer in her little eddy pool. He quickly scanned downstream.

He saw Sonia, still on her back and apparently lulled herself, drifting along with the current toward the lip of Nevada Fall. Javier scrambled to his feet and rushed downstream. But too late. Sonia floated serenely over the waterfall.

Three months later, Javier Caceres threatened to sue the National Park Service for $1 million in damages. He claimed that his wife had floated over Nevada Fall because the NPS had not posted the warning signs in Spanish. For reasons now lost, Caceres did not prosecute this suit.

Years passed in Yosemite during which no one fell off one of its big waterfalls. During this time rangers were grateful for the public's belated but seemingly growing awareness of the danger they posed. They crossed their fingers and hoped the era of fatal errors at the brinks of the Park's waterfalls had finally ended.

On July 11, 1991, the NPS was forced to feed this wishful thinking into the shredder. On this day a 29-year-old Austrian named Werner Beinstingl hiked to Upper Yosemite Fall. Beinstingl was, of all things, a "rocket scientist" living in Goleta, California. He had been visiting with a friend whom he now told that he was going to climb to a higher spot above the fall for a more perfect photo.

On a mission, Beinstingl began scrambling onto ever more perilous terrain exposed to a truly monumental 1,430-foot drop. Finally he reached a sketchy little perch located *above* the normal overlook area beside the fall. Here, while trying to take that perfect photo, the scientist lost his footing and fell those 1,430 feet—and then some. His lengthy freefall was witnessed by seven other hikers scattered in various locations. Werner Beinstingl died instantly of massive injures, including complete evisceration.

Four years later, another foreign-born visitor met his end at a Park waterfall. On August 15, 1995, 27-year-old Francois Serge Durand De Fontmagne from Lyon, France hiked with Jean-Francois Petit to Nevada Fall. Here yet again the Merced appeared too refreshing to resist. De Fontmagne decided to swim in the pool about fifty feet upstream of the Nevada Fall footbridge.

This location seemed to offer a double opportunity. As his friend swam, Petit, on shore, snapped souvenir photos of him "above" the stupendous scenery. While Petit eyeballed through the viewfinder, the Merced swept De Fontmagne downstream and over the waterfall.

He vanished among the river-pounded boulders scattered at the bottom. Someone spotted his body a few days later, but before it could be retrieved the current shoved it through a twelve-inch-wide crack, which allowed it to vanish yet again. What were believed to be his remains were not rediscovered until nearly four months later. They were trapped many feet down, wedged in a narrow niche under a rockfall so large, unstable, and hazardous that officials decided it was too dangerous to do anything other than leave them in place.

On September 3, 1995, a mere two weeks after De Fontmagne had shot off the lip of Nevada Fall and long before his body was discovered, 31-year-old Daniel Lawrence Rex Kahler from San Diego hiked with Catherine J. Mao to the top of the same waterfall. While Mao sunbathed and soaked her feet, Kahler swam in the small pool twenty-five yards upstream of the bridge. This scenario seemed virtually a cookie-cut repeat of De Fontmagne's behavior of two weeks earlier but without the camera work.

Unlike De Fontmagne, Kahler next hauled himself out on a rock to warm up for a moment and admire the scenery. He then reentered the Merced to wade knee-deep toward midstream—as if trying to cross the river. Witnesses saw him lose his balance and slip into the current. Despite Kahler's "frantic efforts" to regain the shore, the swift moving water pulled him under the footbridge and over the waterfall into that long plunge onto the rocks below.

By now you might have detected a new pattern emerging in this sort of tragedy. Early fatal waterfall errors seemed the province of kids, inexperienced teenagers, and young men in their early twenties who were not "worldly wise" but who *were* feeling their oats. By the mid-1980s and into 2006, however, the victims of Yosemite waterfalls had become older, seemingly more sophisticated, educated, and often foreign men. Indeed, of the dozen victims of waterfall plunges from 1985 onward the average age is 30 years old. Prior to that, during the seventy years between 1913 and 1983, the average age of the thirty-four victims was 20.5 years old. After 2006 most new victims again were young.

Reinforcing this significant new age profile, on July 10, 1999, 31-year-old Siddiq Parekh, an "experienced" Yosemite hiker from Diamond Bar, California had hiked with Imran Dadabhoy and two other friends toward Half Dome. The four men stopped atop Nevada Fall to eat their lunches and to soak their feet in the Merced.

Despite having passed reposted NPS signs warning of the danger of entering the Merced here above the waterfall, Parekh decided to further cool off by lowering himself into the river waist deep. Upon easing into the water Parekh soon slipped on algae-covered rocks and fell. The powerful current pulled him downstream. Now possibly aware that the warning signs he had just passed and ignored had been posted for a good reason, Parekh grabbed at a water-polished boulder and tried to haul himself out.

Parekh's grip proved unequal to the power of the river. The current pried his hands loose. Jim Mohan on the nearby footbridge saw him partially recover by "sitting up like he was going down a water slide" just as the river sucked him over the 594-foot fall. Witnesses above and below the drop stared in horror as Siddiq Parekh rag dolled through space and spray.

As we will see later in this book, all too many tragedies in Yosemite have unfolded simply because a hiker decided to detour off-trail and head cross-country onto an imagined shortcut. Despite any positive connotation of scenic allure that the word "cross-country" might convey to most of us, when a hiker abandons a maintained trail and tries to blaze a new, unscouted shortcut *into* Yosemite Valley from the rim, bad things top the list of possible outcomes.

As foul weather began rolling into Yosemite during the early afternoon of February 6, 1999, 17-year-old Mitch Griffin was hustling down toward the Valley on the Yosemite Falls Trail. He decided the switchbacks ahead did not constitute his cup of tea. Below the base of Upper Yosemite Fall, Griffin detoured into the bed of Yosemite Creek. The creek, he reasoned, took the shortest route down to the Valley. Sure, there were more waterfalls along it, but he could just scramble along the rock beside them and thus also take the shortest route.

This simplistic perspective lured the teenager into Yosemite Creek's "Inner Gorge," a very narrow, shady, wet, cold, steep, deep, and often vertically walled ravine incised into the half-mile-high cliff on the Valley's north wall above Lower Yosemite Fall. The upper sections of the route he chose proved possible to scramble. Not safe or prudent, but doable. Besides, the way led downhill and was therefore easy. Griffin frequently faced small broken cliffs where a little downclimbing and a short jump here and there earned him quick and significant progress toward the Valley. When he looked back up at some of these, he probably realized that climbing back up them would be a challenge. Maybe even one beyond his ability.

But if he kept going down, such concerns would remain academic. He did wish that he could actually *see* what lay ahead. But why worry for nothing? So far so good.

Several hundred vertical feet below his starting point, Griffin faced another drop. A vertical drop down the water-polished granite. It looked short enough to jump. He began his scramble. He slipped and fell. His ankle twisted upon impact. His wrist felt shocked. He got to his feet to take stock. Now his ankle would no longer support his weight. It was broken.

This was bad. But maybe it was not as bad as it might be. Maybe he was close to the bottom.

In a way, he was. Indeed, when he inched forward to peer over the next drop his stomach sank. No wonder the roaring from below was so loud here. He was standing, he now saw, directly above Lower Yosemite Fall. Yosemite Creek plunged from his position 300 vertical feet onto talus below. He glanced to each side of the fall. The wet, polished, but broken granite he had been scrambling down now transformed to wet and vertical on both sides of the waterfall.

No way could he descend from here even with a good ankle. Even with a rope.

Well, he would just have to try to get back up.

He turned around and surveyed the route down which he had just scrambled and fallen. He noticed that his wrist now really hurt. He moved it experimentally. It too was broken. The descent he had just made looked different from this angle. The vertical part was a lot higher. He limped a bit closer. No way could he get back up that thing now. No way.

This ledge above the waterfall was so small that a few steps in any direction led to its edge. In fact, he realized as he looked around him again more carefully, this was a pretty small ledge. And it was the final, very top pour-over for Lower Yosemite Fall.

He looked around. A winter storm now engulfed the Valley and seemed to be moving in at fast forward. Clouds obscured the cliffs. Already it was raining. And he was definitely trapped here. And now that he was no longer moving, the cold began feeling a lot more uncomfortable.

Then a new thought must have intruded in the teenager's mind. What if enough rain fell up there back behind him to raise the creek level high enough to sweep over his ledge?

He looked straight upward into the narrow slice of gray sky framed by the walls of the Inner Gorge and started screaming "HELP!"

There was a trail up there. Yet, as a direct aid to Griffin getting out of his predicament, that trail might as well have been on the moon. But maybe someone was up there and would hear him. And then someone would come and save him.

Someone was up there. And at about 3 p.m. someone did hear him.

Griffin's panicked screams for help emerged even above the roar of the falls.

The visitor who heard them set in motion a SAR mission.

But not an easy one and definitely not a safe one. No helicopter could get anywhere near the trapped and injured kid. The weather and vanishing daylight ruled out the aircraft even as a mere shuttle for rescuers onto a safe landing zone somewhere above. Human beings would have to get to him the hard way. And, Yosemite SAR and Emergency Medical Services Director Keith Lober now realized, the hard way was to become harder with every passing minute. For starters, night was falling. They would have to rescue whoever was down there in the dark. Second, it was pouring rain. The rain was likely to turn to snow. But even if it did not, it would raise the creek level; it would expose the rescuers to hypothermia; it would make every conceivable route to the boy slick and incredibly dangerous; it would loosen the soil and rocks for the approach and make them far more hazardous; and it would also send rocks rolling and ricocheting down the walls of the gorge like random cannon fire.

All in all, this mission was going to be extremely risky. It held the potential to kill rescuers and result in more casualties than if the SAR team did nothing but stay at home in front of a warm fireplace.

In short, Lober concluded, no one could afford to make a mistake on this operation.

Soon Lober mustered the SAR team—Mary Hinson, Werner Braun, Jo Whitford, Jay Salvedge, Mark Garbarini—the best rescuers and/or climbers he could find. These people first had to hike toting fifty-pound backpacks of climbing and rescue gear about 1,000 feet up to a position well above the hidden victim. Once they ascended the terrain above the gorge they veered into it. Already the soil was so wet that it liquefied under their boots. Oozing mud squirted out from their soles with each step. The problems this posed were twofold: First they had to counter the tendency to slip and slide with every step and second, they faced a worse hazard of boulders that began rolling at the slightest nudge.

Any minute now the team would be forced to set up a rappel so that they could descend by rope. In this rain, how long would their supposedly waterproof headlamps last? A brief size-up revealed no straightforward route down to their screaming victim. The SAR team would have to set up multiple rappels and descend in stages, scrambling laterally and downward after rappelling. Ultimately, the rescuers would have to rappel 400 feet of cliff.

Accomplished climber Werner Braun led the way on these. He chose routes and anchor locations and generally blazed a vertical trail in the inky dark and stormy confines of the Inner Gorge.

None of this got done as quickly as anyone hoped. The weather was so violently foul that it seemed an evil force sent to stop them. As Keith Lober would explain:

> There was so much water falling out of the sky that our headlamp reflectors looked like little fishbowls, sloshing half full of water. Almost all of our headlamps and radios eventually failed due to being waterlogged. It was like standing in the flush of a 2½-inch fire hose set on a fog pattern.

As Ranger Mary Hinson followed on rappel, she heard more boulders tumble in the dark. Being out here was like playing Russian roulette. Would one of those rocks hit her? Or perhaps even more cruel, would one slam down on her soaking wet rappelling rope and sever it, thus dropping her into the gorge and then sending her shooting over that same waterfall?

Lober explains how bad things were:

> Huge boulders were washing loose all around us….In the dark we

> could not tell where the sound of the boulder that was crashing down was coming from. We couldn't tell if it was coming from above us or to the side of us. It was truly frightening.

As if on cue, a large shard of plummeting granite cracked like thunder. It was so close! Hinson held her breath. What were the odds, really? She, her teammates, and her rope were such small targets. Despite the odds, the hissing shard now did hit her rope. Indeed boulders hit it in *three* places. These impacts cut through the sheath and most of the core strands of her safety line. But not every strand. Miraculously, just enough of the rope remained intact to support her weight until she joined those below. That had been *close*…

The team struggled onward, hauling their gear and hoping that they and their trapped victim would make it through this night alive.

Eventually they reached Mitch Griffin. The rescuers were amazed to find that he had trapped himself directly above the lip of granite over which poured Lower Yosemite Fall. His injuries per se, they now discovered during their survey of the now lethargic boy, were not life threatening. But he was so hypothermic that his plunging core temperature *would* kill him if he were not transported to a warm, dry place pronto.

As they packaged the injured teenager onto the Stokes litter they had hauled down those cliffs, they masterminded a plan. This plan did not include hauling Griffin back up. Instead they would send him down right next to the falls that had terrified him for these past several hours. Mark Garbarini now climbed aboard the teenager's litter to help guide it. Lober explains:

> We lowered him 300 feet in a litter to a waiting ground team that carried him out of the Lower Falls Amphitheatre. We were all quite miserable.

On October 30, 2000, Rangers Mary Hinson and Keith Lober were awarded Department of the Interior Valor Awards. Rescue climbers Werner Braun, Mark Garbarini, Jay Salvedge, and Jo Whitford each received a Department of the Interior Citizen's Award for Bravery.

Meanwhile Mitch Griffin survived his ill-conceived shortcut and got to live his life.

Thankfully, during the next six years after Griffin's missed appointment with the Grim Reaper, no one managed to get swept off a Yosemite waterfall. But on July 30, 2005, when 24-year-old Chintan Chokshi hiked with several friends toward Nevada Fall, this halcyon spell was about to end. The group stopped for a break at Vernal Fall. Here Chokshi, a native of Ahmedabad, India but residing in Sunnyvale, California as a Silicon Valley engineer, decided to wash his face in the river. He crawled through the safety fence. As he did, 52-year-old Rich

Hendler saw him. Appalled at the risk the man was taking, he asked Chokshi pointedly, "What the f— are you *doing*?"

Chokshi simply looked at Hendler then walked down toward the slick rock twenty yards upstream of the waterfall. He slipped almost immediately in his Nikes, but caught his balance.

Next, instead of taking a lifesaving lesson from this near mishap, he continued closer to the river. At the edge Chokshi slipped again, fell on his butt this time, and slid into the flow. He frantically tried to regain his feet in the stream, which according to the incident report was "extremely swift on [this] date," but he failed. His now-alarmed buddies watched helplessly as the river poured him over the waterfall into the pool far below.

Compounding this tragedy, on September 24, the day Chokshi's body was finally located, NPS Special Agent Dan Madrid suffered a fatal attack of asthma near the Vernal Fall footbridge while participating on the mission to extricate the body.

A month before Chokshi was found and Agent Madrid died, the mother of all photo-ops-gone-bad unfolded. On August 22, 2005, 21-year-old Shane Michael Kinsella of Dublin, Ireland hiked to the top of Upper Yosemite Fall with his buddies, 21-year-old Stephen Anthony Flynn and Nicholas O'Reilly. The trio arrived at about two in the afternoon. There the three ate lunch and went swimming in the pools. More importantly, each visitor from the Emerald Isle also drank "three or four tumblers of wine."

Next two of the men walked to the lip of the waterfall. Here Kinsella took Flynn's photo as he posed atop the falls.

This done, the two men swapped positions. Kinsella now posed for a photo. He decided to make it more dramatic by clowning and pretending to be falling into the waterfall. Flynn took the snapshot then he stared into the camera's LED display. This photo, he now saw, had not worked out.

So Flynn asked Kinsella to pose for it again. Kinsella obliged by hopping up and down and spreading his arms out over the water with even more exaggeration of a comical mishap about to happen. As he again pretended to fall he actually *did* fall into the river and shoot over the falls into that very long drop into eternity.

Even in the face of articulating the obvious, these all-too-many episodes of accidental waterfall plunges compel us to reiterate some lessons learned in the hardest way. Proximity above any waterfall incurs a predictable high risk. Entering any significant stream which flows over a waterfall—regardless of any sense of security inherent in what might seem like a "safe" distance between one's entry point and the fall—is a proven killer. Any sense of security imagined in such a situation is chimeric and illusory. The power of moving water, even knee deep, has carried hundreds of people to their doom in the Sierra Nevada. That said, falling into such a stream accidentally instead of entering purposefully does not make it any less deadly. How easy is it to fall in? The shorelines of these streams are of finely polished rock which is smooth and very slippery even when dry. When wet the rock becomes extremely slick. When wet and also with algae growing on it the water's edge becomes unbelievably tricky, worse than a melting sheet of ice. Hence the warning signs and safety railings so far from the actual stream. The bottom line? Be smart, stay alive by staying a safe distance away. It is probably safer to jump into the ocean with a great white shark than to tempt fate above a high waterfall in Yosemite.

TABLE 1. ACCIDENTAL FATAL PLUNGES OFF WATERFALLS IN YOSEMITE. (All episodes are discussed in the text unless otherwise noted.) Words in bold are key elements of incident.

Name, age	Date	Location	*Circumstances*
Austin Ramon Pohil, 21	May 20, 1913	Snow Creek Falls (100+ feet)	*U. C., Berkeley student Pohil* ***tried to cross*** *the head of Snow Creek Falls during spring runoff by scrambling over a wet boulder. He lost his footing and fell.*
Lucille Duling, 16	August 22, 1924	Vernal Fall (317 feet)	*Duling of Hollywood, California arrived atop the fall with her parents and friend Riva Straub. The girls crossed the guardrails and the Merced* ***for a photo****. Lucille* ***tried to rock hop*** *back "just above the fall." She stumbled, fell, and was swept over.*
Forest Case, 12	June 29, 1929	Vernal Fall (317 feet)	*Case of Burlingame, California hiked with Edward Shoemaker atop the fall. The boy* ***waded 20 feet into the river, stopped to admire the scenery,*** *lost his footing, and fell. Shoemaker tried to help but the current swept Forest shrieking over the brink. He was never found.*
Louis Kitzes, 24	June 16, 1934	Nevada Fall (594 feet)	*Kitzes of San Francisco was hiking with 4 friends. He waded into the Merced and jumped onto a rock at the brink of the fall to* ***pose for a photo****. He slipped off and was swept over. His body was found 9 days later.*
Albert Alan Muff, 31	June 17, 1944	Snow Creek Falls (100+ feet)	*Muff of Los Angeles* ***scrambled solo off-trail*** *at the head of the falls to take a* ***photo****. He "apparently slipped on the wet rocks into…Snow Creek" then vanished for 60 days in a deep pool below.*
Mary Majdick, 20	July 20, 1945	Nevada Fall (594 feet)	*Majdick of Oakland lost her footing while trying* ***to retrieve a dropped canteen****. The river swept her over the brink. A hiker found her body in a logjam below Emerald Pool 10 days later.*

Keen Freeman, 11 Orville Dale Loos, 21 (would-be **rescuer**)	July 9, 1946 Vernal Fall (317 feet) *Freeman of Washington, D.C. tried to fill his canteen 60 feet upstream of the fall. He dropped it then tried to retrieve it but* ***slipped*** *into the river. Navy veteran Loos plunged in and caught Keen 15 feet from the brink. He fought for a shoreline rock but the current yanked him free and carried him, holding Keen, over the lip. Freeman's body was found a week later. Loos' 12 days later.*
William C. Hansch, 40	June 3, 1947 Vernal Fall (317 feet) *Hansch of Sacramento* ***solo hiked*** *toward Nevada Fall then* ***mysteriously vanished off-trail****. His knapsack sat 65 feet from the brink. 54 days later Hansch's body was found at the base of the fall.*
John Bernard Thomas II, 16	August 11, 1964 Upper Yosemite Fall (1,430 feet) *Thomas of Bellflower, California hiked to the top of the fall with buddy Robert Perry. Thomas "climbed down to* ***slide on sloping rock*** *to the top of the Upper Yosemite Fall...he was unable to stop and plunged over the precipice [falling] 1,400 feet" to a pool 250 feet from the bottom.* (not in text)
Daniel R. Duda, 12	July 8, 1965 Vernal Fall (317 feet) *Duda of Brilliant, Ohio went over the fall for unknown reasons. His body was found on October 16.* (not in text)
Roberta Mary Hurd, 7	June 21, 1968 Vernal Fall (317 feet) *Hurd of Jackson, California was* ***playing solo*** *from her parents in the water near the fall.* ***Unseen****, she slipped in. She was spotted in the river 20 feet from the brink. Her body was found on July 4th.*
James William Gibson, Jr., 19	July 5, 1968 Upper Yosemite Fall (1,430 feet) *Gibson of Whittier, California had been sunbathing with Luis Ortega, who saw him get up and walk* ***solo*** *and* ***off-trail*** *toward the fall. His body was found at the base of the fall the next day.*
Evelyn Consuela Rosemann, 24	October 18, 1968 Nevada Fall (594 feet) *After 3 days in Yosemite, Rosemann of San Francisco was found by 3 hikers on October 19, 200 feet from the base of Nevada Fall in suspicious and unique circumstances. Whether her death while* ***solo hiking*** *was due to an accident, suicide, or murder was never determined. Rosemann had been raped pre- or postmortem, the latter more likely.* (not included in waterfall statistics but instead is discussed in Chapter 14. Homicide)
Christine Fuentes, 9 Yolanda Delia Fuentes, 30 (would-be **rescuer**)	June 18, 1970 Vernal Fall (317 feet) *The mother-daughter Fuentes of La Puente, California had scrambled* ***off-trail*** *past the safety railing with a family party to sit on rocks and/or* ***wade in the river and pose for photos*** *less than 75 feet upstream of the brink. Christine tried to retrieve a lost hat and was swept over. Yolanda went after her but shot over the brink too. Her body was found 56 days later. Christine was never found.*

Christopher Selden Goldman, 14

June 19, 1970 Staircase Falls (300 feet), Ledge Trail
*Goldman of Davis, California scrambled the closed Ledge Trail with 2 buddies from a YMCA group who detoured **off-route** to nearby Staircase Creek **to drink**. The 2 stopped at the stream but saw Goldman being swept down it past them and over Staircase Falls 300 feet. He was found the next day, 500 feet below.* (not in text)

Nicholas Michael Cordil, 19

July 27, 1970 Upper Yosemite Fall (1,430 feet)
*Cordil of Los Angeles separated from Donald Echenberg to **solo hike off-trail**, saying he was "going to look at the fall." His body was found in pieces in the pools at the bottom, 3 days later.*

Steven Hurston Brown, 9

July 1, 1971 Waterwheel Falls (340+ feet)
*Brown of Hillsborough, California had hiked 10 miles with 4 family members from Tuolumne Meadows to Waterwheel Falls at 6,500 feet. He **solo hiked off-trail** on the sloping granite **for a better look**. He slipped into the river. His body was recovered on August 31, 2 months later.* (not in text)

Victor Vega, 21
Kathleen Ann Alvarez, 16 (would-be **rescuer**)

July 10, 1971 Nevada Fall (594 feet)
*Alvarez of Torrance, California **waded off-trail** into midriver and stood on a rock 50 yards upstream of Nevada Fall **to pose for a photo** with Vega, who followed. Vega fell and was swept downriver. Alvarez reached out to rescue him but slipped off her rock. The current swept both over.*

William Ramirez, 22

July 11, 1971 Vernal Fall (317 feet)
*Ramirez of Gardena, California climbed over the guardrail with his brother then continued **solo to swim** 175 feet upstream of the waterfall. The current sped Ramirez seemingly "in shock." His brother tried to rescue him but could not. He was found 10 days later.*

Randy Friedman, 16

July 20, 1971 Vernal Fall (317 feet)
*Friedman of Hartsdale, New York was with a tour group. He climbed over a guardrail **solo off-trail to fill his canteen**. He slipped into the river and was swept over the fall. Friedman was the fifth victim to die in a Yosemite waterfall in 20 days. He was never found.*

Gregory A. Bershaw, 18

May 28, 1972 Snow Creek Falls (100+ feet)
*Bershaw of Fremont, California had hiked with 2 companions to Snow Creek then continued **solo off-trail** across mossy rocks **to wade in "to refresh himself."** Returning to shore, he lost his footing and was swept over the cascades.* (not in text)

Leah Oliver Good, 49

April 30, 1973 Vernal Fall (317 feet)
*Good, ill with cancer and wife of the Park's assistant superintendent, left a note for her husband that she was **solo** hiking the Mist Trail near Vernal Fall. She never returned. The next day hikers spotted her body in a pool 50 yards downstream of Vernal Fall. She had not drowned but had died from impact.* (not in text and not included in waterfall statistics; also listed in Chapter 13. Suicide)

Patrick J. Rose, 21

October 13, 1973 Nevada Fall (594 feet)
Rose of Cleveland Heights, Ohio hiked with Thomas Stropki atop Nevada Fall. Both men saw NPS warning signs. To ***go swimming****, Rose crossed the guardrail* ***off-trail solo*** *and entered the Merced. It swept him downriver. Rangers recovered his body 5 days later.*

Gregory Edward Brazil, 22

May 19, 1975 Eagle Creek Falls (25 feet)
Curry Co. employee Brazil of Clovis, California walked with Deborah Morgodo ¼ mile up Eagle Creek near the Three Brothers. There Brazil, apparently influenced by drugs, doffed his clothes and ***stood in the creek****. Morgodo heard Brazil scream then saw him slide on his back, feet-first over the lip. CPR failed.*

Harold A. Corwin, 19

July 17, 1977 Hidden Falls (65 feet), Tenaya Creek
Curry Co. employee Corwin of Irvine, California was hiking with friends. Despite their warnings, Corwin ***sat in a water-carved, steeply down-sloping****, 45-foot chute. Unable to stop himself on the polished granite, he slid over a 20-foot cliff/fall. He died shortly after reaching the local hospital.*

David Kingseng Chu, 21

August 18, 1977 Vernal Fall (317 feet)
Chu of Fresno, California climbed over the guardrail and past warning signs to wade midstream to ***take a photo looking straight down over the lip****. Belatedly alarmed, Chu tried to leap to the shore but slipped on the polished, algae-covered rock and shot over the brink. He landed in a crack 250 feet down the cliff face, behind the fall, requiring a challenging rope recovery.*

Dennison Taylor, 23

May 27, 1978 Hidden Falls (65 feet), Tenaya Creek
Taylor of San Carlos, California was camped upstream of Mirror Lake with 5 friends. He wandered off ***solo*** *and* ***off-trail*** *and did not return. His body was found the next day in the second pool within Hidden Falls. The only way to have ended up in this car-sized hole was to have dropped from above the waterfall.*

Richard E. Dix, 26

July 30, 1978 cascades at base of Wapama Falls (1,400 feet)
Dix of San Mateo, California was ***solo*** *backpacking near Hetch Hetchy. Possibly under the influence of drugs, Dix left his gear on the trail between Tueeulala and Wapama Falls and entered the creek where the trail crosses it near the base of Wapama. A helicopter search found Dix's nude body in the cascades.*

Greg D. Taylor, 20

August 2, 1979 Hidden Falls (65 feet), Tenaya Creek
Taylor of Orange, California was a ***solo*** *hiker. Witnesses saw him slip while* ***traversing off-trail*** *around the polished lip of Hidden Falls. He fell 50 feet into a 10-foot wide plunge pool in a series of short waterfalls.*

Kenneth J. Mendonca, 18

August 2, 1979 The Cascades (500 feet)
Mendonca of San Ramon, California and Terry Whelan ***scrambled off-trail*** *into the gorge below Big Oak Flat Road and*

"crawled" barefooted on butts and hands ***for a vertical view down*** *The Cascades. Mendonca slipped down the mossy granite off the edge into the waterfall and fell 200 vertical feet into the next water-filled chasm.*

Mark F. Trifiro, 27

April 20, 1981 Silver Apron area
While trying to ***take a photo****, Trifiro of Hartford, Connecticut slipped* ***solo*** *and* ***unwitnessed*** *on wet, water-polished granite as he* ***walked off-trail*** *along shore above the footbridge over the Merced. The river swept him 250 yards over Silver Apron. He soon died due to internal bleeding caused by bashing during his "swim."*

Omar Antonio Morales, 15

July 1, 1984 Nevada Fall (594 feet)
On a family outing, Morales of San Francisco ***jumped off a slab*** *into the Merced 120 yards upstream of the fall. The current swept him. His brother-in-law leapt into the river to rescue him but had to be saved himself. Morales plunged over the edge.*

Sonia Del Carmen Caceres, 27

June 14, 1985 Nevada Fall (594 feet)
Caceres of Lynwood, California hiked with her husband, Javier, their infant son, and 2 sisters atop Nevada Fall. Noting no "Danger" signs, Sonia ***floated on her back in current*** *125 feet from the brink. When Javier saw her drifting toward it he rushed to save her. But Sonia floated over the fall.*

Kenneth C. Sorenson, 28

October 4, 1987 Bridalveil Fall (620 feet)
Sorenson of Simi Valley, California ***scramble-climbed*** *with Kenneth French to the top of the fall. Sorensen* ***waded in the pools ever closer*** *to the edge to stand 10 feet left of the lip. For unknown reasons Sorenson was next seen 5 feet lower and falling "in a freef-all position…face down and arms spread eagled and screaming" into the pool below.* (accident or suicide?) (not in text)

John Eric Ofner, 20

August 13, 1989 Upper Yosemite Fall (1,430 feet)
Ofner of Santa Barbara hiked with 2 friends atop the fall and went swimming. Ofner walked ***off-trail to the brink for a vertical look****. Turning around he lost his footing and fell facedown into the stream. It swept him over the edge. The impact decapitated him.*

Werner Beinstingl, 29

July 11, 1991 Upper Yosemite Fall (1,430 feet)
Beinstingl, a "rocket scientist" from Goleta, California but originally from Austria, hiked to the top of the fall with a friend. While trying ***to take a "vertical" photo off-trail*** *from the cliff* above *the overlook area, Beinstingl lost his footing and fell over the waterfall.*

Kenneth D. Fawcett, 59

June 4, 1992 Wildcat Falls (about 100 feet), Wildcat Creek
Fawcett of Manhattan Beach, California, his wife reported, had ***scramble-climbed*** *next to the falls.* ***Trying to peer over the brink****, he slipped on the polished granite and fell nearly 100 feet.*

Francois Serge Durand De Fontmagne, 27	August 15, 1995	Nevada Fall (594 feet) *De Fontmagne of Lyon, France hiked with Jean-Francois Petit. De Fontmagne* ***swam*** *in the pool 50 feet upstream of the bridge as Petit* ***photographed*** *from shore. The river carried De Fontmagne over the fall. His probable remains were found nearly 4 months later.*
Daniel Lawrence Rex Kahler, 31	September 3, 1995	Nevada Fall (594 feet) *Kahler of San Diego hiked with Catherine J. Mao atop the fall and* ***swam*** *in a small pool 25 yards upstream of the bridge (as De Fontmagne above had done). He waded knee deep toward mid-stream, lost his balance, and he sped over the lip.*
Zhiming Li, 35	July 5, 1997	Nevada Fall (594 feet) *Li, a software scientist from Irvine, California, hiked with 11 friends atop the fall. He* ***swam*** *above the bridge (as De Fontmagne and Kahler above had done—spring floods had washed away the NPS "Danger" signs). Li fell and was swept downstream. A friend tried to snag him from the bridge but missed. Li went over the brink. His body was found 3 months later 600 feet downstream of the base of the fall and wedged 6 feet down against a rock.* (not in text)
Siddiq Parekh, 31	July 10, 1999	Nevada Fall (594 feet) *Parekh, an "experienced" Yosemite hiker from Diamond Bar, California, hiked with 3 friends. They stopped at Nevada Fall for lunch and to soak their feet. Parekh* ***dunked*** *waist deep (despite warning signs)* ***to cool off****. He slipped and was swept over the fall.*
Chintan Daksheshbai Chokshi, 24	July 30, 2005	Vernal Fall (317 feet) *Chokshi, a native of Ahmedabad, India but residing in Sunnyvale, California climbed through the safety fence and past warning signs* ***to wash/cool his face****. He slipped twice, fell on his butt, and slid into the flow 20 yards upstream of the waterfall which poured him over.* ***One member of the investigative team, Special Agent Dan Madrid, suffered a fatal asthma attack during the recovery of Chokshi's body on September 24.***
Shane Michael Kinsella, 21	August 22, 2005	Upper Yosemite Fall (1,430 feet) *Kinsella of Castle Park in Dublin, Ireland hiked to the top of the upper fall with 2 friends. After drinking a lot of wine, Kinsella* ***posed for a photo****, clowned and pretended to be falling into the waterfall. This shot did not work out, so Stephen Flynn asked Kinsella to pose again. He again pretended to lose his balance, and actually did tumble into the river and shoot over the waterfall.*
Paul Dong Jin Kim, 25	September 6, 2009	Merced Fall (drops 30 feet in 150 feet) *Kim of La Cresentia, California slid down Merced Fall into a pool. Bystanders retrieved him in 3 minutes for CPR but to no avail.*
Ramina Badal, 21 (would-be **rescuer**) David "Nenos" Hormiz, 22 Ninos Yacoub, 27 (would-be **rescuer**)	July 19, 2011	Vernal Fall (317 feet) *All 12 members of the Assyrian Church of the East based in St. George Church in Ceres, California, including leader Genard Lazar, climbed over the safety railings while ignoring warning signs and several onlookers' verbal warnings not to do so. For 30 minutes they visited the river (which due to a 200 percent snow-*

pack and a mild spring, was flowing at a high, 1,000 cfs.) and the lip of the fall, all within the NPS "closed" area. Badal of Modesto, Hormiz of Turlock and Yacoub of Modesto, California, all students, ate, ***played****, and* ***took photos****. Standing to leave, Hormiz slipped, lost his footing, and fell in. Badal reached out to him. He grabbed her hand. She lost her footing and toppled in with him. Hugging one another, they sped toward the fall. Yacoub, now 20 feet behind them, jumped in to rescue them but also lost control. As onlookers screamed in horror, all three shot over the edge. This triple fatality set the record for any group going over a waterfall in Yosemite and also brought the fatal tally at Vernal Fall up to 16, also a record for any Yosemite waterfall. Hormiz was found on August 5, 80 yards downstream of the base of the falls and Yacoub on November 29, 100 yards downstream of the Vernal Fall Footbridge. Badal was found on December 3, 140 yards below it.* (not in text).

Kenneth Norman Stensby, 73

May 6, 2013 — Vernal Fall (317 feet)

Stensby of Edina, Minnesota ***solo hiked*** *to Vernal Fall. He did not arrive back at the Ahwahnee Hotel where he had left a note that he would return by noon. Rangers found his backpack, minus his camera, by the guardrail adjacent to the top of the fall. Two days later helicopter searchers spotted his body near the base of the fall. It seems Stensby did not wash over the fall but,* ***unwitnessed****, somehow fell adjacent to it (trying to take a photo?).* (not in text)

Aleh Kalman, 19

June 1, 2013 — Nevada Fall (594 feet)

Kalman of Sacramento, California was a member of a Second Slavic Baptist Church group who went ***swimming*** *about 150 feet from the lip of the fall. He was swept over it by current driven by about 500 cfs. 3 dog teams and 20 searchers failed for weeks to find Kalman. They discontinued until lower water. On August 2, Kalman's body was found 2 miles downstream.* (not in text)

Andrew Thai, 21

June 18, 2016 — Carlon Fall (~20 feet), South Fork Tuolumne River

While ***hiking****, Thai of Elk Grove, California* ***slipped on wet rock*** *at the edge of the top of Carlon Fall then fell over the falls into the pool below, drowning after suffering impact trauma.* (not in text)

Tomer Frankfurter, 18

September 4, 2018 — Nevada Fall (594 feet)

Atop Nevada Fall, hiker Frankfurter of Jerusalem ***handed his phone*** *to a young woman hiker and asked her to take his* ***"selfie" photo as he "posed" by dramatically clinging to****, and* ***dangling from****, a granite precipice perched, exposed, above 600 feet of air next to Nevada Fall. Bystanders yelled at him that his astoundingly bad plan was "too dangerous," telling him to come away from the cliff. But as the strangely obliging woman with Frankfurter's camera "snapped" photos and bystanders watched in horror, he blurted, "I need help!" Heroic Good Samaritans hurried at their own peril to grab his arms and wrists slippery with sweat. But he slipped from their grips, lost his own, and fell.* (not in text)

James Jerome Youngblom, 64	late June (?), 2021	LeConte Fall (229 feet)
	*Youngblom of Turlock, California embarked on a **solo backpacking hike** from White Wolf to the Glen Aulin trailhead but vanished. His body was found in the waterfall, the second highest on the Tuolumne River, on June 25.*	
Eric R. Freedman, 64	September 25, 2022	Nevada Fall (594 feet)
	***Hiker** Freedman of Folsom, California mismanaged his footing and was swept over the fall.*	
Killian Axel Brocker, 21	July 21, 2023	Vernal Fall (317 feet)
	*Brocker was **swimming** in the Merced above the fall at a near maximum flow and was swept over the fall.*	

Chapter Two

SNOW

Although the year 1932 proved to be a classic year for Ford coupes, it was also a year in the midst of the Great Depression. This was a year when many people could not afford even an old Model T and instead were often forced to hoof it or else remain where they were. In early June of that year Charles Miller, described by the *Mariposa Gazette* (June 9, 1932) as an "aging lumberjack," set off from Mono Lake (east of the Park) on a solo, trans-Sierra hike. His destination was Yosemite Valley. Although it was June, Miller's route crossed a lot of very high country, the road through which had not yet been opened, an event that normally followed the big snowmelt.

For his trek Miller had loaded into his swag one box of pancake flour, grease, and a few handfuls of ground coffee. His first day of walking went well; even though the east side of the range was steeper than that to the west, it happened to be the rain shadow side of the Sierra. Thus the terrain here did not force Miller to slog through deep drifts. He camped that first night in Lee Vining Canyon. The stars rotated crystal clear across the heavens and put on a spectacular show. The Milky Way appeared solid enough to grab. So far so good.

The next day Miller climbed up to Tioga Pass at 9,945 feet. Then he began plodding down the snow-covered surface of the old road toward Tuolumne Meadows. With each step, it seemed, the depth of snow increased.

The previous winter had dumped a lot of snow in the high country. Indeed, as Miller slogged along toward the west he also had gazed in awe across the many square miles of virginal white, blazing bright in the high altitude summer sun. He marveled at the amount of ice out here even while he strained to see the elusive road itself. Snow, snow everywhere. So much snow in fact that by the time he reached Tuolumne Meadows blue flames started shooting up across Miller's eyes.

As his eyesight vanished due to snow blindness, the mostly buried Tioga Road became ever more difficult for him to see. Next his ability to feel it with his increasingly less sensitive, soggy-booted feet also diminished.

Miller tried to stay on the road. But in places drifts had buried it five feet deep and then the sun had semi-melted it into a consistency that all too often resembled wet concrete. Tromping blindly over this white landscape, which offered far fewer navigational clues now than it later would when its granite reemerged, Charles Miller soon found himself inadvertently slogging cross-country. No longer on the road, he soon found himself lost.

As the going became increasingly awkward and exhausting and as the sloping granite grew ever more unfriendly, he next began not just falling, but tumbling downhill fifty feet at a time. Several times he managed to stop his fall only by slamming into a tree.

When Miller at last managed to descend to bare patches of ground he still could not see what it—or his surroundings—looked like. Because of this he repeatedly found himself plunging into pools of snowmelt, sometimes hip deep.

All in all, Charles Miller had trekked himself into pretty serious trouble. Miserable, he bivouacked that night, and then stumbled all the next day, falling, sliding, slamming into rocks and trees and downed timber, getting soaked by ice cold water, but making progress, he hoped, toward Yosemite Valley. His days and nights soon blended into an endless ordeal. On his fourth day out from Mono Lake he ate the last bit of flour from his box. It made only one small pancake.

That day and the next he continued struggling downslope. He no longer stood and walked on two feet. During many stretches he crawled on his hands and knees, groping his way toward the Valley like a wounded bear.

Late on the afternoon of his fifth day, a group of hikers found him crawling along the "Tenaya Trail" (likely the Snow Creek Trail). One of them immediately hurried back down to find help. The next morning a team of rangers reached the 65-year-old Miller. Due to his surprising ability to navigate despite near total blindness and also due to his good fortune of having encountered other hikers, Miller survived his ordeal in the snow and also retained all of his body parts. Maybe the lesson here is: Even if you cannot afford a car, do procure a pair of sunglasses. In reality, Eskimos long ago solved the problem of snow blindness without such lenses. They did this by making an eye shield by creating a blindfold of leather (or cloth) and slicing a pair of slits in it to permit entry of only a tiny fraction of light and of the normal field of view. By moving one's head around one can see enough of the world to navigate but not enough snow reflection to blind oneself.

And maybe Charles Miller should have known this.

Indeed, there exists an eerie prequel to Miller's ordeal and rescue. It occurred seventeen years earlier and yet again during another early June trip over the Old

Tioga Road. During that month in 1915, Ranger Forest Townsley also jumped the gun on the snowmelt. His mission was to check on conditions in the high country. Lakes in the area, he soon found, were still iced over. And almost everything in view remained buried in snow. Once in Tuolumne Meadows, Townsley made his way to Soda Springs, one of John Muir's favorite camps.

Here the ranger found a box upon which someone had very recently written a last desperate letter, a forlorn farewell to the world. Its author noted in it that while hiking he had lost the Tioga Road in the snow at Soda Springs but he was planning to make one more stab at finding it instead of just sitting here and dying.

Because the message scrawled on the box seemed new, the duty-bound ranger thought he should look for the poor wretch lost out there in the snow.

Amazingly, Townsley spotted the man relatively soon. When he got to him he found the wayward snowman acting dazed. He appeared exhausted enough to be struggling along literally on his last legs. What was this poor devil's name? Miller. Where had this Miller been coming from? Mono Lake. And what was the first name of this lost vagabond named Miller? Unfortunately, the *Mariposa Gazette* for June 12, 1915, and perhaps Townsley himself, never reported Miller's first name. We're betting, though, that it was Charles.

Less than three years after Charles Miller's 1932 episode of snow blindness, in January of 1935, yet another serious episode of "man-meets-snow" unfolded in Yosemite's high country. The hiker this time was German-born Carl Bantel. He had been "working" and camping near Lake Eleanor during autumn of 1934. While this may sound industrious enough, residents of the area had expressed concern that after his legitimate work was done he continued to linger and seemed up to no good. Furthermore he was rumored to be carrying a pistol and other weapons.

Rangers immediately located Bantel but found no firearm. He was, though, carrying a sharp hatchet and about fifty pounds of food and other gear. He informed the rangers that he was planning on hiking across Tioga Pass. Bantel next told John Myers of White Wolf that he planned to hike east over the mountains. Myers had grubstaked Carl Bantel with salt pork and other groceries but now tried to dissuade him from his trek by explaining how an early winter storm, even during November, could trap him. Myers felt compelled to explain this because he held reservations about the man's mental acuity. Bantel, he noted later, was not merely a German from the Russian border and not a born Westerner but also seemed a bit mentally unbalanced.

Notwithstanding John Myers' well-meaning misgivings, Bantel had crossed the Sierra multiple times before; hence his doing so yet again may have seemed routine. At any rate, as his footprints later would reveal, Bantel started for the summit despite the man's warnings.

As fortune would have it, soon after Bantel began his tramp up the Tioga Road, it began snowing. Hard. So hard that between November 15 and 21, the white stuff had piled up to a near-record level. More to the point, this "instantaneous" snowpack evidently trapped Bantel.

More than six months later, on June 11, 1935, Government workers plowing the Tioga Road found Bantel's diary near the recently half-burned barn of the Yosemite Creek Ranger Station. The sad entries he had penned described forty-one cold and hungry days between November 25 and January 4. He had arrived at this unburned (at the time) building, he noted, with 2½ pounds of coffee and only the same weight of salt pork. This was not much grub to sustain a person during a five-month winter.

Bantel's entries, identical every day for his first week, reveal the quality of his fare when it was most sumptuous: "Coffee; water off [of] salt pork." After that first week ended, by December 2, Bantel wrote that he was now eating, "water from boiling grain dust." This dust he likely had found in the stable area as left-over feed for horses—if you ever have watched horses as they habitually vacuum clean the ground for every last grain of oat, then you know how pathetically thin Bantel's "dust soup" must have been.

Making his situation even more painful at zero temperatures, Bantel had not even been carrying a blanket. In an attempt to stay warm he had filled a couple of gunnysacks with hay and used these as his bed in the corner of the building. He also had stuffed oiled scrap paper into the cracks between the boards to better insulate the barn to retain heat from the wood stove. To prevent yet more loss of his own dimming body heat he tied rags around his wrists and ankles.

After December 10, Bantel had nothing left to eat except salted water.

On day forty-one, January 4, his diary entries ceased. His journal includes no mention of his having made, or seriously contemplated making, a final effort to hike back to "places of habitation [he knew to be] not far away." In his final throes of starvation Bantel may have decided to burn the barn—still well stocked with firewood—possibly as a signal to attract rescuers.

The road workers five months later found his starved and nearly mummified body sprawled on a rock ledge (and on the cover of this book) sixty feet from the cabin in which he had been bivouacking. Inside it the rude table still stood set with a pan of saltwater with a spoon in it. *The Superintendent's Monthly Report* for June, 1935, referred to Carl Bantel as an "eccentric mountain hiker."

The tragic saga of Carl Bantel's last trek is unusual but not unique. As early as January 18, 1886, white pioneers ended up with cold, snowy obituaries in Yosemite. Fifty-two-year-old John "Saw Mill" Johnson provided the earliest known record of this sort. Johnson was a Norwegian immigrant who worked as a saw miller for Snyder and Company at Hites Cove on the South Fork of the Merced River. Not being able to afford a horse, he walked solo along the "old" Coulterville Road near Foresta with his destination as Yosemite Valley. Somehow—no one knows the exact details—Johnson became hypothermic and froze to death while still on the route.

In light of the many generations of wilderness seekers, skiers, loggers, herders of sheep and cattle, deer hunters, gold prospectors, cavalrymen, and pilgrims of other persuasions to visit Yosemite after its "discovery" in 1849 (see Chapter 14 for more on this), it remains remarkable that so few people have managed to trap themselves in the monster snowpacks that blanket its high country in winter. Of course, "few" is a relative term.

One reason why far fewer people have met tragic ends in Yosemite in the winter than during other seasons is that for many decades most people interested in the place possessed the good sense to get the heck out of the high country before the snow buried them there. The common wisdom for years held that only a fool would dally up there and wait around to be frozen to death. The sport of skiing, of course, transformed that latter classification to one of "winter enthusiast."

An early example of this sort of metamorphosis began on March 18, 1937, when 23-year-old Eleanor Bricca of San Francisco, an "enthusiastic skier," went skiing at Badger Pass. She shot off solo from the "up-ski" hill and shooshed down the slope. Toward the bottom Bricca zigged where she should have zagged. More specifically, she turned to the right toward Peregoy Meadows instead of left toward the Ski House.

Once committed, she continued sliding along in the wrong direction. As the day waned and no familiar landmark revealed itself, it dawned on her: "I knew I was lost.... And as I thought I was on or near one of the ski runs, I figured the best thing to do was to wait until someone came along."

As dusk dimmed the slopes, Eleanor did what most men would never do, she admitted her dilemma to herself, stopped where she was, and sat down on a tree trunk to await help.

Night fell. So did the temperature. Still she sat on her log. She then wondered again and again: Would she have to wait until morning before someone showed up? It was cold out here and daylight would not arrive for a long time.

Oddly—but fortuitously—searchers had set off fairly soon once Bricca failed to return; an army of more than 100 people began scouring the surrounding hills. These included rangers, skiers from the local Winter Club, and young men from the CCC (Civilian Conservation Corps) camp in the Valley. Using flashlights, they prowled the slopes and the woods around Badger Pass. In fact, sitting there on her tree trunk, Bricca saw their lights playing peek-a-boo between the pines a few hundred yards away.

She yelled to them for help. Then she waited. No one answered, no lights pointed in her direction, and no nocturnal skier veered toward her. She cried out again. Still, no one seemed to notice.

Indeed they did not. For whatever reason, Bricca seemed unable to alert her many potential rescuers. Even so, she remained in place. To stay warm she walked in circles around her log, she later would admit, and "sang songs throughout the night to keep awake and to keep my spirits up."

With the coming light, Eleanor found herself half frozen and still wedded to that same tree bole. At least now she could see. Meanwhile yet another party of searchers led by Ranger Jerry Mernin noted a ski trail deviating from the regular run. With daylight now an ally, they followed these fresh tracks down the mountainside for two miles. There they found Bricca: shivering uncontrollably. She was still sitting on her log.

For another illustration of winter enthusiasm gone cold, consider the bizarre misadventure of 25-year-old college student William P. Jacobs. On February 8, 1946, he went skiing with a few companions at Badger Pass where he lost his glasses in the snow. Being severely nearsighted without them, he looked around for a familiar landmark or a face he recognized. He "saw" neither. Meanwhile his companions veered off in some unknown direction. To compound matters, as Jacobs headed the way he reckoned the ski lodge must be, a blizzard started dumping huge, white flakes across the landscape.

In the whipping hurricane of flurries, Jacobs skied off in the wrong direction and into a white no-man's-land.

Jacobs' friends had lost sight of him. But by the time they realized this and started looking for him, his tracks had already been obliterated by blowing, falling snow. This storm, the first of two that would bury the Nearsighted Mister Jacobs, lasted 36 hours and dropped 32 inches of snow. The temperature sank to five degrees.

Plunging through this new powder, searchers soon combed the region for William Jacobs. They peered into every suspicious-looking, snow-blanketed nook and cranny. None of it produced the lost skier. William Jacobs, it seemed, had vanished. And his prognosis appeared anything but positive. Veteran trackers concluded that no one in that beautiful but frozen mess out there could survive more than two days without shelter.

When the weather finally cleared, Jacobs' parents joined the expanding search effort. Despite dire predictions that the young nearsighted skier could not still be alive, rescuers continued probing the region in earnest. They hunted until a second blizzard rolled in and dropped even more snow. Overall the searchers continued for ten agonizing days over a twelve-mile diameter of terrain. Eventually almost everyone gave up. Even Jacobs' parents now began to cope with the inescapable loss of their son. He was out there, somewhere, frozen and buried under several feet of snow. Crushed with despair, his parents returned home. They resolved to return in the spring when the melt began and look then for his body. And for closure.

On day eleven, District Ranger Duane Jacobs (no relation) and Assistant Chief Ranger Homer Robinson, spied a suspicious looking hump well off the skiing route. The two searchers veered over to investigate. Maybe it was the lost kid's body.

Indeed it was. But the body greeted them weakly with a "hello." Lost and nearly blind, William Jacobs had bumbled the wrong way through that first storm but had stumbled upon a small, wooden NPS cache containing a rescue toboggan and blankets. Using these he had constructed a lean-to shelter in which he bivouacked, awaiting rescue.

No rescuers, however, had come. Days had passed. Many of them. One after another. Snow continued to fall. Lots of it. Overall, things looked pretty bleak even to a nearsighted college student. But he continued to lay there in his improvised cocoon for a very long and miserably cold and hungry eleven days...hoping for the best and waiting for the sound of a human voice.

Somewhat stunned by their find, the rangers reported that despite Jacobs being ravenously hungry and despite his long ordeal—and two frozen toes—the young, and now skinny, Mr. Jacobs still possessed the strength to walk out under his own power.

As the years passed the number of winter visitors to Yosemite multiplied. But not all of them flexed the survival muscles in their heads hard enough when faced with the backcountry. An example of this involved 34-year-old Arthur Vern "Jern" Klingenberg. On March 2, 1970, the Kern-Kaweah Chapter of the Sierra Club had planned to begin an eight-mile snowshoeing trip along the trail from Badger Pass over Horizon Ridge to the Ostrander Ski Hut (empty and phoneless at this time). But after Ranger James Holcomb warned its members of impending moderate to heavy storms the club reluctantly cancelled this trip. Better safe than sorry, some of them muttered to each other in disappointment.

Four members of the club, however, muttered something else. "Jern" Klingenberg of Bakersfield, California decided with three others—Martin Clark, age 43, James Holly, age 29, and Ramona Rickles, age 35—to go snowshoeing anyway the next morning (Saturday) on the same planned route. Once Ranger Holcomb learned of this foursome's intentions, he strongly advised them yet again to not go.

They went anyway. And, as predicted, it snowed. As if actors in a contrived training film intended to portray what not to do in the winter, the four found themselves slogging along all day in a blizzard that dumped a one-day total of twenty-three inches. Worse, seven miles out, a mere one mile short of the ski hut, Klingenberg, who had been experiencing problems with his shoes and with falling back, collapsed. He seemed unable to continue. Because his three companions were tired anyway, all four decided to bivouac dinnerless in their tent and sleeping bags.

So far, things could have been a lot worse. Then they headed that direction fast. Klingenberg, who had been complaining of heartburn two days before, now vomited and complained of suffering upper abdominal pain. His companions—one of whom, Rickles, never had been on snowshoes prior to this outing—decided to return seven miles to Badger Pass in the morning to fetch help. So, on Sunday at 7:15 a.m., the three Sierra Club members left Klingenberg suffering alone in his tent. Why did they simply leave him alone?

"It was a soul-rending decision," said Martin Clark, M.D. at home in Delano (as quoted in *The Fresno Bee* on March 4, 1970). "We did what we thought was the best thing under extremely trying circumstances."

Ten more inches of snow now fell, adding to Saturday's twenty-three inches. This ever increasing snow depth slowed the trio immensely. It took them twelve hours to return those seven miles. By then it was dark.

That evening Ranger Holcomb asked Clark to help him locate Klingenberg during the following morning. Both Clark and James Holly now told Holcomb that they could not help because they had preexisting commitments. When Holcomb flatly told both men they had a responsibility to Klingenberg and "I expect one of you to go," neither man responded positively (noted in a March 11, 1970, Yosemite National Park memorandum). Instead both men merely reiterated that they had obligations. Clark did add to Holcomb that his directions to Klingenberg's tent were exact and no problems should be encountered in finding it.

Ranger Holcomb arranged for the Tucker Snow Cat to locate and then evacuate the incapacitated Klingenberg. The machine, Holcomb soon heard, had sustained damage to its steering shortly after setting out to help. Next Holcomb learned that repair parts for the vehicle would not be immediately available. In that no other vehicle could replace it in a timely way, Holcomb set out alone on skis on forty-two inches of new snow to search for Klingenberg. By now it was late morning.

Behind him men worked to repair the Tucker and, as Holcomb had also requested, to order a helicopter. Holcomb had also requested borrowed use of the Curry Company's Trackmaster. Meanwhile, after Holcomb had set off on skis, Ranger Dick Marks nixed the helicopter in favor of that surface vehicle. This decision turned out to be yet another burden for Holcomb to bear. With late timing, the Park learned that the Curry Company's Trackmaster also had broken down. Now it was too late to use a helicopter. Yet again Holcomb was on his own. It almost made one believe in fate.

By 5 p.m., Ranger Holcomb had plowed his way by skis to the area where Clark had indicated. But, circling in the thick cover of heavy, wet snow, he could find no sign of the tent. Search as he might, nothing tent-like appeared in the fading light. He now radioed in his report that he could not find Klingenberg in the area where his buddy Clark had indicated. Finally, the Park ordered Holcomb to bivouac at the Ostrander Ski Hut a mile farther then return in the morning to try again. Holcomb did so.

Up early, he donned his skis again and skied back into the search area, arriving by 7:50 a.m. During the evening before, the Park had also "ordered" James Holly (another of Klingenberg's snowshoeing buddies) by phone in Porterville to return to Yosemite to help locate his now missing, "impossible- to-miss" companion. Holly arrived back in the Park at 7 a.m. to accompany other rangers riding in on the now-repaired Tucker Snow Cat.

Late during that Tuesday morning Ranger James Holcomb, still alone, finally found the elusive tent. It had collapsed and had been partly snowed under. This explains his difficulty in finding it. As Holcomb neared it, he next saw that the door of the flattened tent lay open. Klingenberg, hatless, lay sprawled within this opening. Eclipsing any hope that Holcomb had arrived in the nick of time, snow now covered the prone man's lower body. The autopsy revealed Klingenberg had died of "cold and exposure" a day earlier, on Monday morning.

Compared to outings made during temperate seasons, those done in high country snow pose several extra challenges to winter enthusiasts. At the risk of belaboring the obvious: Snow is cold enough to kill. It soaks clothing and increases vulnerability to hypothermia. Snow is more exhausting to traverse—whether via cross-country skis, snowshoes, or just plain boots—than hard ground. It "conceals" trails, particularly from people lacking route awareness. Snow also "irons out" the topography, makes it "featureless" and easier to get lost in. Exposed routes on cliffs become drastically more slippery when snow melts then refreezes on them. Snow also conceals the path's true edge—where the rock ends and thin air begins. Snow under a bright sun can blind a person. As if all this were not enough, snow also lowers the flammability of natural tinder precisely when a fire is most desperately needed—as dramatized so perfectly in Jack London's classic tale "To Build a Fire."

For yet another illustration of how snow beguiles seekers of scenery in Yosemite consider the January 14, 1973, experience of 21-year-old Robert "Robin" Baxter of Santa Rosa, California. Baxter decided to solo hike to Little Yosemite Valley. To embark on this trail he first had to deliberately step over the cable that held the sign that read "TRAIL CLOSED." Due to a recent heavy snow and to the reality that this section of the gorge gets no sun for months on end during winter, the trail is often officially closed to travel (at these times an alternative winter route exists).

Nearing the top of Nevada Fall in a spot where the trail was carved from bedrock, Baxter stopped to take a photo of the partly frozen waterfall. Looking through the viewfinder, he realized he needed a better location for the ideal shot. To get it right, the young man inched over the snow-shrouded path onto its icy edge. Yes, he thought as he inched toward infinity, this looks about right.

As Baxter's eyes focused on beauty, his smooth-soled cowboy boots slipped.

Maybe "slipped" is putting it mildly. Robin Baxter actually slid off the path and tumbled 200 feet down the steep snow-covered, granite talus, bouncing and banging all the way. Grinding to a stop was no picnic either. When he tried to move his body at the bottom, various nerve endings screamed at him to remain still. Although X-rays had yet to confirm it, he had fractured all five of his lumbar vertebrae. He also had sprained one ankle and dislocated the other. On top of these injuries his multiple hits against the granite had abraded and bruised several other parts of his body.

Being crippled and stranded off trail at nearly 6,000 feet elevation in the middle of winter was bad. Really bad. But on the good side, he knew he was within a couple of hundred feet of the trail. Someone would surely happen along, he thought, and when they did he could yell to them. On the bad side of the scale again, aside from his many injuries, he could not even see the trail. Worse, in addition to his now too tight, circulation-reducing cowboy boots, he was dressed only in a pair of corduroy jeans and a light, water repellant windbreaker. And, of course, even worse yet, that trail upon which a Good Samaritan must happen along if Baxter were to survive was, again, closed.

Thus began for Robin Baxter an almost unbelievably long ordeal of yelling—and of freezing. In his pocket he had a small bag of dates, less than twenty of them. Having no idea how long he might be stuck here, he immediately rationed himself. Only four dates every two days. For water he gnawed on ice like some sort of giant crippled beaver.

Meanwhile the cold days and the absolutely freezing nights passed, one then another, then another, then another, and yet another…

An appallingly miserable nine days after Robin Baxter fell, three Bay Area teenagers hiked the frozen Mist Trail. The trio thought they heard faint yelling from above them. They followed these desperate sounds. Finally they edged close enough to establish good voice contact with someone who seemed to be in trouble (though they never did reach Baxter physically). They next hiked back down the trail after yelling a promise to him that they would go for help.

At long last Robin Baxter's ordeal of pain and hypothermia seemed to be over.

Rangers Joe Abrell and I (Farabee) were first to arrive on site. The kid was a mess. Even so, at first, we doubted he had been trapped there as long as he said because he seemed to be in such surprisingly good spirits. We quickly discovered, however, that Robin's feet were frozen solid in those thin, tight fitting cowboy boots. And despite his bonhomie of the moment he admitted that if help had not arrived that very day, he was seriously thinking of slitting his wrists with ice.

Although he would soon lose one foot to frostbite, Robin Baxter was, despite seriously bad odds, alive.

For reasons some people understand perfectly while others find unfathomable, Yosemite's backcountry in winter acts as a Siren. And the outcome of following the voice of this Siren can prove as surprisingly unpleasant as during the days of Odysseus.

Consider the saga of 20-year-old David Heiller. In 1973, he set out on a cross-country backpacking trip through the Yosemite backcountry. This journalism student from the University of Minnesota had allowed himself two weeks to cover the ground between Yosemite Valley and Snow Creek. Having made a shakedown hike shortly before, he had learned a few things. Apropos of his new insights, for this solo trek he had packed plenty of rice, dried soup, and pancake mix, and of course, vital for a budding journalist, books and writing materials.

What Heiller failed to pack was a map. Indeed, not only did he not carry a map, he did not even study one in advance for routes between the Valley and Snow Creek. Along with a vacant space in his gear where his map and compass should have been Heiller also failed to tote a reliable waterproof container for his matches. To make his prospects dicier yet, the young would-be journalist neglected to inform anyone in the Park that he would be hiking the high country in general, let alone tell anyone about his specific destination or particular route.

How important is any of this? We'll see.

David Heiller started up the iron-hard granite on November 3. Had the Gods of Backcountry Weather been smiling at Heiller during his November quest for a painlessly pleasant nature experience, his "planning" might have played out without a hitch. But asking for dry skies for two straight weeks during November, one of the four snowiest months of the year in the Sierra, is asking a bit much of the Gods.

Despite the odds, Heiller had a great first week. But on November 10, snow started flopping out of the sky. It quickly blanketed the entire landscape. The flakes did not merely flurry; they poured from the sky incessantly and with an apparent vengeance—for nine days. Trails grew murky then repeatedly eluded him for long stretches. Drifts transformed each walk in any direction into a calorie-draining slog. Then the trails vanished.

David Heiller pressed onward. He irrevocably committed himself to getting someplace where other human beings could and did live. He knew otherwise he would die. To find such a place it seemed immaterial whether he continued ahead or retreated by backtracking; he was halfway "there" whichever direction he chose. Inconveniently, he was also halfway away.

Almost as soon as the first white stuff carpeted his neighborhood, Heiller decided to begin rationing his food. This was a smart move. This became even easier to live up to when his matches grew too wet to light a fire. In that the idea of devising a bow-and-drill set-up to build a fire by friction also eluded him (to many people this seems like an almost supernatural ability, but it is merely a matter of technique—and friction), he found himself eating cold, soggy uncooked rice and dried soup glued together with snow and occasional pancake batter. This fare held limited allure despite the large metabolic demand of slogging ever onward through deepening snow.

Eventually, however, no measure of sheer determination and icy uncooked rice balls could substitute for good prior planning, fire-building skills, or for the ability to orienteer with a topo map and compass. Nor could these compensate for the fact that no one knew that Heiller was out there somewhere and/or that he was supposed to show up at Snow Creek by November 17.

Not surprisingly, after several days of trudging through the snow, punctuated by evenings with his pen, his books, and his prayers, David Heiller finally admitted to himself the Big Truth—he was lost.

This insight hit him on November 19; this was sixteen days after he had begun his two-week hike. This also was the day when the seemingly unending storm finally did end. While this switch in the weather may sound promising, even liberating, the snow-buried landscape now offered the mapless Heiller no clue as to where he was. This insight into being lost was not a good moment. Even so, whatever books he had been reading and whatever thinking he had done had imbued in him a positive attitude—a survivor's attitude.

"I decided that I wanted to live," Heiller later admitted, "and I was not going to let some snow stand in my way."

Continuing to slog, trudge, push, kick, and wade along, breaking trail with ice-cold boots while using the sun as his compass, the young man made very slow progress. He painfully inched into the lodgepole pine forest and granite knolls near May Lake, a mere fourteen miles from Yosemite Village, by late November. Although still uncertain about where he was, Heiller refused to give up. "What kept me going [was] reading, writing, and praying, and luckily I managed to keep my wits about me."

On November 30, twenty-seven days after David had hiked out of Yosemite Valley, three cross-country skiers came across the exhausted and still lost youth. They fed him hot food and assisted him to the relative security of the comfort station built of cinder blocks at Tenaya Lake. From there he was taken to Snow Creek—his original destination. A helicopter from Lemoore Naval Air Station eventually shuttled him to Lewis Memorial Hospital in the Valley.

Those three Good Samaritans truly saved David's life and in the nick of time—the very next day in the high Sierra it snowed yet another fourteen inches.

Obviously a person solo in the backcountry during winter need only fail to cope with one or two of the "extra" challenges posed by snow to sink into serious trouble. Consider next the strange story of 68-year-old Edgar Gordon. On April 4, 1975, Gordon, a medical doctor and dedicated jogger from Madison, Wisconsin, went cross-country skiing on the Dewey Point Trail with his 28-year-old son Stuart. Intending to be out for only a few hours, the pair carried no trail map, no food, no heavy clothing, and likely no compass. Nor did they sign out on the trail register.

Where Dewey Point Trails #14 and #18 intersect, Dr. Gordon stopped and told his son that he was tired. Instead of continuing on, the elder Gordon now added, he planned to return to their car up at Summit Meadow via Trail #18. Meanwhile Stuart could continue skiing on #14.

To both men this seemed a reasonable plan. After all, the parking area was not far away, the slope back up to the car not too steep, and while the weather was not exactly clear, neither was it a blizzard. Yet.

Stuart continued skiing only for about twenty minutes beyond that last intersection. Something clicked in him at this point; he decided to return. Back at the junction he veered onto Trail #18 and began following tracks he assumed to have been made by his father's rented skis. Maybe he would catch up with him even before reaching their car.

When Stuart Gordon arrived at their vehicle he looked around for his father. Dr. Edgar Gordon was nowhere to be found. This place was unequivocally their rendezvous point. The elder Gordon's not being here alarmed Stuart. He now wondered: Had he truly been following his father's tracks in the snow or instead been following someone else's? At this point there existed no way to be certain.

Stuart could not endure merely sitting at the car and waiting for his missing father to appear. His dad, he now reasoned, should have been here. If he was not here, then something unplanned must have happened. Maybe that something required Stuart's presence to fix. Now unable to stop wondering what sort of reason best explained his father's failure to show up, Stuart Gordon left a marker at the car then he began retracing his route on Trail #18 to search for the missing man. He now stopped to ask each person he met whether he or she had seen his father.

None had. And by the time Stuart reached the intersection where they had separated, his anxiety and frustration were rubbing together to produce alarming friction. But maybe a harmless explanation still existed. Had his father simply detoured onto a different route back to the car? A longer, slower route? And, if so, was he now there at the vehicle, perhaps impatiently waiting for his son? To check on this, Stuart now returned again to his car.

His father was not there. And no note or signal had been left to communicate his having been there. This situation had now deteriorated to bewildering. Stuart hurried back to the intersection of Trails #14 and #18 yet again. He stood and searched around him. He stared down at the crisscrossed tracks left by skis in the snow. As newly falling snow filled in these long channels he wondered: What could this now vanishing maze of tracks really tell him? He gazed around. He yelled out for his father. He listened for a response. None came. By Stuart's third return to their car—now being buried by a serious storm—he had run out of ideas for finding his missing dad. He seemed to have utterly vanished.

Desperate, Stuart Gordon finally contacted the Park.

Badger Pass Ranger Rick Smith became the "Search Boss." As acting SAR officer at the onset of the operation, I (Farabee) helped coordinate Rick's efforts. Both the NPS and Curry Company snowmobiles became the search vehicles during the now on-going storm. We followed each suspicious track departing from either trail. Finding no lost skier on any of these, we next followed the Bridalveil Creek Trail. By now darkness had fallen. The air pierced by the beams of searchlights appeared as that classic black field populated by an endless bewildering blizzard of dazzling, streaking white flakes. While visibility now was not exactly nil, neither was it in our favor—or in Dr. Gordon's.

We reached McGurk Meadow. Still we found no sign of the missing man. By 9:30 p.m., we had a dozen SAR personnel out there hunting in winds gusting to forty knots, genuine blizzard conditions. We strung ourselves across the white-out landscape in a straight-lined, true grid search to pick up every conceivable lead. Hour after hour we combed the primary trail.

No one called in his having located Gordon. In fact, the only thing we found that was alive was a cinnamon teal duck I spotted that had been forced down onto the ground by the storm. I placed the duck in the front pocket of my water-proof cagoule. With its head poking out of this shelter, we kept moving forward, farther along the search grid. (Eventually another ranger released the bird, alive and well, in El Portal.) By 3:30 a.m. we had run out of new ideas that could work in the dark during a blizzard. We next asked for assistance from the Rescue and Coordination Center at Scott Air Force Base. They promised to send help as soon as the weather broke.

Meanwhile it did not break; instead thirteen inches of new snow fell.

The next morning we hit the snowfields again to resweep every local trail. We expanded our search to other trails. We continued looking under every tree canopy and sheltering rock. At some point, we reasoned, the lost doctor, despite mild hypothermia, must have realized he was lost and that he had no hope of finding his way back in the dark, especially during a blizzard. At that time, he most likely would have sought sanctuary by huddling under any natural feature that offered a hope of shelter.

The blizzard continued, making all of our work nasty work. We scoured the landscape all day long. Again no one found any sign of Edgar Gordon. We finally terminated our efforts again—temporarily—at dark that night. We resumed at dawn on day three. Despite how lousy the weather had been so far, now every condition worsened. Skiing and then even snowshoeing proved nearly impossible. With each new inch of snow, hope for finding the lost 68 year-old dimmed.

We decided to fly in famed search-and-rescue strategist Bill Syrotuck and his team's well-trained avalanche dogs from Seattle—courtesy of the United States Air Force. Their three dog teams joined the existing searchers and began looking again on day four. Meanwhile it snowed yet another seven inches.

No doctor.

Ditto for the search results on day five.

Finally, on day six, we faced a harsh reality. We had no choice but to release the dog teams to return to Seattle. Despite having used dozens of searchers and having employed every tool we could lay our hands on, after almost a week of effort we still could not find Edgar Gordon.

In spite of how well he had eluded us—however inadvertently—he failed to remain lost forever. Seven weeks later, on May 26, while flying in a Lemoore helicopter over territory well outside the original wide search area and now working on another rescue mission, Ranger Dan Sholly was offered a belated opportunity to scan for the missing man. The pilot soon lowered a corpsman to the current accident site. This phase of their operation incurred a fifteen-minute interval during which everyone had to wait. Sholly asked the pilot something like: Since we've got this time, let's use it to take a look at the rim area above the waterfall (Bridalveil). Within a very few minutes Sholly spotted a patch of light blue nylon emerging from under melting snow.

Sholly instantly knew what the nylon implied. The Lemoore helicopter crew now lowered him by cable fifty feet into the low brush and manzanita. Here he found Gordon kneeling upright and facing uphill, from whence he came. The lost man's position was fifty yards from the Valley rim and about 100 yards west of Bridalveil Fall. Sholly radioed up to the hovering airship to lower him a body bag. The Lemoore team ultimately raised Sholly and the now half-preserved Dr. Gordon back into the aircraft. The team then completed their original rescue mission.

How, we wondered, had Dr. Gordon gone so wrong as to end up here?

Instead of going south on that fateful day to their parked car, Dr. Gordon had gone directly in the wrong direction, due north. To do this he had to deviate significantly from any existing trail and then strike across virgin snow. And to go this way he also had to decide to proceed downhill instead of uphill—he had originally skied downhill with his son, so logic alone would have impelled him to choose only a return direction that led uphill. How had he managed to make so many lethal mistakes a mere hour away from his car?

The postmortem revealed no injuries. Edgar Gordon, likely hypothermic and definitely disoriented, had simply taken the path of least resistance, one leading downhill. He had skied north to the south rim of Yosemite Valley. Once overlooking the Valley, he next had decided to drop down into an ever more rugged lateral drainage not far from the top of Bridalveil Fall but miles away from Trail #18. Finally the worsening route and the creeping cold overwhelmed him; he stopped, kneeled, hunched over, and died. How far off-track had the elder doctor veered to become so lost?

That summer, aided by a helicopter, Ranger Sholly and Stuart Gordon revisited the site where the latter's father had died. They found one of the elder man's ski poles. Retracing the lost man's ill-fated route on foot, they found, would have taken all day to cover this same terrain.

Not every mishap due to snow happens in the backcountry, or even off-road. Indeed the roads themselves can present some of the Yosemite's most intense snow dangers. Once the Tioga Road was built, for instance, it required regular maintenance. The same hazards incurred during construction had to be faced again repeatedly. Seasonally for decades Yosemite roads and trails have been buried by landslides, blocked by hundred-ton rocks, and strewn with dozens of downed trees scattered as if in a giant game of "pick-up sticks." Both winter snows and summer rains have carved holes that undermined the pavement. On top of these, floods have washed away huge sections of road, as have week-long downpours blowing in off the Pacific Ocean.

One problem here is the Tioga Road was neither designed nor engineered for winter. This is because even though its route had been discussed and planned for decades, it was surveyed and built during a series of drier years. And even though winters halted road construction, which should have been a heads-up, these seasons were mild enough that they failed to raise additional concerns about routing. The issue of winter arose only when planners proposed to relocate the road away from locations where snow lay unmelted longest to thus facilitate earlier openings. Some people feared that a new Tioga Road would be opened year-round to bring in a winter sports complex and additional infrastructural development to Tuolumne Meadows. Most opposition to this road focused on its impacts on scenery and from increased access. True, construction techniques were heavy-handed. Conservationists still abhor the great scars gouged for the road across the open granite at Olmsted Point and Polly Dome near Tenaya Lake.

The process of seasonally opening any road crossing a mountainous high pass after its winter closure is both a science and an art. Road crews in the Sierra can testify to this. So can those who routinely tackle clearing the sixty- to eighty-foot deep drifts on the Going-To-The-Sun-Highway in Montana's Glacier National Park. Indeed there is nothing that anyone does in Glacier that is more demanding or more hazardous than this months-long job.

As might be expected—although hoped against—in Yosemite, employees have died while maintaining the Tioga Road. These were Barry Lee Hance and Sammy Lee Smallwood. (Smallwood is discussed in Chapter 4. Park Builders.)

Ever since the new road was dedicated to the public in June 1961, the Park's road crews have faced learning the hard way what opening and maintaining the road required. And while those performing snow surveys could (and did) routinely avoid Olmsted Point west of Tenaya Lake because of near-constant avalanche danger, maintenance crews possessed no such luxury. The pavement at Olmsted Point crosses a broad shelf of sloping, open granite. At its bottom, or toe, the rock had been blasted and chiseled to cut out a roadway. This cut, it turns out, lies at the foot of an avalanche path. When driving here during summer we can take the safety of the route for granted. But this is not the case during winter or even late spring. Conditions here then turn far more ominous.

Plowing the snow aside here means carving out heavy drifts piled directly across an avalanche run. Crew members have all sensed the extreme danger. Following the record-breaking winter of 1969, opening this road proved somewhat similar to laboring under the blade of a guillotine. When Olmsted Point was partially plowed through during the following spring, an avalanche swept loader operator Lem Barnett off the road and over the side of the mountain. Luckily the snow was so deep that it held him and his machine long enough that both could be rescued. While this was a happy ending, it also had been such a close call that many a road crewman afterward felt in his gut: "Someday somebody's gonna die at Olmsted."

Trial and error learning here led to a pattern of first plowing open the outside lane, then slowly narrowing away the snow holding back the avalanche poised above the inside lane. The tactic became: Let it melt as much as possible but work on it in the mornings while it is still frozen so that when it does loosen and slide no one will be caught in its path. If the mass of potential avalanche snow up there looks too ominous, try explosives to bring part of it down. This blasting, however, precipitated some close calls and otherwise failed to work well. Often it seemed to increase the danger of yet another slide. During some of these early experiments, no avalanche experts were called in to advise procedure during openings of Tioga.

In 1983, yet another extremely heavy winter, the snow piled to depths both huge and heavy. The crew tried blasting several sections of the road. This failed. When ordered to go up to shoot at Olmsted, one explosive expert demanded first the help of an avalanche expert. A Maintenance Division manager responded to this hesitant blaster, "If we have to ask for help, we're not very professional, are we?"

A strong chief ranger now supported this cautious explosives man by bringing in an expert from California's highway department. Backed by his expertise and by safety provided by rangers, the blaster successfully removed the dangerous snowfield. Most of it cascaded downslope after one large shot.

In 1988, Barry Hance became Mather Road Foreman with the responsibility for maintaining the Tioga Road. He was a helpful guy with a big grin who seemed to make time for everyone. Those who knew him best said he was also an excellent and safe operator who would never shove someone else into a job he was not willing to undertake himself. During this era, however, dry years had taken the pressure off the dreaded openings of Olmsted Point. And as each year passed, 1983 increasingly seemed an exceptional year rather than one seminal to redefining the practices of road opening there.

Many national parks characterized by seasonal road openings similar to Yosemite's—Yellowstone, Glacier, and Rocky Mountain—face tremendous pressures from neighboring small communities and localized political constituencies. An open road means money to them. A closed road means lean times. Unfortunately and generally, there often exists little regard for what it takes for Park Service personnel to accomplish the high wire balancing act of keeping these peripheral communities happy without killing anyone. The pressure can be intense. Each community has a favorite politician whom they call upon to lean on park managers.

The winter of 1995 dumped less snow than had fallen during 1969 or 1983, but it still piled up a lot more than any normal year. This snowpack then lasted well into summer. Again, Hance was in charge of opening the Tioga Road. He and his crew had opened one lane and had begun working on other sections. Next they slowly peeled back that inside lane at Olmsted Point. Meanwhile politics reared its head to the point where different directions from management began to complicate the crew's work. For one thing, managers decided not to blast the avalanche.

For another, Maintenance had borrowed less than ideal equipment for this job. Worse yet, no avalanche expert had been enlisted to consult on the challenges now presented.

On June 11, Hance was ordered over the phone to have the road ready and opened to two lanes by June 16. As eventually would be reported in the Park's official Board of Inquiry into this death, according to Barry Hance's wife Kathy (present during the phone call), Barry was told "It *will* open, regardless."

On the morning of June 13, 1995, Hance, admitting that he "had to take some chances" to get the road open in time. He tried peeling away more of that inside lane poised below the avalanche. He plowed it using a bulldozer unequipped with a protective cage for the operator. The avalanche soon lurched downslope and buried him and the machine. An autopsy revealed that Hance had died of major blunt trauma to the chest which caused "rapid suffocation."

Consequently OSHA, the federal government's safety arm, cited the Park twice for "willful" violations of the Occupational Safety and Health Act (of 1970). Among other things, one citation was for lack of job safety analysis, poor avalanche training, inadequate lookouts and rescue capability, and lack of an avalanche consultant for the road opening. The second citation was for the use of an open, unprotected bulldozer when no avalanche assessment had been made. The Park challenged these citations. Ultimately, the next spring, this second citation was reduced from "willful" to "negligent"—not knowingly in violation of the law.

Even so, the Park soon made changes for the next year's opening of the Tioga Road. The Park adopted a road opening policy which included avalanche safety training, hazard assessment based on historical snow records, and stationing nearby emergency response capabilities.

Following the funeral of Barry Lee Hance, his wife Kathy received a specially carved headstone. What effigy had the stonemason carved into it? A bulldozer.

Not long after this, the Park established a Barry Hance Memorial Award: "given to an employee who personifies Barry's hard work, excitement for life, concern for fellow employees and reverence for Yosemite National Park."

What is the upshot of the risks posed by snow in Yosemite? Few to none exist to those who have prepared themselves realistically for the dangers that snow can and does pose to those in Yosemite's backcountry (or on its roads, for that matter). On the other hand, people who enter the high country between October and May wishfully thinking that snow will not pile one or two feet deep on (or during) their outing and therefore have not prepared themselves for the challenges that snow can pose mentally, emotionally, physically, or in equipment needed, are gambling with their lives—and with those of the rescuers sent to find them. Being prepared is more than a motto, it is vital.

TABLE 2. FATAL OUTCOMES FROM BEING TRAPPED OR LOST IN, OR FOOLED BY, YOSEMITE SNOW. (Incidents not discussed in the text are noted.)

Name, age	Date	Location	*Circumstances*
John "Saw Mill" Johnson, 52	January 18, 1886	Coulterville Road near Foresta	*Johnson was a Norwegian immigrant who worked as a saw miller at Hite's Cove on the South Fork of the Merced River. He became hypothermic and froze to death while **walking solo** along the "old" road into Yosemite Valley.*
Carl Bantel, 35	January 4, 1935	Yosemite Creek Ranger Station	*German born Bantel (a.k.a. Otto Miller) hiked the Tioga Road. Near-record snowfall from November 15 to 21 **trapped** him. Six months later, on June 11, 1935, government workers plowing the road found his starved and almost mummified body sprawled on a rock ledge. His diary of 41 days from November 25 to January 4 told of slow starvation.* (Bantel graces the cover of this book.)
Hugh McFadden, 59	December 24, 1935	Wawona	*McFadden had been **drinking alcohol** on Christmas Eve when he fell into the shallow creek bed near his cabin then failed to self-extricate. He was found 2 days later, dead of hypothermia.* (may not have been a snow-related fatality, not in text)
Arthur Vern "Jern" Klingenberg, 34	March 2, 1970	1 mile from Ostrander Ski Hut, Horizon Ridge Trail	*Klingenberg of Bakersfield with 3 others embarked on a planned 8-mile snowshoe trek from Badger Pass to the ski hut. 7 miles in, he collapsed. They bivouacked. In the morning, after 23 inches of new snow, the other 3 **left him alone, sick** in a tent, and returned for help. Klingenberg died of "cold and exposure."*
Edgar Gordon, 68	April 4, 1975	north of Dewey Point Trail	*Gordon, an M.D. from Madison, Wisconsin, cross-country skied with his 28-year-old son Stuart. Tired, Dr. Gordon said he would return south to their car at Summit Meadow while Stuart continued onward. On May 26, 7 weeks later, Ranger Dan Sholly aboard a helicopter spotted Gordon's parka. He had **skied the wrong direction**—due north and downhill, off-trail, to the "rim" of Yosemite Valley not far above Bridalveil Fall—and died of hypothermia.*
Joseph Howard Krischke, 41	December 29, 1993	Badger Pass	*Krischke of Camarillo, California **skied** with 2 teenagers he had just met. He suggested **deviating off the trail** for a more challenging route. They did so. Both boys slowed down when they saw a large bump ahead. Krischke did not. He hit the bump, left the snow, lost control, and **fell head first** against the base of a ski lift tower. He sustained a severe head injury and died in St. Agnes Medical Center in Fresno the next day.* (not in text)

Barry Lee Hance, 43	June 13, 1995	Tioga Road
	NPS employee Hance of Groveland, California was operating a bulldozer 400 yards east of Olmsted Point when an avalanche of snow collapsed and buried him and his machine. The autopsy revealed he died of major blunt trauma to the chest which caused "rapid suffocation."	
Lee McCarthy, age?	April 1 (?), 2011	El Portal Trailer Court #E5
	After having been arrested multiple times, McCarthy was found long deceased and semi-sitting on sleeping bags on a futon among piles of trash in the fenced backyard of Trailer E5 where he had been camping out. McCarthy had medical problems and may have died of possible ***exposure (?)****.*	

Chapter Three

BASE JUMPING

On October 2, 1926, Captain Harold D. Campbell—who happened to be the current United States record-holding pilot for the most hours in the air without a mishap—and Lieutenant W. J. Wallace of the Marine Corps Aviation Station headquartered in San Diego flew two DeHaviland biplanes over Yosemite Valley. This was not the first human flight over the Park, but it would be the first in which someone exited from a perfectly good airplane to take his chances with a mere gossamer canopy of silk. The two pilots circled and took photos. Next they hosted a Yosemite first: Sergeant A. P. Atherton leaped from Campbell's ship from 3,000 feet up and parachuted down between the granite walls to the Valley floor. Even as early as 1926, Atherton was already a bit of a skydiving addict; this was his thirtieth jump. And this jump went off as smooth as silk.

Over the years, people bent on escaping the humdrum have pummeled Yosemite with bizarre ways to play. So bizarre that John Muir, a risk-taker himself, has likely rolled over in his grave so often that he has caused a local seismic phenomenon. But perhaps no form of recreation has proven more controversial than BASE jumping (parachuting from a Building, Antenna, Span, or Earth). In the case of Yosemite we specifically are interested in Earth, or to be more precise, cliffs.

Perhaps not surprisingly, the first recorded BASE jump in any national park area occurred off Yosemite's El Capitan. It took place on July 24, 1966. Who did it? Brian Lee Schubert and Michael Pelkey, both 26 years old and from Barstow, California. At about 5 p.m., both experienced sky divers leaped off the big rock, each to earn a near brush with death. Pelkey sustained a broken ankle and abrasions. A motorist found him limping alongside the road. When rangers responded to this motorist's report, Pelkey informed them that his partner lay more seriously injured at the base of the monolith. Schubert, the rangers soon found, had sustained a broken leg and a broken foot.

For many years, perhaps the most remembered BASE jumper in Yosemite history was Rick Sylvester. After clandestinely building a small ski jump of packed snow at the edge of El Capitan, on January 31, 1972, this accomplished Yosemite climber and skier sailed off the summit. He kicked free of his skis and headed his parachute to the meadow below. He made an unplanned—but relatively safe—landing in a tree. On this, Sylvester's first try, however, his camera had given him trouble. So he stole a second jump to get that footage. Five years later he duplicated his feat by skiing off a cliff in Canada while doubling as 007—James Bond—in *The Spy Who Loved Me*.

Since 1966, at least thirteen other national park areas have "hosted" BASE jumping. The sport gained enough momentum in the 1970s to pose environmental and safety problems in Yosemite. Indeed, more than this, BASE jumping highlighted a fundamental question of values influencing how Yosemite should be managed as a National Park.

Despite these uneasy dimensions of BASE jumping, the Park granted a trial period three months long (August 1 to October 31, 1980) during which jumps were legal. As it had done with hang gliding, the Park required BASE jumpers to obtain a permit, one of a dozen issued per day, and only for El Capitan. The intent here was to have the parachuting community itself somehow self-regulate who was capable of, or qualified to, make such jumps safely. Anyone violating the Park strictures would be prosecuted under Air Delivery 36 CFR 2.36 and under the Endangered Species Act 16 USC 1531 due to seasonal nesting by peregrine falcons on the cliffs.

The experiment did not go well. The Park discontinued it after only sixty-eight days "due to frequent injuries, resource damage, illegal jumps, and spectator management problems experienced during the trial period." The final straw that may have broken the camel's back was the day when I (Farabee) detained a dozen or more would-be parachutists standing, jammed like cattle, in the bed of a big stake truck as it detoured off the Tioga Road to creep past a barrier and onto an officially closed road en route toward the top of El Capitan. The group's intent was to perform a mass BASE jump to be filmed for the popular TV show *That's Incredible*. Only the driver of the truck was culpable (because the parachutists had not yet made any BASE jumps) but this single citation bogged down this project to such a standstill that it fizzled out altogether.

In the bigger picture, some BASE jumpers during this trial period ended up injured. These included broken pelvises and snapped femurs—serious damage, not mere scrapes.

Indeed, on the very first day on which the Park had okayed "trial" BASE jumping, a female nurse and parachuting enthusiast had humped her rig along the trail to the top of El Capitan. Immediately after she flung herself off the huge cliff into thin air and pulled her release cord, her chute tangled. With her canopy poorly deployed she found herself unable to control her descent.

She slammed into the monster granite face. Speeding downward and unable to gain complete control, she whammed against the cliff again several times in swift, glancing collisions. Each hit added to her growing list of "owies." It seemed amazing that when she hit the ground she was still alive.

Park Rangers carried her to the Valley Clinic. There Dr. Jim Wurgler went to work to piece her back together.

One of her many problems was the traumatic, near-total amputation of her nose. It was still present, Wurgler later told me (Ghiglieri), but it now dangled off her face by a thread of skin—like some useless appendage that her body was attempting to reject.

Wurgler, trained as a surgeon and with experience as a military physician in Viet Nam, explained that never before in his medical career had he been called upon to reattach anyone's nose. And now as he racked his memory from medical school and from journals he had read in an attempt to do a functionally and cosmetically good job on this poor woman's face, he felt repeatedly struck by the irony of her garb. She was wearing a unique T-shirt. Now a very bloody T-shirt.

Despite all the gore spattered across it, the shirt's bold print remained all too legible. It proudly read something like: "FIRST WOMAN TO BASE JUMP OFF EL CAPITAN."

Someone at the clinic proved unable to resist the urge to photograph her. Her ironic and grisly snapshot hung on the wall there for years.

The mayhem the Park experienced from BASE jumping during (and after) that trial, noted Chief Ranger Steve Shackelton, posed an important question: Should Yosemite National Park be managed as an "anything-goes circus" with a large force of rangers to pick up the pieces or does its image demand placing limits on activities that notably detract from wilderness values?

The Park opted for the latter.

Although Yosemite experienced no fatalities from jumpers during the trial period, a half dozen have since occurred among those parachuting illegally. In addition to these deaths, more than a dozen other jumpers have been seriously injured. Interestingly, compare this with the sport of hang gliding. Not only has sailing off a cliff with a kite remained legal and permissible since 1974 (though descents are regulated to early mornings and with a permit), the sport had been blessed for decades by a notably nonfatal and almost injury-free history. In 1974, for example, 170 flights went off Glacier Point without a serious glitch.

Again, unfortunately, the same cannot be said for BASE jumping in Yosemite.

James Dale Tyler, a 35 year-old from La Puente, California, was a professional movie and TV "stunt" parachutist. He had already made more than a thousand jumps. Some of these were performed for television programs such as *Daredevils*,

That's Incredible, and *To Tell the Truth*. One of his trademark stunts was the seemingly "chuteless" dive that he had personally innovated by creating a concealed rig whose design he guarded very closely as a trade secret. Another of his highly paid stunts was a scenario in which two skydivers—one seemingly without a chute—fall into the void from two separate aircraft, rendezvous in midair, and then descend under one canopy. This latter trick might have come in handy for its innovator on August 4, 1982.

At 6:30 p.m. on that day, Tyler prepared for an illegal leap off Half Dome with fellow thrill seekers 27-year-old Howard G. Dunklin and 20-year-old Patrick Tierney. Because of the late hour, the trio had already attracted a small crowd of climbers and hikers atop Half Dome. One of the three asked one among these to shoot pictures of the divers using their camera. Tyler asked another guy if he would carry down a small amount of Tyler's trash.

The crowd soon metamorphosed into an audience who, according to witness accounts in the Park's incident report, now listened to a brief but cocky lecture by James Tyler on what the three would be doing once they skydived off the world-famous rock. It went something like: "We will dive into a short freefall, three or four seconds, because prevailing wind conditions won't allow us to make the seven- or eight-second jump otherwise possible from Half Dome. We'll coordinate our jumps at five-second intervals. It will take us four or five minutes before we land on the meadow north of Half Dome."

Tyler, witnesses would later report, next asked the crowd to please not say anything to others about this triad of jumps because parachuting was illegal in Yosemite and he did not want to spoil the opportunity here in the future for other clandestine jumpers.

As Dunklin and Tierney stood alongside Tyler during his plea for silence, witnesses were certain these two had heard his "illegal" disclaimer.

The three adventurers made their final preparations and then held hands. Tyler next pulled out a walkie-talkie and confirmed with a feminine voice below that she would be ready to pick up all three within two minutes after they hit the landing zone.

At about 7 p.m. Tyler threw himself off Half Dome. Dunklin quickly followed. Tierney, who had retrieved the trio's camera, spiraled down last. The latter two men made good landings east of Mirror Lake. Witnesses atop Half Dome said that Dunklin very quickly collected his gear then hurried off the meadow and out of sight. Tierney, they reported, popped his chute after a very short free fall. But when he landed, witnesses below said, instead of hurrying off the sward as Dunklin had done, he immediately looked back and up toward the cliff face as if searching for, or staring at, something that he had passed during his descent. Was that something Tyler?

Unlike his two younger companions, Tyler had fallen about a tenth of the vertical distance from the summit to the Valley floor and—as witnessed by climber Kevin Phillips at the base of Half Dome—then had deployed his yellow and orange chute. Bizarrely, his canopy almost immediately "cartwheeled" vertically, spiraling possibly due to wind. This out-of-control descent slammed Tyler into the granite wall where his rig continued to malfunction. He "bounced repeatedly into the cliff" with his canopy still deployed.

The crux came about 600 feet up from the cliff base. Here his chute caught on a ledge and immediately folded up. Tyler now plummeted into the talus at high speed.

Phillips and his climbing partner scrambled to Tyler's position within a minute. These two first responders found him doubled over a rock and face down. He was coughing up blood but he still exhibited a strong pulse. The partner quickly scrambled back down over the rough terrain (it was now about 7:30 p.m.) to seek help. After dark he returned with two more climbers, the closest other human beings available. An NPS Trail Crew also happened to be nearby. They too climbed up over the talus and arrived at about 9:45 p.m. Trail Crew Foreman Tim Ludington joined them a few minutes later.

He now gently turned Tyler over so he was face up. The seriously injured jumper made weak, wet breathing sounds.

Phillips and Ludington worked together to perform CPR. The pair compressed his chest and blew into his mouth for the next hour. Rangers Bob Elliot and Sue Smith arrived. The expanded rescue team continued CPR for another ninety minutes.

Supervisory Ranger Butch Wilson arrived after midnight. He examined the large amount of dried blood on the right side of the victim's head and then searched for a pulse. He found that Tyler now lacked even a carotid pulse (the last pulse to vanish). Wilson instructed the team to go through all of the CPR protocols again. Then he radioed their findings to the Yosemite Medical Clinic, far below.

At 1:10 a.m., six hours after Tyler whammed into the rocks ahead of his trailing streamer of nylon, Dr. Bryan Roberts ordered CPR to be halted. James Dale Tyler had become the Park's first BASE jumping fatality.

Much earlier that evening, when Kevin Phillips had first found Tyler, he believed that had a helicopter been immediately available for—and capable of—whisking the stricken BASE jumper to advanced care within thirty minutes after his impact, Tyler may have had "a fighting chance." Whether Phillips' assessment was accurate or not will never be known. By midnight it was a moot point. Sadly, however, perhaps it need not have been so moot.

Tyler's partners—Dunklin and Tierney—safely below in the meadow, must have suspected that something had gone wrong. This was especially likely with Tierney, who had stood in the open and stared back toward where Tyler had slammed the talus. Even so, these parachutists made it about as difficult as possible for the rangers there to extract even the very simple information that Tyler existed and had made a jump, let alone that he was likely in need of the medical help the rangers could muster.

The encounter between the jumpers and rangers unfolded adversarially shortly after Phillips and his buddy had scrambled to Tyler's impact point to help. Fifteen minutes after the jump, Rangers Neil Williams, Bill Patton, and Dan Dellinges experienced the devil's own time trying to gain vital information from the missing man's two companions. As the rangers approached, Tierney and Dunklin refused to stop walking to answer their questions. Neither man would even make eye contact. And instead of coming clean about what they had just done, they denied everything—including the fact of Tyler's jump. Dunklin brusquely told Williams, in passing, "We're not the parachutists." No surprise, this utterance sounded suspiciously like a guilt-laden evasion.

When Williams, Patton, and Dellinges explained that they needed to check the two packs for parachutes, Dunklin told them to "Blow off!" He flatly denied that the rangers held any right to examine his or Tierney's loads. He said, in essence, that he would not allow a search.

Ranger Williams replied that, on the contrary, he had probable cause for a search. He punctuated this statement by pulling Dunklin's pack off his back. He immediately yanked from it a blue parachute. Another extracted a chute from Tierney's pack. Williams felt a strong concern for the condition of BASE jumper number three who had not made it to the meadow. So he next took Dunklin aside and impressed upon him the Park's need to know whether to mount a rescue mission for the missing man. He asked Dunklin again point-blank what he knew about the owner of the ill-fated yellow canopy which witnesses had said seemed to be in trouble. At this point, instead of providing potentially lifesaving information, Dunklin told Williams: "I'll sue you for police brutality."

Amazingly, despite all this prodding, neither young man would admit they had seen a parachutist in trouble. Nor would either even hazard a guess about where such a person might now be. This delay explains why rock climber Phillips' belief (admittedly, a hunch) that Tyler might have possessed a real chance of surviving had he been evacuated within thirty minutes became moot. Neither Dunklin nor Tierney would give up their comrade. Perhaps they truly believed that protecting Tyler from being cited for BASE jumping was a more important service to their friend than medical attention might have been.

Nonetheless, this denial and de facto "sacrifice" of Tyler failed to pay off. Just before midnight, for violating 36 CFR 2.36(a) and 2.2(a) [illegal parachuting, Case #82-11,144] the two live BASE jumpers went to jail. Meanwhile, Tyler went to the morgue.

This story would seem to end at this point. But as retired Park Historian Jim Snyder notes, *Newsweek* magazine for March 28, 1983, suggested that the ill-fated Tyler was an IRS agent engaged in some sort of sting operation to stop a money-laundering ring for cocaine dealers. The magazine further suggested that he might have been a double agent. More detailed specifics on this have so far eluded us. Muddying the picture, Snyder notes, an *Outside* magazine article during that next month (April) focusing on Tyler's BASE-jumping death did not mention any such covert background. But if *Newsweek's* information was accurate, it suggests the possibility that Tyler's jump gear may have been sabotaged in some way to prematurely end his career. Whether any of this cloak and dagger stuff is even remotely accurate remains unknown.

Despite the Park arresting twenty-eight parachutists in 1984 alone, getting them convicted, fining each one $500 and confiscating their expensive parachuting equipment, thrill seekers continued jumping from Yosemite's cliffs.

The next hairy episode involved 35-year-old Mitchell Reno of Antioch, California. On October 23, 1988, Reno leapt first off Half Dome. Two others followed him. Again, these BASE jumps were clandestine.

Far below the trio of jumpers a pair of climbers—Dave Bengston and Scott Stowe—had been working their way up the granite about 300 to 400 feet from the base of the cliff.

These two heard what they thought was the whoosh of a rock coming at them. They quickly looked up, hoping they would not be forced to try to dodge a granite meteor. Instead they saw Reno plummeting down and trailing a colorful, cylindrical streamer of nylon. The ill-fated adventurer whistled past them, his arms and legs flailing in the air.

A second before he hit, both his chute and his shroud lines stretched upward to their full length. But they never caught air. Reno slammed at high speed into the boulders and brush strewn about the base of Half Dome. He died instantly.

The doomed jumper's error was most likely due, in the parlance, to a case of "brain lock" (a.k.a. stimulus overload) and not to equipment failure. Why is pilot error the far more likely cause? The Park gathered up Reno's equipment and took it to a Forest Service Smoke Jumper parachute specialist for analysis. This expert examined the main canopy and found it to be unmodified and undamaged. More importantly, he found Reno's spring-loaded reserve chute intact, functional, but undeployed. These findings shout pilot error.

The experience of Susan Alaine Oatley, a 40-year-old research scientist from Solana Beach, California, seemed even less equivocal than either Tyler's or Reno's. She jumped off the New Dawn Wall of El Capitan with three others at sunrise on September 25, 1993. Three of the four parachutists safely spiraled down to the meadow below.

The first inkling to the Park that BASE jumpers had dived off the big wall—and that one of them might not have done very well at it—came from Keith Jones who had driven to the Park offices afterward and reported that he had seen a fourth body leap from the top, but never saw a canopy blossom. He said this last skydiver had fallen all the way into the tree line. Upon being eclipsed by trees, Jones added, he had heard an immediate minor "explosion."

Jones next showed rangers where he remembered seeing the plummeting form vanish from his sight. The searchers soon found the woman's badly mangled body. Her brain had been avulsed on impact. Immediately above her splattered remains dangled two canopies—one pink and one blue—badly tangled in the stunted oak trees.

Oatley had indeed popped her chute(s). But she apparently had done so either far too late—literally a moment before she impacted the ground—or else she had attempted to release them so close to the wall that neither properly deployed. Which was it? Oatley, as one of her partners later described it, had failed to at first adopt a "boxman" (horizontal) position from which she next could assume a forward-tracking, head lower position that would slide her across the air and away from the wall. Instead she adopted, probably inadvertently, a reverse-tracking position. This error of allowing her head to be the highest part of her body with her legs lowest while they still were aimed at the wall would have directed her into it. She knew she needed to deploy her chute to survive and therefore did so. But her immediate proximity to the face would not allow her canopy to fill with air. This may explain the ultimate streamer condition of her chutes in the trees above her point of impact with the ground. The other, less likely, interpretation for what went wrong here is she simply failed to pull her ripcord in time due to "brain lock" during free fall.

One of Oatley's other partners on this foray was her boyfriend from Australia. What's interesting about this is: He fled the scene and allegedly used her ATM card to expedite his future expenses incurred while vanishing. Indeed, as far as the Park is concerned, "he still officially remains a fugitive."

Despite the occasional fatal fall, or maybe because of them, Yosemite's walls remained a magnet for BASE devotees. Jeff D. Christman, a 42-year-old professional parachute instructor from Buckeye, Arizona had made his very first such jump (an illegal one) off the massive, 7,042-foot-high El Capitan years earlier. He returned for a replay on the morning of October 21, 1996, with two buddies. The trio was part of a group of six other Buckeye residents who had traveled to Yosemite together. Now, at 7 a.m., Christman's two other partners-in-crime deployed their chutes just fine.

Witnesses watched these two make good landings.

These same witnesses reported, though, that after Christman jumped off the 3,000-foot cliff he popped his chute "much higher than is typical for jumpers at this site." This quickly proved to be a big mistake.

Probably facing the wrong way when he opened, Christman immediately slammed into the cliff face. He hit so hard that he may have instantly brained himself. At any rate he subsequently hung limp in his harness during his descent as his canopy repeatedly careened back into the wall. He and his rig narrowly missed bumping and snaring two climbers bivouacked on a ledge. Eventually, after ricocheting off the granite several times, he jerked to a halt, hung up on a rocky salient on El Capitan Tower. He was now snagged 1,300 feet above the Valley floor and dangling like a Halloween prop for a haunted house.

Twenty-five minutes later one of Christman's buddies phoned 911.

To avoid a 1,600-foot rappel from the top, the rescue (read "recovery") team instead used the Park helicopter to hover fifteen feet from the wall above Christman's position. From there Rangers Chris Robinson and John Roth rappelled down 250 feet from the chopper to the ledge. Here, halfway down the mammoth face of El Capitan, they found the BASE jumper dead from massive trauma to the chest and head.

The two rangers packaged the victim onto a litter. Then they waited on the huge wall for the arrival of a Lemoore Naval Air Station helicopter to transport the body off the face.

By the time it arrived, the retrieval of Christman had become a touch-and-go proposition due to strong updrafts now buffeting the machine. These turbulent air masses prevented the navy pilot from holding his airship close enough to the cliff and simultaneously keeping it stable enough for either ranger to grab its jerking, swinging cable. To make matters worse, the rescuers knew the machine's rotating blades were generating an electrical shock that would seriously jolt them were they to grab the cable wrongly. They had to carefully ensure that the metal cable first touched the granite and grounded out, or else risk being shocked and knocked off their holds.

After several misses at accomplishing this, the pilot gave up and asked the rangers to move the body fifty feet lower to a better ledge system. This was far easier said than done; Christman weighed more than 200 pounds. The litter and the rangers' gear brought their total load to 300 pounds. Even so the two started moving Christman as instructed. One man lowered him. The other pulled him downward and inward. After winning this struggle the rangers had now placed themselves in position.

But when the crew chief tried to lower the cable yet again in this new improved pickup location, the winds and squirrelly updrafts again batted the machine too badly for either ranger to grab it. Finally Robinson solved this problem by attaching himself to a fifty-foot rope and "running" fifty feet up the cliff. From there he snatched the swaying hook (carefully enough to avoid being electrocuted). Chris next towed the cable back down to that new, lower ledge.

Here Ranger/Park Medic Roth hooked the litter to the cable and prepared for it to lift him and the dead man off the face of El Capitan.

Wind continued to buffet the big helicopter unmercifully. It swayed erratically. Getting off this ledge was sizing up to be an increasingly serious challenge. To dampen this swaying, John Roth had brought with him 300 feet of 7 mm rope. He now attached one end of this to the litter and gave the other end to Robinson so he could feed it out under tension to control the dangling litter holding the victim and Roth. This seemed like a reasonable plan. Until the chopper began to lift them.

Almost instantly the litter started spinning and wrapping Roth's thin tail rope around himself like a silkworm weaving its cocoon. It also wrapped around the dangling cable's hook. Robinson, still on the wall, now imagined what would happen if he were to let go of his end of this rope and then the rising air currents allowed it to suck upward and entangle the helicopter's giant rotors.

Racing against this scenario playing out in a spectacular crash against the face of El Capitan, Roth frantically struggled to free *his* end of the rope. He got it loose and let it drop. The Lemoore crew then hoisted the two people—one alive, one dead—into the airship.

Robinson now policed up their ropes and their other gear. Next he clipped into a piton on the Tower and waited. The Lemoore crew soon returned and lowered their cable, this time to lift him off the ledge. While hooking the machine's thin hoist line into his nylon harness, Robinson could not help feeling haunted by the image of what would happen if the aircraft were to be blown badly off its hover just as he clipped onto this cable while he was *still* fixed to the granite face. It would severely stretch his resources, so to speak.

Triumphing over this macabre—but also all too real—imagery, Robinson unclipped from the piton. The crew hoisted him with all that NPS rescue gear dangling down between his legs up into the machine.

Park rangers arrested everyone in Christman's party for 36 CFR 2.17 (a) (3) and charged them in U.S. District Court for participating in, and assisting, an illegal parachute jump in Yosemite. "Under a plea agreement," notes the *Yosemite National Park News Page* for July 28, 1998, "the five defendants each received a $2,000 fine, one year of supervised probation, and they must split the $4,690 cost of the recovery of Christman's body."

The prospect of losing "style points" due to these sorts of legal prosecutions vexed Frank Peter Gambalie III, a 29 year-old from Zephyr Cove, Nevada. He had built a career of sorts out of jumping off improbable platforms—buildings, bridges, et cetera. He was the kind of daredevil who would make the local TV news as a mystery parachutist who would leap from this or that tall building in some huge metropolitan city and then vanish like the Lone Ranger. As his career evolved, he made a pact with himself to never allow himself to be arrested. This promise—not the risky business of BASE jumping itself—would turn out ironically to be a fatal one.

During one illegal inner-city leap off a tall building, one allegedly sponsored by a "power drink" distributor, Gambalie executed a flawless skydive followed by a good landing. Then he fled. He managed to flee successfully partly because he had prearranged for a friend to act as a decoy for the police. The buddy allowed himself to be arrested because, after all, it would be nearly impossible for prosecutors to prove he had made a jump that he in fact had not made.

Once locked up, the decoy became something of a local hero (at least a jail cell hero) for having possessed the *cojones* to have made that televised daredevil jump (which in fact, he had not). This ruse allowed Gambalie yet again to keep his pact with himself to never be arrested. The sponsoring company's lawyer soon freed the "heroic" decoy. All in all, no real harm was done. At least this is how it might have seemed at the time.

At 5:10 a.m. on June 9, 1999, Gambalie made an illegal BASE jump off El Capitan. Gambalie's jump would soon evolve into an epic error born of his promise to himself.

One complication here was that before Gambalie leaped, someone had tipped off the Park that a jump would be attempted that morning. In response, the Park had staked out rangers to monitor the gigantic face of El Capitan.

Indeed, just after dawn somebody jumped. As Ranger John Stobinski reported:

> I saw a parachute, with a single person attached, descending in the air from the top of El Capitan near the Salathé Route. He made several turns and appeared to be headed for a landing near the west end of El Capitan Meadow. I started running in that direction from my location, a distance of about fifty yards. When I got thirty yards away I saw Ranger Tom Schwartz running toward where I was running...[He yelled] "Stop, Park Ranger. You're under arrest. Get down!"
>
> I then yelled: "Stop. Park Ranger. You're under arrest. Down, down, down!"
>
> —The subject, a white male, about 5'8"-5'10", 150-170 pounds, with dark collar length hair, wearing baggy black pants, and a baggy white turtleneck, looked at Tom and me. He then reached up to both his shoulders and released his parachute. He then turned and ran into the trees at the west end of El Capitan Meadow. Ranger Schwartz ran after him at a distance of about 15-20 yards. I heard Schwartz radio that the subject was running south. I started running south along the tree line toward the Merced River. When I reached the river [now in a stage of seasonal maximum flood], I heard Schwartz radio that the subject had jumped into the river.

Meanwhile, from the perspective of Ranger Schwartz, while still in the meadow:

> He [Gambalie] then looked at Stobinski and me again, smiled, and began to run away from us to the south into the woods. I continued to run after the individual for approximately 400-500 yards around

> trees and over downfall while at the same time dispatching over the radio my location and direction of travel...50 yards behind the individual. As we got closer to the river, I saw him reach up with his arms to release the shoulder straps of his pack. I then looked down to jump over a log and a ditch, looked up and saw him dive into the river and begin swimming toward the opposite bank. He was swimming with his head above water ferrying at an angle slightly upstream.
>
> I walked closer toward the bank and he quickly glanced back at me then continued to swim across the river. Within two or three seconds he was getting pulled toward the middle of the river where the current was swifter and moving around a large rock. He disappeared behind the rock so I ran downstream around a pile of rocks and trees so I could better observe downstream. I saw no signs of him in the river or on either bank. I went down the riverbank and walked out on a tree that stuck out approximately 15 feet into the river and looked up and down both banks and the river.
>
> Other park rangers continued downstream and came upstream on the opposite side of the river continuing the search for the parachutist. I stayed on the tree observing the river and both banks until approximately 0615. I then walked upstream along the north bank through El Cap Meadow and met with other Park Rangers at the El Cap Crossover Bridge. We returned to the Law Enforcement Office by 0730.

Several search teams, helicopter crews, and five dogs looked for Gambalie. On July 7, four weeks after his illegal leap, Frank Peter Gambalie III's body was recovered from the Merced River, a mere 300 yards downstream of where Ranger Schwartz had last seen him. A postmortem investigation revealed death by drowning. Gambalie died trying to swim across the Merced while wearing baggy sweat clothes in an attempt to escape arrest and to keep that pact with himself (and maybe also to avoid paying a $2,000 fine?).

That Yosemite's cliffs dangled temptingly as forbidden fruit galled many people in the BASE jumping community. One of them was Jan M. Davis. At age 58, Davis was a longtime Hollywood professional stuntwoman with sixteen years of skydiving experience. On October 22, 1999, she leapt off El Capitan as the fourth of five people in a planned act of civil disobedience to protest the National Park Service's policy of prohibiting BASE jumping as a legal recreational activity. She jumped with fellow demonstrators Mark Knutson, Henry Boger, and Joseph Weber.

This promotional protest had been well planned. The enthusiasts had contacted the Park ahead of time, even requesting that authorities be present to witness their planned act of civil disobedience against Park policy. This monitoring would include videoing from the top as well as being observed by rangers below. The protestors' companions were also recording from above and below. These cameras were to run as all five adventurers threw themselves off the nearly 3,000-foot cliff.

In contrast to rumors that Davis gave a protest speech before jumping, the videos show she did not address the cameras or onlookers. All business, she simply got her gear ready then ran off into thin air.

Davis possessed significant experience, including about seventy-five BASE jumps. She had also parachuted from aircraft well over a thousand times. As a Hollywood stuntwoman, she had performed challenging jumps in several movies including *Point Break*, *The Puppet Masters*, *Goldeneye*, and Michael Crichton's *Congo*. In 1988, she also became the first woman to parachute off Venezuela's Angel Falls—at 3,212 feet, the tallest of the world's big, continuous waterfalls.

The first three protestors—Knutson, Boger, and Weber—all made good jumps, one at a time. The crowd of at least 150 people below observed each man. Cameras caught every second of the action. Each landed on the meadow and was given roughly thirty seconds by rangers to make his media statement. Afterward each was arrested for 36 CFR 2.17 (a) (3), handcuffed, and led away to jail. These short speeches adamantly stressed the safety of BASE jumping and the prehistoric attitude of the Park in not allowing it.

Next came Davis. The crowd, which had gathered to witness this epic five-part act of protest now expected to see another brief freefall, a chute popping open and then a soft spiral descent to a gentle landing in the tall grasses of El Capitan Meadow. This floating demonstration would then be followed by yet another brief media interview.

Instead, they saw something else.

Again, all five jumpers had agreed in advance not to flee from the rangers. Indeed, they would submit to peaceful arrests, forfeiture of their equipment, and to appear in Magistrate Court. Herein lay the seed of disaster. For there is parachuting gear and there is well, *better* parachuting gear. The painful question for the BASE jumper practicing civil disobedience is: If one protests with one's convictions held deep in the heart—as Henry David Thoreau would sanction—does this also require one to forfeit really top notch equipment?

Jan Davis equivocated on this and decided the answer must be: No, it is perfectly acceptable to practice what you preach with less valuable gear. So, while she decided to use one of her own parachutes, she elected not to use her own rigging. She borrowed some items, a few of which were different to what she was accustomed. Her own setup had a back-mounted, bottom-of-the-container (BOC) pilot chute release. This is what she had accustomed herself to use most recently. But the rigging she elected for El Capitan instead had its pilot chute in a leg pouch, with a leg release location.

At 2:32 p.m., she stood above the North America Wall of El Capitan, a 2,800-foot freefall. In the crowd below, her common-law husband Tom Sanders stood with his camera to his eye ready to shoot an historic video that finally would help prove the Park was unfair—if not downright wrong—by prohibiting BASE jumping. And his 58-year-old wife would be one of the pioneers to make this happen. Standing beside Sanders was NPS Special Agent Jeff Sullivan.

The multiple tapes being shot would reveal something no one expected. It would show a professional stuntwoman as she repeatedly tried to reach for and release her BOC pilot chute. Remember, she was *not* wearing her normal BOC-chute rig. She had a leg sheath pilot chute. Strangely, the Park's video—repeatedly analyzed by Sullivan and others—does not show that Davis ever reached for the release on her leg.

Because Agent Sullivan believed it was possible that she might in fact have been trying to reach her leg-mounted pilot chute but perhaps had been doing so out of the angle of view of the Park camera, he made repeated requests to the civil disobedience group for their own footage. When they finally complied, Sullivan was able to see something the Park's film had not shown. In this new tape, Davis did appear to reach for her leg release at least once. But when no chute popped open to slow her descent, instead of again making positive contact with the rubber, knob-like handle at the top of the pilot chute which juts out from the leg sheath, she apparently assumed that her pilot chute had deployed but that it had then fouled or tangled somehow against her back container or instead was delayed or caught in the dead-air burble immediately above her back.

The "civil disobedience" video next shows the 58-year-old daredevil plummeting at more than one hundred miles per-hour as she repeatedly swiped at her back chute container in the somewhat standard procedure to clear a pilot chute from being fouled or delayed. The problem here again is she had never deployed her pilot chute at all. Therefore *it* never had a chance to foul or—more importantly—to deploy her main chute.

In short, Davis never released her chute. She dropped almost 3,000 feet and impacted the rocks at terminal velocity and then rolled at high speed down the slope.

She hit so hard, noted Sullivan, her impact sounded like a sonic boom. It sounded shockingly explosive—so loud "it set off alarms of the cars parked at the Meadow."

The crowd stood there stunned.

A thorough postmortem examination revealed nothing was wrong with the equipment Davis had been wearing. Both her pilot and main chutes had been packed properly (Davis and her rigger together had packed them). To be absolutely certain of this, Investigator Sullivan hauled the dead woman's gear to the 66th Air Rescue Wing for expert technical analysis. They too found that neither chute had any defect. Nor had anything been tampered with or sabotaged in any detectable way. Indeed, after her terrific impact with the ground Davis' leg-mounted pilot chute had remained halfway out of her leg sheath; it bulged out, its black tubular grab knob now looking very easy to grip.

Jan M. Davis had died due to pilot error.

The Park's SAR bill for her body recovery came to $6,155.32. Individual fines for each jumper were $2,000.

BASE jumping and sport parachuting in general remain illegal in Yosemite National Park. Indeed, the Park itself came under heavy criticism for even having allowed this one planned act of "civil disobedience." But from the Park's perspective this is tricky ground. The United States Attorney and the Solicitors Office both decided that BASE jumping was not illegal until a person actually jumped. In other words, it is not illegal to walk to the edge of a Yosemite cliff while wearing a parachute. The crime of BASE jumping only takes place once the person jumps. Thus the Park could not be held culpable for "allowing" these civil disobedience jumps. They could only arrest the perpetrators after the fact. Even so, no one exited this episode alive with something really positive scrawled on their ledger.

Do lifesaving lessons reside within these half dozen fatal events that are anything other than obvious? Parachuting in any circumstance, even from something as mundane as a well-controlled training aircraft, is a thrill. One that allows a skydiver to practice and perform a wide array of skills. Why then must one leap off El Capitan instead? Is it because Yosemite Valley appears as such an enticing fantastic natural spectacle from that elevation? Or is it instead to test oneself against the BASE jumping challenges inherent to pulling off this sort of dive in this far tighter, less forgiving environment? Maybe it is for both reasons. Either way—and legalities aside—for those half dozen discussed above at least, it does not seem to have been worth the risk.

Remember Brian Lee Schubert? As mentioned at the start of this chapter in 1966, at age 26, he and his buddy Michael Pelkey became the first BASE jumpers to leap off El Capitan—and the first known to BASE jump in any national park. Forty years and hundreds of jumps later Schubert participated in the infamous annual plummeting extravaganza called "Bridge Day" hosted by West Virginia at the NPS New River Gorge National Scenic Riverway. On October 21, 2006, more than one-hundred thousand spectators lined up on or next to the 1,700-foot-long New River Gorge Bridge looming 876 feet above the river to see the action. This is the world's second highest single span, free-standing bridge. At any rate, Brian Lee Schubert, now 66 years old and living in Alta Loma, California, BASE jumped off this bridge into the gorge while nearly a quarter million eyes watched him. By the way, he had not made a BASE jump now for decades. And he had only practiced jumping into a swimming pool.

He deployed his chute far too late. It opened only twenty-five feet above the river. The crowd atop the span emitted a sudden gasp of shock. Schubert died upon impact with the water. This not only ended his career and his life, his death—one of about 100 BASE jumping fatalities overall since 1981—also put a damper on the festivities. But apparently not for long. As noted by the October 21, 2006 Associated

Press article "Parachutist Dies Jumping Off Bridge at W. Va. Festival," Fayette County Sheriff Bill Laird said: "After Schubert's body was recovered and taken to a funeral home, jumping at the festival resumed [for a total of 804 jumps]."

TABLE 3. FATAL BASE JUMPS IN YOSEMITE. (All episodes are discussed in text unless noted.)

Name, age	Date	Location	*Circumstances*
James Dale Tyler, 35	August 4, 1982	Half Dome	*Tyler, a professional stunt parachutist from La Puente, California with more than 1,000 jumps, made an illegal jump. His chute "cartwheeled" vertically and uncontrollably, slamming him repeatedly into the cliff face. His canopy caught on a ledge and folded up 600 feet from the base. Tyler plummeted onto the talus.*
Mitchell Reno, 35	October 23, 1988	Half Dome	*Reno of Antioch, California made a clandestine leap off Half Dome. Two climbers 350 feet up observed him whoosh past them flailing and with his canopy deployed in a "streamer" (a tangled, non-inflated chute). Just before he hit the talus, his chute and shroud lines stretched to their full length. A Forest Service parachute expert found all of Reno's gear to be functional.*
Susan Alaine Oatley, 40	September 25, 1993	New Dawn Wall, El Capitan	*Oatley, a research scientist from Solana Beach, California, illegally jumped off El Capitan with 3 others who spiraled down safely. A witness saw her leap but not successfully deploy a chute. She crashed into the trees explosively. Her most probable error was failing to achieve a forward-tracking position. Instead she assumed a position that took her into the wall.*
Jeff D. Christman, 42	October 21, 1996	El Capitan	*Christman, a professional parachute instructor from Buckeye, Arizona, made an illegal jump off El Capitan with 2 buddies. He opened "much higher than is typical for jumpers at this site." He repeatedly slammed into the cliff. His chute hung up on El Capitan Tower, 1,300 feet above the Valley. A rescue team was inserted by Park helicopter to package him for extraction by a Navy helicopter.*
Frank Peter Gambalie III, 29	June 9, 1999	Merced River, El Capitan Meadow	*Gambalie of Zephyr Cove, Nevada built a career out of BASE jumping off improbable platforms and had made a pact with himself to never be arrested. He made an illegal jump off El Capitan and landed safely. While fleeing rangers, Gambalie dove into the Merced (in spate) to escape, but* **drowned**. (not included in BASE jumping statistics but instead in drownings)

Jan M. Davis, 58

October 22, 1999 El Capitan
Davis was a Hollywood professional stunt woman of 16 years experience, 1,000+ skydives, and 75 BASE jumps. She leaped off El Capitan as the 4th jumper in an act of civil disobedience protesting the Park's policy of prohibiting parachuting. Davis' error was in failing to release her leg mounted pilot chute. An examination of her gear revealed nothing wrong.

Dean Potter, 43
Graham Hunt, 29

May 16, 2015 off Taft Point, 7,500 feet
Extreme free soloist and BASE jumper Potter (who in 2001 climbed El Capitan's Nose in 3 hours and 24 minutes, and who was the first climber to free solo both El Cap and Half Dome within 24 hours) of Yosemite, California had childhood dreams of being able to fly (and of falling) and was inspired while climbing by seeing a ***wing-suited BASE jumper*** *whiz past him. Potter and Hunt of El Portal, California made a dusk wingsuit BASE jump off Taft for their 20+th time to thread a V-shaped notch above Lost Brother. During their approach, partly* ***un-witnessed****, Potter was lower and straight. Graham, however, veered away, left, then veered back rightward to re-join Potter but at a diagonal angle that smacked him into the far wall. Potter made the notch but impacted rocks beyond it. Why? Only conjecture. Neither chute was deployed. (not in text)*

Chapter Four

PARK BUILDERS

Although Yosemite is America's first region to be legally set aside strictly for the sake of its scenery and for the enjoyment of people, the years since have proven it to be far from sacrosanct. It gained park status only by a thread which today sometimes seems as thin as gossamer. In February of 1864, San Francisco shipping magnate Captain Israel Ward Raymond wrote a letter to California's junior senator, John Conness, urging him to persuade Congress to grant to the State of California Yosemite Valley and the Mariposa Big Tree Grove "for public use, resort, and recreation." To make his point about how spectacular these two chunks of landscape were, Raymond included an album of stunning photographs.

Both photography and Yosemite were relatively "new" at this time. But a dedicated pioneer in both had very recently combined them with an innovative and impressive technique. A storekeeper self-taught in photography, Carleton E. Watkins, had designed and then specially built an 18- by 22-inch box camera to master the area's scenic challenges. Between 1862 and 1864 he had hauled his heavy and cumbersome gear around the Valley, taking carefully composed and technically advanced, large format, high quality photos of a locale that existed mostly as a sort of fantasy place by the few outsiders aware of its existence.

Senator Conness took Raymond's proposed project to heart—and to Congress. Inspired in part by Watkins' superb photos, Congress then President Lincoln approved the Yosemite Grant Act. It consisted of two, noncontiguous sections: the Yosemite Valley Grant (36,111.14 acres) and the Mariposa Grove Grant (2,589.26 acres) which contained the Mariposa Big Trees. The total reserve added up to a bit more than sixty square miles. Signed into law on June 30, 1864, the act stipulated that both these tracts were now "owned" by the State of California.

The classic "campfire" version of how the larger region of Yosemite shifted into a national park seemed to pivot on a camping trip. Robert Underwood Johnson, editor for *The Century Illustrated Monthly Magazine* (formerly known as *Scribner's*), inveigled John Muir into acting as his guide in Yosemite. Muir, already a well-paid contributor to the magazine, jumped at this. In 1889, the two tromped the area's scenic backcountry. One evening, sitting around their campfire near Soda Springs in Tuolumne Meadows, Johnson suggested to Muir that he should strongly consider popularizing the ongoing campaign to secure national park status for Yosemite. Muir could do this, Johnson continued, by writing illustrated, persuasive articles for *The Century*.

Muir loathed the process of writing for publication, despite writing being his main source of income. Even so, he started whacking away at it. In June of 1890, Muir's articles— "The Treasures of Yosemite" and "Features of the Proposed National Park" —appeared in *The Century*. In this pair of hortatory writings, Muir urged for protection of a Yosemite National Park that he hoped would include the mountainous watersheds and sources for the two rivers—the Tuolumne and the Merced—flowing into the area's two major glacial valleys: Yosemite and Hetch Hetchy (these proposed boundaries followed the rectangular township lines and did not include the irregularly shaped headwater regions of both rivers). The legislation introduced into Congress shortly after Muir's articles saw print was contested bitterly. Lobbied heavily by Editor Johnson and others, however, it passed both houses and was signed into law on October 1, 1890, by President Benjamin Harrison, a surprisingly pro-environment chief executive for that era. The boundaries of the nation's new park largely followed the expansive yet well-considered recommendations that Muir had popularized.

Yosemite Valley itself remained a state-owned enclave—and a poorly funded and marginally managed one at that. Muir and others continued lobbying to include the Valley into the National Park. Muir's efforts were aided by greater apparent solidarity when, on June 4, 1892, twenty-seven influential allies formed themselves into the original Sierra Club. Their campaign to secure the future of Yosemite as a large, more or less self-sustaining park would prove to be a long one. Ironically it too would be won in part during a camping trip.

In May of 1903, at President Teddy Roosevelt's personal and impassioned request, Muir took T.R. on a four-day horseback trip into Yosemite's backcountry. Muir, among other things, lobbied with Roosevelt against the hodgepodge run by California in Yosemite Valley. This ultimately proved helpful. Less than three years later, California ceded the Valley back to the Federal Government. On June 11, 1905, Roosevelt signed the Federal Government's formal acceptance, written to go into effect in 1906.

Muir now felt more than mere relief, he felt ecstatic. He exulted over his success, writing to editor Robert Underwood Johnson, "You don't know what an accomplished lobbyist I've become under your guidance. The fight you planned by the famous Tuolumne campfire seventeen years ago is at last fairly, gloriously won, every enemy down."

Sadly, Muir's overall set of victories would prove to be, in one sense, pyrrhic. This is because, notes Alfred Runte in his *Yosemite the Embattled Wilderness*, as part of the process of redesigning Yosemite National Park, Congress directed Secretary of the Interior Ethan Allen Hitchcock on April 28, 1904, to figure out where the boundaries should be drawn to best serve the public interest. More specifically, this was to determine "what portions of said park are not necessary for park purposes, but can be returned to the public domain." To follow this Congressional mandate, Hitchcock appointed a three-member boundary commission: Major Hiram Martin Chittenden of the U.S. Army Corps of Engineers; Frank Bond, Chief of the Draft Division of the U.S. General Land Office; and Robert Bradford Marshall, a U.S. Geological Survey topographer. This trio toured the Yosemite region and by June had masterminded its fate.

Chittenden and the commission faced an extremely complicated review. One of the main issues they needed to consider was the great number of preexisting private claims and inholdings already sewing up much of what lands might be inside any proposed boundaries for Yosemite. These land owners possessed "the right to build roads and in some cases railroads, take out ditches, use a certain amount of timber, drive stock across government land, etc."

The commission also considered that the Army which patrolled the Park was experiencing difficulty in performing many of its duties due to a confusing array of previously existing resource claims. Troopers were often unsure of exactly where they were in relation to these private properties. The boundaries along township lines cut through canyons and crossed streams in ways such that their precise property lines could not be determined by cavalry patrols. Thus handicapped, the soldiers often could not eject trespassers. To help illustrate this complexity, there existed nine claims under the Pre-Emption Law of 1841 in Yosemite Valley established between 1856 and 1862. Each was 160 acres in size. Outside the Valley itself a similar problem prevailed.

One amazing (admittedly, when viewed through the lens of today's values) guiding principle by which this Congressional commission operated was: To save the scenic portions of Yosemite, they should excise from it lands rich in natural resources that potentially could be mined or timbered by private industry. And as Runte says, "Nor would the outright purchase of every claim solve the problem indefinitely." Were harvestable natural resources kept in the Park, noted Major Chittenden, "there would still remain the knowledge of the presence of precious metals in these mountains, and this would form a temptation of the strongest kind to trespass on the reservation and seek to cut it to pieces." The Sierra Club, Chittenden noted in his report, regretted any reduction of the Park, but he added that even *its* members understood the necessity of doing this due to those extensive private inholdings. Indeed the commission recommended excising from the Park "all that can be spared without serious detriment [to scenery]." Unfortunately, in the long run, application of this must-be-worthless-except-for-scenery principle would end up gutting the Park as a functional ecosystem.

The original Park lands to be sacrificed and given back into the public domain, according to Chittenden's arithmetic, added up to 543 square miles (347,500 acres) for logging and mining. Giving away this much of Yosemite National Park—one-third of it—the commission said, would thus *protect* it. (A year later Yosemite National Park lost yet another sixteen square miles. Today, Yosemite contains 747,956 acres, or 1,169 square miles).

To its credit, however, the commission did also recommend that all private holdings within the remaining Park be purchased from individual ownership by the federal government. A second positive recommendation by the group was to *add* to the Park 114 square miles. These included nearly all the watershed of the South Fork of the Merced, all of the main fork of the Merced, and all of the upper Tuolumne River. This was done to protect it from cattle and sheep. Furthermore, the commission noted, parts of what would remain in Yosemite were definitely "features of great scenic beauty, notably the Hetch Hetchy Valley on the Tuolumne—a second Yosemite—Lake Eleanor, and the Tiltill Valley."

Congress quickly approved Secretary Hitchcock's recommended boundaries and the return to the public domain of Yosemite's timber and grazing lands. A bit more surprising, pro-conservation (which a century ago meant something very different from "preservation") President Teddy Roosevelt signed part of this into law on February 7, 1905. A new, almost one-third smaller, Yosemite National Park was born, one with the Valley inside it, but also one stripped of much of its ecosystem capability. The ecological mistakes incurred due to these new boundaries would soon prove major. Although some historians note that our word "mistake" can be used only due to the clarity of hindsight, before even a year had passed, noted Acting Park Superintendent Major H. C. Benson, large mammals within Yosemite began noticeably decreasing because the now reduced Park had lost hundreds of square miles of lower elevation forest and meadows. These lost Park lands, it proved, had been winter range for Yosemite's deer and other mammals. Now the Park's wildlife was being slaughtered in this new degraded and "de-parked" habitat by hunters who waited literally just beyond the Park's new boundary.

One of the biggest casualties within the "new" Yosemite National Park was something that did not even possess the ability to flee—Hetch Hetchy Valley (named after the Miwok word *hetchetci* for the edible-seed-bearing, waist-high grass that once grew there in profusion). The Park's second great valley was known to probably only a few thousand Americans. Fewer yet had ever troubled to go there. Those who had seen it claimed it rivaled Yosemite Valley in splendor and uniqueness. John Muir called it "the Tuolumne Yosemite…a wonderfully exact counterpart of the Merced Yosemite…with wide variations it is a Yosemite Valley all the way." California State Geologist Josiah Dwight Whitney recommended in 1868 to visitors that they take the trouble to see Hetch Hetchy "if it be only to see how curiously nature had repeated itself." As John Muir notes in his 1912 book *The Yosemite*, artist William Keith insisted, "in picturesque beauty and charm Hetch Hetchy surpassed even Yosemite."

Notably, due largely to Major Chittenden's appreciation of the great valley, Hetch Hetchy had remained inside Yosemite National Park. Even so, despite Hetch Hetchy (and much of Yosemite in general outside the Valley) encompassing wild lands known personally to a relatively tiny number of Americans, the water that flowed out of it was quite well known to many more Californians.

As early as 1870, the city fathers of San Francisco recognized that future growth would be crippled without more dependable water. Over the next three decades, engineers considered, however briefly, at least fourteen possible sources including Lake Tahoe, Blue Lakes, Clear Lake, the Yuba, Eel, and Feather Rivers, and even Calaveras Valley in southern Alameda County as future sources for the liquid gold. In 1882, J. P. Dart, an engineer working for the fledgling San Francisco and Tuolumne Water Company, drew up then filed in the Tuolumne County Courthouse the first, albeit little known, plan to divert water from the Tuolumne fifteen miles northeast of Groveland. Dart's plans included an aqueduct from there across the San Joaquin Valley to a reservoir in the East San Francisco Bay hills. Six years later George M. Harris offered San Francisco his rights to the Tuolumne River from the head of the Grand Canyon of the Tuolumne to its confluence with the San Joaquin. His price? $200,000. Despite Harris' offer representing for San Francisco a rescue from many years of being held hostage to the Spring Valley Water Company—a rapacious and privately held company that had monopolized every significant source of water on the San Francisco Peninsula and charged the city the highest water prices known—the leaders of the water-starved city declined. In 1894, Harris reiterated his offer. He explained that not only did the Tuolumne offer the purest water on earth but also its upper canyon could easily store a million gallons (a drastic underestimate). Again, surprisingly, San Francisco balked.

At the precise turn of the century, San Francisco created a Board of Works and gave three men one year to research and then formulate a solution to San Francisco's festering problem of securing a reliable and adequate source of water. The three—civil engineer Marsden Manson (a founding member of the Sierra Club), U.S. Army engineer Colonel George H. Mendell, and A. B. Maguire—evaluated several Sierra Nevada rivers. None did the trick. Meanwhile Board of Supervisors Engineer Carl E. Grunsky, a loyal coworker who shared Mayor James Duval Phelan's imperial dream of a San Francisco remodeled on the style and scale of classical Rome, identified the Tuolumne River as the city's most preferred source. It drained a watershed of more than 650 square miles, the vast majority of which lay above 6,000 feet in elevation. Grunsky also noted that Hetch Hetchy would be the best canyon in which to store its water. The rub here? Marsden

Manson identified only one: the high cost of diverting all that water from Yosemite to San Francisco. The fact that Hetch Hetchy was *in* Yosemite National Park and belonged to the American public was not yet considered important. Even the U.S. Geological Survey (USGS) itself, in its 1899-1900 *Report*, had already concluded that a reservoir in Hetch Hetchy could "furnish the city of San Francisco with an unfailing supply of pure water."

When the city fathers read this report, they apparently quit looking elsewhere. This was despite the USGS 1890-1891 *Report* also listing dozens of other sites in California. This was also despite USGS Director John Wesley Powell warning that Hetch Hetchy was "such a wonder spot of nature," that damming it should only be done as a last resort. "Hetch Hetchy Valley is a mountain meadow 3,700 feet above the sea," Powell's *Report* read. "It is a veritable Yosemite Valley on a small scale. The Hetch Hetchy Falls, near the lower end of the Valley, are fully equal in beauty and grandeur to many of the falls in Yosemite Valley."

The austere beauty of granite-walled Hetch Hetchy Valley now led to what would become a prolonged political ping-pong match between preservationists dedicated to keeping Yosemite undamaged versus businessmen intent on converting it into an economic asset. Not only was this locale ideal for building a cheap, narrow, high dam that would store a lot of water, the elevation itself of Hetch Hetchy also facilitated "head" for hydropower. As David Brower writes (in his Foreword in the 1988 reprint of John Muir's *The Yosemite*): "What the city really wanted [besides the water itself] was the difference in elevation between Hetch Hetchy Valley, at 3,800 feet [sic], and Moccasin Creek power house at 800 feet. If the city could control the flow of the Tuolumne River over the course of that drop, a substantial amount of profitable hydroelectric energy could be generated."

In short—and this aspect of Hetch Hetchy's fate often has been neglected in the telling—San Francisco was not battling merely for its own survival as a viable municipality, it instead was also lobbying for a site in which to build a dam *as a municipal investment* from which power and water might be sold to nearby municipalities to generate financial profit for the city itself.

On February 15, 1901, Congress passed the Right of Way Act. This rescinded Congress' 1890 prohibitions against building dams and felling timber in Yosemite. The Right of Way Act said dams might be authorized and it listed Yosemite National Park as a candidate location—"only on the approval of the chief officer of the Department under whose supervision such park or reservation falls, and upon a finding by him that the same is not incompatible with the public interest." In October of 1901, Grunsky, Manson, and the city's Mayor James Duval Phelan aimed at this new loophole by petitioning the U.S. Government for water rights to the Tuolumne River and for a permit to build dams at the mouth of Hetch Hetchy and at Lake Eleanor. They petitioned not for the city, nor even in the name of the city's mayor, but instead in that of Phelan as a private citizen. Meanwhile Phelan and the San Francisco City Council ordered engineer Grunsky to prepare a plan for a Hetch Hetchy dam and for the aqueducts and tunnels necessary to deliver the Tuolumne River to the city. On July 28, 1902, Grunsky handed in his forty-six-page plan. He did note that expanding the capacity of nearby Lake Eleanor (again, not only located inside Yosemite but also listed as one of its outstanding scenic wonders) plus tapping Cherry Creek (nearby but outside the Park)—which, as an engineer, he favored as much as Hetch Hetchy—would fully satisfy San Francisco's need and would flow to the city via the same planned aqueduct. To deliver sixty million gallons of Yosemite water per day from Hetch Hetchy, he added, would cost the city $39.5 million.

In 1903 Secretary of the Interior Hitchcock officially denied San Francisco's request. Among other things, he pointed out, the city's surveys of the areas to be used "had been made surreptitiously and without securing the consent of the Department" for San Francisco's purposes. Hitchcock also felt that such a dam in Yosemite National Park was not what Congress had in mind when they had gazetted it, despite the Right of Way Act. ("It is inconceivable," he wrote in 1903, "that it was intended by the Act of February15, 1901, to confer any authority to be exercised for the subversion of those natural conditions which are essential to the very purposes for which the park was established.") In short, he explained, such a dam was "not in keeping with the public interest."

Secretary Hitchcock's refusal might seem to have spelled *finis* to San Francisco's obsession with Hetch Hetchy, but his decision to preserve the glacial valley—as is ultimately the case with virtually all decisions to conserve nature—never constituted more than a mere delay of destruction. Seldom are conservation victories truly permanent because human greed remains unrelenting. Meanwhile, even some of the most preeminent professional guardians of America's public lands at the time proved myopic with regard to America's ecological and conservation future. No less a luminary than Gifford Pinchot himself, "father of the U.S. Forest Service" and an aggressive proponent of its multiple use, would say in 1913:

> I am fully persuaded that...the injury...by substituting a lake for the present swampy floor of the valley...is altogether unimportant compared with the benefits to be derived from its use as a reservoir.... The delight of the few men and women who would yearly go into the Hetch Hetchy Valley should not outweigh the conservation policy, to take every part of the land and its resources and put it to that use in which it will best serve the most people.

Only a year after Secretary Hitchcock said no to a dam in Hetch Hetchy, in 1902, Congress passed the Newlands Reclamation Act. As would become apparent, Nevada Congressman Francis Griffith Newlands had sponsored this bill with at least partial self-interest in mind. By working in concert with state engineer William Hammond Hall and others, Newlands would soon amass a fortune by speculating in water rights and land acquisition whose values would be escalated via water developments born of his act, which established today's Bureau of Reclamation. Decades earlier, the Bureau had been a brainchild of John Wesley Powell, the famous explorer of the Green-Colorado River system who served from 1880-1894 as the second Director of the USGS. Now, in the year of his death, his brainchild finally had become law. The Newlands Reclamation Act sanctioned the building of large storage dams on federal land—albeit not *within* national parks.

Phelan and other San Francisco city fathers now (1903) lobbied with Gifford Pinchot. Two years later, Pinchot formally recommended to President Roosevelt that Lake Eleanor and Hetch Hetchy be given to San Francisco as sites for reservoirs. Torn, T.R. responded that it was a matter for the Secretary of the Interior to decide. In that Hitchcock had in fact already done so in favor of Yosemite National Park, Pinchot's recommendation became a moot point. So, in 1906, San Francisco gave up. It passed Resolution 6949 stipulating that the city spend neither time nor resources in continuing to seek Hetch Hetchy as a site for a dam. The dam was a dead horse.

At 5:12 a.m. on April 18, 1906, this dead horse was shaken back into life. The Pacific Plate snapped twenty-one feet north along the San Andreas Fault (one of seven faults surrounding the city) and jerked past the North American Plate. An earthquake that would have registered between 7.7 and 8.3 on the Richter scale (local seismic measuring devices at the time waggled completely off the chart) shook the western Bay Area for nearly a minute. As noted by Sid Perkins in his "Region at risk: a look at San Francisco's seismic past and future" (in *Science News*, April 15, 2006), at this time San Francisco was not merely one of the big cities in California or on the West Coast, it was *the* city. One quarter of all Americans west of the Rocky Mountains lived in San Francisco. City residents totaled 400,000. And these represented most of the richest people around. Banks in the city held deposits exceeding $1 billion, "more than all other western banks combined."

The quake not only rattled 28,000 of the city's buildings into rubble, it yanked, bent, and severed gas lines and also broke most of the iron pipes providing San Francisco with water. So the scores of fires ignited during the quake remained unquenched due to lack of water. (The 1906 fires in San Francisco burned so unabated that Ghiglieri's Phi Beta Kappa grandmother, Alice Margaret Gallagher, told him that she and her college friends at the University of California in Berkeley had sat on the roof nearly all night to watch the massive spectacle of the city across the bay burning to the ground. The next morning she took an illegal ferry across the bay to tour the still burning city.) Estimates of property loss sat at $524 million. The official death toll, notes Perkins, stood at about 300 people killed. But, he adds, subsequent interviews with survivors suggests that as many as 3,000 might have died.

In response, Teddy Roosevelt soon appointed former Mayor Phelan as sole trustee for the $10 million in relief funds for the city. For Phelan, beyond the devastation and loss suffered by himself and the thousands of others in the city there shone a silver lining. The new city to rise from the ashes of the old could emerge in an image of classical Rome. And the one thing this new city would need most was pure and copious water from a storage dam in Hetch Hetchy Valley. After overseeing the conviction of the current corrupt Mayor Schmitz and the city's equally corrupt Board of Supervisors, Phelan re-launched his campaign to secure Hetch Hetchy. Gifford Pinchot now pledged to Phelan and engineer Marsden Manson his greatest level of support.

A year after the big San Francisco quake, Ethan Hitchcock, at age 72, resigned his position as Secretary of the Interior. Roosevelt appointed James A. Garfield to replace him. Pinchot now wrote to Manson, the original Phelan civil engineer (and, again, a founding member of the Sierra Club), a letter advising him to reapply for San Francisco's Hetch Hetchy permit through Garfield. Manson now became Judas (at least as far as Yosemite National Park is concerned) by making that application. Meanwhile San Francisco's new Board of Supervisors hurriedly repealed Resolution 6949.

Despite other available, non-Park sources of water having been identified for San Francisco in the Sierra Nevada by the USGS and others, in May of 1908, Garfield awarded the city the permit it had repeatedly sought to dam Hetch Hetchy Valley. The city was to possess this section of Yosemite on the amazing condition that at least two-thirds of San Franciscans voted "yes" on developing Yosemite National Park for their water needs. Like Pontius Pilate, Garfield had thus seemed to have absolved himself of the responsibility for judging whether or not Hetch Hetchy indeed was San Francisco's only viable option (what Garfield did was unprecedented [and possibly illegal]; he abdicated his own responsibility and passed off to San Francisco—instead of to himself or the federal government or to the people of the United States—the responsibility and authority to decide the fate of this scenic portion of Yosemite National Park). Garfield also imposed the condition on San Francisco that it fully develop Lake Eleanor first, before beginning any part of construction of a dam in Hetch Hetchy.

Led by John Muir, the Sierra Club began lobbying in Congress against the dam. "Dam Hetch Hetchy!" Muir would exclaim on the final page of *The Yosemite*. "As well dam for water-tanks the people's cathedrals and churches, for no holier temple had ever been consecrated by the heart of man."

Efforts by Muir and his allies, and even a surprising last minute plea by Roosevelt to Congress that in Yellowstone and Yosemite both "all wild things should be protected and the scenery kept wholly unmarred," led to the House Committee on Public Lands tabling San Francisco's Hetch Hetchy application in 1908, thus avoiding a final decision.

Incensed by Congress' lack of approval, 86 percent of San Francisco voters in

November of 1908 said yes to the city's plan to dam Hetch Hetchy. In 1910-1911, the City was forced by another of Garfield's conditions to pay $1 million to former California State Engineer/Surveyor William Hammond Hall (and to a trio of speculators who were "silent" Pacific Gas and Electric [PG&E] founders and who had bought in with Hall). Hall had speculatively acquired the competitive water rights around Cherry Creek and the outflow from Lake Eleanor in 1902—right after Phelan, Manson, and Grundy had filed for similar rights. Again San Francisco seemed poised with a green light to monopolize and transform Hetch Hetchy into a water tank.

In 1909, William Howard Taft replaced T.R. as president. Taft appointed Richard A. Ballinger as his Secretary of the Interior. Both men now decided that Hetch Hetchy was better used as a scenic portion of Yosemite National Park than as a reservoir for San Francisco. Further, Taft's new Director of the USGS, George Otis Smith, studied the problem and concluded in 1910 that Lake Eleanor alone was "amply sufficient to meet the present and prospective needs of the city."

Yet again San Francisco's claim on Hetch Hetchy became a dead horse.

San Francisco Engineer Marsden Manson attacked Smith's report and found irregularities and errors that he used to lever Ballinger into ordering a second study, this time by the U.S. Army Corps of Engineers. Over the next two years engineer John Riley Freeman prepared a 400-page, highly detailed and technically sound analysis on San Francisco's specific plans to dam Hetch Hetchy and to use Lake Eleanor and Cherry Creek and also to build a 172-mile aqueduct capable of delivering 400 million gallons of water per day. While technically sound, Freeman's 1912 report again failed to seriously consider or evaluate alternate, non-Yosemite sites in the Sierra Nevada to satisfy San Francisco's needs. Worse, it insisted that it was an economic error to dam Eleanor before damming Hetch Hetchy (*the* engineer's dream canyon).

When the Democrats ran Woodrow S. Wilson in 1912 against a now dividing Republican Party in which the warring Taft and Roosevelt factions split their votes in twain, former Mayor James Duval Phelan acted as the Democratic Party's state treasurer in California. Wilson won. And Phelan was owed a favor. Meanwhile the Army Corps' 146-page report, using Freeman's data, agreed with Freeman's assessment that Hetch Hetchy offered San Francisco the cheapest and biggest source of water. Outgoing Taft's recently appointed Secretary of the Interior Walter Fisher, however, agreed with his predecessors Hitchcock and Ballinger that he did not possess the authority to permit only what Congress could: The excision of a major scenic portion of America's most famous scenic national park for use as San Francisco's water cistern.

President Woodrow Wilson now appointed as his Secretary of the Interior Franklin K. Lane—formerly the San Francisco city attorney who had handled the city's original proposal to dam Hetch Hetchy.

Interestingly, it was already apparent at this time that it was not true that San

Francisco's need for water could *only* be met by damming Hetch Hetchy. One of Manson's assistant engineers, Max J. Bartel, delivered to him on April 24, 1912, a plan to dam and deliver the unprotected and available Mokelumne River (well north of Yosemite) to San Francisco for less money than what the Hetch Hetchy project would cost. The Mokelumne, explained Bartel, would and could satisfy the city's needs. Manson ignored Bartel. East Bay cities instead developed the Mokelumne during the Roaring Twenties—in time, ironically, to sell some of its water to San Francisco for years before the city finally completed its own system diverting the Tuolumne.

Despite the notoriety of Bartel's report, on August 5, 1913, the House pushed forward California Representative John E. Raker's bill to give Hetch Hetchy to San Francisco. The Senate followed suit on September 24. Despite anti-dam publicity published by magazines and newspapers and despite tens of thousands of letters written to Congress in protest of the dam and despite impassioned arguments against it delivered on both floors of Congress, on December 6, the Senate passed, 43 to 25 (with 29 abstaining), San Francisco's "emergency" request to build a dam in Hetch Hetchy as soon as possible.

On December 19, 1913, Woodrow Wilson signed Raker's act into law. After all, its proponents pointed out, San Francisco would add a beautiful lake to the other 111 lakes in Yosemite. Moreover, the dam and reservoir would actually improve the local scenery over the natural grassy floor of the valley by the impounded waters reflecting images of the majestic cliffs.

John Muir had railed in his book *The Yosemite* prior to the final vote:

> Nevertheless, like anything else worth while, from the very beginning, however well guarded, they have always been subject to attack by despoiling gain seekers and mischief-makers of every degree from Satan to senators, eagerly trying to make everything immediately and selfishly commercial, with schemes disguised in smug-smiling philanthropy, industriously, sham-piously crying, 'Conservation, conservation, pan-utilization,' that man and beast may be fed and the dear Nation made great.

On December 9, 1913, the *New York Times* summed up Washington, D.C.'s work with the headline: "One National Park Lost." The editorial went on to ask:

> Any city that would surrender a city park for commercial purposes would be set down as going backwards. So far as we are aware, such a case is unknown. Any State Legislature that would surrender a State park would set a dangerous and deplorable example. When the Congress of the United States approves a municipal sandbagging of a national park in order to give some glamorous city a few dollars,

> against the protest of the press and the people, is it time for real conservatives to ask: What next?

A year after Wilson signed the Raker Act, 76-year-old John Muir, by his own admission stricken "to the heart," died. Arch-conservationist and future Sierra Club Executive Director David Brower believed that Muir's having lost Hetch Hetchy to dam builders "might have instilled the huge grief that hastened his death."

After the Congressional vote, proponents of the dam wasted no time utilizing a $45-million bond previously approved by the citizens of San Francisco. In 1910, loggers clear-cut Hetch Hetchy. Indeed, Alfred Runte notes that the city cut more than six million additional board feet of timber within the Park (illegally), aside from what was removed from Hetch Hetchy's floor to create a clear bottom for the reservoir.

Construction of O'Shaughnessy Dam (named after the project's Chief Engineer Michael Maurice O'Shaughnessy) was given to the Utah Construction Company, which began the job in 1914 and finished in 1923. According to local newspapers, San Francisco's project was to furnish 400 million gallons of water daily to four million people, as well as "200,000 Hydro-Electric Horsepower for general use for lighting, heating, rail transport and manufacturing purposes."

In 1938, San Francisco would add yet another eighty-five feet of height to the dam to create a total height of 312 feet. This brought the full pool elevation of the reservoir to 3,796 feet and extended its length a bit farther to eight miles. Framed by spires, cliffs, and domes looming nearly 2,500 feet higher, Hetch Hetchy became a beautiful reservoir in what had been a Shangri-La. This reservoir sat in an irreplaceable glacial valley that geologist Josiah Dwight Whitney (namesake for the tallest mountain in America's contiguous forty-eight states) had remarked was so stunning that "if there were no Yosemite, the Hetch Hetchy would be fairly entitled to a worldwide fame."

In that this book chronicles death in Yosemite, the Hetch Hetchy dam story had to be told here. This dam and its 167 miles of aqueduct send an average of 220 million gallons of the Tuolumne per day to the Bay Area. San Francisco uses only a third of this water—it sells the rest elsewhere. These sales of water plus hydropower sales to PG&E net the city about $130 million per year. Hetch Hetchy, again as David Brower notes, was in fact sought more for its elevational advantage of generating hydropower; viable sites outside the Park offered less head. San Francisco's economic colonization of Yosemite National Park also entailed significant collateral damage to the humans who labored to build the Hetch Hetchy Project itself.

Looked at from a perspective of pure engineering, O'Shaughnessy Dam and its attendant works comprise an impressive achievement. It could be said that, for its time, the completion of this ambitious effort was second only to building the

Panama Canal in 1914. Yet today O'Shaughnessy Dam situated at the west end of Hetch Hetchy Valley in Yosemite National Park may also be the most controversial dam in the United States, rivaling for this dubious honor with much larger Glen Canyon Dam, which was completed in Northern Arizona in 1963 (incurring significant environmental damage to more than 400 miles of the Colorado River upstream and downstream of the concrete).

The Hetch Hetchy Grant (a.k.a. the Raker Act) signed into law by President Woodrow Wilson on February 19, 1913, authorized use of public lands along a nearly 130-mile route between Yosemite and San Francisco. It also authorized construction of O'Shaughnessy Dam in Yosemite. At 430 feet above its foundation (312 feet above the streambed), this dam is relatively short by today's standards; it no longer even ranks within the world's tallest one hundred. But when it was dedicated on October 16, 1938, it was the tallest dam in California. The state now holds others that are higher. The 777-foot Oroville Dam on the Feather River in northern California, for example, stands tallest in the United States. Nor is O'Shaughnessy even the tallest dam within the system of lands administered by the National Park Service. Hoover Dam (the 24th highest in the world) in Lake Mead National Recreation Area stands 726 feet high barely thirty miles from Las Vegas and backs up its reservoir into Grand Canyon National Park. Glen Canyon Dam impounding Lake Powell in Northern Arizona (also outside Grand Canyon National Park) tops out at 710 feet. For perspective, the tallest dam in the world is in Tadjikistan on the Vaksh River. It is earth and rock filled and towers a stunning 1,319 feet high.

Who oversaw the design and construction of San Francisco's project? Michael Maurice O'Shaughnessy, for whom the dam is named, graduated from the Royal University in Dublin in 1884. When handpicked in 1912 for the job of City Chief Engineer by the Mayor of San Francisco, the 48-year-old O'Shaughnessy left San Diego with an already impressive twenty-five years of experience under his belt. In 1918 he was made overall general superintendent for the Hetch Hetchy Project. His name was not bestowed on the dam until its dedication on July 7, 1923.

Built primarily to trap and store water, at full pool the reservoir behind O'Shaughnessy Dam holds 52,000 acre-feet. By comparison, Lake Mead behind Hoover Dam originally held more than 32 million acre-feet (now 28 million due to siltation) and Lake Powell, extending 186 miles behind Glen Canyon Dam, holds 27 million acre-feet of water. In short, among the big boys today, O'Shaughnessy isn't. But in the 1920s it was.

Surveying on the Hetch Hetchy Project began in 1908—before being officially authorized. Construction faced a major problem at its onset merely in getting men and materials into the wild mountain areas where needed. To get to the dam site, only accessible by trail at this time, the first thing necessary to build was a nine-mile stretch of road from Hog Ranch to Hetch Hetchy Valley. To grade this road, San Francisco contracted the Utah Construction Company in late 1914. As specified by the Raker Act, its width had to be twenty-two-feet so that it could later be used as a vehicular road (some of this original roadbed remains the current paved road into Hetch Hetchy).

Ted Wurm, in his detailed and comprehensive *Yosemite's Hetch Hetchy Railroad*, chronicles the human casualties. He names sixty-eight people who died overall while working on the project but admits his "list is incomplete." Wurm also notes a 1934 article in the *San Francisco Chronicle* which states that eighty-nine lives were "checked off" as the price of construction, though not all names are listed. At least two men were killed in the Park while building this road from Hog Ranch (now called Camp Mather, Hog Ranch was inside Yosemite National Park from 1890 to 1905). Probably these men are the very first two to die while working on any aspect of the Hetch Hetchy Project. Both were part of a crew of eight. According to Sonora's *The Union Democrat* (on January 16, 1915), Tony Marich met his end on January 7, halfway from Hog Ranch.

> It seems that Marich, with other men, was engaged in blasting rock; that after loading, the fuses were lighted and Marich retired the usual distance considered safe to await the explosion. When it occurred a piece of rock was projected through the air which struck him back of the head and caused a fracture at the base of the skull. The doctor was on the scene shortly, but Marich expired 30 minutes after receiving the injury and without regaining consciousness. He was a native of Austria and 29 years of age.

The old cliché "misery loves company" soon took on a new meaning in Yosemite. As *The Union Democrat* reports further:

> When Deputy Coroner [C. Harry] Burden reached home, word was awaiting him that another fatal accident had occurred at a camp two miles above the one where Marich met his fate, and he started out early the next morning to cover the same ground over which he had just completed a disagreeable trip, in company with Mr. Shaw in an automobile. [Harry Burden also operated at least one funeral parlor in the town of Sonora.]

On January 9, again according to the same January 16 news article, 45-year-old Claudius Cendon:

> ...was one of a crew engaged in removing a huge boulder, where a cut was being made. They had sprung the rock out of its natural position, and were picking beneath it to facilitate its removal from

> the roadway. Sam Neksich saw the rock, which measured three cubic yards, moving and he shouted a warning, but Cendon was caught beneath it and borne to the earth, nearly every bone in his body was broken. His death must have been instantaneous.... He was 45 years of age and a native of Spain, in which country a wife and two children survive him.

Wages paid during the complicated series of construction projects in and near Hetch Hetchy lured many transient laborers. Some were recent immigrants from Europe where World War I raged. Details as to the lives of these men, sometimes even their full names, often were limited to only the sketchiest bits reported in a brief and sometimes obscure news article. Many of those killed while working on O'Shaughnessy Dam were buried with little fanfare in nearby Sonora. We suspect some of these men's families, particularly those living in the Old Country, might never have learned of the full circumstances of their loved one's death.

Beginning in September of 1915, workers started erecting camp buildings and related infrastructure high on the canyon's north wall overlooking Hetch Hetchy Valley. Construction of a 1,000-foot long, twenty-foot wide diversion tunnel soon followed. This was accompanied by building a small diversion dam in the main gorge. Meanwhile the valley floor had to be cleared of trees. The main part of this beautiful valley was about a mile and a half long and two-thirds of a mile wide. By the end of June 1916, between 400 and 500 men were hard at work here dismantling much of the valley's beauty.

Vital to supplying all of this construction effort was the Hetch Hetchy Railroad and later the Sierra Railroad. Ted Wurm notes in *Yosemite's Hetch Hetchy Railroad* that it cost $2 million, or about $29,000 per mile, to build its 68 miles of roadbed (in today's dollars this would equal almost half a million per mile). The Utah Construction Company accepted the completed railroad line from its builder in October of 1917. The quality of the graded bed and rails and rolling stock were such that it was still occasionally used until 1948 or later. At least seven men were killed during one or another phase of the Hetch Hetchy Project's railroads. Though records are sketchy, it seems none of them were killed within Yosemite.

With so many people working under dangerous conditions for years on end, the contractor needed a modern medical facility. Utah Construction situated its main center, a twenty-six-bed hospital, hours and miles away in Groveland. They equipped it with operating and X-ray rooms. Its primary physician (he also treated local families) was Dr. John Degnan, born in Yosemite Valley to a pioneer family. Degnan took charge of the hospital in April of 1921 and remained its key doctor until 1934, by which time construction had mostly ended. During at least the first phase of the dam's building, the Utah Construction Company also maintained a smaller hospital at Hetch Hetchy.

The next major phase for the Project in Yosemite was not O'Shaughnessy

Dam itself but instead the multi-arched, low Eleanor Dam a dozen miles north of Hetch Hetchy and also within the Park. This little known structure was begun in August of 1917 to raise the level of the original, tiny Lake Eleanor by thirty-five feet. San Francisco placed it into service a mere ten months later. (The namesake for "Eleanor" was the daughter of Josiah Dwight Whitney, state geologist in the 1860s and, again, director of California's first State Geological Survey.) Eleanor, the first of at least five dams on the Project between Yosemite and San Francisco, was intended to aid in generating year-around hydropower for the Moccasin Powerhouse, which transmits it via a ninety-eight-mile line to the city. Thankfully, no one was killed while working on Eleanor Dam.

It may sound strange, but O'Shaughnessy Dam, the key Hetch Hetchy structure, was actually completed twice. This "two-dams-in-one" concept had been planned in advance. Again, on August 1, 1919, San Francisco awarded a contract to the Utah Construction Company to erect the initial structure at a cost of slightly over $6 million. The first concrete for this phase was poured in September of 1921. Pouring continued until late spring of 1923. More than 500 men labored on this, often going day and night during summer and winter. The finished phase one structure was dedicated on July 7, 1923. But the cost had exceeded mere money. At least sixteen hardworking men had been killed on or near O'Shaughnessy Dam. (As a comparison, Hoover Dam [a.k.a. Boulder Dam]—the biggest thing built in the history of the world until after World War II—cost $49 million and about 110 lives of the 3,500 or so men working on it.)

Initially, most casualties on the job at Hetch Hetchy were due to rock falls precipitated by blasting the gray granite of the valley's north and south walls. At least four workers were killed this way. The first, on April 25, 1920, was 20-year-old Jose Zurana. Learning the specifics on poor Zurana, though, has proven anything but easy. Indeed, he may be the poster boy to illustrate just how confusing it often was to accurately determine even simple facts for this book, even to the spelling of a man's name. The Park's *Superintendent's Annual Report for 1920* has Jose's last name as "Serrano." The California Death Certificate #19339 has it spelled as "Zurana." *The Union Democrat* for May 1, 1920 has it as "Zurano." This same Sonora newspaper goes on to say, "He was at work operating a drilling machine at the base of a hill when a large rock loosened and fell from a higher point, striking him on the head, crushing in his skull. His death was almost instantaneous." We trust this account was accurate.

"ARM TORN FROM SHOULDER" reads the front page of Sonora's *The Union Democrat* on December 2, 1921. The article following this macabre headline illuminates the dangers these workers faced. It also highlights the loneliness of their lives.

> Another tragedy occurred on the Hetch Hetchy works last Saturday in which Ed Castraine was the victim. He was employed at

> the rock crusher plant at Camp 2 and was engaged at the rock distributor when he received his fatal injuries. In some way his sleeve caught in the revolving belt, and when his co-workers found him he was minus his right arm, which had been severed at the shoulder and his shoulder-blade was broken. The injured man was rushed to the hospital at Groveland, but his death resulted 12 hours after the accident and was due to shock and loss of blood....
>
> Deceased was about 37 years of age. Nothing was known about him among those with whom he worked. He was buried Wednesday in the city cemetery by Undertaker O'Beirne.

Construction continued despite fatalities without skipping much of a beat. And as the dam itself was built, its ever-increasing height became the most dangerous element of the workplace. As listed in Table 4, over time, eleven men died from falls here, some plummeting more than 200 feet. Between 1921 and 1923, as the phase one dam was erected, nine men fell. The last two plunged to their deaths in 1935 and 1936 as the dam was being raised to its present-day height. The critical mistakes that killed them varied from the victim simply losing his balance to instead being sent spinning into thin air when cables or bolts or other infrastructure broke.

But height and rocks were not the only dangers. Two workmen drowned in the Tuolumne River, one while on the job and another who went swimming just downstream of the dam on his day off. Four more died when hit by falling equipment. At least one worker died of a heart attack. The psychology of working here apparently also took its toll. On October 19, 1927, John Hill, known in his homeland of Finland as Johannas Helhikla, took a straight razor to his own throat.

The planned second phase of the dam—raising it eighty-five feet higher—began in 1935 and ended early in 1938. Chief Engineer O'Shaughnessy had anticipated this adjunct with the idea of increasing the reservoir capacity behind the dam by 75 percent to possibly escalate its electrical output in the near future. The Transbay Construction Company made the lowest bid ($3,219,965) to win the contract for this project.

By this time the United States now sagged in the midst of the Great Depression. Thousands of hungry jobless men roamed the country looking for any kind of work at any rate of pay (this accounts for the nightmarishly high death toll incurred while building Hoover Dam between 1934 and 1936). The second phase on the Hetch Hetchy Project now incorporated President Franklin Delano Roosevelt's relief efforts for the unemployed. This "Alphabet Era," named for its many government programs known by their abbreviations—the ECW, CCC, NRA, and WPA—placed a blizzard of welfare and put-men-to-work programs into motion. Luckily, due to increased safety awareness, better supervision and labor relations, less blasting to do on the unstable cliffs, and also lessons learned from the first phase of building in Yosemite, "only" four more men died working on the dam. More advanced and refined techniques and equipment also must have contributed to this improved safety record. As an example of this, and as noted by retired Park Historian Jim Snyder, "Electric blasting was adopted after 1923, greatly reducing deaths and injuries. Although still inherently dangerous, it is less so."

Typical of these deaths is that of 35-year-old Leonard S. Bailey, a San Franciscan. On October 24, 1935, he was secured by a sling to the high line (cable) above the dam. Possibly due to Bailey having given the signal to stop the cable too late, or else due to too much slack in the cable and ropes, he was slammed against the granite face of the cliff. Upon hitting the granite Bailey was thrown loose from his sling and fell to the ground below. He was killed "almost instantly."

On November 22, 1935, 26-year-old William Baker, of Pitcher, Oklahoma, was knocked loose by a section of two-inch diameter air line attached to a steel skip on a high line above him. The pipe hit Baker and fractured his skull.

Twenty-one years after Tony Marich became the first to die (in 1915) in Yosemite while working on the Hetch Hetchy Project, James N. Covington suffered the ignominy of being the last. *The Union Democrat* (October 30, 1936), notes that 29-year-old Covington:

> —died at the Hetch Hetchy Hospital [in Groveland] late last Friday night [October 23, 1936] as the result of an accident that befell him the evening before while he was working…at O'Shaughnessy Dam. Covington, who was a signal [single?] man, in some unaccountable manner, fell from his station a distance of fifteen feet fracturing his skull. He remained unconscious until his death twenty-four hours later. He was a native of Mississippi but had resided in Sonora for the past twelve years where he finished his high school education, and was quite prominent in…football and basketball teams. He was a likable fellow and his sudden and premature death is very much regretted by his many friends.

Thirty years and many millions of dollars after the start of construction of the dam at Hetch Hetchy and its associated structures, San Francisco now operated one of the greatest water projects ever undertaken by a municipality. As a postscript there seem to be only two persons who died in Yosemite while employed on the finished product. On July 2, 1939, Fred T. Powell fell off it while doing some chore. On October 12, 1944, O'Shaughnessy Dam Caretaker James Gray became a conduit for lightning when the bolt struck a nearby power line then passed through him.

As big as this project was in Yosemite, O'Shaughnessy Dam and the Hetch Hetchy Reservoir constituted only one part of San Francisco's very complicated system to generate hydropower and to store and deliver Tuolumne River water to a destination 167 miles away. The attendant aqueduct system required a huge amount of construction—one of the Coast Range tunnels, for example, was bored a record-setting twenty-five miles in length—and incurred even more than its share of injuries and casualties. In one such tragedy on July 17, 1930, a dozen men were killed in the Mitchell Ravine Tunnel through the Coast Range due to an explosion caused when a spark of unknown origin ignited natural methane gas seeping into the shaft. The *Superintendent's Monthly Report* for July, 1930, notes:

> It is the consensus of opinion that this disaster was due to the ignition of a large volume of methane gas. Safety experts of the State advise that recommendations in use of safety appliances and machinery were not complied with by the engineers in charge of this work. On July 25th City Engineer M. M. O'Shaughnessy signed an agreement not to resume work on the Hetch Hetchy tunnels in Alameda County until every safety requirement recommended by State and Federal engineers has been installed in the tunnels.

Every person who died while working on the Hetch Hetchy Project, within Yosemite National Park or not, like James N. Covington, had friends, a family, as well as a real life and a personal story. We hope we have done at least partial justice to their sacrifices.

At 10:12 a.m. on October 24, 1934—six years after James Duval Phelan died, two years after Freeman died, and a mere twelve days after 70-year-old Michael M. O'Shaughnessy died—the Tuolumne River finally flowed into Pulgas Water Temple after a passage of 167 miles from Hetch Hetchy through the new aqueduct system. (Oddly, the engineer is often included in the total number of eighty-eight men and one woman—a nurse caught in a fire in the company's hospital in Groveland—to die building the Project.) The Pulgas was a Roman Renaissance revival pavilion built at Crystal Springs Reservoir about thirty miles south of San Francisco.

The financial cost of all this turned out to be $142.1 million during a time when gold was worth $20 per ounce. To keep the Tuolumne flowing through this new plumbing would cost several billion dollars more by the turn of the century. The environmental cost was the loss of a second, albeit smaller, Yosemite Valley. Was this loss of Hetch Hetchy Valley and of the lives of so many workers there worth it? That's up to you to decide.

Beyond the Hetch Hetchy Project Yosemite is laced with hundreds of other construction projects for the needs, use, or convenience of visitors and employees of the government and concessions. Buildings dot the Park. Most of these are connected via roads. These roads have been surveyed, blasted, carved, graded, leveled, paved, and then resurveyed, realigned, rebuilt, resurfaced, et cetera, for nearly a century and a half. Mercifully, given the amount of granite dynamited into the air to create Yosemite's road and trail systems over the decades, deaths have been relatively few: seven workers have died while building or maintaining them.

None of these few deaths, however, proved painless. On April 23, 1926, William P. Walsh, a laborer for the V. E. Dennis Construction Company, was working at the top of an embankment in El Portal when it collapsed. The sliding earth and rock pummeled then buried Walsh, breaking five of his left ribs, four of his right, and puncturing his left lung. A week later, on May 1, Walsh died in the Yosemite Hospital from his injuries. In 1930, Lewis Memorial Hospital replaced the Yosemite Hospital. Five years after this switch, on May 25, 1935, 41-year-old William Anderson Combs, a powderman for the Bureau of Public Roads, was setting off multiple detonations to loosen rocks for construction of the Big Oak Flat Road. Several boulders tumbled down the hill onto Combs and two other employees. The latter sustained survivable injuries while Combs died en route to the Valley's Lewis Memorial Hospital.

Building the Tioga Road in several phases down through the years was dangerous. The workers faced a host of hazards, any of which could kill in the blink of an eye. They routinely worked with explosives to blast boulders out of the way or off the cliffs above. They rode and wrangled bulldozers, graders, front-end loaders, and steam shovels—and in the early years did the same with mules and donkey engines. Men were forced to dodge falling rocks too many times to count. Landslides had to be cleared. And huge and ancient pine trees had to be dropped with crosscut saws and, more recently, large chainsaws. Much of this effort was made during blizzards, lightning storms, or torrential rains. Given the amount of hazardous work performed in constructing the Tioga Road (and all the other roads and trails in the Park), we are probably fortunate that the safety record is as good as it is, and it *was* very good.

Even so, a few accidents did happen. In the category of those slightly more complicated than mere bad luck we tally 25-year-old William C. E. Arnold's run-in with a large compressor. On May 24, 1939, on the Tioga Road near White Wolf, Arnold was working with the compressor. Somehow he misjudged things very seriously while the machine was operating and got caught between its large belt and the pulley. He survived long enough to arrive at the hospital alive but died soon thereafter.

Dynamite claimed another road worker nearly half a century later. On May 17, 1984, 52-year-old Sammy Lee Smallwood, a National Park Service maintenance man of thirty years, was working on a crew moving a rock at Little Blue Slide on the Tioga Road, one mile east of Tuolumne Meadows. After detonation, a rock from the blast flew into the air and struck him in the head; his hard hat did him little good against the force of the blow. Smallwood died en route by helicopter to Modesto Memorial Hospital.

Considering that by now thousands of people over a century and a half within

Yosemite National Park have worked on the job under hazardous conditions to build more than 360 miles of road and 800 miles of trail plus many hundreds of other diverse facilities—offices, hotels, houses, stores, museums, ski lifts, bridges, tunnels, campgrounds, scenic lookouts, and turnouts—the death toll here for non-dam construction is astounding not for the few who died, but instead for the very high percentage who lived. The potential in all this building for many more of these workers to have suffered fatal accidents—and for the rest of us to have chalked up their deaths to mere bad luck during a dangerous enterprise—was far higher than the reality. Let us hope that the future unfolds at least as well for the next generations of builders.

TABLE 4. DEATHS WHILE BUILDING IN YOSEMITE. (Incidents discussed in text are noted.)

Deaths During Construction of O'Shaughnessy (Hetch Hetchy) Dam:

Name, age	Date	Location	*Circumstances*
Tony Marich, 29	January 7, 1915	Hetch Hetchy area, 4 miles from Hog Ranch (Camp Mather)	*Despite seeking shelter at what he thought a safe distance, Marich was killed by a* ***rock*** *blasted through the air.* (in text)
Claudius Cendon, 45	January 9, 1915	Hetch Hetchy area, 6 miles from Hog Ranch (Camp Mather)	*While building a road to service the dam, a* ***rock*** *"which measured three cubic yards" was loosened by construction. Cendon "was caught beneath it and borne to the earth, nearly every bone in his body being broken. His death must have been instantaneous."* (in text)
Jose Zurana, 28	April 25, 1920	Hetch Hetchy Dam Site	*Zurana, an "industrious and frugal" Spanish laborer, was working a drill when struck and killed instantly by a* ***falling rock****.* (in text)
D. O. Robinson, 56	May 4, 1920	Hetch Hetchy Dam Site	*Utah Construction Company assistant superintendent of construction Robinson of Denver was struck by a* ***loose cable*** *on May 3.*
Arley Kellam, 50	May 3, 1921	Hetch Hetchy Dam Site	*Kellam of Kansas* ***drowned*** *in the Tuolumne River while working below the dam. His body was recovered on May 18th.*
Pat McCarthy, 39	May 8, 1921	Hetch Hetchy Dam Site	*McCarthy died instantly when struck on the head by a* ***falling concrete bucket.***

P. H. Kilker, 45	August 4, 1921	Hetch Hetchy Dam Site
		Kilker "was instantly killed…by ***falling out of a bucket*** *in process of being hauled to the top of the [170-foot] tower." He was being hoisted in the bucket with 4 other workmen. When they reached the top they "observed Kilker was missing."*
S. Cotter, adult	September 12, 1921	Hetch Hetchy Dam Site
		Cotter was struck fatally by a ***rolling boulder.***
Ed Castraine, 37	November 26, 1921	Hetch Hetchy Dam Site
		Castraine's ***sleeve got caught in the revolving belt of a rock crusher*** *"and when his coworkers found him he was minus his right arm, which had been severed at the shoulder…" He died 12 hours later of "shock and loss of blood."*
Mike Cheski, 38	December 1, 1921	Hetch Hetchy Dam Site
		Cheski ***fell 30 feet*** *from the upper construction area to the base of the dam's foundation.*
A. Juiz, 34	July 7, 1922	Hetch Hetchy Dam Site
		Juiz was ***struck by the boom of a derrick****. "His ribs and chest were so badly crushed that it caused an inward hemorrhage…"*
Horace C. Thompson, 34	September 11, 1922	Hetch Hetchy Dam Site
		Thompson, a rigger, ***fell 150 feet*** *from one of the concrete construction towers and died 30 minutes later.*
George H. Carlson, 32	January 28, 1923	Hetch Hetchy Dam Site
		Carlson of San Francisco, and foreman of the rigging crew, was in one of the dam's chutes with 4 others when safety bolts broke. They all ***fell 60 feet****, but only he died.*
H. K. Nickols, 24	February 10, 1923	Hetch Hetchy Dam Site
		Nickols of McAlister, Oklahoma ***fell 25 feet*** *while moving about covering freshly laid concrete with canvas to keep it from freezing.*
Joe Dower, 30	February 22, 1923	Hetch Hetchy Dam Site
		*Dower, a native of Russia and a carpenter's helper, "****fell on the steps*** *at the back of the dam, and* ***rolled down about 70 feet****." He died 90 minutes later of a fractured skull.*
Mike Aracic, 29	February 24, 1923	Hetch Hetchy Dam Site
		*Aracic of Austria, was "****struck by the shute*** *[sic] of a concrete spout and knocked from the concrete forms…" and* ***fell 40 feet****. A witness said "Aracic was not looking, or he could have squatted down and let the shute pass over him…"*
Amico De Iullo, 41	April 7, 1923	Hetch Hetchy Dam Site
		De Iullo, along with Bailey (below) and a third worker (who survived), ***fell about 100 feet when a cable chain broke.***

James Bailey, 24	April 7, 1923 Hetch Hetchy Dam Site *Bailey, (along with De Iullo, above) "found everlasting sleep" when he was "dashed to death in a long fall caused by a chain becoming separated from a cable."*
Leonard S. Bailey, 35	October 24, 1935 Hetch Hetchy Dam Site *Bailey, a San Franciscan, was secured by a sling to the high line (cable) above the dam. He* ***was slammed against the cliff,*** *thrown from his sling, and fell 20 feet to the ground. He died "almost instantly."* (in text)
William Baker, 26	November 22, 1935 Hetch Hetchy Dam Site *High above Baker of Pitcher, Oklahoma a steel skip on the high line knocked loose a section of 2-inch diameter air line pipe. The* ***pipe fell and hit Baker*** *and fractured his skull. By November 1935, about 350 men were at work on this project.* (in text)
Peter G. Achats, 23	October 12, 1936 Hetch Hetchy Dam Site *Achats was* ***crushed between a loose concrete bucket*** *and the dam.*
James N. Covington, 28	October 20, 1936 Hetch Hetchy Dam Site *Covington of Sonora, California* ***fell 15 feet off a ladder*** *and died the next night of a fractured skull.* (in text)
Fred T. Powell, 37	July 2, 1939 Hetch Hetchy Dam Site *Powell of Los Angeles, California was working on the dam and fell.*

Deaths During Road or Trail Construction:

William P. Walsh, 26	May 1, 1926 El Portal Road *On April 23, Walsh, a laborer for the V.E. Dennis Construction Company, was working atop* ***an embankment when it collapsed.*** *Sliding earth and rock pummeled* ***then buried Walsh,*** *breaking 9 ribs and puncturing his left lung. He died a week later.* (in text)
Michael Rhodes, 61	September 8, 1930 trail between Vernal and Nevada Falls *Rhodes, originally from Ireland, was a tool nipper of 17 years' government employment (since 1913). Probably near the "Ice Cut," notes historian Jim Snyder, and while carrying tools up the trail to the crew, a rockslide swept him over a 300-foot cliff. It was suspected that recent blasting may have incited the slide.*
William Anderson Combs, 41	May 25, 1935 Big Oak Flat Road *Combs, a powderman for the Bureau of Public Roads, set off multiple detonations in a road cut. Additional* ***rocks tumbled down the hill onto Combs and 2 others.*** *The latter survived. Combs died en route to Lewis Memorial Hospital.* (in text)
Ernest Mossien, 44	June 3, 1937 Big Oak Flat Road *Mossien, a Park resident and government engineer, "died at the hospital of pneumonia, which was brought on by an injury*

		incurred when ***he fell*** *[off a cliff on May 12] while working on the new Big Oak Flat Road."*
Hilmar Heldal, 32	August 2, 1937	Big Oak Flat Road
		Heldal, working on the "new" Big Oak Flat Road, died when a ***large dump truck wheel rolled over his body*** *[July 21]. The driver had not seen him under the truck where he had sought refuge from nearby blasting.*
William C. E. Arnold, 25	May 24, 1939	Tioga Road near White Wolf
		Arnold of Cathay, California was working with a ***large compressor*** *and was* ***caught between the belt and a pulley****. He was alive when arriving at the hospital but soon died.* (in text)
Sherman D. McDaniel, 37	May 27, 1966	2 miles west of Crane Flat
		McDaniel, a contractor from Crows Landing, California, while building the new Big Oak Flat Road, operated an earth mover but lost control and was either tossed from it or jumped off. He landed in its path and ***was crushed beneath it****.*
Sammy Lee Smallwood, 52	May 17, 1984	Tioga Road, 1 mile east of Tuolumne Meadows
		An NPS maintenance worker of 30 years, Smallwood was on a crew using dynamite to move rock on Little Blue Slide. ***A large flying rock struck his head.*** *Despite his hard hat, he died en route by helicopter to Modesto.* (in text)

Chapter Five

AIRCRAFT DOWN

On July 13, 1924, L. R. Hyman and Dr. Stetlerm of San Francisco flew into Yosemite in a biplane. They circled the walled Valley, dropped into it, then lined up for an approach on Leidig Meadow, near the Village. By now residents and tourists alike were watching rapt. To the relief of just about everybody, the small craft touched down safely. Although a few other pilots had landed before in the Park, people still jostled to admire the novelty. Flying that sort of thing into a place like this, people likely said to one another, took guts. The spectators now crowded the plane and expounded on the courage—or the idiocy—of its two occupants.

This successful landing is the happy part of this tale. During Hyman's attempted takeoff, he failed to gain enough lift in the hot summer air. Yank back on the stick as he might, the machine refused to lift enough. It crashed into a tree.

Amazingly, both men escaped serious injury. That too is a happy part of the story because, as we will soon see, many others who have crashed in the Park have experienced worse outcomes. Yet while Hyman himself emerged relatively unscathed from this mishap, his plane was wrecked. Apparently Mr. Hyman was an indefatigable, can-do kind of guy. He ordered the plane dismantled then shipped by freight back to San Francisco for repairs. He planned on flying it again.

The first plane wreck ever in Yosemite was not Hyman's. Instead it had occurred three years earlier on July 23, 1921. No one was injured when the craft nosed over during takeoff and suffered only minor damage. The owners repaired the tattered machine on the spot and safely flew it back to San Francisco.

Two years earlier yet, another aerial milestone took place in Yosemite. On May 27, 1919, Lieutenant J. S. Krull, of the United States Army Signal Corp, landed a

Curtiss biplane in the Valley. This was "after much discussion as to the feasibility of the proposition and considerable negotiation with officials at Mather Field [commissioned as Mills Field in Sacramento on February 21, 1918]…"

Apparently a paramount concern on this maiden landing was how the small plane would handle the tricky winds as it powered down between the rims of the Valley. Well, there was only one way to find out…

With one hand on the throttle of the 150-horsepower Illspane-Suiza engine, Krull tested his uncertainty of the air currents. Once satisfied that making a landing down there was doable, he flew in from the direction of Half Dome. He made a perfect landing on the field that had been prepared for him in the meadow. The crowd of spectators there applauded with approval. After this christening, Leidig Meadow would serve as Yosemite's "official" airfield for years to come.

Just after dawn the following morning Lieutenant Krull executed an equally successful take off. The only glitch in this entire "mission" for the Army pilot was he had to make a "forced landing due to gasoline trouble" at Mormon Bar, west of the Park. Even so, he made the roundtrip of 150 miles from Merced in less than two hours of actual flying time. Darned good flying for 1919.

Within three months after Krull daringly proved it could be done safely, a second and a third landing occurred in Yosemite. The success of these pilots prompted Park Superintendent Washington B. Lewis to write glowingly of the future of Yosemite aviation in his *Annual Report to the Director*:

> There seems no reason why, after complete aviation maps have been prepared of the surrounding mountain country, showing all of the possible landing places (and there are many of the countless high mountain meadows suitable for this), this method of transportation in the Valley will now become popular, and I believe that before very long definite preparations must be made to provide proper landing places, not only in Yosemite Valley, but in other places of interest in the park, such as Tuolumne Meadows and Lake Tenaya. I believe also that feasibility of the use of the aeroplane for fire patrol from the Valley is one that should be immediately considered.

With increasing air traffic in a region with weather as changeable and potentially dangerous as in Yosemite, a serious crash was inevitable. The first happened on July 25, 1926, in Wawona—on what is now the golf course. On this flight noted author, climber, mountaineer, and explorer 48-year-old LeRoy Jeffers of New York City rode as a passenger with Dr. Sterling Bunnell of San Francisco at the stick. The latter was a noted orthopedic and plastic surgeon, who, as an amateur aviator with his own plane, had become one of the first "flying surgeons." His work in flying mercy missions up and down the length of California had earned the respect of many. This flight to Yosemite from Redwood City, though, had no medical purpose. Instead it was intended to offer Jeffers a bird's eye view of the central Sierra Nevada, about which the mountaineer-author was writing a magazine article.

Jeffers was no hack. He boasted an unusual history. Educated at Harvard and now a senior librarian for the New York Public Library, he had turned to mountains as an avocation. His list of amateur accomplishments in this arena became increasingly impressive. In 1920, he bagged a first ascent of 12,100-foot high Mount Moran in what is now Wyoming's Grand Teton National Park. To pull this off he had made the final critical moves to the summit after dark—which revealed a combination of guts, confidence, and perhaps even recklessness. To his credit, Jeffers' passion extended well beyond merely climbing mountains in Europe and North America. Jeffers had also become an outspoken proponent for the conservation of America's resources, especially its scenic wonders. He extolled in print and during lectures the idea that every citizen should appreciate and protect these, their precious natural assets.

In recognition for his contributions to science Jeffers was made a Fellow of the Royal Geographical Society. He also became the organizer and secretary of the Bureau of Associated Mountaineering Clubs of North America. In addition, he was a member of the National Park Commission, the National Institute of Social Science, the California Academy of Sciences, and he also worked as librarian for the American Alpine Club. In short, LeRoy Jeffers was a one-man whirlwind of outdoor appreciation.

Now trying to land before an audience of 200 local residents and guests of the Hotel Wawona, Dr. Bunnell twice circled the landing field. He cautiously worked his way down between nearby tree-covered ridges. Abruptly, only 100 feet off the deck, he banked hard for his landing. The plane suddenly lost lift and slipped out of his control. It plunged almost straight down in a nose dive and slammed the ground in a sickening crash.

Explorer Jeffers died instantly. Bunnell survived the impact with head injuries and a fractured hip. He was evacuated from his ruined aircraft back to a San Francisco Bay Area hospital where he spent a lengthy convalescence.

This crash was not only the first fatal aircraft incident in what is now Yosemite National Park, it also seems to be the first anywhere in the National Park System.

A year later, in 1927, J. L. Mayberry, an entrepreneur from Fresno announced his proposed airplane service between Merced, Wawona, and Yosemite Valley. He also planned to build a landing field. This never got off the ground, so to speak. But for more than ten years after his announcement air travel in and over Yosemite went smoothly. Unfortunately, when it finally became unsmooth, it became very unsmooth.

After more than a decade had passed since Mayberry's optimistic announcement, the worst happened. On March 1, 1938, 35-year-old Pilot John D. Graves from Palo Alto, California lifted his Transcontinental and Western Airlines

(TWA) flight off a San Francisco runway at 6:30 p.m., en route to Winslow, Arizona by way of Burbank. His departure was ominously timed from the onset. Immediately to his south, that paradise called Southern California was being hit by its worst storm in sixty-four years.

Graves' copilot was 29-year-old C. W. Wallace. Their flight attendant was 23-year-old Martha M. Wilson. Also on board was an off-duty TWA pilot, 31-year-old Harvey Melvin Salisbury. Otherwise the Douglas-manufactured "Sky Queen" (NC-1299) was carrying only five other passengers. The DC-2 Sky Queen held fourteen passenger seats. It was sixty-two feet long and flew on eighty-five feet of wingspan. The aircraft was powered by two, 730-horsepower propeller engines which offered a maximum speed of 210 mph, a range of 1,085 miles, and a service ceiling of 22,000 feet.

Company ground control figured the transport could clear the area before the storm moved into its intended flight path. Even if true, this flight still would be touch and go. After reporting in over Modesto then Fresno, Graves radioed that weather conditions were deteriorating rapidly. They were flying at 10,000 feet, he said. He was now between Tejon Pass and Saugus, forty miles south of Bakersfield. "Ice is forming on the wings," Graves reported, "and I am turning back."

This was a good decision. But Graves had made it a bit late. Fifty-five minutes later, Graves radioed again he was still at 10,000 feet and that conditions were terrible. He was, he said, between cloud layers in the dark and was uncertain as to exactly where he was (this was before the era of radar).

The dispatcher at Union Air Terminal at Burbank radioed Graves instructions to detour back to Bakersfield and to land there if possible—or else set down anywhere he could. This too was good advice, but again it came late.

After sending instructions to Graves, TWA Control heard in response only silence.

The small airliner carried fuel for six hours. This could easily get the nine people aboard to Winslow or to a good number of alternative emergency destinations. That is, it would get them there had the weather been okay. But it was not okay.

The plane never arrived in Winslow. Nor did it touch down in Bakersfield or Burbank or on any other known airstrip.

The radio silence from the lost Sky Queen now became deafening. The next morning the search began. A woman whose name was never learned telephoned from thirty miles east of Fresno to say she had seen the lights of a plane flying low at 9:20 p.m. Authorities took her report seriously. Conditions, unfortunately, proved anything but propitious for a search. The snow level had dropped to 2,000 feet elevation and cloud cover hovered only 500 feet higher. Two inches of rain had pummeled the immediate region. None of this was good.

Six planes took off to begin the hunt. Almost immediately bad weather forced them to turn around. They were down on the tarmac again only half an hour later.

The following day, "mystery lights and a white object were reported," noted the *San Francisco Chronicle* for March 3, "sighted at nightfall near a mountainside scar in the area where the plane was last seen [sixty miles northeast of Fresno]." In reality, huge ambiguity characterized the location and path of the Sky Queen.

On day three, a party of twenty ground searchers, including TWA personnel, tried to reach this "mystery lights" area. Horrible weather turned back these rescuers too. This record storm had already dropped seventy-seven inches of new snow in the high country (meanwhile thousands of people had been driven from their homes in Los Angeles and twenty-one other people had been killed there by floods). Several search pilots on this day almost lost their lives and those of their crews due to flying in this anomalously hazardous weather. This storm made all SAR efforts touch and go—with far more touching than going.

Conditions finally improved on day four. Now the search was expanded to include fifty planes. Some were hired by TWA, some were private planes volunteered by the Los Angeles County Sheriff's office, some were U.S. Army, and some Navy. They combed a rather small area of 88 square miles located 30 to 40 miles northeast of Fresno near Shaver and Huntington Lakes. Based on reports of sightings during the night of the crash, this area still seemed the best bet. The search coordinator had divided it into twenty-two sectors. Each pilot of this armada had his or her own four square miles of very rugged, snow-covered topography to scour. A few additional craft prowled the periphery, increasing the total area searched to 100 square miles. Unfortunately, even if these planes had been in the right place and even if the Sky Queen had been directly below them, the several feet of new snow almost certainly would have completely camouflaged the downed aircraft in white.

Meanwhile more than 400 other foot searchers, 300 of them young men from the Civilian Conservation Corps (CCC), combed the foothills closer to Fresno. Perversely, the weather continued to be wet, windy, cold, and miserable. Yet again, this army found nothing.

As the future would reveal, it would have been impossible to have located the lost Sky Queen where they were looking. It was not there. The aircraft, it would turn out, had crashed in the south central section of Yosemite, more than thirty miles north of the designated area. Those "leads" by apparently well-meaning civilians had been misleading.

Making matters far worse, new clues, mostly proving innocently or even deliberately wrong, popped up like weeds. One of these insisted the plane had landed near Bakersfield and everyone aboard was okay.

The mystery deepened. For more than three months, the $1,000 reward offered by TWA went unclaimed.

As days then weeks passed, people asked again for the umpteenth time: How could an airliner vanish altogether over land? Maybe it really had not crashed over land. Perhaps, instead, as other Sierra Nevada crashes in the future would do, this

TWA flight had the incredible bad luck to plunge into a lake and sink. As the months passed, the mystery of the lost Sky Queen became ever murkier.

Meanwhile a 23-year-old CCC worker from Fresno named H. O. Collier, who was stationed in the Wawona Camp, took it upon himself to systematically comb the backcountry on his days off. He had a hunch, he said, that the flight had gone down nearby. Of Collier, Ranger John W. Bingaman wrote—in his 1961 *Guardians of the Yosemite: A Story of the First Rangers*— "Each weekend he would take off from his camp with a few supplies and a blanket and would systematically take a set course and cover as much distance as possible. This particular trip, he told me later, would have been his last."

Despite the heavy snow of that March storm, by June the sun had melted much of the high country at least semi-clean. Now, 104 days after the crash, on the warm Sunday afternoon of June 12, 1938, a dozen miles northeast of Wawona in Yosemite National Park, Collier hit pay dirt. Two-hundred feet below the summit of the 9,709-foot Buena Vista Peak, he stumbled across the missing plane. It sat sadly smashed and crumpled and still partly buried in snow. Heartbreakingly, had the Sky Queen been flying just a little higher, it would have cleared Buena Vista Crest (east of the peak and the trail).

Investigators from the Civil Aeronautics Board concluded that Captain Graves, "while seeking his bearings, was attempting a steep bank. He struck three pine trees, shearing them off, and then plowed into the mountain on its southern side."

Eight of the nine people aboard still remained inside the fuselage. Recovering their bodies required sixteen hours using Curry Company pack animals. At one point in this operation one of these hardy horses was nearly lost in a raging creek.

One complication in all this revolved around Collier's position. The question was: If he was still on the federal payroll, would he be ineligible to claim the $1,000 reward offered "to the person leading a (TWA) company officer to the location of the downed ship?" Interestingly, at the time when the young man said he "discovered" the lost plane, he in fact no longer worked for the CCC, having just been honorably separated.

The next question soon arose: Did this ex-CCC worker truly locate this lost aircraft for the first time on June 12 or had he found it earlier? Nearly seventy years later, long-retired senior Park Ranger Tom Tucker—who worked in Wawona in 1938—still vividly recalls rumors that Collier had actually discovered the crash sooner but had kept it secret until he was eligible to claim the reward. This rumor then went on to say that only then had Collier revealed its location.

Was the rumor true? What actually did happen here? We doubt that, at this point, we will ever know for sure. For one thing, when found, the plane was still half buried in snow. How long prior to June 12 could any telltale part of the Sky Queen have been visible? Not long. Regardless, we believe Collier deserved the reward. After all, he did continue systematically to do the difficult footwork on his own initiative and on his own time. In fact, he found the plane and its nine occupants that everyone else had not only failed to find but also had virtually quit looking for.

Two months after Collier's discovery, the mother of 22-year-old Jay Tracy and 19-year-old Mary Lou Dirlam arrived in Yosemite. Both of this woman's children had been on board the ill-fated flight (the remaining three people aboard had been 49-year-old Victor Krause, 35-year-old Anna B. Walts, and 35-year-old Lucius B. Walts). Brother and sister had been popular Stanford students who had been en route home to Mansfield, Ohio, to visit their 45-year-old father, Jay N. Dirlam, because he had just suffered a heart attack. Mrs. Dirlam arrived now to make the trip up the Chilnualna Trail to the crash site to place a small bronze plaque on Buena Vista Peak to commemorate her loss. Her husband and her children's father, it turned out, had died of that heart attack before even learning of the TWA crash. Thus, in a matter of hours, poor Mrs. Dirlam had lost her entire family.

Thankfully, this TWA crash constituted the first—and only—fatal commercial plane crash in Yosemite. It also remains the Park's largest accident of any kind in total casualties.

During the summer of 1941, Yosemite Valley experienced such a rash of low altitude "buzzes" by Army Air Corps pilots feeling (and burning) their oats, that they became a dangerous nuisance—especially to hikers and equestrians. On July 11, two planes buzzed the treetops for half an hour, plenty long enough for their serial numbers to be recorded by irritated civilians and rangers on the ground. The Superintendent then reported these nuisance aircraft to Stockton Field where they were based. The commanding officer soon promised the Park he had ordered disciplinary action "which it was felt would prevent recurrences of low flying by Army personnel over the Valley." The Park's goal at this time was to restrict all flights to at least 1,000 feet above the Valley rim. As it would turn out, this might have played a role in saving a few lives of future military pilots who flew over the Yosemite region.

Unfortunately, it did not save all of them.

A few months later, just prior to October 24, 1941, a flight of nineteen P-40 "Warhawk" planes of the 57th Pursuit Squadron, made up of the fastest aircraft in the U.S. Army at this time, had just crossed North America from Connecticut to Southern California en route to Washington. This fighter's water-cooled 1,090-horsepower engine was rated at 357 miles per hour. The plane was normally armed with twin .50 caliber plus twin .30 caliber wing-mounted machine guns. This model of aircraft had already gained notoriety in China as the famed "Flying Tigers" squadron acclaimed by Colonel Robert L. Scott's World War II bestseller *God is my Co-Pilot* and by John Toland's later book *The Flying Tigers* and by the movie of the same title starring John Wayne. Now flying out of March Field near Riverside, California and bound for McClellan Field near Sacramento, the 57th Squadron's formation hit heavy cloud banks and fog. "We were flying in close V-formation," reported Major C. E. Hughes, commanding the flight. "We were close together when we hit the cloud. We were in the cloud two or three minutes. During that time we split up."

Of the original nineteen P-40s, five continued onward as planned and made it to McClellan Field. A sixth, low on fuel, was forced to land in Tulare. Seven others continued to follow Major Hughes as he detoured to Smith Valley, Nevada. "I tried to call them back by radio, but it was no use," the major noted of his other missing planes. "After we separated [and dropped 2,000 feet lower to get out of the clouds], I looked down, thinking I was over the San Joaquin Valley [many miles to the west], but I was over the [Sierra Nevada] mountains with only twenty minutes of gasoline." Hughes' squadron of eight, less than half the number he had under his wing (yes, pun intended) a mere half hour earlier, now landed on a strip on the east side of the Sierra. Inconveniently, this strip in Smith Valley was too short for them to take off from after refueling.

Ultimately a road grader would be required to lengthen that strip to 3,000 feet. Once this was done, only six of Hughes' eight P-40s would manage to fly from Smith Valley to Reno then over the Sierra Nevada to Sacramento (this was because one P-40 in Smith Valley would be too damaged to take off; the other P-40 would be forced to return to Smith Valley due to engine trouble).

Thus far in this saga of the scrambled 57th Pursuit Squadron we have accounted for only fourteen of its nineteen aircraft. These five remaining P-40s fared far worse.

One of these missing pilots, Lt W. H. Birrell, was a graduate of West Point. When Major Hughes and his seven followers vanished within that cloud, Birrell also entered the High Sierra at the controls of his new P-40. He flew in company with four other pilots. These five also disappeared almost immediately, at about 2 p.m.

The next day, Birrell's "demolished ship" and severely burned body would be discovered by searchers on the slope of 5,000-foot Grey's Mountain, in the Bass Lake region south of Yosemite. His plane, they would note, "had apparently crashed into the peak with terrific force."

Lt John H. Pease, one of the remaining four missing fliers, was in the air northeast of Tehachapi when visibility became nil in a "blinding snowstorm." Abruptly his fuel pressure dropped, even though he still had "plenty" of fuel. He climbed to 16,000 feet. Now his oil pressure suddenly dropped. As the young aviator wondered what the hell was going wrong with his P-40, his Allison engine caught on fire. Pease, who had been trying everything he could think of to baby his new machine along with each new malfunction, now knew he had to draw the line at catching on fire. Besides, whatever else could go wrong with his equipment on this flight by now had become something he would just as soon pass up experiencing. Better to bail out while it was still possible. Pease ejected.

He hit a hurricane force blast of freezing air. He counted off the seconds he had been trained to wait then he pulled the rip cord on his parachute.

His rip cord broke.

Despite this, Pease managed to deploy his parachute—even if he had not managed to successfully cajole his very expensive new pursuit plane through its chain of malfunctions.

Another flier, Lt E. F. Carey, who had stayed with those four *other* pilots who eventually made it to Sacramento safely, saw Pease bail out. Carey would soon report his companion's situation. Meanwhile, the young lieutenant floated downward under his canopy.

"I ran into a snow storm," Pease would later report, "on the way down."

He now drifted to a landing considerably south of Yosemite. Despite freezing due to inadequate flight clothing, Pease landed unhurt. Fortuitously, he missed a forest of big trees punctuated by boulders. Instead he came to rest squarely in a cushioning "mesquite" bush. "It must have been the only mesquite bush," Pease would later joke, "in miles." Although he did not know it yet, he and his "mesquite" were in Wild Rose Canyon more than a hundred miles southeast of Yosemite.

Pease unclipped from his rig, then started hiking. For luck, he carried his broken rip cord in his hand. About five miles downcanyon he found an old cattleman's cabin. He stopped here for the night. He built a fire, ate some canned cheese and "old pancakes" then slept on some ancient bedding. Except for the cold, this bailing-out business really was not all that bad.

The next morning Pease hiked two more miles and reached the Willoughby Ranch near Kennedy Meadows. Mrs. Mabelle Willoughby fixed breakfast for the lieutenant while they listened to a radio broadcast explaining that a search had been mounted for him. After the meal, Mr. Willoughby drove Pease twenty-eight miles to a telephone at Little Lake, a village on Highway 395 more than thirty miles northeast of today's Lake Isabella. There he phoned the U.S. Army Air Force to report in. His P-40 (serial #39-213), he would learn, had augered into the granite a dozen or so miles from where Birrell's plane had.

Still missing were Leonard C. Lydon, Richard N. Long, and Jack C. West and their three aircraft. Twenty-two search planes, mostly bombers, combed the vast region between the small Mother Lode town of San Andreas, well south of Lake Tahoe, all the way south through and beyond Yosemite to Owens Lake. This region had been divided into twenty sections of 525 square miles each. Unhelpfully, new snow had already blanketed much of the Sierra, the same snow that Pease had parachuted through, making the search job much more difficult. Harder yet, a Douglas B-18 search bomber also crashed on October 24 en route to the search area, killing an additional five airmen. Next, on October 29, a Vultee BT-13 crashed near Balch Camp east of Pine Flat Lake in eastern Fresno County during this same search, killing another two airmen.

On November 1, five weeks before the Japanese would surprise attack Pearl Harbor and one week after Birrell had died and Pease had escaped from his burning fighter, searchers discovered Lieutenants Lydon and West on the slope of Barton Peak in Kings Canyon National Park. Both pilots' motors had failed. Each had bailed out unknown to one another over the remote southern Sierra. Luckily they bumped into one another while crossing Sugar Loaf Meadow one day after having jumped from their ailing Warhawks.

The downed pilots had flashed their lights as SOS signals. Against the odds, someone in a search plane had spotted them. Both men were rescued unscathed but ravenously hungry—no hospitable ranch woman had made *them* breakfast during their week in the wilderness.

Oddly, while Leonard Lydon himself had been rescued from a more or less well known area, his wrecked P-40 still never has been found.

Worse, despite every effort, both Lt Richard N. Long *and* his Warhawk aircraft both remained missing. Had he crashed in Yosemite? This utter mystery would persist unsolved for many long years. Finally in 1959, a pair of backpackers hoofing it at 11,000 feet near Kings Canyon's South Guard Lake solved it. There, eighteen years after the ill-fated young pilot had vanished, the two hikers found the almost-unrecognizable wreckage of a P-40. Intermingled with the mangled fuselage were pieces of bleached and weathered human bones. Among these was a gold Second Lieutenant's bar. Investigation revealed this pursuit plane and the skeleton—and the tarnished gold bar—as Long's.

Poignantly, Long had not been initially detailed to make this cross-country flight with the 57th Pursuit Squadron. The fateful day of October 24, 1941, was originally scheduled to be his wedding day. For Second Lieutenant Richard N. Long, a change in flight orders had changed *everything.*

Between October 24 and November 2, 1941, the US Army Air Corps locally experienced thirteen plane wrecks during training missions—incurring thirteen dead and three missing. Such mishaps continued in the Sierra Nevada throughout World War II. A few were in Yosemite. Based on research by Gary P. Macha for his book *Aircraft Wrecks in the Mountains and Deserts of California: 1909-1996* (second edition), on June 21, 1943, one of the worst occurred. Lt William E. Hunt piloted a USAAF B-24E bomber (#42-7188) over the sierra and the eastern portion of Yosemite. For reasons still unknown to us Hunt was flying at 12,800 feet but trying to clear a ridge at about 12,900 feet elevation. The bomber hit hard between Koip and Kuna Peaks on the Park boundary at 12,800 feet. Also on board were co-pilot 2nd Lt Keith E. Delp, navigator 2nd Lt Dwight G. Beacon, bombardier 2nd Lt Clair Hartzell, engineer TSgt Sam Meyerhoff, radio operator SSgt Elmer Swaving, and photographer Pfc Maurice A. Smith. The entire crew died in Inyo National Forest, although two propellers bounced into the Park.

World War II was raging fiercely in both theatres by the time Yosemite hosted its next air tragedy. This one happened on April 13, 1944, when a 4th U.S. Army Air Force P-70A-1 Nighthawk (AF #42-54132) from the 450th AAFBU Group stationed at Hammer Field, Fresno vanished while executing a night training mission. This model had two 1,600-horsepower engines and could fly almost 330 miles per hour at 14,000 feet. Its service ceiling was 28,250 feet, its combat range a thousand miles. It was intended to be a night fighter but saw very little combat use in WW II because it was heavy and relatively slow.

The unit's Flight Plan #22 was a simple joint exercise with one other plane. The orders involved tracking and pursuit. Weather at the time was high overcast with possible light precipitation. Their mission called for one pursuit plane to track a target aircraft at 15,000 feet altitude during a short but circuitous flight from Fresno to Stockton.

Things started going awry quickly when the pilot of the target craft, Lt Michael O. Gard, began experiencing trouble regulating his oxygen. Preoccupied, Gard became uncertain of his heading as he flew. He led the twin-engine fighter behind him—piloted by 25-year-old Lt Jack Forest Marlow of Illinois (and with 550 hours of flight time) with radar observer 26-year-old Lt Edward P. Schlieter from Long Island, New York—up into the foothills near Friant Dam thirty miles north of Fresno. This location was okay in that it was the pilots' assigned rendezvous point. But Gard next strayed severely, leading Marlow into wispy clouds over Yosemite's high country.

Both aircraft leveled out at 14,500 feet (this was despite Flight Commander Robert E. Franklin having stipulated that all aircraft were to fly at 15,000 feet for this mission). Moreover, Gard's flight over the High Sierra—again with Marlow and Schlieter following him—was, as the Air Force accident report (# RAL 076) would later note, "considerably off course."

Gard's radar observer, Lt M. L. Mosley, reported to Gard that the fighter was successfully following them as they turned westerly back toward Fresno. Mosley watched as Marlow passed through a wisp of cloud, then reappear. Then the trailing aircraft abruptly disappeared. When Mosley reported that Marlow had failed to reappear, Gard circled back to the site where Marlow was last seen. They orbited the area for about ten minutes and tried to reestablish radio contact.

They heard only silence.

Gard next decided his fellow aviator may have returned to their original rendezvous at Friant Dam. So he returned there. But no, Marlow and Schlieter were not here either. They had truly vanished.

Subsequent searches for the lost plane proved unsuccessful. On April 22, after ten days, the Army Air Corps gave up. The Nighthawk had disappeared with both men aboard.

Seventy days later, on July 2, Archie Westfall, a packer working for Curry Company, was guiding a party of fishermen into the southern part of the Park near the junction of Moraine Meadows Trail and Givens Creek. Westfall, concerned with fish, instead discovered Marlow's wrecked P-70.

An initial investigation could determine no cause of the crash. But the Army ultimately concluded the plane had been "in a flat spin when it struck the earth."

They suspected instrument failure, but the plane had caught fire and incinerated the cockpit, making a reconstruction of instrument readings impossible. Indeed almost everything in the front half of the aircraft had burned up. Lt Marlow was only identifiable via dental records.

Investigators found Lt Schlieter halfway out of his escape hatch with his parachute at the ready. This suggested the two airmen knew their pursuit craft was failing them and had at least a few seconds of forewarning. Unfortunately, they hit the granite a few seconds too soon for either man to escape. The question now arose: Would those "lost" 500 feet of altitude not available to them due to Gard's choice of a 14,500-foot, not 15,000-foot, altitude have allowed Schlieter, or even Marlow the extra few seconds he needed?

This incident prompted Air Force command at Hammer Field to subsequently warn its pilots to: "strictly avoid conditions where malfunctioning of any equipment may jeopardize the safety of the aircraft and it occupants particularly over the hazardous mountain terrain which renders rescue practically impossible in the region of the Sierra Nevada Mountains."

Major John C. Doherty, Investigating Officer on the crash, wrote further: "It is recommended that 1st Lt Michael O. Gard be reprimanded for violation of AAF Regulation 15-23 for negligently though unintentionally deviating from a contact flight plan."

Only four months after Marlow and Schlieter died, on August 28, 1944, 20-year-old Lt Eugene K. Wicks (with 729 hours of flight time, despite his youth a solid resume at this time in the war), piloting a P-70B Nighthawk (#42-39742) with 21-year-old Lt Richard O. Davis onboard as radar operator took off from Hammer Field in Fresno well after midnight. Their mission was to fly with two other planes on an "Intruder Training Mission" to Don Pedro Reservoir (on the lower Tuolumne River) then east over the Sierra Nevada to Mono Lake, then south to Bishop, then return across the Sierra to Bakersfield, then fly north to land again at Hammer Field. Wicks had already flown a mission with this same Nighthawk to Lake Tahoe and back that evening. The aircraft had performed well. The altitude for this operation was 20,000 feet, using supplemental oxygen from the ground up.

Flight Commander James V. Du Pratt described Wicks as "a very steady and confident pilot and very conscientious about his Night Fighter Training. Before the take off I watched him go over this particular XC [cross-country] with his Radar Observer, checking all headings, time and distance information that the R/O [radar observer] had plotted."

Based on all this—and with fifteen miles of visibility that night—no one would have expected problems on this mission. Even so, Wicks crashed eighty miles out of Hammer Field, a mere five feet below the top of 11,161-foot Quarry Peak, on its west slope a dozen airline miles northwest of the Tuolumne Meadows Ranger Station but fifteen miles short of his checkpoint at Mono Lake. A tandem pilot flying higher saw the "terrific explosion" then the plane's "fiercely" burning pieces scatter in the dark like Fourth of July fireworks.

The airplane split in two. The front section bounced over the top and disintegrated "in small pieces scattered for about one-half mile down the East side of the peak." The impact had been so severe that in his report, forward observer Arthur C. Sawyer noted, "The aircraft was in a multitude of very small pieces and the one piece of radar equipment that was found intact was destroyed [internally]. No other confidential equipment left intact. The pieces of the wreckage that at some future date might be seen from the air were thrown [by Army Air Force recovery men] down a deep cavern so that they would never be visible."

What went wrong here? Wicks' and Davis' low altitude—11,156 feet instead of 20,000 feet—implies an abrupt failure of either a critical component of the P-70B or of Wicks himself. The USAAF accident report filed by Major Charles W. Hailes notes:

> Lt. Lester, pilot of one of the searching aircraft, reported that in the line of flight of direction indicated by the point of first contact and the wreckage, higher peaks exist than the one struck, which indicates that the plane was losing altitude at the time of crash. The cause for loss of altitude may have been motor trouble, failure of oxygen equipment at higher altitude for which they were briefed to fly, or error on part of pilot but such cause cannot be determined.

The SAR team consisted of District Ranger Frank Givens and Ranger "Two-Gun Billy" Merrill. The pair were accompanied by four packers plus thirteen U.S. Army soldiers from the 922nd Signal Company stationed in Fresno but currently bivouacking in the Valley. They required several days to locate the wreckage and remove Davis and Wicks, one of whom was still recognizable and one not at all. The packers hauled both bodies out to White Wolf and the Tioga Road, arriving on September 3, a week after the crash.

For the next fifteen years the air above Yosemite proved safe. This long halcyon spell ended when yet another military craft went down. On March 24, 1959, 36-year-old Commander Peter N. Rippa of Sunnyvale, California sat at the controls of the 2,700-horsepower, single-engine Douglas AD-6 Navy Skyraider in "formation" at 7,500 feet with two additional planes piloted by LTJG K. Fox and Ensign H. J. Pennel. They were making a "routine" flight inside, of all places, Tenaya Canyon, the rim of which was partly obscured by clouds.

Commander Rippa underestimated the elevation of the rock-hard topography and at 2:40 p.m. tried to fly under a cloud. With an available maximum speed of 325 miles per hour and a cruising speed of 240 miles per hour he slammed his forty-foot-long plane head first into the granite at the upper rim of Tenaya Canyon four miles northeast of Half Dome. A fellow pilot witnessed the crash despite the clouds and noted that the World War II-era aircraft (serial #139669) exploded into flames upon impact.

The Civil Air Patrol (CAP) located the wreckage and provided rough coordinates for a recovery party. Four rangers were dispatched via a Sno-Cat to the site. They spent a difficult and fruitless day searching during a snowstorm. The following day, on March 27, the SAR crew finally reached the wreckage and located Rippa's severely burned body. On the return trip the Sno-cat inconveniently broke down on Snow Flat. So the Rangers were forced to carry the burned body by hand for several miles, including down the steep, icy Snow Creek Switchbacks. Thankfully, a second team showed up and assisted them.

Although most of Rippa's Skyraider has been cleaned up, its radial engine still lies near the top of what is now called "Airplane Gully."

About three years later, on July 19, 1962, 27-year-old Ben Amergin, who was to be ordained a minister the following week in Sacramento, had been begging his friend 26-year-old Alvin Taylor, also of Sacramento, to fly him to a Billy Graham revival in Fresno. Taylor, rated as a commercial pilot, rented a Piper Commander (N5069P) in Sacramento. Then he flew Amergin and two other friends—23-year-old Paul Sokol and 17-year-old Nick Lokteff—south.

The four buddies made it to the revival just fine. Billy Graham filled Amergin with the fire and the light. Indeed, all went well until their return flight to Sacramento. Alvin Taylor took off from Fresno at 11 p.m., having filed no flight plan. The weather held clear. Their liftoff looked good. Taylor flew north…then he deviated in radio silence with the rest of the world and banked the little plane off the shortest route and over the Sierra Nevada.

That night Taylor's brother, Glen, experienced a lucid dream in which his brother seemed to be talking to him but was complaining that Glen would not listen. "I woke up shaking," Glen Taylor reported, "and scared."

During this dream Glen's brother Alvin and the other three men vanished.

Their fates remained a mystery for the next thirty-two years!

The day after the four disappeared, the search began. The rescue coordinator divided up the missing pilot's possible flight route into grids. "Literally hundreds of airplanes" scoured this path. All to no avail. Glen Taylor drove a lot of that route on roads, hunting from the ground. His nightmare-turned-reality now haunted him. He later said, "I nearly wore out my Oldsmobile looking. It was all I thought about."

Eventually all the searchers were called back and thanked. They then went about their other business. Even so, Glen continued to hunt for his brother for years afterward. He typically followed up every report of a discovery of a small plane crash anywhere in California south of Sacramento and north of Fresno. "Then [after thirty-two years] I picked up the paper and opened to the page where it [a crash discovery article] was," Glen said. "As soon as I read the year [1962] I knew. I knew."

On August 7, 1994, a Park Trail Crew worker, Richard Miller, on his day off went hiking in Stubblefield Canyon in north-central Yosemite. He came across the twisted, melted fuselage between 9,100 and 9,300 feet on a steep, thirty-five to fifty-degree slope. Bleached, charred, fractured bones littered the crash site. The number on the cockpit instrument panel remained legible. It read "N5069P."

How had things gone so wrong on this flight? The Piper Commander was not a powerful airplane. It could climb, even fully loaded as Alvin Taylor's had been, but it would be "like pulling a heavy trailer up a hill," noted Glen Taylor. "You'd have to give yourself plenty of room to make the altitude." Evidently, Alvin Taylor had not given himself quite enough room. Also obvious, Taylor was flying drastically off the shortest route between Fresno and Sacramento. Why? Perhaps he had decided to do this to treat his three passengers to a night time overview of Reno, "the Biggest Little City in the World." This was a sight, Glen Taylor noted, that his brother had always considered well worth seeing.

Only not this time.

A few years passed after Alvin Taylor's lost flight before another aerial mishap in Yosemite. Yet again it was a military pilot. On July 10, 1966, 34-year-old Captain Kenneth Danison, a U.S. Marine Reserve officer from Ross (Marin County), California, piloted a Navy A-4 Skyhawk out of Alameda Naval Air Base en route to Fallon, Nevada for training exercises. The A-4, made famous in the 1986 movie *Top Gun* starring Tom Cruise, was just over forty feet long, gained its lift from a mere twenty-six-foot wingspan, and could punch a hole in the air at 675 miles per hour. At 2:05 p.m., Danison crashed due to unknown causes three-quarters of a mile north of Tilden Lake, again near the northern boundary of the Park. The impact disintegrated the jet, scattering wreckage and igniting several small fires later extinguished by NPS fire crews. Data on the cause(s) of this military crash were not available.

Almost a decade passed before Yosemite rangers were called upon to respond to another serious plane crash. On February 8, 1975, 37-year-old Donald Barnes of Modesto, California, with 30-year-old passenger Charlotte Ann Bacon from Waterford aboard, tried to fly his single-engine red and white Cessna (#N51678) from Las Vegas to Modesto over the Sierra Nevada. Barnes committed the serious pilot error of thinking he could nurse his small plane across the high peaks during a heavy snowstorm. He flew barely more than halfway across the mountains before icing up.

Faint emergency signals from Barnes' Cessna, first heard by a commercial airliner passing far overhead, suggested the downed plane was inside the Park. The Yosemite SAR machine shifted into high gear. Special small, handheld emergency locating devices were flown in from Tacoma, Washington overnight by the military. Satellite radio communications—possibly a first ever for non-military search and rescue—were installed in the Park's Command Post by noon of February 9th. Despite heavy snows and a serious storm forecast for yet more snow, a four- and a five-person rescue team started into the very remote area by skis late that afternoon. A pair of additional four-person teams was poised to also leave on skis the next morning. They all faced tremendous avalanche hazards the following day. Indeed, thirty-two years later one SAR member Joe Abrell recalls, "We had a hell of a time because the snow was so deep."

The next day, February 10, blessed everyone involved on this SAR mission with a small, unforeseen, several-hour window of marginal but better weather. Piloted by the aptly monikered "Stormin" Norman Hicks, a Lemoore Huey "Angel" was able to make its way into the Valley to join the search. Rising above the Valley Rim, these airborne searchers almost immediately picked up the signal then skillfully zeroed in on the Cessna's fading electronic beacon.

Minutes later they saw the lost plane half buried in snow at 11,000 feet on a steep ridge of Post Peak, just above Ward Lakes. The four rangers onboard quickly realized they were now slightly outside Yosemite's boundary. Unable to set the Huey down here due to the weight aboard it and to the high altitude, Stormin' Norman instead put the ground team on terra firma a mile away. From there they skied to the crash. Meanwhile Lieutenant Commander Hicks flew back to Lemoore to refuel.

As awkward—or even silly—as bureaucratic boundaries may seem in a case like this, the NPS rangers on skis now lacked legal jurisdiction to act. One inch beyond the Park's boundary was as good as a hundred miles. Indeed, these people knew they held no authority to serve as coroners or official investigators despite their being the only SAR personnel on the ground. And because of a new blizzard predicted to bury the region—and the wreck and the victims—in just a few hours, these rangers would likely be the only officials on this scene for days, maybe weeks.

To split the horns of this legal dilemma and forge a practical solution, Captain Berkeley of the Madera County Sheriff's Department got on his office phone and, patched through the Park's Radio Communications Center, quickly deputized Ranger Ron Mackie from afar as he stood beside the mangled aircraft. Berkeley next urged the Park team to remove the two frozen bodies and get off that mountain ASAP.

Mackie got moving again. And just in the nick of time. Within the hour of the team leaving Post Peak, the downed aircraft would be covered with deep snow and stay buried for the rest of the winter.

True, Donald Barnes and Charlotte Bacon had died when their plane hit Post Peak *outside* of the Park. As for crashes *inside* Yosemite, Captain Dannison in his Navy Skyhawk had been the last to be killed (in the summer of 1966) for quite a while. Indeed more than ten years passed before Yosemite's next fatal crash.

This one happened on December 9, 1976. And despite it being a doozy of a crash, one that would become legendary, only two people knew when it happened—but they knew it only for a few seconds.

For the rest of the world the first clue regarding this wreck came six weeks later, on January 25, 1977. At the time four backcountry winter hikers—Ron Lykins out of the San Francisco Bay Area and three friends—were trudging through the snow at 9,000 feet elevation a dozen miles south of Yosemite Valley. There in the snow they came across a strange find. It was the nearly complete right wing of an airplane. The wing tip had been painted with red and blue markings. This wing had lodged on edge between two trees. This white wing did not look like it had been there long.

Upon Lykins' return to the Valley, he and his buddies reported what they had found to Ranger Randy Cooley. Cooley in turn radioed SAR Ranger Tim J. Setnicka and asked: "Do you have a map showing all the plane crashes in the park?"

"Yep, sure do," replied Setnicka, "on my office door."

"I'll meet you there in ten minutes," Cooley said.

Cooley soon explained that the four backcountry skiers had contacted him while he was on road patrol. During their trip they had come across an aircraft wing in a tree. "They said it looked like it hadn't been there for very long," Cooley added. "It had the N number on it." Cooley now produced his pocket notebook and read the number aloud: "N80BD."

"Where do they think it is," asked Setnicka.

"They were east of Ostrander Lake."

Setnicka and Cooley looked at the map. Plane crash sites dotted the park but none were close to Ostrander Lake.

"Huh?" said Setnicka. "There's nothing close. Do these guys know where they were?"

"Yeah, they seemed squared away," said Cooley.

Setnicka and Cooley hashed out the possibilities a bit more then decided to call the Air Rescue Coordination Center (ARCC) at Scott Air Force Base in Illinois. All inland military search and rescue activities in the United States were coordinated through this military facility. Therefore the ARCC would likely know about any ongoing searches for currently missing aircraft. Moreover, whenever the Park needed military assistance for SAR work, they had to request a mission through the ARCC. For this reason, the phone number was already included on the SAR Ranger's telephone speed dial.

Setnicka hit the speed dial. He next explained Lykins' find of a wing in a tree to the duty officer—a sergeant. The man responded that the Air Force was not engaged in any ongoing search. Nor, he added, did his office have a report of a missing aircraft in the West. The sergeant now jotted down the wing's N number. He promised to call back.

Five minutes later Setnicka's phone rang. An Air Force captain on the other end asked him to recount what he knew about the mystery aircraft. He next asked Setnicka to verify the N number. Then he asked him to verify it again. Without divulging anything from his end, the captain said he would call back. Sertnicka began wondering what all this cloak and dagger melodrama was about.

Fifteen minutes later his phone rang again. This time a U.S. Customs Agent from Washington, D.C. identified himself on the other end. This agent wanted details of the crashed aircraft. To avoid all possibility of a mis-identification he now verified the N number with Setnicka. Then he verified it yet again. The agent now wanted to know the aircraft's location. "Where," he asked, "is the nearest road to the crash site?"

Setnicka explained the reality of the wing's location—there was no road. The agent did not seem particularly happy about this. And when Setnicka asked why Customs was interested in this plane crash, the agent refused to give him any details.

What the heck, both rangers now wondered anew, was so important and so hush-hush about this lost aircraft?

Twenty minutes later Setnicka's phone rang yet again. It was the Customs Agent. This time he had his supervisor on the line with him. This supervisor asked Setnicka to repeat his entire story of the wing in the trees. Setnicka complied, hearing his own, now oft repeated, words on the phone yet again. How many times would he have to tell this story? And to how many people in the chain of command?

Once the agent had heard the wing-in-the-trees story for himself, he set about determining that Setnicka and Cooley were indeed Yosemite National Park Rangers. Now he finally explained why Customs was so interested in Lykins' discovery. As soon as the agent cleared the phone line, Cooley phoned Yosemite Chief of Law Enforcement Lee Shackelton.

This mysterious wing wedged in the trees became the seed for Case Incident Report #77-0133—soon to be a high country legend.

The Park now dispatched two rangers into the snow-covered backcountry to investigate. To do this a Lemoore Naval Air Station helicopter inserted Joe Evans and Bruce McKeeman onto a ridge about five miles east of Ostrander Lake. Flying in, the team had spotted the thirty-foot long wing.

Once on the ground Evans and McKeeman found two other pieces of a fairly big airplane. One section, only fifty yards from Lykins' wing, was a vertical stabilizer with "N80BD" painted on it in black letters a foot tall. The final piece, yet another fifty yards farther, was a ten-foot-long horizontal stabilizer from the tail. It too was white.

All three pieces lay in a straight line almost in the bed of Illilouette Creek about two-thirds of a mile above and northwest of Lower Merced Pass Lake. In fact, the fragments led like a proverbial trail of bread crumbs directly toward the now frozen lake.

Once this updated information was relayed to the Air Rescue Coordination Center, Major Duane Farnham informed the Park that the tail number came from a World War II-era Lockheed Lodestar missing since December 9, 1976. Not only would the fate of this particular Lodestar turn out to be convoluted, it would also turn out that it was not even a Lodestar. As research by Rick Schloss in 2006 would reveal, the aircraft was actually a Lockheed PV-1 Ventura built originally as both a light bomber and a submarine patroller. Approximately 1,600 planes of this model had been delivered to the military beginning in 1942—few pilots, however, made positive reports of it once they flew these clumsy, sluggish aircraft during combat. Be that as it may, sometime between 1958 and 1963 this particular plane had been retrofitted into a "Howard 500." Only seventeen of these models were ever converted by adding two 2,500 horsepower engines which offered a cruising speed of 325 miles per hour and a range of 2,200 miles. The Howard 500 carried 1,500 gallons of aviation fuel, was 60 feet long, and held aloft by a 72-foot wingspan. This upgrade considerably enhanced its cargo capacity above the original 5,000-pound limit.

This aircraft, Farnham now informed the Park's investigating Ranger Norm Hinson, had been piloted by 31-year-old Jon Scott Glisky of Seattle. Aboard too was 29-year-old Jeffrey Carl Nelson, also of Seattle, as sole passenger.

Here is where the plot thickens. It seems that after the plane had been missing for ten days, Pamela Glisky, the pilot's wife, had called the Coast Guard in Seattle. At this point she shared some of the details about her husband's business in the air.

Major Farnham now further informed Ranger Hinson that the plane in question had taken off from a remote beach landing strip in San Quintin, Mexico, 250 miles south of Tijuana and 600 miles south of Yosemite. At this point the plane was loaded with marijuana, thousands of pounds of it. Glisky had been flying this drug cargo north to a rendezvous somewhere in the Black Rock Desert east of Reno, Nevada. The importer's plan then called for off-loading the tightly jammed bales, each one up to 140 pounds, of "green gold" onto trucks. The plane would then lift off again. The street value of this contraband at the time was at least half a million dollars and likely far more than a million.

The now cargo-less Lockheed was next to fly onward to a normal landing in Boise, Idaho.

But, Major Farnham explained, the old Ventura had not arrived in the Black Rock Desert. Nor had it landed in Idaho. Nor had it been spotted anywhere else—until Ron Lykins and his friends had gone cross-country skiing south of Yosemite Valley. Several federal agencies had searched for the missing plane for eleven days in December before finally giving up. (Later investigation would reveal that when the aging aircraft had crashed on December 9th, it and the two-man crew aboard had been making their *second trip of that day* from Mexico.)

So *whose* plane was it? Major Farnham also divulged that the registered owner was Red River Ranch, Inc. of Fort Lauderdale, Florida. According to Pamela Glisky, the "ranch" had purchased the aircraft with cash.

Okay, so far, so good. But exactly where was this Lockheed and its close-to-million-dollar load now?

What would eventually become clear was that for some combination of reasons—the aircraft's age, its prior maintenance, and its probable overloading and the incorrect, hasty distribution of loose cargo—the vintage Lockheed's starboard, muscular 2,500-horsepower engine had fallen off its wing. And the wing soon followed the engine. Lee Shackelton would eventually learn that this engine had developed a serious oil leak sometime during its first run of the day. After pilot Glisky had made his first drug delivery that day in northern Nevada, he had flown back south and landed in Las Vegas. There he had hastily purchased an oil line. For whatever unknown reason, Glisky had not taken the time to have the new oil line installed. It may have been the lack of this minor repair that explains why he lost that still-bleeding engine in midair many hours later over the central Sierra Nevada. With nearly three tons of cargo aboard, Glisky had possessed no real chance of easing the now vibrating Ventura to a safe landing on just one remaining engine. And absolutely no chance at all on just one wing. All of this explained the Lockheed's no-show for its second planned delivery in Black Rock. What was a little harder to pinpoint was the final resting place for the dismembered aircraft itself.

Now, because the machine had been carrying contraband and was doing so by air and was doing so internationally and it had crashed in Yosemite National Park, five different federal agencies coordinated their efforts in this investigation.

Because the pieces of the aircraft—again like a trail of bread crumbs—led directly to Lower Merced Pass Lake, this is where the search focused. Searchers quickly found other parts of the aircraft. Pieces of jagged metal, ripped electrical wires, scattered insulation, and torn hydraulic lines festooned the trees in tangles on the edge of the lake. Another hodgepodge scatter of nondescript debris lay frozen amongst and under the freshly sheared-off branches. Investigators also found a few burlap bags filled with marijuana mixed in with this miscellaneous junk. Searchers also spotted yet other burlap bales bulging through the layers of snow just offshore. These had frozen tightly locked into the foot-thick ice. Clearly, the bulk of the plane—and its illicit cargo—lay submerged somewhere under the ice of this six-acre lake.

Over the next two days a dozen of the Park's staff set up shop on or near the lake. A Customs helicopter brought up from San Diego ferried these personnel back and forth from El Capitan Meadow. Despite it being early February the weather here during this winter of drought was now shirt sleeve. Even so, the glare off the frozen, snow-covered lake became blinding. Everyone wore dark glasses and slathered on sunscreen as if they were vacationing in Waikiki. Unlike a Hawaiian vacation, some of the rangers now handled chainsaws to cut holes in the ice and free the half-submerged marijuana. Others loaded the hundred-pound bags onto the dark blue Huey as its blades rotated nearby in seeming impatience.

Other investigators yet collected evidence and began reconstructing what had gone wrong here.

A team of Yosemite divers donned cold water gear to search the icy depths for the bodies of the two men known to have been aboard. After chainsawing holes through the ice, these divers also wallowed through the now slushy water of the lake's shallows to grapple with the huge wet bags of marijuana dotting it—and to recover anything else that did not belong there.

The government had enlisted as team leader for this SCUBA effort Bob Tostenson. He was not only a commercial diver and owner of Bob's Dive Shop in Fresno, he also possessed the warm dry suit and two-way underwater radio and, more to the point, the experience and specific training for this sort of thing that we—Rangers Mark Forbes, Rick Smith, Bill Wendt, and I (Farabee)—lacked. We "SCUBA rangers" were working on scene primarily to back up Bob.

Lest any of this begin to read like a federal picnic at the lake, I have to say that, in my entire fifty years of diving, the several dives that I made in Lower Merced Pass Lake during those two days at the beginning of February were done under the worst conditions I have ever experienced. We were diving at nearly 9,000 feet elevation in thirty-three-degree water. Our neoprene wetsuits were not designed to function in this sort of cold for more than a few minutes. Our only entrance into the lake was by sliding down through a manhole-sized opening sawed through foot-thick ice. The surface here looked black and greasy with hydraulic fluid and aviation fuel. It also tasted that way. Visibility in the water below the ice was less than two feet. We groped our way around in the fifteen-foot deep water like blind men exploring a strange room booby trapped with knife blades. Razor sharp pieces of ragged metal jutted down from the ice above us and up from the muck below. Those overhead had floated up (buoyed by attached insulation, et cetera) to be frozen in place and now hung down, guillotine-like. Beneath us lay the mother of all jungles of sharp edges, the mangled fuselage itself. During our searches we remained linked to the surface tender on the ice with a thick manila rope—a nylon line would be too easily severed on a jagged edge of the plane. A lost tether, of course, could easily spell death under the opaque ice. All of these tricky and extremely hazardous conditions added up to very good reasons for us to have brought in a professional diver like Bob Tostenson.

Again, Major Farnham had told us that two aircrew members likely were down there somewhere beneath the ice. Search as we might, we found nobody. Maybe this was because we could not get into some of the wreckage deeper on the bottom. Maybe, instead, these guys had parachuted out in time and then hoofed it to anonymity. Instead of dead bodies we ultimately recovered more than a ton of high-grade marijuana.

Before we could accomplish more, on February 4th, a blizzard hit the Sierra. This severe storm forced us to shut down the recovery operation. Regional newspapers thus far had been sensationalizing our progress from one day to the next.

Now they published our exodus.

Concurrent with the other four agencies involved—the National Transportation Safety Board (NTSB), Drug Enforcement Agency, Federal Aviation Administration, and Customs—the Park elected to let the winter and isolation safeguard the site. Anyone trying to reach the wrecked Lockheed to loot it, their reasoning went, would be forced to slog at least a dozen miles through very rugged country and snow. And not only was the wrecked plane sequestered deep under frigid water, this water was capped by a foot of snow and ice. In short, the plane and its remaining cargo seemed as safe as if in a locked vault.

Despite the logic that these barriers would prove too arduous for looters, in the real world reason does not always dictate peoples' decisions. In fact, as soon as it became known that the Park and other agencies had left the scene of the wreck unguarded and were waiting until the spring thaw before revisiting it, the Lockheed might as well have been parked behind the Ahwahnee Hotel. It was now an open season for entrepreneurs. As if to facilitate their unique opportunity, this winter would be one of the very driest on record. While snow did exist in the high country, it lay packed at a minimal level.

The first looters to venture to the wreck probably felt tickled to find themselves staring into a deep freeze of high-grade marijuana left completely unguarded. These guys probably were climbers, although employees of the Yosemite Park and Curry Company also had been quick out of the starting gate. At any rate, when the first of these few salvagers returned to the Valley toting a heavy load of dope (never mind that it was water soaked and laced with oil) they triggered a minor gold rush for the bonanza of marijuana that already was being called "Lodestar Lightning."

Two enterprising climbers allegedly free dived into the freezing water and chopped a man's jacket out of the fuselage. In it was $1,600 in brown-stained fifty-dollar bills plus a little black book peppered with "drug underworld" contacts and phone numbers. For some reason, the diver tore these pages to shreds and scattered them in the snow. But he kept the cash. (Two months later, investigators dug the shredded paper out of the snow and reassembled them into pages that would prove useful.)

A couple of the luckiest salvagers allegedly cashed in their hauls for sums that likely reached five-figures. At least one now famous climber bought a new vehicle based on one trip. A couple may have funded dream vacations to Europe. No doubt at all, several Camp 4 former scroungers and poverty-level seasonal concession employees were now regaling themselves to pricey steak dinners in the Valley's best restaurant. Some of the biggest names in Yosemite climbing had reputedly cashed in on the lost Lockheed and upgraded their lifestyles. Facts and figures on this, it seems, have been grossly distorted down through the years. Even today the myth of who pulled off what and how much they profited from it continues to grow.

One tip off (of several) to the Park that the doomed Ventura was being looted came from Bob's Dive Shop. Tostenson reported several granite-loving, big wall climbers had dropped in to rent SCUBA gear. Soon officials had to admit that, despite the forbidding elements and isolation, several "adventurous individuals" had made it to Lower Merced Pass Lake to conduct their own free market salvage of the cargo. And unless the Park hit the brakes on these entrepreneurs, they would salvage and smuggle out the whole enchilada.

Today it is hard to say how long this frenetic harvesting lasted. Most of those profiting from it have proven too "shy" to speak up for the record. But finally, on April 13, 1977, sometimes referred to as "Big Wednesday," six heavily-armed rangers onboard a U.S. Customs helicopter dropped in on the lake to halt this commerce in contraband. Paul Henry still grins over the mayhem as he and his fellows flew in just above tree line to suddenly pop up over the ridge bordering the lake. "Boy, they were surprised," Henry admitted. "There were maybe a dozen or so people working out there on the ice, and when they saw us they scattered just like a covey of quail. They left everything: sleeping bags, packs, pickaxes, sleds, and dope."

That day only two Raiders of the Lost Lockheed were arrested, Vern Clevenger, age 21, and a juvenile of 16. A talented and now very successful photographer, Clevenger recalls (today, fondly) being stopped by Ranger Ron Mackie that afternoon.

> We were booking down the snowy trail with a chainsaw sticking out of my pack when we ran into Ron. He knew us, we knew him. We reeked of oil-soaked grass. He knew it, we knew it. With no practical way to cuff us, Ron commanded us to report directly to the U.S. Magistrate the next day. We did and Judge Pitts ended up throwing the "case" out of court as an illegal search. We never did make a penny off that plane.

For the next two months, Park Rangers guarded Lower Merced Pass Lake 24/7. Even into May and then June, more bales of marijuana popped to the surface like delayed bubbles. Meanwhile the lure of easy money never quite fizzled out. On one very early patrol, Ranger Dennis Burnett found a "kid" hiking toward the drowned Lockheed on his quest to score some of that now famous Lodestar Lightning. Dennis detained the shivering young man. Law enforcement informed him the city of Santa Cruz had an outstanding warrant for the kid's arrest, "so I placed him in cuffs for the night," Burnett explained. "And since he was soaked from hiking through the snow, I stripped him down and put him in Mark Forbes' wetsuit for the night in my tent. I went in for seven days but got snowed in and [I] stayed for twelve days. Because of the storm we couldn't get a helicopter in, so I had to hike him out the next day."

During another long, boring afternoon of exile at Lower Merced Pass Lake in late April, as Rangers Ray Kennedy and Mike Osborne were doing their ten-day guard stint, they spotted movement across the water. Ray went around one way and Mike the other. They closed on six young men, none over 21.

When confronted by the two rangers pointing Colt .223 rifles, the teenagers dutifully responded with polite "Yes, sir" and "No, sir" answers. Osborne soon became intrigued with these guys. He could hardly believe their story. They had been struggling to get to this wreck site for two weeks. It soon became apparent to Mike that they were "not the brightest bulbs on the tree."

This six-pack of would-be salvagers now explained how they had just spent a week trying to find Merced Lake, roughly ten miles of torturous terrain distant from Lower Merced Pass Lake. En route to this wrong lake via a wrong trail they had run into a Park Service Trail Crew. These hard working federal employees traditionally look as if razors and barbers are anathema. As the six hopeful entrepreneurs passed this sun-browned platoon of workers slaving like a chain gang they had quipped: "Why are you guys working so hard when there is a ton of dope to be had up the trail?"

The Park Service crew members looked at each other and raised a collective eyebrow. The deeper in the woods you work, the more nuts you find.

None of the six hopefuls held any concept of where they were in relation to their imagined bonanza. Worse, when they finally did figure out which lake was which and then managed to trudge to the correct location of their imagined gold rush, they arrived so late in the game that for all their labors they gained nothing but the opportunity to explain to Osborne and Kennedy how inept and naïve they were.

By the afternoon of June 16, the small "mom and pop" salvage company contracted by the Park had already spent several days on site and now was winding down their efforts at removing the wreck itself. Making a shallow dive and wrapping chains around plane parts to be winched to shore was an 18-year-old worker who only recently had been SCUBA certified. The crew had just removed several chunks of metal and had uncovered the cockpit, revealing it the first time. It lay there only about fifteen feet down and broken open.

Nearby, Bob Howard, Don Coelho, and I were sitting on shore in our wetsuits. By this time we had begun to believe that the two men who had been flying that plane had somehow gotten out of it before it sank in the lake. In fact, I was convinced by now that we would never find them. At this moment the 18 year-old shot out of the water like a Trident Missile.

His eyes through his face mask looked as big as saucers.

No doubt existed in our minds about what the boy had just seen.

Indeed, only a moment behind the panicked teenager the well-preserved body of a dead man bobbed to the surface like a stunt man for a zombie movie.

Ranger Howard volunteered to enter the lake and haul the corpse to shore. Next we hitched on our air tanks and dived in to find and haul out the pilot. He must be down there too.

He was. And once we got him onto shore Don Coelho and I faced the repugnant task of amputating all of the men's fingers so they could be shipped to the FBI lab for printing. These loose fingers would confirm that the pilot indeed had been Jon Scott Glisky. And that his passenger was indeed Jeffrey Carl Nelson.

Whose airplane was it? Even by late June, official "attempts to locate the owner of the plane," reported the *Mariposa Gazette* on June 16, 1977, "have proved futile."

True, investigators had determined that "Red River Ranch, Inc." was a fictitious corporation. But whose? To get to the real buyer the feds indicted the broker of the sale of the aircraft in Florida State Court on drug charges. As part of a plea bargain, this broker-turned-informer identified the true owner/buyer as a California attorney who lived near Santa Barbara. This may sound pretty clear cut, but soon the United States Attorney subsequently declined to prosecute. Why? Because this broker abruptly lost his incentive and now refused to cooperate. What sort of pressure had changed his mind? The answer remained unclear.

Despite this setback, the Park—along with Customs and the National Transportation Safety Board—did initiate a civil recovery action to collect the $20,000+ cost of removing the wreckage from the lake. The lawyer-owner of the dope plane was personally served with this Bill of Collection. He never paid it.

All in all, the wreck of the lost Lockheed became a legend that continued to grow instead of shrink. In 1987, Jeff Long drew from this Lower Merced Pass Lake episode for his book *Angels of Light*. Years later, in 2002, mystery author/Ranger Nevada Barr also used it as background for her novel *High Country*. As we go to press with *Off the Wall*, Rick Schloss, a longtime friend of Jon Glisky and his wife Pamela, is writing what may promise to be the definitive book on the crash in Dope Lake. His working title? *Lodestar Lightning*.

In short, this saga is likely to remain an alluring legend of Yosemite's high country. The crash proved to have a silver lining for many of the varied characters who had gotten to it early in the game (although, admittedly, not much good came to Glisky and Nelson). Indeed, as one climber put it, "Dope pulled out of that plane financed quite a few climbing expeditions to the Himalayas." Unfortunately the same cannot be said of other air crashes in Yosemite.

Only a year and a half later, on the Fourth of July of 1978, 30-year-old Gregory Parker of Los Angeles piloted a twin-engine Piper Seneca (#N56954) from Burbank to the Yosemite-Mariposa Airport. He arrived around 6 a.m. Despite the early hour, Parker's arrival was actually late because he had deviated off course to fly over, then into, Yosemite Valley to buzz the face of El Capitan. This, of course, constituted a violation of Park air regulations, but this breach was revealed only later when film was developed from Parker's Kodak camera.

In Mariposa that morning airport manager Bill Neighbor refueled the Piper with 60.1 gallons. Parker expressed concern to Neighbor over the now heavier weight of the plane. The full tanks plus five occupants and their luggage added up to the maximum load this aircraft could lift during the heat of the summer. Later that evening the plane would be carrying Parker, his 26-year-old wife Deborah, and their three friends—Sally Lou Barret, age 42, Donald Allan Bryant, age 20, and 19-year-old Kathleen Hopson—home to southern California.

These five now rented a car from Neighbor to tour the Park to "have some fun." Parker planned to return to Mariposa from Yosemite by 8 p.m., during daylight, and then fly south. Instead Parker and company did not return until a few hours after dark. Mrs. Neighbor heard the five returning at about 10:25 p.m. A second witness, Mrs. Ringrose, reported she saw an aircraft lift off the runway at 11:28 p.m. that night. Curious because of the late hour, Ringrose watched the plane. She saw it barely clear a hill at the end of the strip and then fly unusually low over the houses nearby.

Parker, it turned out, had taken off short from the 3,310-foot runway. In so doing he had allowed himself scant distance to clear the nearby mountains. With the darkness, they were unable to see how close they were to the ground—or to the tree tops. Luckily, Parker had kept the heavily loaded plane in the air.

Later investigation would reveal that Parker had only recently acquired his pilot's license and had logged slightly more than the minimum required hours before flying into his Yosemite "adventure." Unfortunately, Gregory Parker had just made yet another poor flight decision that would prevent him from ever logging additional hours.

After barely clearing those houses at the end of the runway, Parker and his twin-engine plane and everyone aboard vanished. The Civil Air Patrol spent six days searching for the missing Piper and its occupants along Parker's original flight path. No one spotted any sign of it.

A couple of days later, on a Monday morning, a maintenance man making a routine examination of the Red Fox chairlift at Badger Pass found the wrecked Piper. The scene was a mess. He could see too that he had not been the first to visit this crash. Bears had been here before him. They had devoured various body parts of the casualties. Indeed, the only things here to have survived intact were Parker's cameras.

The investigating ranger on this Yosemite incident (#78-1958), Guy Whitmer, concluded Parker had displayed a chain of careless errors: he failed to notify air control of his change in flight path from Burbank to Mariposa; he failed to abide by altitude limits over Yosemite Valley (being inside it); he flew recklessly close to the face of El Capitan; then, tired and possibly exhausted from being busy for nearly twenty-four hours straight, itself a "game plan" exhibiting poor judgment, Parker committed his final fatal set of errors. He deviated from his flight plan to Long Beach to fly over Yosemite again, this time at night, and he meanwhile carried in his plane its maximum possible load.

Aviation accident investigators examined the widely scattered wreckage. Meanwhile, Park rangers recovered what remained of its occupants. The Piper's propellers revealed they had been rotating under power right into the ground "just under the crest of the mountain" (about fifty feet below it) while going westerly at approximately 8,000 feet. The NTSB told Park Coroner Don Coelho they found that from the exact location where the aircraft had hit a red fir tree one could just see the runway lights of the Mariposa airport. This visible landmark, not visible from the right or left of the crash location, may have tricked Parker into believing that he was flying high enough. Unfortunately, the topography and trees immediately surrounding this little window of visibility were not in his favor. This finding tends to eliminate aircraft failure as an extenuating factor. Instead it places responsibility on the pilot, who obviously had been flying too low. Why so close to the ground? Was it due to that heavy load?

Probably not. The Piper was rated for a maximum of five people with light luggage. So what had happened? And why too had Parker deviated from his flight plan south? Was it just for one more scenic view of the Valley? Again, the pilot had carried multiple cameras onboard. In his collection was an infrared camera. Upon learning that Parker had a fascination for Yosemite's topography, investigators began to suspect he had flown over the darkened landscape to photograph it with his special equipment. If true, then he was crowding in one more recreational "task" into his very long Fourth of July. Also if true, this turned out to be the straw that broke his Piper's back.

The next air crash involving the Park's SAR personnel occurred less than four years later—on January 3, 1982. But when 38-year-old Robert J. Vaughn, a chemist for Chevron Oil, with his wife Lee Vaughn, age 36, and his stepson Donald Priest, age 11, took off that day from Mammoth Airport in his Grumman American AA-5B Tiger (#N28912) they were mere minutes away from setting into motion a now legendary search and rescue mission. The Vaughns had just done a ski trip around Tioga Lake. Intermittent flurries had added an element of authenticity to their Sierra experience in winter. Now, upon takeoff at 4:30 p.m. that Sunday afternoon, the day was already cold. But it was about to become a lot colder en route home to Orinda, California. Indeed Vaughn's flight was about to become the quintessential epic of cold.

Flight control had informed him that he could not fly the short route across Tioga Pass due to bad weather (which turned out to be the storm of the decade) but instead must fly north to Reno before detouring west. But now Vaughn, despite having filed this Reno flight plan, decided to ignore it and flight control to instead fly over Tioga Pass anyway. Less than an hour after liftoff, radar contact with the plane abruptly ceased. This occurred near Tioga Pass. Two minutes later, Vaughn radioed to Oakland Air Traffic Control that he was losing altitude due to severe downdrafts despite his 180 horsepower and probably off course. Also, he added, he was probably in trouble.

Indeed.

The Grumman with all aboard failed to reappear on radar screens.

Vaughn had made his bid for a safe flight by taking advantage of what appeared to be a break in the weather. It had been snowing off and on for two days. As soon as it stopped, he decided to fly. As luck would have it, within an hour or so of his last radio contact, a new storm began dumping nineteen more inches of snow during that first night alone. For almost three days the storm raged on, dropping more than four feet of new snow. On January 5, Yosemite Valley recorded a record snowfall, 29.5 inches. This prolonged bad weather restricted search efforts solely to ground personnel. Yet try as they might under these punishing conditions, no one found any sign of the plane.

Finally, on Wednesday, January 6, three days after the crash, the storm abated. The Civil Air Patrol (CAP) now began a search over a whitened, high-elevation landscape. Even so, for two more days rescuers found no sign of the missing brown and white aircraft.

True, that last radar contact with the Grumman indicated the missing plane would most likely be somewhere close to a 12,000-foot contour. While helpful, this "prime" zone still encompassed a lot of very white, almost featureless terrain now buried four feet deep—about 100 square miles of terrain, by the way—over which these past two days of aerial hunting had yielded nothing.

On Thursday evening, four days after the crash, the frustrated search coordinators huddled together to review all the information thus far compiled. Things did not add up. Some felt certain the mission had indeed covered the entire 12,000-foot contour possibilities and they somehow had missed the plane solely due to it having been buried in new snow. Others reckoned the aircraft had gone down elsewhere, outside their search area. After all, the CAP search's overall tracking and flight plan was one interpreted by the new Interim Track Analysis Program (ITAP). This program had been the "electronic guru" the CAP had relied upon implicitly.

But SAR Ranger John Dill, in Yosemite Valley, doubted this ITAP plan. His lifelong interest in science had instilled in him an attitude of critical analysis when it came to anything technology was touting as foolproof. Dill now sat down and painstakingly reanalyzed where the searchers had been directed thus far in relation to where the radar said Vaughn's plane had last been. He compared these with the real world topography out there. Lo and behold, his analysis revealed a heretofore overlooked small but crucial error in the ITAP's plan.

Dill convinced almost everyone that they may have not looked for the downed aircraft where it actually was even though it might be parked right in their "prime" search zone. But finding that holes existed was only step one. He now sweated to devise step two, a new and better search plan for tomorrow (Friday) morning. Despite the passage of seemingly enough time to guarantee no survivors out there, the SAR team still felt determined to fill in the gaps created by their original efforts. In essence, this meant re-searching their original prime zone on the area of the Sierra Crest between Tioga Pass and Mount Conness.

By now everyone on this search knew that if anyone aboard that missing plane had survived the crash itself, their chances of living through January Sierra blizzard temperatures for five days at 12,000 feet in a broken airplane would be infinitesimal—if not zero.

Be those odds what they may, five days after Vaughn's aircraft vanished, on Friday, January 8, the CAP/Mono County Sheriff's Department Search and Rescue patrol using Lemoore Naval Air Station helicopter "Angel Three" with Yosemite rangers aboard took off for a new round of searching. The airship flew against winds of thirty miles per hour toward White Mountain. Those aboard again scanned the blinding landscape below for any trace of the missing aircraft.

At 11:35 a.m., during their fifth pass over the same barren ridge, Ranger Jim Sano and Crew Chief Gerald B. Balderson, Jr. spotted Vaughn's plane on the east slope of the 12,000-foot White Mountain in Mono County, north of Tioga Pass and just outside Yosemite. It became immediately obvious the plane's Emergency Locator Transmitter had failed (shattered upon impact). The aircraft sat "nose-in to a 40+-degree snow slope about three-quarters of a mile east of the summit of White Mountain," noted Ranger Anne Macquarie in Incident Report #82-0030. "The vertical stabilizer and the back top part of the fuselage were the only parts of the plane we could see, the rest was buried in the snow." The plane had hit 800 feet lower than the crest that it had to clear.

The undisturbed blanket of white around the wreck led those hovering above to conclude "no apparent survivors." After Anne Macquarie assessed the level of avalanche hazard, the SAR chopper returned to Tuolumne Meadows to drop off Ranger Sano and to pick up Ranger Chas Macquarie plus additional specialized gear, including avalanche probes, two PIEPS (avalanche beacons that emit a radio frequency allowing searchers to zero in on a buried victim), a grain scoop shovel, and skis. All of this was to allow him and his wife Anne to ski from a landing site on White Mountain to the downed plane.

Pilot LCDR Daniel Ellison set down on one skid on a small ledge at 11,200 feet elevation, 100 feet higher than the plane itself. The ranger couple plunged through waist-deep snow toward the wrecked Grumman. They paused to evaluate a possible avalanche separation. At first, only Chas, now roped, descended to the plane. After he shoveled his way to the cockpit, he heard something surprising.

A cry from inside the plane.

Chas now called to Anne that he had found the impossible. She now joined her husband atop the aircraft and, with sudden urgency, helped clear part of it.

Chas peered inside. Eleven-year-old Donald Priest was in there and he was still alive. He sat wedged inside the fuselage behind his frozen mother and stepfather, neither of whom was wearing a hat, gloves, or heavy clothing at all. "They had made no attempt," Chas Macquarie would later report, "to dress warmly." Donald was dressed in a parka and long underwear but he too had neither hat nor gloves. He had, however, draped an ensolite pad over his lap. The windchill during this long ordeal plummeted to minus thirty degrees.

Donnie Priest later told rescuers what happened after the plane crashed:

> When I woke up it was light, but the top of the plane was covered with snow...windows were broken and the snow had come in the plane, mostly the front seat. I was very cold and very, very hungry. I tried to put my boots on, but my pants were frozen to my legs. I called to my mom and Ron and shook them, but they did not respond. I knew that they had died. I tried to get a sleeping bag out, but all of the luggage had frozen together. I curled up some sleeping bag pads and tried to get warm. Once I looked for my Mother's purse to see if she had some crackers but there was too much snow. I ate some snow but did not know where any food was.

"How do you feel?" Chas, still atop the snow-covered plane, now asked the half-frozen boy.

"My feet are cold," the boy answered.

"Think you can climb up here to me?" Chas asked.

Donald started to rise out of his seat but slumped back into it. The ranger now saw to his horror that the boy's feet were bare and severely frostbitten.

Chas quickly broke out the rear window, reached through, and with Anne's help hauled the boy out. The Macquaries put Chas' balaclava on Donald's head and Anne's fiberfill jacket on him. Next they stuffed his entire lower body into her sleeping bag. Assessing his condition, they found he had no spinal injuries or other major trauma. These were amazingly positive findings, but again the boy was severely hypothermic and frostbitten.

The two radioed the helicopter. Its pilot soon hovered over the wreck. Crew Chief Baldeson tossed down a fishnet "screamer suit." He followed, rappelling. The trio worked to harness the boy into it. They clipped him to the hoist cable. Those above winched him up. Donnie's eyes rolled back in his head as he fell into an apparent coma. His body's core temperature was 84 degrees F.

The chopper crew now left the Macquaries behind at the wreck and rushed Priest to the Yosemite Medical Clinic, then to a hospital in Fresno.

At 3 p.m. that day, John Dill radioed the couple at the downed Grumman to inform them that no machine was available to return and pick them up. The two rangers now skied from the crash site back to Tuolumne Meadows, arriving "home" at 7:30 that night.

The Park saluted John Dill for his competence—and confidence—in reanalyzing the search information and for insisting that their efforts be focused on researching the prime area that supposedly had been ruled out.

A week after this, the boy endured surgery above the ankles to amputate both of his severely frostbitten and gangrenous feet. His father, Donald Priest, Sr., stayed with him at Stanford University hospital throughout this medical nightmare. Less than five months after his five-day ordeal of cold, Donald Priest stepped out of a Lemoore Naval Air Station helicopter on his new prosthetic feet to meet and to publicly thank the Park rangers and helicopter crewmen who had found him against such daunting odds.

Twenty-five years after Donnie Priest's nearly miraculous escape, he is in Vacaville running Precision Orthotic Prosthetic Solutions where he builds and fits prosthetic limbs for amputees. "It's the most challenging and rewarding thing I've ever done," Donnie admits. "It's carpentry, sculpting, automotive bodywork, pre-med biology, psychology and physics."

Even before the Viet Nam War, helicopters facilitated difficult rescue operations. Soon these machines—and their crews—became indispensable, as illustrated by the rescue of Donald Priest and by hundreds of other operations referred to in this book. Helicopters in national parks alone have performed many thousands of successful SAR missions.

Even so, helicopters are not magic carpets. They remain machines subject to material failure. On October 4, 1979, a Marine Boeing CH-46 helicopter made an unscheduled stop in Tuolumne Meadows, while flying from Mather AFB in Sacramento to China Lake from the west. The rear engine lost power. A crewman noted fuel leakage. The chopper crash landed a mere hundred yards west of the Tioga Road and an equal distance from the Tuolumne store. The five-man crew abandoned the aircraft just as it burst into flames. In retrospect, this incident had unfolded in a nearly perfect way to avoid human casualties.

A far more nightmarish episode of a helicopter operation going sour occurred on July 7, 1984, when Pilot Will Benda and crewman/observer Randy Byerley of the California Highway Patrol had just picked up an injured hiker, 26-year-old Thomas Wayne Fenion of Oakland, California. Fenion had broken his leg during a hike in Yosemite. At 2 p.m., not far from their original pickup point and now just outside the Park's northern boundary, things went wrong.

With Fenion still secured onto a backboard, itself strapped to the single-engine Bell Long Ranger helicopter (with a rating capacity to haul seven people), the ship apparently lost power. Pilot Benda struggled with the machine, flying about 2,000 feet above its service ceiling for density altitude, but could not prevent plunging into the forty-five-degree water of Peeler Lake.

The windshield burst on contact. This allowed both CHP officers a way out. The two fought their way free of the Bell as it sank forty feet deep with Fenion strapped aboard. Benda suffered vertebral compression fractures and could not swim. Byerley assisted him to shore. Thomas Fenion, however, remained trapped, strapped onto the helicopter on the bottom of the lake where he drowned.

Despite a few helicopter crashes in Yosemite, the majority of fatal incidents would involve fixed wing aircraft. On July 26, 1986, 53-year-old David C. Feiler of Paradise, California piloted a Piper Cherokee Six with himself plus five others aboard en route to Death Valley. For reasons unclear, Feiler crashed his aircraft at 6:11 p.m. at 10,400 feet in Gaylor Lakes Basin, immediately west of Tioga Pass.

Before a witness could radio the crash to Park Dispatch, the plane exploded into flames. Feiler and 60-year-old Thomas C. Nutting of South San Francisco were killed instantly and incinerated. A third person aboard, 67-year-old Mathilde T. Nutting, was critically burned over 65 percent of her body. She survived in a Reno Hospital for eighteen agonizing days. Of the last three passengers, Ray and Kathie Nutting suffered burns over 30 percent of their bodies. The third and last, David Nutting, sustained less severe burns.

As soon as the radio distress call went out, Ranger/Paramedic Mead Hargis decided to divert the medical helicopter run on which he was currently engaged. He next stopped to pick up another ranger. This man's wife was a physician too; she volunteered to accompany the mission. Then Hargis beelined to the wrecked plane. Within twenty-three minutes of the crash these rescuers had arrived on scene. This quick response by Hargis, the doctors, and the pilot of his "hijacked" machine facilitated not only their own quick arrival but also that of two other helicopters as well. The prompt evacuations of the three survivors to burn centers in Fresno and Modesto, then to the University of California, Davis Medical Center saved at least one injured passenger's life. Mead's independent decision making in this emergency earned him a Department of Interior Exemplary Act Award.

How bad is the number of air crashes in Yosemite? Overall, they cannot be considered more than moderate: a dozen wrecks over nearly eight decades ending before 2013 have killed forty-three people. Crashes very close to but outside Yosemite's boundaries—requiring Park assistance—consist of several more aircraft down with at least six victims killed. Roughly half of these sixteen or so crashes were "weather-related," which can be considered a euphemism for pilot error. The prime rule for pilots is "you don't *have to* get there" (the meaning being that instead of continuing to fly toward a destination through bad weather, one should instead turn around and seek a safe landing elsewhere).

For comparison with Yosemite's statistics, consider those from Yellowstone National Park. It is almost three times larger than Yosemite and far more isolated. Between 1943 and 2013, when its fatal air mishaps happened, only seven aircraft crashed. These resulted in twenty-one deaths. This tally is roughly similar to Yosemite. But for a more shocking comparison, consider Grand Canyon (twice the size of Yosemite but far larger yet when other Canyon-connected jurisdictions are added in) where 25 percent of America's tour flights operate. Between 1956 and 2018, sixty-six aircraft went down fatally inside Grand Canyon National Park or on nearby plateaus killing 385 people. This nine-fold higher tally makes Yosemite air space seem quite safe.

TABLE 5. FATAL AIR CRASHES IN YOSEMITE. (Episodes not described in text are noted.)

Name, age	Date	Location	*Circumstances*
LeRoy Jeffers, 48	July 24, 1926	Wawona	*Jeffers of New York rode in a small aircraft piloted by Dr. Sterling Bunnell, an amateur aviator from San Francisco. While trying to land in Wawona, Bunnell lost control. The aircraft plunged 100 feet and crashed. Jeffers died instantly. Bunnell sustained major injuries.*
John D. Graves (pilot), 35 C. W. Wallace (copilot), 29 Harvey Melvin Salisbury (off-duty TWA pilot), 31 Martha M. Wilson (flight attendant), 23 Jay Tracy Dirlam, 22 Mary Lou Dirlam, 19 Victor Krause, 49 Anna B. Walts, 35 Lucius B. Walts, 35	March 1, 1938	Buena Vista Peak, 12 miles northeast of Wawona	*Pilot Graves of Palo Alto, California lifted his TWA Douglas "Sky Queen" from San Francisco at 6:30 p.m., en route to Winslow, Arizona, during the worst storm to hit southern California in 64 years. The plane vanished. On June 12, 1938, H. O. Collier finally found the wreck 200 feet below the top of 9,709-foot Buena Vista Peak.*
Lt William E. Hunt (pilot) 2nd Lt Keith E. Delp 2nd Lt Dwight G. Beacon 2nd Lt Clair Hartzell TSgt Sam Meyerhoff SSgt Elmer Swaving Pfc Maurice A. Smith	June 21, 1943	between Koip & Kuna Peaks on Park boundary at 12,800 feet	*This USAAF B-24E bomber (#42-7188) crashed due to flying 100 feet below the crest. Why pilot Hunt was flying at this altitude remains unknown to us. The bomber impacted the ridge in National Forest where the entire crew was killed. The impact was so close to the Park that the bomber's propellers bounced into it.*
Lt Jack Forest Marlow (pilot), 25 Lt Edward P. Schlieter (radar observer), 26	April 13, 1944	Moraine Mountain, east of Wawona	*A 4th U.S. Army Air Force P-70A-1 (type A-20) Nighthawk from Hammer Field, Fresno crashed during a training mission flown by Marlow of Illinois with Schlieter of Long Island aboard. 70 days later a Curry Co. packer/guide discovered the wreck near where Moraine Meadows Trail hits Givens Creek.*
Lt Richard Davis (pilot), 20 Lt Eugene K. Wicks (radar observer), 21	August 28, 1944	Quarry Peak, northwest of Tuolumne Meadows	*Davis, piloting a P-70B Nighthawk, crashed 5 feet from the top of 11,161-foot Quarry Peak. Both aviators died instantly as the plane split in half. Observations by 2 other nearby pilots suggest Davis was losing altitude when they hit. The cause "could have been motor trouble, failure of oxygen equipment, and/or error on part of the pilot." Two days later rangers located the wreck.*
Commander Peter N. Rippa (pilot), 36	March 24, 1959	eastern end of Tenaya Canyon	*Rippa of Sunnyvale, California, piloted a single-engine, Navy Skyraider in "formation" with 2 other planes on a "routine" flight in Tenaya Canyon, whose rim was partly obscured by clouds. Rippa underestimated the topography and tried to fly under a cloud. He slammed head on into the granite, exploding.*

Alvin Taylor (pilot), 26
Ben Amergin, 27
Paul Sokol, 23
Nick Lokteff, 17

July 19, 1962 Stubblefield Canyon, northeast Yosemite
Taylor of Sacramento rented a Piper Commander (#N5069P) and with 3 friends took off from Fresno at 11 p.m. to return to Sacramento. The Piper with all aboard disappeared for 32 years! On August 7, 1994, a trail crew person on a hike came across the Piper's melted fuselage at 9,200 feet on a steep slope.

Captain Kenneth Danison (pilot), 34

July 10, 1966 ¾ mile north of Tilden Lake
Danison, a Marine Reserve officer from Marin County, California, flew a Navy A-4 Skyhawk out of Alameda Air Base en route to Fallon, Nevada for training exercises. At 2:05 p.m., he crashed due to unknown causes. The jet disintegrated.

Donald A. Barnes (pilot), 37
Charlotte Ann Bacon, 30

February 8, 1975 south of Post Peak, outside Yosemite N.P.
Barnes of Modesto, with passenger Bacon of Waterford, tried to fly his single-engined red and white Cessna (#N51678) from Las Vegas to Modesto over the Sierra during a heavy snow storm. He crashed. His emergency transmitter brought a Lemoore NAS helicopter team to the plane just outside the Park. Deputized Park Rangers recovered the bodies. (not included in statistics)

Jon Scott Glisky (pilot), 31
Jeffrey Carl Nelson, 29

December 9, 1976 Lower Merced Pass Lake, southeast of Glacier Point
A WW II-era Model Lockheed PV-1 Ventura (#N80BD) piloted by Glisky with Nelson aboard (both from Seattle) was flying 5,000-6,000 (?) pounds of marijuana from Mexico to Black Rock Desert, Nevada. The plane lost its starboard engine and crashed into the lake. A variety of Yosemite-ites salvaged possibly a ton of contraband before being stopped.

Gregory Parker (pilot), 30
Sally Lou Barret, 42
Donald Allan Bryant, 20
Kathleen Hopson, 19
Deborah Parker, 26

July 4, 1978 Badger Pass
Parker of Los Angeles piloted a Piper Seneca with 5 onboard from Mariposa en route to Los Angeles at 11:28 p.m., after a 20+ hour day. He veered into Yosemite and vanished. A new pilot, Parker had logged "minimum" hours and made several careless errors. A 6-day search failed. His wrecked twin-engine airplane was later found at Badger Pass Ski Area.

Robert J. Vaughn (pilot), 38
Lee Vaughn, 36

January 3, 1982 White Mountain, north of Tioga Pass and east of Yosemite N.P.
Vaughn, his wife Lee and his stepson Donald Priest, age 11, took off from Mammoth Airport in his Grumman aircraft (#N28912) en route home to Orinda, California. Within an hour the plane vanished from radar. Searchers took nearly 5 days to find the wreck and Priest, its sole survivor. (not included in statistics)

Thomas Wayne Fenion, 26

July 7, 1984 Peeler Lake, north of Yosemite N.P.
Pilot Will Benda and crewman/observer Randy Byerley of the California Highway Patrol picked up Fenion of Oakland, who had broken his leg in the Park. Minutes later, the single-engine Bell Long Ranger lost power and plunged into Peeler Lake. Both CHP officers, injured, made it to shore. The Bell sank 40 feet in the lake with Fenion still strapped aboard. (included in statistics due to initial injury in Park)

David C. Feiler (pilot), 53
Thomas C. Nutting, 60
Mathilde T. Nutting, 67

July 26, 1986 Gaylor Lakes Basin, west of Tioga Pass
Feiler from Paradise, California, piloted a Cherokee Six with 5 others en route to Death Valley. He crashed at 6:11 p.m. at 10,400 feet. The aircraft exploded into flames, instantly killing Feiler and Nutting of South San Francisco. Mrs. Nutting survived 18 days. Three other passengers were burned but, due to a rapid emergency response, survived.

William D. Ross (pilot), 69
John Thomas Hunsicker, 30
Stephen Charles Aldrich, 41
Constance Minor, 45

May 28, 1993 Mount Lyell, SSE of Tuolumne Meadows
At 1 p.m., Ross of Incline Village, Nevada flew his twin-engine Beechcraft Bonanza (#N2R) from Visalia, California with friends from Gardnerville and Reno and headed east over the Sierra into overcast weather. Hours later Ross' emergency locator transponder was broadcasting. SAR mission #93-1253 found the aircraft had plowed long furrows in the snow on the west face of Mount Lyell (at 13,114 feet, Yosemite's tallest mountain) at 11,800 feet on a forty-five-degree slope. All aboard had been killed. The cause of the crash is uncertain but pilot error by deciding to fly into bad weather instead of turning around remains suspect. (not in text)

Richard Zuccato, 43

June 13, 2002 Braille Book, Cathedral Rock
While climbing, Zuccato of Baytown, Texas fell. During his rescue Navy helicopter Rescue 2 lost power then snapped its hoist cable when the litter holding him hit a tree. The machine landed damaged with Zuccato dead and Corpsman Jason Laird injured. (described and listed in Chapter 9. Big Walls)

Nicol Struan Wilson, 68

December 17, 2012 near Vogelsang High Sierra Camp
Wilson of Solvang, California was piloting ***solo*** *his single-engine, low-wing Mooney M20 aircraft from Santa Ynez Airport to Mammoth Mountains Airport when he disappeared over the high-country of Yosemite. Severe weather impeded an intensive search by the Civil Air Patrol, California Highway Patrol, and others. On July 6, 2013, hikers discovered the mostly-intact aircraft near the Vogelsang camp.* (not in text or text statistics)

Geoffrey "Craig" Hunt, 62

October 7, 2014 near Arch Rock entrance.
While piloting Cal Fire S2T air tanker # 81, Hunt, a 13-year veteran with Cal Fire from San Jose, California, was flying ***solo*** *and about to drop 1,200 gallons of chemical retardant on the 252-acre Dog Rock Fire as the aircraft climbed a steep canyon wall the near the Arch Rock entrance. Federal investigators said the aircraft's wing might have hit a tree and fallen off before the fatal crash.* (not in text or text statistics)

Chapter Six

FALLS WHILE SCRAMBLING & HIKING

"*Haste makes waste.*" On August 19, 1958, 17-year-old Will Beeghley from Long Beach, California should have had these three words scribbled in big letters on the toes of his shoes. That afternoon Beeghley was hiking downhill with three buddies on the notoriously ultra-steep Ledge Trail route located on the west edge of Glacier Point. It had been a long day. The teenagers had already hoofed it for an unaccustomed distance. And by now it was hotter than—well, it was pretty hot.

The water in Beeghley's canteen was history. As he half slid down the loose granite and dirt in the heat he began to feel that the trail below looked endless. Okay, if not exactly endless, then at least too long. Loathing the route's weaving little detours as it dropped into the Valley, he stared at the steep slope in front of him and made a really bad decision.

Beeghley now told his companions that there should be a faster way down and that he wanted to take it. All three tried to dissuade him. After all, as they pointed out, this route was already miles shorter than any other, and he was only talking about a few minutes of difference in descent time. But to an immature brain, such minutes matter. So Beeghley abandoned his companions and started scrambling down the 2,500-foot series of broken cliffs. Will Beeghley's decision to detour off the Ledge Trail to instead wing it alone down the cliff was about to lead to an epic that, before it ended, would suck in a cast of hundreds—no, make that thousands.

At first he probably felt a sense of triumph in how quickly the distance between him and the longed-for Village was diminishing. The difference in elevation seemed to melt away—as did the butt of his new Levis jeans as he slid down the rough granite.

According to the *Fresno Bee* (on August 20, 1958), "the boy was about 1,500 feet above the Valley floor directly down from the [Glacier] Point." Here his scramble had degraded into very serious terrain requiring protection with rope and hardware. Soon Beeghley's shortcut fizzled out into a one-foot-wide ledge. This shelf nestled a few feet below an overhanging projection of granite that prevented any person on it from standing up straight.

Here the teenager had to hunker down just to avoid falling off. A foot or so ahead, he peered over its edge for a view of the next section of his invented route. To his vast disappointment, he saw that his ledge ended in a sheer drop that would kill anyone who fell off it. In short, no feasible option existed down from here. To arrive at the bottom alive, he needed hundreds of feet of rope or else a pair of sturdy wings from a *Quetzalcoatlus northopi* (the huge pterosaur with a thirty-nine-foot wingspan).

Beeghley looked down the yawning vertical cliff and felt his emotions tumble over themselves. The first, that the world was not accommodating itself to his needs, was smothered by a sudden fear of physical peril. Hell, he'd have to go back up and find a better way. The teenager now surveyed the immediate route that he had taken down to this ledge. Looking at it now he suspected he might not be able to *get* back up.

Even so, he tried. Then he tried it again. Nope, he could not manage to get back up. Yep, he had trapped himself. And not in a particularly pleasant spot.

Will Beeghley had stranded himself on a short, one-foot-wide ledge that led nowhere in all directions. Worse, he could not stand up, sit down, squat, nor lie down on this perch. He could not even place both feet on it at the same time. This awkward arrangement was already proving a strain after even just one minute. Yet if he failed here, he would fall into 500 feet of air. Not only was he trapped on this horrible little spot nearly 1,500 feet above the Valley floor, worse yet, no one even knew about it.

Sheer terror probably understates Beeghley's mental state.

Meanwhile, back on the trail, his companions reached the bottom with a minimum of drama. Once there they looked for him. Slowly it became clear to his buddies that he had never made it down. His shortcut must have turned out not to be.

Could he still be up there somewhere? They scanned the cliff face. Could that dot up there be *him*? Yes, the figure was waving his T-shirt. He must have been stuck on that cliff, they realized, for quite a while now.

Beeghley's cousin, Bob Bauman of South Pasadena, reported his predicament. By now it was 8:30 p.m. Park rangers soon arrived on scene. Night had fallen. They puzzled over a way to get to Beeghley. The era of sport climbing was still in its infancy at this point (see Chapter 9). The rescuers knew that climbing the cliff from near the bottom was impractical. On the other hand, no way could they climb more than a thousand feet, scout a lateral way across the face, traverse it, set safety protection and a belay anchor, rig a rescue harness, descend by rappel, haul the stranded kid and his rescuer(s) back up, and then retrace their way back to the trail—all in the dark.

Therefore they planned their rescue effort to begin before dawn the next morning. Meanwhile the SAR team—Rangers Rick Anderson, Frank Betts, "Buck" Evans, Dick McLaren, John Merriam, Vern Nichols, Don Potts, Dick Stenmark, and rescue leader John Townsley—knew they had to keep the kid awake or else he would doze off and fall. One wink, in fact, and he would be dead.

Enter the Park bullhorn.

Methodically, Ranger Vern Nichols vocally blasted up to Beeghley their plan. Although stating the obvious, he repeatedly reminded the boy that he needed to hang on up there until morning, when the rangers would rig some way to reach him. By the way, he added, "Do *not* fall asleep!" To help him stay awake, Nichols told him, he would continue to yell up using his bullhorn.

Because the Park was loaded with summertime visitors, many had already gathered to rubberneck Beeghley's unbelievable predicament. These onlookers presented yet a new problem. Voices travel and echo from a long distance in the Valley. It soon became imperative to literally silence everyone within a mile or so. Beeghley needed to hear exactly what the rangers wanted him to know.

Once the rescue team had issued this new mandate for Valley-wide silence, instead of nine rangers, a few of Beeghley's buddies, and a slowly growing gaggle of spectators, now seemingly *everyone* in this vicinity who had been instructed to practice noise discipline quietly gathered in a cluster to squint up at the teenager and whisper in hushed voices their opinions about him. Meanwhile, Ranger Vern Nichols bullhorned frequent admonitions to the kid not to fall asleep. He repeated this all night.

To stay alive Beeghley stood hunched and leaned back on one foot, then he stood hunched over in the opposite direction and leaned back on the other foot, then he switched and stood hunched on just the first foot again, and then, well you get the picture. Hour by hour he shifted his feet and his body. Fatigue hit him in waves, assaulting his consciousness with soporific demons sent by Morpheus, the Greek God of Dreams.

Nod off for an instant and die.

Nichols' bullhorn blared yet again in the starlight: "Will, are you staying awake? Hang on up there. You can get through this. Just *stay awake*."

The area near and above where Will Beeghley had marooned himself had for years been called the Firefall Cliff because of the Curry Company's summer exhibits. Curry, however, was not the originator of this very "un-wilderness" circus act. The original firefall from Glacier Point was innovated by James McCauley in the 1870s as a Fourth of July show. Spurred by guests who had asked him about shooting fireworks off the cliff to celebrate Independence Day, this Yosemite pioneer had countered by building a huge bonfire and then shoving off the blazing wood. Fanned to dazzlingly bright flames by the rush of oxygen during the 1,500-foot drop, the falling embers had produced a mesmerizing spectacle.

Decades later, in 1899, two school teachers from Indiana—David A. Curry and his wife Jennie—arrived in Yosemite and set up several tents on the Valley floor below Glacier Point as a commercial camp. They managed to book about 300 guests during that first summer. The Currys spent the next three decades building a concession operation in the Park, alternately innovating attractions and amenities in Yosemite and then lobbying in Congress to protect their gains and/or to inveigle lawmakers to allow expansion. The single greatest spectacle that these quintessential entrepreneurs concocted for their summer guests was the evening "avalanche of fire from Glacier Point," an extravagant display that stymied competing concessions. To keep the embers blazing, Curry hired a "firefall man" to each morning prepare a massive bonfire of half a cord of bark from fallen red firs, ignite the pile at 7 p.m., then, two hours later—upon the ceremonial and stentorian call being yelled from Camp Curry to "Let the fire fall"—shove the heap of walnut-sized embers off the cliff.

In 1913, the Assistant Secretary of the Interior abolished the firefall. In 1917, Secretary of the Interior Franklin Knight Lane granted David Curry a five-year lease and allowed him to resume the firefalls. The Curry Company—which in 1925 would be merged with the Yosemite Park Company and be renamed the Yosemite Park and Curry Company—managed to keep this very popular public spectacle going until 1968, when the National Park Service itself finally abolished it. But not without opposition. Consider Robert Scharff's glowing (pun intended) prose penned in his 1967 book *Yosemite National Park*, a book published "In cooperation with the National Park Service" and with an approbative foreword penned by then Secretary of the Interior, Stewart L. Udall. Scharff writes gushingly:

> Each evening during the summer season the stream of glowing embers pours from the edge of Glacier Point, 3,254 feet above Camp Curry. This sight of *unsurpassed beauty* is visible from most open areas in the eastern half of the Valley. Sometimes the embers pour straight down the cliff, gradually spreading fanwise as they approach the ledge below; again the stream of fire waves back and forth in its descent in the manner of a windblown waterfall. It continues for several minutes, and as the last mass of embers is pushed over the cliff a shower of sparks and flame arise momentarily. Thereafter the glow fades very gradually and dies away, leaving the cliff to darkness and many a watcher close to tears. [italics ours]

Tonight, despite no firefall, Beeghley too was likely "close to tears."

Before dawn the rescuers toted 2,000-pound-test ropes and other gear down from Glacier Point via LeConte Gully to a spot about 500 feet above the trapped teenager.

Hundreds of campers rubbed the sleep out of their eyes and now watched transfixed. They passed their binoculars back and forth and muttered about what kind of a kid gets himself stuck up there like that, perched above certain death. To the tune of "Won't you come home, Bill Bailey," at least one of them might have been softly humming a more insidious "Don't you fall down, Bill Beeghley; don't you fall down…"

The rescuers now worried about the passage of time. After all, this kid had been stuck on his tiny perch now for about eighteen hours.

How bad was it for the trapped teenager? "If I would have moved forward, I would have fallen," Beeghley would later admit, "I almost fell asleep three or four times, but the rangers kept calling me and that kept me awake."

The rescue team did find a viable route down and across the Firefall Cliff. Again, it positioned them 500 feet above the trapped young man. This was a lot higher than was desirable. From here three of the rescuers—Betts, Stenmark, and Anderson—rappelled about 250 feet lower from a fixed anchor (a tie-in point around a solid tree or the rock of the cliff face). From here, as Ranger Frank Betts still remembers it, as they stood at the base of the Firefall in a pile of dead embers deposited over the years, the trio lowered 250 more feet of half-inch nylon utility rope with a bowline tied in its end. They now yelled down to Beeghley instructions on how to sling the rope around himself and told him what they were planning to do to get him back up. These plans included their hauling him up hand over hand as he assisted them by scrambling upward on his own power. To secure the desperate but now hopeful climber, the three rescuers above moved him in stages and used a Prusik (a short moveable loop of rope used as a safety tie-in to a main rope) to tie him in short on the rope, anchored to a six-inch thick pine tree. This first raising took about twenty minutes.

The crowd of perhaps a thousand spectators held their collective breath as they watched the trapped teenager inch back up the cliff. Once the trio of knights in shining armor had Beeghley "safe," and standing with them on those Firefall embers, they were poised to begin phase two. The next stage of the operation would be safer yet, but also would prove time consuming. The five rescuers positioned higher on the cliff now began a block and tackle operation to crank Beeghley up the cliff. Next the five also lifted his three newfound best friends. This took hours. But it all went perfectly.

All nine of the above-mentioned rangers on this SAR operation were honored with the Department of the Interior's Unit Award for Excellence of Service by Secretary of the Interior Fred A. Seaton. An almost cutting-edge rescue for its time and an augury of things to come, pulling Beeghley off that cliff, noted Park

Superintendent John C. Preston, required "a superb demonstration of the most skilled techniques of rock climbing and mountain rescue practices."

Interestingly, only two years earlier in Rocky Mountain National Park, then Seasonal Ranger Frank Betts had climbed while carrying a litter with three other rangers to rescue yet another 17-year-old boy (Patrick Dwyer) who had fallen off rappel on Hallet Peak and was seriously injured above a sheer precipice. The trio reached him and then lowered him by rope during four hours of darkness to safety. For this 1957 effort Betts and his three co-rescuers became the first National Park Service employees ever to be awarded the Department of the Interior Valor Award.

Déjà vu.

One final detail that Frank Betts recalls from this incident may merit mention. When Beeghley started on this adventure, he had been wearing that new pair of Levis jeans. By the time he was safely back up at Glacier Point, the butt of his new jeans had been worn through to his, well, whatever was under those Levis. Clearly, the kid's not-too-smart shortcut down was made by the seat of his pants.

Admittedly, Will Beeghley's descent had played out a bit longer than he had anticipated. But unlike what many other less fortunate young men who have attempted shortcuts and then suffered, survival had been the bottom line of this teenager's ordeal.

Again, the decision to abandon a good trail or route and forge instead onto an unscouted, "shortcut" is not unique to Beeghley. Shortcuts have been taken countless times before 1958, and countless times since. Yet this single decision has killed innumerable people. Most have been young men in the outback who, feeling tired and/or hurried, have indulged their impatience and jettisoned their common sense. Their thinking likely goes like this: "I'm tired and if I use this trail it will take me hours to get to camp; there has to be an easier way." Just how serious a danger can shortcutting pose? No one knows how many times an impatient person has detoured onto a hoped-for shortcut and survived unscathed. No doubt tens of thousands of times. On the other hand, detouring off a proven route when uninformed or merely in a hurry has gotten a lot of people into big trouble. We know from the records that of 133 fatal falls through 2012 that occurred while hiking in Yosemite *at least* 25 percent of them (at least thirty-four victims) occurred while the person scrambled somewhere off one of Yosemite's 800 miles of high quality trail on an imagined shortcut. Revealingly, every one of these fatal mistakes was made by a male—no woman in Yosemite is known to have shortcutted and paid for it with her life. Even these figures on males very likely underestimate the total. Forty-four percent (fifty-seven males and two women) of those 133 fatal falls were in fact *solo* hikers whose errors went unwitnessed. It is unclear from postmortem evidence just how many other deaths probably involved attempts to shortcut. Our guess is this decision has led to more than half of Yosemite's many hiking-scrambling falls.

As a comparison, these statistics are only a bit lower than those within Grand Canyon. For example, of forty-nine fatal Inner Canyon falls up through 2006 (as opposed to falls off the rims), thirty-two of the people involved (64 percent and again nearly all men) were solo hikers. At least nineteen of these people (38 percent, which includes only one woman) were shortcutting when they fell to their deaths off a cliff somewhere in that park.

One of the earliest notable incidents of shortcutting in Yosemite happened a century ago. On October 7, 1906, a young man named Henry W. Tupper of Fresno, California had hiked with two companions from Wawona to Glacier Point. While descending into the Valley via the dangerous LeConte Gully route of the soon-to-be "Ledge Trail," the 24 year-old told his buddies that he had decided to try a shortcut. Despite their reservations against this, Tupper headed off alone. His erstwhile fellow hikers made it down to the Village safely. Tupper never showed up.

The next day searchers followed Tupper's footprints "to a point where it would have been impossible for him to return, and to go on, as he doubtless did, would have been fatal." This may sound a lot like what young Beeghley's shortcut had yielded. Only Tupper's played out differently. A day later somebody found his hat several hundred feet below the spot where his footprints had led. Noted Yosemite artist Chris Jorgensen used a powerful field glass to finally locate Tupper's battered body on a cliff face behind a tree, 600 feet below where searchers had stopped.

Three years after Tupper's demise, on August 6, 1909, 17-year-old Horace R. Logan of Berkeley also suffered an unwitnessed fall of about 900 feet from this ultra-steep route while trying to descend solo from Glacier Point. The teenager's disappearance spurred his family to offer a $1,000 reward for his discovery.

Six other young men from Berkeley headed by Adolph Bohnack began an exhaustive search. They crawled all over that cliff for eight days, peering in every crevice they could. Finally, on August 14, they found Logan's body "in a sort of crevasse or cave at the foot of Staircase Fall, torn and battered almost beyond recognition and badly decomposed." The searchers had risked their lives to share that $1,000 reward. Even after being split six ways, in 1909 this was big money.

The "Ledge Trail" route became infamous quickly during the early 1900s for the inordinate number of casualties among its users. As noted by recently retired Park Historian Jim Snyder, this trail had been used as a route from at least as early as 1870, despite its perils. It descended 3,250 feet in a mere 1.75 miles. It was unimproved, steep, and in places so narrow and sketchy that officials had long since placed warning signs at its top and bottom posting it as "dangerous." By 1872, the Park (still a California park at this time) had sanctioned the construction of the nearby Four-Mile Trail by entrepreneur James McCauley (John Conway was the man who actually did the work building this toll "road"), making the shorter route obsolete.

To most, 1.75 miles does sound shorter than four miles (somewhere on the endless road to wisdom is a billboard reading: Not all miles are created equal). As time passed it became a minor Badge of Honor to have hustled up or down this steeper route despite—or maybe precisely because of—the far greater danger it posed. Yet the footing was so bad that Valley entrepreneur David Curry told his employees in 1910 that they could hike anywhere else in the Valley they pleased, but if they hiked that 1.75-mile LeConte Gully—which began right behind Camp Curry—he would fire them.

Regardless, on July 27, 1914, and despite that promise to terminate, 27-year-old Albert Shaw, Jr., a Curry Company photographer from San Francisco, ignored his boss, as well as the Park's warning signs. He hiked the steep route anyway. And he did so alone. But firing him turned out to be unnecessary. Albert Shaw failed to negotiate the trail and died when he slipped and fell off the cliff face.

The Ledge Trail route was finally improved in 1918 into a bona fide trail to afford a steep but reputedly "safe" route to Glacier Point. It remained less than two miles long. On June 13, 1924, 35-year-old Everett E. Shields of San Francisco hiked down it alone. He somehow fell off above Camp Curry. Only two years later, on August 4, 1926, 16-year-old John Henry Meherin of Alameda, California experienced a similar fate but with an obvious reason why. Meherin's companion, who witnessed the mishap, said: Meherin was "*running* down the trail" during their descent from Glacier Point. He missed his footing (probably near its exit from LeConte Gully) and ran right into thin air. Meherin became the *third fatality from the same point* along the Ledge Trail.

Again, despite these deaths (or perhaps because of them), the Ledge Trail exuded an allure to thrill seekers. On July 11, 1928, 24-year-old Joseph R. Hurd of Burlingame, California had hiked with Richard Ham to Glacier Point via a safe route. Upon their return, Ham prudently decided to take the Four-Mile Trail down. Hurd countered by telling Ham members of his family had instead insisted to him, "to experience a real thrill he must come down the Ledge Trail."

Ham argued with Hurd about the dangers—by this time the Ledge Trail had been prohibited by the Park for downhill travel—but Ham could not dissuade him from his decision. On top of Hurd's bad judgment, he also now taunted his friend that he would reach their car at Happy Isles first. "In his eagerness to beat Ham to the Valley Floor," the Park report noted, "Hurd was traveling pretty fast and failed to make the right turn at the watercourse [Staircase Creek], plunging to his death on the rocks below."

By 1952, the National Park Service made an even more serious effort to prohibit all *downhill* travel on this trail. Within ten years the trail had vanished from maps of Yosemite and was officially abandoned and not maintained except for warning signs reading "Trail Closed" at its top and bottom. Despite its defunct status, hikers would continue to use it with fatal results in 1965, 1970, 1972, 1976,

1993 and possibly also in 1998. Overall, about fourteen young men have died while traversing or shortcutting to or from this trail. They represent more than 10 percent of all fatal hiking/scrambling falls in Yosemite. Their deaths make the Ledge Trail route the third most fatal geographical "entity" in the Park after El Capitan and the Merced River.

Returning to the "shortcut" syndrome of hiking, particularly when doing so alone, consider the next brief examples. On May 27, 1956, 28-year-old Robert Franklin Johnson, a doctor from San Francisco, scrambled out of the Valley up Indian Canyon with a companion. Once on top and east of Lost Arrow, Dr. Johnson left his partner for what he said would be a "short hike" back down. He was attempting to blaze a new route back to the Valley down through Castle Cliffs and the Yosemite Point Couloir. Johnson never arrived. Rangers looked for him for five days. Their effort included only the third use ever of a helicopter in Yosemite. When found, he had fallen eighty feet and landed on a narrow, obscure sandy and brush-covered ledge. The searchers buried Dr. Johnson where he had died. Making only minor variations on this same theme, on May 6, 1985, 22-year-old Fredrico Hernandez of Los Angeles and 15-year-old Jesus Cortez hiked down the Four-Mile Trail and decided to shortcut it about three-quarters of a mile east of the Sentinel Creek crossing. The two Angelinos scrambled down a gully then hit a vertical drop off that baffled them. As Cortez sat and stared at it he held a branch for support, Hernandez simply sat on the edge of a rock and looked down into the Valley not far below. Hernandez shifted his weight slightly, inadvertently lost his friction, and fell off his rock into 300 feet of air.

The promise of easier or faster passage across unscouted terrain has lured males for many decades. An early yet more complicated incident of this unfolded on October 6, 1934, when three friends from Berkeley hiked to North Dome. Because it is a short daylight month and the three wanted the most mileage while heading out but the shortest mileage coming back, 34-year-old V. N. Borsoff, his 30-year-old brother Nick, and 47-year-old L. N. Jacovless elected to shortcut their way back down to the Valley. Their plan was to "slide" down the cracks and chimneys of the very steep gully toward Mirror Lake, 2,500 feet below.

No surprise, the three stranded themselves on the forbidding terrain and were forced to spend a very cool night perched on the cliff like three Gelada baboons hunkered on an outcrop in Ethiopia. At dawn they resumed their difficult descent. As each man continued to pioneer routes, they all became separated. And as their paths proved ever more ridiculous, each one experienced mishaps and suffered injuries. Two of them battered themselves so badly that, incapacitated, their injuries finally forced them to stop. Both older men had gotten stuck in difficult locations.

Somehow Nick Borsoff succeeded in making it all the way down. He soon requested a rescue for his brother and his friend.

By midday the rescue crew had reached Nick's brother. Their task had not been a breeze. They had found him more than halfway down the steep gully but now exhausted and with one knee fractured. Despite having to package him onto a litter and lower him laboriously by ropes from dangerous cliffs, he turned out to be the easy victim. Jacovless, on the other hand, proved to be far more of a problem. For one thing, no one could even find him.

The ranger team continued climbing cliffs and traversing ledges. They used ropes as they ascended ever upward. Each time they topped a yet higher ledge they hoped to find their missing third man huddled there. But so far, no dice. Where *was* this guy? As the day waned, not only did it appear that their lost man was truly lost, it also became clear that the rescuers themselves were doing all of this the hard way. By now they had climbed so high via challenging terrain that they realized rather than having made this series of climbs *up* this daunting gully they would have done things better and faster and easier had they instead accessed North Dome Gully from above then descended it in the staggering footsteps of the three naïve shortcutters. Unfortunately, this realization was a moot point. Like it or not, the rescuers were now committed to continuing this arduous ascent.

After nearly an entire day of exhausting climbing, the team finally found Jacovless about 1,500 feet above Mirror Lake. Battered, he had curled up in a shallow pocket in the granite cliff. He had somehow loosened a rock almost a day earlier while scrambling down. It had fallen on his head, seriously hurting him. As if that injury was not bad enough, Jacovless had also managed to break his leg.

The rescuers stabilized him and strapped him into a stretcher. As if acting out some black comedy of wilderness tribulations, they were soon to learn that their entire miserable day thus far had been a cakewalk compared to what came next. To get Jacovless to the Park's hospital, the rangers now had to lower him from ledge to ledge in short, challenging stages for well over a thousand feet. "The rescue of these two men," noted the *Superintendent's Monthly Report* for October, "was one of the most difficult and dangerous ever undertaken here, as that cliff is very precipitous with only narrow and slippery ledges, and there were only a few trees to which ropes could be tied in slinging the men down."

Happily, through the Herculean and apparently indefatigable efforts of these rescuers, both hikers who had stranded themselves on their deceptively easy looking shortcut lived to be wiser men.

Most of these shortcutting incidents above proved tragic and, in hindsight, most of the victims seem to have been oblivious to the hazards to which they went out of their way to expose themselves. A few of these people seemed naïve to a fault. Consider the more recent case of 21-year-old Henry Tien. On March 24, 1997, this Stanford University student went day hiking up the Yosemite Falls Trail with his girlfriend of a year, Susie G. Wu.

The two had not done much hiking together. After roughly an hour, and now near Columbia Point, Wu, who wanted to "get there," decided to go ahead because her boyfriend was moving much too slowly. He told her this was because he just wanted to "take in more of the sights." After separating, both became solo hikers.

Susie Wu hiked uphill at a normal pace. Even so, she intermittently stopped to wait for Henry Tien. She stopped for what she considered to be an inordinate time. Despite her pauses, he never caught up with her. By 3 p.m., she had hiked well past Columbia Point, but because she still had not seen her friend, she turned around to go find him. Along the way down, she stopped twice to carefully write him a note. She weighted down each of these with a stone in a conspicuous place just in case they somehow inadvertently passed each other.

Wu's notes would prove sadly unnecessary.

Farther down the trail at 4 p.m., she found Tien lying bashed and unconscious with serious head injuries incurred during a long fall. He was already under the care of a ranger medic and attended by twenty-nine other people.

No one had witnessed Tien fall. Yet Wu thought she knew him well enough to make a close guess as to what had gone wrong. She suspected that after being dilatory to indulge his aesthetic needs, he had probably tried to execute a burst of speed to catch her. If true, he also very likely tried shortcutting the switchbacks (maybe even, investigators would suspect, to the point of rock climbing). This may have fostered his fall. After his air evacuation to Modesto, Tien was pronounced dead in the emergency room.

Again, at least thirty-one young men have lost their lives in Yosemite while trying to shortcut maintained trails and/or established routes. Table 6 at the end of this chapter lists many others whom we have not discussed individually. Many of these were solo hikers who died from falls while deliberately off-route. Yet more fell due simply to getting lost.

An epic illustration of this occurred on July 9, 1974. Sixteen-year-old Erick James Stakkestad of Aptos, California began a hike with Kevin Croskey, age 17, and Chris Boulerice, age 16. The trio's plan was to walk from Tenaya Lake to Yosemite Valley via the thirteen-mile Mount Watkins Trail. This was a reasonable plan. But when they crossed the wide section of bare granite below Olmsted Point on the Tioga Road their route was obscured by fog. Here they lost their way. Inadvertently, the teenagers now blindly descended into the treacherous Tenaya Canyon. As the terrain became ever more unfriendly, the trio realized that if they continued they might land in big trouble. So they wisely decided to bivouac for the night.

They awoke in good spirits but now surrounded by even thicker fog. They did not like where they were, and they also began to feel ever more impatient about just sitting there in the fog without making any sort of progress. So they chose to keep heading downhill. After a short distance they hit terrain so scary (and still foggy) they again reevaluated this "hike downhill" option as being too perilous.

They were so becalmed in dense fog that all they really knew for certain was they were perched on a slope in a mystery canyon that they could neither see nor locate with certainty on a map.

Stakkestad now volunteered to continue onward for help. His buddies Croskey and Boulerice told him he should not try it. Instead, they insisted, they all should just wait here until the weather cleared so they could see. Despite these two voices of reason, Stakkestad, low on sleep and short on calories, decided to try it anyway. He told his friends he intended to continue west (the correct direction but on hazardous terrain) and would stop periodically to yell for help. He now dropped his backpack and departed alone.

Croskey and Boulerice soon heard him shout. After a while they next thought they heard him cry, "Croskey!" More time passed. But now they heard nothing.

Worried about this silence, Croskey and Boulerice decided to follow what they believed was Stakkestad's trail down a gully. It soon ended in an abrupt drop-off. To continue down this chute lay beyond the pair's abilities, so they returned to their bivouac site. Two hours later the fog lifted.

Now finally able to see, the two prudent hikers left Stakkestad's pack as a marker of his last known position then worked their way back up to the trail. They then hiked over to the Snow Creek Switchbacks and into the Valley, reaching the Village by sundown. Rangers now organized a SAR mission and planned a helicopter overflight at dawn.

With Croskey aboard at seven the next morning, searchers quickly spotted Stakkestad's backpack where the two teenagers had wisely left it to mark the site. Within ten minutes the team also spotted the young man's body almost directly below his gear, crumpled on a steep slope below a high vertical face. Erick Stakkestad, in his self-assigned mission to get the three lost hikers out of this nightmarish landscape, had walked right off the sloping rock into nothing but fog and had fallen almost 400 feet.

As this teenager's fatal outcome hopefully illustrates, feeling lost—and experiencing the fear and panic it engenders—can prove to be a brain drain of the first magnitude. Maybe this tendency is exacerbated by the reality that, during many treks, even in stupendously beautiful terrain, people can be lulled into a mental state wherein they simply focus on dredging up the energy to put one foot in front of the other while fighting their impulse to sit down and take the onerous weight of their packs off their backs and feet. The existence of the trail itself alleviates not only the worry about which way to go but also allows the hiker to not be concerned with critically analyzing the specifics of the terrain surrounding him. This freedom allows backcountry novices to survive hike after hike unscathed. This is a good thing. A problem with well-marked trails, however, is they do not foster a critical spatial sense of topography and route-finding ability. Because of this, when some people do become lost they often react emotionally and intellectually much as a 4-year-old child does who has lost its mother in a strange city. They become more or less incapable of making the logical, informed decisions needed to extract themselves. They panic.

Often getting lost begins in an innocent way. On May 27, 1979, 18-year-old Daniel S. Wilson of San Rafael, California climbed to the top of the Royal Arches with three other teenagers. Long before getting lost, the four had first made the cardinal error of not turning back while sufficient daylight remained for them to safely return. Instead, the peer-pressure mentality of "making it to the top" probably eclipsed this sort of decision-making.

The foursome topped out at 7 p.m. To accomplish a descent with less than two daylight hours remaining, they traversed east along the Valley rim to the nearly 2,500-foot descent down the ultra-rugged North Dome Gully. Admittedly, this gully is the standard—albeit very dangerous—descent route used by technical rock climbers in this area. Although very steep, a well-beaten "path" does descend it. The four also planned to rappel the vertical sections of this route "as needed."

At a brief glance, there was nothing inherently wrong with this plan. Until one examines the details of its execution. Surprisingly, the four young men had decided on this specific plan even though none of them had ever descended or even seen North Dome Gully before. Ironically, they were not about to see it now either. This is because, despite their belated haste, the four scramblers had run out of light. Dusk had retreated to starlight. Now, at 10:30 at night and having not brought headlamps, the adventurers could neither find nor scout their way down. Descending now over unknown and un-seeable vertical terrain after nightfall was, not to put too fine a point on it, reckless.

The climbers found themselves perched and stranded on a slab that offered an uncomfortable but feasible sanctuary. The teenagers also found themselves in disagreement. Two of the young climbers wanted to bivouac here until dawn, less than seven hours away. The other two, including Daniel Wilson, insisted instead that they continue dropping down to the Valley. Within moments of expressing his adamancy, Wilson stepped toward what he was guessing was their best descent route. His feet slipped on a wet, gravel-covered rock. Unable to brake, he slid ever faster down the slab for 150 feet then shot off a ledge into thin air to fall almost 100 feet.

To the three still stranded above, the chances that Wilson could survive a fall that had sounded so lengthy seemed infinitesimally small.

At about midnight, they began yelling for help. Within an impressive mere two hours Rangers Craig Patterson and Jerry Reynolds had not only responded to the shouts, they had scrambled up to and joined the stranded young men near the top of North Dome Gully. Both rangers now spent another sunless hour searching for Wilson by climbing and peering into crannies and hidden brushy pockets in the highly broken cliff face. After not finding Wilson, Patterson and Reynolds decided that doing what they were doing in the dark was just too unsafe to continue. Instead they would return in the morning. After all, Wilson likely had been already dead for hours.

The two rangers now escorted the three surviving teenagers down North Dome Gully along the "patented" route to the Valley.

At 7 a.m., within fifteen minutes after launching the helicopter, searchers spotted the missing fallen teenager. By 10 a.m. Rangers Peter Fitzmaurice and Patterson reached the crumpled body. Not surprisingly, they had assumed the victim was dead. Now, however, they were surprised to find him alive—barely. Wilson was unconscious, and had sustained a plethora of battered body parts, but maybe there was hope.

The helicopter hurried to sling in emergency medical gear for his extraction. Meanwhile, Lemoore Naval Air Station scrambled and launched their rescue ship to fly in and haul the teenager out.

Before this could happen, at 11 a.m., Wilson quit breathing. His collection of high impact injuries had taken too serious a toll. Patterson began chest compressions as Fitzmaurice delivered breaths on him. Relatively soon thereafter, a Lewis Memorial Hospital physician assessed Wilson's many injuries. Convinced the fallen young man's prognosis was hopeless, he instructed the rangers to cease their efforts at resuscitation.

The dynamics of getting lost and then suffering a fatal fall such as Daniel Wilson's is so common it might deserve its own terminology, perhaps something like "semi-vertical terrain testosterone poisoning." No, you're right, SVTTP will probably never catch on. But while you try to think of a better one, consider a few more examples of how this sort of tragedy happens.

On February 23, 1980, 20-year-old Steve Leroy O'Neal of Salt Lake City, and two fellow airmen, Manfred Schoenhoefer and Michael S. Kepler, chose to hike up from Yosemite Valley. None of them possessed any previous experience in the Park or in climbing elsewhere.

Bushwhacking off-trail, the young trio aimed for the top of Lower Yosemite Fall. They crossed a small stream on the north side. Gaining elevation fast, they next scrambled up a series of moderately-sloping granite ramps. Eventually they made "near" the top of the fall. Here they decided they could go no higher.

After taking in the views and admiring what they had accomplished, the trio started back down. Not far into their descent of several hundred feet they lost their original route. Rather than backtrack up the very steep slope to relocate it, the airmen decided to continue down by "winging it."

The three soon hit a long vertical drop. Kepler and Schoenhoefer decided it would not "go." O'Neal, wearing leather-soled cowboy boots and otherwise unequipped for scramble climbing, disagreed. He insisted that it would. Furthermore, he added, it would go safely. O'Neal's friends again both yelled down at him that the route was impossible, or at least far too dangerous. To emphasize how convinced they were of this, they began retracing their steps upward to seek a safer return.

O'Neal ignored them. His behavior next resembles that of a testosterone-driven solo scrambler committed to an imagined shortcut. Ten minutes later and unseen by his more cautious colleagues, O'Neal lost his holds and fell at least 300 feet. He died when he hit in an oak tree about twenty feet from the bottom of the climb that Steve Roper's *Climber's Guide to Yosemite* called "The Commitment YDS II, 5.9."

Consider the next variation on this theme of getting lost and then making desperate, rather than thoughtful, patient moves to self-extricate. On March 20, 1980, 19-year-old David Mark Bixler of Somerville, New Jersey and Daniel M. Mitzsche, age 20, tried to backpack down from Glacier Point. They had illegally ascended the officially closed (for winter) Panorama Trail. But they did not want to return that way. The good news was when they got lost they were *very* close to the Four-Mile Trail they had been looking for. The bad news was they failed to see it.

To search for it—or for any other route that would go—the two soon began bushwhacking downslope. The terrain quickly worsened and steepened but, like a dangling carrot, their route still appeared "promising," or at least not impossible.

The scramblers now hit a vertical chute dropping about twenty feet. It barred their progress. Beyond this crevice, however, the route continued to look okay. But first they had to get past this drop…

What happened next is termed in psychology the "sunk-cost effect." Another term for this might be the "used car syndrome." It develops when we buy a used car that proves to be a lemon. As we continue to pay dearly to repair one breakdown after another the logical option to dump this vampire never seems reasonable—we have invested too much to be willing to write it off. Something similar occurs when we begin investing in a new route of our own invention that continues to deteriorate to become ever more dangerous. Our reluctance to stop and turn around and retrace our steps and to write off our "route" completely and thereby chalk up our investment of time, energy, and pain as a total loss grows with each step, each grunt, and with each new handhold found. This conflict metastasizes into a duel between our ego and the terrain. Somehow we convince ourselves that it makes the most sense to invest just a little more effort and faith in this crummy route. After all, we think, I *know* I am getting so much closer.

Bixler and Mitzsche now stared longingly at the more promising terrain just below the granite chute that had stopped them cold. Whatever doubts about the grave deterioration of this route that might have entered their minds at first, their personal investment in it (which in reality was fairly minimal) now took precedence. Bixler decided to cross the rock crevice by jumping down off the cliff into the top of a tree growing from the steep hillside below. The two discussed this tactic and somehow agreed that leaping into this tree made sense.

To them.

David Bixler jumped first. He fell through the branches of his target as planned. But in so doing he hit his head. Hard. He also hurt a few other body parts. He plopped onto the ground semiconscious at best.

Amazingly, Mitzsche followed Bixler. He now leaped off the cliff into the same tree. The impact fractured his arm and his skull—so hard that he too knocked himself out.

Both young jumpers regained consciousness in dimming light and, feeling pretty bad, elected to bivouac there for the night. At about 3 a.m., David Mark Bixler died from intracranial bleeding and swelling due to his head injury.

After dawn, the seriously injured Mitzsche saw other hikers on the nearby Four-Mile Trail. He soon reached it, only to report the death of his friend.

Ironically, this pair of battered cross-country scramblers had tortured themselves—one of them fatally—by being lost a mere seventy-five yards from this well constructed trail leading down to the Valley. This was in fact the path they had originally wanted to hike. The lesson? There exist many, but one might be: An earnest investment in dedicated reconnaissance for a sound route can avert tragedy.

A more epic episode of excessive reluctance to reevaluate a perceived route while trekking over unknown terrain occurred on August 7, 1993. Forty-six-year-old Mark Conley of Merced, California and Greg DiCarlo decided to launch a cross-country scramble-hike-climb from Mount Hoffman across the "saddle" to Tuolumne Peak. From there they planned to descend its "far side." Two and half air miles separate the two peaks. On the ground the hike is at least eight.

The first error the pair made was in using a Park brochure as their guide instead of an actual topographical map. Despite this self-imposed handicap the two, who previously had never attempted a trail-less hike before, made the 10,850-foot top of Hoffman okay. It was the descent that proved a challenge.

Because Conley and DiCarlo were aiming cross-country, they wanted to continue down off the mountain in the direction providing the shortest route. Detouring away from that direction seemed like defeat. Their problem was in figuring out a way down the, to them, "unknown" side of Mount Hoffman. Had they been better prepared, say, with a topographic map and by consulting a backcountry ranger or hiker who had done this route before, planning a good itinerary might have been reasonably straight forward. But without either, and also without the luxury afforded by physically looking *up* at the perils of a potential route, they were partially blindfolded. As they now looked down from Mount Hoffman, their view of the promise versus peril of a possible descent route toward Tuolumne Peak appeared foreshortened and partially hidden. The two felt tempted to just wing it.

To complicate matters Conley was wearing "worn" hiking boots. Soon, after descending about a quarter mile northeast of the summit, he ventured out onto a small, wet ledge. He had just told DiCarlo that he intended to downclimb off it to a lower shelf.

DiCarlo glanced at all the air visible below Conley's precarious spot and experienced a moment of clarity. "Mark, this is too dangerous, don't do it."

Conley responded, "Yeah, I can do it."

As these words left Conley's mouth his worn-out soles started sliding down the wet granite. As he slid toward the edge he uttered a panicked, "Oh, my God!"

As his old boots glided off the edge he exploded a single expletive, and then he screamed as he fell 100 feet through empty air. (Later, searchers would find that when Mark Conley hit bottom his momentum was so great that it had wedged him into the bergschrund—the carved gap above the head of a glacier—like a spike pounded by a hammer.)

With a sick sensation now perfusing him, DiCarlo carefully edged up to the drop-off in a safer location to peer below for his friend. He could not see him.

So he found a better route down then circled back to where he thought Conley should be. But search as he might, he still could not find him. Finally, he gave up and started working his way along what he thought must be a beeline to help. Again DiCarlo was using nothing but that brochure as a map. This was still his first-ever cross-country hike.

DiCarlo got lost. Getting unlost ate up time and calories. As the raven flies he was only a few miles from the South Fork Trail or, in another direction, from May Lake. Even so, these few miles grew rather than shrank due to false starts on wrong bearings beset with daunting obstacles. With each, DiCarlo became even more confused. Nightfall forced him to bivouac without gear.

By late morning of the next day he finally made it to the Glen Aulin High Sierra Camp, several miles farther.

When interviewed by Park Rangers, DiCarlo admitted: "I think we were stupid…we shouldn't leave trails…tell people to stay on trails."

One of the more amazing misadventures in the annals of Yosemite bushwhacking and in search and rescue here occurred on June 20, 2003, when 18-year-old Graham Becherer-Bailey decided to hike solo from Tenaya Lake to the Valley. To avoid the "beaten path" (as if one exists down Tenaya Canyon…), Graham consulted about alternatives with a couple of friends who worked in the Park. They told him that an infrequently done but doable route existed down the Canyon and it crossed mostly second and third-class terrain (Class 3 translates to "scrambling, a rope might be carried"). This route also paralleled the creek for much of the way. The rub here was that a couple of spots might demand rappels. But by staying to the right of the stream, his friends added, these drops could be avoided.

Graham intended to make this hike in one day. If he avoided making mistakes, this day hike would indeed be only a day hike. As almost everyone does, Graham wanted a light pack. He took only the barest of essentials. These did not include any canyoneering hardware or a helmet. But he did toss in a single rope—and his cell phone. The teenager intended to address any vertical drops by using natural anchors and then going hand-over-hand down his doubled line.

A common practice that has led to many fatal accidental falls is that of young men hiking alone. Wanting to do this is understandable. When hiking solo into the wilderness a young man must rely only on his own devices and his native intelligence for survival. Among other reasons, such hikes also become classic rites of passage. Australian Aborigines even have a name for it: "going walkabout." A critical difference between American culture and traditional Aboriginal culture Down Under is: Young Aborigines grow up in the bush. Just about all of their lives they live in it, forage in it, travel through it, and due to parental training they understand virtually every nuance and denizen of "their" bush far better than American teenagers know even their favorite video games. In contrast, most Americans do not grow up in the outdoors; nor do most even walk through it with bush-savvy fathers as mentors. So, by comparison, young solo American hikers often prove to be relative babes in the woods, ones far more vulnerable to mistakes. Also, because most of the errors committed by these hikers go unwitnessed, understanding exactly what went wrong proves far more of a challenge.

Graham Becherer-Bailey's first few hours in Tenaya Canyon proved straightforward. The route seemed beautiful, fun, and exclusive. Next the creek abruptly dropped over a waterfall fifty- to seventy-five-feet deep and then crashed through a narrow gorge. His buddies had warned him about this section, but now in person it looked far more difficult than what they had described.

Decision time. Rappelling here was doable. But what if the next section below it was not? How hard would it be to climb back out? Prudence now spurred Graham to stick to the right on easier terrain and hope for the more obvious, slightly simpler way down to the stream that he had been told about. In search of this he bushwhacked for quite a distance through manzanita along a mountainside route that lost little elevation. He soon found himself hundreds of feet above the creek, which had descended in a series of waterfalls.

As if sympathetic to his problem the terrain coaxed him down several slabs that fed into a small side drainage. He followed it. It waterfalled out into a vertical cliff. This was pretty clear cut alright, but it was not Class-3 terrain.

Graham stared down the Class-5 (again, vertical and needing ropes, protection, and training or experience) face of the cliff with its long misting drizzle of water. Yes, this wall was possible to rappel (or, in this case, descend hand over hand). And if he were at the bottom, the terrain beyond looked so good that he should be able to easily scramble to the creek. From there it was only a couple of miles to the Valley. Again, that is *if* he were already down there.

Inconveniently, this drop totaled more than a hundred feet high. Graham now looked around for an easier, safer descent route. He spent an hour searching his side of the canyon only to conclude that this cliff in this side drainage still appeared his best option. At this point, the thought had not yet reared its head that retracing his way back upstream through the brush and manzanita to that first fifty- to seventy-five-foot waterfall might be his best option.

So Graham now doubled his rope around a tree near the cliff and grabbed it. He peered over the edge. His line did not even come close to reaching the bottom. But it did hit a substantial slab that angled steeply down for dozens of feet to a broad ledge with a pool of water on it. Getting down from that shelf did not seem to pose a problem.

Decision time again. Once he started down this rope he was committed. If the rest of the route did not go with just this one rope he would be trapped—without ascenders of some sort he could not climb back up.

Even so, it did look to the 18 year-old as if he could hand-over-hand his way down to that slab. And from there simply climb down to the granite with the pool. He might even be able to use his rope again from the tip of the slab. Again, from the ledge going down farther to the creek looked pretty easy.

Graham now descended his rope using only his hands and feet—no Prusik, no safety hardware, no harness—but he did possess confidence. He had practiced this sort of thing before, and it was going well despite the somewhat overhanging nature of the cliff.

As oft has been uttered, the devil resides in the details. As Graham lowered himself and felt a sense of well-being because his skill level matched this task, he noticed his rope was changing. The drizzling water falling from above was quickly soaking it. As he clutched the wet line with one hand and moved the other, his gripping hand slipped down the rope an inch or two. This was bad. To combat this increasing slipperiness, Graham now tried to move faster. In his race against an increasingly soggy and slick line, his momentum built up. Only ten feet from the end of his doubled rope and another five feet above the top of the slab, he lost his grip altogether.

Graham slid off into the air.

He fell then hit the top of the steep granite. From above, this slab had appeared to have been maybe forty feet higher than the shallow pool. It instead proved to be eighty feet high and nearly straight down.

He bounced, fell, rolled, bounced again, fell again, and with each second built up speed despite friction against the granite. Then, after eighty-five feet of this, he hit. Hard.

He opened his eyes.

"Holy shit, I fell! Holy shit, I'm okay!" Graham touched his head. It hurt, but at least he could feel it. His hand came away bloody. He tried to stand up in the pool to survey his situation. His right leg shot excruciating pain up to his brain. He stared at it. There was now a joint between his hip and knee—a new bend in his leg that should not be there. He knew this was extremely bad news. Its gravity grew in his mind as he painfully crawled twenty feet to haul himself out of the water.

Once on the dry granite it slowly became clear that, crippled as he was, he could not get himself off this ledge. He was trapped! He would be stuck here forever unless he purposefully fell off or else some huge storm created a big enough waterfall to wash his bones off it.

So now what?

Despite how lightly he had packed for this day trip, Graham had included his cell phone. But he had fallen and tumbled close to a hundred feet onto hard rock then landed in shallow water. Was it possible that the phone even worked after all that abuse?

Graham dug it out of his pack. Its LED lit up as it was supposed to. Amazing! That his cheap plastic phone had emerged unscathed from the crushing trauma which had crippled his body seemed miraculous.

He dialed 911. As most of us who have toted cell phones into the backcountry have learned, being deep in a narrow canyon and between solid rock walls almost always precludes hitting a repeater. In short, cell phones do not work in places like this. In retrospect, Graham's dialing 911 seems naïve. In fact, had the teenager crawled only a few *feet* in any direction on this remote ledge deep in Tenaya Canyon, he would have lost his thread-thin line of sight to the only existing repeater station. Having just tumbled eighty-five feet and made a bloody, broken mess out of himself might make Graham seem a poor candidate for being termed "lucky," but now he was indeed incredibly lucky; he had inadvertently crawled to exactly the right tiny little pinpoint place for his phone to work.

"Park Dispatch," came the official voice.

Graham described the trouble he was in and tried to provide a detailed description of where he was.

The helicopter and SAR team found him quickly. After sizing up the steep terrain, the pilot determined that he could land only in the canyon bottom several hundred yards distant. Two ranger-paramedics scrambled from there with their medical kits up to Graham's ledge. They stabilized and splinted his snapped femur. Once he had been packaged for transport, a second helicopter, this one from the California Highway Patrol, hoisted him off the ledge in a "short haul" to the Valley. There the doctor quickly transferred him by yet another air ambulance to Modesto. Graham's X-rays and MRI revealed he had suffered a lumbar vertebrae compression fracture and a broken pelvis, and the upper portion of his right femur had shattered into pieces.

Less than a year later, Graham Becherer-Bailey had healed to the point at which, as he describes it, he is able "to do whatever activities I choose, but I'll probably lay off contact sports a little longer." In retrospect Graham noted to us more than a year later:

> This was the most traumatic thing that has ever occurred to me,

> mostly because I did it to myself. I still have dreams about it, and the accident is never far from my mind. I have never been as embarrassed as when I had to call for help and put people in danger for my sake. I almost didn't call for that reason. I can hardly be classed as a beginner—I've had the benefit of 18 years of outdoor education from my family, have been climbing my whole life, and have had extensive canyoneering experience elsewhere. It sounds crazy even to me now, but I was really comfortable going hand-over-hand. It was standard procedure back home, but on a cliff this steep and this high it was a dumb thing to do. I could easily have turned around and hiked back to Tenaya Lake, even if I had to spend the night en route. But the greatest lesson learned was humility. I needed a big slap in the face because I was getting way too cocky with my climbing. I definitely got a BIG slap in the face.

More analytically, SAR Ranger John Dill notes on Graham's Mission Report:

> Graham was extraordinarily lucky, first that the fall did not kill him, second that his cell phone survived, and third, that his call got through. Tenaya Canyon is a notorious no-service zone—as is much of the Park—**and his own rescuers were unable to call out from the scene**. Otherwise we don't have much to say but the obvious. First, regardless of your route description and its source, once you are out there—on trail or off—you have to use your own judgment every step of the way. The advice from Graham's friends may have been correct, but it was insufficiently detailed to keep him on track in such rough country, and he had actually wandered off route. A map will sometimes help, but it, too, will lack the necessary resolution. Second, if you are taking a rope, take the gear to go down it safely. Add to this some Prusiks and lightweight foot loops for ascending your line again if you find yourself at a dead end. Graham would have hardly noticed the weight of this gear in his daypack, and it would have been far cheaper than all those helicopters and hospital bills. Tenaya Canyon has been the scene of many strandings, injuries, and fatalities, all involving parties without the skills and/or gear for the terrain. [bold ours]

Again the devil lurks in the details. On September 27, 1994, 20-year-old Graham S. Turner of Scotland and Joanna Childs from England hiked the trail from Wawona Tunnel about two miles, gaining roughly 1,000 feet of elevation to Old Inspiration Point. They wanted to watch the sunset. Predictably, the spectacle turned out to be dazzling. The problem here was inherent in the pair's idea to watch the sun vanish from a place where they neither intended to bivouac nor planned to safely exit. Turner and Childs had not brought flashlights.

Old Inspiration Point is impressive. It is the overlook where Major Savage and his Mariposa Battalion—while trying to round up and dispossess the Yosemite Indians on March 27, 1851—first saw the Valley (see Chapter 14 for details). The identities of the original person—or persons—who masterminded the name "Inspiration Point" remains murky. Many apocryphal stories exist to explain how the name came to be but the actual naming event remains elusive. According to Peter Browning in his *Yosemite Place Names* the first publication of the name Inspiration Point is now attributed to James Mason Hutchings in his *Scenes of Wonder and Curiosity in California*. In reality, Hutchings had already published the name "Inspiration Point" in his *California Magazine* in 1860. In 1871, he says, "Almost before the gratifying fact is realized, you have reached 'Inspiration Point' and are standing out on a bald promontory of rock....in all my life, let it lead me where it may...I think I shall see nothing else so sublime and beautiful, till, happily, I stand within the gates of the Heavenly City."

It may be understandable that 1994 visitors Turner and Childs tarried over-long for that sunset. What seems less comprehendible is they had not brought flashlights to facilitate their return. During their hike back the two got lost despite having the somewhat visible old Wawona Stage Road to follow.

Inadvertently the pair soon veered off-trail. And as often happens, they took the path of least resistance by going downhill more than they should have. When they spotted the headlights of vehicles passing along on roads below them, the lights looked closer than they should have been. The two hikers realized they had lost too much elevation too fast. This cue prompted them to start back up.

Childs soon slipped and fell. She tumbled in the dark then hit something hard. The impact knocked her unconscious. When she awoke she found herself alone, still in the dark, and injured. To cap it off, when she next groped around to assess her location she found herself perched on a small ledge above one cliff and below another. Her continual groping blindly only confirmed her fears.

She was trapped.

Desperate, she called out to Turner.

No answer.

Crying out again convinced her that he was either out of earshot, or else...

Childs began yelling into the darkness for help.

She yelled all night.

Just after dawn someone below heard her screams. This witness triggered a SAR mission into motion. Using a spotting scope from Highway 140 to zero in on the screams, a searcher finally located Childs. Then the team moved in to rescue her. A team member also found Turner. He too had fallen. Less lucky, he had tumbled 150 feet beyond and below Childs' ledge and had died on impact.

An old saw exists which explains how for loss of a nail, the war was lost. While admittedly this is an extreme example of what a bit of poor preparation can inflict, it nonetheless has been proven sadly prophetic in the wilds all too many times. Perhaps the worst sorts of lack of preparation are those that ultimately lead to diminished mental capacity. Not mere fatigue, but actual diminished capacity.

Just how bizarre this can get occurred on July 12, 1980. Seventeen-year-old Victor Robinson Zenoff of Atherton, California had hiked with Evan Dean Maloney up to Columbia Point via the Yosemite Falls Trail. On their return, Maloney would later report, Zenoff began to giggle and act "silly." He asked everyone they met on the trail: "Who am I? Where am I? What am I doing?"

About 5:30 p.m., Maloney grabbed Zenoff and told him the reason he was acting so strange was he was tired and had nothing to eat for two days. Maloney emphasized they should continue down to the Valley. In short, the pair was hiking together but the two had not planned to meet their physical needs. While some people can perform heavy labor without food for days and still retain some clarity of thought, others exist who, for metabolic reasons (hypoglycemia), are incapable of doing this. Victor Zenoff, it would turn out, was about to prove himself a candidate for this second group.

Zenoff now responded by saying, "I know how we can get down faster—" After saying this he started running, almost sprinting, down the rocky trail with its sharp switchbacks.

Alarmed, Maloney hurried after him. He wanted to catch Zenoff and stop him before he hurt himself. But Zenoff, as silly as he was, was now hauling butt at a ridiculous pace.

As Maloney ran to catch up, he rounded a corner and "saw Zenoff's body in mid air, just south of the trail five feet below the level of the trail." Just before Zenoff disappeared through the brush and over the edge, Maloney screamed, "Victor!"

Maloney next started yelling "Help!" as he frantically descended the path. He stopped at various exposed edges to search for his friend. Failing to spot him, Maloney then abandoned the trail. But just as he started to scramble down the bare granite, he heard a voice from far below yelling that he just found someone badly hurt.

Maloney climbed back up to the maintained route then hurried down it. When Maloney reached Zenoff he saw he had fallen and tumbled 600 feet and now was unconscious and suffering massive head injuries. Despite this huge fall Zenoff was still alive. His respirations had dropped to about four per minute from a normal adult's fifteen or so, but his heart was still beating.

Having been alerted by another visitor, a rescue team arrived in less than an hour and began to provide assisted breathing. Victor Zenoff soon died anyway due to the extreme severity of his injuries. Indeed, had the doomed young man fallen 600 feet into the best surgical center in the world, one equipped with state-of-the-art life-support instead of onto bare Yosemite granite, his prognosis likely would have been no better.

Loss of mental acuity due to metabolic problems caused by poor sleeping or eating really differs very little from loss of mental acuity fostered by environmental problems such as heat or cold. In either case, the result is impaired judgment. Impaired judgment and vertical terrain are not good bedfellows.

Consider the odyssey of 38-year-old Stephen Eric Lyman, one of Yosemite's more renowned artists. On April 17, 1996, Lyman of Sand Point, Idaho went scramble-climbing on a day trip into the Cathedral Rocks area across the Valley from El Capitan. Lyman embarked on this photographic foray not only despite the fact that a storm was approaching the Valley but perhaps *because* the approach of the storm would create dramatic atmospheric changes in color. How true this latter conjecture might be remains a moot point; Lyman failed to return that night as planned.

The Park initiated a SAR operation the next day but found no sign of him. Later they learned that during the night of the 17th someone had been heard calling for help somewhere up among Cathedral Rocks. Motorists below had heard the mysterious cries, but none of them could pinpoint their source in the dark. In hindsight, these yells for help seem likely to have been Lyman's.

To better understand why and how such an experienced mountaineer as Lyman went missing hundreds of feet above the Valley floor during a storm it might help to gain partial insight into how the artist's mind might have worked. Was there something about Stephen Lyman that may have gotten him into this predicament?

He was a talent of inspired ability—so much so that he had earned the kind of reputation that made each of his paintings worth not just a good price but a better price than the previous one. Lyman loved Yosemite and he painted it in glowing detail, and he painted it often. As the Park Historian Jim Snyder noted in his article "Remembering Steve Lyman in Yosemite" (in *The Yosemite Association, Fall 1996 Quarterly)*, Lyman's "Yosemite Alpenglow" painting of the Valley was done in a perspective from Eagle Peak and done flanked by surrounding peaks while making it appear even more roadless than when John Muir first saw it. This painting was so good and so nearly perfect that it fooled people—even those familiar with the Park—into assuming it was a gigantic and superlative photograph.

For years the artist had been somewhat a protégé of John Muir. In the famed conservationist's heyday before the twentieth century, Muir frequently had made sojourns into the Sierra Nevada equipped almost as lightly as if he were strolling in a city park. Intrigued by Muir, arguably Yosemite's most influential and well known "pioneer," Lyman visited John Muir's old home, preserved by the National Park Service in the Bay Area town of Martinez.

Here Lyman sat in Muir's "scribble-den" to absorb the spirit and essence of the man he admired. Muir had written about his exhilarating adventures. These often seemed enhanced by what appeared to have been Muir's reckless behavior. His feral experiences in the wilds and his lightweight, almost devil-may-care preparation alluded to in *The Mountains of California* seemed to have influenced Lyman, who also appeared to recognize himself as a kindred spirit. Lyman revealed this perceived intersection of identities by cryptically saying to Historian Jim Snyder, "Muir wrote; I paint."

And what Lyman seemingly liked most to paint was a Yosemite whose landscapes were highlighted by fire, water, light, and lightning. These dramatic dimensions constituted the highest-energy elements of nature in head-to-head conflict.

On April 19, two climbers descending from the East Buttress Route found Lyman's battered body in the steep gully between Upper and Middle Cathedral Rocks at an elevation of 5,700 feet. He was clothed only in his underwear. The climbers found no other equipment or clothing nearby. Additional searching by Park SAR personnel finally revealed a ledge 180 feet higher with the victim's cotton clothing, piled intentionally with other possessions. The clothing had been doffed and piled when soggy—Lyman, they guessed, had likely removed his wet clothes in hopes of stalling his rate of accelerating hypothermia. (Indeed, because paradoxical disrobing during the late stages of hypothermia is not uncommon, another interpretation here is that he had performed his "decision-making" to remove his clothes with a "cold operational brain.")

Not very Muir-like (John Muir likely would have worn wool)—except for one lightweight pile jacket, all of Lyman's clothing was of cotton, again, now very soggy. He had not been carrying a rain parka or other foul-weather gear. That he had not re-donned his pile jacket (it would have helped him retain heat despite being damp) at this point possibly reveals how impaired his mental capacity might have been.

Reconstructing Lyman's demise, it became clear to the SAR team that when he had embarked on his venture he probably had done so with good—or at least survivable—weather in mind. But he had taken no backup gear and seemingly had made no plan "B" for bad weather.

Because of Lyman's decision to travel light, he had left himself vulnerable to the mind-sapping effects of hypothermia on that ledge where he had dumped his clothing in a wet, soon-to-be-frozen, heap.

Why was he even up there in that chute?

His decision to descend this way may have been a last-minute one. More likely, however, this return route had been his intention from the start of his trip. It offered a safer way down than his original route up, which at the beginning required Class 4 climbing and would necessitate a rope to get back down.

Why had he stayed up there so long that the weather caught him? His camera revealed he had remained high on the notch between Upper and Middle

Cathedral Rocks to photograph storm clouds passing over the Three Brothers. This chute is a natural way down from his perch. He probably realized he had overstayed his time. He needed to make an appointment at 8 p.m. in Sacramento this same evening for a radio interview (this was to be followed by staying the night in nearby Davis at the home of his friend Park Historian Jim Snyder).

Several lessons reside here. One is: No matter how bad the weather gets, the option to bivouac in full survival mode (possibly by trying to light a fire and/or by hunkering under any sort of natural shelter to remain as dry as possible) should never be dismissed. Bivouacking probably occurred to Lyman although he did not decide to do it. Soaked by rain and sleet, his judgment was soon very likely failing due to hypothermia. All of this was probably compounded by fading daylight and plunging temperatures.

Worse, hand-in-hand with undermining his ability to think, hypothermia also would have sabotaged his physical prowess. Whatever competence on rock he might have exhibited on a good day became moot now that both he and the rock were cold and wet.

As with many hikes spurred at the end by a sense of urgency, Lyman's too proved a trap. He had become "ledged out" both to the right and left after removing his wet clothing. He next probably tried to downclimb that rock face. He seemed to have quickly lost his holds on the slick, cold granite. Stephen Lyman then fell nearly 180 feet.

What might have motivated him to make such a poorly prepared quest? Was it simply a mistake of over optimism, the sort that a lot of us have made but survived through luck? A mere four days prior to his tragic fall he had written in his journal:

> These mountains have felt and seen so much; their rise into the sky millions of years ago, the glaciers slip over them, the carpet of trees springs forth as a garment, the native ones hunt grizzly, deer, and woodpeckers, the falcons nest, the waterfalls boom, and a million tourists ride in shuttle buses! We are simply a blink in their stone eyes. This is a GRAND place.

Stephen Lyman's last published painting "Cathedral Snow" reveals almost exactly the location *and* the conditions that he failed to recognize and to prepare for in real life during his April hike. His lack of simple preparation became his undoing.

At the risk of harping, we feel compelled to reiterate that the solo aspect of many victims of falls in Yosemite and Grand Canyon and elsewhere often looms salient. The important lesson here—repeated far too often by tragedies—is that risks of going solo should not merely be "calculated," but instead should be managed via care and preparation and self-control measured objectively and conservatively—not romantically—against these the risks of the terrain. Otherwise, all too often, wishful thinking proves to be the last act of cognitive thought one's brain experiences. Ever.

Veteran trekker and climber George Steck put this lesson to us more succinctly: "A solo hiker often has a fool for a companion."

Although *Off the Wall* chronicles a surfeit of examples illustrating this to be true, we felt tempted to toss in one of the most famous recent examples of Steck's maxim. It is provided by Aron Ralston. He made his big splash into America's pool of notable outdoor enthusiasts in 2003 by canyoneering solo into Utah's Blue John Canyon, trapping himself in its bottom by dislodging a chockstone that, as he fell off of it, rolled atop and pinned his right hand. He finally escaped after nearly five days by snapping the bones of his wrist and sawing off his gangrenous hand with a dull, cheaply made multi-tool. Of course he next wrote his biography *Between a Rock and a Hard Place*. Admittedly this is an inspired title for a story such as his. It chronicles how he had set off alone, told no one where he was going, and did not even mention where in the United States. Then he had gone into Blue John poorly prepared to counter his mishap. His story of survival, despite reading as apparently candid, however, fails to paint him as a good role model for wilderness travel (unless one offsets this disapproval by approbation for his next cashing in via the American tradition of selling his macabre story for more than a million dollars).

Again, in the more recent era of Americans' love affair with entering the wilds as a rite of passage or simply for solitude, trekking or climbing alone must be seen objectively as incurring higher risk than doing so with a buddy. And for some people with limited experience, going solo incurs inordinate risk (again, sixty victims, nearly half of all fatal falls, were solo). This can be reduced somewhat by leaving detailed information about one's itinerary prior to one's departure. Even so, the romance of being out there "conquering peaks" (or one's sense of insignificance?) will always be alluring. The reminder we would like to include here is that when things do go wrong during this alluring experience, *one heck of a lot of other people risk their lives to pick up the pieces*. These days we are all in the wilderness together as a social species which sends its members into harm's way to rescue those who take such risks but underestimate them. If one decides to venture onto dangerous terrain, especially solo, but then things go wrong, one should also know in advance that one's rescuers will be made up of living beings who value their own lives. Knowing this compels each of us to answer in advance the same question: Am I responsible for making decisions which minimize the risk to myself—and therefore also to my potential rescuers?

Hopefully we all will answer "yes."

Beyond the increased risks of hiking or scrambling alone there lies a more obvious one. This one is inherent in the nature of the terrain a person chooses. About half of Yosemite's fatal scrambling falls occurred after the hiker involved had chosen to climb on a landscape verging on vertical. A very youthful version of this occurred on May 25, 1992, after 7-year-old Eric Shawn Dillon traveled past the junction of the Horse and the Mist Trails with his adult neighbor Linda Castro and with 9-year-old Jennifer Farrell. The trio continued up the Mist Trail to the top of Vernal Fall, with the boy leading. Castro frequently had to yell to him to wait up and not get too far ahead. They continued toward the Silver Apron and stopped west of the Clark Point Junction for a five-minute rest and a snack (next Castro planned on returning to the Valley where the kids could rest and eat a real meal). Here Shawn climbed up on a large rock and ate his candy bar. Then he quickly vanished from view on the boulder's backside.

Linda Castro got up to check on him. She found him about forty feet farther at the base of a sloping section of bedrock. She told him to stop right there and wait for her. Then she turned to help Jennifer down the slope because her shoes were slippery. When Castro turned back toward Shawn he had vanished yet again. She was worried, but she also suspected he might be playing a hide-and-seek trick on them. She parked Jennifer on a rock with instructions not to stray from it and then headed back to look again.

She searched for several minutes in several directions, on trail and off. She called out his name but heard no response. And found no sign of him. Finally she concluded he had been so hungry that he had passed her and headed down the trail. Castro retrieved her young friend and resumed her search downhill.

She soon met half a dozen backpackers and recruited them into helping her find her missing charge. Instead of finding Shawn they soon stumbled on another hiker who had found a young boy badly injured from a fall. He had lain crumpled there, the hiker said, for about twenty minutes.

As it turns out, instead of waiting when he had been instructed to, Shawn had scrambled around atop an overhanging cliff. Now off-trail and atop the upper staircase above Vernal Fall, between the Mist Trail and Clark's Point Trail, Shawn's athletic abilities failed him. He fell off the rock for an astounding 100 feet. But not through thin air alone. Shawn had plowed into the tops of trees above the Mist Trail, crashing through their branches. Then he had hit the ground twenty feet below the trail.

Park Ranger/EMT-1 Dan Horner responded by helicopter with the SAR team. He found the boy not merely alive after his 100-foot fall, but verbally responsive. Shawn, it would turn out, had broken his tibia and fibula and, although thrashed severely by the trees that saved his life, he had suffered no other real injuries. Ranger Horner would later exclaim that of all the survived falls of which he knew, Shawn's big adventure remains the most amazing.

After all is said and done, what do we know about scrambling falls in Yosemite? Most of the critical facts are known for most of these fatal events. Their details sift quickly into patterns that stand out as if embossed. First, of 133 known fatal scramble-hiking falls through 2012, 120 of the victims were male.

During more than a century, only thirteen women are known to have died this way. Of the 93 percent who were men, we should ask: What sort of males were they and what sorts of errors had they made? A revealing answer is: They were young men. Overall, their average age was 24 years old.

Without knowing much more than this, one might conclude this young average age may equate to a profile. Indeed it does, but the profile is even more crisp than it appears at first glance. This is because no one who died in these falls was under 10 years old. That's right, no young children. A similar pattern exists at Grand Canyon where forty-nine people who died in accidents off the rims (through 2006), none was under 13 years old. The upshot here is, when it comes to fatal heights and avoiding falls most children (other than the unusual Eric Shawn Dillon, above) are generally a lot smarter and more capable than adults give them credit.

Of Yosemite's 120 male fall victims up through 2012, about 90 were evenly split between the two age groups of 10 and 19 years old and 20 and 29 years of age. Clearly, fatal falls are mostly a young man's province.

Along with this profile of youth is the disturbing total of twenty concession employees who have suffered fatal falls, all while off-duty. Comparing these twenty (which comprise nearly one-sixth of all of these types of fatal accidents) against only two National Park Service employees who have died this way leads one to suspect striking differences. Over the years more than fifty other concession employees have also died traumatically in Yosemite (2 went over waterfalls, 4 fell while technical climbing, 3 vanished in the backcountry, 1 died of a recreational drug overdose, 2 were killed by treefalls, 8 drowned, 14 were driving cars or motorcycles, a dozen committed suicide, and 4 were homicides). These seventy concession employees killed while *off-work* compares unequally with about ten NPS employees who died in these ways (six of whom were driving).

Why this difference? For one thing, concession employees outnumber NPS employees at least three to one. On top of this, more NPS employees than concession employees (for decades) lived outside the Park and thus had their off-hours there, and hence might be "invisible" to us when they died of traumatic causes. Even after making all these adjustments, the difference remains striking. Additionally, at least seven National Park Service employees in Yosemite have died due to accidents while *on duty*. Records from the 1920s and 1930s, however, remain unclear as to whether a few of these men were contractors to the government or instead federal employees.

At any rate, if young men are the ones who make most of these fatal errors, exactly what *sorts* are they?

As we have seen in the many episodes thus far in this chapter, the major behavioral risk factors (in descending order—and these are minimum estimates) for all fatal falls are the victim's decision to: hike *off trail* (64 percent); *scramble-climb* without adequate experience or equipment on exposed faces (52 percent);

hike *solo* (45 percent); take a *shortcut* (26 percent), scramble in the *dark* (8 percent), and allow himself to get truly *lost* (more than 6 percent). Of course it is possible for one person to make every one of these risky decisions during a single foray into the wild.

Hampering this process of analysis is the inconvenient reality that not every victim of a fatal fall in Yosemite has left behind sufficient clues for investigators to reconstruct exactly what happened to them. At least a dozen remain mysteries.

One mystery occurred on July 20, 1970, when 20-year-old Jonathan L. Wirt, a Yosemite Park and Curry Company employee from Sunnyvale, California needed to visit the doctor in the Valley to have his recently broken collar bone checked. But he was housed up on the Tioga Road, well away from Lewis Memorial Hospital. Wirt decided to hike solo to the Valley by dropping into Tenaya Canyon apparently via the Snow Creek Trail.

He never arrived.

His disappearance spurred a SAR mission using sixty searchers plus bloodhounds. For several days the team scoured what they presumed was Wirt's potential route. Despite their efforts, they failed to locate him. Finally the Park scaled back. (Technically, when a person is not found, regardless of the span of time after he or she disappears, the search is never officially terminated.) For weeks and then months after Wirt vanished, no one stumbled across any sign of the lost hiker.

Three months later, on October 18, Lee Spencer and two hiking companions were nosing around four miles up canyon from Mirror Lake. Well off the beaten track they found Jonathan Wirt's decomposed body in a jumbled heap of granite boulders. His remains were identified by dental records and also by personal possessions. He had apparently fallen from 500 feet higher up on the canyon wall. How he had gotten so lost and fallen such a serious distance remain unknown to this day.

Similarly befuddling is the experience of 19-year-old Bradley Eldon Hoffman of Simi Valley, California. Hoffman was visiting the Park with a companion, Terry St. John. Allegedly Hoffman had set off by himself on August 4, 1972, to scramble from the Valley. Hoffman, St. John later noted, never returned. St. John said he waited three days for Hoffman then simply drove home to Simi Valley. Ominously, he left without telling Park officials about his companion being missing.

No missing person report was filed for Hoffman until August 22. St. John apparently never got around to it. Instead Hoffman's father, when he finally learned from St. John what had happened, called the Park. Suspicious due to St. John's feckless and bizarre behavior, the senior Hoffman reported his son had been carrying $300 and that, according to mutual friends, St. John, "suspected" to have had illegal dealings in Simi Valley, had been acting "very strange since his return from Yosemite without Brad."

In short, the father suspected foul play. No help at all in allaying his suspicions, searchers failed to locate Brad Hoffman. Their efforts were severely hampered because he had not left his exact hiking itinerary with anyone except perhaps St. John, who seemed clueless. As might be guessed, no searcher found the missing man.

More than three months later, on November 10, local climber Charlie Porter accidentally discovered Hoffman's scattered skeleton on the talus slope between and above Swan Slab and Camp 4, not very far north of Yosemite Lodge. In the victim's jeans were his wallet and sixty-two dollars in cash. Again, what went wrong here remains a mystery.

Brad Hoffman's location prompts questions: Had he tried a bit of scrambling near the popular Swan Slab face but fallen? Had he started up to the Yosemite Falls' Trail and then lost his route and fallen? Or had he not been solo after all and instead, as his father suspected, been the victim of foul play? And if so, why would the culprit have left money in Brad's jeans? Frustratingly, despite further investigation by the Park no clear answer surfaced to any of these questions.

Another mystery unfolded on June 20, 1977. Three days before this, 22-year-old Timothy John Clark left the Merced Lake High Sierra Camp at 7,216 feet elevation with gear but without a map or compass. His stated intent was to backpack roughly five miles to and then summit 11,522-foot Mount Clark. Late on June 19 Clark returned to the camp. He told its manager Karl Vidt that he had summited the mountain but had found no register there. Clark added that even on top of Mount Clark he was surrounded by higher peaks. An electrical storm, Clark added, had spurred him to flee the summit. He had fled in so much haste that he had slipped and fallen. His urge to escape had prompted him to abandon his gear so that he could move faster and farther out of the range of the lightning bolts flung by Thor.

Because no higher peaks "surround" Mount Clark—except in the quadrant to the southeast—Vidt concluded that Clark had been on the wrong mountain, one closer and lower than Mount Clark.

On June 20, Clark declined the offer of breakfast from Vidt but told him he planned on hiking down to Yosemite Valley (about fifteen miles). Clark was now more or less gearless due to his pell-mell flight off the peak.

Alone again, he hiked for nearly ninety minutes down the well-defined trail. Chuck Butler, a hiker going uphill, found Clark there sitting down. As they talked casually, Clark asked Butler the reason why Jesus had died. Butler, feeling sympathetic to Clark's physical hunger but not wanting to become embroiled in his spiritual conundrums, gave Clark some of his food then continued hiking uphill.

Shortly thereafter, at 1 p.m., another group of hikers discovered the body of a young man a half-mile from Twin Bridges between the second and third Bunnell Switchbacks. Whoever this dead guy was, he had fallen about 300 feet.

The fallen man lacked anything that might identify him. So the Park sent a composite drawing of the mystery body to newspapers in hopes that someone out there would recognize him. The victim's brother saw the *Fresno Bee* drawing and called the Park to tell them the face in the paper looked a lot like that of Timothy John Clark.

To determine what might have led to this tragedy, investigators found that Clark's footprints had veered off-trail to continue cross-country. How he managed to fall, whether he simply had been wandering about and then tried to shortcut back to the trail, or else his fall resulted from something more pathological unfolding in his mind, remains uncertain. Suicide, however, cannot be ruled out.

The following year yielded yet another mystery fall. On September 28, 1978, 21-year-old Larry Lee Jordan, a Yosemite Park and Curry Company stable hand originally from Pontiac, Michigan, embarked on a solo scramble up the cliff base of Glacier Point. What happened next pivots on what one decides what might have been Jordan's motive for having made this ascent.

A week earlier, Jordan had been investigated as a larceny suspect in the Park. The investigators found enough evidence to file a warrant for his arrest on September 22. Eventually, after yet another law enforcement interview with Jordan, a ranger set off to take him into custody. Just before this could happen, Jordan vanished—possibly en route to a fissure-like cave in a lower cliff of Glacier Point.

On October 3, David Anderson was scouting for a new climbing route. He happened upon Jordan's bloated, maggot-riddled body at the top of the talus at the base of Glacier Point. It appeared that he had fallen about 150 feet.

How and why did Jordan die where he had? In Incident Report #78-3238, Ranger J. D. Moncada concluded:

> —Jordan had determined that evidence and statements were being gathered that would charge him with the larcenies. He therefore gathered the items that we found him with and was going into hiding in the area where his body was found. While climbing up the crack, darkness was probably approaching (he had left the Park's Law Enforcement Office at approximately 5 p.m.). Being excited and most likely in a hurry, he lost his footing and/or handhold and subsequently fell.

A chain of again mysterious errors apparently occurred on July 7, 1998, when 16-year-old Miguel E. Lopez of West Covina and 17-year-old Manuel Castillo of Hacienda Heights, California went scrambling above Staircase Falls. They may have initially used remnants of the perilous old Ledge Trail. Ironically, if the two boys had stuck to this notoriously dangerous path they might have fared better than they did.

A couple of hours after the teenagers left for their hike, concession employees well below in Curry Village heard someone from above them yell: "Oh no…Oh my God!"

A few of these employees equipped with two-way radios started scrambling upslope to see if they could help whomever had been screaming in fear. But the terrain soon proved too difficult.

Ultimately, Park Helicopter 551, returning from another assignment, conducted a search. Observers onboard spotted two bodies 1,500 feet above the Valley floor. The pair lay sprawled helter-skelter on an unnamed buttress just west of Glacier Point Apron.

This cliff face hosts a tiered waterfall called Staircase Falls. Its upper section is bordered on the west by LeConte Gully and on the east by the old, and long since closed, Ledge Trail. The bodies of Lopez and Castillo and their battered personal effects had ended up scattered across very challenging terrain on the ledge system that forms the base of the first three levels of Staircase Falls. The scramblers had fallen more than 200 feet and had died from unsurvivable injuries. What they had been doing and how they had fallen, however, remain a mystery. We only know that at least one of the two teenagers saw it coming in time to scream coherently.

Lopez and Castillo were almost the last teenagers to have died from scrambling falls in Yosemite up until the year 2004. Since 1984, during the final twenty years of our analysis of falls sustained while hiking/scrambling, the average age of victims took a leap (as it also did with waterfall falls—see Chapter 1—and with falls from technical climbing, see Chapter 9). During the seventy-five years from 1909 until 1983, the average age of the ninety fall victims was 22.5 years old. From 1984 to 2025, sixty-three more people died from scramble or hiking falls, but their average age was about 34 years old. Why this shift toward ever older victims instead of what previously looked (statistically speaking) like a doomed "herd" of very young people? Hard to say. But not only did more older people (of the baby boom generation and the one following it) fall fatally during the most recent forty years, fewer young people did.

Several separate sociological trends may act in concert to explain this. One might be that more recently "we" have been creating better educated and more realistic, survival-oriented young people who choose to venture into the outdoors than before 1984. If true, this would be a pleasant reality. Another possibility is the slick "outdoor magazine syndrome:" Wilderness-type pursuits have been presented in the past two decades as far more appealing and fulfilling to an ever greater number of older, urban, but less experienced and less wilderness-skilled adults. Boomers going boom. A third possible influence is that during the past two decades the process of middle-class adolescence in America has been lengthened by many years. Far fewer teenagers go out on their own at age 18 as before and consequently are not in the mountains and canyons in as high numbers and making as many naïve errors.

Instead their home-dependency has been lengthening and with it, so has more sober advice to be more careful. Indeed this may dovetail into yet another set of trends. The "Index of Child Well-Being" for 2005 noted the following trends since 1975. First, test scores for kids nationwide have remained stagnant (the population is apparently not getting any smarter in general); second, childhood obesity has risen dramatically; and third, childhood safety has risen 40 percent. These statistics, though admittedly murky, prompt one to ask wryly whether Yosemite has seen fewer young people in fatal falls partly because so many of them in the past two decades have become too fat and pampered to step off the pavement and get into trouble. Maybe computer video games have replaced the wilderness as a provider of fulfilling challenges.

You can weigh these possibilities yourself. Perhaps we have missed the critical element and you can pinpoint it.

This chapter closes with one of the more bizarre mysteries in Yosemite, one that occurred in apparent conjunction with a far more notorious backcountry air crash that made news in America from coast to coast. Indeed, a lot of this has become the stuff of "(sub)urban legend." On May 23, 1977, two ill-prepared young climbers—26-year-old Larry Day of Lexington, Kentucky and 22-year-old Don Evans of Orlando, Florida—had stranded themselves on the Yosemite Point Buttress (the "YPB Route") just east of the Upper Yosemite Fall, in drizzling weather. Desperate, at 2 a.m. they had started screaming through the dark and gloom for help.

I (Farabee) happened to be Acting SAR Ranger at the time and was home asleep when I heard the cries for help coming off the cliff above and behind my house. I contacted the Communications Center, which in turn alerted the after hours, on-call ranger. The task of organizing this rescue fell on Ranger Ginny Rousseau. To get mission #37 going she rousted out several of the climbers who lived in the Camp 4 Rescue Site. These young "rock jocks" lived here semi-permanently under the arrangement that they be available to assist on climbing rescues. They responded to this middle-of-the-night intrusion with good attitudes, and by 3 a.m. six of them had moved into action.

With their headlamps bobbing in the misty rain the team started up the Yosemite Falls Trail, a highway as trails go. All six knew a rescue on the YPB probably would be simple despite the miserable wet.

Walking a minute behind the main group of SAR personnel was 30-year-old John "Jack" A. Dorn of Utica, New York. He now tromped uphill under the yellow glare of his YOSAR ("Yosemite SAR") headlamp. Watching his feet hit the dirt and granite, he flicked the "play" button on his Walkman and listened to tunes as he ascended the switchbacking trail.

At about 3:30 a.m., something odd happened. Dorn, a big wall veteran of numerous challenging technical climbs, made a mistake east of Columbia Point and fell 600 feet to an instant death.

How does a climber of this caliber stumble off a tourist trail? Just about everyone wondered. A few posed hypotheses. Maybe Dorn had partied too long or too hard the night before. Or maybe he was just plain tired. Or maybe he missed seeing where the winding trail had turned left instead of right. Or maybe he had ducked off the trail on purpose to relieve himself but had miscalculated his footing and fallen.

Which was accurate? Were *any* of these accurate? In the stretch of path where Dorn had vanished the trail bed was good except for one shoring rock now missing from the edge. Instead of the rock along the outside margin of the trail there now existed a small hole, like the empty socket after a tooth has been pulled. Had Dorn stepped on this rock just to have it fall out?

The rescuers ahead of Dorn had in fact heard a rock fall at about the time of his accident.

Adding up all of the known facts in this unwitnessed tragedy led investigators to conclude that Dorn had indeed been the victim of a freak mishap wherein the shoring rock on the outer edge of the trail had failed as he placed all of his weight on it. But *why* would he have placed all of his weight on an artificially placed rock poised above such a critical exposure?

Maybe fatigue had dulled the edge of his normal wariness. Or maybe it was a case of momentary inattention while punching a button on his Walkman. Or perhaps it was just because he was feeling too casual.

Despite these reasonable hypotheses, weirder rumors multiplied like rabbits. Dorn, it turns out, was one of those hardy winter entrepreneurs who had only a couple of months earlier may have reaped some of the loot from the "Dope Lake" air crash. As was detailed in Chapter 5 (Aircraft Down), a doomed World War II-era Lockheed had been carrying several thousand pounds of high-grade marijuana when it lost an engine in midair on December 9, 1976. It crashed through the trees then sank to the bottom of Lower Merced Pass Lake. Winter hikers discovered part of the wreck six weeks later, and soon the nature of its cargo flashed across local newspapers. The Park removed much of the marijuana within the first three days of this discovery, but the Sierra winter froze the lake so thick that officials decided to wait until the spring thaw before further salvage.

Soon spontaneous entrepreneurs from among the Camp 4 climbing fraternity and elsewhere in the Park made a snowy dash a dozen miles with chainsaws and maybe even SCUBA gear to lighten the Park's workload by roughly a ton.

The rumor mill later had it that a few Valley locals believed that Dorn's demise on the Yosemite Falls Trail at 3:30 a.m. on May 23, 1977, was not due simply to his own error or to a loose shoring rock but instead was the fruit of foul play emanating from disagreements over dope salvaging shares from that sunken Lockheed. As far as we have been able to ascertain, no evidence exists to support this hypothesis. Thus it tumbles back into the realm of mere rumor.

Meanwhile, by the way, those two stranded climbers on the YPB route were safely rescued by the SAR team ahead of Dorn.

Most of us feel special. Not special in the sense that the silver spaceships are coming from the planet Zorb just to pick us up for an exclusive cruise across the Milky Way galaxy to decide the fate of the universe, but special in the sense that bad things happen to *other* people, not to us. Lessons of survival may pass into one of our ears and then exit from the other. Heck, we've heard it all before. We've learned our lessons. We do things intelligently. We *know* what we're doing.

Maybe we are right about ourselves. Once we step off the pavement, life is good. On the other hand, life can turn not so good—or even get extinguished—if we make the wrong mistake in the wrong place. Some of these basic errors are so simple that to mention them might seem insulting. Always take survival gear appropriate for the season (this would be in addition to the basic map and compass and GPS and perhaps a cell or satellite phone, fire-starting materials, headlamp, knife, first aid supplies, poncho, and so on). Always leave your planned itinerary, including your return time and date, with someone responsible (including the Backcountry Office) before you hit the trail or the rock climb. Adhere to your planned itinerary unless it proves unsafe due to snowpacks, rock slides, or whatever. Reassess your plans objectively and early when changes in the weather threaten to convert your terrain to hazardous. Resist temptations to shortcut or to execute spur of the moment climbs on exposed terrain. If you are hiking solo, take nothing for granted. Along the same line, remember George Steck's maxim about a fool for a companion. Two heads usually are better than one.

TABLE 6. FATAL FALLS IN YOSEMITE WHILE SCRAMBLING OR HIKING. (Incidents discussed in the text are noted.)

Name, age	Date	Location	*Circumstances*
Giacomo Campi, 50-60	May 28, 1871	Vernal Fall	*While climbing a rickety ladder beside Vernal Fall, Campi, a restaurateur from San Francisco, stopped to offer assistance to a lady. She declined his hand. He stepped back to bow graciously but stepped into empty air and fell 35 feet to fracture his skull. That summer the ladders were replaced by wooden stairs and a railing.*
"young man"	late May, 1872	"one of the falls"	*"A young traveler exploring among the rocks by one of the falls, had fallen down a chasm....the poor fellow was a corpse. His friend...fastened his body upon a mule, and so they journeyed back to San Francisco." (James Cropper, A Month in California. London: Society for Promoting Christian Knowledge, 1873: 27-28.)*
Henry W. Tupper, "young"	October 7, 1906	Ledge Trail to Glacier Point	*After walking with 2 others from Wawona to Glacier Point Tupper of Fresno tried a* ***solo-scrambling-hiking shortcut*** *to the Valley. Searchers followed his footprints "to a point where it would have been impossible for him to return, and to go on, as he doubtless did, would have been fatal." Tupper had fallen 600 feet.* (in text)
Horace R. Logan, 17	August 6, 1909	Ledge Trail to Glacier Point	*Logan of Berkeley was a student of St. Matthews School in San Mateo,*

*California. While trying to **hike solo** down from Glacier Point on the forbidden, steep, and unimproved route despite it being posted "Dangerous" he fell unwitnessed 800 feet.* (in text)

Albert Shaw Jr., 27

July 27, 1914 — Ledge Trail to Glacier Point
*Curry Co. photographer Shaw of San Francisco ignored warning signs advising against using the Ledge Trail and also ignored his boss's threat of being fired if he used it, and **hiked it solo**. He lost his hat, tried to retrieve it, but fell off the cliff.* (in text)

Everett E. Shields, 35

June 13, 1924 — Ledge Trail to Glacier Point
*Shields of San Francisco **scramble-hiked solo** down the Ledge Trail. Veering **off-trail**, he fell off the cliff above Camp Curry.* (in text)

John Henry Meherin, 16

August 4, 1926 — Ledge Trail to Glacier Point
*Meherin of Alameda, California **ran** down the trail during his descent from Glacier Point. He missed his footing, ran into thin air, and fell off the cliff. He became the **third fatality from the same point** on the Ledge Trail.* (in text)

William Keleman, 25

July 9, 1927 — above Upper Yosemite Fall
*Keleman of Oakland was **scramble-climbing** and lost his footing, falling about 50 feet.*

Joseph R. Hurd, 24

July 11, 1928 — Ledge Trail to Glacier Point
*Hurd of Burlingame, California had hiked to Glacier Point with Richard Ham, who decided to take the Four-Mile Trail down. Hurd, **solo**, used the Ledge Trail because his family had told him it was a big thrill. Trying to reach Happy Isles first, "In his eagerness to beat Ham to the Valley Floor, Hurd was **traveling pretty fast** and failed to make the right turn at the watercourse, plunging to his death on the rocks below."* (in text)

Reinholt Pfauter, 21

July 11, 1928 — below Lower Yosemite Fall
*Pfauter of Germany had been in the Park only one day when he tried to **scramble-climb** the wall at Lower Yosemite Fall. He fell from a ledge.*

Cecil Allen Morrison, 30

September 22, 1928 — Valley Cliffs near Grizzly Peak
*Morrison of Los Angeles went **scramble-climbing** and lost his footing, falling 200 feet.*

Tom Lupton, 70

April 15, 1931 — Four-Mile Trail
*Lupton, an American Indian and resident of Yosemite, disappeared during a **solo hike** on the trail. Rumors had it that Lupton's mind had become "deranged." His body was discovered 6 months later at the foot of the cliff near Union Point.*

Costello C. Chase, 39

August 8, 1932 — Cathedral Creek
*Curry Co. manager of the Glen Aulin Hikers' Lodge Chase set off on a **solo hiking** mission to discover a safe **shortcut** route into Cathedral Creek. He vanished. After 3½ days searchers found him at the foot of a 200-foot cliff.*

Ernest Mossien, 41

June 3, 1937 — Big Oak Flat Road
Mossien, a German-born Government engineer assigned to Yosemite road construction, fell from a cliff adjacent to the road on May 12. He caught pneumonia and died in Lewis Memorial Hospital. (also listed in Chapter 4. Park Builders)

Carl A. Pellum, 22
April 27, 1940 Sierra Point, above Happy Isles
Pellum, a private with the Ninth U.S. Field Artillery at Fort Lewis, Washington, was in the Valley for a Fort Ord Army Base road march. He ***scrambled off-trail*** *hundreds of feet up Sierra Point onto a cliff face with Gerald U. Stevens. Pellum slipped. Stevens tried to block his fall. Both men fell. Stevens landed with minor injuries in a tree. Pellum bounced from ledge to ledge before slamming 600 feet below.*

John Alexander DeSerpa, 27
July 23, 1942 base of Upper Yosemite Fall
Curry Co. manager of the Lodge Grill DeSerpa of Ventura, California ***scramble-hiked*** *down the base of the fall on mossy, mist-sprayed rock with Eugene Bare to swim. He lost his footing and fell about 50 feet.*

Charles Robert Kahn, 18
July 28, 1945 between the Four-Mile Trail and Ledge Trail
Kahn of Chicago tried to ***scramble-hike*** *a* ***shortcut*** *near Glacier Point. He slipped and fell 150 feet.*

Donald Bennard Boyd, 14
May 31, 1947 Sunnyside Bench
Boyd of Oakland tried to descend the cliff with Lawrence F. Franke by ***scramble-hiking off-trail*** *behind the Government Maintenance Yard after dark. He slipped and fell.*

Martha Lee Helwig, 16
June 7, 1947 base of Cascades Falls
Helwig of Sebastopol, California was ***scramble-climbing*** *up from the base of the falls with other family members when she slipped on the wet rocks and fell 100 feet.*

Chalmers Judson Groff, 19
July 19, 1948 base of Half Dome
Groff of Washington, D.C. plus a fellow NPS Blister Rust Crewman were ***scramble-climbing*** *down mossy rocks below the face of Half Dome. He slipped, nearly taking his buddy with him.*

Paul Harrington Garinger, 41
September 15, 1948 Half Dome cables
Garinger of Burlingame, California ***descended the cables solo*** *off Half Dome. A witness saw him stop 1/3 of the way down and put his head in his hands. He next toppled over 1,000 feet.*

Darrel Joyce Warren, 21
November 11, 1949 Lower Yosemite Fall
Warren, a soldier from Merced, California, was ***scramble-climbing off-trail*** *when the rock beneath him dislodged. He fell 75-feet.*

Alan Teviotdale, 24
September 11, 1953 gorge below Upper Yosemite Fall
M.I.T. exchange student Teviotdale of Tyne, England was ***scramble-hiking off-trail*** *with Henry H. Plotkin down to a pool to swim. He slipped off a smooth ledge and fell into the shallows, fatally fracturing his neck and skull.*

Donald Lee Genereux, 14
July 1, 1955 Lembert Dome
Genereux of Stockton, California ***scramble-climbed*** *the dome with his brother James from the SE side, then descended the SW side. Donald lost his footing atop a 75-foot cliff and fell nearly 400 feet.*

Robert Franklin Johnson, 28
May 27, 1956 Yosemite Point Couloir east of Lost Arrow
Dr. Johnson of San Francisco ***scramble-hiked*** *with a buddy up Indian Canyon. Here Johnson said he would make a "short hike"* ***solo shortcut*** *to the Valley. He vanished. The 5-day search included the third use of a helicopter in Yosemite. Johnson had fallen 80 feet onto a narrow, sandy ledge. Rangers buried him there.* (in text)

Ronald Walter Beck, 19 | August 29, 1956 | Grizzly Peak

*Beck of Forest Park, Illinois tried to climb the 6,200-foot peak but felt vexed by switchbacking. He **solo scramble-climbed off-route** to **shortcut**. He took off his shoes to traverse slick rock and fell 50 vertical feet then tumbled another 100 feet.*

Leon Ellis Erdman, 16 | July 17, 1958 | east of Indian Canyon

*As part of a "California Bible Conference Church" group, Erdman of San Lorenzo tried to **scramble** up the cliffs above Church Bowl with Willard Dugan, age 22. He fell behind, became **solo** and fell.*

Alvin Douglas Griggs, 16 | November 1, 1958 | above Sunnyside Bench

*Griggs of Fairfax, California and Nelson Zeigler detoured off the Yosemite Falls Trail at the base of the upper fall to **scramble** a **shortcut** about 700 feet above the Valley floor east and above Sunnyside Bench near the base of Lost Arrow. Zeigler heard a noise and "turned in time to see Griggs fall" 250 feet onto Sunnyside Bench.*

Robert Irion Jr., 10 | June 22, 1959 | cliffs above Camp Curry

*Irion of Los Angeles **solo scramble-climbed** the cliff behind Camp Curry for a "better view" of the Firefall. At 8:30 p.m., after dark, he failed to return to his family's campsite. Five teenagers from the next site located the boy, dead from a 100-foot fall.*

Thomas Feiss Farber, 29 | June 12-14, 1963 | Yosemite Falls Trail

Backpacker Farber of New York City went missing, was found 3 months later "presumed to have fallen [about 1,000 feet] while hiking or climbing" west of Yosemite Falls.

Benjamin Gruber, 50 | October 24, 1963 | Sierra Point, above Happy Isles

*Gruber of San Francisco **hiked** down the trail from Sierra Point with his son and another on July 12. He slipped and fell 200 feet.*

Richard William Parsons, 19 | August 23, 1964 | base of Lower Yosemite Fall

*Parsons of West Peabody, Massachusetts **scrambled** on the cliff near the fall's base, slipped, and fell 80 feet onto talus.*

Michael Ray Barr, 17 | August 10, 1965 | Tenaya Peak

*Barr of Roseville, California left his parents' camp and vanished. Searchers found him "badly smashed" the next day 100 yards below Tenaya Peak and an estimated 200-foot fall, apparently while **free-soloing**.*

Ronald Terrance Hayes, 13 | October 9, 1965 | Ledge Trail to Glacier Point

*Hayes of San Jose, California hiked with Bob Archibald up the Ledge Trail, closed for 5 years. The boys became thirsty and **shortcutted off-trail** in search of water. Both slipped. Archibald self-arrested. Hayes fell 400 feet.*

Quin Charles Frizzell, 31 | June 4, 1966 | Tenaya Canyon

*Frizzell, a scientist at California's Livermore Lab, vanished while **scrambling solo** in Tenaya Canyon. A massive search failed.* (discussed and statistically counted in Chapter 12. Lost)

Patrick Michael Kearns, 19 | April 13, 1968 | between Washington Column & Royal Arches

*Wearing street shoes, Kearns of Redwood City, California **hiked** to the top of Washington Column with Stan Crouch and Dean Hathenbic via the Falls' and Rim Trails. Halfway, his buddies turned back. Kearns continued **solo**. Returning via a chimney between the Arches and Column, Kearns, **off trail**, slipped off the steep rock and "plunged 1,800 feet from the top of Washington Column."*

Joseph Edwin Rothe, 18 — July 21, 1968 — Chilnualna Fall, Wawona
Rothe of San Jose hiked ***off-trail*** *with Dan Guaraldi, age 21, "in an area of polished granite where Chilnualna Creek flows over a series of small waterfalls." Rothe slipped on the wet rock and fell about 30 feet.*

Angelita D. Kisto, 22 — August 4, 1968 — area below Upper Yosemite Fall
Curry Co. employee at the Lodge Kisto of Bapachule, Arizona ***scramble-hiked off-trail*** *with a girl friend and slipped on wet rock. She fell about 45 feet.*

Peter Anthony Ullrich, 17 — August 21, 1968 — east end of Yosemite Valley
Ullrich of Santa Rosa, California and 3 companions ***scramble-climbed*** *a semi-vertical face well above Tenaya Canyon Bridge. Ullrich lost his holds and fell.*

John Michael Wrightsman, 21 — November 4, 1968 — Sunnyside Bench
Curry Co. bellman at the Ahwahnee Hotel Wrightsman of Alamogordo, New Mexico ***scrambled solo*** *from the bridge below Lower Yosemite Fall to ascend Sunnyside Bench. He fell.*

Alice Grier Ranson, 21 — June 21, 1969 — Cascade Falls, Triple Peak
Ranson of Burlingame, California ***scrambled*** *up nearly vertical rock and fell 500 feet, dying from impact on a cliff adjacent to Cascade Falls. She was found 2 miles downstream a week later.* (discussed in Chapter 10. Drowning)

Jerry Alexander Stevens, 18 — July 25, 1969 — Sunnyside Bench
Stevens of Hollywood set off from Camp 4 on a "short" ***solo*** *hike of the Yosemite Falls Trail and vanished. A 5-day SAR found him* ***off-trail*** *below a 100-foot fall on wooded slabs east of the gorge.*

Donald Michael Miehls, 20 — May 9, 1970 — above Church Bowl
Miehls of Omak, Washington died from a fall during a ***solo scramble-hike*** *off-trail above the Church Bowl, west of the Ahwahnee Hotel.*

Brian John Rochelle, 20 — June 21, 1970 — Ahwahnee Buttress, Devil's Bathtub
Rochelle of Canoga Park, California ***hopped from rock to rock*** *in the nude on the ledges. He lost his balance and fell 150 feet. An investigation suggested Rochelle was on an LSD "trip."*

Gary William Riley, 21 — July 3, 1970 — Sunnyside Bench
Riley of Anaheim, California ***scramble-climbed*** *the Sunnyside Bench and fell 150 feet.*

Jonathan L. Wirt, 20 — July 20, 1970 — Tenaya Canyon, 4 miles east of Mirror Lake
Curry Co. worker Wirt of Sunnyvale, California disappeared during a ***solo hike*** *from the Tioga Road to the Valley via the Snow Creek Trail. On October 18, 3 hikers found Wirt's body off the beaten track. He had fallen 500 feet, maybe lost or attempting a* ***shortcut***. (in text)

David B. Wentworth, 29 — May 21, 1971 — Pywiack Cascade, Tenaya Canyon
Dr. Wentworth of Olympic Valley, California ***solo hiked*** *from Tenaya Lake to the Valley. He tried to* ***scramble*** *a trailless* ***shortcut*** *via the rock slabs of the Pywiack Cascade, "extremely hazardous and can be traveled only by people experienced and equipped for technical rock climbing," noted Ranger Ron Mackie in the Park's Incident Report. "Dr. Wentworth was neither." Hikers found his body 10 days later below a fall of about 375 feet.*

Mary Ann Ruth Hoefer, 19 — May 22-24, 1971 — Illilouette Canyon
Curry Co. front desk clerk at the Lodge Hoefer of Belvedere, California was last seen at 2 p.m. wearing jeans and hiking boots at the Lodge Meadow Annex. She vanished during an apparent ***solo hike****. On July 10 a hiker found skeletal parts of Hoefer's body below a 700-foot cliff near Illilouette Canyon. Had she been lost (in the Valley…) and died of exposure or instead had she taken a small fall?*

Rick Alan Mallory, 19 — August 31(?), 1971 — inner gorge of Tenaya Canyon
Curry Co. employee Mallory of Martinez, California left Tuolumne Meadows to ***solo day hike*** *roughly 20 miles to Yosemite Valley. 15 days later a hiker found Mallory's body on the north side of the inner gorge, midway down Tenaya Canyon, below a 150-foot fall.*

Clifford Pope Thompson, 19 — March 31, 1972 — Lower Yosemite Fall
Thompson of Fresno, California with Howard Thompson and John Skellie ***scrambled*** *the 300-foot cliffs east of Lower Yosemite Fall. Just below the top, Thompson slipped and fell 200 feet. He bounced twice and landed upside down in a tree, his skull fractured.*

Lionel James Kerian, 18 — April 23, 1972 — above Mist Trail
Kerian of Sacramento hiked the Clark Point Trail above Vernal Fall with Paul Devitt and Keith Tanner then ***scrambled off-trail.*** *Devitt and Tanner decided to return to the Vernal Fall's Trail. Kerian, unwitnessed and* ***solo****, slipped off the rocks and fell 600 feet into a tree that nearly bisected him.*

John Robert McDaniel, 15 — June 3, 1972 — LeConte Gully, Ledge Trail to Glacier Point
McDaniel of Salto, California hiked the Ledge Trail with Robert Baker and another. At 6 p.m., McDaniel became a ***solo*** *hiker and vanished. A 4-day SAR mission found him at the base of LeConte Gully. He seemed to have left the Ledge Trail to* ***scramble*** *a perceived* ***shortcut*** *"and attempted to downclimb a fifth class climb with no means of protecting himself, lost his footing, and fell 700 feet."*

Bradley Eldon Hoffman, 19 — August 4, 1972 — above Swan Slab
Hoffman of Simi Valley, California ***solo scramble-hiked*** *from the Valley but never returned. His "buddy" Terry St. John said he waited 3 days then went home without reporting Hoffman's missing status. On Nov. 10, Hoffman's skeleton turned up on the talus slope above Swan Slab, about 100 yards north of Yosemite Lodge.* (in text)

Estelle Berra, 18 — October 2, 1972 — Matterhorn Peak
Curry Co. employee Berra of Yonkers, New York fell while ***scrambling*** *Matterhorn Peak and slid out of the Park on a glacier.*

Robert M. Travis, 26 — April 19, 1973 — Nevada Fall area
Travis of Castro Valley, California ***solo hiked*** *to Nevada Fall but never returned. Six days later searchers found his body below the "Ice cut," a 200-foot cliff very near the top of the fall.*

Phillip L. Utz, 14 — June 25, 1973 — Sunnyside Bench
Utz of Newhall, California went ***scramble-climbing*** *unprotected with Desmond Wells. While descending to the Valley floor Utz fell about 200 feet.*

Brian R. Quinn, 18 — July 16, 1973 — Sunnyside Bench
Quinn of Fresno, California led 3 companions on a ***scramble-climb*** *up some steep slabs. All 4 lacked technical experience and carried a "common clothesline" in case a rope was needed. Quinn slipped and fell 150 feet.*

William M. Penny, 43

July 21, 1973 Grand Mountain, northeast of White Wolf

Penny of Sunnyvale, California was embroiled in a contested divorce from his wife of 19 years, was having financial problems, and had discussed ("but not seriously") suicide and/or disappearing to assume a new identity. He vanished on a ***solo scramble-hike****. A major SAR effort found his body on a narrow ledge at 8,800 feet elevation, 350 feet above the base of Grand Mountain and Upper Ten Lake. Death was due to a head injury from a fall. Penny's gear indicated that he was planning for survival, not for suicide.*

Mark G. Weaver, 17

October 21, 1973 base of Upper Yosemite Fall

Fisherman Weaver of Portola Valley, California was ***scramble-climbing*** *with Thomas Weaver, age 14, and James Stillman, age 15. Witness Robert F. Wigington saw Weaver lose his holds and fall 150 feet, hit rock, then plunge into the creek. Wigington dove in and hauled him unconscious to shore. He died 2 hours later.*

Erick James Stakkestad, 16

July 9, 1974 Tenaya Canyon

Stakkestad of Aptos, California ***hiked*** *with 2 partners from Tenaya Lake to Yosemite Valley via the Mt. Watkins Trail. The trio, in fog, lost the trail to Snow Creek. They bivouacked but awoke to thicker fog. Against his buddies' warnings, Stakkestad went for help* ***solo****. He yelled periodically to maintain contact then screamed. He had walked off into a 400-foot fall.* (in text)

Bruce Lester Bartman, 18

August 3, 1974 Bridalveil Fall

Bartman of Ann Arbor, Michigan began a ***barefooted scramble*** *of Bridalveil Fall with Jonathan Dreyfus. Partway up the pair quit and down-climbed. Bartman missed his footing on the wet, mossy rock in the mist and fell 35 feet, hitting his head on impact and continuing into the pool.*

Jacklyn M. Donahoe, 21

September 27, 1975 Cascade Creek

Donahoe, an Air Force nurse from Atwater, California, visited the Cascade Creek Bridge on the Big Oak Flat Road with friends and ***scrambled*** *to sit on a rock at the edge of a 70-foot cliff. To move to a different site above the brink she rose and grabbed a dead, 3-inch thick limb of a Jeffery Pine to* ***swing around*** *it to her new spot. The dead branch broke. It was her only hold. She silently fell 70 feet.*

Daniel Martinez, 20

September 27, 1975 west of Ahwahnee Hotel on Ramps

Curry Co. caretaker of vending machines Martinez of Brentwood, California ***solo scramble-climbed*** *steep rock in* ***rubber-soled sandals after dark*** *to "view the moonrise." His search took 42 people and 250 man-hours before rangers found his body 6 days later at the base of a 175-foot cliff.*

John Shiner, 22

February 13, 1976 North Dome Gully

Shiner of Palo Alto, California with Michael R. Majors and Mark W. Pryor ***scrambled*** *up the steep North Dome Gully and bivouacked. In a foggy dawn they descended the same steep rock scattered with wet gravel. Shiner lost his footing here, bounced on his back, slid about 10 feet across a small ledge, and fell off a 400-foot cliff.*

William L. Gooch, 22

May 19, 1976 Ledge Trail to Glacier Point

Curry Co. employee Gooch of Garden Grove, California ***solo scramble-hiked*** *down the Ledge Trail—officially closed and posted: "Danger! Do not attempt to follow this abandoned trail…" Gooch next detoured* ***off-trail*** *to try to* ***fill his water bottle****. Two other Curry employees saw him sliding down a wet slab and heard him mutter "Oh, Shit!" then fall 600 feet.*

James L. Mumolo, 17

June 1, 1976 Snake Dike, West Buttress of Half Dome
New Curry Co. employee Mumolo of Fremont, California ***scramble-climbed solo and at night*** *(wearing a down parka and carrying a flash-light) up to the base of the Snake Dike climbing route on Half Dome but fell 150 feet.*

Phillipe P. Delorme, 23

July, (?) 1976 west of Ahwahnee Hotel on Ramps
Delorme of Paris, France vanished as part of an international tour group while ***solo****. His body was found weeks later on August 17, badly decomposed but with massive head and chest injuries. He had been* ***scrambling****.*

Alan H. Fields, 20

May 15, 1977 Sunnyside Bench
Fields of Modesto and Roger Sanderson, age 19, detoured off the Lower Yosemite Fall's Trail to the base of Sunnyside Bench. Partway up the first pitch of the Regular Route (rated 5.0, and posted with warning signs), Sanderson told Fields it was too steep for him. Fields ascended anyway ***solo****. As Sanderson studied the route down, Fields, about 10 feet below the second bolt and sling, fell* ***unseen*** *past Sanderson and another 100 feet to the bottom.*

John "Jack" A. Dorn, 30
(would-be **rescuer**)

May 23, 1977 Yosemite Falls Trail, east of Columbia Point
Dorn, a climber from Utica, New York and resident of Camp 4, was on SAR Mission #37 on the Yosemite Point Buttress, just east of the Upper Yosemite Fall. At 3:30 a.m., during drizzle and mist, Dorn fell ***unwitnessed*** *600 feet off the trail.* (in text)

Timothy John Clark, 22

June 20, 1977 Bunnell Switchbacks, Merced Lake Trail
After fleeing a lightning storm, Clark of Dearborn Heights, Michigan departed the Merced Lake High Sierra Camp to ***solo hike*** *to Yosemite Valley. Clark's footprints veered* ***off-trail****. His body was found by hikers between the 2nd and 3rd switchbacks at 1 p.m. of the same day below a 250-foot fall.* (in text, also listed in Chapter 13 as a possible suicide)

Timothy L. Zuspan, 31

May 11, 1978 Grizzly Peak
Zuspan of Turlock, California made a ***solo****, cross-country* ***scramble*** *above the talus slope on the south side of Grizzly Peak. He lost his footing and fell hundreds of feet to the base.*

Larry Lee Jordan, 21

September 28, 1978 base of Glacier Point
Curry Co. stable hand Jordan of Pontiac, Michigan ***solo scramble-climbed*** *the cliff base of Glacier Point then vanished. On October 3, David Anderson, scouting for a new climbing route, found Jordan's body below a 150-foot fall.* (in text)

Peter James Meyer, 21

May 13, 1979 above Sunnyside Bench
Meyer of San Francisco separated from several friends and ***solo hiked*** *up the Yosemite Falls Trail then vanished on a scramble. Searchers found him above the Sunnyside Bench, dead from a fall.*

Daniel S. Wilson, 18

May 27, 1979 North Dome Gully
Wilson of San Rafael, California climbed to the top of the Royal Arches with 3 teenage friends, summiting at 7 p.m. They descended the previously unseen North Dome Gully. At ***10:30 at night*** *and with* ***no lights****, they failed to find the route. Two teenagers wanted to bivouac; Wilson insisted they continue. He next slipped on wet rock and fell 100 feet off a ledge.* (in text)

Steven Anthony Sereda, 22, August 16, 1979 between Clouds Rest/Little Yosemite Valley
Curry Co. food service worker Sereda of Castro Valley, California went ***solo scramble-climbing*** *and apparently fell about 40 feet—"it seems probable," notes Ranger Mike Fink (in Incident Report #79-8359), "that the victim attempted to free-climb the over-hanging, exfoliating granite ledges along a thin crack, ascending vertically toward the summit, and fell backwards."*

Steven Craig Ennis,19 September 16, 1979 Castle Cliff above Sunnyside Bench
Ennis of Turlock, California and Paul Anderson ***scrambled*** *300 feet up Lost Arrow Fall (dry) on "unstable" rocks. Ennis, following Anderson, lost his footing and fell 75 feet.*

Steve Leroy O'Neal, 20 February 23, 1980 "The Commitment," Lower Yosemite Fall
O'Neal of Salt Lake City and 2 fellow airmen inexperienced in Yosemite and in climbing ***scrambled off-trail*** *up second-class ramps near the top of Lower Yosemite Fall. They lost their route down. O'Neal became a* ***solo scrambler*** *trying a* ***shortcut*** *in cowboy boots. He fell 300+ feet.* (in text)

David Mark Bixler, 19 March 20, 1980 Glacier Point near Four-Mile Trail
Bixler of Somerville, New Jersey and Daniel M. Mitzsche, age 20, backpacked down from Glacier Point. Lost, they bushwhacked ***off-trail.*** *Bixler tried to cross a rock chute by jumping into the top of a tree from a steep hillside. He fell, injuring his head. Mitzsche followed. He fractured his arm and his skull and knocked himself unconscious. Bixler died at 3 a.m. while bivouacked only 75 yards from the Four-Mile Trail leading into the Valley.* (in text)

Victor Robinson Zenoff, 17 July 12, 1980 Yosemite Falls Trail
Zenoff of Atherton, California ***hiked*** *with Evan Dean Maloney to Columbia Point. Returning, Maloney* ***ran down the trail.*** *Maloney "saw Zenoff's body in mid air, just south of the trail 5 feet below the level of the trail." Zenoff tumbled 600 feet.* (in text)

Vance Kendall Cook, 21 August 14, 1980 base of Bridalveil Fall
Cook of Alta Loma, California and David L. Donaldson ***free-scramble-climbed*** *a large wet rock below Bridalveil Fall. Cook lost his holds and fell about 50 feet, suffering massive head injuries.*

Adam David Berry, 16 December 30, 1980 Snow Creek, Tenaya Canyon
Berry of San Francisco and Eugene Mendicelli ***scrambled up*** *the Snow Creek area in "near vertical" and "difficult" terrain. Berry sat on a large, crumbling rock ledge scattered with dead leaves. As Mendicelli ascended toward him, he saw Berry "slide off the rock on his buttocks feet first" then fall about 40 feet.*

Michael A. Higa, 14 May 3, 1981 North Dome Gully
Higa of San Jose and Victor Leong left an Andrew Hill High School group to ***scramble up*** *to the North Dome Gully area. The pair separated. Leong slipped, fell, was severely injured, and spent the night gearless. Rangers located Higa's body the next morning in a side ravine of North Dome Gully; he had fallen* ***solo*** *400 feet down a 60-degree slope.*

Stephen Kyle Goode, 18 July 8, 1981 base of Washington Column
Goode of Arlington, Texas visited Yosemite with 5 friends as a high school graduation gift from his family. Goode and James Hornaday ***scramble-climbed*** *a cliff at the base of Washington Column. Goode lost his holds and fell 100 feet.*

Judith D. McDade, 23 — August 7, 1981 — Tenaya Peak
Curry Co. cook McDade of Williamsville, New York ***scramble-climbed a Class-5 route*** *up Tenaya Peak with Bennett Johnston but with no ropes or gear. The pair stalled out on a cliff from which McDade fell 100 feet. Johnston required rescue.*

David E. Boyden, 19 — October 9, 1981 — Sunnyside Bench
Curry Co. worker Boyden of Granada Hills, California vanished during a ***solo hike****. On May 16, 1984, $2\frac{1}{2}$ years later, a Park visitor found Boyden's skeleton, fractured consistent with a fall, above Sunnyside Bench below Lost Arrow.*

John Allen Wilson, 30 — August 10, 1982 — Lower Yosemite Fall
Wilson of South Lake Tahoe, California and his wife hiked to Lower Yosemite Fall. Despite the sign: "Dangerous to scramble on surrounding boulders and cliffs," Wilson ***scrambled solo off-trail*** *east of the Waterfall Route to a ledge. He stranded himself 200 feet up. As witnesses called for help, Wilson shifted position during an attempted downclimb and fell off backwards 150 feet.*

Richard Alan Rudolph, 18 — June 20, 1983 — Nevada Fall
Rudolph of Mission Viejo, California tried a trail-less ***scramble*** *from atop Nevada Fall to Starr King Lake, beginning $\frac{1}{8}$ mile southeast of the Nevada Fall's Bridge. His 2 brothers and sister judged his shortcut dangerous. He* ***solo*** *ascended a steep talus slope, crossed a stream, and tried climbing 45-degree, exfoliating slabs of granite wet with running water. He paused to get a drink but fell 20 feet, hitting his head and dying instantly.*

Michael Sedlack, 14 — June 23, 1983 — Washington Column
Sedlack of Lakewood, California with Dave Steward and Todd Heiss, both age 14 and from a church group, ***scramble-climbed*** *a cliff on Washington Column. About 9:30 p.m. (after dark) they got stranded. Sedlack tried to* ***solo*** *climb down but fell more than 200 feet. Steward required rescue. Heiss made it down safely.*

Christopher Melgard, 21 — July 27, 1983 — east side of Grizzly Peak
Melgard of Pinole, California was an epileptic subject to grand mal seizures. He ***solo scramble-hiked*** *and apparently tried to* ***shortcut*** *upward to Half Dome. It took 200 searchers from 13 SAR teams plus helicopters and 13 trained dog teams 4 days to locate his body below a 600-foot fall about 1,000 feet west of Vernal Fall.*

Jeffrey Lee Dyer, 26 — October 22, 1983 — Cathedral Lakes
Dyer of Atlantic Beach, Florida was a non-climber who, with 2 buddies, ***scrambled*** *along a cliff near the Cathedral Lakes Trail. He fell 200 feet.*

Tony Iavello, 18 — June 18, 1984 — Camp 4 Wall, above Camp 4
Iavello of Simi Valley, California and Dave Menchaca, age 18, ***scramble-hiked*** *up to Eagle Peak and next tried to descend the Camp 4 Wall. They* ***got lost*** *and strayed* ***off-route.*** *Iavello slipped on a ledge and fell 1,000 feet into Eagle Peak Ravine. Menchaca stayed on the ledge and yelled for a rescue.*

Avital Bar-Gil, 22 — June 29, 1984 — east of Columbia Point, Upper Yosemite Fall's Trail
Bar-Gil of Bat Yam, Israel went ***scrambling off-trail****, fell, and sustained lethal head injuries.*

Dirk Barnes, 23

October 13, 1984 west of Ahwahnee Hotel on Ramps
Barnes of Long Beach, California and Carlos Alvarez, age 24, ***scramble-climbed*** *the sloping lower ramps above the Ahwahnee Meadow. Alvarez slipped; Barnes was in his fall line and either tried to stop Alvarez or was simply "taken out" by him. Both men tumbled 200 feet down a 45-degree slab and landed on a ledge. Both were helicoptered. Barnes soon died. Alvarez survived.*

Fredrico Hernandez, 22

May 6, 1985 Four-Mile Trail
Hernandez of Los Angeles and Jesus Cortez, age 15, ***scramble-hiked*** *down the Four-Mile Trail and decided to* ***shortcut*** *it ¾ mile east of Sentinel Creek. Descending a gully, they hit a vertical drop that baffled them. As Cortez sat and stared down he held a branch for support. Hernandez sat on the edge of a rock, moved slightly, and slipped off into a 300-foot fall.* (in text)

Daniel Eric Howard, 18

June 25, 1985 east of White Wolf
Howard of Simi Valley, California ***backpacked*** *with 3 teenagers from White Wolf to Ten Lakes but fell behind and got lost. For 5 days, up to 120 searchers combed the area. They found Howard's body in a side drainage of the Grand Canyon of the Tuolumne where,* ***unwitnessed****, he had* ***scrambled solo off-trail*** *to fall 300 feet.*

Juergen Hugo Karl Kahl, 52

July 31, 1986 Cathedral Peak
Kahl of Palo Alto, California made a ***solo scramble-climb****. That afternoon 3 hikers on Cathedral Peak Saddle spotted his body 300 feet below. His watch had stopped at 7:42 a.m. Rangers concluded he had fallen 100-200 feet* ***unwitnessed*** *during his ascent.*

James Terrance Cassidy, 40

September 1, 1986 Ribbon Fall area, El Capitan
Cassidy of Mariposa, California and Jo Ellen Bradley, age 44, ***got lost during a day hike and bivouacked****. The next morning Bradley refused to continue due to rough terrain. Cassidy descended as a* ***solo scramble-climber****. An hour later Bradley heard a rockslide—Cassidy falling 600 feet off a cliff. Sixty searchers aided by the Park helicopter rescued the stranded Bradley 28 hours later.*

Dean A. Flack, 20

September 21, 1986 above Yosemite Chapel
Flack of Sacramento and John Rogers, age 19, ***scrambled*** *200 feet up a talus slope. Flack climbed* ***solo*** *another100 feet above the talus then,* ***unwitnessed****, fell 100 feet.*

Wendell Blakeney, 28

July 27, 1989 North Dome Gully
Blakeney of Chino Hills, California left friends in the Valley to ***solo hike*** *up the Yosemite Falls Trail then across to the Snow Creek Trail en route to Mirror Lake—then he vanished. A major search located his body on July 30 in North Dome Gully, dead from a long* ***unwitnessed*** *fall, apparently while shortcutting.*

Chad Austin Youngs, 17

February 18, 1991 Camp 4 Wall, above Camp 4
Youngs of Davis, California ***scramble-hiked,*** *then climbed with Kevin Ashley Morris, 22, into the cliffs above Camp 4. While descending a chimney in a ledge system northwest of the campground, hastily due to sunset, Youngs lost his footing and fell 300 feet.*

Carter L. Phelps, 49

May 13, 1991 North Dome Gully
Phelps of Northridge, California and Ron Merkes, age 23, climbed Royal Arches overnight then tried to return to the Valley down North Dome

Gully. Soon after starting their descent, Phelps, who was unroped (despite carrying ropes) and following Merkes, lost his footing and yelled "I'm off!" and fell 175 feet.

Walter G. Little, 68

September 27, 1991 west of Ahwahnee Hotel on Ramps
Little of Denair, California began a ***solo, day hike*** *of the Snow Creek Trail to North Dome but failed to return. After 4 days searchers found his body at the base of the Ahwahnee Ramps. Little had likely lost the trail then had* ***scrambled*** *down, but lost his footing* ***unwitnessed*** *and fell.*

Charles B. Feinman, 49

May 18, 1993 LeConte Gully, Ledge Trail to Glacier Point
Feinman of North Miami, Florida asked several local climbers about "easy" routes not requiring technical equipment then set off on a ***solo scramble-climb****. On May 25, climber John C. Ross discovered Feinman's decomposing body below a 300-foot fall.*

Mark Conley, 46

August 7, 1993 Mount Hoffman, northwest of Tenaya Lake
Conley of Merced, California and Greg DiCarlo ***scramble-climbed off-trail*** *from Mt. Hoffman to Tuolumne Peak. Conley, in "worn" hiking boots, ventured out on a small wet ledge he intended to downclimb but slid and fell 100 feet.* (in text)

Jon Paul LaFrance, 19

August 15, 1993 Sunnyside Bench
LaFrance of Laguna Beach, California and his brother Robert ***scramble-climbed*** *east from the Yosemite Falls Trail across Sunnyside Bench. Descending, they hit a cliff. They traversed upward to search for a trail. LaFrance slipped on a slab, twisted, slid on his back 50 feet, and vanished over the edge about 200 feet.*

Graham S. Turner, 20

September 27, 1994 above Wawona Tunnel
Turner of Scotland and Joanna Childs of England hiked the trail from Wawona Tunnel to Old Inspiration Point to watch the sunset. Without flashlights, they got ***lost*** *on their return in the dark and became* ***off-trail scramble-hikers.*** *Both slipped and fell. Childs was knocked unconscious. Turner fell 150 feet.* (in text)

Kelly Gleeson, 33

May 30, 1995 100 yards downstream of Hidden Falls, Tenaya Creek
Yosemite Medical Clinic nurse Gleeson led 2 friends on a ***day hike*** *via a muddy, slippery section of an un-maintained footpath toward Hidden Falls. She started* ***sliding****. Her friends tried to reach her but failed and watched her fall 100 feet into the ravine.*

Synne Storlein, 28

June 4, 1995 Yosemite Falls Trail, above Columbia Point
Storlein, a Norwegian woman from Ann Arbor, Michigan, ***scramble-hiked off-trail*** *about 200 feet above the Yosemite Falls Trail at a dangerous "viewpoint." She fell* ***unwitnessed*** *40 feet.*

Michael W. Gerde, 57

August 29, 1995 Half Dome Cables
Gerde of Huntington Beach, California was ascending Half Dome behind Matthew Lorenzini and felt a loss of energy. Lorenzini told Gerde, "We don't have to do it..." Gerde responded, "I really want to; I want the T-shirt (printed with "I hiked to the top of Half Dome"). Half an hour later Gerde collapsed (of acute heart failure), lost his grip, and fell.

Stephen Eric Lyman, 38

April 17(?), 1996 gully between Upper and Middle Cathedral Rocks
Lyman, a noted Yosemite artist from Sandpoint, Idaho, failed to return from a ***solo photographic foray*** *as a storm approached. On April 19, a*

pair of climbers descending from the East Buttress Route found Lyman's body clothed only in underwear in the steep gully. He had fallen 180 feet. (in text)

Alejandro Fernandez, 22

July 5, 1996 Airplane Gully in upper Tenaya Canyon
Fernandez of Vigo, Spain ***solo scrambled*** *in search of a route around a waterfall and steep cliffs in an area "extremely hazardous to hike in." He fell 150 feet. Hours later his brother Guillermo found his body.*

Henry Tien, 21

March 24, 1997 Yosemite Falls Trail below Columbia Point
Stanford University student Tien day hiked with Susie G. Wu. She had gone ahead up the trail because Tien was moving so slowly—now as a ***solo hiker****. At about 4 p.m., Wu returned to find Tien unconscious on the trail with head injuries from a long fall. Tien might have tried* ***shortcutting*** *switchbacks.* (in text)

Charles V. Richards, 67

August 10, 1997 West Face of Mount Conness
Richards of Derbyshire, England ***scramble-hiked*** *from Saddlebag Lake up Mt. Conness with his wife on an* ***off-trail*** *route traversing a series of the steep West Face slabs exposed to nearly vertical drops. Richards slipped and fell 250 feet, dying of massive head trauma.*

Miguel E. Lopez Jr., 16
Manuel Castillo, 17

July 7, 1998 Staircase Falls, above Curry Village
Lopez of West Covina and Castillo of Hacienda Heights, California ***scrambled*** *above Staircase Falls (via the old Ledge Trail?). Park Helicopter 551 spotted both bodies 1,500 feet above Curry Village on a triangular buttress west of Glacier Point Apron and east of the (closed) Ledge Trail. Lopez and Castillo had* ***mysteriously*** *fallen more than 200 feet.* (in text)

Timothy M. Shirk, 20

June 24, 2001 gorge below Upper Yosemite Fall
Concessions employee Shirk of Tahoe City, California hiked with co-worker Olivia Ouimette. Below Upper Yosemite Fall they ***scramble-climbed off-trail*** *down polished, wet, algae-covered, sloping granite. Ouimette changed her mind and retreated. Shirk,* ***solo****, slipped unwitnessed, fell 40 feet, and hit his head. An autopsy revealed THC in Shirk's blood; his backpack held marijuana.*

Larry Gene Schlenker, 60

July 24, 2001 Matterhorn Peak near Burro Pass
Schlenker of Valley Springs, California was ***mountaineering*** *at 11,000 feet with Roderick and Gregory Davis. Father and son stopped for food and to tend their 3 pack goats. Schlenker, "determined to reach the top," forged up* ***solo*** *and summited alone. While* ***scramble-climbing down*** *a 50+-degree cleft in the ridgeline covered with seeps and moss and slime, Schlenker fell* ***unwitnessed*** *30+ feet and died of head injuries.*

Paul D. Sharp, 17

April 23, 2003 Castle Cliffs, above Sunnyside Bench
Sharp of Castro Valley, California led a ***scramble*** *with Charles Homer and Robert Burton and "were hiking in the Castle Cliffs, a rugged, steep, trailless area on the north side of Yosemite Valley." He slipped, slid, and tumbled about 15 feet then vanished over a cliff. Homer and Burton said they next heard Sharp falling and hitting for another* 10 seconds!

Donald Anthony Cochrane, 48

June 23, 2004 Half Dome Trail
Cochrane of Saratoga, California hiked down from Half Dome via steps on the rock to the Half Dome Trail. He complained of chest pain. He asked passing hikers to go for help. Shortly afterward, Cochrane fell off, tumbling 300 feet down the steep granite slabs.

William Wagner, 55

June 24, 2005 east side of Lembert Dome

Wagner of Tucson, Arizona hiked with his wife Andrea and daughter Charlotte but became angry and separated during their descent. With knee problems, he eventually went ***solo off-route*** *then vanished. Ranger Eric Gabriel found his body on the base of the upper East Face below a 200-foot fall down a climbing route called Fatted Calf (5.10c). It took four 300-foot lowers to recover his body.*

Hyundo Ahn, 25

June 26(?), 2005 inner gorge of Tenaya Canyon

On June 20, Ahn of Dae-Gu, Korea embarked on a ***solo,*** *multi-day* ***hike*** *then vanished. In the Backcountry Office he had seemed "real confident" despite being warned that deep snow hazards blocked his planned Yosemite-to-Whitney Portal route (the John Muir Trail). Ahn had said, "I will see how far I can make it." On August 5, searchers found his backpack hung up on a snag and partly emptied in a pool below the Pywiack Cascade; the next day they found his body a mile downstream, beyond the route's second rappel station. His demise remains a mystery.*

Michael Gresham, 24

July 14, 2006 Royal Arches, west of the Ahwahnee Hotel

California Conservation Corps trail worker Gresham of Eureka, Montana was assisting in moving camp from Yosemite Creek Campground to Snow Creek but somehow ***got off trail solo*** *and fell about 1,000 feet to near the base of the Royal Arches.*

Stephen Daniel Demchik, 17

August 3, 2006 base of Bridalveil Fall

During a ***scrambling*** *descent with Matt McCarty from the base on large boulders scattered below, Demchik of Phoenix, Arizona lost his footing on the slippery rock and slid off. He hit another boulder then slipped off it into a 30-foot fall. He hit on rock and injured his head and abdomen. He remained conscious and responsive for about 20 minutes. Paramedics arrived to no avail.*

Patrick Noah Watt, 28

October 28, 2006 southeast of Grizzly Peak

Watt of Missouri had been seen ***solo scrambling*** *up Grizzly Peak Gully east of and above Happy Isles. Searchers found his body above the treeline between Vernal Fall and the Vernal Fall footbridge. He had fallen 400 feet. His specific error remains a mystery.*

Emily Sandall, 25

November 10, 2006 Half Dome cables

During cloud-shrouded weather Sandall of New Mexico was descending the Half Dome cables (in October the cable hand lines are laid down on the rock and the stanchions which hold them up are removed to prevent damage by avalanches) when she slipped on the wet granite, lost her grip on the cable, and slid/fell 300 feet.

Jennie Bettles, 43

April 21, 2007 Half Dome cables

During damp weather Bettles of Oakland, paused on the cables, which were in their non-lifted, lay-flat positions for the winter. Passersby asked her if she was okay and were answered with a "yes." A moment later, they heard her screaming as she fell 675 feet.

Hirofumi Nohara, 37

June 16, 2007 Half Dome cables

Nohara of Japan was ascending the upheld cables with four fellow hikers about 2/3 up the steepest pitch. He lost his footing, slipped, hit and caught on a pole, was spun outside the cables head first, then fell 300 feet, hit a ledge, then fell another 1,000 feet.

Luis Ramirez, 12 — February 16, 2008 — Munginella Route, off Yosemite Falls Trail
Boy Scout Ramirez of Modesto, California detoured with fellow scout Eric J. Gonzales away from his troop in a quest for a ***shortcut*** *down. Gonzales slipped and fell almost immediately but arrested his slide and short fall by grabbing a tree. Gonzales then saw Ramirez lose control on the steep slope and fall 300 feet to near the base of Lower Yosemite Fall.*

Manoj Kumar, 40 — June 13, 2009 — Half Dome cables
Kumar of San Ramon, California was descending the cables during a sudden rain and hail storm. He slipped on the wet granite and fell 500+ feet. His death led to a new regulation system reducing cable climbers to 400 people per day based on a 7-day advance registration and a $1.50 fee.

Katherine Marie Brizzard, 53 — August 14, 2009 — Cloud's Rest at 9,900 feet
As Brizzard of North Hollywood, California was hiking an ascent just below the summit, witnesses saw her lose her footing while passing a friend, Jaime Conte, on a narrow part of the hiking trail. Brizzard fell and tumbled about 90 feet down broken terrain.

Jorge A. Nuñez, 61 — July 17, 2010 — Lower Yosemite Fall Trail above Columbia Pt.
Nuñez of Los Angeles, California was scrambling ***off trail and cross country*** *and had cliffed-out. As people tried to help and a SAR team was en route, he refused to wait, slipped and fell.*

James Jason Dunbar, 34 — May 13, 2011 — Upper Yosemite Fall Trail
Dunbar of Berkeley, California was ***running down the trail****, slipped, and suffered a head injury that proved quickly lethal.*

Robert Barth, 75 — June 27, 2011 — Housekeeping Camp, Tent #220
Barth of Yorba Linda, California fell in a ***household accident*** *and died of a head wound.*

Haley Paige LaFlamme, 26 — July 31, 2011 — Half Dome Cables
At noon during white-out conditions of mist caused by a storm of heavy rain and lightning, LaFlamme of San Ramon, California ***lost her grip*** *on the cables due to an apparent* ***conduction of lightning*** *and slid down 600 feet of steep granite. Other climbers using the cables also were mildly electrocuted but retained their grips.*

Kao Kue, 17 — August 10, 2011 — Mist Trail below Vernal Fall
On an August 6th ***day hike****, Kue of Fresno, California was* ***running and hopping*** *down a steep section of trail ahead of his 10-member family hike and,* ***partially witnessed*** *by his brother Pao, stumbled and lost his footing. He struck his head and died 4 days later. His family asked about suing the Park for $20,000 funeral costs.*

Ryan Leeder, 23 — August 22, 2011 — Half Dome Summit
As two climbers at the base of the Direct Northwest Face Route prepared dinner they heard a scream and spotted Leeder of Los Gatos, California falling "uncontrollably" from above. Leeder's initial fall was ***unwitnessed****. He had a history of schizo-effective disorder and drug abuse, was jobless, but was acting upbeat and positive prior to his fall. Nothing suggested suicide. The investigating ranger found Leeder's dropped Double Diamond cigarette 6 feet from the edge immediately above his fall line. His stepmother noted Leeder as "****clumsy****." Toxicology revealed a cocktail of* ***drugs*** *in Leeder's blood that causes dizziness and poor balance during his* ***day hike****.*

James Michael Millet Jr., 39

August 11, 2015 base of North Dome, Valley Rim
Millet of Burlingame, California parked his car off Tioga Road at Porcupine Camp Campground and set off on a ***solo day-hike*** *on the Upper Yosemite Falls Trail. 19 days later a ranger found Millet's note inside his car stating his destination. 2 days of searching located Millet dead from an* ***un-witnessed*** *1,000-foot fall at the base of North Dome (3 weeks after having set off).*

Mathew Kern Baldwin, 24

August 28 (?), 2015 El Cap Gully, El Capitan
On September 5, a hiker found a backpack belonging to Baldwin of Reno, Nevada on the trail atop El Cap Gully. Airborne rangers spotted his body about 900 feet down the cliff: ***un-witnessed*** *fall(?).*

Kevin Golden, 23

January 6, 2017 Four Mile Trail, then LeConte Gully
Golden of Long Beach, California and his hiking partner ***passed/violated an NPS "TRAIL CLOSED" sign*** *(closed due to snow and ice) then tried to detour past a 30-foot wide snowbank via a very steep (60 degrees) route ending below in a cliff drop-off. His partner said they should turn around. Golden, however, continued* ***off trail*** *but slid and fell 1,000-1,500 feet into LeConte Gully's box canyon. His remains were recovered on May 12, 2017.*

Joseph A. Strekall, 33

July 7, 2017 Dawn Wall, El Capitan
Strekall of Portland, Oregon & Helena, Montana ***backpacked solo*** *to camp atop El Capitan. At sunset, climbers at the base witnessed him* ***falling 3,000 feet*** *from near the top of the Dawn Wall. Strekall had no parachute but was wearing climbing shoes and a chalk bag and his camera was in his pocket. Investigators found that Strekall was a novice lacking the skills to free solo El Capitan; he had told other hikers that he wanted a selfie depicting himself as if he'd soloed El Cap. Had he tried to position himself on the cliff to take that selfie but then fell? His autopsy and witnesses both suggest intoxication.*

Asish Penugonda, 29

May 21, 2018 Half Dome Cables
Penugonda, a native of India and living in Milford, New Jersey, was ***climbing on the cables*** *during an approaching thunderstorm and lost his grip. He fell about 400 feet.*

Meenakshi Moorthy, 30
Vishnu Viswanath, 29

October 24, 2018 Taft Point
Self-described "ardent adrenaline junkie" Moorthy and husband Viswanath, who took "wow-worthy photos" for their obsessively traveling, daredevil blog "Holidays & Happy Ever Afters," were natives of India living in the San Francisco Bay Area. After being seen unnervingly close to the edge, the pair vanished ***unwitnessed*** *from Taft Point, their camera stood on their tripod and aimed for a* ***"selfie" photo*** *on the cliff's edge. YOSAR personnel found the pair's remains 800 feet below. Postmortems indicated intoxicating alcohol levels. Significantly, on Moorthy's previous, standing-on-the-edge-in-a-Wonder-Woman-suit Grand Canyon blog segment she asked rhetorically, "But did you know that wind gusts can be FATAL? Is your life worth one photo?" Now we do.*

Joshua Brock Connor, 32

December 25, 2018 Silver Apron, Emerald Pool off Mist Trail
On Christmas during a partial national park shutdown, Connor of Los Angeles, California & Lima (Lakeview), Ohio was ***hiking solo*** *and died of head injuries sustained during an accidental* ***unwitnessed fall off-trail*** *(on ice?) down Silver Apron into the Merced.*

Lucian Miu, 21

July 31, 2019 foot of Bridalveil Fall
Miu of Romania ***bypassed NPS "Stay on Trail" signs*** *to scramble* ***off-trail***

solo up loose talus and boulders nearing the waterfall's foot then climb huge boulders. He slipped on wet rock, and fell about 20 feet, sustaining a fatal head injury.

Danielle Burnett, 21 — September 5, 2019 — Half Dome cables
Burnett of Lake Havasu City, Arizona ***lost her grip on the cables while ascending****. She fell about 500 feet.*

Anthony E. Viglione, 77 — October 2, 2020 — Sentinel Dome Trail
Viglione of San Jose, California was hiking with family members and fell at ground level, dying unexpectedly (was this medical due to high elevation or trauma?).

Daniel Range, 30 — May 5, 2021 — Taft Point
Range tried to leap across a large cleft at Taft Point, underestimated the distance, and fell.

Dennis Nelson, 71 — July 22, 2023 — Chilnualna Falls Trail near the Trailhead
Hiking, Nelson fell near the trailhead, fracturing his femur, then suffered a heart attack.

Steven Elden Trvalik, 26 — July 29, 2023 — Tenaya Peak (10,301-feet) descent trail
While descending, Trvalik of Arlington, Massachusetts & Los Altos, California fell and suffered fatal skull and neck trauma.

John P. Klear, 55 — October 21, 2023 — West Gully of El Capitan
Descending via a scramble/downclimbing combination the mixed 4th and 5th Class route of West Gully approximately 700 feet, Hiker Klear of Toledo, Ohio fell.

Jian Chu, 42 — May 19, 2024 — Valley Rim at Taft Point
Hiker Chu (female) fell approximately 900 feet.

Grace Rohloff, 20 — July 13, 2024 — Half Dome Cables
After mentally crossing off Half Dome from her "bucket List," Rohloff of Phoenix, Arizona began descending the 400 feet of cables following her father. An unanticipated storm slickened the granite. The soles of Rohloff's new hiking boots slipped free. She fell 200 feet.

Peter Thomas Lak, 51 — August 8, 2024 — Mist Trail
While hiking up the steps below Vernal Fall, former professional soccer player Lak of Huntington Beach, California collapsed due to cardiac failure.

Mathew James Mullen, 20 — August, 8, 2024 — Sunnyside Bench, east of the Yosemite Falls
Mullen, a resident assistant cook in the Camp Mather kitchen, day-hiked with a group but slipped while traversing a social trail serving as an approach to a climbing route.

Kirk S. Thomas Olsen, 61 — August 23-27?, 2024 — Ostrander Lake area ½ mile S of Glacier Point
Searchers found solo backpacker Olsen of San Luis Obispo, California deceased unwitnessed off-trail on September 14. Olsen apparently lost track of the trail and had failed to re-locate it.

John Joseph Buckingham, 30 — May 4, 2025 — Sunnyside Bench
"Jack" Buckingham of Escalon, California was scrambling the 3rd-4th class slabs en route to Fern Ledge but fell. His autopsy stated death to exsanguination due to femoral artery injury.

Kyungtae Park, 31

December 17, 2025 terrain upstream of Upper Yosemite Fall
*Park was witnessed **scrambling** for fun on semi-vertical terrain when he fell 50 feet down bedrock into a pool well upstream of Upper Yosemite Fall.*

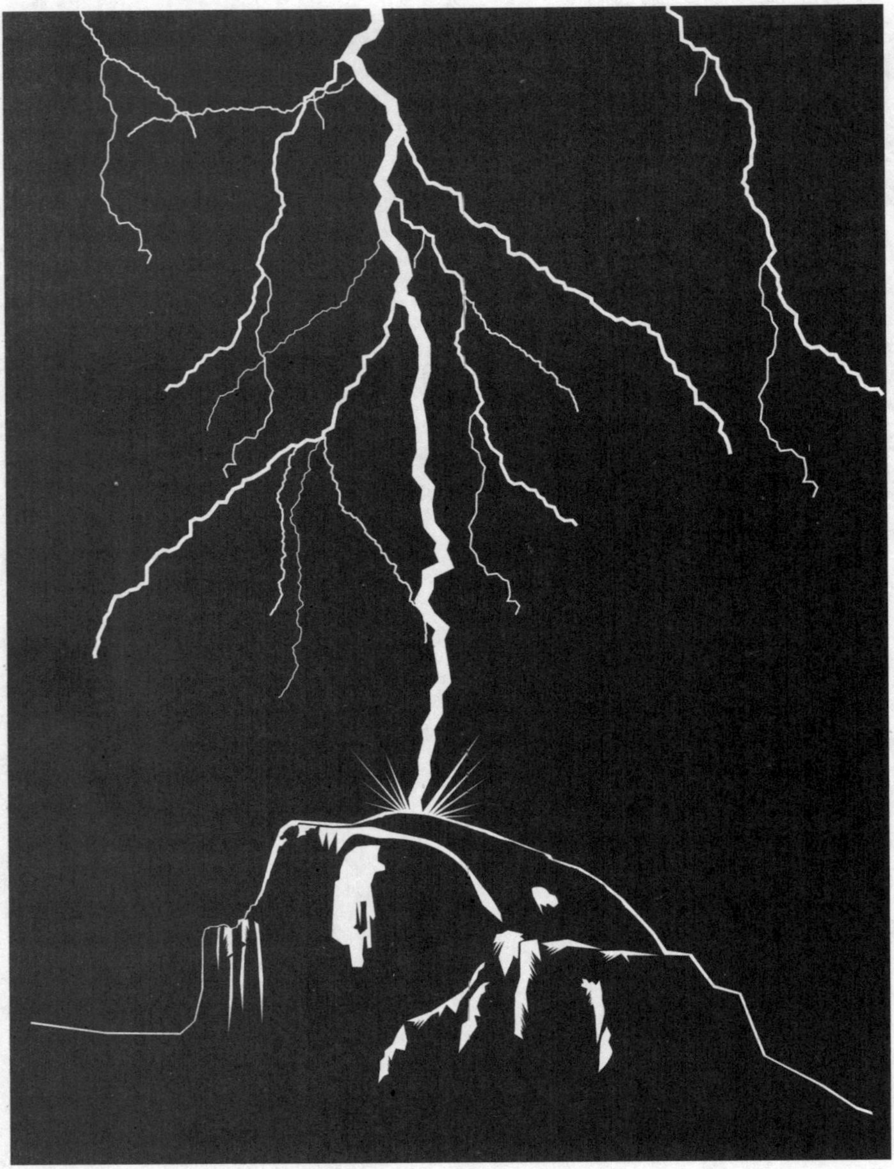

Chapter Seven

FREAK ACCIDENTS & ERRORS

LIGHTNING

In early September of 1971, 26-year-old Steve McRee of Lakewood, Colorado had descended about two-thirds of the way down the metal cable stairway of Half Dome with his buddy William Howsman. This portion of the hike is no cup of tea even under perfect weather. And today was not perfect. A summer Sierra storm now choked the sky. The air crackled with electricity.

Bad luck, a bolt of lightning struck so close to McRee it "jarred" him loose from the ultra-steep trail. He slid more than 200 feet down a frightening, out-of-control descent along the glacier carved face of steep granite. He slammed to a halt in the talus at the bottom. Howsman stared down at McRee. He half expected his friend to be killed. But to Howsman's relief, McRee started moving. Moving a lot more than a dead person could. On the other hand, McRee was now moving a lot less than a healthy person would.

Steve McRee's impact with the rocks had broken both of his knees plus an ankle and a wrist. Half Dome itself also now sported a lot more human epidermis. Howsman climbed the rest of the way down the cliff and ran for help. McRee survived.

One statistic, likely accurate, is that lightning is hitting some part of this planet at least every *second*. This translates to about forty million strikes per year. Some experts claim the rate may be even ten times higher yet. It is difficult to count such phenomena accurately on a global scale. Either way, a bolt of lightning cannot be called unusual. More the opposite. Nor does any law of nature prohibit it from striking the same place twice. Ghiglieri has a 350-year-old ponderosa pine behind his house on almost level terrain in Flagstaff, Arizona that has been struck at least twice. And it is not the tallest tree nearby. So yes, lightning not only can, but often does, hit the same place twice. Or thrice. In fact, it can strike probably hundreds of times in the same place over the years—if that place constitutes a prominent natural "lightning rod," such as Half Dome.

Lightning is generated because, as the turbulent clouds in a violent storm build up a negative charge of static electricity in their lower levels, the ground below them becomes positively charged. When the difference in the polarity of these two masses becomes great enough, the negatively-charged electrons in the sky abruptly overcome the normal insulative properties of the air between them and the ground. When these negative electrons ground out they can do so at up to two billion volts in a mere one-tenth of a second, thus violently canceling that polarity between cloud and earth to something more neutral. This grounding-out process—lightning—seeks not only the shortest path but also that of least resistance. Part of this path can be a tall tree, a flagpole, a prominent spire, or more to our point here, a hiker or climber perched atop a high salient.

One of the earliest records of lightning versus visitors in Yosemite was July 16, 1911. On that mid-summer day fourteen people were riding on horseback in a line. By the time they started toward Glacier Point from Illilouette Fall a thunderstorm had built itself into an atmospheric pyrotechnic spectacle. The riders, obeying some primal but misleading urge, took refuge in a tight bunch within a small grove of pines.

One rider dismounted. As if he had flicked a cosmic switch, lightning instantly struck the trees above. In a flash, nine horses were stricken dead. The riders stared in shock at the animals collapsing underneath them. Then each rider stared at one another. Amazingly, none of them were hurt. Not even slightly. "The horses seemed to wilt right under the riders, giving them ample time to get out of the way." Five horses survived. Inexplicably, one horse, in the middle of the cluster remained unhurt. Why had most of the horses in the grove been killed, but none of their riders?

These unlucky—but lucky—equestrians attributed the vulnerability of their mounts to the iron shoes on their hooves which, they hypothesized, must have facilitated conduction of the high voltage to the ground. The riders also attached their own immunity to the insulation of their leather saddles. Why one very fortunate horse in their midst had survived has evaded explanation.

As mentioned in a previous chapter, the damming of Hetch Hetchy Valley incurred a significant number of casualties during construction. Lightning killed one of these workmen. On May 23, 1921, 54-year-old John A. Sandahl, a San Francisco electrician for the "Hetch Hetchy project" was standing in the doorway of the South Fork compressor building above Groveland (outside of the Park) when lightning struck. As the bolt passed through him he collapsed to the floor, already dead. Burns were visible between his fingers and on one leg. The second workman to be struck down by Thor was James Gray. On October 12, 1944, Gray, a Yosemite resident, was on the job at O'Shaughnessy Dam when lightning hit a nearby power line. It broke, fell, and hit him. The bolt of electricity "used" the unfortunate man to complete its path to the ground.

Again lightning can strike almost anywhere. Consider this next example. Although the "Bear Show" feedings in Yosemite (which consisted of feeding American "black" bears at the dump sites, with nearby bleachers set up and lights aimed to illuminate the bruins) would be officially terminated in the fall of 1940, four years before this would happen, on July 18, 1936, 42-year-old George Block had ambled down to the lower Tuolumne Meadows dump site to take a gander at the "bear pit." Block, a camper from Los Angeles, had chosen to reconnoiter the Park's bear attraction during a thunderstorm. As he stood gazing into the pit, a bolt of lightning struck him. He died instantly.

Three decades would pass in Yosemite before lightning would kill again. On August 27, 1972, 19-year-old Edward Jules Willems of Greenbrae, California, had hiked to the 8,842-foot summit of Half Dome with Randall McLean Boone, also age 19. Late afternoon thunderstorms had dominated the skies for the past several days. The teenagers had read—and then walked right past—the signs advising visitors against hiking Half Dome during spells of electrical weather.

The two reached the summit at 3:42 p.m. The view proved stupendous—despite the darkening clouds now sinking ever lower. Ten minutes later rain pelted down. The pair hurried to join others seeking refuge under a rock overhang near the very the edge of the 1,800-foot cliff. They made it to cover without getting soaked.

Just a few minutes later, a bolt of high voltage electricity slapped their apparently snug, safe position. Unbeknownst to this coterie of hikers, they were crouching literally directly beneath a lightning rod.

An 18- to 24-inch long, rusted shaft of a jackhammer drill stood permanently embedded in the granite only inches above their heads. Perhaps the drill bit had gotten stuck in the hard rock many years earlier when workers were trying to erect a sign. No one today remembers. For whatever reason, however, the long-forgotten and now almost invisible metal shaft stuck slightly out of the boulder above the young people's heads.

The path of least resistance...

The billion-plus-volts of energy passed through Willems. It exited his foot with a sizzling smell and probably killed him instantly. Neither Boone nor the others, all of whom still huddled under the ledge miraculously unscathed, knew CPR. Willems' cardiac arrest—which sometimes can be reversed by cardiopulmonary resuscitation—went un-reversed.

Soon after this tragedy, workers sawed off this accidental lightning rod flush with the rock to prevent a repeat incident. Or so they thought.

Tempting fate—and also inadvertently testing that old adage that lightning never strikes twice in the same place—on July 27, 1985, 16-year-old Brian Jordan of Hayward, California reached Half Dome's rounded top with 25-year-old Robert Frith of Mountain View, California. The pair had loosely attached themselves to other visitors during much of their eight-mile and 4,737-foot climb up to the 8,842-foot summit. As many visitors do every summer, the party walked past the sign warning people of the danger of lightning strikes and advising them to stay off the rock and cables during the presence of storm clouds. It was as if the warning sign had been placed there for reasons that had nothing to do with them.

A thunderstorm slowly rolled in. Even so, as Bob Madgic details in his book *Shattered Air* (2005), some of the visitors remained on top of the giant monolith of granite instead of hustling off for safety. Frith, Jordan, and several others took refuge in the same exact overhanging shelter in which Willems and Boone had hidden thirteen years earlier. This time no stub of a lightning rod protruded above them.

Feeling both safe and exhilarated, the new companions fished into their packs and broke out food and cans of beer. They were hosting a "thunder party" atop Half Dome.

Lightning cracked nearby. The granite dome buzzed like a transformer. The air filled with a zillion frantic electrons. Everyone's hair began to stand on end like Elsa Lancaster's in the 1935 classic black and white production of *Bride of Frankenstein.*

More bolts struck. One hit the ledge overhang and, in an apparent "splash effect," shot through both Jordan and Frith. It also sought its path of least resistance by entering 28-year-old Tom Rice and 24-year-old Bruce Weiner at their hips and exiting via their feet. Another huge electrical discharge also diverted through a fifth person under the ledge, Adrian Esteban.

One super-high-voltage bolt had struck Frith in the forehead. He collapsed into convulsions. These became so violent that his less injured companions feared that he would flop right off the monolith. Two of them grabbed Frith by his sweater to secure him. Repeated lightning strikes caused Frith to slip from their grasp. As if in some *Final Destination* movie scene in which fate inexorably wins the last hand, Frith rolled off the summit into 1,800 feet of freefall. The bolt had also hit Jordan and killed him instantly. His limp body toppled dead, wilting in place—as had those unfortunate horses on the Glacier Point Trail so many years earlier—under the group's "protective" ledge.

Both Rice and Weiner had sustained serious injuries. If they were to survive, they had to be rescued. Esteban assessed his own injuries. He soon realized that he was the lucky one; his injuries paled compared to what had happened to the four others with him. Somehow, he knew, he had to get help. But how?

Well down the monolith of granite other hikers—21-year-old Mike Hoog, 22-year-old Linda Crozier, her 21-year-old brother Dan, and Rick Pedroncelli — had decided to camp at a sub-base camping spot and wait for the storm to clear. Their decision to halt here had been prompted at least in part by reports by other hikers descending who said that the summit seemed too dangerous. After the storm passed, Hoog decided to clamber to the top to view the sunset. Behind him

Pedroncelli followed. And behind him Linda Crozier.

Hoog summited first. Instead of finding a scenic spectacle, he happened onto a triage challenge. Fortunately for those injured, Hoog had earned an associate degree in emergency medical services and was also an EMT-I. As he now began sorting out victims and tried to administer first aid, Pedroncelli cleared the horizon behind him. Once he saw how lightning had transformed Half Dome into a disaster zone, he turned and yelled down to Linda Crozier to hurry because they needed help. Crozier, a recent graduate of U.C., Davis in physical education and a graduate student in exercise physiology, also seemed a lucky arrival for the surviving victims of the lightning strike.

Even so, Hoog could see that the injured people up here needed a lot more medical help than he and his two companions could provide. And if they were to get more, he would have to get off this rock now and contact the Park.

So, as Pedroncelli and Crozier remained to attend to the injured victims, Hoog downclimbed for help. Several minutes later he picked up Dan Crozier in camp. Together they hustled through the dark to find a ranger with a radio.

Meanwhile, a couple of miles away and nearly half a mile lower at the Little Yosemite Valley Ranger Station, 30-year-old, mounted Backcountry Ranger Colin Campbell was ready to call it a day. The storm had been an extravaganza of thunder, lightning, and rain. Sure, it was good to have the rain, but even better when the storm finally quit. Campbell had picketed his horse of five years, John Paul (named, as one story goes, after the famous Revolutionary War sailor John Paul Jones). Campbell's evening would consist of a bowl of Spaghetti-O's followed by a relaxing hour or so sitting with his cowboy boots propped up in front of the campfire alongside Park Backcountry Maintenance Specialist Scott Jackson.

Thoughts of how early they would have to get going in the morning prompted both men to abandon the fire and the moonlit panorama surrounding Little Yosemite Valley to instead go hit the sack.

As Campbell brushed his teeth, Mike Hoog and Dan Crozier emerged from the darkness. Out of breath, the two "blurted out" a terse explanation for their hasty trek. Lightning had struck Half Dome, Hoog explained, one guy had gone right off the summit and another guy killed. Three more had been badly injured. They needed help. Dan Crozier added that his sister was trying to help them, but they needed more help than she could provide.

Two men killed and others badly injured demanded an immediate response. It also required one heck of a lot of emergency medical equipment. Ranger Campbell thought about taking John Paul to haul some of this. But, again, it was dark and he had no packsaddle and the trail was horse-feasible only for part of the way. Nope, John Paul would have to remain picketed. Instead, he and Jackson would have to carry the litters, oxygen, ropes, critical victim gear, food, and other survival equipment on their backs and—because the loads were too bulky even for their backs—also in their hands.

Over his radio Campbell learned that the nearest other rescuers to follow them would also be on foot but they were miles farther away. Following even farther behind them would be a team of rescue climbers from Camp 4.

Now, wearing cowboy boots while hauling his loads uphill, Campbell considered the route ahead. Why, he asked himself, did it *have* to be Half Dome?

Riding on John Paul, Campbell felt at home. He did not feel at home, however, on ultra-steep granite. Never had. In fact, he was not fond of heights. And the summit of Half Dome was thousands of feet up: 4,737 feet above Yosemite Valley and a couple of thousand feet above his present position. Worse, a big chunk of that ascent was via that cable ladder. Why did people feel they had to stand on top of this rock? Worse yet, he would be wearing his slick, leather-soled cowboy boots to climb that thing, wet and in the dark, for several hundred feet, while hauling all this heavy gear…

But duty did call. And he *was* a National Park Ranger.

Duty or not, these boots likely were going to get him killed. Already they were proving a handicap in trying to keep up with Jackson. He was an animal when it came to hauling gear uphill.

Near Liberty Cap and where the timber ended, Colin spotted a lone tent. *Eureka.*

He heard himself yell through the nylon: "Hey, in there, you got any boots?"

An invisible male answered, "Who's asking?"

"I'm a ranger and I need a pair of shoes. I don't have time to explain it all now, but there's been a major medical emergency on top of Half Dome and I have to climb up there with rescue gear—and all I've got right now are cowboy boots."

"Well, I've got some tennis shoes."

"What size are they?"

"Size twelve."

"That's exactly my size." (This was an arguably lifesaving coincidence.)

It was quiet for a moment in the tent. The camper poked his head out in the dark. "I suspect," Campbell later remembered, "that if I had not been wearing my uniform, he would not have believed me."

Next came the moment of truth; the mystery camper became a Good Samaritan; he handed over his shoes.

Campbell thanked him, dropped his loads of rescue gear, and tried on the shoes. They were of white leather with a red stripe. They did not have Vibram soles, but what soles they did have constituted an immense improvement over his boots. "They felt *good*," Campbell would later admit. "If I hadn't been wearing these, I never would have made it."

Leaving the helpful camper with his less-than-helpful old cowboy boots, Campbell and Jackson resumed their uphill trek in the moonlight. Pretty soon it got steep. Indeed, this rock ultimately became so steep that for years every expert on Yosemite proclaimed that no human being would ever set foot atop Half Dome. There simply existed no way to get up it. But on October 12, 1875, George Anderson did the impossible by becoming the first person to reach the summit. It had not been easy. He had spent weeks drilling a row of holes into the granite into which he then jammed metal pins to use as a ladder. In 1919, the Sierra Club provided funds to replace the rope cable with permanent, waist-high metal cables raised on pipe supports with wooden foot-rests every ten feet, pretty much as it is today. Even with these new cables, admits Jeffrey P. Schaffer in *Yosemite National Park: a Natural History Guide to Yosemite and Its Trails*, "Half Dome is certainly not for acrophobics."

Now, partway up the cables, on that forty-five-degree slope of granite, Campbell received a radio call advising him that the Park was now planning to make a night-time helicopter insertion on the top. They were scrambling to get personnel and gear ready and they would wait for him to reach the scene before attempting to land a machine up there. By the way, Incident Commander Reilly had added, we can only pull this off while the moon is up. And it won't stay up there all night.

Nothing like a little extra pressure…

Campbell and Jackson hit 8,842 feet at roughly midnight.

They quickly surveyed the scene, assessed the victims, and radioed their findings.

Soon the airship came in and landed on the huge, still moonlit dome estimated at the size of seventeen football fields. The French-made Aerospatiale Twinstar was a Medic Flight, thirty-seven minutes out of Modesto. Its pilot, 35-year-old Al Major, sported a huge handlebar mustache. Major, Campbell now saw, looked calm and very focused.

For good reason. Al Major had learned to fly at age 19—courtesy of the U.S. Army. In 1969 the army had then sent him to Viet Nam where he flew for nineteen months. There Warrant Officer Major had flown helicopters for 1,700 combat hours. The army had awarded him the Bronze Star, the Distinguished Flying Cross, and fifty-three air medals. Nobody lives through something like that without developing the ability to control his emotions and to focus tightly on the task at hand.

Campbell watched Linda Crozier as she helped Flight Nurse Maggie Newman and Paramedic Bill Bryant now caring for and packaging Adrian Esteban. They were, Colin quickly determined, professional, competent, and on the ball.

Al Major's machine first lifted off the worst cases during two, back-to-back, twenty-minute round trip flights into the Valley. Again, flying at all was possible only because the moon was still visible in the sky, albeit low on the horizon.

By the time it was Campbell's turn to be relieved and shuttled to the Valley on the helicopter's third rotation, the moon had set. Campbell explains:

> As bad as this night had been, the scariest part of that whole experience was my flight off. We had lost the moon. It was *dark*. We

> were now evacuating the least critical person. It was like flying into a black envelope.

Despite the black hole below, Al Major pulled it off.

The next day, that Good Samaritan in the isolated tent near Liberty Cap would complain to the Park that some ranger had robbed him of his good shoes during the storm and had left him with these ragged leather cowboy boots. The Good Samaritan then handed over Campbell's size-twelve beauties. (Indeed, this camper's having worn Campbell's exact shoe size became an inside joke: "Hey, Campbell, you can't even find shoes that fit at the store, but you found them on the only camper up there…")

After this flight, Campbell eventually made it back to Little Yosemite Ranger Station. John Paul, standing there still picketed, gave him a nicker and that pointed look that every stable hand knows can be only translated as: "Where's breakfast?"

"Somebody somehow got my cowboy boots back to the station at Little Yosemite Valley," Campbell added, "I never figured out how." Campbell eventually became the Superintendent of Texas' Padre Island National Seashore, a relatively flat place with nothing higher than a fifty-foot sand dune.

Ultimately the effort to retrieve Frith's body mangled in the talus below proved to be yet another challenge. That bolt of lightning had caused him to roll off into an isolated section of steep rock surrounded by extremely difficult terrain. This required a team of expert climbers. The retrieval proved so difficult that they had to work for fifteen hours to secure Robert Frith's body and carry it to the Valley.

This epic storm had also hosted another SAR mission at the same time. It was up Tenaya Canyon to find four lost people, two of whom were epileptic but without medication. Ultimately, fifty-nine people of the Yosemite rescue teams were named in a Department of the Interior Exemplary Act Award for these two simultaneous missions. The storm would of course not be the last one to hammer the high granite cliffs of Yosemite. On June 25, 2000, for example, during yet another wild summer Sierra tempest, 24-year-old Andrew Betts, Brad Betts, age 28, and Gerard Meade, also 28, were climbing the final pitch of the Southeast Buttress of Cathedral Peak. Above them, already on top, stood 23-year-old Bojan Silic and Wolfgang Ertel, age 42.

As (bad) luck would have it, a bolt of lightning cracked onto the summit. It zapped four of these climbers, inflicting at least minor burns. Three of these burned people now lay injured—or dangled unconscious—off the wall.

This storm proved so turbulent and violent that it precluded a helicopter insertion. Rangers Jeff Webb and Paul Austin started hiking to the area. Soon four more SAR personnel followed on foot. Once the weather allowed, Rangers Keith Lober and Steve Yu heli-rappelled onto the wall.

Meanwhile the injured climbers had kept their heads and begun assisting one another. Because the weather and terrain continued to prohibit a helicopter evacuation, the growing SAR team hand carried out the Betts brothers, who had been hit the worst. From the trailhead an ambulance next transported them to the Mammoth Lake Hospital. Toughing it out, the other stricken climbers declined treatment.

Do practical lessons exist about protecting ourselves from lightning? About a third of Americans killed by lightning are standing in the open in places such as soccer fields, baseball diamonds, or golf courses. But running for cover under a big tree can be even worse than standing in the open. This is because as lightning strikes this natural "attraction," it can jump laterally from the more resistant wood to other, shorter, more conductive rods nearby (us) as it "seeks" a path of even less resistance. This is why about a quarter of Americans killed by lightning were seeking safety under the "protection" of trees. Entire kids' soccer teams have been felled by one strike while "hiding" under a tree. So what does one do instead? Where *does* one go?

To use a tree to our advantage, the experts say, we have to hunker down low about twice as far from the tree as its height. And toss those aluminum hiking poles away. In general, being lower is better. The difference here is illustrated by the fact that no one has ever been struck by lightning while boating the Colorado at the bottom of Grand Canyon despite thousands of violent monsoonal thunderstorms, yet on the Canyon's rims strikes have claimed many victims. So, if caught in a high place, descend to a safer one. Hiding under a thick dry rocky ledge is almost ideal—unless, as we've seen, it happens to be atop a natural lightning rod such as Half Dome. The lesson? Be smart and avoid becoming one of the 62 people yearly in America killed by lightning.

OFF THE WALL: NATURAL & OTHER ROCKFALLS & SLIDES

Equally as terrifying as a bolt of lightning zapping from the heavens are chunks of Yosemite bedrock detaching from above and then accelerating down on you like a rain of high-speed bulldozers. At least lightning usually restricts itself to the accompaniment of thunderstorms. Compared to a rockfall, those high-voltage events seem almost comfortably predictable. If it is afternoon during stormy weather and you are out on an exposed peak, then you are begging for it.

On the other hand, most rockfalls remain far less predictable. More often than the electrical "events," rockfalls do seem to come out of the blue. If you are in their path, you're toast.

Since the first non-Indians wandered into Yosemite Valley in 1851 about 400 notable rockfalls have thundered off its cliffs. Some have proven lethal.

In mere seconds at about 2 p.m. on October 23, 1949, one humongous rock slab fell from the west shoulder of Sentinel Rock. Its impact sent up a thick mushroom cloud of dust that reduced visibility to literally a few feet in the eastern end of the Valley. Half Dome vanished from view. Cars in motion abruptly slowed to a snail's pace. Drivers poked their heads out side windows and blinked away dust-stained tears while gasping for breath through handkerchiefs. Many motorists panicked, thinking that Yosemite Valley was about to be filled with rubble—with them smashed flat under the bottom of the pile. Claustrophobia reigned supreme. The slide that caused this nuclear fall-out look-alike closed the Four-Mile Trail. Fortunately, no one was killed.

Probably the number one process giving birth to falling slabs is "frost heaving" when rain or melting snow percolates into a crack in a cliff face and freezes. Each time ice forms, it expands the water's volume ever so slightly. This expansion nudges the fissure a bit wider, much like a hydraulic jack might do. Repeated hundreds or thousands of times frost heaving acts like a wedge, splitting one rock from another. Such separated flakes can exceed thousands of tons.

A second process facilitating natural rockfalls is the simple one wherein water acts as a lubricant in the joints between rocks. "Oil" this surface interface with enough water to reduce the friction between masses and gravity will do the rest. Driving on any mountain road after a heavy rain will provide inconvenient examples of this.

The third process creating erratic mass movement, one common in California, is an earthquake. Though these create rockfalls far less often than one might expect, when they do, the results can be spectacular. Consider John Muir's episode from *The Yosemite.*

> I was now convinced before a single boulder had fallen that earthquakes were the talus-makers and positive proof soon came. It was a calm moonlit night, and no sound was heard for the first minute or so, save low muffled, underground, bubbling rumblings, and the whispering and rustling of the agitated trees, as if Nature were holding her breath. Then, suddenly, out of the strange silence and strange motion there came a tremendous roar. The Eagle Rock on the south wall, about a half mile up the Valley, gave way and I saw it falling in thousands of the great boulders I had so long been studying, pouring to the Valley floor in a free curve luminous from friction, making a terribly sublime spectacle—an arc of glowing, passionate fire, fifteen hundred feet span, as true in form and as serene in beauty as a rainbow in the mist of the stupendous, roaring rock-storm. The sound was so tremendously deep and broad and earnest, the whole earth like a living creature seemed to have at last to have found a voice and to be calling to her sister planets. In trying to tell something of the size of this awful sound it seems to me that if all the thunder of all the storms I have ever heard were condensed into one roar it would not equal this rock-roar at the birth of the mountain talus.…A cloud

> of dust particles, lighted by the moon, floated out across the whole breadth of the Valley, forming a ceiling that lasted until after sunrise, and the air was filled with the odor of crushed Douglas spruces from a grove that had been mowed down and mashed like weeds.

In addition to the ways just listed, simple erosion can also cause rockfalls. When masses of rock become unsupported due to erosion below them they may simply break off and fall. Not as spectacular as John Muir's earthquake episode, but none the less effective.

As might be obvious, many of the processes that lead to rockfalls in Yosemite would not happen unless the rock was already cracked. Most Yosemite granites began as gigantic, mushroom-shaped, igneous plutons intruding upward 85 to 150 million years ago beneath a much more ancient mountain range of sedimentary rocks. Thereafter for millions of years continuing up to today the Pacific Plate subducted under the Sierra Nevada, shoving this range upward. This uplift continued into the Pleistocene and fostered massive erosion of the original, overlying sedimentary rocks. It also aided the carving of canyons into the newer granites, which *expanded* due to removal of the overbearing weight atop them. As the rock expanded, it cracked. Glaciers during the Pleistocene buried the exposed granites yet again, compressing them. During the subsequent melt-off about 13,500 years ago the reexposed granites expanded yet again. And cracked yet more.

In the Valley, experiencing periodic rockfalls is simply a price of being there. They always have been. Even for the Indians. On June 11, 1860, "A large mass of rock" fell from "the high cliff near the Great Fall" in Yosemite Valley and killed an "Indian boy" whose name went unrecorded. Why this slab fell, especially during the normally dry month of June, remains unclear. The cause of the next fatal episode, however, is clearer.

Seventeen-year-old Florence "Floy" Hutchings had been born and raised in Yosemite. She was the daughter of Yosemite literary and hotel pioneer James Mason Hutchings and his composer wife, Elvira. From the time she learned to crawl, Floy had enjoyed a free run of the Valley as her play yard. As she grew she soon became such a wild spirit that her parents nicknamed her "squirrel" for her lightning fast reflexes.

These must have helped her survive: Her early playmates were lizards, wasps, and rattlesnakes. John Muir called Floy "a rare creature" and "a smart and handsome and mischievous topsy."

Even as a small child, she would gallop her horse at full speed across Yosemite's meadows. Later, on September 26, 1881, still at the tender age of seventeen, Floy Hutchings was guiding (or possibly following below) a group of tourists to Glacier Point via the very steep LeConte Gully/Ledge Trail route. By one account she paused to pick ferns. Meanwhile some person on the route above her dislodged a boulder. It tumbled down on Floy. Her quick reactions now proved inadequate. The granite struck her fatally.

Author Benjamin F. Taylor, a family friend of the Hutchings had suggested in his book *Between the Gates* four years earlier, "Let us give the girl…some graceful mountain height, and let it be called 'Mount Florence.'" Ultimately a 12,561-foot peak west of Mount Lyell, along with one of its streams and with the lake it fed, all were named "Florence."

The next death to a rockfall followed not long afterward, on March 21, 1886. As John Henry Allen, a 57-year-old Canadian, was visiting the lower end of Yosemite Valley, in the Merced River Canyon probably not far from Arch Rock, a rockfall of unknown origin caught him. A survey team later found him. Other than he was subsequently buried in the tiny Foresta Cemetery, we found no information on exactly what Allen had been doing or what caused this accident.

The number of National Park Service personnel who have been killed accidentally by any natural cause in Yosemite could be counted on one hand. One of these rare unfortunates was 49-year-old Charles R. Scarborough of Michigan. For the year prior to June 21, 1954, Scarborough had been working as Assistant Chief Ranger of Yosemite National Park. On this summer solstice he rode on horseback well behind Ranger Herb Ewing. The two men and their string of six mules were packing supplies to the Merced Lake Ranger Station, thirteen miles farther east. Their ride went to hell three miles up from Happy Isles, just below Clark Point.

It was just after noon when, from a few hundred feet above them and sounding like a loud cannon booming, tons of granite exfoliated from a cliff. The disintegrating slab accelerated, breaking into ever-smaller chunks as it ricocheted down slope. The big pieces sheared off small oak trees as they cascaded. Ewing, leading the mules, quickly dismounted and tried to flatten himself against a rock face. As he tried to melt into the wall, he hoped for the best.

Meanwhile Scarborough was positioned as sweep on the trail, ten feet behind the last mule. With a bit less advance warning than Herb Ewing got, he entered the path of the rockslide precisely at the wrong instant. The avalanche knocked him and his doomed horse off the switchback and down the brush-choked slope nearly 100 feet.

When Ewing got to him, it appeared that Scarborough had been killed instantly by a head injury—possibly even before falling. Amazingly the slide injured none of the other animals. Ewing himself emerged unscathed. Even so, in the future nothing would ever convince Ewing to again use the Nevada Fall's Trail.

Sometimes the victim creates his own rockfall. On July 5, 1969, 24-year-old Dean Hobbs Pickett of Davis, California decided to scramble off the Tioga Road down onto a steep slope below Olmsted Point. He stepped on a 2,000-pound slab of granite; his balance was precarious. With the flat rock sitting on a 40-percent slope mostly covered with snow, Pickett's situation suddenly became far more tenuous. Like a bulldozing snowboard, the rock began to slide with him aboard.

Trying to maintain his balance, he shifted his feet. Instead of improving his predicament, he inadvertently tipped his perch just enough to flip it like a coin. As the granite rolled, Pickett fell downhill and forward, ahead of it. The boulder plowed over the top of Dean Hobbs Pickett, crushing him.

Eleven years later, beginning at six minutes after noon on November 16, 1980, an epic Yosemite tragedy unfolded. A slab of granite some 200 feet high and 60 feet wide—about 1,000 cubic yards—peeled from the "Forbidden Wall." This thousand-foot-high and almost completely vertical cliff hangs directly above nearly a mile of switchbacks of the upper stretch of the Yosemite Falls Trail. The cliff got its name in the 1960s when it was officially declared off limits to climbing because of the hazard to those passing below.

Now cabin-sized boulders roared down and across the very popular trail, erasing half a mile of it west of Upper Yosemite Fall—and, unfortunately, slamming into at least twenty-two hikers.

Before the huge dust cloud even settled, a four-ranger "hasty" team led by Bryan Swift was already hustling up to the scene. This unit was quickly followed by Jim Reilly and a seven-person medical crew. As these first responders ascended, they tried to recruit every able-bodied visitor they passed as helpers.

The very first rangers to enter this devastation sent reports down of finding an ever-increasing number of serious injuries. Upon hearing these, Chief Ranger Bill Wendt dropped the litter he was carrying and began sprinting uphill. He toted a set of MAST pants (Military Anti Shock Trousers designed to pool a victim's blood in his core area and brain to avoid or delay the effects of shock due to traumatic blood loss from the victim's lower extremities) for any victim of severe shock. As he moved upward, he triaged victims into classes of more or less urgent. Well up the slide, he came upon 53-year-old Dieter Frost of Ammerland, Germany. Frost was lying on his side. He looked bad. Really bad.

Wendt checked for a pulse. None. Pupils? Fixed and dilated and glazed. Fifty feet away, almost completely buried by boulders, lay 37-year-old Hans Michael Wagner, also of Germany. He, the Chief Ranger now saw, was dead too. Wendt climbed higher.

Above, on the unstable heap of sharp granite, Wendt found Ranger/Paramedic Mead Hargis working on James and Meg Black from Hillsborough, California. Both had been badly injured by the cascade of granite. But they were still breathing.

James Black was, as Mead had radioed down earlier, indeed severely shocky. The two rangers now fitted those MAST pants on him and inflated them to shift the blood in his legs and pool it in his core and thus raise his blood pressure to a level that might help him survive. Eventually rangers hoisted the couple off the newly formed rock pile and airlifted them to the helicopter staging area in Ahwahnee Meadow. There the arriving Fallon and Lemoore Naval Air Station ships would eventually carry them to advanced trauma care. Both husband and wife would survive.

Still early in this SAR challenge, at 1:15 p.m., other hikers-turned-Good-Samaritans directed Ranger Bryan Swift and rescue team member Kelly Repp to help Kirt Williams. He lay half buried and unconscious under a shattered heap of sharp rock. The young man had been hiking with Jason Pulis. Careening boulders had rolled the two 16 year-olds from Concord, California downslope. The slide blended them with broken rocks.

The rangers grunted while trying to excavate and free Williams from the scattered anvils of granite. Next the crew carried him to a large, somewhat level rock to stabilize his wounds. The rescuers now saw how badly the rockfall had mashed Williams; he had suffered fractures of both arms and both legs. Moreover, a boulder had half scalped him. To the rescue team's additional shock, when the men had initially moved Williams, they got their first glimpse of Jason Pulis buried beneath him.

Pulis, they now found, was covered almost entirely by one very large boulder. With a sinking sensation in his belly, Ranger Swift checked for a pulse in the young man's extremities, one after another. He detected none.

At 3:24 p.m., a navy helicopter evacuated Williams from the Valley, the first of many to be lifted out of the Park. Earlier in this incident, to keep the air uncluttered for emergency flights, Chief Law Enforcement Officer Lee Shackelton had instructed the FAA to close the local airspace above the rockslide and its scattered human victims. Despite this closure, one news helicopter from a San Francisco TV station continued to hover not only in the restricted airspace but also actually in the way of emergency flights (later, using a section from NPS regulations, the Park cited its pilot). Notwithstanding this interference, the navy machine managed to lift Williams out. Amazingly perhaps, given his many injuries, he lived.

Other hikers coming down from above the rockfall now were stopped by the lack of trail. Helicopters would eventually shuttle them over the large avalanche and down into the Valley.

Search teams from the California Rescue Dog Association soon arrived to look for additional victims. They found none. Based on the testimonies of survivors, which indicated no missing people, the team called off their efforts.

Due to the amount and size of rock burying Pulis and Wagner, neither body could be excavated until the next day. To dig out the two men required a Park Trail Crew. Wagner had been buried not only by several big boulders but also by fallen trees.

In terms of casualties, this stacked up to be Yosemite National Park's worst rockfall. It killed three hikers and injured nineteen others, five seriously.

On top of the human toll, more than forty of the trail's switchbacks had to be reconstructed. Rockfalls in Yosemite would continue.

At 6:52 p.m. on July 10, 1996, a huge chunk of granite more than twenty times the size of the one that killed Frost, Wagner, and Pulis detached from the arched face of Glacier Point. The 495-foot-wide, 130-foot-high, and 20-foot-thick slab detached from 800 feet below Glacier Point at an elevation of 6,600 feet. It roared and plummeted down more than 2,000 vertical feet, pushing a 150-mile-per-hour blast of air in front of it so powerful that it flattened nearly 2,000 trees near Happy Isles.

Upon slamming into the Valley floor, the 60,000-ton slab blew itself into smithereens with the explosive force of hundreds of tons of TNT. Pulverized rock soon would blanket fifty nearby acres with dust up to an inch deep. Flying debris and falling trees injured eleven people. Sadly, one of these trees crushed 20-year-old Emiliano Morales.

The cataclysm was so Armageddon-like it spooked some people to panic. Visitors sprinted for their cars in terror. Their ensuing traffic jammed into a line of stalled vehicles all trying to flee in slow motion through the dense cloud of fine granite and escape before being buried alive.

In March, 2009, 43,000 cubic meters of rock peeled off the wall near Half Dome, more rock than during the 1996 rockfall, but with no human casualties.

LOGGING or FIREFIGHTING

As happens anywhere people live, work, play, travel, build, and conduct their lives, unspectacular, garden-variety accidents also kill in Yosemite. The largest loss of life in this varied category is from, of all things in a National Park, logging. Less like acts of God than acts of poor judgment, fatalities due to felling of trees have left their victims as dead as those from an avalanche or lightning. Of the fifteen killed during some phase of logging, most were men.

The two women—38-year-old May Weisgerber (on September 23, 1912 at Glacier Point) and 63-year-old Amy Elizabeth Miller (on September 18, 1982 in North Wawona)—were curious people simply watching a tree being felled. In both cases they stood in what ended to be the wrong place. Miller, a Park resident, was one of at least ten people who had been watching a six-hour felling operation by Patrick Hicks, age 44, done in the riverbed of the South Fork of the Merced. The five-foot thick Douglas fir fell in the wrong direction and crushed Miller as she tried to flee.

Through the years different types of logging operations have worked within the Park. These do not count routine removal of trees for roads, campgrounds, and buildings but do include removal for safety in such places. They also include eliminating trees for control of Blister Rust (an organism/spore that parasitizes and kills sugar, western white, and whitebark pines—all native to Yosemite) in the 1930s and 1940s. The biggest felling operation, and in today's environmental climate, certainly the most controversial one, was the large scale removal of commercial timber on the western edge of Yosemite from 1912 to 1942 in the astounding amount of 1.25 *billion* board feet of lumber! Nearly all of it, notes historian Hank Johnston in *Yosemite's Yesterdays*, was felled within the original,

1890 boundaries of Yosemite National Park.

For decades people had thought that a large proportion of these lands were too remote to be logged. Things changed in 1907, when the railroad arrived in El Portal. Financial visionaries could now see that options for profitable felling had dramatically increased.

This new level of cutting could happen because when the Park had been created it had contained within its boundaries a preexisting 40,000 acres of inholdings already in the possession of timber companies. But because the federal government had not allocated money in the 1890s or early in the 20th century to buy back this extent of previously awarded logging properties within the Park from these companies, Congress came up with a "solution" to do just the opposite. It instead authorized a three-person commission to reconsider the Park's boundaries (see Chapter 4) with the goals of shrinking Yosemite to excise most of those inholdings. In 1905 and 1906 Congress cut out more than half these acres from the Park's 1890 boundaries and thus removed impediments to these lands being logged. This is how the bulk of the logging would take place in what was no longer the Park but instead either the neighboring Stanislaus or Sierra National Forests. Large as these "adjustments" were in reducing Park inholdings, they still left about 20,000 acres of lumber lands unsafely ensconced within the now shrunken Park.

In 1910, the Yosemite Lumber Company formed itself as a legal entity to cut these trees. But to do this the company first had to lay nearly 100 miles of train track, much of it deep into the Park. In several places, this railroad penetrated up to two to three miles *east* of the present Wawona Road as well as between Crane Flat and the present Park boundary. Thus, between 1916 and 1923 alone, company loggers cut an estimated 6,000 acres of the Park.

On top of the sheer ecological impact of cutting these trees, the presence alone of work crews also was significant. An example from the *Superintendent's Monthly Report* states that in the first half of November of 1926, before the two logging camps located in the Park had closed for the season, an average of 105 men resided at Camp 15 (near the Merced Grove) and 223 more men were living at Camp 16 (near Crane Flat).

Again, the impact of the trains also became pivotal in the decision-making process over which (and how many) trees were felled and which escaped. With no train, moving much of this timber would have been uneconomical. With it, more could be cut and transported for a profitable sale. Timber cut by loggers from these camps was soon stacked up in loads that totaled up to fifty log cars in length in one haul. Trains carried these trees from El Portal along fifty-four miles of track to the mill at Merced Falls not far north of Mariposa. Again, most of this timber was felled inside the *original* boundaries of the Park as it was created in 1890. Despite the legality of this cutting, resentment by parts of the public began to emerge. As historian Hank Johnston notes, the first major voice was that of conservationist

Willard G. Van Name of the American Museum of Natural History. He wrote:

> It is a piece of legalized and officially conducted vandalism that transcends anything committed by the German Army against the monuments of art and architecture in Belgium and France. It is a disgrace to our nation, to the century in which we live, and to our civilization.

Despite its articulate and reproving message, Van Name's published denunciation of the logging practices in and around Yosemite seemed to act only as a solitary beacon on the shoreline of a sea of relative indifference. With only a few blips due to repeated financial difficulties, the Yosemite Lumber Company continued to denude these local forests. In November 1942, the last commercial logs felled in Yosemite rode the rails to the mill in Merced Falls.

At least eight men are believed to have been killed in the Park while working for the Yosemite Lumber Company. Most died in or around Camp 15 or Camp 16 between 1920 and 1927. Another died from a large crew of men ensconced at Camp 14, also located near the Merced Grove but just outside the Park. Five victims were hit by a falling limb from a felled tree or the tree itself. Two others were caught under the rolling logs of the downed trees. The seventh man was killed by a falling gin, or loading pole. We found no fatal accidents that occurred south of the river within the Park.

At this time the company owned and operated a hospital in Merced Falls. It is probable that some workers suffered accidents within the Park and subsequently died in this hospital yet Park officials never knew of it. Hence our record of men killed logging for this company in the Park is likely incomplete.

The ninth logging victim was 18-year-old Louis F. Miller, a Civilian Conservation Corps (CCC) worker from Toledo, Ohio. On November 6, 1934, Miller was tending the rewinding of a steel cable onto its drum for a log drag in Wawona's CCC Camp YNP-7 (during the life of the national CCC—1933-1942—the organization set up and used six separate camps at different times in the Park). Although his mistake went unwitnessed, its aftermath made it easy to dissect seconds later. Miller had somehow slipped and allowed his body to be trapped between the rewinding cable and the drum hoist. The cable trapped and crushed him like a steel anaconda: "Death," the report read, "was instantaneous."

At least four other CCC young men died during their periods of service in Yosemite, three from motor vehicle accidents (see Chapter 8. Wheels), the fourth from pneumonia.

Until the "Let Burn" and "Prescribed Fire" philosophies matured in the 1970s and 1980s, fire suppression had reigned for generations within the National Park System almost as an obsession. Yosemite holds some pretty big forests. And hundreds of fires have burned parts of these over the years. Knowing this, one might expect to lose several firefighters over a century or so of fighting fires. Surprisingly—

pleasantly so—this is not the case. Only two have died in the line of duty.

On August 14, 1944, 17-year-old Jerome Stearman from the Stanislaus National Forest was employed with three hundred other men to battle a fire near Little Nellie Falls in the Foresta area. He somehow positioned himself in exactly the wrong place at the wrong time: A large burning log rolled onto the teenager, killing him instantly. Although the falls on Little Nellie Creek are about 400 yards outside of the Park's boundary, the record is unclear as to whether Stearman's demise occurred within or outside of Yosemite. The fire did involve the Park, and Jerome Stearman's death was included in the *Superintendent's Monthly Report*, so we include his unfortunate death here.

Fifteen years later, on July 14, 1959, 63-year-old Rube Phillips, a foreman on the Park's Blister Rust Crew, became a second firefighting casualty. He suffered a cerebral hemorrhage while suppressing a fire in the Tuolumne Grove. It remains arguable that the fire itself did not cause Phillips to die; instead, one might posit, he died a natural death during a challenging moment. While this might be true, he did die while trying to control a wildfire. Be that as it may, thereafter, Yosemite fire officials set an upper age limit of 50 years for personnel working on the front line of a burn.

FREAK ERRORS

The causes of freak accidents in Yosemite—as they do in most places—run the gamut from very bad luck at one end to abject carelessness on the other. In the former category is 16-year-old Janice Moreland's experience. On August 4, 1937, Moreland, from Hollywood, was camping with her parents in Tuolumne Meadows. A gasoline stove exploded in the tent and severely burned her. A ranger administered first aid and radioed for help. The ambulance took three hours to arrive at this very isolated area then took three more to transport her to the Valley. Once she had arrived there, the doctor felt certain she would survive. Instead, on September 3, after four weeks of apparent recovery, the young woman abruptly died (possibly of a blood clot causing a pulmonary embolism, but this remains conjecture).

Once upon a time cars were built such that the owner could access his engine components—and maybe even understand how to fix the thing when it was not running right. This simplicity of those days was often a blessing. But on August 3, 1965, it instead proved a curse for Kenneth Richard Standiford. The 34 year-old had been driving with his wife Ruth and their infant when his car stalled near Crane Flat. After having it towed to the Yosemite Park and Curry Company Garage in the Village, the quote to fix it there seemed too steep.

At 9:30 p.m., Standiford tried to fix it himself. He borrowed a container of gasoline, removed the air cleaner from his carburetor, and began priming it by slowly pouring in gas. Meanwhile his wife pumped the gas pedal and turned the ignition key.

The starter whirred. The engine sputtered, coughed, and maybe even caught.

Then it backfired. Flames belched out from the carburetor perched atop of the motor. Standiford recoiled and jumped backward. As he did so, the open container of gasoline in his hand sloshed onto him. In the blink of an eye, he was on fire.

He screamed and then did one more thing completely wrong: He started running around in circles in the dark. The wind lit him up like a human torch. Ruth Standiford yanked off their baby's blanket so fast that her infant spun in its cradle. Then Ruth chased down her husband. She threw the blanket over him as he fell to the ground. Garage mechanics had also witnessed this spectacle. They now ran to the human torch with a fire extinguisher. With dry chemicals they knocked out the last of the flames.

Ranger Lee Shackelton, the Valley Fire Chief at the time, still clearly recalls the tragedy from forty years ago:

> I was at home and off duty when the fire phone rang in my bedroom. The caller was reporting a man on fire at the Curry Garage. I immediately jumped into my Firehouse pickup and, going Code Three, arrived at the scene in less than two minutes. I was the first responder there. I found the victim on the ground, moaning with pain with burns over about 40 percent of his body. His shoes were leather and still smoldering and emitting smoke.
>
> None of the responding ranger patrol vehicles were rigged for a litter transport. Without a stretcher, I directed six men there to lift him into the bed of my pickup and I hurriedly drove him to Lewis Memorial Hospital. Fortunately, it was but a minute away.
>
> I can still see the doctors trying to undress him, but his nylon T-shirt had melted into his flesh, and they could not remove it without taking skin with it.

Despite prompt action by Ruth Standiford, by the quick mechanics, and by Park rescuers, Kenneth Richard Standiford succumbed to "bronchitis and bronchopneumonia due to thermal burns" on August 11 at the Peralta Hospital in Oakland.

Yosemite also hosted a classic smoking-in-bed death. On December 19, 1967, Nathaniel Brederman fell asleep and dropped his lit cigarette. The sofa upon which he was dozing went up in flames, as did the entire five-room home. One catch here: The 60 year-old happened not to be dozing off in his own home. Instead he was visiting his neighbors, the John Browns, and at their house in El Portal while they were away. Some homecoming…

Four people in Yosemite have asphyxiated due to carbon monoxide poisoning. In one case a vehicle leaked CO from its exhaust into a camper in which the owner was sleeping. In the second tragedy, on May 21, 1977, Tina E. C. Castro and her 3-year-old daughter Myra E. Campos and Tina's boyfriend Roberto A. Vitaurre died in the Valley's Upper River Campground by leaving an hibachi burning inside their camper van when they went to sleep. The small charcoal fire was unventilated. Carbon monoxide from the slow combustion was absorbed by the victims' red blood cells, preempting the attachment of oxygen. They all died of hypoxia and were not discovered until the next evening.

In the category of fatal errors closest to the Darwin Awards is 19-year-old Charles W. Edwards' August 22, 1948 adventure with a handgun. Edwards, of Edgartown, Massachusetts, was playing with a pistol with 12-year-old Janet Jackson. Why, exactly, he was doing this was never adequately explained. Perhaps he was showing off. At any rate, as the two sat in his car near the Yosemite Lodge, he held his gun against his right temple and, assuring his young friend the pistol was unloaded, told her to pull the trigger. She did so. The gun fired. The bullet killed the teenager instantly. The *Superintendent's Monthly Report* stated: "A thorough investigation of this accident fixed the verdict as an accidental shooting." Even so, in this episode it is difficult to firmly rule out suicide.

This next episode also smacks of suicide, but you can judge for yourself. After midnight on January 14, 1992, 28-year-old Miguel Cavazos, a "known drug user" and recently terminated employee of the Yosemite Park and Curry Company, left his temporary residence. Cavazos, of Fresno, had just ingested a large quantity of "crank" methamphetamine and smoked some marijuana and washed it all down with beer. (Investigators later seized methamphetamine, marijuana, psilocybin, plus other narcotic paraphernalia from his room.) Six hours after he left his room, he was found unresponsive and prone on a floor of the Yosemite Lodge Annex. Labored breathing and his comatose condition indicated an immediate trip to the Merced Community Medical Center. Despite constant rescue breathing en route, he died the next day of an "accidental drug overdose."

The next strange episode occurred well out beyond any buildings and beyond easy understanding, but not beyond the infrastructure of civilization. About a mile up the Four-Mile Trail from the Valley Floor and 100 yards to its side stands a forty-foot tall, galvanized steel electrical transmission pole. This tower-like structure is perched on a huge boulder surrounded by others "some as large as small houses." Near its top emerge two cross arms that allow three electrically energized cables to travel around the main beam. Numerous guy lines stabilize this pole-tower to its boulder and to the surrounding slope. The tower's lowest ladder peg sits about four feet above ground level. Recently this structure was posted with a sign indicating "High Voltage." On another note entirely, the view from high up on this pole is unobstructed by nearby trees and encompasses all three Yosemite Falls on the far side of the Valley. It is, by some reports, "spectacular."

At 7:37 a.m. on May 7, 2004, Jay David Muchhala from San Francisco entered the Park alone at Arch Rock. The 27 year-old spent that night in Camp 4. Two days later, at 4:10 p.m., Muchhala somehow found this pole standing not far from the Four-Mile Trail.

And then he climbed it.

Near the top of the power pole, Jay Muchhala made contact with the high voltage lines. Instantly electrocuted, he fell forty feet to the ground, narrowly missing a large boulder. In a quirk of chance, Steve, Sue, and Michael Whittier witnessed Muchhala fall. Michael ran down to the Valley floor for help.

The initial radio call described the situation as an electrocution with a downed, electrically energized wire. Prudently first responder Ranger Ed Visnovske did not simply rush up to the crumpled victim. Instead he held back a moment to assess the situation. *Was* there an electrical wire on the ground? Visnovske walked a half-circle around the pole to examine it and the immediate area. He quickly determined that, despite several obvious black burn marks on the tower's upper section, all the wires were in fact still intact and attached at the top. Bizarrely, one of the cross arms up there held a small piece of skin. Nearby it hung melted nylon. Macabre as these were, it seemed safe to approach the victim.

Muchhala, the ranger now saw, had come to rest on his stomach with his feet (encased in rock-climbing shoes) toward the pole. Within seconds, Visnovske discovered that the downed man had a very faint pulse and was still breathing—eight to ten breaths per minute. Despite an impressive amount of blood on the man's head and face, his head position was assisting in keeping his airway open. Large burn areas blackened the victim's left torso, hip and thigh (investigators would later find burn marks on both feet), and his pants had melted.

As bad as all of this looked, maybe this guy still had a chance.

Advanced therapy by additional rangers included oral intubation to maintain an airway, IVs, drug therapy, and CPR—but the automated defibrillator advised against shock and indicated instead that Muchhala's heart was in a state of "pulseless electrical activity." About this same time Visnovske noticed "brain tissue" on the ground. Almost immediately everyone on scene knew the man's injuries were far more complicated and serious than believed at first. Among the later responders in the SAR team was Dr. Jay Friedman from the Yosemite Clinic. He finally pronounced Jay David Muchhala dead at "1730 hours."

On June 11, 2004, Special Agent Steve Yu, the accident investigator, received the autopsy report from the Merced Pathology Medical Group. Jay David Muchhala had died due to "high voltage electrocution." Moreover, it went on to say, the head injuries suffered when Muchhala fell from the power pole were "lethal in extent."

Investigators wracked their brains to figure out a reason why the San Franciscan had climbed that obviously fatally hazardous pole. Maybe his alleged interest in photography and in drawing by pencil allowed him to be seduced by that spectacular view from up there. Maybe. But if so, this failed to explain why investigators never found his camera or sketch gear despite making an exhaustive search. Either way, it had proved a view "to die for."

TABLE 7. FATALITIES IN YOSEMITE DUE TO LIGHTNING, ROCK FALLS, LOGGING, FIREFIGHTING, AND FREAK ACCIDENTS. (Incidents discussed in text are noted.)

Name, age	Date	Location	*Circumstances*
Lightning:			
George Block, 42	July 18, 1936	Tuolumne Meadows	*Block, a camper from Los Angeles, stood near the garbage dump to look at the "bear pit" during a thunderstorm. Lightning killed him instantly.* (in text)
James Gray, adult	October 12, 1944	Hetch Hetchy area	*Gray, a Yosemite resident and dam caretaker, was electrocuted on the job when lightning hit a nearby power line, then struck him.* (discussed in Chapter 4. Park Builders)
Edward Jules Willems, 19	August 27, 1972	Half Dome summit	*Willems of Greenbrae, California hiked to the top of Half Dome with Randall McLean Boone, age 19, after having passed and read the sign advising against Half Dome during electrical storms. When rain began both hikers plus 2 others hid under an overhang near the summit—almost directly under an inadvertent lightning rod. Lightning struck Willems fatally.* (in text)
Brian Jordan, 16 Robert Ward Frith, 25	July 27, 1985	Half Dome summit	*Jordan of Hayward and Frith of Mountain View, California hiked with other visitors, passing posted signs warning of lightning dangers. A thunderstorm rolled in. Lightning strikes killed Jordan and Frith and severely injured 28-year-old Tom Rice and 24-year-old Bruce Weiner. Frith, hit in the forehead, rolled off the summit into a 1,800-foot fall.* (in text)
Natural & Other Rockfalls, Icefalls & Slides:			
unnamed "Indian boy"	June 11, 1860	"Great Fall" Yosemite Valley	*"A large mass of rock" fell from "the high cliff near the Great Fall" in Yosemite Valley and killed an "Indian boy" whose name went unrecorded.*
Florence "Floy" Hutchings, 17	September 26, 1881	LeConte Gully below Glacier Point	*Floy Hutchings, born and raised in Yosemite as the daughter of Yosemite pioneer James Mason Hutchings and his wife Elvira, was hiking to Glacier Point via the Ledge Trail route. A person above her dislodged a boulder which struck her.* (in text)
John Henry Allen, 57	March 21, 1886	near The Cascades, above Arch Rock	*Allen, a Canadian laborer looking for work, was walking up the Merced Canyon when hit fatally by a rockfall that buried the trail. A survey team found him.* (in text)
Mary E. Wilson, 75	July 2, 1948	Sierra Point Trail	*Wilson of Los Angeles was killed by a falling rock while hiking ⅔ of the way to Sierra Point. Why this rock fell remains unknown.*

Charles R. Scarborough, 49	June 21, 1954	Nevada Fall Trail at foot of Clark Point *Assistant Chief Ranger of Yosemite Scarborough was on horseback 3 miles up from Happy Isles on the Nevada Fall's Trail. From 750 feet up, tons of rock fell. As Scarborough entered the path of the slide, he and his horse were swept 100 feet off the switchback.* (in text)
Dean Hobbs Pickett, 24	July 5, 1969	below Olmsted Point *Pickett of Davis, California was* ***scrambling off-road****. He stepped on a 2,000-pound slab of granite supported by snow. The boulder slid down the 40-percent slope with Pickett aboard. The slab flipped, throwing Pickett downhill then sliding over him.* (in text)
Sheila V. Erskine, 13	March 15, 1974	Mist Trail below Vernal Fall *Erskine of Carmel, California hiked the Mist Trail with 14 other kids when "a ton of ice" fell on them from 400 feet above. Erskine's head injuries proved fatal 2 days later.*
Jason S. Pulis, 16 Dieter Erichwalter Frost, 53 Hans Michael Wagner, 37	November 16, 1980	Upper Yosemite Fall's Trail *At noon a slab of granite 200 feet high and 60 feet wide—about 1,000 cubic yards—exfoliated from "The Forbidden Wall" above the Upper Yosemite Fall's Trail. Huge rocks hit 22 hikers, killing Frost and Wagner, both of Germany, and Pulis of Concord, California. This was Yosemite's most fatal rockfall.* (in text)
Emiliano Morales, 20	July 10, 1996	Happy Isles *Granite exploded off the arched face 800 feet below Glacier Point. The 60,000-ton slab slid more than 2,000 vertical feet and roared into Happy Isles at 150 mph. Flying debris and falling trees injured 11 and killed Morales of Montebello, California.* (in text)
Peter James Terbush, 22	June 13, 1999	Glacier Point Apron, above Curry Village *At 7:35 p.m., a 550-ton slab slid 2,000 feet as Terbush of Gunnison, Colorado, and 2 buddies climbed the Apron Jam Route. Terbush was killed.* (in text and table of Chapter 9. Big Walls)
Xuan Wang, 56	February 24, 2019	Mist Trail up to Vernal Fall ***Ignoring an NPS "TRAIL CLOSED" sign****, Xuan Wang of Cupertino, California continued hiking past/violating the closed gate up the Mist Trail. A heavy mix of falling snow and ice hit her.*
Georgios Theocharous, 51 Ming Yan, 35	December 27, 2022	Hwy 140, ½ Mile East of Arch Rock Entrance Station *185 tons of natural rock fell 1,000 feet onto the San Jose, California couple's rented Dodge camper crushing and shoving it and them into the Merced River.*

<u>Accidents While Logging or Fighting Fires:</u>

May Weisgerber, 38 — September 23, 1912 Glacier Point
Camp Curry employee Weisgerber of San Francisco was hit by a tree intentionally felled.

Charles W. Nutter, 31 — September 4, 1915 near Wawona
Nutter was hauling logs to the Quigg sawmill when a loose log rolled over him. He survived only 2 days.

John Moore, 40 — August 7, 1919 unspecified location
Yosemite Lumber Co. employee Moore died instantly when struck on the head by a falling gin, or loading pole. Because Moore and eight other employees of the Yosemite Lumber Co. who are listed here below were all mentioned in the Superintendent's Monthly Reports, *we assume their deaths occurred within Park boundaries.*

H. Lindstrom, 37 — October 29, 1920 unspecified location
Yosemite Lumber Co. feller Lindstrom was struck by a falling limb.

John May Lewis, 40 — May 13, 1923 Yosemite Village
While working in a sawmill during December, 1922, a large splinter thrown from the saw hit Lewis of Madera and injured his skull. He underwent surgery and almost fully recovered, but an abscess formed on his brain. During repeat surgery, he died.

Jesse McGill, 21 — June 26, 1924 working out of Camp #14
Yosemite Lumber Co. feller McGill from Georgia was killed when a tree fell on him. During this multi-year era hundreds of acres were cut within the boundaries of Yosemite but on company land.

Gilbert J. Turner, 32 — March 25, 1926 working out of Camp #16
Yosemite Lumber Co. limber Turner, one of more than 220 men working at Camp #16, was caught beneath a rolling log.

Frank Phillips, adult — April 19, 1926 working out of Camp #16
Yosemite Lumber Co. feller Phillips dropped a tree and was struck by one of its limbs. He died the next day.

Frank Merill, adult — May 3, 1926 working out of Camp #16
Yosemite Lumber Co. feller Merill was struck on the head by the limb of a falling tree. His skull fractured, he died the next day en route to the company hospital at Merced Falls.

John (Rudolph) Splatzdoffer, 56 — May 1, 1927 working out of Camp #16
Yosemite Lumber Co. woodsman Splatzdoffer, a German, was hit on the head by a falling tree, or one of its limbs, and died instantly.

Joe Carr, 40 — July 14, 1927 working out of Camp #15
Yosemite Lumber Co. bucker Carr of Mendocino, California was

trapped on June 20 beneath a rolling log pinning his legs and lower abdomen. He died of his injuries in San Francisco.

Louis F. Miller, 18 — November 6, 1934 near Wawona CCC Camp YNP-7
CCC worker Miller of Toledo, Ohio was tending the rewinding of a steel cable onto its drum for a log drag. He somehow slipped and was trapped between the moving cable and the drum hoist. "Death was instantaneous." (in text)

Jerome Stearman, 17 — August 14, 1944 near Foresta
Forest Service firefighter Stearman worked with 300 other men to contain a fire near Little Nellie Falls (just outside the Park boundary). A large burning log rolled onto Stearman, killing him instantly. (in text, but he may not have been in the Park)

Ruben Carl Phillips, 63 — July 14, 1959 Tuolumne Grove
Foreman Phillips of the Park's Blister Rust Crew suffered a cerebral hemorrhage while suppressing a fire in the Big Trees of the Tuolumne Grove. (in text)

Amy Elizabeth Miller, 63 — September 18, 1982 North Wawona
Park resident Miller, was with 10 people watching a 6-hour tree felling by Patrick Hicks in the river bed of the South Fork of the Merced. The 5-foot diameter Douglas fir fell in the wrong direction and crushed Miller as she tried to run away. (in text)

Freak Accidents and Miscellaneous Fatal Errors:

Agnes Armour Leidig, 2 — December 21, 1868 Yosemite Village
Leidig, the daughter of the Lower Hotel proprietor George Leidig, died from eating spoiled peaches.

Effie Maud Crippen, 14 — August 31, 1881 Mirror Lake
Yosemite resident Crippen (and girlhood friend of Floy Hutchings) cut her foot on a broken bottle while ***wading*** *in Mirror Lake and* ***severed an artery*** *so badly she bled to death during the 3 mile ride back to the Village. Mrs. Hutchings explained, "Effie slowly drooped and faded from our sight, 'till her life passed away."*

Leonard L. Fisher, 14 — July 11, 1910 Yosemite Valley
Fisher of Napa, California had climbed 75 feet up into a tree during a contest of "who can climb the highest" and fell.

Clayton H. Nesbitt, 31 — July 6, 1931 Yosemite Valley Campground
Nesbitt of San Gabriel, California was hit during the explosion of a camping-type gas stove.

Louis Giffin, 23 — May 22, 1935 Merced River, El Portal
On May 19, Giffin of Los Angeles ***dived into the river and broke his neck*** *by hitting a boulder. He died 3 days later in Lewis Memorial Hospital.*

Owen Ramberg, 35 — August 28, 1936 Yosemite Village
Curry Co. head bellman Ramberg of Milwaukee, ***climbed 30 feet***

up a pine tree *at home to repair a radio aerial. He fell off a limb and broke both wrists and both legs, suffering internal injuries. He survived only a few hours.*

Janice Moreland, 16 — September 2, 1937 Tuolumne Meadows
Moreland of Hollywood was camping with her parents on August 4 when a ***gasoline stove exploded and severely burned her****. After 4 weeks of apparent recovery in Lewis Memorial Hospital, she abruptly died.* (in text)

Charles W. Edwards, 19 — August 22, 1948 Yosemite Lodge
Edwards, of Edgartown, Massachusetts, sat in a car and played with a pistol with 12-year-old Janet Jackson. He ***held his gun against his right temple*** *and, assuring Jackson the pistol was unloaded, told her to pull the trigger. The bullet killed Edwards instantly. Investigation ruled this as an accident.* (in text and is possible suicide listed in Chapter 13. Suicide)

Lynn Draper Butler, 37 — December 2, 1956 cabin in Wawona
Butler of Wawona died of a cerebral contusion and basilar skull fracture sustained during an unwitnessed fall during which he hit his head on a stove.

Clyde L. Given, 40 — July 21, 1960 Tuolumne Meadows
Given of Akron, Ohio died of environmental heat problems.

Marvin Booker Crawford, 69 — May16, 1962 Lewis Memorial Hospital
While Crawford of Sun City, Arizona was parked in his pickup camper in the front parking lot waiting for his wife to be released, he asphyxiated due to ***carbon monoxide poisoning****.*

Kenneth Richard Standiford, 34 — August 12, 1965 Yosemite Park and Curry Company Garage
On August 3, Standiford was trying to repair or start his car motor by pouring from an open container of gasoline. His carburetor burped on him. He recoiled and spilled the gas on himself. It ignited and burned him and his nylon shirt, impacting more than 40 percent of his body. He survived 9 days before succumbing to his burns at Peralta Hospital in Oakland. (in text)

Nathaniel W. Brederman, 60 — December 19, 1967 El Portal Administrative Site
Brederman, visiting the home of El Portal neighbors that were away, fell asleep while ***smoking****. The sofa he was on went up in flames, as did the entire 5-room home.* (in text)

Charles Hyler Ludwig, 50 — April 30, 1971 Ahwahnee Hotel Dining Room
Ludwig, a psychiatrist from Fresno, was eating dinner in the Ahwahnee while attending a conference of physicians. He died by ***choking on "a large piece of steak."*** *An emergency tracheotomy removed the chunk of beef but too late.*

Roberto A. Vitaurre, 23
Tina E. C. Castro, 21
Myra E. Campos, 3 — May 21, 1977 Upper River Campground
These Los Angelenos overnighted in a small van and let a ***charcoal brazier/hibachi*** *continue to burn. In the unventilated van all 3 asphyxiated due to* ***carbon monoxide poisoning****.* (in text)

Miguel Cavazos, 28	January 15, 1992 "H" Dorm restroom, Yosemite Lodge Annex *Terminated Curry Co. employee Cavazos of Fresno, a "known drug user,"* ***ingested a large quantity of methamphetamine, marijuana and beer****. He died the next day of* ***drug overdose****.* (in text)
Norman Hatch, 76	April 7, 1997 Upper Pines Campground *Hatch of Escondido, California was working underneath an Itasca Sun Cruiser recreational vehicle lifted up by 3 hydraulic jacks. The* ***RV rolled off all the jacks onto Hatch****.*
Jay David Muchhala, 27	May 9, 2004 1 mile up Four-Mile Trail *Muchhala of San Francisco climbed an unposted 40-foot high metal electrical pole 100 yards off the Four-Mile Trail. He made contact with the charged line near the top. Why he climbed the high voltage power pole remains a* ***mystery****.* (in text)
Evan Anderson, 20	May 26, 2006 Glacier Point *While standing at the safety railing at the Overlook, Anderson of Capitola, California dropped his digital camera over the edge. It landed on a ledge about 15 feet down. He leaned or climbed over the railing to assess retrieving his camera but fell 1,600 feet. Witnesses saw him fall in a spread-eagle, almost skydiving position which led investigators to suspect suicide. His lost camera became the clue convincing investigators it had been a freak accident.*
Kevin Kay Buletti, 60	November 30, 2009 New Curry Housing *Concession employee Buletti of Yosemite was reported by her roommate, upon returning from a vacation, as deceased and decomposing. Cause of death was an apparent accidental overdose of 7 different drugs. Buletti was a former drug abuser on medical leave after surgery with an apothecary of pain killers.*
Terry Robert Axelson, 65	January 8, 2013 Wawona *While eating, Axelson of Henderson, Nevada* ***choked on a piece of meat.***
Kathryn Erlene Hopkins, 20	March 17, 2014 Mirror Lake Trail *With buddies, Hopkins of Martinez, California was* ***longboarding*** *(skateboarding) and accelerating downslope on the paved trail due to gradient. She swerved to miss some pedestrians, hit a pile of pine needles, lost control, and flew off her board. She hit head first and died within minutes due to* ***cranial impact****. CPR failed.*

Chapter Eight

WHEELS

On June 25, 1979, I (Farabee) responded to the most bizarre car crash of the thousand motor vehicle accidents I worked during my career. The location itself of this collision was not so much bizarre as it was ominous. The accident happened on the Big Oak Flat Road 1.6 miles uphill from the turnoff to Foresta—at a bend known then as Deadman's Curve.

On this hot summer day construction on the road had slowed traffic to a crawl. The George Reed Company had won the government's contract for its routine repaving. The company's game plan was pretty standard: Close one lane and repave it while allowing traffic to continue to use the other. This of course led to one direction of traffic traveling while those going the other direction waited in their stopped cars. This arrangement tended to stall nearly everyone in a parked line in the heat while a long line of travelers rolled happily past from the opposite direction. Luckily, such annoyances rarely prove fatal.

Working this day was Wilbur Selfridge. He drove George Reed's 1962 International truck tractor. At this soon-to-be critical moment, his 17-year-old rig hauled two bottom (belly) dump trailers, each about thirty feet long. Both trailers brimmed full with hot asphalt. The 52-year-old tractor driver from Modesto was heading inbound to the work site to spread this load he had picked up outside the Park.

To assure some sort of workable order and safety among the several large construction vehicles and to keep all those summer visitors rolling along in one direction at a time in the opposite lane, flagmen and ubiquitous yellow advisory signs stood at both ends of the half-mile long work zone.

Selfridge now drove downhill along a gentle curve about half a mile from, and toward, Deadman's Curve. On his way into the Park, Selfridge had stopped to pick up Carol Willett. She had been hitchhiking with her 4-year-old son Arlo. Little Arlo and his mother made not a whisker of difference for Selfridge's massive load, one that the front page of the next day's *Fresno Bee* (June 26, 1979) would describe as "40 Tons of Steaming Asphalt."

En route to the job site little Arlo had watched curiously as Selfridge had pulled over to check his brakes. At these check stops they had seemed to be working all right.

Yet at four o'clock that afternoon, during the hottest time of the day, those brakes failed. Carol Willett felt her anxiety level rocket from none to stratospheric when Selfridge suddenly "became panicky about the brake system as he kept pumping the brakes, stopped talking to her, and tried to down shift but couldn't, and [said] that the truck could not be stopped."

Frighteningly, the southbound, downhill, curving grade ahead continued to impart greater speed to the massively-loaded old International. Willett now grabbed little Arlo. As they rounded the curve a bit more, they saw one of the least desirable of all possible scenes directly ahead of them: In their lane stood a line of vehicles stopped dead.

Carol tried to guess their odds of surviving. What the heck had she been thinking to hop onto this sort of ride with Arlo? She glanced at the line of blurring trees alongside the road. Next she sensed how much bigger each car in that stalled line ahead of them was growing in her vision. She guessed that they must be moving at least thirty miles per hour, maybe even forty. In just a few very short seconds, she realized to her horror, all hell was going to break loose.

Mustering years of experience behind the wheel of one or another large rig, Selfridge quickly swerved into the open, opposite lane. He almost made it clean. His speeding truck clipped one car then sideswiped a camper. These two hits may as well have been Tonka Toys. Both vehicles snapped aside upon impact.

Worse, these collisions subtracted close to zero momentum from the tractor and its heavy trailers. Indeed, gravity continued to add speed as the rig rolled south.

Selfridge frantically struggled to downshift to take back command from his runaway. But the transmission refused to shift into a lower gear. Carol now held Arlo in a death grip with one hand and clamped her door handle with the other.

Downhill half a mile away and hidden by the curve, their predicament was about to take a big turn for the worse. The flagman down there who controlled the uphill traffic rotated his sign around from STOP to now read SLOW. He next began methodically waving the long line of northbound cars into the lane originally designed to be southbound, the one down which Selfridge's still unseen and out of control southbound behemoth now approached.

The first vehicle in this line of tourists now aiming head-on toward the still invisible Selfridge was a Chrysler sedan rented from the Park's Avis Rental

Car office. Twenty-six-year-old Peter Gunter sat behind the wheel. His attractive fiancée, Annette Beckmann, also 26, sat beside him. These two from West Germany were touring the American West. As their car drove slowly uphill, the still unseen monster truck with the load of hot asphalt rolled out of control toward them. Both drivers were now aimed for the blind Deadman's Curve. They would arrive there at the same time. And when they did, only one lane would be available.

As if the road here had been designed by a fiend, the mountainside on the outside of this curve dropped steeply out of sight. The road's edge offered less than two feet of shoulder. Barely enough room for a motorcycle driven by a stunt driver to pass.

On the opposite side of the road a brushy ravine yawned about forty feet deep. At its bottom extruded a large metal culvert.

When Gunter and Selfridge simultaneously saw they were heading directly at one another in a sudden game of "chicken," they both reacted. In the same way. And in the same direction. The drivers yanked their steering wheels to veer their vehicles off the road and toward that manzanita-clogged ravine.

Both the Chrysler and the International left the pavement, pitched forward, and flew diagonally downslope. The truck with those forty tons of asphalt abruptly hit and bulldozed the doomed sedan over the embankment then nose dived on top of it.

Meanwhile, in midair, Selfridge bailed out his door. Due to the truck's angle and the steepness of the slope below, the man dropped at least twenty feet onto forgiving downhill terrain and rolled to a halt only slightly injured. Carol Willett, still holding little Arlo in a death grip, also leaped into space. Unbelievably, given their speed and the length of the fall before hitting the slope, neither she nor Arlo were hurt.

Tim Dallas was the first Park ranger to arrive on scene. Only a few minutes had passed since the International had violently hammered the Chrysler. One glance at the hellish scene below was all it took for Tim to yank his radio and broadcast a plea for *all* the help he could get. Tim did not know it at this time, but he had not only met this now-buried driver before, he had assisted him at yet another accident. Only the previous day Peter Gunter had hit a deer on the road while driving this same Chrysler rental car.

Responders started moving toward Deadman's Curve from every direction. Driving Code-3, Ranger John Daley and I arrived within fifteen minutes of Tim's call. When we had started our dash from the Valley, we had known the need was serious—but we had no idea how convoluted and ugly this wreck would be.

The Chrysler, we now saw, was literally flat. It was unrecognizable as to what type of vehicle it had been. The whole thing was now only as thick as its engine. The nose of the smashed truck cab had penetrated into what had been the rental car's roof. On top of this tractor, the two belly dumps reinforced by grimy six-inch-thick I-beams all the way around had stacked themselves almost vertically one on top of the other. Both now stood perched at a precarious seventy-five-degree angle aimed up toward, and past, the edge of the ravine. The end of the second belly dump was so high that it rose ten feet above the level of the road. It seemed to be balancing solely on the other now partially empty one beneath it.

As if this arrangement weren't hideous enough, tons of heated road material jolted loose by the sudden stop had shot forward to bury everything in its trajectory—including the flattened car.

The black sands that had been funneling down as if from a giant hourglass had stopped. Now the asphalt was solidifying onto the lowest parts of the wreck below. The stuff still looked super-hot. Moments earlier it had flowed almost like a liquid. Now heat waves rippled the air above it. Nightmarishly, the flowing sands had piled ever higher around the passenger compartment of the buried sedan and had sealed in whoever might be within. As this "hell" had cascaded down from above, it had spread and begun to cool—and to harden. The scene reeked of oil.

We groped for a rescue plan.

Within moments, we found ourselves—still in our uniforms—frantically digging into the black blob of the buried car with shovels we had borrowed from the road construction crew. We had to get whoever was trapped in that pancaked sedan out of it now, or else forget it. These shovels constituted the best plan John and I could come up with. We had to do *something*. Sure, more help was on the way. So was bigger and better equipment. But this stuff was not *here*. It remained many minutes away.

I was standing on top of the crushed Chrysler and had been shoveling for a good ten minutes before it finally dawned on me what it was that I was perched on. The soles of our hiking boots now stunk as they burned. The buried car was so hot that Daley and I soon began to suffer heat exhaustion. The air we were breathing could not have been less than 140 degrees.

Fortunately for both of us—and for Tim and for several other rangers who had since arrived and begun to assist—before we collapsed from heat exhaustion onto the smoldering asphalt, the first of the Park's fire trucks arrived. We yelled up to them to throw our protective yellow firefighting gear down to us.

We were not about to give up.

Neither were the other responders who were arriving. Firefighters above quickly engaged the truck's pump and began hosing the vehicle—and us—with water. Each second of spray cooled the area more. This spray felt great. But this improvement came at a price. It further cemented that alluvial flow of asphalt.

People and resources continued to arrive. Soon at least twenty Park employees and six pieces of heavy equipment worked on task. These included two huge, earth-moving front-end loaders poised for action but waiting for a safe plan. One critical tool still remained unavailable. The Park did not possess a "Jaws of

Life" extrication device for ripping open a deformed car. Eventually the Merced Fire Department, ninety miles away, sent up two of these powerful lifesaving tools.

The Chrysler's doors were not only crushed and deformed but now sealed shut with hardened asphalt. Frustratingly, these proved so solid and stubborn that we eventually broke both Jaws of Life trying to pry the car open.

This setback did not change the reality that someone had been driving that car. And that someone was still in it. And if *we* did not get them out soon, they'd be toast.

As each plan we put into effect failed, I thought about the Giant Sky Crane. It was flying in our vicinity to lift trees on a nearby forest-clearing project. Now desperate and trying to "think outside the box," I asked the Park's Fire Dispatcher to request the huge Sikorsky be put on standby in the event we might need it to stabilize the precarious belly dump trailers. It got dark, however, before we could implement that idea. In hindsight, the danger of doing things that way probably made this lack of availability just as well.

We now had almost every available on-duty ranger involved in trying to untangle this nightmare in time to save lives. Yet while we did know that at least one person was trapped, what we did not know was whether or not the victim (or victims) inside was still alive. And as each of our efforts failed, we reevaluated the likelihood that whoever was stuck in there was already dead. If the victim, or victims, were dead—and this seemed ever more probable—we could take the time to work more safely.

Kathy Loux, Head Nurse at the Valley Clinic, had driven the Park's ambulance. She and Tim Dallas scrambled down into the ravine and wriggled their way to the only small opening in the Chrysler. She stretched her arm inside and groped for a victim. That she could find someone alive in that squashed hellhole now seemed increasingly farfetched.

Abruptly Loux screamed: "You guys are not going to like this, but I found a *pulse*!"

For an hour now about five of us had been digging and scraping at this buried wreck, trying to uncover what we now knew were two people trapped in the flattened car. Truth to tell, we *had* assumed that absolutely no one could be still alive under all of this. So time had ceased to be so critical. Kathy's discovery now dictated a renewed sense of urgency.

Even so, we became even more frustrated. How *do* you get to someone who is sealed in a crushed car buried under a ton of now almost hardened asphalt that is situated under a tractor that itself is situated under a pair of giant steel trailers perched tandem and ready to topple? Loux's groping had indeed discovered an oil-hidden foot (later we determined it to be Annette Beckmann's) inside the crushed wreck. And she *had* felt a pulse in the victim's ankle. Our problem was we could reach this ankle but we could not get to the rest of the woman.

Thirty minutes later, as daylight faded and finally disappeared, so did Beckmann's barely perceptible pulse. After her amazing and lengthy survival in this brutally miserable trap, Annette Beckmann had finally died.

Several large spotlights mounted on the two fire trucks now beamed down into the gully and the sepulcher of a wreck. To make the buried car safe to dismantle we needed first to stabilize the highest, somewhat balancing end trailer by securing it with half-inch cables hitched to the Park's immense front-end loaders. Not being particularly smart about my own safety, I volunteered to work my way up and around the belly dump's jungle-gym-like, I-beam framework to set a cable. Nervously clinging to the near-vertical trailer with one hand, I hurried and fumbled with my other hand to wrap the hook-ended cable around something strong enough to hold it. Working with one hand like this was a bear.

Suddenly the thirty-foot-long dump trailer shifted. It felt like a major earthquake, although the trailer likely moved only an inch or two before settling. But there was no way I was going to wait around for that thing to take a big fall with me clinging to it. Instinctively I threw myself into space and hoped for the best. My left shin smashed into a sharp edge of angle iron then I dropped fifteen feet into a large manzanita bush growing on the slope of the ravine. The excruciating pain almost instantly sent me into shock. Nurse Loux—not only a friend of many years but one who had helped deliver my children—arrived at my side in a flash. This injury took me out of the game.

By 9:30 that evening the expanded rescue crew had finally dug Peter Gunter from his flattened rental car. He had been trapped in there for five and a half hours. For him, it turned out, time had not mattered. He had been crushed upon impact and had died immediately. In contrast, Annette Beckmann, the crew now found, had somehow ended up in a small, semi-protected gap created by the foot well in the backseat. Despite finding her here, it still took yet another ninety minutes to finally free her. The young woman could not have met her end in a more gruesome way. She had not been killed immediately. Instead the heat had slowly cooked her. Meanwhile her throat had gradually filled with oily grains of loose asphalt and suffocated her. We could only hope that she had lost consciousness very quickly.

"Deadman's Curve" is now known as "Asphalt Curve."

THE FIRST ROADS & WAGON TRAILS INTO THE VALLEY

Even though Yosemite Valley was America's first park, for years getting into it remained far from easy. During the decade following James Mason Hutchings' inaugural party of tourists into the Valley in July of 1855, there averaged but eighty-five tourists per year. Until the summer of 1874, three horse trails provided the only practical entry. Even these had proved a challenge to construct. If you left San Francisco bound for Yosemite, you needed to board a ship and travel twelve hours up the San Joaquin River to Stockton. Next you climbed into a stagecoach for a weary, dusty, bone-jarring ride to Mariposa, Coulterville, or Big Oak Flat. Then you began a two- or even three-day ride on horseback into the Valley.

The first horse trail was a forty-mile toll route that began at Mormon Bar, near Mariposa. It climbed east over Chowchilla Mountain to Wawona and then veered north. Next it meandered across the headwaters of both Alder and Bridalveil Creeks before winding down into the Valley at Old Inspiration Point, above what is now the Wawona Tunnel. This route reached the Valley floor near the base of Bridalveil Fall. Named the Mann Brothers' Trail after the three men who built it, the whole thing cost a whopping $700. When the trail opened for business in August of 1856, if you were on foot, you paid $1 for the privilege of walking it. If you were riding a horse and/or led a pack mule, the toll doubled. Two of the brothers who built this trail, Milton and Houston, had been members of one of the four parties of tourists the previous year.

The year 1856 also saw a second pathway blazed into the area—the Coulterville Trail. It followed a coarse, preexisting mining road running from Coulterville to Black's Ranch via Bower Cave. From there the relatively level route ran east and north along parts of Bull and Deer Creeks, eventually reaching Hazel Green just north of the Merced Grove. It then worked its way over Crane and Tamarack Flats. This toll-free stretch of thirty-three miles reached the Valley rim at what would come to be known as Gentry's. From there the trail dropped dizzily. It leveled onto the Valley floor near El Capitan Meadow.

Only a year later, the Big Oak Flat Trail became the third and last of these early ways to be opened. This one was pioneered by a pack train operator out of the mining hamlet of Big Oak Flat, ten miles north of Coulterville. Its thirty-three miles ran east through Groveland, Buck Meadows, and across Harden Flat. At Crane Flat it intersected the recently completed Coulterville Free Trail (where these two trails followed a common route, it was also known as the Big Oak Flat Trail).

Noteworthy here, despite the rough grades and primitive quality of these three early routes, no one managed to get killed on any of them in the vicinity of Yosemite. On the contrary, an ever-increasing number of mule trains used them safely to haul in supplies for an ever-increasing number of visitors to the ever-more-famous Valley. Despite this success, early entrepreneurs in tourism here believed their ships would not come in until good wagon roads—not mere trails—existed. A big stumbling block to building these, however, came not from lack of desire but instead from California State's Yosemite Board of Commissioners. In its 1867 *Biennial Report* the commissioners stated: "We do not consider it any part of our duty to improve the approaches to the Valley or Big Trees. This may safely be left to the competition of the counties, towns, and individuals interested in securing the travel."

Despite California's disclaimer, even before the dust raised by constructing these trails had settled—well, the dust never really did settle—road building began anyway. By the late 1860s, several turnpike companies formed in the foothill communities west of Yosemite. Local historian Hank Johnston's *Yosemite Yesterdays: Volume II* chronicles the fascinatingly cutthroat competition and convoluted construction complexities incurred while building the first three wagon roads into the Valley.

Wagons rolling into the Valley symbolized progress to such a dominating extent that June 17, 1874, became a red letter day. On that Wednesday Dr. John Taylor McLean and his financial supporters drove the first wheeled vehicle into the Valley (at least two wagons already existed in the Valley but they had been hauled in piecemeal on the backs of mules, then reassembled). McLean had driven in on the 17th to prepare for the grand opening the next day of their much anticipated Coulterville Road. "It was determined," boasted the *Mariposa Gazette*, "that every wheeled vehicle, horse, mule, and jack in the Valley should be put to use by the people, who would one and all go out and meet the Coulterville delegation….We understand that 50 carriages passed over the road on June 18, and the procession was over a quarter of a mile long. Great enthusiasm prevailed…"

This stretch of progress originated in Coulterville and went to Bower's Cave, where it became a toll road. Then it wound beneath the giant trees in the Merced Grove, down around Big Meadows, and then passed through what is now Foresta. It soon dropped into the Merced River Canyon on a very steep (grades of up to 16 percent) and narrow bed to near The Cascades. Leveling off at the bottom, the road then followed the river to El Capitan Meadow where it joined already existing Valley roads. The main Coulterville Road ran thirty-one miles from Bower Cave. The cost of the entire project was $71,000.

The next wagon route into the Valley—the Big Oak Flat Road—saw completion on July 17, a mere twenty-nine days after Dr. McLean's Coulterville Road had enjoyed its major fanfare. It more or less followed the trail of the same name. It started in Chinese Camp and passed through the small mining camp of Big Oak Flat. From there it wound through Buck Meadows and east to Hodgdon Meadows. It next penetrated the Tuolumne Grove then continued on to Crane Flat, Gin Flat, Tamarack Flat, and Gentry's Station. This second road into Yosemite dropped down across the huge talus slope on the Valley's north side and emerged near the base of El Capitan. The "road averaged 13 feet in width," notes *Yosemite Yesterdays: Volume II*, "with an average grade of 8 percent and a maximum grade of 16 percent. Total construction cost was about $56,000."

The Wawona Road—the third wagon road into Yosemite—officially opened a year later on June 24, 1875. Its twenty-seven miles cost $51,000 to build. This cost included building the still extant 130-foot-long, covered bridge across the South Fork of the Merced River. Despite what one might expect, the Wawona

Road did not follow the Mann Brothers' Trail. Instead it led northerly and westerly from Wawona to Chinquapin Flat, following more closely the route of the current Wawona Road. It next climbed up to Inspiration Point (above the Wawona Tunnel). From there it shot down a 12 percent grade in a few short miles to flatten out near the current location of the Bridalveil Fall Parking Lot. Remaining on the south side, it soon joined existing roads and followed the Merced upriver into the Village.

With these roads came not only progress and the potential for wheeled travel but also the opportunity for those wheels to elude the control of their driver.

MISHAPS WITH WAGONS & STAGE COACHES

All three of the early highways into the Valley were dangerous and demanded great skill by a driver. They also required fortitude by the passengers. Amazingly—considering the rugged and winding downgrades of these roads coupled with the unpredictable nature of the large animals that drew wagons along them—only six people in Yosemite died in wagon wrecks.

Perhaps the saddest of these deaths was also the first. It took place on September 20, 1888, when 6-year-old J. Sanders "Harry" Wright somehow fell out of his mother's carriage as it rolled across the rocky road near Bridalveil Fall. The Sanders were from San Francisco. Little Harry was the grandson of the Cooks, who ran a local hotel. Be that as it may, fate apparently decreed that despite the slow roll of the carriage, every one's response would come too late to prevent baby Harry from being fatally crushed beneath the wagon's iron-rimmed wheels.

A far more "historical" mishap of this sort—but at higher speed—occurred on October 31, 1902. This one unfolded as 78-year-old James Mason Hutchings and his third wife (of about ten years), Emily Ann Edmunds, descended the final portion of the Big Oak Flat grade in their wagon. Detouring from their longer trip to San Francisco from their home in Calaveras, they intended to camp in the Valley, a place that for decades had been the most significant and formative influence in Hutchings' life.

Indeed, for forty-seven years James Mason Hutchings may well have been the most important human presence in the early development of Yosemite Valley. In 1855, the British-born Forty-Niner had been not only one of Yosemite's first visitors, he also had led the first of four groups of tourists (together totaling forty-two people) into the Valley. Hutchings' passion for the place had soared to the point that within a year he was publishing the *Hutchings' California Magazine*, a monthly that highlighted his adopted state's "wonder and curiosity." In the pages of his periodical he effusively extolled the delights of his first visit to this marvel.

To good effect. Hutchings also became one of Yosemite's first hotel managers.

On April 20 of 1864 (only ten weeks before President Lincoln signed Yosemite in as America's first natural park), he purchased the Upper Hotel, which soon became known as Hutchings' Hotel. As the years passed (fifteen of them in Yosemite—he sold his hotel in 1874; its new name became the "Sentinel" Hotel), his influence and importance grew. California appointed him "Guardian of Yosemite" from 1880 to 1884. He meanwhile worked as a tour guide in Yosemite and, again, as one of the Park's few pioneer authors. In addition to his magazine he also penned his book *Scenes of Wonder and Curiosity in California.*

Hutchings would spend more of his long life in Yosemite than in any other place. During his periods of residence and his visits there spanning nearly half a century he remained a passionate and outspoken champion of the Valley and the wilderness surrounding it. It is ironic, then, how his final visit would play out.

Late on the afternoon of Friday, October 31, 1902, he and Emily Ann drove their wagon down toward the Valley. They had nearly completed their descent of the steep, 2,500-foot drop of the Big Oak Flat Road to the Merced River. Although almost near enough to touch the Valley floor, as Emily Ann would later report, it instead turned out that they were perilously distant:

> Coming down the grade we were impressed beyond all expression, and when we reached the point where El Cap first presents itself, my dear husband said, "It is like heaven." There was no apparent danger, as we had already passed the worst curves and were nearing the bottom. Suddenly one of the horses shied, either at a large rock above the road or because a wild animal was near at hand, and dashed down the road.

The spooked horse jumped entirely over the wagon tongue and started running full speed down the grade. Instantly the second horse joined this downhill sprint.

Neither the wagon's brake, nor Hutchings hauling in on the reins managed to slow the equines or the vehicle below breakneck speed. It swerved from side to side on the narrow road and bounced and jostled. Hutchings yelled to his wife that the galloping team was out of control.

Near the base of El Capitan one wheel hit a boulder on the side of the track then popped over it. The wagon bucked hard. The lurch sent Emily Ann flying in an arc to the ground where she tumbled and sprawled.

Meanwhile Hutchings gripped the reins and stayed aboard the wagon for another twenty feet. Then another jolt sent him flying. He slammed head first into a cluster of granite boulders.

Emily Ann, "only" scratched and bruised from her impact with the ground, rushed to him. She found him still conscious. "I am very much hurt," constituted his only utterings to her. His self-diagnosis proved accurate. His skull had been fractured against the granite. Emily Ann propped him up and dribbled a shot of whiskey into his mouth. This failed to revive him. Indeed, he died within a mere five minutes of having flown through the air. Eventually Mrs. Hutchings gave up trying to revive him.

Next she hiked for two sad hours to the Sentinel Hotel where she relayed her tragic story. On November 2, mourners buried Hutchings in the Valley next to his second wife, Augusta (who had died of natural causes) and next to his 17-year-old daughter, Florence "Floy" Hutchings, who had been killed twenty-one years earlier in LeConte Gully by a rockfall. Their graves in the Valley's Pioneer Cemetery are marked by a large piece of granite and a stone cross. As historians Hank Johnston and Martha Lee note in their *Guide to the Yosemite Cemetery*: "His funeral was held in the famous 'Big Tree Room,' which adjoined his original hotel building in Yosemite Valley. As she was about to leave Yosemite on November 8, Hutchings' widow wrote the following account in the register of the Sentinel Hotel:"

> On Sunday, November 2, 1902, my dear husband was borne from the Big Tree Room and its time honored memories. The residents of the Valley and many of the Indians, who had long known him, followed—we laid him to rest, surrounded by nature in Her most glorious garb, and under the Peaks and Domes he had loved so well and explored so fearlessly.

Roughly eight years passed before another spectacular wagon wreck. On July 10, 1910, a somewhat similar accident occurred in Yosemite. The *Mariposa Gazette* (for July 16, 1910) described how the out-of-control stage coach:

> —went over a cliff into the Merced River, falling 100 feet [sic].... One man and three women were carried down with the stage. The other passengers (eleven total) and the driver jumped in time. Two horses were killed....The coach was rounding a sharp curve known as Devil's Elbow [today called Windy Point]...between Yosemite and El Portal. One of the leaders stumbled and knocked the outside leading horse over the cliff....When the driver saw that the coach was going over he called to the passengers to jump for their lives, at the same time leaping to safety himself. Those who were carried over with the coach were able to extricate themselves [from the coach and the river] in time.

Amazingly, those passengers who failed to jump in time and were carried off the road into the Merced River survived. Horses, in this case, proved the only casualties.

Less than a year later, on June 3, 1911, another spectacular wagon wreck occurred. The stagecoach was rolling along near Artist's Creek, not far from today's Wawona Tunnel. There 25-year-old Eddie Gordon from Wawona ran into a hornet's nest. Literally. As the wasps swarmed, his team bolted.

Gordon's stagecoach had been designed with a kingpin that would pop loose to allow the axle and wheels to separate and go with the horses rather than continue to drag the carriage. The kingpin now popped loose. The freed team of horses charged on for only a short distance. Meanwhile the coach overturned.

Somehow Gordon, a veteran driver for the Yosemite Stage and Turnpike Company, stayed with his errant wagon throughout this tumult until it crashed and was partially flattened. Unfortunately, R. S. Leisenring, a 70-year-old man from Allen Park, Illinois was crushed in this wreck and died outright. Five days later, 65-year-old Sarah Diefendorfer, also aboard and from Allen Park, too, died from her injuries.

Relatives of the deceased filed a suit against the Washburn Family, who owned the stage line. But after the surviving passengers reportedly wrote glowing letters commending the driver's dexterity and daring in handling the emergency, these relatives dropped their suit.

MOTOR VEHICLES INVADE YOSEMITE

Automobiles have created what has proved to be the most significant—and, some would add, the most unfortunate—impact among all the human enterprises thus far in Yosemite National Park. Significantly, they have also revealed themselves to be the single most lethal "location" for a human being to place oneself while in the Park. More than a century has passed since the first incursion of a combustion-driven vehicle into the Valley. On June 23, 1900, the very first car to enter *any* national park chugged into Yosemite Valley by way of Wawona. Thirty-six-year-old Edward Russell drove the brand new, ten-horsepower Locomobile owned by Los Angeles photographer Oliver Lippincott. In the snapshot of the pudgy Lippincott sitting triumphantly aboard, he dwarfs the skeletal, bicycle-like vehicle. Be that as it may, after their steam-driven contraption accomplished this first, neither Yosemite nor any other American park would ever be the same. (Lippincott also spent days driving another new-fangled horseless carriage—a Toledo Eight-Horse—to the South Rim of the Grand Canyon, arriving on January 6, 1902. This too was a first for what would become a national park in 1919.)

Despite Russell's and Lippincott's feat, motor vehicles remained primitive, tiny, and unreliable during this era. In contrast, railroads stood tall as proven winners. On May 15, 1907, scheduled passenger service began on the Yosemite Railroad's new seventy-eight-mile line from Merced to El Portal, ten miles west of the Valley. Then to transport arriving tourists from there into the Valley, entrepreneurs spent $73,260 to build a difficult six-mile wagon road up and along the Merced to the Coulterville Road, two miles above Arch Rock—today's road still uses some of this original roadbed. The price for a ticket on this short train ride in 1907 cost a sizable $18.50 roundtrip, but at least it included the wagon ride into the Valley. Moreover, this cost in money and time was less than half of any of the longer, more arduous horse-stage trips. This far easier access to the wonders of the Valley also heralded the end of the era of toll roads.

Again, automobiles remained such novelties that only the most intrepid of drivers were willing to tackle one of the three long, dusty, rugged wagon roads into the Valley. But even back then, and despite their rarity, these noisy and fume-belching gadgets instantly posed big problems for the Park. In June of 1907, Major Harry C. Benson, Yosemite's Acting Superintendent and an officer in the Cavalry, found motor vehicles so dangerous—despite only about a dozen ever having reached the Valley—that he summarily banned all of them from the Park. He considered the existing roads too steep and narrow to be used simultaneously by horse stages and autos. Benson also found automobiles so offensive that those few vehicles that actually did manage to somehow get into the Valley were allegedly ordered to be chained fast to a log until their hour of departure.

Benson's successor, Major W. W. Forsyth, continued what the *Mariposa Gazette* (on August 8, 1912) termed a "war game" against the emerging powerful California automobile associations. By now, notes historian Hank Johnston, California already had 100,000 motorists driving its roads. Even so, Forsyth also successfully fought the state's congressional delegation to keep Yosemite free of exhaust fumes.

But this ban on America's freedom machines would not last.

In October of 1912, notes Johnston in his *Yosemite's Yesterdays*, at a National Parks Conference held in the Valley John Muir was called upon for his opinion on whether or not these contraptions should be allowed into the Valley:

> All signs indicate automobile victory, and doubtless, under certain precautionary restrictions, these useful, progressive, blunt-nosed mechanical beetles will hereafter be allowed to puff their way into all the parks and mingle their gas-breath with the breath of pines and waterfalls, and from the mountaineer's standpoint, with but little harm or good.

On April 23, 1913, the clerk for the Wawona Hotel—still outside the Park at this time—recorded their season's first vehicle, a Packard. Before the snows would fall late that year, Wawona would tally 215 vehicles carrying 696 passengers. In short, the touring public had demonstrated their preference for driving their own cars to get to Yosemite. The writing was on the wall. No fortune teller was needed to foretell the role cars would soon play in California. Bowing to pressure a week later, on April 30, 1913, new Secretary of the Interior Franklin K. Lane announced that he would rescind the Park's six-year ban on automobiles. On August 23, cars finally gained regular readmission to Yosemite. The first one to enter drove the Coulterville Road.

Even so, motorcycles continued to be banned until 1917. As we will soon see, this prohibition probably saved a life or two.

By November 19, 1913, the White Motor Stage began making "bus" runs into the Valley from the train depot in El Portal. Horses would still pull coaches from Wawona until June of 1915, when auto tours to the Valley began. The Army posted speed limits of 15 mph in the Valley, of 10 mph in "rolling, mountain country," and of 5 mph on steep descents. Moreover, horses and horse-drawn wagons retained the right of way to the point that motorists were required to pull to the shoulder and cut their engines if "approaching animals manifest signs of fear." Despite the Army's sixty or so restrictions on driving, 739 vehicles registered in the Valley in 1914. A year later this tripled to 2,270 cars using Yosemite's then 152 miles of road (106 miles were either toll roads or privately owned). One by one, each of America's national park areas soon capitulated to what appeared inevitable. Probably reluctantly, on August 1, 1915, autos were finally allowed into Yellowstone. For park visitors, the role of horses shifted from utilitarian to recreational.

No surprise, Yosemite's first car crash was not long in coming. On July 7, 1914, notes the *Superintendent's Annual Report*, "Mr. Van Aiken of North Fork, California was driving down the Coulterville Road and in attempting to provide room for the passage of an up bound automobile his wagon was overturned, throwing Mr. Van Aiken and breaking his leg. His injuries were attended to at the Post Hospital."

Anything involving an automobile during this era was so novel it was newsworthy. Even so, it is impossible today to ascertain whether or not Yosemite's second wreck was the May 19, 1915 mishap described three days later by the *Mariposa Gazette* as "an auto containing five persons turned turtle [rolled over] on the road between Wawona and Yosemite....The doctor at Sugar Pine was called to attend those injured."

The first arrest for drunk driving was not long in coming either. On July 13, 1918, Frank Wirick, a motorbus driver on the run from Yosemite to Wawona earned the ignominy of becoming the first person in Yosemite to be arrested for causing an accident due to "driving while intoxicated" (now termed DUI for Driving Under the Influence). "The arrest was due to the fact that Wirick in making a turn in the road did so at such speed as to cause Mrs. J. C. Bruce and baby to be thrown from the machine and painfully injured." Oddly, this well-publicized case was dismissed when the Mariposa County Prosecutor failed to provide any witnesses.

In contrast to car accidents themselves and to episodes of drunk driving, several years of driving would lapse before a Yosemite driver would sink to the level of hit and run. The *Superintendent's Monthly Report* for March of 1927 noted:

> Yosemite had its first hit-and-run case on the evening of March 26, when Mr. A. R. Rente reported that a car had struck him and knocked him to the pavement while he and a friend were walking toward the Sentinel Hotel, near the intersection of Cedar Lane. The only information that they could give was that it was a light car and it had very poor lights or no light at all. They thought the car was a coupe, either a Chevrolet or a Ford. The rangers made a complete tour of the parking spaces around the floor of the Valley where cars could be inspected but no car that answered the description could be found. Mr. Rente was quite severely bruised, but not seriously injured.

As we know all too well, worse outcomes are possible. Yosemite's first fatal car crash occurred on September 26, 1918 (for perspective, the first fatality due to a motor vehicle accident in any national park happened in Yellowstone three years earlier on September 3, 1915, when a large Maxwell touring car rolled over). On his way up from El Portal Charles A. Clark, a 42-year-old government foreman for road construction in Yosemite, lost control of his Ford truck at a sharp curve just below the Pohono Bridge. The Ford rolled over and threw Clark free. An instant later a large boulder the truck had loosened rolled on top of Clark and pinned him to the earth. He lay trapped for nearly twelve hours before someone spotted him there dead the next morning. Clark had failed to negotiate a curve on a part of the road that had been built in 1874.

Since Charles Clark's ignoble first, more than 177 other people have died due to motor vehicle accidents (MVAs) in Yosemite. Although the normal number of victims killed per accident is one, up to four have died in a single accident. This big one happened on September 23, 1926, after fourteen laborers working for the Dennis Construction Company had crammed themselves into the back of a Ford truck en route to their work site on the lower El Portal Road. As the old Ford crested a hill in the Pohono Bridge area, at the Power House intake, the driver downshifted but missed the gear. This miss was because the truck's Ruckstell axle had slipped into neutral, cutting out the low and reverse gears and also obviating the transmission brake. The driver groped to find any low gear but failed. The gear shift lever, it would also turn out, had been improperly fastened to the frame of the transmission. The Ford picked up speed. Next its brakes failed. The driver yanked on the emergency brake. It not only proved sluggish, it proved altogether useless. The truck freewheeled down the grade and accelerated out of control. It rolled 1,800 feet in the same area where Clark had died before it overshot a curve and crashed into a huge rock. This impact ejected every man from the open vehicle. it injured all of them. Two men died instantly. A third succumbed en route to Mercy Hospital in Merced. These first three casualties included Grant Hagerman, Johan Karlson, and Thomas Martin. A fourth man, William Larsen, died of his injuries five days later.

Since then and through 2011, the ages of all victims of vehicle accidents in Yosemite range from 2 months old to 89 years old. With regard to the gender of those killed, again males predominate; 144 of the known 183 victims as of 2025 were male (78 percent). Moreover, half of all victims were also young, 29 years old or younger (20 percent of them were teenagers; another 26 percent were between the ages of 20 and 29). The average age of all male victims was 31 years; that of women was 34. Interestingly, about half of the women killed died as victims of male drivers. For a larger perspective on these deaths, by 2016 America still led the world's top 20 high-income countries with motor vehicle fatalities per capita, 10.3 per 100,000 people, for a total of 32,894 deaths.

The salient points to emerge here pivot on which deadly human errors were made behind the steering wheel (or behind the handlebars) to rack up such an impressive death toll in Yosemite. Unfortunately, inadequate records prevent us from identifying every reason why many of these crashes occurred. Other reports, however, do include causes. At least 41 people died because the drivers, for example, were speeding before they killed someone. At least 14 drivers were drunk. Seven drivers slid on ice. At least a dozen people died because the driver dozed off then crashed. As far as we can tell, no one has been killed by hitting wildlife, but 7 Yosemite accident victims died due to crashing into boulders. More than 40 people died when they slammed into a tree. Some so hard that their vehicle broke in half.

Given that literally tens of millions of motor vehicles have by now driven into Yosemite with the outcomes of only about 183 fatalities, it is noteworthy that motorcycles, entering the Park in numbers only a tiny fraction of what cars total, have led to an inordinate death toll (this holds true in national parks in general). Yosemite's first motorcycle ever entered on June 26, 1905, after a two-and-a-half-day trip from Stockton. For the next 30 years two-wheelers entered the Valley, a few illegally, with no one being killed. On June 20, 1934 this changed when 27-year-old Earl Merrill Clough of Watsonville, California earned the distinction of becoming the first easy rider to crash fatally. Employed by a road contractor on Glacier Point, Clough was speeding on his motorcycle along Wawona Road near Bishop Creek. He failed to retain control of his machine and slammed head-on into an oncoming Ford.

Since then, in one or another part of Yosemite, 31 people have died during motorcycle mishaps (including one on a motorbike): 29 men and 2 women—both of the latter were passengers riding behind male drivers.

An often overlooked detail of car fatalities is that one need not be in a vehicle to become a victim of a motor vehicle accident. Among the most tragic and senseless of motor vehicle deaths in Yosemite was that of the three members of the Walls family. On February 28, 1970, 40-year-old James L. Walls, Joy Walls, age 39, James D. Walls, age 10, and his 14-year-old sister Susan were doing what tourists are supposed to do, enjoying the breathtaking vista from Discovery View. In a case of very bad luck, as they stood in the chill air at the downhill end of the parking lot farthest from the Wawona Tunnel, 22-year-old Richard Cornelius sped out of the 4,230-foot long tunnel, emerging behind them.

Cornelius' speeding car swerved left. He and his three passengers bounced off their seats as it crossed the cement curb separating the parking area from the roadway. The driver hit his brake pedal for fifty yards, but due to his speed, he hit the brakes far too late.

The out of control car slammed into the father, mother, and son and pinned all three against the rock wall bracketing the parking lot. One small shred of mercy: They did not know what hit them. The car crushed them so fast and so hard that it cut all three pedestrians in half. Fourteen-year-old Susan abruptly became the lone surviving member of her family—and a witness to their most horrific and senseless killings.

The Sacramento driver responsible for this carnage claimed he was reaching for an item in the backseat when he lost control. Even so, statements by witnesses suggest instead that he was driving far too fast. A Federal Grand Jury indicted Richard Cornelius for Vehicular Manslaughter; he was soon found guilty. His victims, the Walls family, became three of a total of nine people in Yosemite who have died as pedestrians hit by drivers.

One need only travel the Park roads once to appreciate how critical the need is for every driver to maintain constantly undivided attention. Countless trees and rocks edge the roadside a few feet from the narrow pavement. Even with Yosemite's generally lower speed limits, when one is in motion on the road potential tragedy lurks microseconds away. The bottom line here is: No one can safely "drive and gawk."

An eerie outcome due to a driver's brief lapse of focus on the road ahead occurred on September 23, 1986. Eighty-three-year-old Hilda Meyer was riding in the backseat of her son Ben's new Ford Aerostar van. She was visiting California from her home in Iowa to attend her granddaughter's wedding (which had taken place two days before) in nearby Modesto. Since she had traveled all that way and was now so close, her family decided, she might as well take this golden opportunity to also see Yosemite.

The day proved beautiful. Five members of Hilda's party enjoyed a quick picnic in Wawona. From there Ben drove them toward Glacier Point. At 3:30 that afternoon, as they approached Washburn Point, the loving son glanced into his rearview mirror to see how his mother was doing at this elevation. Great, he thought to himself, she looks fine.

Barely more than a second later, she was dead. Ben, who had allowed himself to be momentarily distracted for a purpose he had decided was worthy, had failed to keep the Aerostar on the pavement and had slammed it head-on into a fir tree thirty inches thick. The National Highway Traffic Safety Administration Report dated April, 2006 notes that nearly 80 percent of all U.S. crashes involved driver inattention. "Simply looking away from the road for longer than two seconds doubles or triples the risk of a crash." In Yosemite, of course, with minimal shoulders and with trees and rocks very close to the pavement, inattention for even one second not only can be, but all too often has been, fatal.

It might seem a bit strange but at least eleven motor-related fatalities in Yosemite happened *after* the victims' vehicles lost the road and rolled down into the Merced River where they drowned. A particularly tragic example of this happened just before 6 a.m. on May 25, 1991, as Elaine Watson, a 44-year-old legal secretary from Compton, California, dozed off at the wheel of her Toyota Camry. She had been driving on Southside Drive, 300 yards east of the Bridalveil Fall Junction. Here the Merced River flows only a few feet from the pavement. It was now a time when runoff from the high country snowmelt swells the river to its seasonal spate. Elaine Watson was driving about as dangerously close to hazardous water as she could get while in the Park and yet still be on pavement.

Watson was not alone in her Camry when she nodded off. Riding with her were her mother Pearl Jordan, age 62, her two nephews, 3-year-old Mario and 5-year-old Lance Thomas, and also Watson's 7-year-old niece, Sequoia Thomas.

When Watson fell asleep the Toyota veered off the pavement and bounced down the boulder-strewn riverbank. It splashed into the Merced at the head of a long rapid. The river here flowed deep and fast. It carried the still-floating car for sixty feet before lodging it against a log jammed about twenty-five feet from shore. The car stopped in a position facing upstream. Almost instantly the strong current swept over the submerged engine compartment and began shoving the vehicle to the bottom of the river.

Bill Perry, a visitor to the Park, arrived almost immediately. He saw the family climbing out through a window and up to the roof of the half-sunken car. He yelled instructions to them to stay put while he went for help. Moments later, four more tourists stopped to help. One of them soon threw Watson a rope. These Good Samaritans yelled from the bank that they would pull the stranded victims to shore, one-by-one.

Elaine Watson, now thoroughly awake, hurriedly knotted the line around Sequoia. The 7-year-old girl jumped into the numbingly cold snowmelt. Before the rescuers had even hauled Sequoia all the way to safety and before either of the older women atop the sunken Toyota could stop Lance and Mario, the two little boys leaped into the river "with" Sequoia. They may have assumed in their young minds that they were supposed to follow their older sister.

Both tiny boys quickly disappeared downstream on the foaming two-foot high waves of the high-flowing Merced. Watson stared in horror and immediately plunged into the river to save her nephews.

Onlookers and would-be rescuers on shore now watched helplessly as Watson too, was sucked downstream to also vanish underwater in the rapid.

Meanwhile Ranger Dave Panebaker happened to be up and at work in the Valley early that morning. Ironically, he was busy writing paperwork for the natural fatality of a hiker in the Park during the previous day. When he heard the Dispatcher broadcast "A VEHICLE IN THE RIVER" (due to Good Samaritan Bill Perry's quick alarm) he dropped his reports as if it had caught fire and sprinted for his car. Only thirteen minutes after the alarm had sounded Panebaker arrived as the first ranger on scene (he probably set a speed record to accomplish this). In a fortunate coincidence for the still stranded Pearl Jordan, Panebaker was a veteran who carried his whitewater rescue gear in his patrol car. He immediately wiggled into his wetsuit and, dragging a rescue rope behind him, swam out to Jordan.

Watson's mother, still immersed to mid-thigh in the river, proved unhurt except for her increasing hypothermia. She had managed to avoid being swept off the sinking Toyota because the force of the rushing water had scissored her legs tightly between the body of the car and its front door. Dave now cradled her to warm her. He also positioned his body as a shield between her and the relentless current. Other rescuers soon joined to haul the 62 year-old, now bereaved, grandmother to shore.

The Park immediately accelerated its massive hunt for the three missing swimmers into high gear. While some rangers searched literally *in* the water, many others walked the rocky shoreline with greater speed to scour a wider area. Two dogs owned by Park staff soon added their efforts. So did the Yosemite helicopter.

Two hours after Elaine Watson had dozed off behind the wheel and then dived into the Merced to save her little nephews, searchers found her body submerged half a mile downriver. The rescuing Ranger-Paramedics initiated immediate CPR. Minutes later the hospital staff continued these efforts. Despite all this prompt action and hours of attempted resuscitation, at 10:20 a.m. the attending physician reluctantly pronounced her dead.

Rescuers dread nothing more than the death of a child. Being forced to accept the deaths of *two* children would prove more than doubly hard. Their determination to circumvent this sort of tragedy fueled a huge, several-week-long search effort. Sadly, two weeks after 5-year-old Lance was seen being swept like a leaf through the Merced's whitewater, on June 7, his body was found. No amount of searching ever managed to turn up little Mario. Finally, three long months later, on August 27, the boy's skull was discovered lodged like driftwood among shoreline boulders.

Glancing through Table 8 reveals a lot about car accidents in Yosemite, but one salient factoid from the past several decades is the seemingly inordinate number of deaths at the El Portal Administrative Site. At least eleven fatal motor vehicle accidents have happened here, accounting for a dozen deaths, several of them by drowning in the Merced. The place itself has a late history as a federal acquisition. In 1958, the NPS acquired 1,200 acres just beyond the Park's western boundary along California State Route 140 where it parallels the Merced River for 1.8 miles before entering the western end of Yosemite Valley—sixteen miles from the Valley's center. This stretch encompassed most of the small community of El Portal, within Mariposa County. The reason for acquiring this land was to relocate utilities, maintenance shops, housing, offices, and other support infrastructure out of Yosemite Valley so as to stay in keeping with the Yosemite National Park General Management Plan. Congress codified El Portal in Title 16, United States Code, Section 47-1 and in Public Law 85-922, Sections 1-6, September 2, 1958, 72 Stat.1772. This Act provides that the laws and regulations of Yosemite National Park shall not apply within the site. Even so, the Secretary of the Interior still regulates its wise use, management, and control. The Park and Mariposa County share jurisdiction there, with the latter having the primary responsibility for higher level criminal cases and coroner's duties.

Notwithstanding this, Park search, rescue, fire, and emergency medical services' personnel frequently are the "first-in" responders to incidents—fatal or otherwise—within the El Portal Administrative Site and also in the greater area of El Portal town along both sides of the Merced River stretching for several miles. Indeed, rangers staff a Ranger Station *on* the administrative site while neither the Mariposa County Sheriff's Office nor the California Highway Patrol now staffs a substation in El Portal. Thus, the Park plays a significant safety role both on and near the El Portal Administrative Site. None of this, however, explains how so many drivers have failed to negotiate the curves here and to crash off the highway, often into the nearby Merced and a watery grave, to the extent of labeling it the most lethal stretch of road in or near Yosemite.

On another tack, not every accident in Yosemite has emerged from an "innocent" mistake—or even from culpable negligence. A few accidents have spun out of purely criminal acts. The front page of the August 15, 1915, *Mariposa Gazette* explains how W. S. Riddell "stole a large automobile at Wawona [on July 25]. In making his getaway the machine was ran [sic] over a bank and abandoned." The record subsequent to this news flash is unclear as to whether or not Mr. Riddell, who survived, ever felt the "long hand of the law." During that era—as it remains today—the "pinch-point control" at the Park's year-around Entrance Stations (coupled with a convoluted system of 360 miles of paved roads) makes it extremely difficult for someone to steal a car from *within* the Park then pull off a successful exit. What happens more often is someone steals an automobile from outside and brings it in.

An unusual instance of this began on October 4, 1994, when a clergyman and his wife in Dana Point, (Southern) California recognized a young "troubled person" and "offered her help as she had no place to live." The person was 18-year-old Theresa May Mitchell of Corvallis, Oregon. The clergyman and his wife not only offered Mitchell shelter in their own home, they also gave her a new Bible and, they believed, a better way to look at the future.

This arrangement lasted four days. Then, instead of accepting sanctuary and perhaps at least doing some serious regrouping, the teenager surreptitiously sought out the couple's checkbook. She then tore two blank checks from the back, forged them for $800, and cashed them. She made her getaway in their 1990 Mercury Sable.

Craving company, Mitchell teamed up with a 20-year-old friend from San Diego named Todd. He was willing to joyride with her to Yosemite, but he soon began wondering why he had been so lax about his own self-preservation. She was such a bad driver that he began to suspect they might never make it that far without crashing. He considered taking the wheel himself, but then had second thoughts about this too. After all, she had "borrowed" this car without asking (he had made her promise, he would later say, that she would return it) and she was driving it. If they got stopped and busted by law enforcement for auto theft he could claim no knowledge of the car or anything else. He'd been hitchhiking, he could claim, and had merely accepted a ride. Were he instead caught behind the wheel he would go to jail without "passing go" and without collecting two-hundred dollars. Nope, she was the one who had to drive.

But to improve their odds of making it all the way to Yosemite, Todd now found that he had to remind her to stop at every stop sign, to slow down in traffic and for speed limits, to not drive down one-way streets in the wrong direction, and so on. Not only did he have to do this, he had to do it carefully because, when confronted, Todd would later explain, "she freaks and makes things worse." Todd's vigilant "backseat" driving was spurred by his conviction that if the police tried to stop them, Theresa would try to evade capture by outracing them. And if she could not manage to drive competently when she was not being chased, well, it would be suicide to be in the car with her when she was.

Theresa may sound like a classic doped-out druggie on the run but, according to Todd, "Drugs were not a part of the picture." Instead, he thought, she had other problems. He had the impression, for example, that she had been a "prostitute" previously and maybe for quite a while. He thought she had been arrested in Sacramento or Oakland when she was only 13 or 14 years old.

It would seem that Todd was working assiduously at keeping a low profile. Even so, a background check on him and Theresa Mitchell would later reveal that both of them had previously managed to collect felony warrants for a burglary in Chula Vista, California that pre-dated this joy ride.

The two made it to the Park on October 14, 1994, with themselves and their wheels still in one piece. They decided to stay in the Wawona Campground. Todd tried to start a campfire at their site but he could not get it to burn.

Frustrated, he asked Mitchell to drive to the Wawona Store for better wood. Agreeing, she drove off alone.

After sunset that evening Ranger Mike Brindero watched a 1990 Mercury Sable make a "California Stop" exiting the Mariposa Grove. The car rolled past the stop sign then cruised through the intersection in front of him. Brindero quickly fell in behind the vehicle. He soon found that it was going 40 to 45 miles per hour in a zone posted at 35 mph. Brindero continued to follow. He gave the driver a few minutes to get his or her act together. When, instead of slowing down, the driver continued speeding, the ranger lit up the overhead emergency lights of his marked patrol car.

Nothing. The young woman at the wheel failed to stop. Instead she cruised by at least two empty turnouts as she hurried north, away from the South Entrance. Brindero continued following, his reds and blues winking.

Within a mile, the Mercury eased in behind a large motor home going the same direction. Apparently its driver saw Brindero's white ranger car. The recreational vehicle now edged over to the side of the road. Instantly the Mercury crossed the double yellow lines and sped around the bigger rig.

As the Mercury continued to accelerate, Brindero finally activated his siren. The car ahead sped up more. The ranger felt his adrenaline level soar as what initially had seemed to him to be a mere inattentive driver now ratcheted up to a high speed chase on a very curvy low speed road.

He glanced at his speedometer. It read just under sixty miles per hour. Yet the Mercury ahead of him continued to pull away. Mere seconds later, the sedan ahead vanished from Brindero's sight on the twisting road.

Halfway between the South Entrance Station and the Wawona Hotel, Brindero, still in hot pursuit, suddenly came upon a large cloud "enveloping both lanes and adjacent property."

Ranger Brindero hit his brake pedal and eased through the dust particles now shimmering so brightly in his headlights as to seem opaque. Beyond the cloud he spotted the fugitive sedan. The Mercury had slid off the roadway and now sat in the dirt right side up.

He positioned his cruiser to help protect the scene. Then he exited it and rushed to the stolen car.

Yes, the sedan sat there upright, but it had been badly wrecked. Its roof was crunched. Brindero quickly saw that the car had hit a tree at high speed. He peered inside. He saw 18-year-old Theresa May Mitchell trapped behind the wheel.

He tried to open the driver's door. It would not budge. He reached through the window into the interior to assess the woman's airway. Even hampered by the dark and the dust and the jammed door, Brindero could see that her breathing was shallow and rapid. She was in shock from her injuries. These likely consisted at the minimum, he guessed, of her chest having been impacted against the steering wheel. She needed medical help and she needed it fast.

Brindero carefully repositioned the injured woman's head to keep her airway open. Soon other responders arrived on the scene. The team quickly stabilized Mitchell, extracted her from the crushed car, strapped her to a backboard, and placed her on advanced life support. This included giving high-flow oxygen by mask and infusing her with an IV.

The Park ambulance rushed Theresa Mitchell to the South Entrance. There they swiftly transferred her to a Sierra Ambulance. Ranger Mike Brindero and Ranger/Park Medic Evan Jones jumped in the rig to assist the attendant as they rushed her to Oakhurst. Before an hour had passed, this team had transferred her aboard a Life Flight to Fresno's Valley Medical Center.

Forty-five minutes after her Life Flight eased down on the helipad at the Level I Trauma Center in Fresno, the physician there pronounced young Theresa May Mitchell dead.

As we have seen, people can die on (or off) the road for the most trivial of reasons—reasons that, were they to be inscribed on the victims' tombstones, would read far worse than ironic to those still alive. Yet another example of this emerged at 1:10 in the afternoon of May 3, 1992, when a passing motorist anxiously flagged down Seasonal Rangers Jose Figueroa and Steve Weinstock. A vehicle, the motorist said urgently, had just gone off the road and over the side near San Joaquin Overlook about half a mile from the Crane Flat Heliport Road. The two rangers hustled. They arrived on scene within three minutes. A few minutes behind them Sub-District Ranger Dave Lattimore also raced to the site of the accident.

Figueroa and Weinstock found a small crowd of onlookers gesturing excitedly as they stared down the steep embankment. Forty feet below the shoulder, a 1984 Ford Ranger pickup truck had wedged with its driver side down against a fir tree. The thin roof of the cab had caved in. The windshield had smashed and now dangled spiderweb-like from its rubber molding. When the roof had collapsed, the rear window had ceased to be. Its former opening now scrunched almost closed. Ominously, as the rangers now scrambled down the rocky slope they smelled the stench of fresh oil and raw gasoline mixed with the odors of disturbed soil and the scent of bruised pine needles.

The rangers also saw a barely perceptible wisp of gray smoke drifting upwards from the front end of the wreck.

Despite the flashy Hollywood pyrotechnics we gape at in movies and on TV shows, statistically few vehicle crashes burst into flames. Fortunately, emergency responders in the real world seldom face rescuing people from a burning car in imminent danger of exploding. Ironic now, Victor Ibsen, the 31-year-old driver of this smashed little truck, was a fireman from the San Francisco Bay Area.

Ibsen and a female buddy, Jill Korte of Redwood City, California, had been rock climbing in the Park and now had been driving out.

A bumblebee had blown into the cab. Instead of pulling off to the shoulder, Ibsen had continued to drive the winding road while trying to herd the venomous winged menace out. As he swatted at and dodged away from the bee, he had swerved off track. Next, trying to get back on track, he over corrected.

Before Korte even knew how, "we were upside down."

As he neared the wreck Ranger Figueroa saw Ibsen. The man was still strapped in his seatbelt. But despite this restraint, his body now partially protruded out the driver's window and lay embedded into the dirt and rocks. Indeed the impact had nearly buried Ibsen's face in the soil. His awkward position suggested that he had been partially ejected at the very moment his truck rolled to a halt against the tree. Then it had jammed him into the ground. Luckily for Korte, she had been able to crawl out her side of the Ford.

Figueroa quickly assessed the sharp, unnatural angle at which the victim's neck now canted. This driver's plight, the ranger now realized, was about as critical as it could get—if this guy was even still alive.

He was. Both rangers now heard his gurgling, restricted breathing in the dirt.

They assessed his level of consciousness. Ibsen proved unresponsive, even to pain. This meant that—if this man was to have any chance to survive—they would have to get him out of the wrecked truck and the dirt and to medical help without delay.

During the mere minute in which helpers had scrambled down the slope and sized up Ibsen's plight, that thin wisp of smoke had turned heavy and dark.

That this mangled little vehicle would explode into a fireball at any second spurred a surge of adrenaline and a frightening sense of added urgency. The rescuers now redoubled their efforts to free this victim. Figueroa, leaning into the cramped, jumbled, crushed cab, twisted and tugged on the man's right arm. Ibsen barely budged. He was truly pinned somehow, but no one could determine how. Not only did the contorted wreckage conceal and confuse their ability to analyze, the thickening smoke boiling out from under the engine hood and through the dashboard transmuted the entire scene into a murky, choking, semi-blind nightmare.

They knew a fire truck was hurrying to their position. But it was not *here*. It was still only en route. They hustled back up the slope for fire extinguishers. The first one they used knocked the flames down. Great. Instantly one of the responders again reached inside to haul out Ibsen. Yet again the man failed to budge. No one knew yet that Ibsen's left arm had wrapped around and under the doorpost, virtually locking him down under the weight of the vehicle. Worse, mere seconds after having used that first fire extinguisher, the seemingly extinguished blaze burst back into life.

Flames now engulfed the entire engine compartment. The fire soon snaked into the cab. The crowd up on the road produced more fire extinguishers. The rangers gratefully used every one, but each proved effective only for mere moments.

Fueled by gasoline draining from the carburetor, fuel lines, and fuel pump under the crumpled hood, the blaze repeatedly redoubled itself. The upholstery began to melt and bubble. These popped and shot hot wads of melting plastic onto the rescuers. Now not only were the responders unable to control the fire, they soon found themselves unable to endure the searing heat enough to even stay near the trapped victim.

A swirl of flames suddenly engulfed the vehicle. The fire continued burning for at least two minutes. The rangers stared helplessly. They felt acutely aware that, despite Ibsen's unconscious state, the man inside those flames had been alive. Being now prevented from helping him and being forced instead to simply stand and watch and imagine what was happening to him proved to be the worst sort of mental torment. The only anodyne for their anguish resided in knowing that the trapped man was unconscious.

The Park fire crew arrived on scene then controlled the blaze. The rangers rushed back to the victim. With enough manpower they finally were able to right the vehicle. Unbelievably, they found Ibsen still alive. But despite the heroic efforts of everyone on this scene, the badly injured man survived only another thirty minutes.

Victor Ibsen's nightmarish death unsettled many of his rescuers. So much so that the Park brought in a Critical Incident Stress Debriefing Team to assist these professionals work through the trauma of having watched the trapped 31-year-old firefighter burn. Ranger Dave Lattimore, for example, was a veteran of many horrible body recoveries and twisted motor vehicle accidents. Yet Ibsen's death had affected even him to the point where, while showering three days after the wreck, he had burst into tears.

Unlike most California roads, those in Yosemite were designed and built to blend into the landscape and to create minimal impact to scenery and ecology. The bottom line for safe driving here may be embodied in one simple statement: When driving in Yosemite, safe speeds are imperative; more important yet, driving should be the one and only activity in which the driver is engaged. Splitting one's attention with any other task or action can all too quickly become lethal.

TABLE 8. FATAL MISHAPS INVOLVING HORSE-DRAWN WAGONS, MOTOR VEHICLES, AND BICYCLES. (Incidents discussed in text are noted.)

Name, age	Date	Location	*Circumstances*
Fatalities Involving Horse-Drawn Wagons:			
J. Sanders "Harry" Wright, 6	September 20, 1888	Bridalveil Meadow	*The boy, a San Franciscan and the grandson of the Cooks who ran a local hotel, was crushed beneath a rear wheel of his mother's carriage (driven by John Caynor) when he fell out onto the rocky road near Bridalveil Fall.* (in text)

unnamed woman

August ?, 1902 — Yosemite Valley

Two women from Stent were riding in their horse-drawn rig. They stopped. One disembarked. As the other started to, her sun bonnet spooked the horse. It flew into a gallop, bouncing the second woman from the speeding wagon. "She was cut dreadfully about the head and one of her ears was torn off," noted the Mariposa Gazette. *"They say she cannot live." Unfortunately the article included neither woman's name nor the outcome of her accident.* (not included in statistics)

James Mason Hutchings, 78

October 31, 1902 — Old Big Oak Flat Road, near base of El Capitan

As British-born 49-er and pioneer Yosemite author, guide, and hotel manager Hutchings and his wife were descending the final part of the road, one horse of his team spooked and bolted. The wagon bucked hard, sending Hutchings flying head first into boulders. (in text)

R. S. Leisenring, 70 — June 3, 1911 — Old Wawona Road, above present-day
Sarah Diefendorfer, 65 — June 8, 1911 — Wawona Tunnel

On June 3 the stagecoach jumped over the road embankment and wrecked. Leisenring of Allen Park, Pennsylvania died immediately. Diefendorfer also of Allen Park died 5 days later. (in text)

James McCauley, 70

June 24, 1911 — Old Coulterville Road, below Foresta

McCauley, another Yosemite innkeeper and long-time Valley resident died in a wagon wreck caused by a runaway horse on the Coulterville Grade.

Motor Vehicle Fatalities:

Charles A. Clark, 42

September 26, 1918 — below Pohono Bridge, near Powerhouse

Park Foreman for road construction Clark died on the road he supervised building from El Portal. His truck veered off a sharp curve and rolled over. Clark lay pinned for 12 hours under a boulder his Ford had loosened. Another driver saw him at 7:45 a.m. (in text)

Dortha N. McCormick, 49 — August 14, 1924 — Old Big Oak Flat Road
Charles J. McCormick, 54 — August 15, 1924

The McCormicks, husband and wife from Chicago, died due to an accident while driving up the controlled incline above the El Capitan Guard Station.

Grant Hagerman, adult
Johan Karlson, 50
Thomas Martin, 50
William J. Larsen, 45

September 23, 1926 — below Pohono Bridge, near Powerhouse

Fourteen men were in the back of a Ford truck en route to a construction site on the lower El Portal Road. The driver missed a gear. The freewheeling truck missed a curve and hit a huge rock. Rangers found the "Ruckstell axle…into neutral…cutting out the low, reverse, or brake on the…transmission…driver only had the emergency brake…and…gear shift lever not…properly fastened to the frame…and…poor condition of emergency brake." Larsen died on September 28. (in text)

William J. Kennett, 11

July 21, 1927 Stoneman Bridge, Yosemite Valley
Pedestrian *Kennett of Los Angeles "was run over by a truck on the Stoneman Bridge and had his legs crushed so badly he died the same day."*

Olive Heisler, 29

December 17, 1927 Lower Valley
Heisler of Kerman, California was ***a passenger thrown from an overturned car****.*

William H. Lansdale, 61

May 9, 1930 Cascade Creek
Lansdale of Walnut Creek, California ***hit a rock****.*

Haig Dalitian, 22

January 15, 1931 Northside Drive, near Rocky Point
Dalitian of Fresno was a passenger when the car went off the road and ***hit a tree****. He died 4 days later in LMH of pneumonia.*

Bert E. Hearn, 26

June 14, 1934 ½ mile north of Chinquapin Junction
Off-duty Park employee Hearn, a local Native American of Bear Creek, California, drove his Model T over an embankment, probably while ***speeding****.*

Earl Merrill Clough, 27

June 20, 1934 Wawona Road, near Bishop Creek
Working for a road contractor on Glacier Point, Clough of Watsonville, California was ***speeding*** *on his* ***motorcycle*** *and hit a Ford head-on in Yosemite's first fatal motorcycle accident.* (in text)

John Quici, 53

May 12, 1935 1 mile south of Chinquapin Junction
Quici of Merced, California died instantly when his ***car rolled over*** *several times.*

Charles Albitz, 32

September 2, 1936 Northside Drive, near Yosemite Lodge
Curry Co. employee Albitz ***hit a tree*** *just west of the Yosemite Lodge due to "****careless driving****."*

Ernest C. Gance, 20
Owen R. Meeks, 19

April 3, 1937 Wawona
Civilian Conservation Corps (CCC) enrollees Gance of Bozoo and Meeks of Stony Bottom, West Virginia drove over a 100-foot embankment.

Marjorie Dellenbaugh, 14

July 9, 1937 1 mile west of Glacier Point
Dellenbaugh of Oakland died pinned under a car that had rolled over because the 17-year-old driver was ***speeding*** *and* ***hit a tree****.*

Ella Gutshalk, 51

July 25, 1937 Old Big Oak Flat Road
Gutshalk of South San Francisco died when her husband drove his Lincoln coupe over a 60-foot bank and landed in an oak tree. No one found them for 3 hours.

Hilmar Heldal, 32

August 2, 1937 Old Big Oak Flat Road
On July 21 Heldal, a ***pedestrian*** *working for a Park road contractor, took refuge under a large dump truck during nearby blasting. The driver did not see him and drove over him.* (also listed in Chapter 4. Park Builders)

Earl Arthur, 20
January 9, 1938 Wawona Tunnel, Discovery View
Buck Meadows CCC man Arthur of Lamar, Oklahoma ***was thrown from the rear of a truck*** *carrying 26 men when it slid into the* ***icy*** *Discovery View area at the Tunnel.*

Mrs. George Gregson, 26
January 2, 1939 between Bridalveil Junction and Wawona Tunnel
Gregson of West Los Angeles died because her husband crashed and drove 150 feet off the road down a steep mountainside and ***hit a large tree*** *on December 26, 1938.*

George D. Evanson, 18
August 27, 1939 Wawona Road
*Curry Co. employee Evanson of Fresno died as a passenger when the vehicle he was in skidded off the road due to "****excessive speed****.*

Clarence Switzer, 19
August 27, 1939 El Portal
Switzer of El Portal, California was riding a ***motorcycle*** *and "hit a car."*

Anita L. Otter, 34
March 3, 1940 between Bridalveil Junction and Wawona Tunnel
Otter of Yosemite died in LMH after an accident the previous day, when her car went off road and rolled 60 feet down a slope.

Jeane Chloe Batson, 52
Nina Della Batson, 49
July 23, 1941 Tioga Road, near White Wolf
The Batson sisters of Clarksburg, West Virginia were killed when Chloe's husband drove his new Pontiac sedan off a straight stretch of road and ***hit a fir tree*** *18 inches thick. The official report noted: "The cause of the accident is unknown."*

Alcid Joseph Guy, 34
September 13, 1941 2 miles east of Badger Pass
Curry Co. employee Guy of Canada died of a head injury when his body was caught underneath his overturned car after he failed to negotiate a curve on Glacier Point Road.

William Henry Dickenson, adult
May 27, 1945 1 mile west of Arch Rock
Pasadena Junior College student Dickenson of Roswell, New Mexico vanished in late March. On May 27, the wheel of his car was found in the Merced. Searching revealed his Model A Ford but not him. (also listed in Chapter 12. Lost)

Robert E. Esparza, 16
February 22, 1947 South Entrance
Esparza of Fresno was ***speeding*** *when his car overturned.*

Martha C. Vissera, 50
Ollie Myrtle Schieck, 49
June 9, 1947 Northside Drive, 1.5 miles west of Yosemite
June 13, 1947 Lodge
Vissera of Los Angeles died of head injuries when her husband Schieck skidded onto the shoulder, lost control, and ***hit a tree****.*

Allie W. Kincaid, 46
June 13, 1947 Old Big Oak Flat Road, near Crane Creek
Off-duty Yosemite Blister Rust crewman Kincaid died of a crushed chest when the car he was riding in skidded off the road and landed in the creek. ***Alcohol use*** *was suspected.*

Frederick Earl Wilson, 25 — June 25, 1948 — Wawona
NPS Maintenance employee Wilson of Wawona died as a passenger when the driver ***lost control*** *and his car overturned.*

Mary Lee DeSilva, 16 — August 13, 1948 — Wawona
Frederick DeSilva, 59 — August 20, 1948
Frederick DeSilva of San Diego likely ***dozed off*** *on a straight stretch of road and* ***hit a tree****. His daughter Mary Lee died immediately. He died a week later.*

Larry Ben Webb, 18 — August 10, 1951 — Cascade Creek Bridge
Webb of Merced, California hit the bridge abutment.

Peter Townsend Wilkes, 17 — July 4, 1952 — 2 miles east of Tuolumne Meadows
Wilkes of Glendale, California was ***speeding*** *when his car clipped another car and overturned.*

Vera Moore Nelson, 40 — July 15, 1952 — Wawona Road, near Grouse Creek
Nelson of Glendale, California died when her husband ***dozed off*** *while driving then rolled 300 feet down an embankment and* ***crashed into a tree****.*

John Conrad Lighthouse, 19 — December 29, 1952 — west of Pohono Bridge
Pedestrian *Lighthouse of Oakland fell on the* ***icy*** *road then a car ran over him.*

Robert Curtis Gibson, 18 — May 29, 1954 — west of Mirror Lake
Gibson of Inglewood, California ***hit a tree*** *on the hill below Mirror Lake.*

Mary Paras Jameson, 36 — September 4, 1954 — 1.6 miles west of Old Village
Jameson of Culver City, California was riding as Mrs. Christiansen drove. At 5 a.m., she ***dozed off at the wheel*** *and* ***hit a tree.*** *Of the 5 people in the car only Jameson was killed.*

Charles Sherman Welch, 39 — May 28, 1955 — Tioga Road into Dana Creek
Welch of Mill Valley, California was in a car driven by Jack MacKechnie who, while ***fighting against dozing off,*** *drove off a 150-foot bank into a rollover. Welch died of a fractured skull.*

Rex Phillip Whitfield, 3 months — July 5, 1957 — Highway 140, west of Arch Rock
Yosemite resident Whitfield's father was driving and got into a 2-car crash.

Donald Lincoln Hibbard, 18 — August 9, 1957 — Wawona Tunnel
Hibbard of West Ridge, New Hampshire survived his August 2nd accident one week, details unknown.

Sverre Gunnar Johannesen, 56 — July 17, 1958 — Wawona Road, near Bishop Creek
Johannesen of Glendale, California drove off the road, injuring his 4 passengers.

Ralph Arancibia, 46 — September 29, 1958 — Big Oak Flat Road, 5 miles from Valley
Park Contractor Arancibia of Merced ***dozed off*** *while driving.*

Gilbert Mancillas, 18	May 21, 1959	west of Mirror Lake
	Mancillas of Fresno ***hit a tree*** *then slid into Tenaya Creek for 4 hours.*	
William Gerald Mouser, 44	July 23, 1959	between Pohono Bridge and Arch Rock
	Mouser of Santa Rosa, California drove solo, east and off the road at 4:45 a.m. and ***hit a tree and rock.***	
Lloyd Delvis Bradshaw, 20	August 25, 1959	Bridalveil Junction area
	Curry Co. employee Bradshaw of Mariposa was ***speeding*** *and* ***hit a tree****, and overturned.* ***Alcohol*** *was a factor.*	
Frank Charles Mason, 21	January 16, 1961	Northside Drive, near Valley View
	Badger Pass ski instructor Mason of Ontario, Canada was ***speeding*** *on an* ***icy*** *road, skidded, overturned, and* ***hit a tree.***	
Donald J. Defendis, 18	June 23, 1961	Chinquapin Junction area
	Defendis of Italy was ***speeding*** *when he crashed.*	
Marion N. Elston, 44	July 6, 1962	Big Oak Flat Road, near Crane Flat
	Road contractor Elston of Riverbank, California was driving a tanker truck, rolled it, was ejected, and the truck crushed him.	
Wayne W. Station, 32	September 29, 1962	north end of Sentinel Bridge
	Curry Co. employee Station of Visalia, California drowned when the car flipped and slid into the Merced. The driver was found guilty of ***drunk*** *driving.* (also listed in Chapter 10. Drowning)	
Douglas H. Thomas, 44	June 23, 1963	near Wawona Campground
	Off-duty NPS Trails' foreman Thomas drove off an embankment.	
Fritz Bertram Lorenz, Jr., 6	September 7, 1964	Village Road, near Happy Isles
	Pedestrian *Lorenz of Fairfield, California darted toward a moving NPS pickup and hit its side.*	
Ramona Ann Hauser, 8	August 15, 1965	1 mile west of Tioga Pass
	Hauser of Los Angeles ***fell off a moving pickup truck*** *and died of head injuries.*	
Terrance Michael Earnshaw, 23	June 30, 1966	Southside Drive, 4 miles west of Village
	Earnshaw of San Francisco was killed when the car he was riding in exited the road at 2 a.m. and ***hit a tree.***	
Dan Allen Jones, 21	August 15, 1966	W of El Portal Administrative Site
	Concession employee Jones of Kingsburg, California was drunk driving his Triumph after midnight on Highway 140, rolled it at a curve and skidded 100 yards upside down. (not in text)	
Minnie B. Ticktin, 58	August 2, 1967	Tioga Road, 2.5 miles E of White Wolf Junct.
	Ticktin of Bronx, New York was driving a car whose accelerator stuck. The car sped out of control, missed a curve, and struck a rocky bank.	

Rae S. Nome, 69	August 10, 1967 Southside Drive, Yosemite Valley *Mrs. Nome of Palm Springs, California was killed when her husband Mourey, age 73, driving, suddenly veered off the road and* ***crashed through brush and hit a tree****.*
William Shiels, 62	September 2, 1968 Tioga Road, near Tenaya Lake *On August 31, Shiels of Australia lost control of his* ***motorcycle*** *and slammed into an embankment.*
Richard L. Cox, 24	September 18, 1968 Big Oak Flat Road N of Hwy 120/140 intersection *Cox of Citrus Heights, California was on a* ***motorcycle*** *that hit a retaining wall then flew over it. His body and the survivor with him likely lay there all night.*
Hugh Mowery, 48	September 24, 1968 El Portal Administrative Site *Off-duty NPS painter Mowery of El Portal failed to negotiate a curve near the incinerator and crashed his* ***motorcycle.***
Emanuel Feibelman, 32	December 7, 1968 Wawona *Feibelman of Fresno was a passenger thrown from a vehicle that wrecked after hitting* ***ice****.*
Enrique Leon Rios, 27 Maria Teresa Valenzuela, 35	July 4, 1969 Tioga Road, at Lukens Lake Trailhead *Peruvian Los Angelenos Valenzuela and Rios "failed to negotiate a curve" and* ***hit a tree****.*
Dale Aaron Brown, 26	January 26, 1970 El Portal Administrative Site *Off-duty NPS Powerhouse employee Brown of El Portal skidded off the road in his VW bus and down a 40-foot bank into the river. He escaped the VW, doffed his clothes, and made it to a mid-river rock where he likely died of hypothermia.*
James L. Walls, 40 Joy Lee Walls, 39 James Douglas Walls, 11	February 28, 1970 Wawona Tunnel parking lot *A 22-year-old man* ***sped*** *his car from the tunnel, jumped the curb, and crushed the 3* ***pedestrian*** *Walls of Merced against a wall at Discovery View. The Walls' 14-year-old daughter Susan was unhurt. A Jury indicted the driver for manslaughter.* (in text)
Howard Clinton Rufus, 64	June 6, 1970 Ahwahnee Hotel Road *While driving a* ***motorbike****, Dr. Rufus of Yorktown, Virginia was hit by a VW van.*
Mary Dodson, 69	June 12, 1970 Tioga Road *Dodson of Ingram, Texas survived her June 4 wreck for 8 days.*
William Richard Shaffner, 22	August 8, 1970 El Portal Administrative Site *Shaffner of Hanford, California drove his car into a rollover.*
Francisco Zarate, 21	August 18, 1971 Wawona Road, near Alder Creek *Off-duty NPS Fire Control Aid Zarate of Planard, California was a* ***pedestrian*** *found dead on the road. At 4:15 a.m., a logging truck ran over him. Zarate was the victim of an earlier* ***hit and run****.*

Ludivina G. Sosa, 15 Elvira Garza, 15	November 14, 1971	Wawona Road, near Mosquito Creek *Both women of Madera, Calif. drove over a 100-foot embankment.*
Johnnie B. Lokey, 42	October 27, 1972	Wawona Tunnel *Lokey of Fresno was driving the dairy truck down the tunnel when engine heat melted the electrical-taped repair of his engine distributor cap. It disintegrated, killing the engine that also powered his brakes. He crashed and became a cottage cheese-covered corpse.*
Oscar L. Craddock, 30	July 11, 1974	Northside Drive, west of Yosemite Lodge *Craddock of Hayward, California failed to negotiate a curve and **hit a tree.** He was **speeding** so fast that the impact shocked and vibrated the tree hard enough to snap off its top 20 feet.*
Phillip Max Kurck, 66	December 28, 1974	Chinquapin Junction area *Kurck of Fresno, driving a small car, **hit a Yosemite Transportation System Bus head-on**, details as to why were not released.*
Rhonda Ann Stumbaugh, 16	June 22, 1975	Northside Drive, 1 mile west of Yosemite Lodge *Stumbaugh of Kettleman City, California was a **passenger** in a car driven by a **drunk** driver who **hit a tree**. This now injured driver had fled from yet an earlier wreck that day.*
Oliver A. Deleissegues, 28	July 6, 1975	Hwy 140 west of Arch Rock *Curry Co. plumber Deleissegues of El Portal was **drunk** driving his **motorcycle** when he struck the rock retaining wall. He flew headfirst over the wall and into boulders below.*
William Wayne Anderson, Jr., 26	July 21, 1975	Northside Drive, near El Capitan Bridge *Anderson of Clovis, California lost control of his **motorcycle**.*
Brian A. Ridpath, 29	July 25, 1975	3 miles north of Chinquapin Junction *Ridpath of Berkeley, California drove over an embankment.*
Todd M. Rinnman, 17 Gregory B. Casey, 16	August 26, 1975	Northside Drive, near Black Springs *Rinnman of Harbor City and Casey of Glendale, California were riding a **motorcycle** when they flew off the road.*
Roderick Marquez, 19 Kirk D. Greenwalt, 19	October 4, 1975	south of Wawona Tunnel *Marquez of Henderson, Nevada was **speeding**, missed a curve, and wrecked. He and Greenwalt of Richardson, Texas were killed.*
Paul A. Carlson, 21	September 18, 1976	below Pohono Bridge, near The Cascades *Carlson of Worchester, Massachusetts was a passenger on a **motorcycle** that wrecked.*
Phillip A. Kruse, 21	May 27, 1977	near Big Oak Flat Entrance Station ***Speeding** his **motorcycle**, Kruse of Hayward, California crossed the center line and hit a car head-on.*
Jane Witucki, 20	July 9, 1977	below Pohono Bridge, near The Cascades *Curry Co. employee Witucki of Concord, California was a passenger in a VW van that **hit a tree** on July 5.*

Timothy W. Ingles, 20

May 27, 1978 Southside Drive, east of Bridalveil Junction
*Ingles of Hayward, California was in a convertible at 3 a.m. which skidded, **hit a tree**, and flipped into the river. He likely drowned under his vehicle. A helicopter hunting for a drowning victim from the day before spotted him.* (also listed in Chapter 10. Drowning)

Alexander Mazen, 81

July 25, 1978 Wawona Tunnel parking lot
*On June 27, **pedestrian** Mazen of Seal Beach, California walked in front of the east tunnel opening, was struck by a Curry Co. tow truck, and knocked 70 feet.*

Richard A. Carlton, 17

August 5, 1978 ½ mile north of Chinquapin Junction
*Carlton of Newark, California was driving a **motorcycle** and hit a motor home head-on.*

Derrol E. Mendosa, 19

August 5, 1978 ½ mile north of Chinquapin Junction
*Mendosa of Newark, California, avoided the motor home that Carlton (above) hit but he still ran his **motorcycle** off the road.*

Peter Gunter, 26
Annette Beckmann, 26

June 25, 1979 1.6 miles north of Foresta Road Junction ("Asphalt Curve")
Driver Gunter and Beckmann of Germany were driving the open lane in a road repaving zone and were struck by a truck and 2 trailers filled with asphalt. Gunter was crushed immediately. Beckmann slowly suffocated and cooked under the hot asphalt. (in text)

Lee Eldon Dawson, 29

July 3, 1979 Crane Flat area
*Californian Dawson wrecked his **motorcycle**. He was evacuated by air to Fresno where he died.*

Young Nom Yang, 19
Won Sohn, 17

August 24, 1979 Village Road, at Curry Four Way
*Yang of Honolulu and Sohn of San Francisco were racing another vehicle at high **speed** (nearly hitting Mike Pass riding his Moped). They next lost control entering the intersection, slid through it, and **hit trees** on the other side. Their car roof had to be cut off to extract them.*

Stephen Cole Hamilton, 32

September 18, 1979 2.8 miles west of Crane Flat
Hamilton of Oakland crashed and was ejected through the roof of his Toyota Land Cruiser as it rumbled down a steep, 75-foot embankment. The wreck was discovered later by a Park visitor.

John DeSoto, 18
Robert W. DeSoto, 50

September 23, 1979 Tioga Road, Crane Flat area
The father-son DeSotos of Fountain Valley, California crashed their motor home off the road and down a 30-foot embankment and were killed instantly.

James W. Karim, 18

September 29, 1979 1.5 miles south of Wawona Tunnel
Curry Co. employee Karim of Sacramento lost control of his car and struck the guard wall. His roof had to be cut off.

Anthony T. Berry, Jr., 18

October 26, 1979 Northside Drive, 1.5 miles west of Camp 4
*Curry Co. employee Berry of Schenectady, New York lost control of his **motorcycle** and **hit a tree**. His passenger survived.*

Lorinda Anne Kimball, 20	April 21, 1980	El Portal Administrative Site
	Curry Co. employee Kimball crashed her VW bug into the Merced River. As her car was towed toward shore, 30 feet from it she was sucked free and carried downstream. Her body was recovered the next day. (also in Chapter 10. Drowning)	
James Duane Wilson, 23	July 16, 1980	below Pohono Bridge, near The Cascades
	El Portal motel employee Wilson of Yosemite ***failed to negotiate a curve****, hit a cement wall, and rolled his car over.*	
Charles C. Oberman, 25	June 13, 1981	Tenaya Lake, at Murphy Creek Picnic Area
	Lieutenant Oberman of George Air Force Base crashed his ***motorcycle*** *at* ***high speed*** *and landed in rocks.*	
Willard Westly Harling, 62	February 16, 1982	6.5 miles north of Wawona
	Curry Co. bus driver Harling died when a supply truck he was driving at 5 a.m. rounded a blind and foggy curve and dropped into a ***15-foot deep, 35-foot long washout*** *created only seconds before his arrival. Several days of heavy storm waters had caused the sudden blow-out of a plugged culvert. An investigation by a soil expert revealed that the fill placed into this curve during CCC days was inappropriate.*	
Mark Bernard Bizzini, 20 Charles Robert Tant, 20	June 9, 1982	1.6 miles north of Foresta Road Junction ("Asphalt Curve")
	Driver Bizzini of Tracy, California and Tant of Prairieville, Louisiana were ***drunk*** *and* ***speeding****. Their Chevrolet pickup rolled down an embankment. They were discovered 12 hours later.*	
Susan Elizabeth Cunningham, 22	July 13, 1982	Tuolumne Meadows
	Cunningham of Columbus, Ohio was a passenger in a vehicle that ***hit a rock****.*	
Stephan E. Singleton, 40	August 27, 1983	Northside Drive, west of El Capitan Bridge
	Forest Service employee Singleton of El Portal crashed his Kawasaki ***motorcycle*** *into* ***a tree*** *at the "20-mph curve."*	
Lawrence E. Welsh, 18	October 15, 1983	2 miles west of Tioga Pass
	Welsh of North Rollings, California crashed his Suzuki ***motorcycle*** *into a car.*	
Vivian Ann Burns, 25	November 27, 1983	3.7 miles south of Big Oak Flat Entrance
	Passenger Burns of Modesto, California was riding in a Fiat driven by her husband, which skidded on ***ice****, rolled over, and rumbled down a 90-foot embankment.*	
Neil Patrick Aldworth, 24	January 11, 1984	Village Road, near LeConte Memorial
	Curry Co. employee Aldworth of Wheaton, Illinois was ***drunk*** *and* ***speeding*** *when he crashed his van* ***into a tree****.*	
James Philip Baker, 38	September 2, 1984	Tioga Road, 2 miles east of Gin Flat
	Baker of Modesto was killed when his ***motorcycle*** *tire blew out and he lost control.*	

Alex N. Villalobos, 21 Linda J. Riley, 19	October 29, 1984 Village Road, near Curry Four Way ***Drunk** driver Villalobos and Riley of Dublin, California were killed while **speeding** after dark on a **motorcycle** at about 6:30 p.m. going the **wrong way on a one-way road into a pine tree.***
Won Tac Oh, 49	July 5, 1986 0.3 mile west of Porcupine Flat Campground *Oh of Azusa, California crashed his Toyota pickup and was crushed beneath it. Two of 5 passengers were injured.*
Joy Rosemary Horgan, 60	August 13, 1986 2 miles east of Crane Flat *Horgan of Kent, Great Britain died when her son drove their rental car on the "wrong side" and hit another vehicle head-on. No seatbelt.*
Hilda B. Meyer, 83	September 23, 1986 Glacier Point Road, near Washburn Point *Meyer of Algona, Iowa died when her son glanced into the rear view mirror to check on her welfare and meanwhile drove his Ford Aerostar off the road and **into a tree**.* (in text)
Debbie G. Brantley, 20 Todd Nels Smith, 20	February 18, 1987 El Portal Administrative Site *Yosemite-ites Brantley and Smith died after being ejected when their car hit the bridge abutment at Crane Creek in El Portal. They may have been **speeding**.*
Mark S. Clemons, 27	March 8, 1987 0.2 mile west of Pohono Bridge *Curry Co. employee Clemons of Midpines, California crashed his vehicle after working a split shift at a local café. **Fatigue** was likely.*
Allen Floyd Webb, 37 Jason G. Cissell, 12	June 15, 1987 Tioga Road, May Lake Junction *Webb and his stepson Cissell of Ridgecrest, California **hit a tree**. **Speeding** was likely a factor.*
Timothy Robert Taggart, 22	August 2, 1987 El Portal Administrative Site *Taggart of Yosemite, California drove his car into a rollover.*
Jill Anne Sharp, 24 Eddie Lee Collins, 40	August 22, 1987 Tioga Road, 0.4 mile west of May Lake Junction *San Franciscans Sharp with Collins died after he crossed the center-line on a curve on his **motorcycle** and hit a pickup truck head-on.*
Eric W. Foster, 25	August 30, 1987 ½ mile east of Arch Rock *Foster of Ahwahnee, California was **speeding**, went airborne off the road, and **hit a tree** 17 feet above the ground.*
Keith H. Voss, 23	July 1, 1988 1.7 miles east of White Wolf *Voss of El Cajon, California drove his car into a rollover.*
Patrick Lehr, 35	August 3, 1988 Tioga Road, near Olmsted Point *Ahwahnee Hotel/Curry Co. cook Lehr rolled his Jeep off the road at 2 a.m. His Jeep caught fire and killed him. Had he **dozed off**?*
Margaret P. Kraenzel, 89	November 3, 1988 Tioga Road, near Olmsted Point *Kraenzel of Groveland, California was a passenger in a **speeding** motor home that crashed.*

Jeannie Beaudet, 64
Marie Paule Martelliere, 52

May 28, 1989 — Tioga Road, 3 miles east of Crane Flat Junction

French passengers Beaudet and Martelliere died when their car ***hit a pine tree****. The survivors sued General Motors with results unknown to us.*

Thomas T. Elkins, 32

October 5, 1989 — Tioga Road, May Lake Junction

Elkins of Albany, California was hit head-on by a vehicle in the wrong lane. John R. Mauldin, the other driver, was charged with Vehicular Manslaughter because of ***speed*** *and* ***alcohol****.*

Ronald A. Brandt, 47

December 29, 1990 — 2.3 miles north of South Entrance

Brandt of Riverside, California lost control of his car and hit an oncoming truck.

Elaine Carol Watson, 44
Lance Brian Thomas, 5
Mario Ernest Thomas, 3

May 25, 1991 — Southside Drive, 300 yards east of Bridalveil Fall Junction

Watson of Compton, California ***dozed off*** *while driving her Toyota Camry and rolled it into the Merced River with 4 other people. Watson's nephews, Lance and Mario, jumped in only to be swept downstream. Watson jumped in to save them. All three drowned.* (in text and listed in Chapter 10. Drowning)

Victor Ibsen, 31

May 3, 1992 — Big Oak Flat Road San Joaquin Overlook

Swatting at a bee, firefighter Ibsen of Mountain View, California drove his Ford Ranger pickup off the road, crashed, and was trapped in it as it burned. (in text)

David K. Gadd, 42

August 15, 1993 — 0.6 mile east of Arch Rock

Concession waiter Gadd of Yosemite was a passenger on a ***speeding motorcycle*** *that* ***hit a rock guardwall****.*

Estelle Walsh, 75
William J. Walsh, 68
Sanford Elkin, 61

July 4, 1994 — ½ mile west of Tamarack Flat

Both Walshes of Sunnyvale and Elkin from Mountain View, California died. Estelle, the driver, was not supposed to be driving due to her history of seizures. She was ***speeding so fast*** *that their vehicle went airborne and* ***hit a tree*** *ten feet above its base.*

Theresa May Mitchell, 18

October 14, 1994 — 2.4 miles north of South Entrance

Mitchell of Corvallis, Oregon ***was fleeing/speeding*** *from Ranger Mike Brindero as she drove a* ***stolen vehicle****. She lost control and* ***hit a tree****.* (in text)

Bepin Mathur, 70

December 29, 1994 — 3.5 miles east of Chinquapin Junction

Mathur of Stanford, Connecticut was a passenger in a van of 7 people. The driver slid it on ***ice*** *into an NPS snowplow, embedding the blade just behind the driver's seat. They sued the Park for $8,100,999 and lost when incident photos showed the snowplow on its own side of the road.*

James David Baker, 35

July 4, 1995 — below Pohono Bridge, near The Cascades

Baker of Modesto crashed his ***motorcycle*** *and was thrown alive into the Merced. He washed downriver and was not found until July 27.* (also listed in Chapter 10. Drowning)

Raymundo Ocampo, 30	March 16, 1996 El Portal Administrative Site *Ocampo of El Portal crashed and was ejected 100 feet from his car, dying immediately.*
Samuel B. Miller, 80	April 17, 1996 west of Arch Rock at Little Windy Point *Miller of Placentia, California was injured in a crash, details unknown, and died in Modesto.*
Chang-Jye Lin, 27 Wen-Chin Chang, 26	December 26, 1996 El Portal Administrative Site *Lin of Troy, New York and Chang of Santa Clara, California lost control and drove their vehicle into the Merced where it submerged upside down.* (also listed in Chapter 10. Drowning)
Chuen Park, 34	December 29, 1996 El Portal Administrative Site *Driver Park of San Jose, California died when his car skidded on oil leaking from a tour bus and crashed into the Merced. He floated free and drowned. Two trapped in the car were rescued by 32 NPS personnel working 3 simultaneous missions.* (also listed in Chapter 10. Drowning)
John Fazio, 58	April 27, 1997 in front of Yosemite Valley Chapel *Fazio of Fresno was killed when his* ***motorcycle*** *was cut off by another car and he was ejected.*
Kevin M. Tucker, 31	July 6, 1998 Tioga Road, 3 miles east of Crane Flat *Tucker of Great Britain was a passenger in a mini-van with 5 other Royal Air Force Personnel. Due to* ***excessive speed****, the driver lost control and* ***hit the same pine tree*** *that Jeannie Beaudet and Marie P. Martelliere hit fatally on May 28, 1989. Three helicopters arrived in response.*
Van Albert Knerr, 35	September 24, 1998 El Portal Administrative Site *Off-duty NPS employee Knerr of El Portal left the roadway with such* ***speed*** *that his Datsun 280 ZX broke in half when it* ***hit a large pine tree****.*
Nuria Pages, 43	June 8, 2000 1 mile south of Big Oak Flat Entrance *Driver Lawrence G. Tomasi, age 56, of Loma Linda, California suffered a* ***fatal heart attack and hit a tree****. His passenger Pages, also from Loma Linda, was killed.*
Shingo Takita, 19	August 26, 2000 Tioga Road, 1 mile east of Yosemite Creek Bridge *Passenger Takita from Japan was partially ejected and killed when the driver,* ***speeding****, rolled down an embankment.*
Mark Gressman, 21	May 28, 2002 El Portal Administrative Site *Gressman of Moorpark, California lost control of his pickup truck and drove it into the Merced just east of Crane Creek.* (also listed in Chapter 10. Drowning)
Peter Mauffray, 47	August 16, 2002 Southside Drive, 1 mile east of El Capitan Bridge *Mauffray of Merced was* ***speeding*** *while* ***drunk*** *and* ***hit a tree****.*

Mark W. Gomes, 38 | August 7, 2004 | below Arch Rock, near Windy Point
Gomes of Oceanside, California missed a curve on his ***motorcycle****, swung into the wrong lane, and hit a tour bus head-on.*

Tor Jensen, 46 | October 7, 2006 | Big Oak Flat Road near tunnel
Jensen of Ventura, California was driving his ***motorcycle*** *downhill, possibly (according to witnesses) over the speed limit. An oncoming car turned across Jensen's lane into a roadside pullout. Jensen collided with it and flew through the car's windshield.*

John Moore, 59 | May 7, 2007 | 0.9 mile east of Merced Grove intersection on Hwy 120
Moore of Groveland, California lost control of his Chevy Astrovan at high ***speed****, skidded 69 feet down an embankment, hit a* ***boulder****, vaulted 17 feet, then 25 feet more, landing upside down. His toxicology report indicated 0.22 %* ***alcohol****.*

Patrick Arthur Westfall, 47 | September 10, 2008 | south of Wawona Tunnel, Hwy 41
Westfall of Belmont Shore, California lost control of his ***motorcycle****.*

Catheryn Friesen, 20 | October 1, 2009 | Tioga Road 9.6 miles east of Crane Flat
Friesen of Fresno, California and Fresno Pacific University was sleeping in a 1995 Nissan Altima driven by Jacob Brotsis, age 20, who ***fell asleep*** *at the wheel, drove off a curve, and impacted head on into a red fir 4 feet thick. Friesen's seat belt apparently was faultily worn. Brotsis sustained minor injuries thanks to an airbag.*

Alena Dennison, 17 | July 19, 2011 | Tioga Highway 120, at Siesta Lake
After 7 a.m., a Chevy Suburban with 7 teenagers aboard near Siesta Lake became a one-car rollover 20 feet down an embank ment, stopping upside down. Six survived with minor injuries. Dennison of Corte Madera, California died.

Denise Hoffman, 59 | July 26, 2017 | lower Yosemite Valley
Details not yet available.

Koji Hayakawa, 28 | March 28, 2018 | Big Oak Flat Road
Hayakawa was involved in a ***head-on collision*** *in the second (middle) tunnel of three between the Valley and Crane Flat on Highway 120.*

Jennifer Anne Marino, 50 | August 24, 2018 | Highway 140 just north of Alder Creek
Marino of Yosemite Valley drove her 2015 Subaru Forester solo and, ***unwitnessed, veered off road*** *then 10 feet down a slope, striking a tree.*

Michael Kevin Morris, 60 | September 9, 2024 | Tioga Road 4 miles W of Tuolumne Meadows
Driving his ***motorcycle****, Morris crashed.*

Christian Brent Smith, 28 — March 11, 2025 — Wawona Road near Campground
No details

Christopher Ireland, 71 — May 9, 2025 — Pentilas Corner
No details

<u>Bicycle Fatalities:</u>

William H. Selby, 52 — September 17, 1973 — hill west of Mirror Lake
Selby of San Carlos, California died of a heart attack while pumping his bicycle up the steep hill below Mirror Lake.

Eleanor Wai Ching So, 39 — August 21, 1986 — hill west of Mirror Lake
On August 12, So of China was on the road riding a Curry rental bike equipped with foot brakes. She tried to stop by using nonexistent hand brakes and ultimately dragged her feet to slow down. She hit pedestrian Irene Palmer who struck her head. So then ran off the road, crashed, and hit her head too. She died 9 days later.

Daniel Freeman, 41 — November 18, 1989 — Village Road, in front of Ranger Club
Freeman of Yosemite was riding his bike when his chain disengaged or broke. His pedals spun freely and he lost his balance, crashed, and died of head injuries.

Sung Mo Ku, adult — May 29, 2009 — Southside Drive, Yosemite Valley
Ku, a German citizen, was riding a bicycle and turned left without first checking the lane to his left. He turned into the path of a Chevy Suburban operated by Frederic Jody Moeckel who was found not culpable.

Marcel E. Watts, 28 — October 17, 2015 — Highway 41, Tunnel View
On October 10, upon exiting the Wawona Tunnel at a ***speed of about 60 mph*** *(according to his 2 passengers), Watts, an Ahwahnee Hotel employee, failed to make the turn, crossed the centerline and the opposing lane, hit the curb, and slid 175 feet farther where his upside down vehicle caught fire. The 2 passengers kicked out windows and, helped by witnesses, freed Watts. The vehicle burned. Watts died of injuries on October 17.* ***Alcohol*** *and marijuana may have been involved.*

Chapter Nine

BIG WALLS AND SMALL ONES, TOO

At the proverbial crack of dawn on September 23, 1972, Neal Olsen began leading the challenging 22nd pitch high on The Nose of El Capitan. Minutes into the climb above Camp 5, he pulled on a slab of granite. With a terrifying grinding sound, it moved. Then it separated. The rock instantly fell, glancing over Olsen's head and hissing across his back. It barely missed crushing his skull and flaying his spine. As if to negate this bit of good luck, the boulder smashed his right leg.

Olsen, now seriously injured and immobile, ended up perched on a ledge 900 feet below the summit and about 2,000 feet above the base of the big wall. His predicament placed him far from a convenient location for a medical evacuation. A lot of yelling by his partner alerted other climbers and then rangers.

By 7:30 a.m., Park SAR Officer Pete Thompson started orchestrating a record-setting effort to get Olsen off the wall before he died. Just one of the problems Thompson faced was that almost all of the Park's SAR gear was gone, up in smoke. This tragedy—and it would truly become one—had come to pass due to the almost unbelievably asinine scheme of a 17 year-old.

Despite his young age, this teenager had already worked on two trail crews. On one under Jim Snyder at Bunnell Point, however, several wasps had stung him. His allergic reaction proved serious enough for him to be evacuated by helicopter to Lewis Memorial Hospital for treatment. Here in the Valley his ability to reason made an illegal U-turn. He decided he wanted to upgrade his apparent standing with the Park. To do this he felt that he needed to show these NPS guys just how useful he was, how good at handling emergencies, and how brave and reliable he was in a tight spot. Displaying all this would require unusual circumstances.

In fact it would demand a genuine emergency as his launch pad. Moreover, the emergency had to be dramatic enough that he would become a hero, but not so extreme that other responders would have the time to take over and eclipse him. An emergency like this—during which he could be the sole responder—might only happen along naturally with the frequency of Halley's Comet.

Just past midnight on August 1, 1972, I (Farabee) responded with just about everyone else to fight a fire in the Park's Maintenance Yard. Coincidentally, Anne Farabee, my wife, was Park Dispatcher that night and sounded the fire alarm.

On fire was the Valley's horse barn and stable. It held many animals, including eight matched patrol horses that Horse Operations and Barn Supervisor Walt Castle had carefully selected during his extensive search across the western United States. Initiated in 1962, the Yosemite Horse Patrol stood as one of the Park's prides and joys.

The fire had almost instantly become huge, certainly for a national park. In a city this blaze would have been responded to by multiple fire stations and numerous machines. As we all scrambled to rescue anything still alive, we found the teenage kid injured. He had been kicked by a spooked horse. He had survived only by sheer luck. I shuttled him to the hospital. All we knew at this point was that he had been in the burning barn trying to save the livestock.

Horses have been a vital component of search and rescue in our western national parks for more than a century. And while helicopters now often replace horses on emergency missions, there still exist tasks that they do well that a helicopter cannot. Dollar for dollar, horses also frequently budget out best in the taxpayer's interest. Ours were both well trained and well tested. And as every equestrian knows, each horse had possessed an individual personality. They were valuable animals. Irreplaceable really. And, again, the boy had been in there, in the smoke and flames, trying—we thought at the time—to save them.

It was only later that we learned this teenager had lit the damned fire himself. Maybe knowing how valuable the animals were, the teenager had torched the stored hay. He intended to rush in as soon as the blaze caught and then heroically release the animals from their stalls. His plan backfired—no pun intended—and quickly spread to at least seven other buildings, including the one in which the SAR Cache was located. His conflagration, fueled in part by 100 tons of baled hay, had raced far beyond his control—and his plans—faster than he had anticipated.

Despite the fierce battle our multiple fire crews waged, our 4,850-square-foot barn and stables burned to the ground. Seventeen horses and mules died horrible deaths, many while trapped in their stalls. The fire also destroyed those seven other wooden buildings (totaling approximately 15,000 square feet). Several were among the oldest historic structures still standing in the Valley; these included two that had been built during the Civilian Conservation Corps-era and a couple built far earlier yet by the U.S. Cavalry.

This disaster also consumed the bulk of the Park's rescue equipment. Just as it is today, it was then the largest SAR cache in the entire National Park System. More to the point here, every rope we had possessed had gone up in foul smelling smoke.

After surveying Olsen's dicey predicament and his challenging location on The Nose, the SAR team brainstormed a plan "A" to get him off the face. Today he would probably be lifted *up* to the summit and then flown to medical help. (In a true life or death race these days techniques and equipment allow a helicopter to directly extract a person at Camp 5 laterally. But because this high risk is only warranted during a dire emergency, by the end of 2006 this procedure has been done only once.) But in 1972 a helicopter extraction was not in the cards, and 900 feet was a very long distance to haul up someone strapped to a litter, especially on El Capitan—even assuming rescuers could get their hands on enough rope.

Plan A quickly became: Lower him *down*. If we actually pulled off this feat, it would probably be the longest, single-stage rope lowering in mountain SAR history. Such a rescue had certainly never been done before in Yosemite. The big hitch in plan A was that an overall 2,900-foot lowering of the victim plus at least one rescuer would take a lot of rope, more than a mile actually. And rope was something we no longer had.

With SAR Ranger Pete Thompson as the overall team leader, the Park made an emergency plea to several sources of equipment, including Tubbs Cordage in San Diego, 400 miles to the south. Everyone responded instantly. Tubbs offered to send more than 7,000 feet of half-inch Goldlon nylon yachting rope. In one of those seemingly rare, "well-oiled" coordinated team efforts, the California Highway Patrol quickly picked up not only the gold marine line from Tubbs but also 2,000 feet of regular climbing rope as well as other equipment and hardware. By late afternoon, a helicopter and crew from Southern California's El Toro Marine Corps Base hovered over the summit of El Capitan. Inside the "Huey" sat three large wooden spools, each wound with 1,200 feet of continuous line each weighing more than 100 pounds. This cargo also included 6,500 feet of additional rope of varying lengths.

Yachting line was acceptable for rescue but useless for technical climbing. Its minimal stretch allowed little "give" to softly brake the fall of someone roped up. In contrast, true climbing rope is dynamic; it stretches over 15 percent to gradually cushion a fall, much like a bungee cord. But necessity now compelled that rope for rigging sails on the ocean would be the name-of-the-game for at least part of the plan to get Neal Olsen off El Capitan.

Efforts to rescue him would drag along for a seemingly endless two days and nights. More than thirty hours would pass after the rock crushed his leg before he saw a hospital. It would take the SAR team that long to rig for the record-making litter lowering.

Climbing Camp 4's world-class Jim Bridwell and Yosemite Mountain Climbing Guide Service Manager Lloyd Price orchestrated twenty additional, experienced big wall SAR climbers as they co-engineered the operation atop El Capitan. Thanks to Tubbs Cordage plus a host of other businesses, agencies, and resources, the team finally found themselves able to do what they needed to. Half a dozen rescuers soon made their way down to Olsen's tiny ledge to render him first aid and to rig the complicated rope apparatus. Conveniently, the route down to the injured man was nearly a straight shot.

The rescuers descended with gear from the summit of El Capitan and then managed their ropes from the victim's beach-towel-sized ledge at Camp 5. At this spot the two rescue ropes (the second acted as a safety backup) passed through pulleys and hardware secured by complicated anchors to make a ninety-degree turn and travel horizontally for several yards to another straight shot down. These lines would hold both the litter and its attendant. The ropes ran through a second directional-change system from the ledge to drop vertically for a mind-boggling 2,000 feet. Much of this descent dangled several feet out from the huge granite wall.

The SAR team strapped the now long-suffering Olsen into the canvas and metal-rimmed stretcher. He and climber Jim Bridwell next endured the extended lowering. Bridwell had a two-way radio rigged to his chest but because he was not always able to let go of the litter at the appropriate time to fiddle with this, Olsen instead pushed the transmit button for him as needed while they descended.

Bridwell would later admit that one of the more interesting experiences during their ninety-minute descent was when they paradoxically went *up* instead of down. Because the surface area of the ropes to which they were rigged added up to such a significant total, the two lines acted as sails. And as the wind blew across the face of El Capitan these "sails" gently floated the two men back upward like gossamer, lifting them smoothly, almost surrealistically, up the granite cliff.

Meanwhile, a dozen additional YOSAR personnel (again, YOSAR is an acronym for "Yosemite Search and Rescue;" the term originated as the result of that recent Barn Fire) positioned themselves on the summit to manage ropes and gear to ensure that the right people went down safely and the correct ones made it back up. Although it seemed to take forever to set up this lowering—again the SAR team had worked straight through the night—the rescue went almost flawlessly.

Ultimately Olsen made it down. And he survived. And for this superlative rescue effort, Secretary of the Interior Rogers C. B. Morton awarded the El Capitan YOSAR Team the Department of Interior's Unit Award for Excellence of Service.

What happened to the kid with the matches? He was placed in a juvenile psychiatric institute in Missouri and given medication for six months. Upon reevaluation he was retained there for yet another six months. At the end of that year he was released on probation—with the stipulation that he continue to take his medication.

BAD RAPS

Since technical climbing first began, using a rope for protection against falls has seemed a good idea. In the old days before World War II these were generally of Manila hemp that not only proved stiff and clumsy but also did not stretch. Worse yet, it wore out and broke. Often the techniques for using these thick lines for safety seemed primitive. Still, using a rope at all frequently defined the difference between life and death.

On February 21, 1932, 23-year-old San Franciscan Henry J. Blank and A. C. Manheim had roped themselves together to act as the other's movable anchor, a common mountaineering technique even today. They ascended the Four-Mile Trail toward Glacier Point on a winter hike. At roughly halfway "up the short trail" they found the steep way buried in snow. Here, in a dicey spot, Blank slipped on the ice and shot off a 300-foot cliff. (Most of the record does not state which trail this was; the February 25, 1932 *Mariposa Gazette* article leaves it open. But one obscure reference does say "Four-Mile" but also lists Henry as "Harry.")

Reacting quickly, Manheim anchored himself to a large boulder—not merely to arrest Blank's fall but also to save his own life. He succeeded. And their rope held.

Immediately awareness hit Manheim that the task of hauling Blank back up would demand Herculean effort…unless maybe he, if able, could climb back up their rope. Could he? Desperate, Manheim yelled questions into the empty air toward his buddy. Unfortunately, communication between them now proved to be limited.

As Blank, injured slightly and likely stricken with terror, dangled over nearly 300 feet of sheer drop, Manheim sweated out a solution wherein he could simultaneously retain his grip on this precious rock yet also haul his friend back up. Was Blank even *trying* to climb back up? Manheim knew he *had* to moor himself—and do it quickly—to be free to use his whole body for pulling. Even inches at a time would do the job.

"If I could just tie myself to this boulder…" Manheim must have thought to himself as he feverishly tried to concoct a plan. Meanwhile, behind him, the sharp granite of the cliff edge chewed into the taut fiber rope. Worse, Blank's swaying body slowly sawed the line back and forth. The clock ticked implacably. With each passing second and each sway the rope abraded deeper. Neither the line nor Blank could endure this gnawing for long.

Sadly, as Manheim schemed for a way to be able to get his partner back up, the jagged granite severed the rope. Henry J. Blank fell, hit, slid, then shot across a small box canyon and struck the opposite wall, crushing his skull.

Episodes early in Yosemite climbing illustrate how roping up may be lethal with the wrong equipment and/or techniques. On March 22, 1949, another roped ascent played out poorly. Nineteen-year-old Kenneth A. Haines and Peter B. Yeazell, age 18, both of Fresno, were practicing rock climbing 300 feet up on a snow-dusted and rain-slicked face alongside Lower Yosemite Fall. These conditions alone read like a recipe for disaster. The two had roped themselves together, each acting as the other's belayer and anchor. What happened next went unwitnessed but the two left enough evidence behind to guess what went wrong.

Apparently one of the teenagers grabbed a rock which dislodged. Having lost his primary hold, he fell. He dragged his partner with him on 100 feet of climbing rope into a two-person, 300-foot fall.

The next mishap occurred more than a decade later, at the beginning of the "modern" era of rappelling and belaying in Yosemite. On March 19, 1960, 17-year-old Irving Franklin Smith had decided to make climbing history. Smith, a blond, crew cut high school junior from Fresno was determined to become the youngest ever to "conquer" Lost Arrow (named after an 1851 incident during which a young captive Yosemite boy deliberately shot one of his "demonstration" arrows so far off target that he could wander out of sight to fetch it and thus facilitate his escape from the invading militia that had captured him—as described in Chapter 14).

A bit of history here. As noted by Yosemite climber/historian Steve Roper in his *Camp 4 Recollections of a Yosemite Rockclimber*, Lost Arrow had been first summited by Jack Arnold on September 2, 1946. This ascent was extremely controversial because instead of having done anything resembling a "free climb," one of Arnold's two companions, Robin Hansen, had first actually lassoed the tip of the Spire from the main cliff then dropped the rope to dangle against The Arrow. His intent was to use this hanging line as an aid to ascend to its top. The controversy over this tactic emerges from the definition of "free-climbing," also called "rope-soloing." Both mean the same thing. And both mean technical sport climbing without using direct "aids" that would include artificial footholds or handholds (such as a dangling rope or a helicopter). Free climbing *does* include rigging—but not climbing *on*—a safety (a.k.a. belay) rope for protection from a fall, and it includes using hardware to keep the belay line itself anchored short enough to safely arrest a fall.

Arnold and his second buddy Anton Nelson next rappelled down to the notch-like saddle between the main wall and Lost Arrow. Despite having unconventionally rigged what initially appeared to be a surefire climbing aid,

GLOSSARY OF CLIMBING TERMS

Aid Climb–to ascend via "hardware" added to the rock instead of climbing the rock itself; a climber might step on and grip a several-rung "ladder" or etrier of nylon webbing.

Anchor–strong supports: tree, boulder, piton, bolt, etc. to which a safety rope is attached then used to rappel or belay from or simply to attach to for safety or rescue work.

Ascenders–mechanical, hand-sized metal devices used for gripping and quickly releasing from an anchored rope to assist in an ascent. **Jumars** are brand name ascenders.

Belay–a "**safety**;" may be a rope serving as a safety attached to an anchor, a person on belay, or a person who is the belayer.

Bolt–up to a 2"-long, ½"-wide metal rod pounded into a specially drilled hole. A "**hanger**" is screwed on to its end and a carabiner or webbing is hooked to it to create an anchor.

Carabiner–palm-sized, oblong metal ring which opens on one side with a spring-loaded gate. It easily attaches to a rope or other gear. Other than a rope, it is the most generally utilitarian of all climbing equipment.

Clean–to remove one's protection as one ascends. Also refers to using protection which does not damage cracks in rocks such as pitons and bolts will.

Climbing Rope–9 mm to 11 mm-diameter nylon line, generally 50 meters long, with a 15+ percent stretch, and able to support 4,000 to 6,000 pounds.

Dihedral–A vertical, more or less right-angled, inset corner within a rock face—like a half opened book standing on a shelf.

Etrier–a ladder-like sling that allows an aid climber to step up from loop to loop.

Figure-8 Knot–simple, quick, "bomb proof" knot used to tie to anchors, harness, etc.

Free Climbing–ascending rock while attached to a safety line. All climbing is done on the rock itself; the rope is never used as a direct climbing aid.

Free Soloing–to climb without a rope, protection, or a belay. Requires a high level of skill.

Friends–invented by Ray Jardine in 1977, these small, removable, self-expanding mechanical devices insert into cracks to anchor or protect a belay rope.

Lead Climber–the first person up a pitch, also called the "**leader**." If this person falls it is called a "leader fall." Leading is more difficult and dangerous.

Nut–a small metal geometric camming device with a sling used to set into a crack and provide an anchor. Similar devices include **chocks** and **hexes**–all of which are removable.

Pitch–a rope length (up to 200 feet). The Nose, for example, is a 31-pitch route on El Capitan.

Piton–up to a 9-inch long metal spike driven into a crack for protection. Replaced in the 1970s by less destructive devices such as chocks and nuts.

Protection–bolts, pitons, Friends, chocks, "stoppers," or other removable aids set in faces or cracks and used to provide anchors for a safety rope and belay.

Prusik Knot–a short, simple loop of rope friction-knotted onto a line. When under tension it will tightly grip a rope as a safety tie-in. When loose it can be slid down or up to ascend a rope. Useful for rescue work.

Rappel–also known as an **abseil**; it is a way to descend a rope at a controlled rate by using friction on it. Usually the rope winds through a descending device, but may instead be wrapped around one's torso in a specific way.

Tyrolean Traverse–maneuver along a rope rigged horizontally from points A to B.

the two soon experienced trouble trying to climb high enough to grab the end of Hansen's lasso rope suspended above them. So Arnold and Nelson resorted to lassoing again with another rope, this time snaring a flake above Salathé Ledge.

Salathé? John Salathé was a Swiss-born blacksmith who lived in San Jose. At age 46 he had become obsessed with climbing—especially Yosemite climbing. A year later, in 1946, he had drilled and placed bolts in one face of The Arrow and then tried to climb *them* to the summit. This was the first known incident in which bolts were used in direct aid climbing in Yosemite. Yet despite these bolts, and despite two attempts to ascend here on them, Salathé had not been able to summit. He had, however, made his way to just beyond this point above the ledge, hence the name "Salathé Ledge."

Back for a moment to Nelson and Arnold. Once they had hooked this flake above Salathé Ledge, they were able to ascend the lower lasso. Arnold, because he was a lot lighter, then made his way up Hansen's higher, original lassoe line to be first on top. Yippee!

Now we return to the quest of young Irving Franklin Smith fourteen years later to be the youngest to ever conquer Lost Arrow. The crux occurred when he and 24-year-old Gerald Dixon descended toward the narrow gap behind the Arrow on their second, 135-foot rappel into the notch. Once off this rappel, they next would have to cross the notch before beginning the actual climb along the route begun by Salathé then pioneered by the rodeo tactics of Hansen, Nelson, and Arnold. The exposure below this rappel point is intimidating—a sheer 1,400-foot drop from both sides of a twelve-foot-wide saddle of rock framed by empty air. Despite this scary exposure, though, the rappel itself descended a clean, very steep slope. It was not quite a vertical wall, and it "should" have been "an easy, 200-foot controlled slide."

Dixon never saw what happened, but he did hear a faint cry from below. He next heard the unmistakable sound of a human body thumping its way down granite at high speed. Somehow Smith had either rappelled off his rope or else messed up his harness or knots, although this latter possibility is less likely because this was Smith's second rappel of the pair that the two climbers were executing and his harness had been working. Unroped, Smith fell nearly 600 feet. His body wedged into West Arrow Chimney—a place author Steve Roper calls "prehistorically dark and damp, a place to avoid. Certainly it is not a good place to die"—700 feet above the deeper base of Lost Arrow.

Ranger and SAR expert Wayne Merry, a member of the first team to successfully climb El Capitan in 1957 and 1958, believed that recovering Smith's body was feasible. Even so, Park Superintendent John Preston said, "No; it's too dangerous" (a half a century later, Merry still disputes his boss' assessment). Preston next took a more radical step. He closed the Lost Arrow area to climbing for a full year.

The upshot? Sadly, instead of becoming the youngest climber to conquer

Lost Arrow, Smith became the first modern-era climber to be killed in Yosemite Valley. Moreover, for several years his remains were wedged in Lost Arrow Chimney as a sort of macabre landmark. A year after the accident, Steve Roper and Yvon Chouinard (who later would found Patagonia clothing) were first to climb the Chimney from the wall's base. As related in his book *Camp 4*, Roper came upon Smith's skeleton, partially clothed by the coat it was still wearing, and (he says to break the tension) yelled down to Chouinard, "Goddamn it! His parka doesn't fit me."

On June 19, 1964, a similar rappelling tragedy occurred. Twenty-six-year-old James F. Baldwin, a Canadian who only two years earlier had done the first aid-climb of El Capitan's 2,400-foot Dihedral Wall, was retreating off Washington Column with John Evans. Baldwin's heart had not been in the climb since even before the onset—he was having relationship problems with a woman named Helen. The problem? It seemed she was not interested in being his girlfriend.

Near dusk, Baldwin gave up on trying to focus on the climb. He stopped and yelled to Evans: "Would you hate me for the rest of my life if I chickened out?"

Evans said no, he would not. Now the two reversed course and began to descend. Somehow, unwitnessed, Baldwin rappelled right off the end of his rope and fell several hundred feet.

In the next few years of the 1960s sport climbing exploded. So much so that it has become necessary to redefine "sport climbing" per se a few times as climbers have successfully pushed the envelope beyond limits previously considered humanly impossible. Much of this change took place in Yosemite Valley—at merely seven square miles it constitutes less than one percent of the Park itself. The Valley looks like very few other places on Earth because of the unusual combination of its immense vertical proportions and iron-solid composition. In short, much of it *looks* impossible to climb.

Which is exactly why people started trying.

The sophistication of techniques and levels of skill evolved rapidly. The quality and innovativeness of hardware and of ropes made almost quantum leaps. More importantly, beliefs and understanding among climbers of what was "possible" repeatedly shattered existing limits. Monolithic walls previously dubbed impossible by earlier climbers now merely fired the ambitions of this generation who tackled the singular challenges of Yosemite's walls with a vengeance.

What singular challenges? Unlike the sorts of rock that people were climbing in Europe, cliffs in Yosemite offered a frustrating dearth of extended vertical crack systems for chimney ascents. These granite faces also lacked traversable ledges. And thanks to the corrasive power of the Sierra's recent glaciers, what holds and jams that do exist prove smoothly polished and slippery. Yet to these mostly young climbers all of these daunting problems became mere obstacles to overcome instead of remaining as road blocks to mastering new routes. Relatively soon during this era, "impossible" walls abruptly became "done" routes, often laced by amusing names for their critical pitches and crucial ("crux") moves.

As Steve Roper notes in *Camp 4*, between 1933 and 1971, Yosemite climbers created 507 new, named routes. The rate of creation accelerated dramatically as Camp 4 (also known as Sunnyside Campground and as "Climber's Camp") evolved into a Big Wall Mecca populated by semipermanent climber-residents. The 1930s offers an illustration. The decade saw only twenty-three routes pioneered. Numbers in the 1940s were much the same. But during the late 1950s and especially the seminal 1960s, a coterie of climbers established new routes as if driven by a maniacal muse. Between 1962 and 1965, Yosemite rock jocks logged 160 first ascents. During the next four years, they made ninety-six more. Those mere eight years of Yosemite's "Golden Age" of climbing account for half of all the first ascents during nearly a forty-year history.

As this pioneering period decelerated, climbing—and establishing more first ascents—did not grind to a halt. By the 1990s, *sixty* routes had been done on El Capitan alone, once considered impossible via *any* route. Jim Bridwell, for example, who began his Yosemite career in 1964, pioneered his most and hardest climbs during the 1970s. In 1975, he, John Long, and Billy Westbay climbed The Nose in less than 24 hours, making the first ever, one-day ascent of El Capitan. In 2010, Dean Potter and Sean Leary climbed The Nose in an astounding 2 hours and 36.75 minutes.

A bit of a surprise to some people, the passage of time and of many thousands of climbers failed to dim the luster of the Valley's appeal. As Don Reid notes in his 1996 edition of *Yosemite Climbs: Big Walls*:

> Yosemite Valley continues to reveal itself as an incomparably beautiful and vast rock-sculpted wonder. Decade after decade, it has been an inspiring dream for climbers, and has also provided the fulfilling reality of a supreme granite-climbing experience. The numbers of climbers attracted to Yosemite, and the level of drama played out in this arena, is testimony to Yosemite's allure, as in the sheer number of routes established by these climbers.

Interestingly, despite climbers forging hundreds of new routes, many of which ascended immense walls previously considered beyond human ability, and despite doing this with new and sometimes unfamiliar innovations in equipment, and despite all of this seeming to be destined to add up to a high rate of casualties, the number of fatal falls during this era was small. During the entire decade of the 1950s, one person was killed while climbing and another due to hypothermia afterward; in the explosion of 1960s, ten died. As Yosemite climbing caught on among the less well trained, however, casualty rates soared. Compare the low numbers in the 1950s and 1960s to those between just June 16 and June 18 in 1975. In three sequential days, three separate climbers died in falls from

CLIMBING CLASSIFICATION SYSTEMS

In Germany during the 1920s, Willo Welzenbach developed a system for rating terrain. This was adopted by the Sierra Club in 1937. Welzenbach's system of six classes escalated in difficulty and danger.

Class 1 is simple hiking.

Class 2 is steeper ground such as a talus slope upon which hands might be used for balance.

Class 3 terrain incurs hand and footholds; looking down from such terrain might make the scrambler nervous.

Class 4 routes recommend a safety rope. Falling could be serious, although a leader here will not use protection for the line.

Class 5 cliff requires placing protection for one's safety rope.

Class 6 was strictly aid-based terrain; this means the climber had no choice but to hang off a piton or bolt or stand on his partner's shoulders to make progress. In Yosemite "Class 6" is considered an obsolete, non-category.

In the early 1950s, pioneer climbers Royal Robbins and Don Wilson recognized that Welzenbach's "Class 5" category was far too nonspecific. It needed to be further sub-defined to reflect the types of climbing being done in Southern California. In about 1956, this new system of subdivision reached the Valley. Despite its origin farther south, it soon became known as the **Yosemite Decimal System** or **YDS**.

YDS Class 5 increments of difficulty escalate from 5.0 for the easiest up to at least 5.14 for the hardest. (Other rating systems are used elsewhere in the world.)

But even the multistage YDS scheme soon proved unable to convey nuances of difficulty in the real world. Hence, climbers in Yosemite tack on a further sub-classification in which **"A" (for aid)** is listed after the Class 5 number. Ratings range from A1 to A5. The more difficult the pitch (usually defined as a rope length between anchors), the higher the number. An A1 would be far less demanding (and intimidating) than an A5.

Nor, it would become apparent, was everything in the above combined system adequate to convey the combination of difficulties. So, in addition to a Class Arabic numeral and an "A" rating, climbs today are also given a **"Grade"** (using a Roman numeral).

Grade I would be a short one- or two-pitch climb that might take an hour or less. The higher the Roman numeral, the longer and more difficult the overall climb. A Grade III will take a half day. A Grade VI, such as most of the routes to the top of El Capitan, used to normally take several days. Some of these routes have over thirty pitches. Even this additional rating standard is compromised, however, because a few climbers now can "whiz" up a Grade VI on El Capitan and then also ascend a difficult climb elsewhere, both on the same day.

three independent climbs. The grand total for the single year was seven climbers killed. During the 1970s as a whole, twenty-nine died. During the 1980s, twenty-six more joined them. During the 1990s things improved a bit; seventeen died in rock mishaps. Within the first seven years of the new millennium the "safer" era backslid a bit. Fourteen climbers have already died through 2006.

Perhaps this upsurge of fatalities in the 1970s was due simply to more climbers on the walls and possibly also due to individuals pushing their own limits on new routes and trying to do climbs faster. Speed—elapsed time on the wall—often deeply impressed the climbing community. The first ascent of "The Capitan," for example, took forty-five days (the route was The Nose). Forty-odd years later top climbers were zipping up El Capitan like Spider Man in hours—and then hustling from the summit down to the Valley to make yet another big wall climb on that same day. In general, speed itself on a route soon became a goal. Faster was better. Faster yet was, well, better yet.

Well before dawn on October 30, 2005, 24-year-old Tommy Caldwell of Colorado began free climbing The Nose (then rated 5.14a), seconded by his wife Beth Rodden. He summited roughly 12 hours later then hustled back down to free climb the thirty-five-pitch The Freerider (5.12c) seconded by Chris (Rocket) McNamara. Caldwell summited shortly after midnight, having logged sixty-five consecutive pitches as lead climber, twice up El Capitan, in one "day." Caldwell's feat, made after brutal training and despite missing half of his left index finger, stands unparalleled. Thus far.

An early example of the quest for speed—at least as personal goals—coupled with a nightmarishly bad rappel revolved around October 15, 1968. Veteran Yosemite climbers Chuck Pratt, age 29, and Chris Fredericks, age 26, were inching their way up El Capitan's southwest facing Dihedral Wall (rated Grade VI, 5.9, A3), at the 6,500-foot level.

We often refer to Class and/or Grade of a climb. Despite the explanation of these systems on the previous page, these classifications still can be confusing. To complicate the process of interpreting ratings, consider the following. In 1964, Steve Roper published *A Climber's Guide to Yosemite Valley*. Updated and enlarged over the next decade, Roper's book was the original Bible for rock climbers in the Park. In it he rates The Nose on El Capitan as VI, 5.8, A3. During the years following, skill levels have risen, techniques improved, and standards have changed. So much so that in the 2005 edition of *Yosemite Big Walls* by Chris McNamara and Erik Sloan, they rate The Nose as VI, 5.13+. This route is now somewhat routinely done without aid, although many climbers do still use it.

Be all that rating history as it may, Chuck Pratt's and Chris Fredericks' goal in 1968 on El Capitan's southwest facing Dihedral Wall was to ascend it in five days. At the time this would seem like a streak of light compared to that first, 1962, heavily bolt-dependent, aid-climb that consumed thirty-eight days over an eight-month period. This had been done by Ed Cooper, Glen Denny, and

Jim Baldwin which finally summited to a Cooper-incited media fanfare. Among other things along the way they had placed 110 bolts and had broken six hammers. According to McNamara and Sloan in *Yosemite Big Walls*, "This is likely the hardest big wall climbing in the world."

Pratt and Fredericks now craved no such fanfare. They simply wanted to climb the sheer, twenty-seven-pitch route—and climb it freestyle, protected with a belay, and to do so without using aids. They had started up on October 9 and intended to return from the summit on the 13th.

Thus far they had done reasonably well. Over four days they had made ten pitches to the first ledge 1,200 feet up. After the 19th pitch, they climbed to the "Black Cave," a wide and welcome chimney with a sloping floor at the 2,100-foot level. Yet another three pitches higher lay "Thanksgiving Ledge." This is the first large ledge on the climb; it is twelve-feet wide at some points and hundreds of feet long. The pioneers on this climb in 1962 happened to have reached it on that holiday. Only another five pitches above this ledge lay the summit.

But in seeming defiance of Pratt's and Fredericks' desire to climb those remaining eight pitches, on Saturday morning of the 12th (day #4) an October storm rolled in. At 6,500 feet, two-thirds of an inch of rain fell. Soon the temperature plummeted to twenty-five degrees. The storm became wintry. The rain turned to snow, then back to rain. To escape the icy foul weather pummeling El Capitan, Pratt and Fredericks spent the night cloud-hidden while standing in their web slings and pressed against the cold, vertical granite. Under these conditions, the possibility arose that their progress on this Grade VI climb might deteriorate to a potentially fatal snail's pace.

In the Valley below, climbing friend James T. Madsen, an engineering student and football player from Seattle, was getting worried. At only twenty, he was already one of the fastest wall climbers around. He also happened to be the only one currently available and experienced with the route that Pratt and Fredericks were attempting in their now "life or death" climb. Madsen, in fact, had partnered up with Kim Schmitz to blaze up the Dihedral Route earlier that year in a mere 2½ days, a time that left the local experts gaping.

Madsen now desperately wanted to help Pratt and Fredericks. He figured they must be bivouacking in Black Cave, which he thought would be dangerously wet. Worse, while his two friends were toting down-filled parkas and sleeping bags, they carried no real rain gear.

On Sunday, the 13th, another 1.31 inches of rain fell. On Monday, their sixth day, an observer spotted the two about 250 feet below Thanksgiving Ledge. They were shaking out their down bags during a couple of hours of full sun. But the three pitches above them to Thanksgiving Ledge were difficult, rated a very serious Class A3 or A4, offering only a few cracks for handholds and footholds and for placing protection. As if an omen to Madsen, that afternoon the rain resumed and then again turned to snow above 5,000 feet. The two climbers attempted the next pitch in this storm, but the weather forced them to retreat. Pratt and Fredericks gave up for the time being, and inched back to Black Cave for yet another night. In Jim Madsen's mind all of this signaled a disaster in the works.

Rangers and other climbers from Camp 4 felt worried too. They seconded Madsen's concern for their friends now stalled out on the wall. Madsen, notes Steve Roper in *Camp 4*, was "an impulsive fellow, not one given to reflection and calmness." True to form, he now cajoled then helped organize rangers into initiating an immediate rescue on the challenging Dihedral Wall. Spurred by knowing that time could prove to be the hypothermic killer, the entire rescue team hurriedly hauled ropes, climbing gear, sleeping bags, food, stoves, et cetera, along the El Capitan trail in the dark and the rain. This rain turned to snow long before their pre-midnight arrival at the summit. All of this took place on foot; using a helicopter was impossible due to the storm and darkness. Drizzle, snow, and sweat had left every rescuer soaked to the skin.

They started a fire, made coffee, and discussed a night rappel to Thanksgiving Ledge. They quickly decided that current circumstances would make such a descent far too dangerous. At dawn, Madsen prepared to rappel far enough to yell to the two men who by now might be literally freezing against the cliff face. He reckoned getting close enough might demand his dropping all the way down to Thanksgiving Ledge. Once he established communications with Pratt and Fredericks, and if they sounded good, then he—and fellow climber Lloyd Price—would leave for them whatever supplies they might need. If they did not sound okay, then he and Price could descend another 600 feet to the tiny ledge on which the pair had last been spotted.

This plan called for Price to haul the survival gear and to follow Madsen down the same rope. In addition, the Park could order a small mechanical lifting winch that, weather permitting, could be helicoptered to the top of El Capitan from Sequoia National Park, 150 miles south.

Madsen tied his anchor to a pine tree three feet thick and growing only six feet from the edge of the cliff. Then he tossed his 150-foot line down the face. He shouldered a forty-five-pound pack of gear, including five more ropes for the rappel, plus jumars, pitons, a radio, and containers of hot soup. He began his rappel *sans* a second, fixed safety rope. Price promptly clipped into Madsen's single rope and watched his friend descend.

Two minutes later, the line below Price went slack. All Price heard from below was Madsen's incredulous utterance, "What the fuck?" and then his scream as he slid off the end of his rope.

Price next heard the unmistakable sound of a body whooshing through the air at high speed. His jaw dropped in disbelief. He turned and, with a look of horror on his face, told the others: "Madsen fell."

Jim Madsen, it turned out, had tied a simple overhand safety knot on the end of this line, but it had proved too small. It traveled right through his carabiner-brake system. Having made what often has been *the* critical mistake, Madsen had not tied a carabiner to the end of his rappel rope. This would have assured a stop. Nor had he attached his ascender to near the end of his rope as a backup (he had one clipped to his gear sling, roughly equivalent to a carpenter's tool belt). Everyone now wondered: How did he screw up like this?

Conjecture aside, the bottom line remains that Jim Madsen, the well-respected climber and would-be *rescuer*, had just plunged a hideous 2,700 feet to his death.

After Madsen's fatal drop, Pratt and Fredericks, who had been holed up invisible from the ground in a deep slot in the wall, continued their ascent of the Dihedral Wall. Aided by their headlamps, they climbed the final pitches to the summit after nightfall. As it turned out, they neither needed nor used the extra gear or assistance that the ill-fated Madsen and the rescue team had so arduously hauled to the summit—although both climbers admitted feeling grateful for the SAR team's presence on top in case conditions worsened.

As may be clear, neither Pratt nor Fredericks were novices likely to need help on a big wall. Indeed, only three years earlier, in 1965, Chris Fredericks had pulled off eleven first ascents in Yosemite, an astounding number in one year that speaks volumes not only about his skill level but also about his survival instincts. Chuck Pratt, Fredericks' frequent partner, stood perhaps in a league of his own—or at least in a very exclusive one. A physics major from Berkeley, Pratt had by October of 1968 already accomplished most of his record forty-eight first ascents. One of these had been Yosemite's major breakthrough climb, the first continuous, committed (no ropes permanently fixed to the wall to allow a quick retreat) climb of El Capitan during seven days in September of 1960 on The Nose with Royal Robbins, Tom Frost, and Joe Fitschen. Standing at five feet, six inches tall, Pratt was a climbing giant; he racked up more Yosemite first ascents by 1970 than any other climber of the time.

And Madsen? As Steve Roper notes further, Royal Robbins would later write: "Had [Madsen] lived and climbed, he doubtless would have written an important chapter in the history of American mountaineering, and probably of world mountaineering."

The lesson? Maybe it is: Friendship matters, but speed kills.

The Park's analysis of the incident concluded that using a helicopter against the face of El Capitan during a break in the weather to visually determine whether or not the two actually needed help might have obviated Madsen's entire rescue attempt. Moreover, a loudspeaker—which Madsen had insisted would be useless—also would have helped. Furthermore, the analysis continued, the mission was marred by unusual emotional haste and tension—with Madsen calling the shots. Ranger Tom Kimbrough concluded:

> In my opinion many of the underlying causes of the accident rested in Madsen's personality. It must be remembered that Madsen at

> age twenty-one [actually 20] was certainly one of, if not the, best and also fastest climbers this country has produced. I was of the opinion that more effort should have been put into an attempt to contact Pratt and Fredericks from the rim. However, Madsen believed strongly that this would be impossible. It is my personal opinion that his thinking on this matter was clouded by a strong desire, perhaps best understood by other climbers, to rappel down to Thanksgiving Ledge, but considering Madsen's knowledge of the area and his very forceful personality I did not feel like making an issue of the matter. Madsen was an extremely active and self-confident person and these qualities which have made him one of the best climbers in the world also, in my opinion, contributed to his death. There are several safety methods which could have prevented his death. However, Madsen, and most other expert climbers as well, would not under normal circumstances such as these use these precautions. Obviously now, the techniques used on that rappel were not sufficient. But Madsen was thoroughly familiar with all safety techniques for rappelling and chose those which he used.

Rappelling, despite potential mistakes such as Madsen's, should be almost completely safe. Safe, that is, if the anchor is solid and the rappeller uses appropriate equipment and correct techniques. Oddly, rappelling is frequently what the public imagines climbing is all about. This misperception persists despite climbing being almost entirely about getting *up*. It is true rappelling plays a very important role in most climbs and is used for retreating due to finishing or because of having no other way down, bad weather, darkness, mishaps, loss of equipment, to reevaluate a route, help a buddy, and so on. Also, to many, rappelling is an entire sport unto itself. Sadly, this technique has seemed so deceptively simple that it has seduced all too many people into making silly and often deadly mistakes. At least two dozen climbers in Yosemite have made fatal errors while rappelling, accounting for 19 percent of climbing deaths.

On June 13, 1973, 23-year-old John William Mokri from Pomona, California was climbing Middle Cathedral Rock in the Valley with Junius Simpson Dean Ketcham, age 28, of Steamboat Springs, Colorado. Mokri soon decided he was not feeling up to the 2,000-foot climb. Ketcham agreed to retreat off the wall. He rappelled to a lower point first and waited for Mokri. Ketcham saw his partner rearranging and cleaning (removing hardware from) parts of the rappel anchor. Although this puzzled Ketcham in a vague way, he was not worried about it. In fact, instead of watching Mokri, Ketcham dug into his pack to get something to eat.

While Ketcham rooted in his pack, Mokri somehow lost his holds and dropped past Ketcham like a rock. Instead of Mokri's rope at least catching in his rappel brake and arresting his fall, he merely dragged the rope which for some unknown reason was not even attached to him. Unroped, Mokri fell about 300 feet. Somehow despite wearing three safety slings—one attached to his swami belt (webbing wrapped around the waist to better distribute one's own weight while it is attached to a rope) and two to his chest—he had unclipped all of it from *all* of his protection and then fallen. "It has to be surmised," notes the Park's incident summary, "that Mokri free-climbed the 5.5 or 5.6 to the baby [an angle piton], cleaned it, and peeled while downclimbing."

As above, it frequently turns out during fatal events that the victim had unnecessarily detached himself from his rope. Approximately sixteen fatal climbing episodes in Yosemite involved either deliberately or carelessly becoming unroped, usually during rappels and while still at an anchor point or while trying to free a snagged line.

How easy becoming unroped can be is scary. Two years after Mokri's demise, on September 21, 1975, 14-year-old Mark Olson of San Carlos, California was attempting a nearly 150-foot rappel off Puppy Dome in Tuolumne Meadows on a 9/16-inch, old-style "goldline" rope. Going over this "beginner's" cliff is how many novices learn to rappel. Olson had clipped in with a commonly-used six-carabiner brake system protected by a Prusik safety loop as a backup. Unwitnessed because his companion was working on another system, Olson shouted and then fell 135 feet with the entire rope, carabiners, and Prusik still attached to him.

The mistake? The critical and pivotal figure-eight knot at the upper end of the teenager's rope, which should have been clipped into his anchor on top of Puppy Dome, wasn't.

A more elaborate rappelling error took place another two years later. On November 3, 1977, 20-year-old Burt Joseph Miller of Dearborn, Michigan climbed to Glacier Point Terrace with 20-year-old Mark Dixon. The two friends of six years had decided to bring only one rope. They summited at about 2 p.m. Fifteen minutes later they began their descent down the 5.9 route. They executed several successful rappels then reached a point for which the rope seemed too short. On this route most of the solid anchors were 150 feet apart, thus requiring two standard ropes for a rappel. For a descent of this length one generally needs to use two connected lines, doubled to allow retrieval from the bottom.

Although both young climbers felt dubious about this drop, Miller thought he could make it. Dixon told Miller that if Miller made it, he would follow. Despite Dixon's statement, he was already entertaining the possibility of yelling for help instead of executing a rappel with too little rope.

Ominously, Miller took off his swami belt and began descending to a fixed pin about fifty feet down. Here he tied his harness webbing to one side and his slings to the other. Several minutes later he yelled back up to Dixon, "It looks like I'll have to do a body rappel [for the next seventy-five feet]." Now using just the friction of the rope running around his body but in fact unroped because no line was attached to him, Miller descended farther. Ten feet above a safe ledge he ran out of line.

Now hanging onto the end of his rope by hand and with a sling clenched in his teeth, Miller tried to reattach himself to the end of his rope. Again, as he dangled far above the ground, he was "attached" only by the grip of his hands.

Dixon stared down at his precarious buddy. He felt worried about Miller being unroped like this. He also knew *he* did not want to do what his partner was now doing. Dixon watched Miller let go of the rope with one hand to reach for a Prusik to attach to it as a safety.

As Miller grabbed for it, his one-handed grip failed. He fell past the ledge only ten feet below and continued plummeting another 600 feet.

Dixon was certain that this accident happened mainly because the two were tired and because Miller had over-estimated his own climbing ability.

Dixon now started yelling for help.

On New Year's Day of 1978, 20-year-old Kendall Ovid West of Santa Ana, California partnered with 13-year-old Marvin A. Johnson. Neither had climbed in Yosemite before or with each other. West, with about six months of experience, chose the lower section of the west shoulder of Half Dome for their one-day ascent. He took the lead. Despite the short day and the winter state of the rock and West having forgotten his climbing shoes so that he was wearing his Cavalier running shoes instead, the pair ascended about 1,000 feet in good time.

Finally deciding to retreat, they traversed west to descend. The rock here, due to its perpetual shade, was moist and mossy. This was an un-scouted, partly overhung rappel route that even experienced Yosemite climbers would have avoided at this time of year—and they would have warned West and Johnson about it had the two asked for advice. Here in the wintry shadow of Half Dome, the young pair made a series of rappels with their single, 165-foot rope for about 300 feet. The second drop ended on a three-foot-wide ledge. Above this point their only rope snagged.

West tried to free it. In the now quickly fading light, he decided their line was "irretrievably" stuck in the trees above. West simply told Johnson—out of view about sixty feet above him—to "stay there." Next, in the dim light of dusk and without having communicated any plan "B" to Johnson should plan "A" (also uncommunicated) fail, West unroped and attempted a twenty-foot downclimb to a much bigger ledge. Within a minute, unseen by Johnson, Kendall West lost his holds and fell 600 feet.

Instead of "staying there" as instructed, the 13 year-old now rappelled on their snagged rope the last sixty feet to that smaller ledge. Here, in a replay of Mark Dixon's dilemma, young Johnson too found himself stranded above a 600-foot exposure, his only rope still snagged. And he did what Dixon had done; he started yelling for help. He yelled all night.

By morning he finally attracted rescuers. A Lemoore Naval Air Station "Huey" rescue helicopter arrived. The team lowered the Crew Chief 100 feet by winch to the teenager's tiny perch. There he secured the terrified, near-frozen youth into a harness and clipped him into their lifeline. Johnson and his rescuer now hung from the cable for a short haul to the nearby Ahwahnee Meadow.

Almost a black comedy, the number of mistakes Kendall West made was critical. Choosing this wet and shady section to climb during the dead of winter was the first error (or not using more expert advice). Not returning down their original ascent route, or at least on one they knew, was another big one. Rappelling off an un-scouted, un-scoutable, and overhung route was yet a third. Carrying only one rope during all of this was a fourth error. Poorly managing and snagging their one rope must also be tallied as a critical mistake. Not stopping to discuss what options they still possessed once their rope got stuck comprised a sixth error. Then not staying safely together and yelling for help was yet one more, huge mistake. Of course West's ultimate error was making the decision to *unrope* and to climb down to a better ledge unprotected and exposed.

Fatal mishaps can happen even to well seasoned, very experienced climbers. Consider the strange case of 26-year-old Karl Ulf Fredrik Bjornberg. On September 13, 1980, Bjornberg of Göteborg, Sweden had just climbed "Wheat Thin" (rated 5.10b). This is part of The Cookie Cliff in The Cascades area. Bjornberg's partner, 23-year-old Bengt Sorvik, was descending first. Bjornberg rappelled after Sorvik who, to save fading daylight, had asked to use the rappel ropes of another group that was also descending from a common ledge.

Before rappelling on another party's rope, for some reason Sorvik added a new, heavy-duty blue sling to the two old-looking pieces of webbing already fixed through three bolts and hangers here. Sorvik tied his new sling with a water knot and then checked it twice. Again, when Sorvik rappelled he did not use this new anchor sling but instead the rope and anchors of the other group. They had clipped into the older slings.

Bjornberg arrived after Sorvik had reached the bottom. Bjornberg then pulled down his own ropes, which landed in a tangle. As he straightened out his lines and threaded them through the anchor in preparation to rappel yet another pitch, he noted to Randall Blake, age 23, from the other climbing party: "Oh, he [Sorvik] rappelled on your ropes." Blake replied, "Yes, he did."

Bjornberg then stepped to the edge and "fell"—actually dropping off into a rappel.

Sorvik now heard a strange noise from above. He looked up to see his partner falling more than 100 feet toward him. Bjornberg slammed into trees head first then hit the ground with all of his climbing gear piling around him. He suffered a severely broken neck and palms burned from trying to grab other ropes. Sorvik rushed to him and found him pulseless.

What went wrong here?

Sorvik reported that Bjornberg was one of the best climbers in Northern

Europe. "He was very safe and lived a very clean life." But, Sorvik added, Bjornberg had very poor vision due to astigmatism.

Was impaired eyesight the problem? Up on the ledge from which both men had just rappelled lay Sorvik's new blue sling, its water knot now untied and gone. The knot had apparently failed instantly by slipping free as Bjornberg's weight yanked on it. Unfortunately for our understanding, no one but he had seen how he had anchored himself. Whether or not he had clipped into Sorvik's new blue anchor sling remains conjecture, though it would have been inviting to do so given that the other group had already rigged their rappel using the older, preexisting webbing.

Sorvik said he could not imagine Bjornberg knowingly rappelling off just one sling; he insisted that Bjornberg must have thought he was threading through multiple lengths of webbing. All the preexisting slings at this belay point, however, remained intact. More ominous, Sorvik further admitted that when he had added that new blue sling he had at first tied the knot incorrectly. He had caught himself and almost asked the nearby Blake to help him. He had, instead, counseled himself to re-tie the knot correctly on his own. He had left inches of free ends and tightened the knot.

To complicate matters, Bjornberg had clipped into the system—again, using an unknown number of slings—with only one non-locking carabiner. This could have unclipped itself; this sort of glitch has occurred in other climbing mishaps involving similar hardware when slings or ropes tangle and twist together as soon as tension hits them (as with Louis Raymond Beal, in Table 9), and it would have fatally freed Bjornberg from any anchor.

What *does* seem certain is that Sorvik's blue sling failed. Bjornberg very likely did use only it, and when it failed his use of a single non-locking carabiner became irrelevant.

Yet another tiny possibility is that Bjornberg had clipped into several existing slings but *not* to the blue one because he had decided to untie it to take it with him. This possibility is very unlikely given the fact that he did not take it with him. In Incident Report #80-10806, Ranger John Dill concluded: "We will never know what the [critical] error was or who made it. Bjornberg died, however, because he made two additional errors. He did not back himself up with another rappel sling or carabiner and he did not double check everything between his harness and the rock before he stepped off."

For a change, what went wrong is pretty clear in Yosemite's next rappelling mishap. On October 24, 1988, 35-year-old Robert A. Burnham from Vancouver, British Columbia was descending ninety feet down the Red Zinger (5.11d) on The Cookie Cliff on a rappel belayed by Michael Forkash. Forkash reports that when his partner reached the anchor at the top of the climb he fed one of his two ropes through the anchor carabiner and let the second rope dangle free from his belt harness. Then he started his rappel.

When Burnham was about thirty feet east of and above Forkash, Forkash told

Burnham the belay line was running out. Burnham told Forkash to let go of the belay rope.

Forkash tossed the remaining part of the belay rope toward Burnham's projected landing point on the ledge. Burnham then lowered himself by gripping both strands of this same rope, now doubled, which was threaded through the top anchor. Meanwhile he also cleaned the route (removed safety protection).

Forkash said he turned his back for a moment to mess with his own gear. Meanwhile Burnham's doubled belay rope turned out to be about ten feet too short to allow him to descend onto the ledge where Forkash waited. He assumed his partner would soon stop his rappel and then traverse to the left and downclimb the last dozen feet in an easier crack without protection. But he did not actually watch to see if his supposition was accurate.

As Forkash was tying his shoelaces he heard a noise. He turned and saw Burnham fall to his ledge then roll toward him unroped but with the lines now winding around his body. Forkash lunged to grab his friend but missed. Burnham slid off the ledge and fell seventy more feet to the ground.

As might be clear, Burnham had possessed other, better options than the one he used. As his belay rope was running out, he could have connected onto it the second rope that was hanging from his belt harness. This would have allowed him to retain a longer, safe belay while downclimbing and cleaning the entire pitch even after his single rappel rope ran out.

The upshot? Unroping under any similar circumstances of exposure, we can conclude based on the fifteen climbers who have deliberately done this with fatal results, is a bad habit.

This next episode of a bad rappel is so spectacular that it begs one's imagination. On September 17, 1992, 42-year-old Robert Moore arrived in Yosemite from Colorado with the sole objective of rappelling off El Capitan in one fell swoop and on one rope. A world record, continuous rappel of 2,649 feet already had been set on August 11, 1980, off El Capitan by an eighteen-person team made up mostly of eastern spelunkers. Steve Holmes had gone first then, taking a mere seventeen minutes. Eight more, including Farabee, had successfully rappelled the same line; seven even ascended back up it, setting a short-lived record for a continuous rope ascent. In 1982, again with Steve Holmes leading, another world record rappel was set, 3,250 feet off the unclimbed west face of Mount Thor in Canada's Auyittuq National Park on Baffin Island. On November 11, 1993, the Royal Marines would set the currently standing record by rappelling 3,627 feet down the shaft of a potash mine in the United Kingdom.

Now attempting to nearly match the older, one-time world-record rappel, Robert Moore muscled his way inch by inch over the overhanging lip of El Capitan and then started down his specially ordered 7/16th –inch, 2,600-foot line. This nylon rope weighed 150 pounds. Amazingly, given the extreme degree of exposure and the phenomenal vertical length of line involved and the potential for a runaway buildup of kinetic energy due to gravity, Moore apparently was not fully familiar with the dynamics of his U-shaped descending device (a.k.a. "rappel rack")—one of his own design.

To begin his rappel, Moore had to "brute-force" his way over the lip of El Capitan. This is because, to get over the edge, he needed to lift the weight of the rope dangling below him as he forced his way backwards. Once this was done he was suspended on his line. At this point, an "extreme rappeller" must adjust the rack to maintain correct speed. Moore now slowly descended 300 feet. Then he stopped.

It seemed his rappel rack was creating too much friction and slowing him to a crawl. Maybe he had paused here to adjust it. At any rate, a witness above saw him start to move things in his rack. Then, in a blink, everything went wrong…

Ranger Michael Ray analyzed this incident. He looked at everything from group dynamics among Moore's companions in Yosemite to his equipment. Ray even reenacted the descent with the same sort of equipment. Moore, it turned out, was part of a group of eighteen climbers focused on Half Dome and El Capitan, each with personal goals. Some wanted to ascend; some to rappel. Again, Robert Moore had traveled to Yosemite only to rappel off El Capitan.

Ominously, Ray learned further, Moore apparently had exhibited a casual attitude about safety. Ray noted the following: "Moore passed the top edge [of El Capitan] with four bars [of his modified descending rack] engaged. At the base he [still] had four bars engaged. Based on our experience, he would not have been comfortable with less than five bars." When Moore stopped 300 feet below the edge of El Capitan to manipulate his rappel rack, he may have been trying to add that fifth bar. More ominously yet, Ted Farmer, a climber who worked with Ray on the reenactment, "was unable to stop during our tests when he used gear like Moore's." Michael Ray continues:

> If Moore had four bars engaged, he may have lost his grip while trying to add a fifth. He may have been pushing the rope [which, again, weighed 150 pounds] in the wrong direction…[inadvertently] allowing the fourth bar to fall to the bottom of his rack and greatly reducing the friction. His grip may have slipped either immediately or while attempting to bring the fourth bar back up. This mechanism, of pushing the rope in the wrong direction when trying to add a bar, has been implicated in some caving accidents in the Tennessee-Alabama-Georgia area.

Maybe this is what happened. Or maybe not. Despite exhaustive analysis and research, no one could determine which scenario best explained the experience of Robert Moore. After he stopped at 300 feet and manipulated his rappel rack he suddenly plummeted down in an accelerating, uncontrolled, 2,300-foot, rope-melting rappel to his death.

Investigating Ranger Kerry Maxwell hypothesized: "There may have been a flaw in the victim's design of his own descending device as the spacers jammed into the first two bars while he was descending. This would have caused a significant increase in the amount of friction the device provided and may explain why he stopped 300 feet down." What we do know for certain, notes Maxwell, is: "Moore's death…could have been prevented if Moore was using a backup safety device that tied him into the rope while he was attempting to adjust his descending device."

This lesson, that of taking just a moment to clip into protection with a safety strap or Prusik while trying to adjust or fix a snagged rope or a hardware problem that is interfering with a smooth rappel seems like pretty basic safety. Actually it is. But as we have seen, fatigue or emotions or foul weather—any illogic stemming from a climber's desire for haste in a rappel—sometimes can seduce climbers into dispensing with it. Such dispensing, if indulged in too often, can become a habit. But not a good one.

As YOSAR Ranger John Dill concludes about such habits after decades of analyzing climbing accidents:

> The more often you get away with risky business the more entrenched your lazy habits become….Your attitudes and habits can be reinforced by the experiences (and states of mind) of others. The sense of awe and commitment of the 1960s is gone from the big-wall trade routes, and young aspirants with no Grade VI's, or even V's, to their credit speak casually about them. Even for experts, most accidents on El Cap occur on the easier pitches, where their guard is down.

At least equally bizarre was the rappelling experience of Sam Meier, a 24-year-old Curry Company worker. He decided to train a new friend, David Scott Mitten, in climbing techniques. On July 5, 1996, both men hiked to Tenaya Creek's Hidden Falls to get the ball rolling.

Meier first rigged a Tyrolean traverse (a horizontal line from point A to point B) across Tenaya Creek. Both men crossed this a few times to train for a future traverse from Lost Arrow Spire back to the main cliff. Things went fine practicing this technique. Meier next began rigging a rappel of Hidden Falls.

He anchored his 11 mm rope to a foot-thick cedar tree above the waterfall. Meier instructed Mitten in how to act as a safety as he next demonstrated a rappel. Once down, he explained to Mitten, the rope would go slack. This would take only a few minutes.

Instead, however, a startling twenty minutes passed before Mitten felt the rope slacken. He crept forward to see if his friend was off belay, but before he could even see Meier, the rope abruptly tightened again. Mitten figured that, because the rope remained under tension, Meier had not finished his rappel.

Ominously, Meier's line stayed taut for yet another twenty minutes. Not knowing this lengthy time span was unheard of for this short a rappel, Mitten decided to take a break. So, leaving Meier roped to an anchor, he detached himself and walked away twenty-five feet to smoke a cigarette.

After yet another twenty minutes, Mitten returned to the rappel anchor again, then to the brink. Having waited, in his opinion, more than long enough for this lengthy rappelling business (which should have taken a mere minute or two), Mitten yelled down to Meier to climb back up.

Hearing no response, Mitten crept forward to peer over the edge. He finally saw his partner below for the first time after his having been on the rope for at least an hour.

Meier was dangling from his line, partially submerged in the pounding water of Hidden Falls. He was yelling for help as he repeatedly tried to push himself out from under the falls in a vain attempt to swing to safety. Sam Meier had been battling inside this waterfall all of this time. Mitten now belatedly realized that Meier was in trouble.

Mitten ran down the trail to Mirror Lake and reported to a couple near the restroom that his friend was stuck on a rope in Hidden Falls and needed help. Mitten's run for help went quickly. He then ran back to Meier. At 7:45 p.m., within twenty minutes of Mitten seeing that Meier was in trouble, Park Dispatch received the distress call. Within fifteen minutes, a "hasty team" was en route, led by Ranger/Paramedic Chris Robinson.

When Mitten returned he dismantled the previously rigged Tyrolean. He climbed back above the waterfall and tried to throw this rope, with ascenders, down to Meier, who was *still* trying to push himself out from under the falls. This was a reasonable rescue plan. And on Mitten's fourth throw he saw Meier grab the rope.

Mitten next heard a moaning sound from below. Mitten had committed a simple but fatal error. He had not secured *his* end of this second, rescue line to an anchor before throwing it off the cliff. Now, as Meier applied tension, the rope slid out of Mitten's grip and dropped out of sight, useless. When this happened, Mitten later explained, he was out of ideas for helping his mentor. So instead of downclimbing and then perhaps wading into the pool to explore other options, he sat down and waited in the dark for the rangers.

When Robinson's team arrived they used lights to spot Meier under the falls. His location was extremely awkward and difficult to see. Robinson yelled several times to establish contact. Now in the dark and hindered by the sound of pounding water, the rescue team could hear no response. What they could see was that Meier had rappelled into a "hole" within the waterfall; he was surrounded by truck-sized boulders, and he was obscured by spraying mist.

Robinson studied the scene and he weighed the non-response of Meier (who had held out well against hypothermia for over an hour because of the hot July weather and relatively warmer water of the creek). Robinson decided that attempting to retrieve a body in the dark under these circumstances was too hazardous.

At nine the next morning, the Park's Criminal Investigator/Coroner Doug Roe hiked to Hidden Falls. He next had to rappel to where, with Robinson, he saw Sam Meier "still attached to his rope, in an arched, supine position with his entire body submerged in the water; his body appeared lifeless."

Understanding what any deceased victim may have been thinking prior to making his or her fatal error is always a chancy exercise. But in Meier's case, perhaps not. When Meier set up his rappel knowing it would end in the creek it is very likely that he believed—possibly from a prior experience in the same location—he would be lowering into a shallow pool. And once down and safely standing, he could simply detach from his rope and scramble to shore. Only this time, the pool was deep. Worse, from the top of the falls neither Mitten nor responding rescuers could see down to this spot. Again, Investigator Roe had to suspend himself from a rope and lower himself to the top of one of the huge boulders that next morning to even see Meier suspended face down in the pool. Thus, in the end, Sam Meier's simple error became a fatal one only because he never communicated a plan B to his novice partner.

As we have seen, even the most simple of errors or lapses of intent focus on a wall can spell out major consequences while rappelling. Consequences that often cannot be reversed. Shortly after noon on June 9, 2006, 27-year-old concession employee Megan Polk of Atlanta, Georgia and her 30-year-old friend Brian Ouday were "cragging" at Arch Rock. The duo was alone on the cliff above a route with a seventy-foot approach of moderate difficulty. Polk, with four years of climbing experience, was about to descend the second pitch of Anticipation (5.11b). She had clipped into a two bolt chain anchor at the top of the route as she fixed her rope preparatory to rappelling to a sling anchor 100 feet below.

Polk looked over her right shoulder as she pulled her rope through the chains. She stopped pulling when she thought she saw the end of the rope pass the anchor below her. Her decision for measuring in this way followed what she normally did on a single pitch route when the rope end was on the ground. She next decided to not pull the rope all the way to its halfway point because, after all, it was a 70-meter rope (about 225 feet) for a 100-foot rappel. More optimistically yet, she also decided not to tie a knot in its end. Although this length looked okay from her perspective—despite a bulge in the face below that detracted from her perspective—the rope's end was in fact about five feet shy of that next target anchor below, at the top of the first pitch. Her partner, with nine years experience, was about seven feet to the left of this same target anchor, but he was engaged in breaking down an anchor the two had built earlier at the start of this pitch. Busy, he failed to notice that Polk's rope was too short to get her all the way down to his position.

Polk unclipped and began her rappel. She was in a bit of a hurry and watched the route itself. Not only was Ouday not monitoring the end of Polk's rope now, neither was she. Ouday finally glanced at her. To his horror, he saw she did not have enough rope.

"STOP, STOP STOP!" he yelled frantically.

But too late. The short end of Polk's line exited through her ATC device. She found herself in midair and unattached to anything.

Emitting what Ouday would describe as an "earth-shattering scream," Polk fell 70 feet. Her scream truncated into a nasty thump as she slammed onto the steep sandy slope on her back. Big rocks studded this terrain as it funneled into a narrow gully about a foot and a half wide carved between two large boulders. Polk bounced twice and slid down slope about ten feet and stopped there.

When Polk hit the ground Ouday's first thought was "Oh my God, she's dead." He looked at her body then at the rope trailing down the cliff towards her. One end of it had snagged on a gear sling hanging from the rappel anchor. He was able to fix this rope and descend on it from his ledge.

Once down he rushed to Polk. Could she have fallen seventy feet and then hit that hard and yet still be alive?

Probably not. With a horrible sinking feeling he approached and examined her. No surprise, she was as inert as a pile of old laundry. A big surprise now, she was still alive but unconscious.

Ouday carefully moved Polk into a secure position to keep her from sliding farther down the slope. He knew he had to go for help immediately if Polk was to have her best shot at survival. But what if she woke up alone here with no idea what had happened, where he was, or what had become of him? He decided to try to wake up Polk.

This worked. He now explained to the dazed and damaged woman that she had taken a bad fall (a thing she did not even know) and that he was going for help. Ouday then ran to the Entrance Station. The rangers there radioed YOSAR.

By the time help arrived Polk was all too aware of what had happened. As she later explained it to us.

> I felt like I'd been run over by a Mack truck, but was fully aware of what had happened; I knew I didn't pull enough rope. I blacked out again until [Ranger] Jo Whitford arrived; she was the first on the scene. It hurt to breathe and I could barely speak. My body was in an extreme state of shock and trauma with spinal damage and internal bleeding so YOSAR made the call to air lift me from the cliff to get me to the hospital as quickly as possible. I credit so much of my survival to the efficiency and swiftness of my rescue and to the competency of the rescue members. I can remember the pain and a feeling of being totally helpless and, at that point my life, was dependent on those around me. I was passing in and out throughout the

> rescue and can only remember bits and pieces. I was trying to talk and give them information they were asking me. One memory is being in a body litter attached to a cable hanging 150 feet below the helicopter with Keith Lober riding on the litter to help stabilize me.

By the time Polk reached the emergency room in Modesto she thought the angels were with her. She abruptly knew she would be climbing again as soon as she was able. Maybe her insight was premature, maybe not. Polk spent ten days in the ICU then stayed in the hospital for eleven more days. Her injuries included three pelvic fractures, a dozen broken vertebrae, both shoulder blades fractured, and two ribs. Despite not having worn a helmet, though, her head and neck were fine. But her lungs had been seriously contused and now had collapsed lobes. Her liver had been lacerated, and the renal artery of her left kidney which carries the blood into the kidney to be filtered had broken. This lesion contributed to much of her internal bleeding. Indeed, she developed a hematoma the size of a football around that kidney before the artery finally clotted itself a couple of days later. Amazingly, none of this armada of injuries demanded surgical intervention.

Sounds pretty bad, alright. On July 2, a mere three weeks after having fallen off her rope, Polk flew home to Atlanta "to finish recovering" at her parents' house for six more weeks. Only five weeks after her fall, Polk started to walk again, now with a back brace and walker. Her muscles had atrophied. She had lost fifteen pounds in the hospital. But sheer will power, it seems, would aid in her recovery, one that appears nearly miraculous. A mere two and a half months after her accident she was back in Yosemite and climbing again—but now with a different attitude:

> —by October I felt as strong as ever. So many people involved in my rescue are responsible for my survival; my climbing partner who kept it together to get me the help I needed, the awesome members of YOSAR, the hospital staff, and my parents who helped me through every step of my recovery. It was an extremely traumatic and life changing experience, one I'm grateful to live through and share with others. So many climbing accidents are caused by human error and are easily preventable. Mine was caused by a lapse in judgment and "going through the motions" without really thinking about what I was doing. I guess the moral of the story is stay aware and always pay attention to your actions because climbing is a serious game without much room for error. A simple mistake can end a life.

Rappelling appears simple but it engenders significant risks and is serious business. Downplaying these for any reason has too often proved a big mistake. The 10+ years from 2015 to 2025 in Yosemite saw 19 technical climbing deaths; 10 were due to errors made during rappels.

ANCHORS AWAY

Climbers all too frequently have taken anchor safety for granted. Indeed, as John Dill notes: "Climbers frequently describe the belaying habits they see on Yosemite routes as 'frightening.'" One of the first serious anchor errors in Yosemite provides a classic example. On June 20, 1968, 18-year-old Ernest Willard Milburn of Oakland and John Gibbons of Piedmont were on the Glacier Point Apron and had completed their ascent of Goodrich Pinnacle, for that era a difficult Grade III, 5.9, seven-pitch climb. On this hot summer day they were on their second rappel. For his anchor on this pitch, Milburn made the decision to attach to a nylon sling left fixed by a previous party much earlier (this is important because largely due to ultraviolet rays, nylon exposed to prolonged sun deteriorates and weakens.) He started his rappel. The weathered and frayed webbing broke. Milburn fell nearly 700 feet. Ironically, Goodrich Pinnacle had been named for Don Goodrich who had pioneered it on May 10, 1959, only to be killed a month later on Mount Conness (described later in this chapter).

Five years after Milburn's mishap, on October 17, 1973, an even worse accident occurred. David Rollo Bryan, a 20-year-old, first-year climber from Oceanside, California and Michael Timothy Harrison, a 24-year-old, 5.10 climber from Bishop, California had just completed the first two pitches of Point Beyond above Monday Morning Slab below Glacier Point. They had used protection that Harrison had placed a day earlier. Things went wrong as Harrison waited for Bryan, "jumaring" (using brand-name mechanical ascenders manufactured by Jumar) up behind him.

Harrison had set an expansion bolt (a one- to two-inch-long, partially threaded metal insert placed into a drilled hole) atop the third pitch with a homemade hanger of ¼-inch-thick, aluminum angle stock (a small piece of metal drilled to attach to a bolt and also to accept a carabiner). As Bryan ascended and was about to join his partner, he unclipped their shared rope from the only other bolt securing their line. This one had been placed to the side of the first. This unhooking now made the upper bolt their sole anchor. It appears, however, that Harrison's improvised hanger, a long one with significant leverage against the center of axis of the bolt holding it, had rotated and turned clockwise repeatedly as each man had ascended. This cranking of their sole hanger had rotated and unscrewed the nut, allowing both pieces of hardware to now detach under the combined weight of both climbers. All of their gear and they abruptly fell into space to their deaths. Even the bolt flew out. The now empty bolt hole was left a bit vertically oblong, much like what you see after a construction nail has been pulled.

As if that dual fatality were not enough, we next have the mother of all anchor failures. This one is not for readers with a weak stomach. But it *is* instructive. On May 14, 1978, three young climbers—Jeffrey Joseph Graves, age 22, John Edward

Nygaard, age 22, and John Paul Garton, age 24—decided to retreat off El Capitan via the long-established Rohr Rappel Route. The three had been about a third of the way up The Nose, a popular, 2,900-foot high, Grade VI route.

Far below them, Matthew Muchnick and Alan Nelson, both from Berkeley, California, were walking along the talus at the foot of the cliff. They heard some strange noises coming from above and looked up. To their horror they saw three flailing figures—one of them trailing a blue, 9 mm perlon rope—hissing down through space toward them. The trio slammed into the talus nearby. Muchnick and Nelson hurried to the impact site and found every climber "obviously dead." Shaken, the two hurried downhill to report the tragedy.

John Dill, Chris Andress, and I (Farabee) investigated the scene. It was the sort of mess no one ever wants to see. Bodies lay crumpled within fifteen feet of one another amidst blood, flesh, and skull fragments. These bodies were partly covered with a blizzard of litter—cans of food, utensils, a pocket knife with the blade half opened, a cut nylon sling, three stress-opened carabiners, a shattered Timex watch, a camera (still closed) and four rolls of exposed film.

The dead climbers were not roped together. Each wore a nylon harness with a six-carabiner brake system for rappelling. Each system was intact and none of the three men had slid off the end of a rope.

Looking *way* up, we saw two ropes still in place, anchored high *above* on the trio's immediate descent route. More intriguing, all of their climbing iron remained in their haul bag. More understandable, every water bottle was empty—this likely explained their retreat off the wall in the first place.

What went wrong here?

Graves had been climbing for three to five years; his experience included several big walls in Yosemite. Nygaard and Garton, their friends later reported, were "into 5.10 climbs." All three shared a reputation for being "cautious, safe climbers." One critical detail in why things went so wrong here is they had run out of water and, now dry, were retreating off the wall from nearly 1,000 feet up during hot weather. In short, they may have been impelled by haste.

An additional clue as to the trio's ill-fated last moments comes from another "almost a witness." At 9 a.m., Karl Mueller saw one of the three climbers penduluming near the Stove Leg Cracks. Mueller's sighting of the three doomed climbers now in itself did not explain much, only their retreat route at Stove Leg Cracks.

About a half-hour after Mueller's sighting, the three were seen lower, about 900 feet up, just below Dolt Tower (this formation was named after the first ascender Bill Feuerer, a.k.a. "Dolt" for his clumsiness by fellow climbers. Sadly, Bill Feuerer had committed suicide a year and a half before this triple fall incident). Photographer Brent D. Nichelin had been below The Nose at this critical moment but he was shooting another, lower, climbing group. He too heard a strange sound; it sounded like "'rip stop' material brushing against rock."

Nichelin now looked up through the 300 mm lens of his camera. In his weirdly magnified view he saw two people plus rope and other gear falling directly toward him. Bodies and gear slammed into the talus a mere thirty feet away. Nichelin did not even glance at the carnage. Instead, shaken, he too fled for help. In fact he was the first and closest witness to the impact but he had already fled before the other two witnesses arrived.

The second party of climbers, those below the trio, had just noted that the team above them had been retreating off the rock. But, focused upon placing their own protection, none of them observed the fatal crux event above them—although they did witness the horrifying sight of three live and thrashing people whooshing past in otherwise empty air.

Our initial thought was that all three men were rappelling on the Rohr Route. We suspected that while all of them were together at a single rappel station, something had failed and the entire party had fallen as one. And while we knew we had to be correct, we also needed to know a lot more: Specifically, what had caused their fall? Indeed, this triple-fatality was important enough to lead to one of the most exhaustive and intensive SAR/death investigations ever done in Yosemite. We combed through every piece of gear the three had and examined each for clues.

What proved invaluable were the four rolls of film. Once developed, they revealed how the men had used their ropes and for which purposes. The film also revealed how they managed their other equipment. From all of this, as Search and Rescue Ranger Tim Setnicka would later write, "we determined that the accident occurred while all three victims and their haul bags were suspended from the bolts at the station which failed but before they had a chance to pull their rappel ropes down."

Why did the bolt hanger fail?

As the official report notes, we suspected "one or two climbers were attached directly to the top Dolt bolt hanger and were standing on their slings." They had attached their haul bags as well as the remaining climber(s) to the same two bolts. These had been set months earlier into the granite a few vertical inches apart. These two hangers were connected with a standard chain of four hardware store links—the upper was a locking link, the lower was a lap link that had been squeezed shut properly, the two in the middle were standard solid links. The climbers apparently had attached themselves and all of their gear by wrapping their ropes and slings and carabiners *around* the chain between the two bolts—but not *through* any link. We do not know why they did not thread through a link. The upshot here is that everything and everyone was hanging *against* that chain not through it. By doing things this way, however, the trio was suspending themselves from just *one* hanger, not two, because if either the upper or lower bolt were to fail, the chain would dangle loosely despite the second bolt remaining secure. The instant it dangled it would have released everything that had been suspended against it. Despite how sketchily they had arranged their anchor, the chain did hold at least until the final climber clipped into it and then also had unclipped from his rappel line. Even with this questionable group decision, a single bolt and its hanger probably would have held even after being subjected to this load. What we wanted to know was: Why didn't it?

Among the wreckage at the bottom we found two more clues that might explain why. First, the fallen knife with a cutting blade open and a "pick/awl" blade partly open, and second, the cut nylon sling. These, in combination, implied that one of the haul ropes or slings may have been jammed. We asked ourselves: Had one of them cut that sling, thus suddenly freeing that haul bag? And if so, had the falling haul bag next been suddenly stopped by another rope? If it had, then the shock/stress of arresting that "minor" drop transferring to the upper bolt hanger—supporting everything and everyone—could have become the straw that broke the camel's back.

This scenario became our working hypothesis. In support of it, we also found a haul line tightly tangled around one of the dead climber's feet so tightly that it had caused burn marks on his boot. This constituted strong evidence that the shock of the haul bag's arrested fall *had* been transferred abruptly through this climber's body and through his gear directly up to the bolt. But even if this is what had happened—and it seemed extremely likely that it had—we still reckoned that the one bolt hanger, placed there only eight months earlier, should not have failed. Or *should* it?

Amazingly, and like a needle in a haystack, among the boulders and trees at the bottom of the cliff, we had found half of the broken steel hanger.

To figure out why it broke, we had to retrieve the other half off the wall and then engage a metallurgist to analyze it for fatigue. Six days after the accident we were able to replace the hangers in the granite wall. Both original bolts—3/8-inch Star Dryvin—looked fine. But the upper Dolt Hanger had snapped in half at both "arms." The lower one dangled every link of the former connecting chain—including the lower, large lap-link—still attached. All of this was intact. This is how we knew the climbers had not tied *into* any of these links, thus fatally negating the back-up function of the lower bolt if the upper one failed.

Strangely, it turned out that we did not have to find a metallurgical engineer. He found us. Gerald P. Fritzke had read about this incident and because his son was a climber, he had been so intrigued he offered us his services, all at no cost to the government, to examine the hanger with an electron microscope, et cetera. We took him up on this. After numerous tests he concluded: "Cracks had been present [in the hanger] prior to the May 14 accident. The strength of the hanger was very low—it would have taken only about 500 pounds to cause it to fail. It was quite soft [10 to 25 percent softer] compared with other bolt hangers I have examined."

The preexisting cracks that Fritzke found in the Dolt Hanger were small and were mostly on the wall side, so they may not have been visible to a climber. How these cracks had formed after being subjected to merely twenty or fewer rappels remained unclear for a while longer. One additional detail muddying this resides in Rohr himself having "modified" the hanger in some unknown way prior to placing it.

Ranger Setnicka concluded: "So a weak mechanical hanger combined with a poor tie-in method added up to a disaster."

That's putting it mildly.

On July 12, 2001, Jacob Quintana was fishing in the Merced. He heard what sounded like a rock fall. He looked up toward the North Buttress of Middle Cathedral to see a person tumbling downward about two-thirds up the face. Quintana also saw another tumbling object, darker and seemingly attached to the falling person. He thought this might have been an equipment bag.

Quintana dropped his tackle, ran to the road, flagged down a motorist, and used the driver's cell phone to call in the incident.

Rangers arrived at the foot of the cliff. They soon found Thomas Vroman Dunwiddie, a 49-year-old climber from Denver, and Myra Monica Elderidge, a 41 year-old from Boulder, Colorado at the base of the cliff. Both were still rigged in their harnesses, dead from massive trauma, and unrecognizable. "Examination of the scene and equipment," reports Ranger Jeffrey Sullivan, "indicated that Dunwiddie was leading and Elderidge was belaying."

How had this tragedy happened? The pair's belay station had been anchored by two pieces of protection at two locations. They had been using a two-rope belay and were still connected by twenty-five feet of climbing rope. Dunwiddie had apparently taken a leader fall and had yanked the anchor protection from both belay points—thus taking Elderidge off the face with him for 1,000 feet. Her left hand was burned by rope, consistent with having tried to arrest her partner's fall. Investigating rangers found the pair's freed belay protection below. It was deeply scarred from having been pulled from the wall by "great force." No evidence was apparent that Dunwiddie had placed his own protection during his leader climb.

An inspection of the cliff face revealed debris from their gear atop the 9th pitch but also possible rock failure points in the 15th pitch. So it remains unclear from exactly where the two fell. How Dunwiddie lost his holds and why he likely failed to set adequate protection during his leader climb also remain mysteries. Fatigue, however, may have contributed to his error(s); the two had made several other difficult climbs during the days just prior to their North Buttress attempt.

On July 2, 2003, anchor integrity came into sharp but belated focus. Mark Howard Lewis, a 48 year-old from Tahoe City, had just begun an ascent of the West Pillar of Eichorn Pinnacle on Cathedral Peak with Aaron Zanto, Brian Dannemann, and Chad Anderson. While Zanto and Lewis were on the second pitch, Dannemann yelled up to them that he could not complete the climb. The whole party decided to retreat.

Zanto, above Lewis, set up a rappel. He used an anchor of webbing and cord that a previous party had threaded behind a constriction in a finger-width crack. Zanto rappelled from this about twenty-five feet down to Lewis. Here he unclipped from the belay rope. Lewis clipped onto it and began his descent. Zanto soon heard him yell. Zanto looked down to see Lewis "spinning through the air with the ropes following him" for 230 feet.

The anchor sling had squeezed through, and yanked free of, the crack. As the *Yosemite Morning Report* for 24 July 2003, written by Tuolumne Subdistrict SAR Coordinator George Paiva, states, Zanto had told rangers "he had evaluated the anchor by tugging on it several times, but did not thoroughly inspect it visually."

An additional lesson here is that anchors can fail *even* with good hardware and a good tie-in method. On August 9, 1992, Alan Wayne Miller, a 39-year-old experienced climber from Stateline, Nevada took 37-year-old novice climber Caroline Lee Kostecki from South Lake Tahoe on the southeast buttress of Cathedral Peak. When Miller was at the top of the 4th pitch he belayed Kostecki as she climbed. She lost her holds and fell. Whatever protection either of these two might have placed (this remains unknown) pulled out. Worse—and this is the point here—Miller's otherwise solid belay anchor failed by yanking clear of the rock because of the tremendous build-up of kinetic energy. Thus Kostecki pulled Miller off the wall with her. Both climbers, still roped together, fell nearly 450 feet.

Another climbing party soon discovered their bodies. Sadly, Kostecki's 10-year-old son, Danny, and a friend Susan Redlong had been waiting for the climbers' return. Instead, SAR team members informed the two of the tragedy and escorted them down from near the accident scene.

Using old pitons or using preexisting bolts, hangers, and/or slings without first critically assessing their integrity may be convenient but may be much like playing Russian roulette. On the other hand, when placing new protection for an anchor, failing to set it with the spectre of a hard fall in mind can result in something that looks cosmetically intact but which might remain as dangerous as a head-on collision with a train.

All tolled, at least twenty climbers (eighteen men and two women) have died in Yosemite due to anchor failures while climbing or rappelling. These account for 20 percent of Yosemite's technical climbing deaths. These failures also account for the majority of Yosemite's eight multiple-death episodes wherein pairs—or, as above, a trio—of climbers all sustained fatal falls while roped together. In short, a solid, bombproof anchor that will hold from all directions of possible tension is in every climber's best interest.

LOST LEADERS
(Protection that Didn't)

To many, leading a climb is what the sport is all about. At the risk of over-romanticizing it, being first up a pitch of any difficulty focuses the powers of observation and concentration with diamond-pure intensity on just one reality, the rock above. Evaluating what's ahead, assessing possible holds, and also understanding one's own hard-won abilities and hard-learned limits, and then testing these by making that next move becomes a clean, adrenaline-drenched rapport between a human and a cliff. Pulling this off with the necessary skill leads to elation and often some pretty fantastic views from above. In contrast to this romance, making a serious mistake while leading can spell the end of all of that—and of life itself.

One of the earliest mishaps of this sort led to a truly hair-raising SAR mission. On September 2, 1963, 27-year-old Earl Hsu from San Jose, California was lead-climbing Cathedral Peak. He was a relative novice. Several hundred feet below the summit he lost his holds and fell. His protection failed. He fell almost ninety feet—past his little brother belaying from below—and rolled to a stop on a small ledge.

Ranger Wayne Merry was leading this rescue. Again, he had been a member of the first climbing team to scale the then "impossible" El Capitan in 1957. He decided that using a helicopter, relatively novel at this time for SAR work in the Park, would be the most efficient tactic.

Pilot A. P. "Mac" MacCloud of Whirl-Wide Helicopters of Fresno controlled the tiny, two-person Hiller-12E to lift Merry's men in a hurry—but only one man at a time. The pilot set each ranger and his gear onto a knife-edged, eighteen-inch wide ridge just below the top. At this altitude, even these small loads strained the limits of the little aircraft.

The first rescuers on scene stabilized Hsu, who was still breathing despite his wide variety of major injuries. Next they packaged him onto a Stokes litter. Wayne and his team now somehow "carried" Hsu 200 yards up to and along that narrow ridge for extraction. They performed this difficult carry immediately above a huge cliff. So far, so good, they all thought.

"The helicopter pilot [MacCloud] was an absolute winner," Merry noted in awe.

> We radioed him in and he put his skid across the crest, and somehow or other we managed to secure the basket to the skid tray without dropping it or falling off in the process. I recall leaning on the skid out over the drop with one hand while lifting the Stokes on with the other—and the skid moving slightly under my hand as we worked. I remember glancing up at the pilot while we were doing that, and I still remember his face—pale, absolute concentration, big beads of sweat on his forehead. Between the time the accident was reported and the time that Hsu was in the hospital, less than three hours had elapsed. After participating in hundreds of other emergencies, whether rescue, ambulance work, structural firefighting, search, or whatever, I have always thought afterward of many ways each operation could have been done better—but this one

> remains in my mind the only one that was almost picture perfect. We did everything we could—but the patient still died.

The biggest killer during leader falls in Yosemite is not from the leaders merely losing their holds. Instead it has been their decisions about placing protection. *Mountaineering: the Freedom of the Hills* advises: "You should protect moves you expect to be hard. Always space the protection to avoid potential falls that are excessively long or dangerous."

How serious are leader falls? Or, put another way, if an accident happens during any phase of climbing and an injury results, what proportion of these occur to leaders? Doctor William S. Bowie worked at the Park's clinic in the 1980s and became interested in the process and causes of climbing injuries (including fatal ones) in Yosemite. He, with Doctor Thomas K. Hunt and Hubert A. Allen, analyzed 220 accidents, 13 of them fatal, over a 3.5 year period beginning in April 1984 and published their findings "Rock-climbing injuries in Yosemite National Park" in *The Western Journal of Medicine* (August 1988, Volume 149). Tellingly, of the known accidents during this time 144 (65 percent) occurred when leaders fell. Although their falls varied in severity, the length of these falls did not always correlate with the resulting severity of injury. One leader who fell a mere six feet suffered a nasty compound fracture of the femur and severe abrasions. In contrast, the trio of analysts also mention a woman climber who took a leader fall for 100 feet, hit almost no rock, was arrested by the stretch of her rope only when it jammed in a carabiner, and emerged with one minor laceration and a couple of small bruises. Yes, she was lucky. This would have been her day to buy a lottery ticket.

More to the point here, during 29 percent of leader falls that led to some sort of injury, the lead climbers' protection yanked out of the wall, lengthening their falls and exacerbating their injuries.

It may seem trite to merely say that always placing proper protection at adequate intervals in a proper manner is an ideal that a climber may aspire to but only seldom achieves. Indeed, the reality is worse. Most climbers rely on their athletic abilities and skills more than on ideally placed protection. This may be as it should be. But many otherwise excellent climbers routinely fail to take the time and effort to adequately protect their belay rope. This is a bad habit. Gravity fails to forgive these climbers; and many poorly protected falls have proven lethal.

According to 20-year-old Frank Edward Johnson, 17-year-old Roger Stetson Parke of Tucson, Arizona rarely placed enough protection. On July 25, 1972, he was leading the Steck-Salathé Route on Sentinel Rock while Johnson belayed him from below. As Parke led the 16th pitch of seventeen he again failed to place enough protection. Maybe the smell of the summit wafted too strongly in his nostrils.

At any rate, Parke lost his holds and fell backwards. Although only a fourteen-foot fall, the teenager hit the wall head first and broke his neck. Johnson tried performing CPR—to no avail. As far as we can determine, Parke still holds the record for the shortest fatal technical climbing fall in Yosemite.

On May 25, 1975, a worse leader fall occurred. Twenty-two-year-old John Fox Schwab from Stamford, Connecticut and 21-year-old Ronald Baum of Hillsdale, New Jersey had nearly completed Selaginella, west of Lower Yosemite Fall. Schwab was leading the 4th—and final—pitch of the 5.7 route while Baum belayed from below. The two had roped together.

According to the incident report, witnesses stated that Schwab had placed only one carabiner and two nuts for protection on this last pitch. Baum, meanwhile, was sitting in a belay seat anchored to two nuts plus a large manzanita bush for backup. Schwab took a leader fall that yanked out both the nuts he had placed. As he continued to build momentum at the end of his safety rope, its inertia yanked Baum's two nuts out of the wall and ripped the bush by its roots out of their fissures. Both men fell about 400 feet, with the unbroken rope between them tangled in the branches of the manzanita.

A few weeks later, on June 17, 1975, James Michael Ottinger, a 30 year-old from Eugene, Oregon, had begun an ascent of Sentinel Rock with 24-year-old Ralph Edward Moore of Corvallis, Oregon. The two had chosen the Chouinard-Herbert Route and were only on the first pitch of the Grade V, 5.8, A2 route not far above the base. Ottinger was climbing above Moore and establishing his own way. At what proved to be the critical moment Ottinger stopped to place protection.

Somehow he lost his footing and fell. His previous protection popped out such that Ottinger fell almost sixty feet onto a narrow ledge. There, crumpled in a heap, he moaned, "Help me..."

Ottinger quickly rolled off this ledge and tumbled another 130 feet over a series of boulders and ledges. *All* of Ottinger's protection, including his anchor, had failed to hold. Moore was eventually able to grab his friend's rope and thus arrest his additional falling. When Moore got to his partner, he was hanging horizontally and head down against the rock by his seat harness. He was delirious and losing a lot of blood from his mouth. Almost immediately he stopped breathing. Moore tried CPR but to no avail.

As if the Grim Reaper had stopped on a whim in Yosemite but then decided he liked what he saw, on the very next day, June 18, 1975, 18-year-old James P. Welcome of Fremont, California was climbing Penney-Nickel Arête between Middle and Higher Cathedral Rocks. His buddy, 19-year-old John Trevino, stood on belay. The pair had completed three 5.6 pitches, although by now they had strayed a little off route. Welcome now led the fourth 5.6, pitch but chose a more zigzag path than needed. Ominously, en route he had set only a few points of protection.

Sixty feet to the left of his last protection point, he stopped on a small mossy ledge to finally set a chock. Welcome had previously been a student in both the beginning and intermediate climbing schools at Tuolumne Meadows, but even so, on this fatal day he had been wearing a new pair of heavy, bulky mountaineering boots incompatible with the demands of this climb. As fate would have it, here he lost his footing on the slippery surface. With so little protection set, he fell seventy-five feet, fatally injuring his head. Bizarrely, Welcome would be the third climber to die in Yosemite over three consecutive days. Ottinger would be the second. The first was Peter Barton, whom we discuss later in this chapter.

Inconveniently, nature fails to design all rock to support perfect placement of protection. Sometimes it is the wall that baffles an otherwise safety-conscious climber. At other times, setting protection is possible but doing so takes a backseat to making quicker progress. Even in hindsight, there remain times when it is difficult to determine which sort of ill-fated situation predominated.

Consider the incredible saga of 22-year-old Robert Bruce Locke of Suisun City, California. On October 5, 1976, Locke was climbing about 1,400 feet below the overhanging summit of the South Face of Mount Watkins. This is a serious nineteen-pitch climb rated 5.8 and A4. Locke's partner was Chris Falkenstein. A good choice, Chris taught climbing for the Yosemite Mountaineering School.

Only a dozen years earlier, this 2,000-foot wall located up Tenaya Canyon and across from Half Dome was first climbed by Chuck Pratt, Warren Harding, and Royal Robbins—the only time these three Yosemite pioneers ever climbed together—on a five-day epic during withering heat. This trio of seriously dehydrated climbers had summited, gaunt and grateful, on July 22, 1964.

Locke, now leading a right-facing dihedral (a roughly right-angled inside corner where two wall segments meet—like a partly open book) during far more pleasant weather, had just set two carabiners onto an already fixed, small Chouinard Hexentric chock, a piece of protection that had been placed and then left behind by a previous climber. He next moved upward and laterally about twenty feet and set two more nuts. He set these in a crack that he knew would not hold them if subjected to a serious jerk. He placed these here anyway, probably—as is often the case—for "psychological protection." In reality, that first Chouinard stopper from long ago was the only true piece of protection thus far on the pitch.

Locke next tried to mantle (a pull-up to one's waist) up onto a ledge. He failed, lost his holds, and fell. His psychological protection exited the granite crack like popcorn. His fifty feet of rope swung him past Falkenstein, who had to duck to avoid being swept off position. Sweeping the belay rope along in front of him, Locke continued swinging into the cliff's knife-edged corner. The impact here dealt him serious injuries. During the fall his belay rope had become entrapped against his hardware. Upon this impact his body acted like a hammer as it slammed the rope against the rock. This impact not only hurt Locke, it shattered a couple of carabiners into shards and, as Falkenstein now saw to his horror, it nearly severed Locke's Edelrid safety line.

Falkenstein, his hands burned badly by the friction of the belay rope while trying to arrest Locke's pendulum fall, started paying out that rope to lower his partner to a ledge. As if in slow motion, over the next several seconds the last strands of the damaged rope elongated nightmarishly as Falkenstein lowered Locke. Then each broke, one after another, plunging the injured climber into the abyss.

After plummeting another 150 feet, by unreasonably good luck his fall was abruptly arrested by an old, accessory, 11 mm line still attached to his haul bag. Below Locke yawned 600 more feet of air.

Falkenstein now unsnapped from his anchor and made his way down to his companion's new position, a precarious one suspended by the badly frayed haul line (Locke's 7 mm Edelrid sling too had been smashed, cut, and soon would fail). When Falkenstein reached Locke he was still conscious. Falkenstein found that his injured partner seemed paralyzed from the waist down and was otherwise barely able to move his arms and hands. Falkenstein laboriously maneuvered him up forty feet to a small ledge. Next he retrieved their gear and stuffed his buddy into his sleeping bag then secured him in place.

Falkenstein then retreated off the sheer face of Watkins in a series of dicey rappels. He knew time was not on Locke's side. So he hurried, connecting ropes together in ways that he would never have trusted under more careful circumstances. Setting his feet onto ground that did not require a rope lifted a huge weight off his heart. He then ran three miles to Mirror Lake and, by 5 p.m., found a phone and called in the emergency.

Ranger John Dill made a recon flight in the Park's Bell B-1 to determine where atop Mount Watkins the SAR team should begin. To fix the best location for a lowering, John memorized the shape of one small bush that seemed a natural marker. Tim Setnicka, the Yosemite SAR Officer, orchestrated the eleven-person rescue team, which included local climbers and guides as well as rangers. Ex-Vietnam military pilot Jim Daughterty began shuttling the team plus nearly a ton of gear to the top of Watkins, an approximately twenty-five-minute round trip, while carrying payloads limited to only 225 to 250 pounds per flight. Five hours of precision flying later, mostly in the dark, Daughterty had set everything and everyone safely atop Mt. Watkins—shaped, as Setnicka notes, like a large scoop of vanilla ice cream with a sheer south face.

All of this was in preparation for what was decided would have to be a 1,500-foot descent to rescue Locke. It was now midnight. The sky was clear and the moon full. As good as that sounds, however, Setnicka reckoned it would not be good enough. To improve on Mother Nature, he had also requested a Coast Guard, four-engine Hercules HC-130H crewed by eight and equipped with a "Carolina Moon." This eight-million-candlepower spotlight, designed for mercy missions on the open seas, runs off its own jet fuel source (good for four hours—

during which its sweltering Coast Guard crew entertain fantasies about shoving the roaring, fuming, heat-radiating contraption out of the plane and into the ocean). Because the huge, slow-flying (100 knots) aircraft needed to circle at a safe altitude above the terrain, the Carolina Moon could be aimed directly at the rescue scene for only sixty seconds at two minute intervals. The Coast Guard claimed that this was the first time a Carolina Moon had been used in mountains and/or on such a rescue.

That is, it *would* be used once the SAR team figured out exactly where the scene would be. One member of the SAR team rappelled off one point. It turned out to be 200 feet too far west. They next tried another spot. It too proved off, this time by fifty feet. The team's position atop the overhanging cliff made the precise location of Locke's Ledge almost a matter of faith based on that one small bush Dill had pinpointed. But by rappelling 100 feet down the slabs while the Carolina Moon lit up the sheer face of Watkins—like God's own private drive-in movie screen—they finally determined where their anchor should go.

Plan "A" was to send down Dale Bard, a "professional" big wall climber, to be followed by a medic, me (Farabee). Each of us would be clipped into one long lowering, managed from the top. Before Dale disappeared I explained, "As you get close, yell to him. If he doesn't answer, as soon as you can, put your hand inside his sleeping bag to test for body heat. Then let me know what you find."

Bard seemed supremely confident despite facing this long descent in the "dark." "Piece of cake," he said. By now it was 1 a.m.

In contrast, I was anything but comfortable with the prospect of following him down. In fact, scared would sum it up.

It took Dale 108 minutes to be lowered those 1,500 feet, all the while scouting and aiming for that sleeping bag. He reached it at exactly 2:48 a.m. Meanwhile, circling at less than 1,500 feet above the rescue scene, the large Hercules continued roaring overhead and played its immensely bright Carolina Moon—hot enough to boil seawater at ten feet—against the cliff. Platoons of black shadows danced, elongated, shortened, and then faded across the wall of granite around Bard and Locke. Again, this weird light show had repeated itself at several minute intervals for more than an hour.

Under this surreal ghostly light of two bright moons, Bard finally was able to yell to Locke, who lay silent in his sleeping bag roped into the small ledge hundreds of feet in the air.

No response.

Dale Bard inched a bit closer, thinking: I'll just stick my hand into his…

Suddenly everyone in Yosemite who had a Park radio heard him screeching: "Butch, you motherfucker, he's dead! Get me out of here!"

Once we calmed Dale Bard down a little we asked some pointed and critical questions. His answers convinced us: Locke was indeed dead.

Now there was no need for me, the Park Medic, to descend those 1,500 feet.

Instead we lowered expert climber Rick Accomazzo with more gear to assist him. The two spent the last hour or two of the night on the posh Sheraton-Watkins Ledge, 220 feet above Locke's body. Shortly after dawn they packaged the dead climber. While this may sound slick, it in fact took many more hours for the entire team of now twenty men equipped with nearly a mile of ropes rigged to hoist Locke—dead due to a broken neck—to the summit by 2:30 p.m.

There is now a nineteen-pitch, Bob Locke Memorial Buttress Route up Mount Watkins. It passes a couple of hundred feet east of where he died.

Of course not all falls attract this much SAR action. Some mishaps occur so quickly that the only possible response is looking at them via hindsight. On April 30, 1977, 31-year-old Suzanne S. Carne of Las Aromas, California extended beyond her ability. She had twelve years of climbing experience, although most of it was with guides. Even so, she had led climbs up to 5.7. She was now leading the Southwest Arête on the Lower Brother (rated Grade III, 5.5). Suzanne's 30-year-old husband John E. Carne, with sixteen years of experience, belayed her during this, her approximately fifty-fifth climb. Suzanne had just admitted to John she was having difficulty. She also had backed off her original route and was now trying a second.

Out of John's sight and 120 feet above and to his right, she yelled to him that she had placed a piece of protection, but she next added that she was not happy with it. She then moved a few feet farther and placed what she said was a better piece. John Carne now felt that the climb was not going well. He yelled for Suzanne to find a good anchor point. Ten feet farther and two minutes later, he heard Suzanne yell, "Falling!"

Several large rocks and rope whistled past him thirty-five feet to his right. Although the cause of her fall went unwitnessed, her husband guessed that she had been trying to place an anchor. Carne fell more than 175 feet, coming to rest at the bottom of the cliff. She died because she had placed poor protection yet had kept climbing farther and farther. Suzanne Carne became the first woman to die during the act of climbing a Yosemite cliff.

Yet another mishap occurred on May 28, 1978, when 21-year-old Gary Gissendaner of San Carlos, California paused 800 feet below the summit of East Quarter Dome, a Grade V, 5.9, A2 route, with 29-year-old Phillip Bard (Dale Bard's brother). Conditions were fine for the polished rock face east of Half Dome. The pair had averaged one pitch per hour. Bard did note, however, that Gissendaner seemed to be a bit impatient. As they continued up successfully, he wanted to climb the next pitches faster yet. Gissendaner, Bard said, had been ruminating over a comment made by another climber that this route offered several "free pitches" which you could ascend without aid. Gissendaner now led the 6th pitch, rated 5.7, A1, and he free-climbed it.

He set three or four chocks en route for his belay rope. Then he found a fixed pin. Above that he placed two more nuts. So far, this sounds pretty good.

Gissendaner next climbed fifteen feet higher and reached a false end of the pitch. He stood there for almost twenty seconds on a small stance offering very difficult holds as he searched for a crack in which to set protection. As Bard watched all of this, he saw his partner lose his footing slightly.

Anticipating a possible fall, he glanced down to recheck his own stance, anchors, and belay. Then he looked back up to see Gissendaner already dropping—his protection popping out of the rock like a giant zipper unzipping. Stopping his companion's fall lifted Bard off his own footing by four feet.

Gissendaner fell sixty feet down the cliff face but stopped about ten feet above his belayer. He now dangled in a semi-prone position, semi-conscious.

Phillip Bard lowered his stricken partner to his own location then moved him to a refrigerator-sized alcove. Seconds later Gissendaner was wracked by a seizure. Bard took forty-five minutes securing his badly injured friend to the cliff. He then executed a single-rope rappel for help, an hour-long job. Two more hours of running got him to Mirror Lake for aid. Ranger Tim Setnicka again became the team leader.

He, John Dill, and Mead Hargis planned yet another lowering operation from the near summit. The Park helicopter recon spotted the victim.

Almost simultaneously the "Huey" helicopter from Lemoore Naval Air Station arrived at the Ahwahnee Meadow, the pre-determined landing site for many SARs within the Park. After speaking with me (Farabee) they indicated that, if I wanted, they would do a "flyby" and assess the situation. Or at least that is what I understood them to be communicating. For some reason they believed instead they had the "green light" to execute an immediate rescue. This unknowingly shoved us from plan "A" to plan "B."

The Lemoore team figured it might be better to try a far quicker but trickier "hanging snatch." To pull this off (literally and figuratively), Pilot Lt John Sullivan had to hover while his rotor blades spun close to the cliff face while Chief Petty Officer Benny Revels rappelled down 250 feet from the airship. Then, dangling at the end of his thin line, this experienced crew chief swung into Gissendaner's alcove. There Revels clipped Gissendaner and himself together and cut the stricken climber loose from his anchor. Now Sullivan cautiously lifted the pair hanging at the end of the swaying rope off the cliff.

Sullivan hauled the two dangling men to Ahwahnee Meadow. But even at a slow speed, the weight at the end of the 250-foot line extended in an arc well behind the Huey. Pulling off a safe landing with this arrangement required delicacy at the controls. One problem here, Revels was unable to communicate with his pilot due to a faulty portable radio. Another problem was Gissendaner now inadvertently hung nearly upside down from Revels' harness. A third problem was the crewman monitoring all of this from the open door of the airship could not accurately judge the altitude of the suspended pair as Sullivan lowered his machine toward open ground. All of these problems added up to a high potential for landing Gissendaner too fast and too hard.

A few hundred feet away about 200 people had gathered to watch all this with bated breath.

As Sullivan lowered the Lemoore Huey, Ranger Paul Henry and I (Farabee) tried to anticipate exactly where he would set Gissendaner on the ground. We had the ambulance gurney out and ready on the muddy meadow. With each new guess we made, we now urgently pushed it back and forth through the mud. We must have looked to the watching audience as if we were rehearsing for a Keystone Cops episode.

Even after Revels dropped a guide rope to us the airship lowered faster than any of us wanted—including Sullivan. Ultimately Revels and Gissendaner, still upside down, splatted onto the ground.

With this pie-in-the-face splat into the tall grass and wet ground, the huge crowd behind us winced and heaved a collective "aaugh" of shock.

After the local clinic stabilized Gissendaner, Lemoore medevaced him to the Valley Medical Center in Fresno where he was treated for a basilar skull fracture and other head injuries. Sadly, he died there on June 3rd, six days after starting his climb.

For their amazing efforts, the five men of the navy rescue crew were awarded Department of the Interior Gold Valor Awards, the only time this had been bestowed on a non-Department of Interior team.

On one end of the protection spectrum might stand a few technical climbers who are such gear hounds they lace pitches with an overkill of hardware intended to arrest every conceivable fall. They worry a lot and they make slow progress. But they survive their climbs. Those more toward the middle of the spectrum tend to be prudent and objective; they protect their routes with care and remain cognizant of the consequences of failed protection during a fall. They do not evaluate the ease of a route by wishful thinking, nor do they delude themselves by believing their climbing skills are infallible. Their speed is solid but not flashy. In contrast, those climbers on the very highly-skilled end of the spectrum may at times be over-confident to the point of denying even the possibility of a fall, let alone the consequences. For many of these "hot" climbers (some of whom may not be as highly skilled as they would like to believe), these consequences—to themselves as well as to their partners, family, and to the SAR and emergency medical crews who must risk themselves during a rescue—may seem academic at best, impossible at worst.

Even great climbers can be undone by wishful thinking. On May 17, 1979, Christopher Shepherd Robbins, a talented 24-year-old climber with 5.11 leading experience from Riverside, California was climbing the Grade VI, 5.9, A4 Tangerine Trip on El Capitan with Randal M. Grandstaff. He seemed a solid partner; he was a 24-year-old, 5.12 leader with eleven years experience. In 1979, *anyone* rated as a 5.12 climber was pretty hot. There existed only a handful of

5.12 climbers in the world. This level of ability was the maximum at that time.

Robbins and Grandstaff decided to each lead alternate pitches. Tangerine Trip would be the first big wall for both of them. They fixed lines on the first two pitches then returned to the ground for the night. The next morning, Robbins slowly jumared up 150 feet to begin leading the third pitch. Meanwhile Grandstaff stood below loading their haul bag. Seconds later, Grandstaff heard a weak scream and looked up. He saw his partner in a tumbling fall. Robbins fell 200 feet and slammed into the ground only thirty feet away.

Grandstaff quickly detected a faint heartbeat and breathing. He began CPR. Within moments he knew his friend needed much more help than he could provide, so desisted CPR and ran down to El Capitan Meadow to get it. Meanwhile Chris Robbins died.

Why had he fallen? An investigation by the Park revealed that Robbins' 11 mm Chouinard rope—a new one used only once before and never during a fall—had parted due to abrasion against the rock. The investigation (Incident Report #79-1338) concluded: "The action of Robbins jumaring caused the rope to slide back and forth on the rock. Apparently the rope's sheath wore through first and then the mantle [the inner core]. Minute rock particles were visible in the broken rope."

This was indeed a tragedy, but surprisingly, a fully preventable one. Only four days earlier, climber Bob Williams had warned Robbins precisely of the likelihood of rope abrasion at that specific anchor location and had told him how to avoid it. But Robbins and/or Grandstaff had either forgotten this or had chosen to not follow Williams' advice.

An unfortunate postscript: While working as a professional climbing guide on June 5, 2002, at Red Rocks outside Las Vegas, a 44-year-old Randal Grandstaff, now with a reputed 800 first ascents under his harness, fell unwitnessed and with his gear 150 feet down the Great Red Book. The reason why remains unknown. His client had just rappelled to the ground. Grandstaff, the client thought, was reconfiguring the belay anchor. An autopsy revealed surprisingly well advanced heart disease but it shed no light on how or why his mishap had occurred during a "routine" chore.

Although it might seem a no-brainer that solid placement is critical, on climbs during which emotions begin to eclipse rational thinking, it really is not a no-brainer. It's a must-use-brainer. Illustrating this, on June 3, 1985, 23-year-old Joseph F. Palmer of Lyndhurst, Ohio was leading a difficult, 5.11b climb named Aftershock on The Cookie Cliff up the canyon from Arch Rock. Ruth Galler, age 23, belayed him. Palmer lost his holds during a lieback move (using one's hands in opposition to one's feet to create a tension counterforce) and fell about sixty feet. He sustained an immediately fatal head injury when he hit the wall.

Galler, helped by two climbers from another party, lowered her partner and then examined him. Although she went for medical help, it was too late. Why had Palmer fallen so far?

After a thorough investigation, Ranger John Dill concluded the cause of Palmer's long fall was his poor placement of protection. He was close enough to his last protection that if he had placed it well it would have stopped him quickly. Instead his stoppers pulled free undamaged and with only shallow scratches indicating they were not "set," but merely touching rock in too-small jutting surfaces. Joseph F. Palmer died strictly because of a weak placement technique.

This sort of error is all too common. At 8:30 p.m., racing against the rapidly failing twilight of the summer solstice on June 21, 1986, 43-year-old Austin Frederick Colley of Yorba Linda, California was climbing the Yosemite Point Buttress east of Upper Yosemite Fall. Meanwhile, 40-year-old Joe Carl Kristy, who had just led the pitch, belayed him from above. Colley climbed up below him but suddenly took a fall. It yanked Kristy off his belay point as two of their three anchors failed.

Kristy had injured his hip and no longer felt competent to climb in the dark, maybe not even during daylight. He now called continually to Colley, invisible somewhere below. Ominously, he heard no response. Again, seriously hurt himself, Kristy bivouacked on a ledge.

Chris VanDiver, a friend of both climbers and a talented climber and an experienced and trained rescuer, missed the pair that night so, after borrowing a Park radio, he hiked up to the Buttress in the morning. He spotted Kristy 100 feet from the top. To help him, VanDiver summited, rappelled down, threw a rope, and helped his battered friend to the top. Meanwhile Kristy explained to him about Colley.

VanDiver requested a SAR mission. A ten-person team recovered Austin Colley. An examination revealed he had died from his mishap the night before. The cause? The incident investigation concluded inadequate protection.

A more strange—and even more spectacular—protection problem occurred two years later. On May 20, 1988, 24-year-old Robert Dietmar Kuhn of Ursenwang, Germany was leading the Pancake Flake Pitch (#24) on The Nose of El Capitan. Kuhn had five years of climbing experience. Peter James Cuthbertson, age 34 and with eighteen years of intensive climbing history, belayed him using a Sticht belay plate attached to his harness.

Minutes earlier Rolf R. Lotz, climbing with another member of the German party, had been doing a lieback on the upper part of the 24th pitch, barely six feet from its top. Lotz had noticed some stones coming out of the crack as he pulled on his rope. Alarmed at this, he tested the ten-foot-long pyramidal block of granite that otherwise looked like a solid part of El Capitan. He could not feel it move. This was a relief. But then he noticed that the Friend (a metal, self-expanding safety device for setting into cracks) he had placed adjacent to the block *had* moved. Seeing this shift, he admitted, with more than 2,000 feet of air below him, scared him to death. So he carefully repositioned his protection to the left of the block and then yelled down, "Don't pull on the flake! It's dangerous!"

Lotz next told the two climbers below him to protect around the flake with a 3- and a 3½-inch Friend and to also use a RURP (a small wedge-shaped removable protection). Lotz and his teammate Chrestian Zelt both felt positive that Kuhn had heard the warning because Kuhn actually shouted back up to them about it. Cuthbertson, below, also admits not only having heard Lotz but also discussing with him how to aid-climb that section to avoid the shaky flake.

Cuthbertson would report that Kuhn had thus far been climbing "very confidently, safely and fast but cautious." Yet despite Lotz's specific warnings, when Kuhn reached the flake he did not switch to aid climbing. Instead he continued to free climb against the adamant recommendations of the climber above him. Cuthbertson watched his partner set a Friend in place then move up to the left in front of the possibly loose pyramid of granite. When Kuhn climbed chest high to it he abruptly seemed a little nervous about it.

Kuhn started to move back down—maybe, Cuthbertson hoped, to reanalyze the hazard. Cuthbertson then glanced down at two American climbers below, on pitch #22. As he glanced down he heard a noise and felt his shoulder get hit "like a slap." He intuitively ducked into the wall as rocks, dust, rope, and Kuhn fell past him. He braced for the weight to hit his belay stance.

It never came.

Kuhn had somehow pulled loose that entire block of granite—about ten feet long by four feet high and probably weighing more than a ton—from near the top of the pitch. The falling flake then hit Kuhn's 11 mm climbing rope and severed it. The rock also sliced through his thinner haul rope that had been attached to their anchor. The dropping, chopping block also knocked Kuhn loose. He and the rock and the now trailing, severed ropes plummeted 2,000 feet.

Five years passed before another spectacular failure to set protection made news in Yosemite. In fact, it made news in the climbing world all the way to England. On Friday, May 28, 1993, 36-year-old British soloist Derek Geoffrey Hersey attempted to free solo (no rope) the difficult fifteen-pitch Steck-Salathé Route on Sentinel Rock.

Over a span of eight years, the five-foot, eleven-inch and 138-pound Hersey had become a Boulder, Colorado legend in his own time. He was so blindingly fast and efficient a free-soloist that a partner on many of his back-to-back advanced climbs might as well have been a lead weight. Hersey typically would study a multi-pitch 5.10 or 5.11 route for several minutes and then blaze up it unprotected in astonishing time. His typical day "on the job" in Colorado would include hitchhiking to El Dorado Canyon with his chalk bag and a few candy bars. He would then solo twenty or so climbs—up to 5.12a, from one end of the canyon to the other. Afterward, he often managed to secure his commute home by haunting the parking lot and exchanging banter in hopes of catching a ride back to Boulder.

His performances after he first showed up in Colorado as an unknown were so hairball and fast that they generated the rumor that he was a rich Brit who had lost his fortune and had come to Colorado to die during a spectacular display of climbing. His unprotected solo ascents earned him the nickname "Doctor Death." When the April/May 1992 issue of *Climbing* featured Derek Hersey, interviewer Annie Whitehouse wrote: "Hersey's climbing style is smooth and intuitive. He moves precisely, with eloquent patience and calm. To compensate for a surprising lack of flexibility, he places his body in creative positions, often using smears and sideways stances. Watching him solo is like watching water flow."

Now, at 11 a.m. on that Friday, Hersey started up the Steck-Salathé Route in his routine, unprotected free-solo manner. His friends waited for his typical triumphant return. He failed to arrive. By evening, they were worried. Enough to report that Hersey had failed to return from his climb on Sentinel.

Rushing to squeeze a final bit of help from the fading light, rangers searched the face using a powerful spotting scope. They saw no one. At nine the next morning, climber Walt Shipley made the same search using binoculars in better light. He spotted a person—unmoving—850 feet above, where the Steck-Salathé and Chouinard-Herbert Routes begin.

Placed into position on a ledge by the Park's helicopter, a SAR team descended a total of 350 feet down to access Hersey's eviscerated and seriously fractured body. The recovery of Doctor Death required technical climbing aids as well as serious team work. His demise, one of several soloists (depending on one's definition, see Table 9) who have died due to falls in Yosemite, had gone unwitnessed.

Sometimes failures can be heartbreakingly minor transgressions of ideal technique. On May 22, 1996, 32-year-old Stephen B. Ross of Pasadena, California demonstrated this. A 5.11, A4 climber, Ross began leading the 5.10a-rated Beverly's Tower on The Cookie Cliff with Jason Holinger (a 5.10c leader). Ross placed his first protection a mere ten feet up into the dihedral. Over his shoulder he told Holinger, who was belaying him, "I'll move this higher later."

Ross did not otherwise comment about his placement, although to Holinger the rock at that spot did look flared. Holinger simply figured his partner knew what he was doing.

As Ross climbed abreast of his aid, however, he lost his holds. Screaming, "Fuck me!" he fell.

Holinger felt almost no upward roll on his belay rope as the protection pulled out of the rock undamaged. The chunk of aluminum might as well have been greased. Ross fell twenty feet then hit another climber, Matthew Pearce—who had been standing unroped while scouting the climb—a hard glancing blow on the head and back. Ross then fell past Pearce (who would survive) and hit the ledge a few feet below, head first. Holinger's safety line finally arrested Ross' fall after only twenty-five feet. This small distance finally proved fatal four days later in the hospital. The cause of Stephen Ross' death was poor placement of protection.

As we have seen, questionable placement is often very risky not only for the climber and his or her partner on belay but also for fellow climbers, Good Samaritans, and SAR personnel. A complicated episode that illustrates this negative domino effect began shortly after high noon on June 13, 2002, when 43-year-old Richard Zuccato of Baytown, Texas was rope-soloing The Braille Book on Higher Cathedral Rock.

Zuccato was using an apparently brand-new "Soloist" device to protect his belay. The instructions for this piece of equipment state that it will arrest the fall of an upright climber in a short distance. They explicitly state that the Soloist is designed to provide, in conjunction with a backup knot, a means of self belay for the solo climber.... "Your ultimate belay is your backup knot," the instructions read. Moreover, they warn, the Soloist "will not lock if you fall headfirst."

Zuccato told Scott Sandberg and Ty Cook, whom he allowed to climb past him as he rigged, that he was "giving the device a go" and that he knew how to tie backup knots for it.

As Sandberg, seconding, climbed then topped out on the first pitch he often looked down to check on Zuccato's progress. He noted the solo climber had placed several points of protection on this 5.8 climb at intervals of roughly fifteen feet. But Sandberg did not see any backup knots for Zuccato's Soloist—a device with which Sandberg happened to possess prior experience.

At 12:35 p.m., Sandberg watched as Zuccato attempted a lieback move high on the first pitch. The Texas climber abruptly lost his holds, fell outward, then inverted into head-down fall. No backup knot secured the Soloist. Nor did any other piece of gear correct for the climber's inversion.

Sandberg heard Zuccato's rope hiss—likely through the Soloist—as the man continued in his inverted fall for more than fifty feet. As Zuccato passed a low tree he seemed to try to grab its branches. He succeeded only to the extent of converting his inversion into a horizontal position. Roughly twenty feet lower, Zuccato slammed on his back onto the ground seventy-five feet below that first lieback move.

While his new self-belay device had, as promised, not arrested his inverted fall, it may have reduced his velocity a bit by friction as he slid down the length of his rope.

Scott Sandberg (who, sadly, would die in an avalanche on New Hampshire's Mount Washington before a year passed) and Ty Cook yelled an alarm to another party above. Next the two retreated off the wall to assist the fallen climber.

By coincidence another party climbing near The Braille Book consisted of

Ranger Jack Hoeflich on his day off and SAR team member Greg Loniewski. These two also heard Zuccato fall and were hurrying to his aid

Amazingly, despite his huge fall, Zuccato was not only still alive but conscious. He was alert and had detached from his harness and Soloist device by the time Hoeflich and Loniewski reached him. But beyond this bit of self-help he was not ambulatory. He had an obvious open elbow fracture and, worse, he informed his first responders that he was experiencing significant abdominal and pelvic pain. Fortunately here, both Loniewski and Good Samaritan Johann Aberger (from the party above Sandberg's) were intermediate-level EMTs. Ranger Jack Hoeflich now left them to stabilize Zuccato. Hoeflich scrambled about a half mile down the Class 2/3 terrain of Spires Gully for help. He soon "hijacked" a passing vehicle and borrowed a cell phone to call Valley Shift Supervisor Ranger Steve Yu. He informed Yu that the 225-pound Zuccato had sustained an open fracture plus internal injuries of unknown gravity.

Yu, now the incident commander, quickly arranged for Park Helicopter 551 to fly in from Crane Flat, fifteen minutes away. This emergency became Incident #02-1435. It would also become one of the more controversial recoveries during which Yosemite and other SAR personnel would risk their lives to rescue an injured climber who apparently had failed to adequately protect his climb.

As Yu coordinated things overall, Hoeflich made his way to the SAR Cache, arriving at 1:43 p.m. Thirteen minutes later, Yu was on the phone with the Air Force Rescue Coordination Center to request emergency assistance from Lemoore Naval Air Station. Within fifteen minutes Yu had the green light for this and was on the phone with Lemoore. The navy air crew scrambled immediately. Their ETA, they said, would be about 3:30 p.m. But by 2:20 p.m., personnel in the Park Helicopter (a Bell "Huey" Super 205) already had made visual contact with the incident site. Helitack supervisor Jeff Power had reported to Yu that a heli-rappel into the gully there was feasible.

Yu next arranged for Helicopter 551 to divert to Tuolumne Meadows to pick up SAR Rangers John Dill, Donna Sisson, and Park Medic Dave Horne from a rope rescue training course in Tuolumne Meadows and return with them for an insertion onto the accident scene.

Meanwhile, Greg Loniewski had managed to borrow a miniature walkie-talkie and was now reporting Zuccato as being increasingly combative—a sign of shock and/or of a possible head injury with concussion complications. Moreover his abdominal and pelvic injuries were swelling.

At 3 p.m., Helicopter 551 landed at El Capitan Meadow to prepare for a heli-rappel of Dill, Sisson, and Horne onto Zuccato's position. Five minutes later the Park aircraft lifted off and inserted the three SAR personnel with their gear. But while Helicopter 551 could perform this heli-rappel of rescuers, it could *not* short haul him out because a vital piece of the aircraft's rigging was currently outside of the Park being modified.

Several minutes later, Ranger Dill radioed from on scene that Zuccato was alert and oriented "times four" (was exhibiting a full level of consciousness), that he had experienced no blackout, that his peripheral motor and sensory functions were intact, and that he was in relatively good spirits (despite earlier combativeness). Horne, Dill and Sisson were administering oxygen, IV fluids, and morphine.

It was, Dill now noticed, a bit breezy at ground level at the pickup site.

At 3:50 p.m., Helicopter 551 returned and lowered a litter and a full-body vacuum splint for stabilizing and evacuating Zuccato. The nine rescuers on scene (the three SAR Rangers, Loniewski, and five Good Samaritans) now worked to package Zuccato in the splint, cervical collar, and head blocks for his short haul. At 4:55 p.m., more than four hours after Zuccato's fall, this team began a ten-minute carry fifty yards over unfriendly terrain to the hoist point atop a big boulder at the base of the cliff. This was also situated nearly in the middle of the gully at about 5,600 feet elevation where a helicopter lift appeared safest.

Meanwhile Lemoore's "Rescue 2" had landed in the meadow. Radio communications coordinated a plan for Rescue 2 to lift the injured climber in the Park's litter.

Rescue 2 soon hovered within the gully bracketing the extraction point. This navy machine was piloted by Lieutenant Bryan Dombrowsky (with 1,700 hours of flight time). Commanding was Lieutenant Commander Patricia Schumacher (with 4,645 hours of flight time). The navy crew also included Petty Officer Gallegos and Corpsman Jason Laird plus one more crewman. At 5:17 p.m., Gallegos, who had a better view downward, guided Dombrowsky to hover off-center over Zuccato. During their approach the onboard crew had been lowering Corpsman Jason Laird. Dill reached out to stabilize the swaying corpsman as he reached the pickup point. Here Rescue 2's cable stopped paying out, but the belay line continued to feed out into a slack pile of about forty or more feet on the ground. Some of this rope even blew into the brush below. Dill pointed this out to Laird and also tried to retrieve it, but it had snagged on something out of sight. Soon, however, the crewman in the machine above had somehow reeled most of this line back into the hovering airship, avoiding a potential catastrophe.

Laird attached Zuccato, now splinted, immobilized, and strapped into the Stokes litter, to the cable and safety rope then signaled for a lift. Soon the crew above had winched the two roughly seventy feet above the pickup point.

So far, so good.

After Commander Schumacher had ordered Gallegos to "Bring 'em up," she saw Dombrowsky positioning the collective "way high" to extract the greatest lift from an apparently dwindling power source (the cause of this loss of power was never determined but it may have been due to wind and/or a downdraft). Alarmed at Dombrowsky's "running out of pedal," a condition that would leave the tail rotor without enough power to prevent the airship from auto-rotating uncontrollably in this narrow gully, Schumacher now told pilot Dombrowsky "Push the nose over." Schumacher, aware that this abrupt loss of power could very quickly prove catastrophic for everyone on scene below *and* inside the helicopter, now assumed control of the airship and pushed the collective down. She aimed Rescue 2 down the narrow gully to gain air speed and, with it, increased control over the rudder. Her emergency response was intended to save the machine and to protect the personnel on the ground, not to protect Laird or to rescue Zuccato.

A moment after dropping Rescue 2 down the gully she heard a "snapping or cracking sound." Just before this, Zuccato and Laird had been suspended roughly seventy feet above the ground, a fairly safe margin for this location.

This cracking sound was the report of the cable breaking. As the helicopter had dropped to regain air speed and control, the middle of the stretcher had slammed into the upper trunk of a Douglas fir growing about 100 yards down the gully. The tip of this tree had naturally forked into three or more trunks, each about six or seven inches in diameter. This impact with at least one of these trunks severely distorted the litter.

This collision with the fir likely also knocked Laird unconscious and, among other injuries, punctured one of his lungs. This injury quickly would develop into a pneumothorax.

As Schumacher continued to push the collective down to regain positive control of Rescue 2, she heard yet another loud snap or crack. This sound was even more ominous. The end of the just broken cable—which had been under the tension of Zuccato and Laird clipped at its end—had just elastically rebounded upward to whip into the rotor blades, entangle in them, then be snapped yet again.

Schumacher now smelled smoke. She next heard Petty Officer Gallegos yelling to her that the hoist cable had broken. He hollered "We've lost 'em!" referring to Corpsman Laird and Zuccato. Commander Schumacher now had to fight to keep the machine flying at all, let alone well. When she "got above forty knots" as they exited the gully she heard Gallegos inform her that they indeed still had the two men suspended on the secondary safety rope, stretched taut beneath their machine but, Gallegos added, Corpsman Laird was now dangling (unconscious) "upside down."

Now the only line securing the two people hanging below Rescue 2 was a safety rope attached to the Sticht plate inside the airship. As the helicopter wobbled, the crew member monitoring the plate somehow lost his stance. Abruptly, this vital belay—normally good for holding only one person at a time anyway—became unattended.

Almost instantly the entire dangling burden fell free from below the belly of the ship as the belay rope hissed out of the Sticht plate, uncoiling like a fishing line off a free reel. Luckily, the line suddenly tangled and knotted at the Sticht plate, leaving about fifty feet of rope still inside the airship. Unluckily, this still left more than 200 feet of line hanging below—with two battered people attached at the end of those 200 feet.

As Rescue 2 exited the gully at a much lower altitude than it had entered, the litter swung so far below that it dragged through vine maples at brush level. This high-speed bushwhacking again pummeled Zuccato and likely whipped the unconscious Laird too.

Schumacher soon lowered the airship toward the meadow. She aimed it into the wind to place the two men suspended below onto friendly terrain. The 200 feet of safety rope (one of these was used during every hoist since April 30, 1975) with its dangling burdens pendulumed from side to side in a long arc.

The pilot thought she was descending slowly but she could not see what was going on below. For one thing, she was positioned on the opposite side of the aircraft from the open door from which the two men hung. In fact, Rescue 2 was descending toward the ground at a safe rate. Commander Schumacher now maneuvered the machine to control the swinging litter so that she could safely set it on the ground.

Gallegos soon stated the litter was "on the deck" and they now needed slack in the rope. Schumacher eased lower. With victim and medic on the ground, Gallegos sliced their errant line from inside the airship. Spookily, about four feet of this line was now missing its protective sheath. The litter's bushwhacking run had been remorseless on that rope.

Yosemite Medical Clinic Doctor Glen Patrigio, followed by two members of an AirMed crew from Modesto sprinted from a third airship, parked on the ground, and extricated Zuccato from the badly deformed litter. One team began CPR on him. Another started working on Laird, who had regained consciousness but otherwise looked far worse for wear.

Meanwhile Commander Schumacher continued flying forward. She flew one circuit of the meadow then set down in the normal helicopter landing spot. Dombrowsky wanted to keep the rotors turning in case their aircraft would be needed to evacuate their injured corpsman to advanced medical care. But Schumacher decided instead to shut down the machine. This was fortuitous. The overhead blades and other critical flight components had been damaged by that snapping cable. Rescue 2, she reckoned, would need repair before it could again safely fly. Indeed the damaged helicopter eventually would be trucked out of Yosemite on a lowboy trailer back to Lemoore where it would be repaired.

Less than fifteen minutes later a ground ambulance, Medic 3, was rushing to Yosemite Medical Clinic with Laird on aboard. Roughly twenty minutes later Doctor Toles inserted a chest tube into the injured corpsman to relieve his increasing pneumothorax.

At 6:25 p.m., six hours after the fall off The Braille Book, Dr. Glen Patrigio pronounced Richard Zuccato dead. When his litter had whammed into that fir tree the impact had severed his spinal column and massively injured his head, neck, and chest.

A bit before 7 p.m. AirMed took off from El Capitan Meadow for Modesto with Laird aboard and still in bad shape. Laird recovered from his broken ribs and other injuries and revisited Yosemite about a month later to thank his lucky stars—and some of the medical personnel who swarmed him after his wild ride.

The bottom line here was it seemed a near miracle that Lieutenant Commander Patricia Schumacher was able to prevent Rescue 2 from crashing at the extraction site and killing those aboard plus some of those on the ground and Laird.

Not long after this denouement, members of Zuccato's family filed a tort claim then a civil suit against the federal government for its failed and fatal rescue effort. Before this suit made it to trial, however, both parties reached a settlement whose specifics remain undisclosed.

Interestingly, the military had activated the Naval Air Station Lemoore Search and Rescue Unit in 1963 and deactivated it on July 14, 2004—as a victim of base reduction. The unit originally flew the UH-34 "Seahorse" airships, but due to the numerous local military operating areas above 10,000 feet elevation, it became apparent that a better performing platform was necessary to rescue survivors in the nearby high Sierra. The unit then transitioned to the HH-1N "Huey" in 1970. With a service ceiling of 15,000 feet, the Huey is capable and has landed upon and taken off from the 14,495-foot summit of Mount Whitney, the highest point in the continental United States. During its forty-one-year history, the Lemoore Naval Air Station Search and Rescue Unit performed more than 950 SAR missions throughout the Sierra Nevada and central California. At least as early as June 21, 1972, the Lemoore "Rescue Angels" were assisting the Park. On that day, Lt Cmdr "Mercury" Morse landed on El Capitan Meadows to evacuate William Lynderman Hendry III, whose skull had been fractured by a rock dislodged by his partner's rope and which fell 80 feet while climbing the East Buttress of El Capitan (see next section below), to Lewis Memorial Hospital. Sadly, Hendry was pronounced dead there. Hence no air evacuation out of the Valley was needed. Pilot Morse instead next flew to the Hetch Hetchy area to lift out hiker Julie Haskins who injured her ankle and could no longer walk.

Incident #02-1435 on June 13, 2002, to rescue Richard Zuccato would become Lemoore Naval Air Station's last rescue flight in Yosemite National Park.

"WE WILL, WE WILL, ROCK YOU"

A nightmare of many climbers is being hit by a falling rock while on a wall. Nearly every rock that falls close while climbing is caused by a climber, sometimes, as we have seen earlier in the case of Robert Dietmar Kuhn on the Pancake Flake on El Capitan, in a self-destructive way. The scary part of rockfalls is, if you are in the fall line, you frequently have neither time nor room to get yourself out of the whooshing missile's path. Indeed, your only option might be to tuck into the wall and simply hope it misses you—or at least hits you less badly. (That is, if you even hear it coming in the first place.) Trying to avoid a rock that is plummeting at you at terminal velocity is as close to a nightmare as you can get and still be awake. A further demon in this situation is a freed rock severing one's rope(s).

In the real world rocks do fall, sometimes unpredictably, and some of these do kill people.

An early example of this happened on June 13, 1959, as 25-year-old Donald Q. Goodrich, a graduate student in math at the University of California at Berkeley and from Susanville, California, was climbing the South Wall of 12,590-foot Mount Conness, five miles as the crow flies northwest of Tioga Pass. Goodrich and his four companions had chosen to not register. At this early point in Yosemite climbing history, climbers were required to register with the Park. This would become a moot issue at 3 p.m. as Goodrich tried to pull himself up onto a block. It turned out to be loose. It instantly tumbled out of the cliff face. The 125-pound chunk of granite knocked Goodrich from his holds and off the wall.

As he fell, his piton yanked out of its crack. This now lengthened his fall to over thirty feet. Far worse, the loose boulder hit him on the head.

Fortunately Goodrich had stalwart companions. His four friends helped the still conscious man down eighty feet to a ledge. There they stuffed him into a down sleeping bag and secured him to the face.

Two of his partners then retreated off the wall *muy pronto*. One of them, John Sheppardson, now ran eleven rugged miles to the Tuolumne Meadows Ranger Station to request a helicopter. Dennis Rutovitz, age 30, followed, arriving an hour later. He reiterated the need for the aircraft.

Uncertain just how critical Goodrich's injuries might be but knowing that no matter how bad they were it was too dark for any pilot to land a helicopter in such treacherous terrain, District Ranger Herb Ewing tried to explain to Goodrich's two faithful buddies how scarce these machines were. The Park did not even possess one. Even if it did, again, the darkness, altitude, and the terrain would prove prohibitive. Yes, he could request one from the Central Valley many miles west, but there would be delays on their end and no guarantee on performance. Finally, flustered because Goodrich's friends considered all of this to be quibbling, Ewing asked Rutovitz: "Who is going to pay for it?"

While Rutovitz fumed over what he now perceived as ridiculous frugality, Ranger Ewing arranged instead for an immediate horseback SAR that night with other rescuers coming in as they could. His plan was this: Once they had ridden as far as they could on four legs, they would scramble higher on two. The SAR team saddled up and rode. Next they hiked. They reached the injured Goodrich atop a 1,000-yard talus slope on Mount Conness at about 1 a.m. Although unconscious, he was still alive, but just barely.

During the next several hours the rescuers hauled Goodrich down—with twenty-seven men helping—by litter out to Tuolumne Meadows. Sadly, he died en route sometime between 2:30 and 4:30 a.m. of a subdural hematoma (a buildup of fluids between the brain and the membrane surrounding it that ultimately inhibits the flow of oxygenated blood to the brain). A Park incident evaluation concluded that a helicopter (remember, this was in 1959) would have made little or no difference, even had one been capable of performing the difficult mission in the dark.

Thirteen years later, on June 21, 1972, a 34-year-old theoretical physicist from Los Alamos, New Mexico named William Lynderman Hendry III was climbing the East Buttress of El Capitan with a friend, Leonard Margolin. By now "The Captain" and many of its routes were standard climbs. But the first ascent of the "easier" East Buttress had been accomplished less than twenty years earlier. Allen Steck, Bill Long, and William Siri, along with soon-to-be-legendary Willi Unsoeld (who, with Thomas Hornbein, would lead the first ascent of Mount Everest via the West Ridge in May 22, 1963, followed by the highest bivouac in history—at 28,000 feet) had made a three-day, boltless but heavily aided climb to the summit there on June 1, 1953.

Now, in the summer of 1972, Margolin was leading above Hendry. As he moved, he dragged his rope over 120 feet of steep granite. He felt his line dislodge something, so he yelled, "ROCK!"

When he looked down, Hendry was already hanging upside down and unconscious, his helmet cracked open. His skull had been fractured fatally by the rock's impact after falling eighty feet. Ironically, while most climbers never even wore helmets, Hendry had been cautious enough to break style by wearing one. Unfortunately, he had failed to get a helmet that fit him properly. Hendry's was so small and fit so snugly that the rock killed him despite the prompt response of the Lemoore Rescue Angels on this, what we think might have been their first Yosemite rescue. Whether a better helmet would have saved Hendry's life remains uncertain.

A more eerie rockfall occurred on May 25, 1977, after 23-year-old Michael P. Cannon of Harwick, Massachusetts and Mark Richey had begun a climb on the Steck-Salathé route on Sentinel Rock. Due to rain and hail, they were retreating down the 10th pitch. Richey was first down. He had stopped next to a large flake (15 feet high by 6 feet wide by 3 feet thick) and began setting a new anchor around a nearby tree for the next rappel.

Cannon stopped next on the same flake. The bad weather prompted him to seek shelter behind it. He stood between it and the wall for about four minutes "squaring away his gear" before he would have to move four feet out into the open to join his partner. He was in no hurry. He had a one-foot wide ledge between the flake and the wall on which to stand. Besides, it was drier here.

Richey glanced over and noticed Cannon leaning his back against the large slab as he unhooked from his rope. As fate would have it, at the instant when he freed himself of both the line and the anchor above, the huge rock slid away from the cliff. Caught off balance, Cannon went with it.

The seemingly "minor" lateral pressure of Cannon's merely leaning against the huge slab had been the proverbial straw that broke the camel's back, or, in this case, dislodged an apparently solidly situated, multi-ton flake that instead had been extremely unstable. When Cannon and the granite boulder hit 600 feet below, both were pulverized.

Again, rockfalls can be killers. And can do so in more than one way. On August 5, 1987, 35-year-old Young Soon Lee tackled Half Dome with five friends from Seoul, Korea. At 8 p.m., Lee was safetying on the second pitch when Shoong Hyun Ji, dislodged a large television-sized boulder. Incident Report #87-2823 explains: "This rock fell straight down severing the belay (climbing rope) and shattering directly above or in front of the deceased. A large fragment impacted Lee's left occipital region resulting in significant tissue trauma." Lee survived for only ninety minutes.

It is now clear that a falling rock does not have to hit a climber to kill him. On May 27, 1997, as 37-year-old Stephan M. Slovenkai of Brisbane, California descended Arrowhead Arête with Eric Henderson, a rock became a problem. They had descended four pitches. There they retrieved a pack they had left earlier. The two then continued their descent, now scrambling down third- and forth-class terrain.

About 1,000 feet below the summit and at about 7 p.m., they tried crossing the granite to the right and then downward. This traverse would allow them to continue down a more direct route than the one they had been following.

Henderson remembers carefully circling around a precariously perched boulder on dicey terrain and then being able to move lower to safer ground. Slovenkai next moved into place behind and above him. But while waiting a few seconds before he would be clear to finish his own traverse, Slovenkai knocked a boulder loose. With incredible bad luck this cascading rock sent both him and his partner into the air. The two now both tumbled down the steep Class 4 slope toward certain death.

Henderson's backpack caught between two boulders—and his pack straps held. This bit of incredible good luck arrested his fall. Slovenkai, however, fell 200 feet.

About eighteen people have died in Yosemite climbing incidents due to rockfalls. They comprise roughly 13 percent of all climbing fatalities. As we hope is clear from the examples above, these fatal events seem to occur more frequently than other mishaps after nightfall and/or during descents when people have "let their guard down" by shifting their focus away from the demands of the moment—in short, by "tasting the beer in the cooler" prematurely.

About 400 known notable natural rockfalls have pummeled Yosemite Valley since Europeans first arrived (see Chapter 7. Freak Accidents). Some of these have been both gigantic and deadly. An event apparently aligned with this pattern occurred on June 13, 1999, as 22-year-old Peter James Terbush of Gunnison,

Colorado and two companions climbed the two-pitch Apron Jam above Curry Village. At 7:35 that evening, a 550-ton slab of granite above them slid 2,000 feet from near the top of the cliff above the Valley. As fate would have it the trio found themselves in the line of fire. Sadly, the flying shards killed Terbush instantly. Somehow, fortunately, his partners received only minor injuries. They were either able to hug the wall closer or else simply lucked out.

After this slide, officials evacuated 1,363 guests and concession employees from their tent cabins in Curry Village.

No secret, some Americans have become litigious and prone to absolving individuals of having made personal decisions that put themselves in harm's way. Instead they seek culpability elsewhere. Illustrating this, Terbush's unfortunate death led to a bit of a "hunt" for a human perpetrator.

Was *this* rockfall a natural event? Or instead was it an anthropogenic one? Chester "Skip" Watts, Director of Radford University's Institute for Engineering Geoscience in Virginia, suggested the leach field on Glacier Point which received up to 5,000 gallons of effluent per summer day, had lubricated and then destabilized the bedrock, perhaps precipitating the slab that killed Terbush. Armed with this interpretation, the young man's bereaved parents sued the Park for $10 million for negligence. In spring of 2004, the plaintiffs altered their argument to suggest that all Glacier Point water system operations contributed to all rockfalls in the Glacier Point area. They argued "The NPS did not follow its own guidelines to determine the hazard level at Glacier Point Apron and thus did not keep its work force and the public safe."

In contrast, Park Spokesman Scott Gediman countered by saying the Park had "been told by several reputable geologists that he [Watts] is way out in left field on this."

On December 12, 2005, a federal judge threw out this $10 million wrongful death suit that alleged the Park had been negligent by allowing people to climb in the Curry Village/Glacier Point area. The judge instead agreed with government lawyers that Yosemite National Park was immune from such lawsuits because Congress has given (and the courts have sustained 16 United States Code 1, Superintendent's Discretionary Authority) agency managers' discretion on locations and operations of public facilities as well as public warnings of potential danger. The court decided to rule on "grounds of assumption of risk" of rock climbing. As of 2024, at least fourteen climbers in Yosemite have been killed due to a rockfall dislodged by a climber. Only two have died due to a natural rockfall.

IT WAS A DARK AND STORMY NIGHT

Regardless of how high-tech and pricey gear has become, weather remains critical during virtually every activity and sport performed outdoors. Indeed, a significant portion of wilderness activities pivots on predicting, preparing for, sidestepping, and/or surviving dangerous weather. Technical climbing is one of the most vulnerable because of the few options a climber possesses when conditions turn nasty. In truly bad storms aficionados of vertical rock normally possess one good option, one mediocre option, and a shaky one. The first and best is to recognize the real danger posed by bad weather settling in and to prudently retreat off the wall when that weather *first* threatens. The second option is to hunker down with appropriate gear wherever a bivouac is possible and wait. The third and possibly most shaky choice of actions is to "sprint" for the top. As with other dimensions of climbing, wishful thinking about the wisdom of the "hunker into the wall" or "we'll do it faster" options often prove fatally seductive.

For an early example, consider 19-year-old Stanford student Anne R. Pottinger. On April 17, 1955, she departed for a climb of Higher Cathedral Spire directly across the Valley from El Capitan with 24-year-old leader Theodore "Jack" Weicker and with Irene A. Beardsley, age 19, also from Stanford. The day before, Rangers Ewing and Evans had warned Weicker against going. He said he knew of the approaching storm and had told the rangers if it stormed he would not make the [Grade II] climb.

Despite snow starting by 8:45 a.m., these three members of the Stanford Alpine Club left for the cliffs anyway. It snowed so hard and so fast in the Valley that by evening snowplows were struggling to keep the roads clear.

Weicker, Pottinger, and Beardsley summited at midday. But bad weather made their descent increasingly difficult. They now found their rappels and downclimbs were all on water- and ice-covered faces. Soon their wet ropes froze stiff. Then they froze against the rock itself. By 9:30 p.m., long after dark, the trio had reached the lower slopes, 700 feet above and an hour from the road. The terrain here was steep and forested, although somewhat sheltered.

By this point Anne Pottinger's light *cotton* clothes had been soaked for so long that she was seriously hypothermic. Indeed, she was so far gone that she simply collapsed.

Here her two companions now made yet another critical error. They did not build a fire. Weicker later said he did not want to use the time which he could spend otherwise by immediately going for help. So instead of building a warming fire, he hurried down slope. Apparently Beardsley, who remained behind, had either decided a fire was unnecessary or wanted to ignite one but failed. Later evidence suggests the former. She too was probably impaired mentally by the cold—for the next couple of hours she basically did nothing.

At 10:45 p.m., Weicker reached the Ranger Office and requested help. Within forty-five minutes and now under a starry and ice-cold sky, a seven-man SAR team carried life-saving equipment as they followed Weicker through the snow to his two companions. The rescuers found both women on the trail where he had left them.

Irene Beardsley, the rangers saw to their relief, seemed to be doing okay. Not so, however, for Pottinger. Instead, they found her "in a kneeling position, forehead resting on a projection of a boulder, cotton clothing 'sopping' wet, her body thoroughly cold, but not yet rigid. Face and hands were palled."

As bad as this may sound, it sounds a lot better than it was. While two of the rescuers quickly built a roaring fire—amazingly they did this under a huge leaning boulder *a mere fifty yards away where the ground was dry*—the others checked her pupils. These failed to constrict in response to light. Next they sought a pulse. They found none. Breath sounds? Again, none.

Despite detecting no discernible signs of life, they performed artificial resuscitation for two hours on Pottinger near the fire. Finally they gave up. Ironically, they were so close to the Valley that it took only an hour to haul in the dead woman.

The *San Francisco Chronicle* (on April 19, 1955) noted that this was Weicker's second fatal expedition; the previous one had been two years prior on Mount Shasta, when Edgar Hopf had fallen 800 feet.

A quarter of a century later, on March 29, 1980, 23-year-old David Thomas Kays also tackled The Nose of El Capitan during the "shoulder" climbing season. Kays of LaVerne, California was an Eagle Scout, a star high school wrestler, a student of Pacific Coast Baptist Bible College, and a man who listed himself as a 5.10 climber who had done Half Dome. Kays, it would prove, was quite driven.

As he slowly rope-soloed the 2,900-foot cliff on his proposed eight-day ascent, he was not merely climbing a big wall. He was in pursuit of a dream.

Kays had made practice rock climbs almost every week for a year on Southern California cliffs in preparation for El Capitan. "He had planned very carefully for this climb," noted his mother. Despite her faith in him, his equipment would seem a bit light for March.

Two other climbers—25-year-old Charles Cole III and Gibb Lewis—caught up with and passed Kays on March 31. During a later interview with Ranger John Dill, Cole noted that Kays had said to them, "I know you; you're famous…and you're famous too….What are your names? It's weird to meet you on this great face."

After introducing themselves, the two noted that Kays told them he had taken a fifteen-foot fall. "He mentioned it several times," Cole remembered, "as if he were proud of it."

Having converged, the three climbed together for a time. As Kays worked his way up the chimney behind Texas Flake, Cole noted that Kays was having as much trouble as either of them but he seemed to be trying to impress them by repeatedly remarking on how easy it was. Cole's impression was that Kays "was naïve and over-confident and seemed to lack a sense of reality, i.e., of the seriousness of the climb. His preoccupation seemed like someone not attuned to what was happening around him. He seemed overly enthusiastic, perhaps obsessed, with his goal and overly impressed with climbing."

Despite whatever mental focus Kays may or may not have possessed, his progress was good. On the end of his seventh day (April 4) he had reached a point only 250 feet below the summit. He told his wife Debbie by CB radio that he planned to summit the next day despite a storm that had already turned from rain to snow at his elevation.

The weather worsened that night. Water flowed down The Nose and froze into ice falls. Winds whipped the imposing granite face and plunged the windchill to abjectly debilitating. Two inches of snow blanketed the Valley floor far below. For David Kays this storm spelled trouble.

Cole and Lewis climbed their final three pitches during this weather. They found it miserable. To keep going at all, the pair first had to spend more than an hour deicing one of their ropes and trying to thaw their frozen metal ascenders. This delay was despite their having the foresight the previous evening to stash a rope in a haul bag to keep it dry. Cole admitted he felt so cold in the freezing and wet weather that "If someone had lowered a rope from the top, I would have jumared out [instead of honorably completing his climb]."

While Cole and Lewis made the summit, Kays failed to show up on this same day, his sixth on the rock. Ditto on his seventh. Ominously, after day seven, Debbie Kays in the Valley below had not been able to roust her husband on his CB radio. Alarmed, she contacted John Dill at the SAR Cache on April 6th.

Dill and Ranger Butch Wilson drove to El Capitan Meadows and studied the wall. Kays, the solo climber, they now saw, lay mostly hidden in the clouds, but he was up there alright. Maybe he had bivouacked to wait out the storm. But two days in the same exposed position during such adverse conditions spelled trouble. Wilson fired questions up the cliff with a bullhorn. No response.

Dill organized yet another top-down rescue. For this one Ranger/Park Medic Craig Patterson rappelled off the lip of El Capitan. By coincidence, this was Patterson's birthday. Two pitches down, about 250 feet, he found David Kays.

Patterson noted the young climber frozen dead against the wall and hanging from his swami belt jackknifed forwards with both his head and feet down. His clothes were bunched half off. Despite this obviously hopeless state of affairs, Patterson dutifully fished for his rectal thermometer and then performed a temperature check "on" Kays. The mercury bottomed out.

Some birthday…

An autopsy later confirmed Kays had died from hypothermia, but it also raised the more complicated possibility that he may have strangled to death after losing consciousness due to this hypothermia. What had been Kays' decision-making processes that he had let this happen?

Investigators found that Kays had dropped his half-full bag of climbing hardware on April 1 (his day #4), yet he still possessed a working radio. On the next day, he had dropped yet another sack containing much of his food and, probably more importantly, his rain gear. His remaining clothing—heavy wool mitts, an inner shirt, a blue cotton sweatshirt, a wool shirt, a down parka part way off, and climbing knickers now drooping down around his knees (again, paradoxical disrobing during the late stages of hypothermia is common)—were inadequate for weathering a prolonged snow and ice storm at 8,000 feet and up on an exposed big wall.

What had fueled Kays' apparently single-minded purpose to the point of dying?

During the summer of the previous year, Kays and a partner had maneuvered themselves into another deadly predicament wherein Kays needed to be rescued off a wall that stood almost directly across the Valley from where he had died. He had trapped himself about halfway up the North Buttress of Middle Cathedral. Only it was not hypothermia and having dropped two of his haul bags that had gotten him into trouble. Instead it was the opposite.

Kays had not brought nearly enough water with him for the blazing August heat. And after he had run out of the precious fluid, instead of promptly retreating to save himself, he had seemingly denied the physiological consequences of dehydration in such heat by deciding to continue upward.

After having climbed higher he had become dangerously dehydrated. (This mistake is common during hot weather climbing. Even so, we wonder: Was Kays' error also abetted by an old habit of having repeatedly dehydrated oneself while trying for lower weight classes for wrestling matches?) His self-created predicament finally became unbearable so he had yelled down that he needed to be rescued.

Ironically, several of the rangers who now helped winch up Kays' frozen body to the top of El Capitan with Ranger Craig Patterson were also part of the team that saved him from death during the heat of that previous summer. Had they arrived much later then, he indeed very likely would have become the first and only Yosemite climber to die of heat and dehydration. It had been a very close thing. Harsh perhaps to point this out, but his "careful" planning for his solo attempt on El Capitan failed to reveal prudence gained from this previous near miss.

Why? YOSAR Investigator John Dill tried to dissect Kays' fatal decision-making. As noted above, Dill interviewed climbers Cole and Lewis. Cole told Dill: "He [Kays] had trouble finding [climbing] partners; he had alienated everyone." Lewis explained why: "Kays had a reputation in Southern California as being too aggressive without the necessary common sense….I could see him telling his wife [over his radio] that everything was alright [despite having dropped his food, rain gear, et cetera] because of his macho outlook."

Incident Report #80-0656 concluded that of additional factors which may have led to his death *other* than the loss of gear during foul weather a prime one was: "Possibly a single-minded purpose that may have clouded Kays' judgment about the possibility of retreat from the route."

Four and a half years later on October 16, 1984, and yet again on El Capitan, wishful thinking struck again. A sudden but not unusual mid-October storm hit

Yosemite. It triggered a massive SAR effort on the Valley's big walls. Two simultaneous rescues were being conducted of three fairly well equipped climbers—Brian Bennett and Norman Boles, as well as solo climber Edwin Drummond—who were divided in two weather-stranded parties on the Zodiac and North America Wall. Although these rescues went well, Incident Commander J. R. Tomasovic notified Mike Murray that fellow ranger Hugh Dougher had just seen what appeared to be two more climbers high on The Nose who seemed not to be moving. At all.

Gary Colliver, leader on the North America Wall Rescue, made a recon flight across the face. He radioed that there existed at least one "11-44" (dead body) and probably a second one, although this one was too hidden to tell.

So a third major rescue (recovery) began. Murray hiked to the top of The Nose and then rappelled 150 feet to the 34th pitch. He found a gruesome scene. Thirty-two-year old Kenji Yatsuhashi and 35-year-old Keiso Sadatomo, both of Hiroshima, Japan, were dead at the end of the bolt ladder (a series, or "ladder," of bolts just below the summit). Sadatomo was dressed in a lightweight down jacket, over a red sweater, blue cotton sweatpants, red "Canyon" climbing shoes, and he had a flashlight attached to his head with a headband. A veneer of ice covered much of him.

An indication of how the freezing weather had clouded the two's thinking is revealed by how they had hunkered into the granite. Sadatomo was held only by a 9 mm yellow rope tied to a sit-harness and then clipped to a bolt. His legs straddled Yatsuhashi, who was frozen in a head-upward position. Yatsuhashi's upper body was covered by a red tent fly. He was wearing a lightweight wind shell over frozen and wet clothing, including red pants. His body hung primarily by a gear sling that ran across one shoulder and beneath the opposite armpit. It was anchored above him to the same, single bolt that held his partner. This scanty tie-in was despite several other good bolts a foot *closer*. Again, the two men, with no apparent bivouac gear other than a tent fly, ended up with icicles hanging off them. Why? The Park's investigation concluded:

> The equipment of the two men, especially their clothing, was very inadequate.... Much of what they wore was cotton. They were in no way prepared to deal with adverse weather. The Park's official Board of Critique for the deaths speculated that the two climbers made a very poor judgment call, believing in the always mild California weather when the basic rule for climbers on extended climbs is to be prepared for anything and not rely on weather reports.

More puzzling yet, the two victims' friend Yoshifumi Teranishi had stationed himself at the bottom ostensibly to visually monitor the pair's climbing progress. Teranishi, the Board concluded, "knew how they were equipped but failed to report any concern for Yatsuhashi and Sadatomo at any time during October 16 *or when he helped to report the request for rescue of the* [other] *climbers on the Zodiac Route* [italics ours]. However, given the weather conditions, it is unlikely that this would have altered the outcome."

The outcome was fatal, but how had it unfolded? The investigating rangers suspected that Yatsuhashi was leading but had already collapsed when Sadatomo reached him. The items still in the stuff sacks that Sadatomo had attached to himself as well as his rigging suggested that he planned to climb beyond his collapsed partner. But then, apparently, the freezing weather also stopped him cold before he could pass him. The gear Sadatomo had stuffed into his sacks included some dry clothes, *a rain suit*, and a dry sleeping bag (none of which Sadatomo had *used* despite his desperate need to). Ominously, a pair of gloves was found clipped well below the pair's final location, again suggesting mental incapacity. As Ranger Murray further reported, the two either were not very logical technical climbers or else both were mentally impaired by hypothermia: "Based on my experience as a climber, the mass of carabiners, slings, and equipment that the two victims were connected to, which in turn were ultimately anchored to the one bolt above the unused, multiple-bolt anchor station presented a confusing, illogical picture that did not follow commonly used techniques."

In short, the pair's poor planning had allowed hypothermia to kill them.

At least ten climbers have died due to hypothermia and exposure in Yosemite National Park. Driven by repeatedly witnessing errors that pivoted on marginal preparation, laziness, and "wishful thinking," veteran Yosemite Search and Rescue expert Ranger John Dill wrote a brief set of preventative recommendations in his Introduction to Don Reid's *Yosemite Climbs: Big Walls.*

> Consider the following gear for each person's daypack: long underwear, gloves, balaclava, rain jacket and pants (which double as wind protection). In warmer weather, all can be of the lightweight variety. If that's too heavy for you, at least take one of those disposable plastic rain suits or tube tents that occupy virtually no space. Take more warm clothes in colder weather. A headlamp with spare bulb and new batteries is very important for finding safe anchors, signaling for help, or avoiding that bivy [bivouac] altogether. Matches and heat-tabs will light wet wood. Food and water increase your safety after a night of shivering.
>
> Keep your survival gear with you whenever practical, not with your partner—climbers get separated from their gear, and each other, in imaginative ways, sometimes with serious consequences.
>
> Standing in slings on poor anchors is not the way to spend the night. If a bivy is inevitable, don't climb until the last moment; find a safe, sheltered, and/or comfortable spot while you've got enough light.

These practical lessons should be well taken. Yet strangely, they seem very difficult for many to take to heart. An all-too nightmarish illustration of a failure to live by Dill's guidelines began on October 28, 1984. That morning two 19-year-old Pasadena residents, Thomas T. Apel and David Dryden, camped at the top of Upper Yosemite Fall to set themselves up for a timely start the next morning to climb Lost Arrow Spire (Grade III, 5.5, A3). Despite their good intentions, it was between 9 and 10 a.m. when the two Stanford students finally reached a position to scope out their route. And noon had come by the time they rappelled down two pitches (130 feet and 115 feet) in their approach to the notch between the main wall and the Spire.

Climbing the next few short pitches (totaling 200+ feet) required several hours longer than the pair had expected. They made the top at roughly 4 p.m. By now the October daylight was about to fade.

Neither had prepared for being stuck atop The Arrow. Their bivouac gear still lay on the main wall near Upper Yosemite Fall.

Dryden had no intention of allowing them to get stuck all night. Enough sunlight remained for him to rig the 125-foot Tyrolean traverse (again, a rope strung more or less horizontally by anchoring it tightly on each end) that he had planned in advance from their position back across the notch to the main wall. This standard method of retreat would eliminate at least 150 feet of rappel to the notch, and it would obviate the need for a 250-foot climb from it back up the cliff on the Yosemite Falls' side.

But by the time Dryden finished rigging it was 7 p.m. Night had long since fallen. Even so, the pair now had their exit route secured. But when Apel tried to cross the Tyrolean it proved too much for him. Dryden would later report that Apel's failure was due to "unexpected fatigue." No matter what concatenation of decisions or unexpected developments had landed these two young men in their present predicament, however, their reality remained that they were now stranded in the cold and dark without bivouac gear atop the tiny, sloping, and wildly exposed summit of Lost Arrow Spire.

As mentioned earlier, Lost Arrow (a.k.a. "The Tip" and "The Arrow") was first successfully ascended in September of 1946. Summiting it then had been a big deal. At least one of the climbers who had pulled it off admitted that he thought it might never be done again. The Arrow of course instead became "routine" and by 1970 more than 200 ascents had been done. Indeed it had been climbed so many times, notes veteran climber/author Steve Roper, many of its small, critical cracks that once had held thin pitons had now expanded or even worn out. In the next fourteen years, hundreds more climbers had made their way up despite deteriorating cracks. One inevitable by-product of so many repeat climbs of a route that "might never be done again" was the engendering of a feeling that Lost Arrow was less hazardous than previously thought.

Now, abruptly, it seemed quite perilous. So dangerous that rather than risk the relatively easy rappel off the top down to the notch in the dark and then climbing the two pitches on the main wall, Apel and Dryden chose to bivouac. To stay warm they planned to do exercises on the tapering, eight-foot-square, naked granite point at 7,000 feet elevation. The two, again, had no sleeping bags and no overnight gear. Nor did they possess even warm clothes beyond one wool sweater.

That night the temperature dropped to twenty degrees Fahrenheit as misting winds created a subzero windchill. The two grossly ill-prepared climbers periodically traded positions to block wind for one another. As early as 9 p.m. both men knew it was dangerously cold. The miserably long night from then on seemed interminable. Lights barely a mile distant in the Valley below played peek-a-boo through the mist, reminding the shivering pair just how close they were to warmth, food, and life itself. And how far…

Dryden somehow survived the nightmare. In contrast, Apel had plunged into hypothermia. At nine the next morning Dryden was trying to revive his partner with CPR. Extremely worried about Apel, Dryden gave up and made his way across the traverse he had strung to the other side. He then hurried down to the Valley for help.

The Park pilot positioned his helicopter directly above the minuscule tip of granite surrounded by nearly 2,000 feet of empty air. Because of the belly of his machine, he could see the granite only poorly. Meanwhile Ranger John Dill rappelled 150 feet on a swaying line from the aircraft and managed to bull's-eye his landing on that same bit of rock not much bigger than an average dining table. It was now noon. Sadly, Thomas T. Apel had long since sunk into irreversible hypothermia. The rescue team quickly "short-hauled" him to the Park's clinic. He was pronounced dead there at 1:10 p.m.

Luckily, eighteen years passed before weather again became a successful predator of climbers in Yosemite.

The first weather fatality of the New Millennium turned out to be an unbelievable cliffhanger. At 6:45 p.m., on December 28, 2002, only fifteen minutes after a serious winter storm had started hammering El Capitan, climbers Matt Robertson and Pat Warren heard cries for help from Zodiac (VI, 5.7, A3). They hitched a ride in the storm to the Park's SAR office. There they reported to Ranger John Dill that earlier, while it was still light, they had seen a climber about 400 feet up on the route. The cries they had just heard in the dark, they added, likely were his.

It turned out that 25-year-old Joseph Emmet Crowe of Azusa, California had taken a stab at a winter solo climb of Zodiac. Maybe he was the one in trouble. By 8 p.m., now well past nightfall, Ranger Jack Hoeflich drove out Northside Drive and used his patrol car's loud speaker to hail whoever might be up there in the darkness.

He heard someone respond but he could not make out any words being said.

Nor could he spot a light—if there was one—through the whiteout conditions.

It did seem to Hoeflich, though, that Crowe's voice was so close that he could not be much higher than the second pitch. Did Crowe no longer possess a working headlight and therefore was unable to get back down on his own? Hoeflich returned to the rescue cache to quickly gear up for the hike up to the base of El Capitan.

By 9:15 p.m., he was scrambling by himself up through the snowy talus and boulder field to the foot of the massive cliff that he knew was there but could not see. An hour later he passed the start of Tangerine Trip. An expert Yosemite climber himself, Hoeflich knew he was only 200 yards from Zodiac even though heavy snow and darkness made landmarks almost impossible to recognize. Ranger Hoeflich tried the megaphone again. Nothing. At 10:56 p.m., he found the base of Zodiac. This is where things evolved from difficult to strange. Hoeflich continues:

> At the base I saw a Portaledge [a rigid, person-sized hammock routinely used for sleeping on a big wall where natural ledges prove unavailable; Crowe's Portaledge had been deliberately attached here much earlier and intended for his end-of-the-day destination after he set ropes on the first, lower pitches] suspended about 3 feet above the ground. I saw three haul bags. I continued to call for CROWE without response. I set up a portable 100-watt spotlight and scanned the wall. [Four minutes later] I saw CROWE hanging about 15 feet from the wall approximately 25 feet above the ground. I did not see CROWE move. I continually called out to CROWE without response. It appeared that CROWE had attempted to descend to the ground, but ran out of rope. It appeared that CROWE attempted to extend his rope by attaching his etriers and slings to the end of his rope.

Without technical climbing gear himself Hoeflich was now confined to the talus at the base of the wall. He radioed for an equipped SAR team. Two hours later, notes Hoeflich, "additional resources arrived on scene and I was able to ascend a fixed line on the Shortest Straw Climbing Route and reach CROWE at 0200 hours. CROWE was cold to the touch. He was hanging by a red Spectra sling, which appeared to be around his arm and neck. I attached a rope to CROWE, cut the sling, and we lowered CROWE to the ground."

The SAR team performed CPR for twenty-seven minutes, but had to terminate when it became obvious that the chilled climber was dead.

Crowe, they saw, was dressed more or less appropriately—in mountaineering boots with inner boots, Marmot gloves, Triple Point fabric parka, bib overalls, polypro/fleece hood, pants, shirt—but he had been "subjected to over four hours of extreme cold and wet weather conditions (wind-driven sleet and snow, temperatures in the mid-thirties)" that had out-classed his gear.

In fact everything Crowe was wearing was soaked through to the skin. Whether this was because he had been hanging directly beneath a steady stream of falling water or instead he had been soaked well before reaching this point will never be known. What is known is the expression on his face was euphoric, even beatific (reports often note that at the last moment, dying hypothermia victims often exhibit signs of profound peace and calm). The autopsy concluded that Joseph Crowe had succumbed to hypothermia an unknown number of hours before his "rescue" while suspended just twenty-five feet from the bottom of the nearly 3,000-foot wall. It seems that the primary errors committed here include having left far too much of his rope in the several pitches above him—perhaps feeling unwilling to lose his investment in climbing and setting protection by cleaning one of these pitches—and, then because of this, during his descent he ran out of rope. Whether or not his decision-making was initially flawed by underestimating the level of threat from cold and wet weather and then his ability to make good decisions was next impaired by hypothermia remain unclear.

After finally lowering him to the snowy ground, rescuers found a small Petzl headlamp nestled in the chest pocket of his water-soaked coveralls. When one of the rangers flicked its switch, the lamp lit up. Hypothermia had apparently impaired Crowe to the degree that he did not "think" to use this vital aid.

Generally, October is a great month for Yosemite climbing; its walls become even more popular. Generally blessed with splendid weather, October climbers relish the reduced heat on the granite faces and are thankful for their need to haul less water up every pitch. But in October of 2004, a not-uncommon early fall blizzard blew in on the 17th and lasted four days. Freezing winds blasted the face of the mammoth El Capitan at fifty miles per-hour. Swirling snow repeatedly created whiteout conditions.

Above, seven climbers in separate parties became stranded on the mile-wide face. Elsewhere in the Yosemite backcountry about twenty hikers, several ill-prepared, became marooned at elevations of up to 9,400 feet and hemmed in by up to four feet of new snow. To make matters more complicated, some had strayed from their itineraries without notifying anyone. All of these simultaneous emergencies created a major strain on the Park's SAR capability.

Among all of this "winter" mayhem a pair of Japanese climbers—26-year-old Ryoichi Yamamoto and 27-year-old Moriko Ryugo—had bivouacked on the wet ledge at Camp Six on The Nose. Photos later viewed from Ryugo's digital camera showed (at least at one point) dry sleeping bags, dry self-inflating pads, even a dry rain fly. Hints as to their mental status at this stage of the climb and storm are revealed by a carefully composed image that Ryugo shot of a tiny red blossom growing out of a crack on their ledge. Her pictures of Yamamoto reveal a somewhat clownish, goofing-off attitude—although it may be that he was clowning only to try to cheer up his partner. One photo he took of her, nestled into a sleeping bag, reveals a woman who may be a bit pensive, but is otherwise in a secure, if not cozy, location somewhat protected (by their tent) from the storm buffeting the cliff face. How bad was their bivouac? When she photographed Yamamoto in his bag, he was only two-thirds inside it, semi-reclining without gloves or hat, and appearing comfortable.

If this was all we knew, we would have little reason to suspect that anything might go wrong from here. But it did. And why it did is a puzzle solvable by only a few clues.

Below the two yawned a vertical drop of 2,000 feet engulfed by a freezing storm whose duration into the future remained unknowable. One line of inquiry as to what the two decided to do next may be embodied in the question: How long can a novice big wall climber (Ryugo) bivouac on a freezing and increasingly wet granite ledge under these terrifying and worsening conditions without developing "cabin fever?"

Thirty-six hours after Moriko Ryugo took her last snapshot of their bivouac at Camp Six, the next photo shows Yamamoto climbing. In fact he had fixed this pitch above Camp Six at least a day before. Another party just ahead that day had watched him set his protection and rope. They later admitted to admiring him as a very capable and fluid climber whose moves proved economical, precise, and quick.

At some point while on the ledge and with the storm still howling unabated, the Japanese couple decided to abandon their ledge for an exposed climb on the face above. Why?

They still had food; they still had water. They had warm clothes (although these may have been getting ever wetter). Indeed they had a survivable—albeit marginal—perch on which to sit out this storm.

Reconstructing other peoples' thought processes is always a chancy business, especially if hypothermia may have entered the picture to diminish their acuity. Investigators initially chalked up the poor decision to abandon Camp Six to the pair having been ill-prepared equipment-wise to remain. But their photos and gear tend to contradict this—at least during the early phase of their bivouac here.

Thus the answer of why they chose to climb in freezing weather rather than remain safe but miserable a day or two longer may reside in the more precise question: How many days—or even hours—can a novice woman climber lie on a ledge high on a world-famously forbidding cliff face during a freezing storm 2,000 feet above *terra firma* before this unfamiliar, uncomfortable, and scary situation slowly nudges her into panic? And, concurrently, how long can an adept professional climber in love with this woman hold out before he decides that his abilities to take care of her are on the line and that he must put his climbing skills where his assurances to her have been?

Whether or not the couple also may have been facing some sort of commitment to be elsewhere at a specific date, which precluded their remaining on El

Capitan, remains unknown.

"From their helicopter," notes Ben Margot of the Associated Press for October 21, rescuers spotted the Japanese pair "blue and dripping with icicles as they dangled from their ropes two thirds up the precipice."

Actually, the two frozen climbers were much closer than that to the summit, on the 28th pitch, only three pitches below the top.

Here, the Associated Press continues, to retrieve the corpses, rangers rappelled down El Capitan and "put the bodies into yellow mountaineering bags and carried them on their backs hundreds of feet to the summit."

Again the Associated Press got it wrong. Ranger Ed Visnovske was lowered down from the top. He confirmed that both people were dead. He cut both loose. Because the two climbers were small, he loaded both into the same litter. Then rescuers on top raised him and the loaded litter back up to the summit.

All of this still fails to explain why this tragedy unfolded as it did. Again, although we will never know for sure, we suspect the pair's decision to climb instead of remain bivouacked was spurred by her panic and by his protective impulse to act "appropriately" by "doing something" about their situation—namely, getting her out of it. In that he was a climber of superior skill, climbing upward may have seemed a reasonable choice of exits from a questionable decision to abandon Camp Six.

The YOSAR recovery photo of the pair's demise reveals what may be the sport's archetypical snapshot of all climbing pathos. In it the two climbers, only two pitches above the ledge at Camp Six, have roped themselves vertically to a cuboidal knob of granite maybe six feet square and projecting about a foot outward from the otherwise sheer face. The two are not standing on the ledge that this embossed square creates. Instead they are strapped to it like butterflies mashed against a car's front grill with their feet dangling more than 2,000 feet above the ground. Yamamoto had wrapped their climbing rope five or six times around the knob to secure it—and them. He had also clipped Ryugo into additional, multiple, bombproof pieces of protection set into the wall itself. Overall, he had weaved an overkill of security. And in this secure position—while strapped into the granite and *dressed for only mildly cold weather* but extremely exposed to the storm—the two froze as solid as the rock.

As the rangers pried the climbers from the cliff they saw that Yamamoto had sawed off a rope only a few inches from his waist. Later the digital photos revealed that this line was the one he had used to dangle their haul bag during the entire climb. Perhaps in an act goaded by hypothermia, he had hacked this rope (very likely his hands were too cold to untie a knot or even unscrew a locking carabiner). Inside this jettisoned haul sack was, among other things, the rest of their rope, neatly coiled, and also a sleeping bag.

Why stop on such an exposed face and tie in at all? Had the two found themselves at a point so many pitches above that Camp Six ledge that it now sat unattainably below them?

No, just a pitch and a half. Only a very few minutes of rappelling would have returned the two to Camp Six. But to return they would need to have been mentally alert enough to make the decision and also physically capable of pulling it off. They were not. Indeed, had they somehow made it to Camp Six, the odds are that they were too far gone already to have survived. In the end only hypothermia adequately explains Yamamoto's decision to secure Ryugo, likely a limp victim of the cold first, to that cuboidal boss on the pitch. After the two—by our count, the 23rd and 24th climbing victims known to die on El Capitan (with two more in 2014)—had left their bivouac during the still raging storm, it must have claimed them very quickly.

ODD ENDS

Early in the history of Yosemite climbing, on June 5, 1905, 55-year-old Charles A. Bailey of Oakland decided to set a record up the west cliffs (but not the "sheer" face) of El Capitan. Bailey was a real estate dealer and a Sierra Club member, but in no way an average one. He had already spent sixteen summers in Yosemite and had "discovered" Sierra Point. He had written several articles on the region, especially ones expounding on its challenging walls. Bailey had also very recently completed a fourteen-month trip around the world during which he "conquered" several major peaks, including the Matterhorn, prior to this particular bid in Yosemite for a first.

Bailey and his 22-year-old partner J. C. Staats of Mount Vernon, Ohio started that morning on what the local *Mariposa Gazette* (June 10, 1905) would describe as the "almost perpendicular face of the cliff where there is no trail and where man has never placed foot before." By mid-afternoon the pair had scrambled up nearly half of the 3,000-foot ascent up El Capitan Gully (a class 4, grade II climb) on West El Capitan.

Here they stopped for a breather; with Bailey on a small ledge and Staats clinging to the face. Abruptly, Staats saw to his shock, Bailey began to slide down the steep rock. Unable to stop himself, he accelerated a few feet toward Staats' left then he shot off into space.

The hapless Bailey fell, slammed his head against the cliff face several times, then plunged headlong out of sight.

Staats stared down horrified. The young alpinist next slowly downclimbed in search of Bailey. He found only the man's hat—and blood stains on the granite. Finally, to extricate himself from the face, Staats resumed the climb to the top. Amazingly he reached the summit (and became the first known person to do this via El Capitan Gully), although he felt "almost prostrated by the physical and mental strain."

The next day, Park personnel executed a 600-foot downclimb to retrieve

Bailey's battered body. In the report of this incident someone noted: "Most of the bones were broken."

Although Charles A. Bailey had used no technical aids or ropes, his death could be considered the first recorded "climbing" death in Yosemite, although his style was clearly that of a free-soloing mountaineer.

Another mishap of this sort occurred on July 24, 1921, to 45-year-old Fred H. Morley of San Francisco while he visited Tuolumne Meadows with a Sierra Club group. He and two companions separated from their comrades to "scale" some of the nearby peaks. Despite carrying ropes, Morley now scrambled alone and unprotected on an exposed flank of Cathedral Peak at about 10,000 feet elevation. He lost his footing and skidded off. Projecting boulders broke his fall seventy-five feet below. His two anxious companions descended by rope and rigged him into a harness to extract him. He was still breathing. Despite this rescue, Morley died the next day of a basilar skull fracture.

A more spectacular incident took place on June 7, 1973. Nineteen-year-old Michael M. Blake from Santa Monica, California was climbing at 7,010 feet on The Nose of El Capitan. He was belayed from above by Jerry P. Volger, age 33, who was positioned out of sight over the curve of the lip. Blake now cleaned this last pitch as he climbed. He may have been "clip-cleaning," that is, clipping his etreir into the next piece up, weighting it, then reaching back and unclipping his rope from the previous protection below and removing it (this would be a bit like lead climbing with a top rope instead of ascending the rope itself by using mechanical ascenders). He did have one ascender on his rig, but it remains unclear how he was using it, or even whether he was using it.

As fate would have it, one of the tie-offs Blake and Volger were using as protection was old. When Blake put all his weight on it, it failed. The bolt also gave way, yanking out from the wall. A critical, take-home error here, Blake had not tied in short. And, again, his jumar ascender seemed not to have been engaged. Next, almost unbelievably, as he fell and built up kinetic energy, the 11 mm Mammut rope (which was only a year old but had a mildly worn sheath from more than a dozen climbs and twenty-four days of use) severed against some unknown sharp salient on the face. The outcome? Literally within 100 feet of finishing the final pitch of this Grade VI route, Blake fell 2,500 feet off El Capitan all the way to the base of the Dawn Wall.

Slipping can be comical in cartoons but on Yosemite's exposed granite a simple slip can morph into a tragic fatal mistake. Consider the following example, one that metamorphosed beyond anyone's imagination: On June 16, 1975, Yosemite local 25-year-old Peter Barton and his buddy Dale Bard had made their way to the base of the West Buttress of El Capitan. Bard, you might recall, is the same guy who the next year (1976) would descend Mount Watkins in the dark for 108 minutes to rescue "injured" 22-year-old Robert Bruce Locke, only to find him dead and cold in his sleeping bag. Be that as it may, early on this next morning the pair made a short climb of two pitches but soon decided it was already too hot to continue. So they started back down.

Still only 8:30 a.m., Bard later would report, Barton was scrambling down an expanse of slick granite partly covered with loose gravel. He grabbed a tree branch to steady himself. It broke off. He slipped and tumbled 150 feet.

His belly filled with dread, Bard hurried down to him. He spoke to him but Barton proved unresponsive, even to painful stimuli. Bard stared at Barton's chest. Was he breathing? Maybe. Wanting to believe a spark of life still burned, Bard now hurried down through the thousand yards of rough terrain to El Capitan Meadow and then reported the incident (which became #75-1107).

By 10 a.m., Bard, accompanied by Rangers John Dill, Dan Sholly, and Mark Forbes, rendezvoused at the west end of the meadow with the Park helicopter. It lifted off to reconnoiter the accident scene with the intent of retrieving the downed climber. They found no landing site near Barton and so had to return.

Sholly and Bard immediately started scrambling back up to Barton on foot while Forbes followed. Meanwhile Dill returned to the Rescue Cache to organize people and equipment. He contacted the Air Rescue and Coordination Center in Illinois to request an airship from the Lemoore Naval Air Station, forty-five minutes south of the Park.

Meanwhile Sholly and Bard clambered up and around boulders, bushwhacked through thickets of gnarled oaks, and climbed 300 vertical feet of numerous Class 3 rock faces to reach the well-liked—but now very seriously injured—Barton.

Upon reaching Barton, Sholly checked for a pulse. He found none. Sholly was not only a Park Ranger; he was also a medic and had been deputized by two adjacent California counties as a deputy coroner. He next checked the victim's blood pressure and examined his pupils for any response to light. Again nothing. Barton's forehead showed a deep indentation. It was bleeding. So too was a wound in his abdomen. Sholly now radioed NPS Dispatch to inform them that the 25 year-old was dead.

Because the body still had to be recovered, and doing so by hand would be hazardous to litter bearers trying to haul it over the terrain below, a helicopter cable hoist remained the safest bet. Ranger Sholly had worked on several dozen helicopter evacuations before; he now considered this one "comparatively rated as one of the easier and safer missions." Even so, he advised the arriving navy crew they should assess the situation personally and conduct their extrication accordingly.

Normally the Lemoore rescue personnel would not respond to a known death; they generally performed risky hoist procedures only when there existed some chance—even if small—of saving the victim. But now that they had arrived on scene and had geared up, this body extraction arguably might save an on-the-ground rescuer from injury. All in all, the lesser of evils seemed to the pilot to be: Use the airship and also hone their skills.

At noon, SAR Ranger Tim Setnicka joined them with a litter evacuation team.

After assessing how dangerous the area was, he sent expert climbers Charlie Porter and Hainrich Majewski upslope to place safety lines. His plan was to get enough people up there to extricate Barton but at the same time expose the fewest possible rescuers to the hazards of the route and the mission.

Recovering the body required enough personnel to rig and then also carry and reposition it onto helicopter-friendly terrain for the pickup. Soon a total of nine rescuers had gathered on scene. With "great difficulty" they hauled Barton 100 feet lower to a spot where Sholly reckoned a cable hoist would be possible. Once there, however, he spotted a second, even better and lower pickup point. This site stood flanked by a steep slope of about 500 feet into a gully. This lower ledge, Ranger Sholly now decided, would be far safer for the helicopter if something went wrong. After all, one never knew…

The nine sweating rescuers now hauled and lowered Barton 100 feet down the next cliff. Once this last move had been accomplished Sholly ordered all unneeded personnel to traverse to safer ground away from the pickup ledge.

Meanwhile, LTJG Tom Stout had landed the U.S. Navy twin-engine helicopter, coded "Angel 6," on El Capitan Meadow. Sholly briefed Stout by radio. Next he ignited an orange smoke grenade to mark their location. Lieutenant Stout said he would fly over their position once to reconnoiter and, if conditions seemed okay, he would then return to hover over the site for the short hoist.

Prior to Angel 6 lifting off Ranger Paul Henry had climbed on board to assist the navy's five-man crew as spotter. The airship soon made its first pass as planned, 800 feet above the smoke. Then it circled away as the crew conducted a standard safety check. Next it returned quickly to hover about twenty feet above and ten feet to the side of the victim.

In this position the rotor tips seemed to have plenty of clearance, at least seventy-five feet. The crew chief lowered twenty of the helicopter's 270 feet of cable. Setnicka and Sholly quickly hooked the line to the litter. They also carabinered a rope to it for use in guiding it from below. All of this went smoothly. In less than three minutes Stout's team was reeling in the last foot of cable. So far, so good.

Suddenly things went south in a hurry.

At the exact moment the crew chief maneuvered the litter into the ship Sholly heard the engine noise change abruptly, as if the million dollar machine had landed on terra firma and its pilot had cut 1,100 horsepower from the rotors. Due to this random mechanical failure, the aircraft wobbled in the air, tilted port to starboard, and sank a few feet. Angel 6's rotor tips suddenly drooped and whirled extremely close to the granite. Setnicka and Sholly dropped to their stomachs on the rock in hopes that they would not be sliced into pieces. Things looked so bad at this point that burrowing into the granite was the only way they would have felt safe.

The Huey stabilized for an instant then it banked hard to port and "rolled" into a spiral descent almost 600 feet down the cliff. The helicopter autorotated two full, counterclockwise turns. The Huey slid and fishtailed as Stout fought to avoid hitting the steep slope. Next the airship turned on its side and weed-whacked into the oak trees then vanished from view.

Some of the rescuers stood agog. All held their collective breath as they waited for the inevitable explosion. Meanwhile Sholly shouted into the radio, "The helicopter is crashing!"

When no explosion came, the team on the ground quickly recovered from their astonishment and hustled to scoop up their gear and start down the fixed ropes to become rescuers yet again.

Thankfully, the airship had not exploded. At least not yet. But smoke now drifted up from the gully. Within minutes Ranger Henry who had been aboard as spotter radioed that the crew had cleared the burning ship. In nearly the same breath he requested a litter for one of its moderately injured crewmen.

The crash site sat about half a mile from the road. A Park fire crew soon rushed upslope to prevent a wildfire spread from the downed machine. Meanwhile Angel 6 and Peter Barton—except for part of his left leg—both burned to ash.

By now Barton's widow was present in the meadow and watching the recovery effort. As the flames and smoke crawled skyward she remarked to Chief Ranger Bill Wendt that the rising smoke from the incinerated Huey reminded her of a "Viking Pyre." She added sadly that, for her husband, it seemed a fitting end. (We suspect that the United States Navy failed to view the loss of their million-dollar UH-1 twin-engine helicopter in quite the same light.)

Noteworthy here, Peter Barton's death would be only the first of three independent climbing deaths in Yosemite that occurred during three consecutive days during that mid-June of 1975 (see James M. Ottinger on June 17th and James P. Welcome on the 18th in Table 9).

Roughly a half dozen mishaps on or below Yosemite's big walls have occurred, ironically, not from slipping after safely accomplishing the most dangerous parts of the climb—as in many of the examples above—but instead from making atypical errors during the climb. It is easy to chalk up these mistakes to fatigue-induced lapses of attention. But it remains not at all easy to fix what gets broken after such lapses.

A unique error unfolded on September 22, 1980, due to a simple lapse of attention. Twenty-year-old Walter Bertsch of Fraastauz, Austria was climbing Magic Mushroom on El Capitan with Albert Vinzens, age 21 of Chur, Switzerland. On day five, Vinzens had just led the 29th pitch (of thirty-one to the summit) of the huge wall. He now waited while Bertsch, ascending from below on jumars, cleaned the pitch.

Bertsch was only three feet from Vinzens' ledge. With three years of climbing experience, the Austrian now unclipped his jumars from their orange and black 11 mm Mammut rope. He did this because at this point the line made several odd angles before being clipped in at its anchor. This setup created severe drag here and would next have forced Bertsch to move laterally before he could then move upward to join Vinzen. To avoid this extra work on this awkward arrangement and instead follow an easier straight shot onto the ledge, Bertsch decided to reattach his ascenders above the piton holding his safety line to the thinner, more conveniently rigged haul line. This smaller rope looked like it would allow him to climb straight up onto the ledge with no detours.

While fully understandable, this decision would soon prove catastrophic. Perhaps preoccupied with the problems posed by the next pitch—again the second to the last remaining on this demanding Grade VI climb—Vinzens had secured this haul line into a piton only via his equipment sling. This sling was a European model held together only by two rivets and intended only for hanging lightweight hardware and rope. It had not been designed to support the weight of a climber. Now, without first asking Vinzens how secure this convenient looking haul line was, he reattached to it.

When Bertsch transferred his weight to the haul line, it instantly broke loose. Bertsch fell 150 feet to the end of the Mammut lead/safety rope and sustained multiple internal injuries.

The equipment sling to which the haul line had been attached snapped and flew into the void and was never even found. Bertsch fell, notes investigating Ranger John Dill, because of the failed haul rope anchor. But more specifically he died because, while jumaring the 29th pitch, he had never adjusted and shortened his lead rope to efficiently act as a safety line even after he moved his jumar to the haul rope. The way he had left it tied in long, it would only stop him after he fell the whole 150 feet.

But at least Bertsch *had* a rope, even if he had made the fatal error of not taking full advantage of it. Unfortunately, while free-soloing ropeless, even the simplest miscalculation can prove terminal. A harsh illustration of this lesson began on July 9, 1981.

The Park doctor at this time, Jim Wurgler, was already a veteran of more than a decade of Yosemite mishaps (he ultimately would log twenty years of service in Yosemite—interrupted by a stint in Vietnam as a military physician—and from Yosemite would serve another ten years at Grand Canyon). Happily, on this day, instead of another strange and urgent injury rushing through the doorway of the Yosemite Medical Clinic (Dr. Wurgler, you will remember, was the physician who reattached the nose of the first woman to BASE jump off El Capitan) he received a pleasant surprise. An old friend had dropped by his house. Well, the friend was not all that old. It was 16-year-old Vik T. Hendrickson of Auburn, California.

Hendrickson's father Roger had been for many years the physician with whom Wurgler had worked in Yosemite, until two years earlier, in mid 1979, when Dr. Hendrickson had moved after fourteen years in the Park to Auburn to start a private practice.

Young Vik, Wurgler now saw, had grown. The doctor had known the boy since he was a baby. He had seen him master the basics, walking, talking, riding a bicycle, and venturing out to explore the challenging world of Yosemite, backpacking, scrambling. Roger Hendrickson had always been proud of the boy for his affinity with the wilds and his mastery of its techniques. Now Vik, with the plastic of his new California driver's license barely dry, had just driven south from Auburn with his buddy Jeff Thompson, age 17, to introduce him to Doctor Wurgler and to show him Yosemite—the place where he was born and also the wild country that had made him the person he now was.

Wurgler was tickled to see Vik. He seemed like he was becoming such a fine young man.

After work the next evening, July 10, Wurgler heard a frantic pounding on his front door. It was Jeff Thompson. But, the doctor could see all too plainly, this was no social call.

"Vik's had an accident!" the 17 year-old blurted breathlessly. "Vik's had an accident."

"Where?"

"Uncle Fanny."

"How bad?"

"Bad!"

With a sinking sensation in his middle, Doctor Wurgler grabbed his Park radio, jumped into his car, and sped toward the Church Bowl. A few moments later he parked in a "no parking" zone then rushed uphill from the car with Thompson as his guide.

Vik had fallen, Wurgler soon saw, and had fallen hard.

After quickly assessing the condition of the barely conscious teenager, Wurgler radioed dispatch to request a Mediflight out of (and back to) Modesto and an immediate ambulance from the nearby clinic.

He glanced around him. The sun no longer lit the cliffs surrounding the Valley. A helicopter pilot would likely balk at landing in the Valley after dark. But Vik's only chance, Wurgler realized, would pivot on his reaching a neurosurgeon soon. Very soon.

The ambulance arrived. The crew packaged Vik and rushed him to the clinic. There Wurgler and Doctor Jeff Fokens tried to administer advanced life support measures. The boy was incoherent and posturing due to cranial injuries. On the positive side of the scale, he was still breathing and even crying out.

Doctor Fokens now expressed his worries over the patient.

Wurgler asked him, "You know who this is, don't you?"

Fokens looked at him, "Should I?"

"This is Roger Hendrickson's son, Vik."

Fokens gave Wurgler a stunned look.

What had gone wrong to cause all this?

Vik had taken his buddy Thompson to the Uncle Fanny climbing route (5.7) at the Church Bowl to show him some free-soloing. Near the top of this climb, Vik had gotten stuck beyond his ability in an extremely exposed position. As seconds, then minutes passed during which he still could not figure out a way to move higher—and he meanwhile remained convinced that he could not descend either (often much harder than ascending)—he developed a case of "sewing machine" legs.

His buddy Thompson had wanted to help but, being so far below, he was not in any position to do anything useful. Besides, didn't Vik have some trick up his sleeve? After all, hadn't he grown up right here, climbing these cliffs and stuff? While trying to solve this dilemma, Thompson witnessed the unbelievable: Vik Hendrickson lost his holds and fell about 100 feet.

Soon the medical flight arrived and flew Vik Hendrickson to Memorial North Hospital in Modesto. The fallen free-soloist arrived there still comatose.

Jim Wurgler now faced making what still remains, after more than forty-five years as a physician, the hardest phone call he has ever made. As he dialed, he tried to keep his composure. He managed it, sort of. *How* could he tell his old friend Roger this sort of terrible news? What words should he use? Could he even manage this without losing it?

"Roger, Vik has been hurt very badly in a fall. I don't know if he is going to make it. I'm so sorry."

Of course these words were met with stunned disbelief, then far worse.

In spite of improvement following neurosurgical procedures made to control intracranial pressure, Vik Hendrickson's condition deteriorated. After "brain death" on July 16, his body was transported to Stanford Hospital where surgeons transplanted several of his internal organs to needy recipients. Young Hendrickson lives on, though not in the way that his friends and family would have chosen.

May 10, 1983 was supposed to be Peter Mayfield's day off. The 20-year-old climbing guide had just spent all night discussing a string of difficult interpersonal issues with his girlfriend. Now, his head still echoing with their disagreements, Peter dropped into the Mountaineering School where he worked. He was there strictly to pick up his paycheck. Well, that, and maybe get some advice on relationships from his best woman buddy, KB, another guide there but also on her day off.

The guide's anticipated "repair session" failed to go off as planned. Their boss Bruce Brossman entered the back room and interrupted, stating, "Some folks want a guide today. Peter, you're up. That's what Chief Guide means: You take the walk-ins when you can!"

Great. With enthusiasm failing to quite bubble, Mayfield grabbed his gear and began what turned out to be a fairly nice day. The middle-aged clients were good guys, and they soon proved more fit and more skilled than most. Mayfield took them to Keystone Corner, Reeds Regular, and Bongs Away Left. Even after all these climbs, the guys were hot for more. So Mayfield decided to take them to Reed's Pinnacle Direct off Highway 120 between the two tunnels.

Because he had free-soloed this 5.10-rated climb umpteen times before and had become inured to the exposure, Mayfield now clambered up the first pitch while trailing the unprotected rope.

This whole thing had become routine. He soon paused to stand on the detached ledge at the top of the first pitch. Here he began to pull up the rope's free end. He planned, as usual, to tie a bowline-on-a-bight to the tree growing nearby. This time, however, while pulling the line it stuck in the flake well below. Crap. Mayfield turned to downclimb to the flake and free the rope. As he turned he bobbled his balance on the ledge. Oh shit…

Those waiting below saw Mayfield make a grab for his unfinished loop around the tree. As fate would have it he grabbed the section of the rope on the wrong side of the tree (not the end that would have created a bight on the tree and held). Off balance and unattached to anything except the dangling rope, which remained unfixed, and now with nothing to hold him, Mayfield toppled backward off the ledge. As he fell into seventy feet of empty air he let out a loud yell that announced he knew he was about to die.

He plummeted toward the ledges below and, to borrow a cliché, toward certain death. One of Mayfield's waiting clients put his hand on the trailing rope where it was running on the ground. The bit of friction this created now allowed the line to sink deeper into the flake crack and stick there. The jammed rope now brought Mayfield up short. After falling about forty feet, he hit feet first on a small ledge early on the pitch. His heel hit it so hard that the impact split his massive heel bone into two separate pieces.

Despite the injury, now high on survivor's adrenaline, he swung back to the crack, untied, and quickly soloed down the lower section to his shaking clients.

> I learned some valuable lessons that served me well over the next 20 years of guiding. One, do not try to get my climbing kicks while working; it can be bad enough at work, pulling the bulge on top of some Tuolumne runout, with rain splattering the stone—so save the soloing for a day off. Second, guiding is never just a job. Gravity never sleeps. So you better not get sleep deprived. The trials of real life may make it necessary to call in sick occasionally rather than put myself or my clients at risk.

A postscript: Twenty years later Peter Mayfield was able to guide the teenaged *grandsons* of the client who saved him, a man they knew but little themselves because he had died of heart failure only a decade after having caused that rope to jam so fortuitously. Mayfield took them up Aqua Knobby and told them about their grandfather.

A very different sort of mishap occurred on September 24, 1987, as 21-year-old Wolfgang M. Schrattner, a 5.10 leader from Scheibbs, Austria was climbing about 2,000 feet up The Nose on El Capitan and following 27-year-old Kurt Schall, a twelve-year veteran climber from Vienna. The pair was moving a bit slower than usual because they had caught up with the party above them. Schall had just topped the Great Roof Pitch (#23) and Schrattner followed, cleaning the route as he ascended.

This pitch arches into a lateral traverse, the route's first horizontal section. As Schrattner moved sideways, he seemed to be having trouble with his ascenders. When Schall was several pieces of protection into this part of the pitch he pulled up their haul bag. Meanwhile he heard Schrattner cry out. Schall turned to see his partner already falling into space.

Investigating Ranger John Dill tried to determine why and how Wolfgang Schrattner had fallen. He noted that Schrattner had seemed to fall close to the free-hanging rope, possibly with his hands or ascenders on it. He was tied to the end of his rope via his seat harness but not to his chest harness. Furthermore, Schrattner had failed to tie in short to this rope. Instead, he had left 130 feet of slack. This mistake allowed him to drop nearly 150 feet down the face and ricochet off a series of small ledges. Either immediately or within mere moments, he was dead.

Ominously, both of Schrattner's ascenders were detached from the rope. Why?

Dill tested these and concluded, "Both ascenders worked perfectly, and I found no indication that either ascender had been forced off the rope, that is, there were no rope fibers caught in the cam teeth, and no parts appeared to be distorted." To figure out what might have gone so wrong for Schrattner, Dill donned the dead man's gear and tried to climb with it.

He found it frustratingly inefficient. "The lengths of the foot & safety slings restricted him to short steps, and the foot loops were too small to tie a clove or girth hitch around his feet to keep the slings from coming off." With no rubber bands to keep them on, they may have repeatedly fallen off his feet, a distracting annoyance. Far more dangerous, Dill found that "the ascenders' safety straps were so short that when traversing horizontally the ascender tended to align itself at a 45-degree angle to the rope instead of parallel to it." Forcing the ascender into a parallel position onto the rope in this situation required a severe wrist bend to manipulate and also caused the rope to run at an angle, *thus disallowing the cam to engage far enough to allow the safety latch to lock*. "By twisting the ascender's frame I could make the rope push the cam back and [improperly] release itself from the ascender." It seems likely that Schrattner, during his lateral traverse with those too-short safety straps, ended up "secured" by one actually unsecured ascender while he tried to move the other one. When he fell he was attached only at his seat harness. Thus Schrattner may have been oriented head downward. He suffered massive head and chest injuries upon impact.

Even with all of these problems, notes Dill, had Schrattner periodically tied in short to his rope, his drop would have probably proven injury free. This climb may have included Schrattner's first lateral traverse. It was also his first (and last) major use of ascenders.

Again, a "small" careless error committed in the wrong circumstances can precipitate a tragedy immensely out of proportion to what one might normally expect. Yet another example of this—albeit a unique one—occurred on September 11, 2003, as 27-year-old Erik Gustav Svensson of Gothenberg, Sweden followed Nicklas Hult, age 30, and Lina Maria Gunnarsson, age 28, to the top of the third pitch of the Nutcracker on Ranger Rock at the base of the Three Brothers. Here Svensson clipped in using two separate slings and two locking carabiners he attached to two anchor points. His buddies asked him why he had clipped in twice. His answer?

"For safety."

Next Gunnarsson began to lead the 4th pitch. Very soon she asked Hult to unclip her locking carabiner and sling for her because she could not reach it from her position. Hult reached back and removed a locking carabiner for her, but he did this without turning around to look at *where* that sling dangling from that carabiner had led.

Almost immediately he heard Svensson scream—a scream whose pitch changed in a Doppler shift. The carabiner Hult had just detached had yanked from his hand as Svensson fell, cartwheeling 250 feet down the face.

Meanwhile Lina Gunnarsson's carabiner and sling remained attached to the wall. Hult now realized to his horror that he had unclipped Svensson by mistake. Even so, he could not imagine why Svensson had fallen—he had been clipped into two points with two slings and two carabiners.

Investigating Rangers Lincoln Else and Leslie M. Reynolds found Svensson's gear to be perfect. He must have been engaged in moving his second safety anchor precisely at the moment when Hult detached his first one in error. It was an almost unbelievable case of incredibly bad timing for a very careless error.

The following episode is arguably the Mother of all adrenaline-drenched, bizarre mishaps from a Yosemite cliff. It occurred on November 23, 1998, from the Leaning Tower beside Bridalveil Fall. Thirty-five-year-old Daniel Eugene Osman, a famous (if not infamous) free- and rope-soloist from Reno and Lake Tahoe was "climbing" with his friend Miles Daisher, a skier and skydiver. Well, he was not really "climbing."

It is true that Osman had built a coast-to-coast reputation for executing a blurring number of amazingly fast and sophisticated and unprotected free-solo climbs. As writer David Foster notes (in his February 7, 1999 Associated Press article "Last leap: gravity conquers"):

> On the rock...Osman was graceful, powerful and precise. He had a simian sense of balance and a gymnast's build, his steel cable legs and arms scratched and scarred from communion with the stone.

> He didn't climb a cliff so much as flow up it, his long black hair dancing between his shoulder blades as he went.

But this was not what Osman was doing on the Leaning Tower on this day. Over the years, flowing up cliffs had proven to be not quite enough. Osman, an archetypical adrenaline junkie, ultimately began to savor the rush of deliberately taking long falls from scouted overhanging faces. He would climb them, sabotage his own protection en route and then deliberately miss a move and fall. His belayer was usually the one to take the brunt. Although this may seem apparent foolery, he was conducting—at least in part—his own brand of psychological therapy. Namely, to conquer your fear, do the thing you most fear.

What fear? In 1989, Osman had taken multiple falls while climbing the crux of a difficult route up Cave Rock near Tahoe. These had scared him to the point where he knew his performance on the rock was suffering. Soon, impressed with how gentle the stop felt after the unbelievable rush of the intentional early drops, Osman began to search for other, greater opportunities to conquer and perhaps ultimately banish his fear of falling.

As writer/climber Kevin Worrall notes in his article in the March 15, 1999 issue of *Climbing*, after his first planned drop Osman told his filmer Mike Hatchett that there existed a "whole world of fun to be had" in these deliberate fallings. Hence Osman's quest to banish his fear gave birth to a new extreme "sport." As David Foster notes, Osman soon expanded his sport to try jumping off anything that facilitated clean falls, natural or artificial. His critical criterion was the "clean" aspect. Osman leaped off over-hanging cliffs, bridges, construction cranes, and natural desert arches. He called his new sport "rope jumping" and also "free flying." It entailed leaping into space while trailing a climbing rope calculated to stop the "free flyer" before he collided with terra firma below, like bungee jumping with climbing rope. Friends whom Osman talked into doing this emerged from their arrested falls buzzing with adrenaline highs and feeling transformed. Osman would chauffeur them back down to Earth with the enigmatic greeting: "Welcome to reality."

As Osman's notoriety and accomplishments and television spots started to earn him money he relied less on his carpentry and stone masonry skills to earn a living. He continued to develop and pioneer this new extreme sport. Dropping into space at the end of a rope remained his obsession. With perfectionist absorption, he analyzed and re-analyzed his techniques, locations, and novel combinations of climbing and traversing gear to push the envelope.

As again writer David Foster notes, Osman softened the terminus of his jumps by rigging his rope in a giant U-shape and then jumping well to the side of his anchor points. This setup softened the halt, but it also demanded plenty of room not just vertically, but laterally, as the U-rig would force Osman into a wide swinging pendulum. Osman called the howling sibilance of the rope whipping through the air behind him at nearly 100 miles per hour "flossing the sky."

Beginning with mere 400-foot leaps, Osman graduated to recruiting a few friends to help him rig a 1,200-foot horizontal line from Yosemite's Leaning Tower to Fifi Buttress and then attach five 200-foot climbing ropes 300 feet out from the anchor. The payoff for this rig was being able to jump down into the air 900 feet off the southwest face of the Tower, from just below the summit. On the Leaning Tower, Osman and his helpers were not so much "climbing" (although climbing was a necessary skill here) as practicing—in a spectacular way—his new passion.

But these 900 feet were only the beginning, the warm-up act. On each subsequent jump, Osman planned to add an additional twenty-five feet. For his "bungee cord," he again used multiple 200-foot climbing ropes tied end to end. It all seemed good, clean fun. And, for the moment, it was legal.

Even so, understandably the Park did not exactly like it. Osman was, they reckoned, planting the seed of a SAR nightmare up there and fertilizing it with adrenaline. To stop him from expanding his new extreme sport into a bureaucratic and rescue nightmare, the Park sent in undercover investigators to watch him. Maybe, they thought, he was doing something illegal, like filming these hairball jumps commercially without a permit.

Nope. He wasn't. Desperate to slow this flying Godzilla down before it began wreaking havoc, rangers resorted to checking Osman for outstanding criminal warrants.

Lo and behold, he had one for failure to appear in court for driving with a suspended license (Daniel Osman's life outside of his carefully calculated vertical excursions allegedly often was chaos). Rangers arrested him in Camp 4. Soon another outstanding warrant bleeped out of cyberspace on Osman, this one on a more serious narcotics violation. Now the Park had no choice at all but to hold him on the felony charge.

Rangers placed him in a "solitary" cell for twelve days—solitary because this was November and the Park's jail was close to empty and also "solitary" because federal guidelines dictated that suspected felons were not to be housed with other prisoners.

Food became an immediate issue with Osman. As David Foster notes, "He ate, drank or smoked anything that felt good…" Indeed he had a reputation for eating anything available from junk food to, to whatever—as long as it was not meat. He told his jailers he was vegetarian. Obligingly, they purchased him special food. Beyond mere nutrition, Osman was also a smokeless tobacco addict. One of his jailers, Ranger Shannon Jay, used Copenhagen smokeless tobacco. Osman asked to "borrow" some. This ranger assiduously kept Osman in chew during his incarceration.

Two weeks later, after his friends raised $25,000 in bail, Osman was free again. The Park told Osman he had five days to remove his ropes and tackle from the Leaning Tower—or else rangers would cut them down and confiscate the whole rig.

Instead of de-rigging his setup, Osman immediately went home to Lake Tahoe to visit his 12-year-old daughter Emma, for whom he reportedly felt a profound, if frustrated (because of his too frequent absenteeism) love. Once there he also regaled his friends with his saga of the immense jumps he had been making before he was arrested. Indeed, it seemed that the arrest had become in his mind a mere inconvenient, non-adrenaline interlude in his quest for record-setting rope jumps.

No surprise then that when he returned to the Leaning Tower with Miles Daisher, his equipment proved Siren-like. By now those ropes had been dangling out there in winter weather for about three weeks.

On November 22, the two men each leaped off Osman's setup—each made jumps of at least 1,000 feet. These two deliberate falls now tallied up to a grand total of sixteen jumps to which Osman's ropes and gear had been subjected. And instead of focusing on the Park's injunction to dismantle his system and stop making outrageous leaps, noted Daisher, his buddy simply focused on the beauty of Yosemite's cliffs and on the immense verticalness of it all. "Look at that golden light on El Cap," he had exclaimed. "That's the future!" What this meant in Osman-ese was he wanted to take his whole set up and hike it up to the summit of The Nose and jump off and maybe push his free-falling record up to an astonishing 2,600 feet.

Instead, on the afternoon of November 23, Osman prepared to jump off his existing traverse for another nine-second-long rush of free-flying. His jump went perfectly. He rappelled off the bottom of his setup on a doubled 4 mm line to the talus slope below then hiked back up for another go. A longer go.

This next jump, Osman decided, would set another record. But not merely a twenty-five-foot increment longer record. Instead Osman added seventy-five feet of line. He was aiming now for a 1,100-foot jump; this one might stretch out to a meteoric eleven seconds of free falling.

He and Daisher pulled the rope up and inspected their knots. They looked and felt as hard and tight as the rocks themselves. Osman sat there on the cliff and hammered them apart, then re-tied them loosely. Daisher, watching this, felt a nervous fear crawl up inside him. Osman's knots were so loose now. "A loose knot," intoned Osman, "is a good knot."

To allow for the longer, lower stretch of this elongated rope, Osman decided to move his attachment on the Tyrolean to another point. After all, at the end of that last leap his nose was only ninety feet away from smacking the ground. This new position for the rope on the Tyrolean would be nearer the Leaning Tower. This time, however, Osman would have to jump north and *over* the static retrieval line (which he used to pull the dangling end of the rope back up to the Tyrolean), instead of next to it as he had done on all previous leaps. This new set up would also require a new jump angle.

Osman fished for his cell phone and dialed up friends—Jimbo Fritsch and Frank Peter Gambalie III—in Tahoe. He enthusiastically explained to them every detail of his changes to his set up. Meanwhile, as he had prepared for and then recounted all of this, a storm rolled in. Now, at 6 p.m., darkness had gathered, softening the harsh craggy details of this vertical world in which Daisher and Osman stood poised to create history. His friends in Tahoe could hear the wind rushing across his phone mic. (One of these two friends on the other end would soon die in Yosemite during an episode that would vie for bizarreness with Osman's own—see Chapter 3.)

As Kevin Worrall tells it, Osman stood poised to leap into the seemingly infinite darkness. He now counted down to Daisher: "Five, four, three, two, one....See ya!" Then he jumped.

Osman dived down at a speed between 105-110 miles per hour. As David Foster writes, Daisher stood above watching—and waiting. "It seemed like twenty minutes," Daisher later admitted, "I was waiting, waiting, waiting." Daisher's eyes followed the shrinking pinprick of light from Osman's headlight for about ten seconds before it vanished.

"I heard Dano let out a yell—'AAUGGH!'" Next Daisher heard trees breaking. "It sounded like a whole massive tree just broke in half. It's echoing across the Valley. And I started freaking."

Daisher tried to contact Osman by radio. When no response came, Daisher climbed down from the Tower and followed the now dangling pendulum line. He finally located his friend in the dark, well below 1,000 feet. Hoping against hope, he checked Osman for a pulse. Nothing. Somehow Dan Osman had plummeted off the system he had designed and had died from impacting the ground while performing the new extreme sport he had created.

Again, something in Osman's rig had failed, letting him drop beyond 1,100 feet. Miles Daisher, standing there in the dark and cold with Osman dead, suddenly felt very alone.

What had gone wrong?

A fellow climber eventually cut down Osman's gear (and for this he was convicted for tampering with a crime scene). The lowest 200 feet of rope had snapped off. It was knotted with a figure-eight follow through tied with the end of each rope doubled back on itself. This knot was double-sized. The outside bends of the knot, notes Worrall, were burned through their outside, protective sheathes. The break itself was hidden inside the knot. Complicating this failure was the possibility the ropes had been wet, the lowest line having moisture wicked down to it via gravity. Such wetness could have shaved the rope's strength. Moreover, the entire system had been hammered by ultraviolet light for three weeks, although that final rope, the one that broke, had been used only for the last ten jumps.

Despite all of this, Kevin Worrall, a friend and expert climber, suspects neither moisture nor UV light constituted the crux. Instead he thinks the static haul line caught and arrested the stretch of the multiple linked 200-foot climbing ropes during Osman's 110-mile per hour fall. By preventing the stretch of the first three or four ropes, only the last one or two ropes were free to stretch. And these two—or maybe even just one—could not withstand the tremendous inertia and build up of kinetic energy of the plummeting daredevil at that speed.

After Dan Osman's death, a tin of Copenhagen was found in his van—along with a note thanking Ranger Shannon Jay, who had kept him supplied.

So how does all of this climbing mayhem stack up? Yosemite, the world's Big Wall Mecca, notes Ranger John Dill who has analyzed Yosemite climbing mishaps for the past 35+ years, hosts an estimated 25,000-50,000 climber-days annually. This "use" leads to roughly 100 climbing accidents per year, half of which involve fractured bones, two of which, on average, include deaths. The 3.5-year analysis "Rock-climbing injuries in Yosemite National Park" by William S. Bowie, Thomas K. Hunt and Hubert A. Allen (mentioned earlier in our section on lost lead climbers) noted fewer injuries, with a total of 220 injured climbers. Who were these guys? The average climbing experience of those injured was 5.9 years. Males comprised 88 percent of injury victims. And the victims' mean age was 27.5 years.

The authors' conclusion? "Injury typically occurred in a highly experienced, usually male, climber who fell while leading a climb....victims requiring immediate surgical intervention or blood transfusion usually died before rescue could be effected."

Reinforcing this gender trend, of the roughly 100 climbing-related fatalities known through 2010, only 7 were women. Comparable to most other types of accidental traumatic deaths in Yosemite, about 94 percent have occurred to males. Interestingly, a close percentage also exists for fatal falls while scrambling (Table 6). This male majority is also similar for waterfall deaths and drownings: males account for about 78 and 82 percent of these victims, respectively (Tables 1 and 10).

Adhering again to the overall pattern in the Park, most victims of climbing deaths were young. In Yosemite climbing up to 1983, fifty-three climbers of known age died in falls, rockfalls, or hypothermia incidents. Their average age was 24 years. Since 1984 and up through 2010, another fifty-two have died in similar climbing-related mishaps in Yosemite, but their average age was 31. From 2007-2019 the average age of all 26 climbing victims was 35 years old. A similar jump in ages exists in all other types of accidental falls in Yosemite during these same eras before and after 1984 (again see Tables 1 and 6).

Why? One hypothesis for the increase in age may be a better outdoor and survival-oriented youth. A second thought might be that greater numbers of older, but more poorly prepared individuals are now climbing and mountaineering because of its relatively new, slick-paged glamour—or whatever; the problem being that more of these individuals possess less acute mental focus due perhaps to having taken up climbing later in life when learning physical skills is more difficult. Or, conversely, it may be that experienced climbers are dying later in their careers when they let their guards down or shortcut on safety through diminishing caution. Maybe instead, this shift is simply due to fewer younger people being out there on Yosemite's granite these days. (Is this because the real world is so much more demanding to challenge than a computer game is?) Given the lack of reliable statistics on who is out there on the rock (climbers do not have to register), it is hard to pin down a cause for this increasing age of Yosemite's more recent victims of fatal climbing accidents. Perhaps appropriate here, there exists a saying among pilots: "There are old pilots and there are bold pilots, but there are no old, bold pilots." Is the same adage true for scramble-hikers and climbers?

Of the dozen men who died utter mystery deaths while climbing (see Table 9), ten were young, between 19 and 24 years old. The other two were 29 and 41. Eight of these dozen were also solo climbers. The lesson: Two heads are better than one. A further tragically learned lesson: haste all too often has made waste.

Most important here, John Dill believes the vast majority of climbing accidents in Yosemite are "easily preventable." A prime axiom of this preventability is contained in his admonition in his essay "Staying Alive" in the Introduction to Don Reid's *Yosemite Climbs: Big Walls.*

> —one of the rules most commonly overlooked: BACK YOURSELF UP. No matter what initially pulled, broke, slipped, jammed, or cut, the incident became an accident because the climber did not carefully ask himself, "What if…?"

In concert with this advice to conscientiously ask oneself "What if?," we considered adding here at the end of this chapter a "lessons learned" sort of summary reiterating the major safety points gleaned from analyzing the many fatal mistakes made while climbing in Yosemite and as described in various sections above. As mentioned earlier, we consider a major value of this book to help to prevent new people from dying due to making the same old mistakes. Despite the worthiness of this goal, however, we soon realized that our attempting a new and pithy summary of lessons learned would constitute hubris on our part. This is because not only does an excellent and timely safety essay for Yosemite climbing already exist, it is a better one than what we would concoct. Roughly a decade ago John Dill invested an unmatched amount of analysis and careful thought to write his "Staying Alive" introduction in Don Reid's *Yosemite Climbs: Big Walls* and in the internet site: *friendsofyosar.org.* Each time we read it, we again find it to be not only one of those seminal pieces of work that offers the tools to make things better but it is also one of those works that approaches the nonpareil.

Therefore we unhesitatingly recommend Dill's lessons-taught article. We also think one would be nuts to continue climbing without having read it. Why? Without mincing his words Dill spells out why:

> By leaving yourself open, you are betting against a variety of unpredictable events. You don't lose very often, but when you do, you may lose very big.

TABLE 9. FATAL EPISODES WHILE TECHNICAL CLIMBING IN YOSEMITE. (Incidents not discussed in the text are noted.)

Name, age	Date	Location	Circumstances
Charles A. Bailey, 55	June 5, 1905	El Capitan Gully	*Bailey of Oakland, California and J. C. Staats, age 22, of Mt. Vernon, Ohio tried to set an ascent record up the west cliff of El Capitan. Halfway up, during a breather,* **Bailey began to slide toward Staats' left then shot off into space.**
Fred H. Morley, 45	July 24, 1921	Cathedral Peak near Tioga Road	*Morley of San Francisco visited Tuolumne Meadows with a Sierra Club group. He and 2 companions* **"scaled"** *some peaks to the east. At 10,000 feet elevation, Morley lost his footing while* **scramble-climbing unroped** *and fell 75 feet onto projecting boulders.*
Henry J. Blank, 23	February 21, 1932	Four-Mile Trail (? to Glacier Point)	*Blank of San Francisco had* **roped** *to A. C. Manheim and was ascending to Glacier Point on snow when he* **slipped off a 300-foot cliff.** *Manheim anchored himself to a boulder, but as Blank swayed suspended over the drop* **the granite gnawed through the rope.**
Kenneth Alden Haines, 19 Peter B. Yeazell, 18	March 22, 1949	Lower Yosemite Fall	*Haines and Yeazell of Fresno were "practicing" rock climbing 300 feet up on a snow-dusted and rain-slicked face when,* **unwitnessed,** *apparently one of the teenagers* **grabbed a rock which dislodged.** *He fell, dragging his partner into a 300-foot fall.*
Anne Reustle Pottinger, 19	April 17, 1955	Higher Cathedral Spire	*Pottinger, a student at Stanford, climbed the spire with Irene A. Beardsley, age 19, and leader Theodore "Jack" Weicker, age 24, who knew a storm was coming and told rangers, "if it stormed he would not make the [Class II] climb." They had trouble descending wet, ice-slicked faces with frozen ropes. 700 feet and an hour above the Valley, Pottinger,* **hypothermic** *in her soaked light* cotton *clothes, collapsed and died.*
Donald Quentin Goodrich, 25	June 13, 1959	South Wall, Mount Conness	*Goodrich of Susanville, California was* **ascending** *with 4 companions when a* **loose 125-pound boulder knocked him off his holds and hit his head. He fell 30+ feet.** *A 27-man SAR team evacuated Goodrich by litter to Tuolumne Meadows but he died. He is the first modern-era climber to be killed in the Park.*
Irving Franklin Smith, 17	March 19, 1960	Lost Arrow Chimney	*Smith, a high school junior from Fresno, was determined to become the youngest to "conquer" Lost Arrow. He and Gerald Dixon, age 24,* **rappelled** *into the notch behind Lost Arrow. On the 2nd pitch Smith,* **unwitnessed, either rappelled off his rope or else fouled up his harness or knots and became unroped.** *He fell 500-600 feet and wedged into Lost Arrow Chimney. Smith became the first modern-era climber to be killed in Yosemite Valley.*

Charles A. Duart, 15

August 20, 1963 east side of Washington Column
Duart of Sacramento, **scramble-climbed** *up Washington Column with Barry Menneffer but slipped on the steep granite and fell 500 feet. It remains unclear whether this is a climbing or scrambling mishap.* (not in text)

Earl Hsu, 27

September 2, 1963 Cathedral Peak
Hsu, a relative novice from San Jose, California, was **lead climbing** *but* **lost his holds**. *His* **protection failed**. *Hsu fell 90 feet. SAR leader Ranger Wayne Merry characterized Hsu's "rescue" from the knife-edge, 18-inch wide ridge just below the summit by the pilot of a Hiller-12E helicopter as "the only one that was almost picture perfect. We did everything we could—but the patient still died."*

James F. Baldwin, 26

June 19, 1964 East Face, Washington Column
Baldwin, a Canadian, was climbing Washington Column with John Evans and asked him if he was willing to retreat. Evans agreed. **Unwitnessed,** *Baldwin* **rappelled off the end of his rope** *and fell hundreds of feet.*

Lawrence Lewis Gee, 15

August 11, 1966 "Valley cliffs"
Gee of Riverside, California and a buddy were technical climbing "approximately 1500 to 1800 feet above the Valley floor." During their descent Gee slipped. ***The cotton clothesline he used as a "dynamic" rope broke.*** *He fell 40 to 60 feet.* (not in text)

Larry M. Greene, 29
Edwin Hermanns Jr., 24

March 30, 1967 between Ahwiyah Point and Half Dome
Greene of Los Gatos, California and Hermanns of Stroudsburg, Pennsylvania climbed near the northern edge of the base of Half Dome and failed to return. On June 17, both bodies were found 50 feet apart, still roped together and slammed into the snow below Class 5 terrain in the saddle. Hermanns was in a sliding, self-arrest position over his ice axe. Greene had rope burns around his waist. Evidence suggests an **avalanche**. (not in text)

Ernest Willard Milburn, 18

June 20, 1968 Goodrich Pinnacle, Glacier Point Apron
Milburn of Oakland and John Gibbons of Piedmont, California were on their second **rappel** *anchored to a* **fixed sling** *left years earlier. It* **broke**. *Milburn fell nearly 700 feet.*

James T. Madsen, 20
(would-be **rescuer**)

October 15, 1968 Dihedral Wall, El Capitan
Madsen of Seattle wanted to help apparently stalled climbers by rappelling the route with rescue gear. He **rappelled off the end of his line on the 1st pitch and plunged nearly 3,000 feet**. *Madsen had failed to back himself up adequately.*

William Ronald White, 22

September 3, 1969 Washington Column
*White of Los Angeles, with James Richmond and Charles Taylor—all inexperienced climbers and members of St. John's Presbyterian Church group—***led** *"a fairly difficult climbing route with absolutely no climbing equipment or the correct type of footwear," noted Ranger James C. Leonard. 300 feet up, both ascending and retreating became too frightening. As Taylor downclimbed toward White to assist him, White moved,* **lost his holds, and fell**. (not in text)

Humphrey Singcheong Shum, 21	December 22, 1969	Gunsight, Cathedral Rocks *Shum of Fresno and Hong Kong was climbing* **solo** *and* **unwitnessed**. *He was found dying with a broken back and lying next to his coiled rope. His accident remains a* **mystery**. (not in text)
William Robert Smith, Jr., 20	April 25, 1970	South Face, Washington Column *Smith of Columbus, Ohio climbed the 1,900-foot South Face with Chad Chadwick, age 23, of Billings, Montana, who was 70 feet above him on the 3rd pitch. As Smith followed,* **jumaring upward unwitnessed**, *he became* **unroped** *and fell 600 feet.* (not in text)
William Lynderman Hendry III, 34	June 21, 1972	East Buttress, El Capitan *Hendry of Los Alamos, New Mexico climbed below Leonard Margolin, who dragged rope over 120 feet of steep rock and* **dislodged a rock which fell 80 feet and fractured Hendry's skull despite a (too small) helmet.**
Roger Stetson Parke, 17	July 25, 1972	Steck-Salathé, Sentinel Rock *Parke of Tucson, was belayed from below by Frank E. Johnson, age 20, as he* **led** *the 16th pitch (of 17). Parke* **placed too little protection**, *lost his holds, and took a* **leader-fall** *14 feet, hit his head, and broke his neck. This is Yosemite's shortest fatal climbing fall.*
Michael Mason Blake, 19	June 7, 1973	The Nose, El Capitan *Blake of Santa Monica, California was* **following** *at 7,010 feet with Jerry P. Volger, age 33, on the final pitch.* **.** *Blake lost his holds and fell.* **The old tie-off failed. The bolt also failed, yanking out. Next his 11 mm rope severed.** *Blake fell 2,800+ feet.*
John William Mokri, 23	June 13, 1973	Middle Cathedral Rock *Mokri of Pomona, California and Junius Ketcham, age 28, of Steamboat Springs, Colorado were on the wall when Mokri decided he was not up to the 2,000-foot climb. He rearranged his* **rappel** *anchor, unclipped from his protection, lost his holds, and fell* **unwitnessed** *and* **unroped** *300 feet.*
Charles Michael Stanbrough, 19	June 17, 1973	Steck Route, Higher Cathedral Spire *Stanbrough of Sacramento was* **solo** *climbing a route never before soloed when he fell* **unwitnessed** *about 100 feet, melting his Prusik belay and breaking his Perlon rope.* (not in text)
David Rollo Bryan, 20 Michael Timothy Harrison, 24	October 17, 1973	Monday Morning Slab, Glacier Point Apron *Bryan, a first year climber from Oceanside, California climbed with Harrison, a 5.10 climber from Bishop, California, who had set an expansion bolt atop the 3rd pitch. As Bryan jumared up toward Harrison, he unclipped their shared rope from the only other bolt. It seems their* **homemade hanger had rotated clockwise repeatedly as they had ascended, thus unscrewing the nut and allowing the hanger to detach** *under their weight. They fell* **unwitnessed**.
John Fox Schwab, 22 Ronald P. Baum, 21	May 25, 1975	Selaginella, near Lower Yosemite Fall *Schwab of Stamford, Connecticut and Monrovia, California.* **led** *the 5.7 climb with Baum of Hillsdale, New Jersey. Witnesses saw*

Baum belay Schwab on the 4th (and last) pitch. As Baum sat in a belay seat anchored to 2 nuts plus a large manzanita, Schwab **took a leader fall that yanked out his protection plus Baum's anchor nuts and the bush**. *Both fell about 400 feet, still roped.*

Peter G. Barton, 25 — June 16, 1975 — West Buttress, El Capitan
Barton and Dale Bard, both Park residents, climbed 2 pitches of West Buttress but decided it was too hot. As Barton **scrambled down an expanse of slick granite sprinkled with loose gravel he slipped** *and fell 150 vertical feet. A Lemoore UH-1 "Huey" helicopter retrieved Barton's body. It crashed and burned with the corpse. One crewman was injured. Barton's was the first of 3 climbing deaths in Yosemite in 3 days.*

James Michael Ottinger, 30 — June 17, 1975 — Chouinard-Herbert, Sentinel Rock
Ottinger of Eugene, Oregon was **ascending** *the* 1st *pitch with Ralph E. Moore as safety when he* **stopped to place protection. He lost his footing and fell** *60 feet onto a ledge, rolled, and fell another 130 feet. The pair's* **other protection had failed to hold**.

James P. Welcome, 18 — June 18, 1975 — Penny-Nickel Arête, between Middle and Higher Cathedral Rocks
Welcome of Fremont, California **led** *the 4th, 5.6 pitch with John Trevino, age 19, belaying. Wearing heavy climbing boots, he led in a zigzag route and* **set few points of protection**. *60 feet to the left of his last protection he stopped on a small mossy ledge to set a chock but* **lost his footing and fell** *75-100 feet.*

Gerald Ceburn Medders, 22 — August 3, 1975 — ridge on Buena Vista Peak
Medders of Fresno set out surreptitiously from Upper Chilnualna Lake to **scramble/free solo (ropeless)** *the ridge west of Buena Vista Peak. He fell 75 feet,* **unwitnessed**. *Church group members found him the next day.* (arguably a scramble incident, not in text)

Mark R. Olson, 14 — September 21, 1975 — Puppy Dome, Tuolumne Meadows
About to **rappel unsupervised**, *Olson of San Carlos, California clipped 150 feet of 9/16-inch goldline rope into his 6-carabiner brake system protected by a Prusik.* **Unwitnessed**, *he next fell 135 feet with the rope and everything still attached to him. The* **figure-8 knot** *at the top end of the rope was not clipped in to his anchor.*

Robert Bruce Locke, 22 — October 5, 1976 — Hook, Line and Sinker, Mount Watkins
Locke of Suisun City, California climbed 1,400 feet below the overhanging summit of the South Face—a Grade VI, 5.10, A3 climb—with Chris Falkenstein. He **tried to mantle onto a ledge, lost his holds, and fell**. *His "protection" ripped out. Swinging on 50 feet of rope, his body slammed his belay rope against the rock and* **severed it,** *plunging him 150 feet lower. The ensuing, innovative SAR included a 1,500-foot, moonlight lowering.*

Jeffrey Robert Hall, 29 — March 23, 1977 — The Nose, El Capitan
Alternating leads, Hall of Santa Clara, California and Shartel E. McVoy, age 36, were on The Nose. As anticipated, the weather turned bad. The pair now decided to **descend**. *En route to Dolt Hole McVoy's* **trailing rope lodged**. *Hall, cold and wet and*

anxious, tried to free it. **Unwitnessed**, *he fell 600 feet* **unroped**. *His ropes and harness were intact with nothing broken, untied, or missing. But his locking carabiner was not locked.* (not in text)

Suzanne S. Carne, 31

April 30, 1977 Southwest Arête, Lower Brother
Carne of Las Aromas, California was **leading** *while her husband John, age 30, belayed. Having difficulty with the route and setting protection, she rounded a corner beyond his sight. Ten feet farther, he heard her yell, "Falling!"* **Unwitnessed**, *she fell almost 200 feet.*

Michael P. Cannon, 23

May 25, 1977 Steck-Salathé, Sentinel Rock
Cannon of Harwick, Massachusetts and Mark Richey were **rappelling** *the 10th pitch under rain and hail. Richey stopped next to a flake (15' x 6' x 3') to set an anchor around a tree. Cannon moved behind the flake, leaned his back* **against** *it, and* **unroped**. **The flake separated from the wall**. *It and Cannon fell 600 feet.*

Burt Joseph Miller, 20

November 3, 1977 Glacier Point Terrace, Glacier Point Apron
Equipped with only one rope, Miller of Dearborn, Michigan **rappelled** *from the 5.9 route with Mark E. Dixon, age 20. At a pitch requiring more rope, Miller took off his swami belt and tried* **"a body rappel"** *for 75 feet but ran out of line 10 feet above a ledge. Miller* **had not tied in to the rope** *at all and now,* **unroped**, *he tried to hold it with one hand while grabbing a Prusik with the other. His one-handed grip failed and he fell 600 feet.*

Kendall Ovid West, 20

January 1, 1978 cliff bands below Half Dome
After lead-climbing with inexperienced, 13-year-old Marvin A. Johnson, West of Santa Ana, California **rappelled** *300 feet of a 1,000-foot, un-scouted descent. Their next rappel ended on a narrow ledge. Their only rope got "irretrievably" stuck. Near dusk West, with less than a year of experience, tried a 20-foot* **unroped downclimb** *to a bigger ledge but fell 600 feet* **unwitnessed**.

Jeffrey Joseph Graves, 22
John Edward Nygaard, 22
John Paul Garton, 24

May 14, 1978 The Nose, El Capitan
Graves, Nygaard, and Garton all from Minnesota fell simultaneously about 1,000 feet. All had anchored around *a chain at the rappel station. The* **bolt hanger, with a preexisting, nearly invisible crack, had failed**. *Ranger Tim Setnicka concluded: "So a weak mechanical hanger combined with a poor tie-in method added up to a disaster."*

James C. Adair, 20

May 30, 1978 Sentinel Rock
Adair, an "experienced mountain climber" from New Haven, Connecticut who had been very recently featured on the cover of a climbing magazine, was **free-soloing** *with George Mandes, age 20, and Ben Ailes, age 20. He strayed unintentionally off route and lost his holds. He fell 330 feet.* (not in text)

Gary Andrew Gissendaner, 20

June 3, 1978 North Face, East Quarter Dome
On May 28, Gissendaner of San Carlos, California was 800 feet

below the summit on a Grade V, 5.9, A2 route with Phil Bard, age 29, on belay as he **led** *the 6th pitch, rated 5.7, A1. He reached a false end, where he* **lost his footing and fell** *60 feet. His* **protection failed**. *He died of a basilar skull fracture.*

Christopher Shepherd Robbins, 24

May 17, 1979 Tangerine Trip, El Capitan
Robbins of Riverside, California was ascending the 2nd pitch on the Grade VI, 5.9, A4 route with Randal M. Grandstaff, age 24, on their first big wall. While jumaring up a line they had fixed the day before, Robbins fell 200 feet. His 11 mm Chouinard **rope had worn through and broken due to abrasion against the rock**.

Jeffrey Lee Drinkard, 19

May 18, 1979 Royal Arches, above Ahwahnee Hotel
Drinkard of Torrance, California had climbed 14 of 15 pitches of the 5.6, A1 route with Steven A. Larson, age 18. At the final pitch, they concluded the difficult sections were over. Both **unroped** *for the 5.4, 200-foot traverse pitch westward across a slab that* **looked easy**. *Drinkard* **slipped and fell about 1,000 feet.** (not in text)

Louis Raymond Beal, 55

September 1, 1979 South Crack, Polly Dome
Despite being warned by Dick DeRusha to wait, Beal of Granada Hills, California continued a 2-pitch **rappel** *without waiting for his 3 partners to catch up. Beal clipped his* **non-locking carabiner** *onto a single piton. He then secured his rappel rope's figure-8 knot onto it. He rappelled.* **His rope unclipped.** *He fell 270 feet.* (not in text)

David Thomas Kays, 23

April 3, 1980 The Nose, El Capitan
On March 29, Kays of LaVerne, California tackled the Grade VI, 5.9, A3 route on an 8-day, **solo** *climb up the 2,800-foot wall. He likely died on his 7th day during a snowstorm due to* **hypothermia** *after having dropped 2 gear bags containing food and his rain gear.*

Donald Raymond Davis, 27,

July 26, 1980 Upper McCabe Lake Basin
Davis of Palo Alto, California camped with 2 buddies on the west shore of Steelhead Lake (outside of the Park) then told them he was going to **scramble-climb solo**. *He failed to return. Searchers found him 4 days later below a 75-100-foot fall on a snowfield just inside the Park.* (arguably a scramble incident, not in text)

Karl Ulf Fredrik Bjornberg, 26

September 13, 1980 Waverly Wafer, The Cookie Cliff
After climbing Wheat Thin (5.10d) with Bengt Sorvik, age 23, Bjornberg of Göteborg, Sweden **rappelled** *second from a ledge above Waverly Wafer.* **Unwitnessed**, *he clipped into an existing but unknown number of slings using* **only one non-locking carabiner**. *It may have unclipped itself. He also may have used* **a new sling rigged by Sorvik that failed**. *Bjornberg's belay rope immediately came loose. With no backup, he fell.*

Walter Bertsch, 20

September 22, 1980 Magic Mushroom, El Capitan
Bertsch of Fraastauz, Austria **ascended**, *cleaning the pitch, on day #5 with Albert Vinzens, age 21, of Chur, Switzerland, who had just led the 29th pitch (of 31) of the Grade VI climb. Three feet from Vinzens' ledge, Bertsch* **moved his jumars from the lead rope to the haul line** *for an easier ledge move. Vinzens had clipped the haul*

		line to his equipment sling, held together only by 2 rivets. It failed instantly. Bertsch fell to the end of his 150-foot rope.
Vik Thomas Hendrickson, 16	July 10, 1981	Uncle Fanny, Church Bowl *Hendrickson, born in Yosemite to one of the Park's prior veteran medical doctors now of Auburn, California,* **free-soloed** *Uncle Fanny (5.7) above the Ahwahnee Meadow. He got stuck in a place beyond his ability, lost his holds, and sustained a 100-foot fall.*
Carol Catton Moyer, 28	September 19, 1983	Tangerine Trip, El Capitan *Moyer of Tahoma, California was cleaning the 4th pitch and* **ascending via 2 jumars** *as Raymond Kovac waited above. As Moyer tried to clear an overhang after unclipping her left jumar, her right jumar failed to hold.* **Unroped** *and with no back-up, she fell 300 feet.* (not in text)
Brian Kenneth Blair, 19	October 8, 1983	Bishop's Balcony, Church Bowl *Blair of Fresno was* **rappelling** *with Brian E. Koepp, age 24. His rope tangled. He attempted to free it and somehow detached himself from it. He fell 90 feet* **unroped**. (not in text)
Donald William Barnett, 39	April 23, 1984	Overhang Bypass, Lower Cathedral Rock *Barnett of Antioch, California was* **rappelling** *with Howard Replogle, age 36. He yelled that the rope was doubled unevenly and he was nearing the short end and he needed to set a piece of protection* **in the dark** *and would try to clip in. Instead Barnett fell 40 feet unwitnessed, then 100 more, after rappelling off the short end of his rope.* (not in text)
Eric Neil Hutchinson, 20	August 8, 1984	Dinner Ledge, Washington Column *Hutchinson of Olympia, Washington had climbed with Todd G. Mazzola and Michael John Daughwerty, both age 22. After bivouacking at 10:15 p.m.,* **another climbing party** *ascending* **in the dark** *above* **dislodged a rock**. *It struck Hutchinson and crushed and severed his spine killing him almost instantly.* (not in text)
Kenji Yatsuhashi, 32 Keiso Sadatomo, 35	October 16, 1984	The Nose, El Capitan *During 2 ongoing SARs in a storm Ranger Hugh Dougher in El Capitan Meadow noted 2 previously unnoticed and now unmoving climbers high on The Nose. Ranger Mike Murray rappelled 150 feet and found Yatsuhashi and Sadatomo of Hiroshima, Japan frozen (***hypothermic***). Both wore inadequate clothing.*
Thomas Taylor Apel, 19	October 28, 1984	Lost Arrow *Apel, a Stanford student, and David Dryden, age 19, both from Pasadena, climbed Lost Arrow Tip (5.12b). Apel then failed to make the Tyrolean traverse back to the main cliff* **in the dark** *due to "unexpected fatigue." They "bivouacked" on the small, naked summit without overnight gear or warm clothes at 20° F. Apel plunged into irreversible* **hypothermia**.
Robert Scott Steele, 24	May 16, 1985	Royal Arches, above Ahwahnee Hotel *Steele of Carmichael, California had been* **free-soloing** *and lost his holds* **unwitnessed**. *He fell 200 feet.* (not in text)

Joseph Forrest Palmer, 23 — June 3, 1985 — Aftershock, The Cookie Cliff
Palmer of Lyndhurst, Ohio **led** *Aftershock (5.11b) with Ruth Galler, age 23, but lost his holds during a layback move and fell 55 feet due to his* **poor placement of his protection**.

Yasuhiro Fujita, 21 — May 5, 1986 — Catchy, The Cookie Cliff
Fujita of Kyoto, Japan, **solo**-*climbed Catchy (5.10d) then* **fell unroped from a sound belay point while wearing a good harness**. *His crotch strap had two locking D-carabiners chained together with a standard figure-eight rappel device. He wore two slings, one loaded with gear, but was not connected to a rope. Apparently he had* **unroped** *from his anchor and/or failed before moving to ascertain that every component of his system was ready.* (not in text)

Austin Frederick Colley, 43 — June 21, 1986 — Yosemite Point Buttress
At 8:30 p.m., Colley of Yorba Linda, California climbed on belay by Joe Carl Kristy, age 40, who had just led the 12th pitch. He fell **unwitnessed** *and yanked Kristy off his belay point as 2 of his 3* **belay anchors failed**. *Kristy was injured but survived.*

Eric Paul Guokas, 23 — June 28, 1986 — Pratt-Kelsey, Higher Cathedral Rock
Guokas of Boulder, Colorado tried the first continuous free ascent, belayed by Douglas MacDonald. On the 3rd pitch about 100 feet above his partner, Guokas lost his holds **unwitnessed, falling** *70-feet due to an* **inadequately protected** *belay rope.* (not in text)

Allan Mitchell Chaneles, 31 — August 30, 1986 — Apparition, Daff Dome, Tuolumne Meadows
After about 5 hours sleep, Chaneles **led** *while belayed by John Gonzales age 30. Chaneles climbed 70 feet up,* **having been "unable" to set protection**. *He tried to reach a bolt 10 feet to his left but lost his holds and fell 140 feet, yanking Gonzales, now injured, off his stance.* (not in text)

Donald Joseph Horten, 29
Fredrick O. Yenny, Jr., 33 — April 25, 1987 — East Buttress, Middle Cathedral Rock
Horten **led** *the 8th pitch (5.6) with Yenny, both of San Jose, California, belaying. Horten started the crux in a dihedral, slipped and fell, knocking Yenny off his stance and into the air as his* **belay anchors failed**. *Both men fell 800 feet. Investigators found no evidence that Horten had placed protection.* (not in text)

Young Soon Lee, 35 — August 5, 1987 — Regular Northwest Face, Half Dome
Lee tackled Half Dome with 5 climbers from Seoul, Korea. At 8 p.m., he was seconding on the 2nd pitch (5.9) when lead climber Shoong Hyun Ji **dislodged a rock** *which severed the belay rope and shattered in front of Lee, hitting his head.*

Wolfgang Manfred Schrattner, 21 — September 24, 1987 — The Nose, El Capitan
Schrattner of Scheibbs, Austria, was 2,000 feet up The Nose following 27-year-old Kurt Schall, a 12-year climber from Vienna who had just topped the Great Roof Pitch (#23). Schrattner cleaned the pitch as he followed but **lost control of his ascenders** *compromised possibly by their safety straps being too short. He fell 150 feet and hit his head and chest.* **He had not tied in short**.

Robert Dietmar Kuhn, 24	May 20 1988 The Nose, El Capitan *Kuhn of Ursenwang, Germany* **led** *the Pancake Flake Pitch (#24) while belayed by Peter James Cuthbertson, age 34. A climber above warned Kuhn of a dangerous loose block and how he should aid climb around it. Kuhn ignored this and began to free-climb past it.* ***Unwitnessed, he pulled the one-ton rock loose****. It fell, probably severing both his ropes. He fell 2,000 feet.*
Dragan Rogic, 28	September 19, 1988 Aquarian Wall, El Capitan *Rogic of Celje, Yugoslavia* **rappelled** *with Boris Cujic, age 26, and Srecko Meic, age 27. While trying to pass a knot joining 2 ropes* **unwitnessed** *he* **unroped** *and fell 400 feet.* (not in text)
Robert Andrew Burnham, 35	October 24, 1988 Red Zinger, The Cookie Cliff *Burnham of Vancouver, British Columbia tried to* **rappel** *90 feet belayed by Michael Forkash. 30 feet from him, the belay rope was running out. Burnham* **lowered himself by gripping both ends of the doubled rappel rope** *threaded through the top anchor. This proved 10 feet too short. Burnham,* **unwitnessed and unroped**, *fell 30 feet then rolled to fall 70 feet more.*
John Lanham, 21	April 7, 1989 cliff bands beneath Half Dome *Lanham, visiting from Shropshire, England, bicycled to Mirror Lake on his first day in the Park and opted to* **free-solo** *the cliffs. Lanham lost his holds roughly 150 feet up the cliff and fell* **unwitnessed** *to the bottom.* (arguably a scramble incident, not in text)
Matthew Wayne Tomlinson, 21	August 2, 1990 Keystone Corner, Five and Dime Cliff *Curry Co. employee Tomlinson of Sacramento was* **leading** *a 5.8 route with Denise Brown belaying. He climbed* **beyond his protection**, *lost his holds, fell 30+ feet, and died of head injuries. Analysis suggested a helmet might have saved his life.* (not in text)
Jonathan Thomas Dawson Morrison, 20	July 28, 1991 northeast face of Mariolumne Dome *Morrison of Pollock Pines, California* **free-soloed** *the Hobbit Book. Searchers found his body at the top of the talus slope. He had slipped and fallen 200 feet* **unwitnessed** *after reaching the top and while scrambling down a cross-country route.* (not in text)
Anthony Michael Brucia, 19	April 30, 1992 Ranger Rock, Three Brothers *Curry Co. employee Brucia* **scramble-climbed** *down with Robert Alan Crawford but* **lost his footing on/in a fall of loose rock** *and fell 140 feet.* (arguably a scramble incident, not in text)
Alan Wayne Miller, 39 Caroline Lee Kostecki, 37	August 9, 1992 Southeast Buttress, Cathedral Peak *As Miller, an experienced climber from Stateline, Nevada, belayed Kostecki, a novice from South Lake Tahoe, at the top of the 4th pitch, she lost her holds and fell. Miller's* **belay anchor failed** *and both climbers fell more than 400 feet* **unwitnessed.**
Robert Eugene Moore, 42	September 17, 1992 near The Nose, El Capitan *Moore of Greeley, Colorado muscled off the lip of El Capitan to* **rappel on his $^{7}/_{16}$-inch, 150-pound, 2,600-foot line** *with the intent of making a single-rope rappel. He stopped 300 feet down,*

maybe to adjust the bars of his self-designed descending device. Next he suddenly plummeted down **the rope** *for 2,300 feet.*

Derek Geoffrey Hersey, 36 — May 28, 1993 — Steck-Salathé, Sentinel Rock
Hersey, a British climber from Boulder, Colorado, tried to **free-solo unwitnessed** *and failed to return. His mangled body was found where the Steck-Salathé and Chouinard-Herbert Routes start, 850 feet above the Valley floor.*

Miroslav Smid, 41 — September 11, 1993 — Direct Route, Lost Arrow Spire
Smid of Metnji, Czechoslovakia tried a 4-day **solo, free-climb** *of Lost Arrow using a solo belay device. Searchers found most of his gear atop the 12th pitch. He had fallen 800 feet* **unwitnessed**. *Smid's mangled body wore a daisy chain tie-in* **severed as if by a falling boulder** *or by the mis-stroke of a hammer.* (not in text)

Gustavo E. Brillembourg, 35 — September 28, 1993 — Northeast Buttress, Higher Cathedral Rock
Brillembourg of New York City, a 5.11 climber, **led** *the 10th of 12 pitches, rated 5.9, with Rui B. Ferreira belaying. Brillembourg lost his holds and took an* **unwitnessed** *leader fall. Both his pieces of* **protection yanked out**. *He fell 120 feet and hit the cliff before Ferreira's Sticht Plate belay could arrest his descent.* (not in text)

Ik Tai Choi, 24 — July 31, 1995 — East Ledges, El Capitan
Choi of Kyeong Ki-Do, Korea **rappelled** *the East Ledges near the base but stopped and* **detached from his climbing lines** *to free a haul bag snagged in a crack that had bothered other climbers. He lost his holds and fell* **unroped** *160 feet to the ground. His adjustable daisy chain safety strap was found clipped to his last anchor—but not to his harness.* (not in text)

Matthew Andrew Baxter, 26 — April 1, 1996 — Zenyatta Mondatta, El Capitan
Park resident Baxter was overdue from a **solo** *climb during a storm. Kristen Ramsey hiked to the base and found he had fallen* **unwitnessed** *300 feet from the 3rd pitch. Several of his* **placements**—*few of which in this case, notes investigator John Dill, "offer[ed] bombproof protection"*—**had failed**. *A carabiner had shattered, and his 10.5 mm Mammut Flash rope had dragged into a ½-inch crack that had pinched and abraded it, weakening it so that it broke 25 feet from the clove hitch he'd been using as an adjustable self-belay. Whether hypothermia influenced Baxter's placements remains a mystery.* (not in text)

Stephen Beames Ross, 32 — May 26, 1996 — Beverly's Tower, The Cookie Cliff
Ross, a 5.11 A4 climber from Pasadena, **led** *the 5.10a route with Jason Holinger. Ross placed his first protection 10 feet up into the dihedral. Waist high to his Camalot, Ross* **lost his holds**, *it* **pulled out**, *and he struck his head fatally.*

Sam Meier, 24 — July 5, 1996 — Hidden Falls, Tenaya Creek
Concession employee Meier was teaching novice David Scott Mitten to **rappel**. *Mitten acted as safety as Meier rappelled, lacking equipment to ascend, to what he may have assumed was a shallow pool. The pool proved deep. Meier trapped himself on his rope within the falls.* (also listed in Chapter 10. Drowning)

Steve M. Slovenkai, 37	May 27, 1997 Arrowhead Arête, east of Upper Yosemite Fall *Slovenkai of Brisbane, California descended the Arête with Eric Henderson. About 1,000 feet below the summit they traversed. Slovenkai, above Henderson,* **knocked loose a boulder**. *It sent both men tumbling. Henderson's pack jammed between two rocks and arrested his fall; Slovenkai fell about 200 feet.*
Darko Dular, 33	July 22, 1997 Hardd Route, The Cookie Cliff *On July 14 Dular of Zagreb, Croatia was* **leading** *the 1st pitch belayed by Elvir Sulich. Dular had set 2 Friends as protection. Applying his weight, they yanked free, and he fell about 30 feet. He survived for 10 days then became an organ donor.* (not in text).
Daniel Eugene Osman, 35	November 23, 1998 Leaning Tower *While* **"rope-jumping"** *with Miles Daisher, Osman, a famous free-soloist from Lake Tahoe, dived off the Leaning Tower, while rigged into 1,100 feet of linked climbing ropes to set a new world record jump. The final rope broke. Osman crashed to the ground at about 110 miles per hour more than 1,200 feet below.*
Peter James Terbush, 22	June 13, 1999 Apron Jam, Glacier Point Apron *At 7:35 p.m., a huge* **slab of granite weighing roughly 550 tons slid from 2,000 feet above the Valley** *as Terbush of Gunnison, Colorado and 2 buddies climbed above Curry Village. Terbush was killed by flying boulders. His companions sustained minor injuries.*
Andrew Jon Morrison, 28	December 3, 2000 South Face, Washington Column *Morrison climbed the 1st pitch above Dinner Ledge last after fellow Australian soldiers Matthew Ryan and Nicholas Thain. Morrison decided to retreat.* **Solo rappelling**, *his ropes became tangled. While pulling one, it abruptly freed. Off balance and* **unroped**, *he fell 500 feet. Morrison, notes Ranger Doug Roe,* **"was not anchored to the cliff face during his attempts to free his ropes."** *He possibly had rigged a single tie-in but had left the carabiner unlocked.* (not in text)
Thomas Vroman Dunwiddie, 49 Myra Monica Elderidge, 41	July 12, 2001 North Buttress, Middle Cathedral Rock *Dunwiddie of Denver* **led** *as Elderidge of Boulder, Colorado, anchored by 2 pieces of protection at 2 spots, belayed. Dunwiddie fell* **unwitnessed and yanked out Elderidge's anchor protection** *(scarring it by pulling it from the rock with "great force"). His fall took her off the face with him into a 1,000-foot fall. Rangers found* **no evidence** *Dunwiddie* **had placed his own protection.**
Richard Zuccato, 43	June 13, 2002 Braille Book, Higher Cathedral Rock *Zuccato of Baytown, Texas tried a layback move high on the 1st pitch while* **rope-soloing with a "Soloist" self-belay device unprotected by a backup knot.** *He fell and slid 75 feet down his rope, sustaining multiple injuries. Navy helicopter Rescue 2 tried to evacuate him, lost power and snapped its hoist cable, and Zuccato's litter hit a tree. The machine landed damaged with Zuccato dead and Corpsman Jason Laird injured* (also listed in Chapter 5. Aircraft Down)

Philip C. Jones, 23

October 15, 2002 Enigma, The Cookie Cliff
Jones of Cornwall, Connecticut was **rope-soloing off-route** *and fell* **unroped** *200 feet, possibly while rappelling or rigging a rappel anchor. His death remains a* **mystery**, *but it may have involved* **stepping and slipping on loose rock**, *precipitating a small rockfall heard by other climbers.* (not in text)

Joseph Emmet Crowe, 25

December 29, 2002 Zodiac, El Capitan
Crowe of Azusa, California **winter solo climbed** *Zodiac but yelled for help in the dark during whiteout snow. He died of* **hypothermia** *several hours before rescue was possible, while suspended only 25 feet from the bottom of the nearly 3,000-foot wall.*

Christopher Price Hampson, 25

May 31, 2003 Overhang Bypass, Lower Cathedral Rock
Hampson of Golden, Colorado had led **"a considerable distance above his last [and only] piece of protection"** *on the 3rd pitch when he* **fell** *80 feet. Sibylle Hechtel stopped his fall out of her sight around a corner. Bob Jensen, free-soloing, climbed within 40 feet of Hampson. Jensen, gearless, downclimbed 800 feet for help. "Blitz team" Rangers Keith Lober and Lincoln Else climbed up only to find Hampson dead due to his* **failure to set adequate protection.** *Hampson became Yosemite's twenty-fourth lead climber fatality of this sort.* (not in text)

Mark Howard Lewis, 48

July 2, 2003 West Pillar, Eichorn Pinnacle, Cathedral Peak
Lewis of Tahoe City, California started a climb with Aaron Zanto, Brian Dannemann, and Chad Anderson. While Zanto and Lewis were on the 2nd pitch, the climbers decided to retreat. Zanto set up **a rappel using a nylon anchor sling left by earlier climbers**. *Lewis* **rappelled** *a few feet from this then fell 230 feet with the ropes. The webbing and cord anchor had been threaded behind a constriction in a finger-width crack and had yanked free. Zanto told rangers he: "had evaluated the anchor by tugging on it several times, but* **did not thoroughly inspect it visually**."

Erik Gustav Svensson, 27

September 11, 2003 The Nutcracker, Ranger Rock, Three Brothers
Svensson of Gothenburg, Sweden followed Nicklas Hult, age 30, and Lina Maria Gunnarsson, age 28, atop the 3rd pitch and clipped in with 2 slings to 2 points. Gunnarsson began to lead the 4th pitch. Hult unclipped Svensson by mistake. Svensson's gear was in working order. He likely had been moving his second safety anchor when Hult detached his first one in error.

Jeffrey M. Cabral, 33

September 8, 2004 Tangerine Trip, El Capitan
Cabral of Leadville, Colorado was cleaning the 5th pitch below 2 buddies while traversing on Petzl ascenders and not otherwise tied into his rope. **Unwitnessed,** *he fell upside down, slid down his rope, and fell 600 feet into the fork of a pine tree at the base of the cliff.* (not in text)

Ryoichi Yamamoto, 26
Moriko Ryugo, 27

October 17-20 (?), 2004 The Nose, El Capitan
A blizzard from October 17–20 blasted winds of 50 mph and white-

out snow conditions. Japanese climbers Yamamoto and Ryugo bivouacked on the ledge at Camp Six. After 2 days and still suffering the storm, Yamamoto led the next 2 pitches. Dressed for only mildly cold weather but tied in and exposed to the storm, the couple froze.

The following entries are not in text but are included in text statistics.

Bela Chris Feher, 35 — September 14, 2005 Slabs Route, Half Dome
Solo *climber Feher of San Diego fell* **unwitnessed** *possibly because his pair of belay anchors pulled loose during his descent. Other than due to a possible* **rockfall** *noted by independent climber Paul Brunner, Feher's death remains a* **mystery**.

Todd Richard Skinner, 47 — October 23, 2006 West Face of Leaning Tower
Skinner of Lander, Wyoming, a world-class rock climber/author with about 300 first ascents in 26 countries—including the 1988 first free ascent of the Salathé Wall (5.13b) on El Capitan and the impressive 1995 first of the east face of Trango (aka "Nameless") Tower (the world's first Grade VII free climb) in the Pakistani Karakorams—fell 500+ feet while rappelling off the nearly 2,000-foot and overhanging "Jesus-Built-My-Hotrod" route on Leaning Tower. The belay tie-in of his old harness broke, leaving his Grigri descent device on the rope and attached to his locking carabiner attached to nothing. Climbing partner Jim Hewitt had warned Skinner 3 days earlier that the loop appeared dangerously frayed but Skinner had replied that the new harness he had ordered had not yet arrived. This seems to be the first fatal consequence in Yosemite resulting from gear failure due to ignored normal wear and tear incurred during routine use. Rangers the next day recovered the lost loop and found it badly frayed from wear at its break point.

Peter Charles Nobel, 44 — November 11, 2007 retreat from Cathedral Peak
Nobel of Oakland with Scott Berry planned to summit during the day and descend Cathedral at night on Nov. 10, but wind, sleet, and light snow stopped their rappels. The next day, hiking within 1.5 miles of Tioga Pass Road on a trail, Nobel collapsed. Berry hiked out for help. Rangers found Nobel dead of **hypothermia**. *The pair had left their bivouac gear in their vehicle.*

Christopher Alan Hale, 23 — June 14, 2009 unnamed cliff above Mirror Lake
Concession employee and lover of **free-soloing**, *Hale of Gainesville, Florida was* **running naked through the woods**—*and likely under the influence of hallucinogenic drugs—toward Half Dome when he vanished. Searchers at the base of a cliff found his body, having "obviously suffered a significant fall."* **Unwitnessed** *fall.*

Jeff Maurer, 47 — August 30, 2009 Third Pillar, Mount Dana
Maurer, a wildlife biologist at Yosemite, and a friend "were climbing Lenticular Limbo on the Third Pillar of Mt. Dana near Tioga Pass. Maurer was lead climber and had placed five pieces of protection before his fall. The friend reportedly felt golf ball sized rocks falling around and realized Maurer was falling." Cause was unwitnessed.

Brian G. Ellis, 31	May 7, 2010	Serenity Creek
	Ellis of Santa Monica, California fell 300 feet while rappelling. His climbing partner noted: "The primary cause of failure was that the knot passed through the rappel rings as Brian was mid-rappel on the single 10.2 lead line.... When Brian set up this system... he forgot to tie the backup knot. When I checked the system for him, I too, committed the same mistake and only observed the main knot. He checked it a THIRD time, and made the same oversight. The only explanation I have for this oversight is distraction and complacency."	
Tyler A. Tompkins, 25	late May, 2010	Lower Brothers, Absolutely Free
	Tompkins of Valencia, California was **free-soloing, solo**, *the Absolutely Free route when he fell* **unwitnessed**. *Hikers Jay Wood and Caryanne McIver discovered his body on May 31. It had been moved and partially eaten by bears and was decomposing.*	
Christina Chan, 31	July 9, 2010	Eichorn Pinnacle, Cathedral Peak
	Chan of Stanford, California was **free-soloing** *and downclimbing with other climbers. She lost her holds and fell 300 feet. Chan was a Ph.D. student and past president of the Stanford Alpine Club—and an instructor with the Stanford Outdoor Education program.*	
Markus H. Praxmarer, 48	September 19, 2011	Regular NW Face of Half Dome
	Praxmarer of Innsbruck, Austria was leading out from the 6th belay and 7th pitch of the route while belayed by Thomas Wanner. 30-40 feet out, Praxmarer **dislodged a large block of granite** *which* **severed his rope** *at the knot at his harness. He fell 700 feet.*	
Michael Ybarra, 45	July 1, 2012	Sawtooth Ridge between Matterhorn and Cleaver Peaks, Tuolumne Backcountry
	After having **solo climbed** *Matterhorn Peak, Ybarra of Rancho Cucamonga, California headed across Sawtooth Ridge.* **Unwitnessed**, *he lost his hand and/or foot holds and fell 200 feet. Ybarra had been a contributing writer covering extreme sports for the* Los Angeles Times *&* Wall Street Journal.	
Mason Robison, 38	May 19, 2013	Muir Wall, El Capitan
	Robison of Columbia Falls, Montana was about 2,300 feet up the Muir Wall (VI 5.10 A2 or C3+, 33 pitches, 2,900 feet) in a stretch listed in SuperTopo: Yosemite Big Walls as "A2 loose, sharp flake." Robison placed a cam behind a triangle-shaped flake in a roof. The cam levered the flake loose toward his waist and shoved him into a fall. The **dislodged rock** *(estimated by YOSAR Ranger John Dill as 3 feet x 3 feet x 2 feet)* **severed his lead rope** *close below his tie-in. He fell 230 feet on his static haul line clipped to the back of his harness and died from his sudden arrested fall. The falling rock missed his partner Marc Venery, age 28, and other climbers below.*	
Felix Joseph Kiernan, 28	June 2, 2013	East Buttress of El Capitan
	While ascending about 600 feet up, Kiernan of London, England was hit by a **falling rock** *about 1 foot x 2 feet in size dislodged from 150 feet above him by his partner.*	

Brad Parker, 36

August 16, 2014 Matthes Crest Traverse

After summiting Cathedral Peak and proposing marriage to his girlfriend Jainee Dial there, then calling his father to tell him "it was the happiest day of his life," Parker of Sebastopol, California went **free-soloing** *on Matthes Crest 3 miles away later on this same day. Other climbers witnessed his fall.* **Fatigue** *may have been a factor.*

Richard Copeland, 50

May 18, 2014 Liberty Cap, near Nevada Fall

Before climbing, Kings Canyon National Park resident and experienced first-ascent climber Copeland stayed while his partner went to fill water bottles. Upon his return, he spotted Copeland at the bottom of a ledge leading up to the climb, a victim of an **un-witnessed, mysterious fall** *of about 300 feet.*

Cody Byers-Long, 24

January 25, 2015 Royal Arches, above Ahwahnee Hotel

Un-witnessed *by his climbing partner, Byers-Long of Fresno, California was* **rappelling** *off a climb he had made 4 times prior but now, via a* **mysterious error**, *he became detached from his rope and fell 400-500 feet—both of the double ropes the pair was using for their rappel followed (?).*

Tyler Keith Gordon, 21

May 27, 2015 The Nose, El Capitan

Gordon of Durango, Colorado was between Camp 5 and Camp 6 with 2 fellow climbers, one of whom dropped a climbing nut onto a ledge below. Gordon **rappelled** *down a fixed line to retrieve it but somehow fell* **due to a mysterious error** *from that ledge about 200 feet, impacting the top ledge of Camp 5.*

Ethan Fair Gillett, 28

October 30, 2015 Dinner Ledge, Washington Column

Gillett of Boulder, Colorado **rappelled off the end of a rope** *fixed to an anchor at the top of Pitch 5. He fell about 120 feet onto Dinner Ledge. The rope belonged to other climbers below. Gillett had secured permission to use it, but apparently did not understand that it went down only about 40 feet.*

Angela Uys, 26

November 7, 2015 3rd pitch, Snake Dike, Half Dome

With relatively little climbing experience, Uys of Berkeley, California with 2 partners was preparing to **rappel** *using a "PAS system" on her climbing harness. Her partners think Uys* **apparently failed to clip a loop of her PAS to the anchor locker** *(or to anything else) and also failed to clip a redundant loop to the anchor before she unclipped from her rope. When she raised her hands up as if relaxing back in harness, she fell backward 400 feet. One possible contributing factor was Uys was carrying her* **camera** *in one hand and periodically taking* **photos.** *Other factors may have been fatigue or haste.*

Sergio Fon, 41

July 10, 2016 Reed's Pinnacle

Experienced climber Fon of Concord, California and his partner had just finished Lunatic Fringe (5.10c). For their **rappel** *they used an 80-meter rope known to reach the ground when doubled. The partner had a Grigri rappel device usable only on a single line. The pair decided to do an uncommon simul-rappel on their rope doubled over an anchor. This requires each rappeller to counter-*

balance the other; both must detach from their rope simultaneously. **Via a mysterious error** *Fon fell 70 feet or so to the ground. The partner suffered an angulated leg/ankle.*

Christopher Vale, 21

September 5, 2016 East Ledges, El Capitan
After climbing the West Face of El Capitan, Vale of Tiburon, California and his partner were descending via the "standard" East Ledges Rappels after nightfall. Other climbers below them had left several fixed ropes for other climbers. Vale **rappelled** *on these first, using an ATC rappel device. He yelled "OFF RAPPEL." His partner soon heard a crashing sound. Possibly one of those fixed ropes had been lodged behind a flake, and when Vale put his weight on it, it loosened, allowing him to fall. Vale had planned to climb El Capitan again the next day and may have been in a hurry (?).*

Matthew J. Price, 34

July 30, 2017 Matthes Crest, Tuolumne Back Country
Price of Oakland, California was leading an ascent using only an 8.5 mm rope (usually used in a twin rope system with a second rope). He **fell 20-30 feet**, *during which his* **8.5 mm rope was cut**, *likely by a sharp projection or constriction. He fell 120 feet to the base.*

Megan C. Kelly, 25

August 26, 2017 Cathedral Peak, Tuolumne Back Country
While climbing, Kelly of San Francisco, California was hit by a **rockfall** *dislodged by a climbing partner above her.*

Andrew Foster, 32

September 27, 2017 foot of El Capitan
On the 4th or 5th pitch of the East Buttress, Foster of Cardiff (Marshfield), Wales and his wife Lucy decided to rappel to the foot. As they hiked away, with Lucy 50 yards behind, a **gigantic slab spalled off El Capitan**, *shattering into some pieces larger than cars. Andrew yelled to Lucy to run. When she tripped on the uneven terrain, he ran back to her and shielded her body with his.* **Rocks** *seriously injured her legs but killed him. Lucy said: "He saved my life."*

Neils Tietze, 31

November 17, 2017 Fifi Buttress, Bridalveil Meadow
YOSAR member and accomplished first ascent climber Tietze of Salt Lake City, Utah was **rappelling** *and apparently experienced an* **unwitnessed** *accident that sent him into a 300-foot fall. Neils was the third and last son of his parents Becky and Chris Tietze. All three sons died young to climbing/alpine accidents.*

Jason Wells, 46
Tim Klein, 42

June 2, 2018 Freeblast, Salathé Wall, El Capitan
Decades-long climbing buddies and "very experienced climbers" Wells of Boulder, Colorado and Klein of Palmdale, California were **simul-climbing** *tethered and ascending about 1,000 feet up when something went wrong on the 5.7 pitch 9 or 10. Klein previously had made 107 one-day ascents of El Capitan, sometimes twice a weekend. Kevin Prince, a third partner on a separate rope, was following but did* **not witness** *the pair's* **mystery** *fall of 1,000 feet.*

Matthew S. Flowers, 36

April 16, 2019 Rhombus Wall, Royal Arches, Valley Cliffs
Flowers had **solo free-climbed** *a pedestal north of, and above, the Ahwahnee Hotel but fell* **unwitnessed** *to the base of Rhombus Wall.*

Patricia "Trish" Stoops, 57

June 8, 2019 Central Pillar of Frenzy, Middle Cathedral
Experienced Stoops of Modesto, California was about to **rappel** *from the top of the climb as lead in an effort to get her group off the face before dark when she made an* **unwitnessed error** *(due to haste?) by mistakenly putting herself on rappel using the long tail of her tied-off, single-strand rope* **then rappelled off its free end**.

Paul Nakauchi, 38

April 27, 2021 Sickle Ledge, El Capitan
Nakauchi of San Diego, California was climbing with a partner. He fell 500 feet when he **rappelled off his rope** *on the Nose Route.*

Frederick James Zalokar, Jr., 61

July 18(?), 2021 Mount Clark (11,527 feet)
Alpinist, climber, winning marathoner & international fanatic Zalokar of Reno, Nevada embarked on a **solo backpacking hike & scramble climb (or free climb?)** *up Mount Clark then failed to return. Searchers found him dead from a 300-500-foot fall below the summit. Previously Zalokar had climbed all of California's 14,000-foot peaks and attempted 6 of the world's "Seven Summits."*

Ryan D. Williams, 32

September 10, 2021 Daff Dome (800 feet), Tuolumne Meadows
While climbing the 70-foot long "Guide Cracks (rated 5.7) Williams of Oakland, California fell somehow while being **belayed**.

Marc Alan Smith Sacks, 50

June 19, 2023 Leaning Tower Rappel Route
The rope used by Smith Sacks of Santa Cruz, California was **cut by a falling rock** *dislodged by his partner. This was the 14th climber fatality in Yosemite due to a* **climber** *loosening a rock into freefall.*

Yongloo Kang, 68

September 28, 2023 below Sickle Ledge, The Nose, El Capitan
*Climber Tom Evans noted that Yongloo Kang, a Korean climbing instructor "went down [***rappelled** *from Sickle Ledge] to fix lines to the deck [base of climb] and went off the end of his rope." Apparently, Kang* **had failed to tie a terminal knot on his rope**.

James Christopher Gay, 39

October 15, 2024 the Hobbit Book, NE face of Mariuolumne Dome (700 feet)
Experienced climber Gay, a YOSAR member, told buddies he was going to **free solo** *the Hobbit Book, a solo he had made previously. The next morning his body was found at the base of the slabs below the route due to an* **unwitnessed** *fall.*

Grant Jeffrey Cline, 18

June 6, 2025 Royal Arches
Free soloing, Yosemite Hospitality employee Cline of Frisco, Texas appeared to have strayed eastward off route, possibly while trying to down climb, and fell **unwitnessed**.

Balin Scott Miller, 23

October 1, 2025 Sea of Dreams, El Capitan
Rope-soloing *on the final pitch, Miller of Anchorage, Alaska tried to free his stuck haul bag by* **rappelling** ***to it on a too-short line, and,*** **witnessed,** ***he*** **rappelled off the end of his line**. *Miller became the 35th climbing victim off El Capitan.*

Chapter Ten

DROWNING

On or slightly before 4:54 p.m. on August 12, 1983, Donna Louise Skinner, age 40, of San Marcus, California and her husband were floating in a small, cheap raft on a swift, deep section of the Merced a quarter mile downstream from the Happy Isles Bridge. This stretch was noted for its hydraulics created by numerous pour-over boulders. The NPS signs posted along the road warned of the dangers here. The navigational skills of the couple—Donna had no real whitewater training—proved unequal to this challenge. Very shortly after putting onto the river, their tiny raft collided with an emergent rock. The boat immediately flipped upside down.

Both husband and wife were dumped into the river. Equipped with a minimal "horse-collar" (or toilet seat-shaped) life jacket, Mr. Skinner managed to swim downstream past the "Big Hydraulic." Luckily, he escaped a series of dangerous strainers of downed, driftwood trees. About 250 yards downriver he climbed out on a big rock in midstream. He scanned the river for his wife. After a minute of not seeing her, he re-entered the stream. Fifty yards farther he paddled into shallow water. From there he yelled for help to a passing Valley Shuttle Bus. He told those aboard that he had lost track of his wife in the river after their raft had upset.

The bus was equipped with a radio. The Curry Company driver now punched his transmit button to get Park Dispatch: "We have a woman lost and maybe trapped in the Merced."

Ranger Peter J. Dalton hurriedly arrived and began his "hasty search." En route he had requested backup with swift water rescue equipment. As soon as he hit the shoreline downstream of where the raft had flipped he also began his size up. Where *is* this woman?

Donna Skinner was not a whitewater rafter. She apparently did not know how to assume a shallow, on-your-back-with-feet-downstream position for self-rescue swimming in current; nor did she know how to maneuver toward shore or away from dangers by employing an upstream ferry angle roughly forty-five degrees to that current. Indeed she likely did not even understand the extreme dangers posed to a swimmer by the old driftwood trees which lay waterlogged and mostly submerged in the river. This lack of training would quickly prove a big problem.

Ominously, at 5:04 p.m. (at least ten minutes after the mishap), Dalton spotted a drifting life jacket. It was a simple horse-collar type not recommended for use in moving water. Either the missing woman had not even been wearing it—or else she had lost it when the current had ripped it off her. Losing it would be easy; only one tie actually held it on. In either case, without a life jacket her prognosis plummeted. At a loss for any other clue, the ranger continued searching upstream. If the life jacket had just been up there, maybe its owner was still up there too.

> I proceeded upstream…checking any strainer that might have trapped [the missing woman]. [Two minutes later] 100 yards upstream on the river right I observed what appeared to be Donna… wrapped around a submerged log 40 ft. from the river bank.

The current had pinned Mrs. Skinner, he now saw, under a foot and a half of swift water and against a partly submerged snag, the star-shaped root ball of a tree, more than a foot thick in one of the main channels. He stared intently. All he could see under the surface were the trapped woman's arms and head. She was completely submerged. He hit his transmit button to Dispatch and told the ranger on duty exactly what he wanted the Swift Water Rescue Team to do once it caught up to him. He then added that he would soon be out of radio contact.

Of the forty feet of channel between Dalton and the trapped woman, twenty were flowing strongly and twelve feet deep. Again, immediately downstream of this point the river narrowed and washed through a series of strainers formed by downed trees and drifting logs. Such strainers are the number one killers of people caught in current. Some of the best kayakers and rafters on Earth who have died in rivers—even while wearing life jackets—died in such nightmare zones. The more one knows about how deadly these are the more one fears them.

Ranger Dalton knew this. He also knew that woman out there would die if she did not breathe air soon. He now removed his equipment belt and entered the river. He tried to swim across the channel to an eddy nearly above her trapped position. He made it:

> —halfway across the channel, using a 45-degree ferry angle until I realized that even with the appropriate gear: wetsuit, fins and life jacket, the exposure to the "strainers" approximately 5 feet downstream of the victim would be high risk.

He now pivoted and swam back to the riverbank. For the next couple of minutes he analyzed the submerged woman's position and planned exactly how to extract her in the least amount of time once the crew arrived with equipment. Less than five minutes later (at 5:09 p.m.) Rangers Gary Colliver and Dan Dellinges did arrive. Ranger Colin Campbell soon arrived on horseback. Everyone on scene knew of cold water submersion cases in which the victim had survived after forty-five minutes underwater. With only about fifteen minutes underwater by now, this woman still had hope—if they could get her out fast.

Geared up, the three men swam out to Skinner's position. Dalton could now see her better. His stomach sank. The woman down there was trapped solidly against the root ball of the submerged, foot-thick driftwood tree by the main force of the river's current—in a textbook example of a strainer-entrapment. Colliver and Dellinges stopped directly upstream of the victim. Dalton now positioned himself behind them. He stood in the very foot of an upriver eddy. He grabbed Colliver to serve as his anchor. Colliver in turn held Dellinges. Here they started their tug of war against the current pinning her. Both downstream men had to fight just to avoid being swept downriver. They knew that being carried down there could turn out to be far worse than an inconvenience. The strainers created by a maze of logs wedged in the river below could not only kill them but also sabotage the sole chance of saving this woman's life. Indeed, both men also knew the risk was high that either of them easily could be pulled right here into Donna Skinner's strainer and trapped *with* her.

But pull now as they might on the trapped victim's limp arms, she refused to budge. They could not even get her head above water. The rangers looked at each other. They *had* to pull her out. As Gary Colliver remembers it, twenty-five years later, at 5:14 p.m.:

> I remember thinking Dan [Dellinges] and I might get sucked under the same submerged log where Donna Skinner was caught. Dan and I, straining together seemed unable to dislodge her. Finally, Dan said, "One last try and we're outa here (or something to that effect). I was skeptical, but said okay. Dan let loose with a huge, growling, extended grunt, and I could feel the effort he was exerting surge—my effort, at best, was no more than I had been able to give earlier; I was getting pretty tired. Dan's enormous effort was what broke her free.

The rag doll of a woman slid upward! After being trapped for at least twenty minutes underwater, Donna Skinner emerged into air. She not only failed to gasp for air (as in the movies) she was pulseless. In fact, by most medical definitions, she was dead.

But not as far as her rescue team was concerned. The three rangers now tugged her upstream to a large eddy on the river's left side. From there they quickly ferried her back across to the right shore. By 5:16 p.m. Park Medic Ranger Charles Fullam was directing aggressive cardiopulmonary resuscitation and additional life support procedures on Mrs. Skinner. Meanwhile the expanding team evacuated her to the Valley Clinic and, with cold water immersion tactics in mind, they continued resuscitation efforts.

At the clinic, Donna Skinner's heart started beating on its own (just like in the movies). Shortly thereafter she began breathing on her own. The medical staff continued, however, to assist her breathing. At this point, despite these extremely important advances, she remained unconscious and immobile and her future remained extremely touch and go.

At 6:30 p.m. (about ninety-five minutes after the boating accident) she was breathing and aboard the Medi-Flight helicopter en route to North Modesto Memorial Hospital.

Nearly three weeks after her rescue, Donna Skinner exhibited such a serious neurological deficit that she was still only manifesting limited motion of her upper extremities. Dr. Jonathan P. Weisul noted, "it appears the time of hypoxia was more extensive than originally believed, and the protecting qualities of hypothermia do not appear to have been enough."

On August 12, 1983, Secretary of the Interior Donald Paul Hodel awarded the department's Valor Award to Peter Dalton, Dan Dellinges, and Gary Colliver. On November 22nd of that same year, NPS Director Russell Dickenson granted a Unit Award for Excellence of Service to all twenty-two members of the SAR team who rescued Donna Skinner.

Despite this award-winning effort being pulled off promptly and as close to perfectly as most rangers involved could remember any rescue being accomplished—and not with high tech gear but with almost nothing but courage and the willingness to invest an all-out physical effort—Donna Skinner never regained consciousness. She remained in a coma for almost eight months. Those many long minutes of entrapment under the Merced had suffocated too many of her intracranial neurons. Eventually, on April 6, 1984, in San Marcus, California (in the San Diego area) her life ended.

Floating the scenic Merced River between the immense granite walls of Yosemite Valley may seem like a recent innovation, say, just in the past forty years or so. In reality, except for possibly the inflatable aspect of today's rafts, it is not. More than a century ago a few adventurous souls were already boating the Merced just for fun. And, as sometimes still happens today, the mishandling of their tiny craft then also led to dire outcomes.

On Sunday, July 7, 1901, 28-year-old Sadie Schaeffer of Packwaukee, Wisconsin took a day off from her waitress job at the Sentinel Hotel to float the Merced with Sadie Young and Johnny Van Campen. Van Campen, a carpenter employed by A. H. Washburn at Wawona, had built a small canvas boat. Locals had warned the trio about the rapids below El Capitan Bridge as being dangerous, possibly even deadly.

For an hour or more all went well as they drifted along in the summer heat. In this stretch the river was swift but smooth, the scenery grand, and ease of the float idyllic. At the lower end of El Capitan Meadow, where the El Capitan Bridge used to be, right above where the whitewater began, Sadie Young prudently asked the boatman to row to shore. He obliged by heading toward the bank.

Once Van Campen had beached his little craft she disembarked. Young turned around on shore and warned her two friends that they should join her and take the boat off the river. It was too dangerous. But her plea fell on deaf ears. Schaeffer and Van Campen pushed off good-naturedly and continued on to "brave" the whitewater.

Soon the oarsman looked downstream and saw the rapids would indeed be too much. Young and the others had been right all along. Van Campen now rowed to shore and groped to grab a branch and stop the boat. He finally gripped a root projecting from the bank and clung to it. He would have to tie his bow line to something…

As he contemplated his options Schaeffer, feeling frisky, grabbed one of the oars. She dipped it, got a bite of current, and yanked. Her stroke tugged Van Campen's grip loose from the root. It also pivoted the little boat back into fast water. Schaeffer playfully announced to her friend they would shoot the rapids anyway.

At this point they had no choice. And no life jackets.

To complicate matters Sadie Schaeffer accidentally dropped the oar into the river. The current floated it out of reach. With only one oar, Van Campen's craft instantly became unmanageable. It broached. Then it capsized. Both people plunged into the chilly river.

As Van Campen swam for his life he also managed to grab Schaeffer's hand. Even so, the violent currents soon smacked both swimmers into a boulder then over it. Next they hit more rocks. As they bumped along in the grip of the current, he lost his hold on his spunky friend. The swift water quickly separated the two. Van Campen managed to fight his way to the bank then crawl onto shore, thoroughly pummeled.

Van Campen never saw Sadie Schaeffer again. Nor did the two men who happened to be watching this mayhem from downstream. Neither saw the spirited waitress surface even for an instant. All they ever found was her hat, half a mile downriver. This 1901 tragedy was Yosemite's earliest fatal boating mishap.

This "hat-only" denouement was, according to one report, despite a platoon of searchers combing the shorelines. This report said she was not found, dead or alive. In another report, though, her body was recovered then buried in the Valley in the south end of the cemetery. Either way, a grave in fact exists there marked with a granite shaft which reads:

AH, THAT BEAUTEOUS HEAD, IF IT DID GO DOWN,
IT CARRIED SUNSHINE INTO THE RAPIDS.

Thankfully, the number of deaths in Yosemite incurred during more than 100 years of boating is small: Seven men and three women have drowned—all but two of these lacked a life jacket. Oddly, this ten-person boating tally is lower than those who have drowned in Yosemite while traveling in an automobile or on a motorcycle. A dozen people (two were women) involved in seven accidents died because their vehicle ended up in the river. Sadly, two victims were young children (discussed in Chapter 8. Wheels).

On the other hand, despite the few boating deaths, the overall number of Yosemite drownings not related to motor vehicles to the end of 2024 is 166 people, a truly appalling number. It rivals the number of victims who have died in motor vehicle accidents. Why so many?

One answer might be just too darn many creeks and sections of rivers that invite swimming and dunking and playing during the heat of summer. Of those 166 known non-vehicular-related drownings (138 males and 28 females) through 2024, only 25 occurred during the eight months from September through April. Or put the other way, 85 percent happened during the four months from May through August. July alone accounts for nearly one third of the grand total. Clearly hot weather plays a role. This finding is not much of a shocker. Summer is also when Yosemite is most visited, especially by younger people.

What were these people doing just prior to dying? A reasonable guess might be swimming. It turns out, however, that only 24 percent (35 men and 5 women) of the drownings were swimmers. Other victims—all men—were fishing when they perished. They account for another 9 percent of the total. As we learned from Sadie Schaeffer's demise, 5 percent were boating. Twenty-two more people (13 percent of the total) drowned unwitnessed. We are not sure how or why they ended up in the water. All of the incidents just mentioned—mysterious or known—account for about half of all non-vehicular drownings. What had the rest of the victims been doing that got them into such trouble?

At least a dozen men and five women were hikers who died while trying to cross a stream or river. These failed crossers account for another ten percent of all drowning victims.

An epic of this sort began on May 29, 1973, when 29-year-old Peter Dike Williamson of Boulder, Colorado, had just completed a difficult technical ascent of the West Face of Leaning Tower with Richard Jack. The two bivouacked overnight along the creek less than half a mile upstream of the lip of Bridalveil Fall. Spring melt now made the stream fast and high. And swift enough to give both men pause to contemplate their options here. After thinking it over all night, Jack decided to safety Williamson with a rope.

Almost every time a line that is tied at one end to a solid object (an anchor of some sort) and is also *attached* at its other end to a person untrained in swiftwater rescue and who enters fast water, a disaster is in the making. As Williamson now entered the cold current it instantly grabbed him and swept him downstream. Both men knew this outcome was likely but both reckoned that the one on shore could pull the other safely back.

Instead, within mere seconds the slack ran out and the line snapped taut. The instant Williamson's leash tightened he began to hydroplane underwater. He struggled, mostly underwater and at the end of his rope, for more than ten minutes as Jack fought the swift water by trying to "reel" him in. Eventually the current washed Williamson into an eddy. But far too late for a happy ending. Despite CPR, Williamson was dead.

The next day, a team of rangers reached the dead climber. They considered the two basic ways to remove him. The easiest and fastest, of course, would have been to lift him by helicopter. The second, less-than-ideal option demanded that at least a dozen rescuers carry him on a stretcher on foot down very rugged and treacherous terrain. Despite the ease of using a helicopter, they quickly were forced to rule it out. This was because all the private ships in the region were now elsewhere working on forest fires. Furthermore, all military aircraft, such as those from nearby Lemoore Naval Air Station, were restricted by policy from responding for a known fatality—unless non-response resulted in a serious hazard to the rescue team.

So the rangers would have to tote Williamson on foot. Then someone mentioned a third possibility: How about getting Peter Williamson to the lip of Bridalveil Fall and then lower him down by rope over the 600-foot cliff?

Despite the allure of this third option it would quickly prove a lot easier said than done. The first part, getting the body downstream to the head of the fall, seemed the easiest. Why so easy? Because after the recovery team secured Williamson in a body bag they tied it to a fifty-meter climbing rope. Rather than try to carry him down the steep cliff and the ankle-breaking shoreline, they planned on simply floating him along on the current and nudging him over the rocks and small pour overs. The distance to the top of the fall would be several hundred yards but this float technique should save them a lot of agony.

God (or, some say, the devil) resides in the details. The rangers set their plan into motion. At first the body bag floated as anticipated. Everyone sighed with relief at the prospect of not injuring themselves during a carry. But quickly the black body bag filled with water. It now became a sea anchor. The same powerful current that killed Williamson now shoved his multiplying mass downstream. As the rangers tried to arrest this ever greater drag the current almost yanked several of them off the steep ledges and into the fast cold water. Like something out of a Hemingway story of man-against-big-strong-fish they nearly lost the bag to the creek—several times.

The line attached to the runaway body bag raced through the team's hands and rope-burned the palms of at least two men trying to stop its wild ride. The crew barely sidestepped further tragedy. Once they had regained control of the several-hundred-pound body bag, they drained it then struggled ever more carefully to haul it to the top of the stunning Bridalveil Fall.

From here came the easy part.

The creek flowed about twenty feet wide and up to two feet deep at the brink. The stream flowed over the smooth granite lip of the waterfall and sprayed down more than 600 feet to pummel a pile of boulders at the bottom. The cliff stood almost completely vertical. In *The Yosemite* John Muir wrote of Bridalveil: "Its brow, where it first leaps free from the cliff, is about 900 feet above us; and as it sways and sings in the wind, clad in gauzy, sun-sifted spray, half falling, half floating, it seemed infinitely gentle and fine; but the hymns it sings tell the solemn fateful power hidden beneath its soft clothing."

Indeed, aiding the task these rangers faced, the waterfall stood overhung in places; this made it seem even more ideal for their planned lowering.

The rescuers tied several ropes together then rigged a brake system to a nearby tree. They lashed the well-drained body bag into a rigid stretcher, attached it to the line, and started lowering it over the edge. Because this descent seemed so straight forward and relatively easy (a lot like what that float had originally seemed), no attendant went along on the rope to help guide Williamson's descent.

Roughly 200 feet down, the stretcher hung up on a small, previously unnoticed ledge. Okay, most of the crew thought, we'll just lift it back off. Frustratingly, repeatedly raising then lowering the body a few feet to free it from the obstacle accomplished nothing—except to eventually break open the bottom of the heavy nylon body bag. The spotter in the parking lot far below radioed up that both the dead man's feet now were poking out.

As the team scratched its heads over this setback, a thunderstorm gathered around them with an apparent vengeance. Thunder popped and lightning zapped almost simultaneously. Here at the top of the waterfall each ranger stood as a potential lightning rod. As the thunder clapped, discretion quickly seemed the better part of valor. Men turned and hustled upstream and away from the exposed top of the waterfall. Meanwhile, Williamson's black body bag dangled conspicuously a dozen feet away from the world-famous natural wonder that the Yosemite Indians had called "Pohono" ("fall of the puffing winds").

Only after the Sierra storms moved on, and the rangers could safely return, did they finish the job of lowering the dead man. Meanwhile, during those two days, Williamson's body swung there beside the scenic falling water. We wonder how many snapshots of Bridalveil Fall were taken during this time without the photographers knowing precisely what they captured in their photos.

Again, and as illustrated above, many Yosemite hikers have died while trying to cross a stream. And some of the worst of these episodes occurred because hikers ended up off route. Getting lost frequently leads to shortcutting or bushwhacking while wishfully thinking. Conversely, sometimes the decision to shortcut to save time or "improve" a route leads to getting lost. Either way, when such trekkers reach a stream and need to get to the other side, they often find themselves not only in a bad location to ford but also nowhere near a bridge. In times of low water, mistakes at otherwise dicey crossings can prove merely wet instead of fatal. But all too many hikers at other times have unfortunately underestimated the power of moving water then not lived to regret it.

Illustrating this, during early June of 1972, 25-year-old Sarah (Sally) Henderson from San Francisco hitchhiked to White Wolf with Matthew Joseph Bard, her partner of three years. Their plan was to hike to the Ten Lakes area. Eight miles into their trek and at about 9,000 feet elevation they lost the trail in deep snow. Being lost in cold, soggy snow was bad enough—although backtracking their footprints to relocate the trail should have been a simple, if not pleasant, tactic—but to make matters more unpleasant a high country hailstorm started pounding them.

The two hikers decided to bivouac just below the snow line. This was smart. The good news was they managed to do this without becoming hypothermic or losing gear. The bad news was that when they woke up in the morning they were still lost. Far worse, they still refused to retrace their original route.

That morning Bard, using a compass but, lacking a topographic map, consulting only a schematic Park brochure, decided to strike off cross-country to the north instead of backtrack from whence they had come. The two were off-trail and traversing a landscape mostly blanketed with snow—in some places *deep* snow. Moreover, there existed no other maintained route to be had north of the Ten Lakes Trail until after one traveled several miles cross-country and dropped nearly a vertical mile down to the Tuolumne River.

To avoid slogging through the icy snowpacks the pair detoured again and again off their compass bearing. Going north did guarantee losing elevation—and escaping these freezing snow drifts—to eventually reach lower, friendlier terrain. Yet faithfully following a cross-country bearing while making detours requires expert use of a compass. Such use would be assisted greatly by possessing, understanding, and referencing an appropriate topographic map that would show safer terrain.

While winging it, Henderson slipped in the snow. The slope was so steep that she slid about a hundred feet down. She collected herself and inventoried the damage, a sprained ankle and scraped back. Carrying her pack now, she found, was torture.

So Bard now carried it (as well as his own). The pair continued hoofing it to the cliffs above Pate Valley. Bard's double-carry was a noble gesture, one that might have worked out okay if the two had been on a trail. But again they were following a rugged and arbitrary compass bearing that did not take hazardous topography into account.

Several miles north of the Ten Lakes Trail, on one of the cliffs above Pate Valley, Matthew Bard lost his balance and fell. He saved himself but lost both their packs over the edge.

At this moment most of their daylight was spent. Despite it being June, a relatively warm month, it would not be a pleasant night here at 5,000 feet of elevation. With little choice, the lost pair was forced to bivouac again. They lit a huge fire. Without their gear, the blaze would be vital to keep them warm. It might also attract help. The fire definitely improved their spirits.

As the flames crackled, Bard gathered a heap of rocks to jettison off the cliff as noise makers over the roar of the Tuolumne River below. This noise, he hoped, might also attract rescue.

In their favor, the roar of the river below now told them they were near Pate Valley. They were not truly "lost" in the sense of "Oh my God, where *are* we?" Instead they simply lacked precise knowledge of where the next reliable path was and where lay the bridge spanning the Tuolumne. They also lacked the skill—and, again, the topographic map—to figure out either of these things.

The next morning Bard grabbed a chunk of charcoal from the smoldering fire and scrawled "HELP" on a nearby slab of granite. Then the pair began bushwhacking down the steep, often cliff-barred slope. Their goal was to work their way down to the trail that existed somewhere along the river.

The topography of the canyon foiled them. They could not find the trail. Having failed at intersecting the route after yet another day of work, they faced yet another bivouac. Without a fire this time, and without food or gear, they shivered the night away in the bushes.

By mid-morning the increasingly desperate couple could see the trail on the opposite side of the river. This seemed encouraging. They continued bushwhacking down the slope. Abruptly, Bard and Henderson dead-ended against a vertical wall. The granite barrier extended down into the river. With this outcrop blocking their progress, they could no longer move parallel to that trail on the far side that they now so urgently wanted.

Despite this disappointment, at this point they still possessed multiple options. One was to retrace at least some of their route back upslope to search for a better way across. Another was to sit tight where they could watch for hikers on the trail and then yell across the river for help.

Neither of these considerations won.

Instead Bard and Henderson hesitantly decided on a more desperate third option. They concluded their only real hope was to swim across the Tuolumne to the trail on the opposite side.

Bard dived into the river first. He "experienced great difficulty in swimming the stream [flowing high and very cold from spring melt-off]," noted the Park's incident report. "At one point he considered himself almost drowned."

As Bard crawled out on the coveted north shore he turned to see his more slender (and therefore more susceptible to hypothermia) partner being swept downstream. He watched her vanish into rapids.

Matthew Bard worked his way down along the rugged shoreline and looked for her. Ironically, he soon passed the Pate Valley Trail Bridge the two had so badly needed. It was a mere 200 yards downstream of where they had decided to swim! He continued to search the seventy-five-foot-wide river for about half a mile. Bard saw no sign of Henderson. He finally gave up and hiked up that long-sought trail to White Wolf to ask for help.

Poignantly, Bard had proposed marriage to Sally Henderson the previous Thursday. She had accepted. Indeed they were planning to be married one week hence. The couple had planned this major misadventure as a "pre-honeymoon" hike.

Several days of searching, including overflights by a low and slow Jolly Green Giant (military helicopter), an NPS Trail Crew finally discovered the lost woman's body lodged in snags fifteen feet off shore, about 200 yards downstream of the bridge. Bard had searched this stretch but somehow had not spotted her. Retrieval would prove to be tricky.

To recover her body entangled in the dangerous "strainer" of tree branches, I (Farabee) was lowered by rope out of a tree above her in my wetsuit so that I could tie a line around her in the powerful current. While doing this I should have been focusing on my onerous task. But instead I could not help but feel the sadness of this unnecessary loss.

The next incident illustrates how murky some of the drowning episodes involving scramblers can be. On July 28, 1967, 19-year-old John Charles Gunn from Richmond, California, and 23-year-old Kenneth Klein, from San Antonio, Texas—both Yosemite Park and Curry Company service station employees—set off on a mildly ambitious trip. It is believed that the two started from the Valley late, at 11:30 a.m., on a hike from Camp 4 to Upper Yosemite Fall and Eagle Peak. They had stashed a motorcycle near Tamarack Flat Campground west of El Capitan. But whether this was the beginning or end of their hike remains unknown. What is known is that they were not experienced outdoorsmen. Moreover, they carried neither bivouac gear nor climbing equipment.

More importantly, they failed to return.

Rangers soon began searching. Tracking the pair proved challenging. As no clues turned up, the SAR team questioned climbers on Lost Arrow. They reported having seen a light atop Eagle Peak late, at 9 p.m. They added that it did not appear to be a distress signal.

So the SAR team investigated Eagle Peak. The searchers found a solo hiker who had hiked it that day. Had he seen Gunn or Klein? Nope, sorry, nobody.

The searchers continued. They interviewed every hiker they could but again found no witnesses. Coinciding with this lack of sightings, the SAR team found too that neither man had signed the registries at Eagle Peak or on El Capitan to the west.

Strongly suspecting the two had left the trail and were now well off the beaten path somewhere, rangers in the Valley began using 25-power spotting scopes to scan scramble routes down off the rim which might have tempted the hikers. Other rangers searched by helicopters. None of them found any sign whatsoever of Gunn or Klein. The searchers added bloodhounds and technical climbers to their effort. Again no sign of either man came to light.

Four days later, on July 31, some backcountry hikers reported having seen two men "wandering around in brush and rocks off-trail on a bench below Eagle Tower." Finally a clue (however vague)! Disappointingly, a renewed effort in this area yielded nothing.

Finally, on September 4, five weeks after the pair had vanished, two hikers—Dennis and Ronald Runyan—found Gunn's body nearly submerged in a deep pool in Yosemite Creek upstream of Lower Yosemite Fall. He had drowned. And he somehow had sustained a broken neck. How he had ended up in that deep pool no one will ever know. His partner Klein seems to have been in no position to shed light on it. Subsequent information never surfaced on Klein. Indeed, so far as we know, he vanished utterly. No death certificate exists for him in the Mariposa County Hall of Records, nor has any relevant newspaper article surfaced.

Equally puzzling is the strange case of Jeanne Hesselschwerdt. On July 9, 1995, the 37-year-old mental health worker from Arlington, Massachusetts set off on an intended "short" solo hike into the woods north of the Glacier Point Road, not far from Badger Pass. When she failed to return, the Park launched a search.

Flying low and slow, a helicopter spent sixty-six hours in the air over the region of her potential route, often skimming at treetop level. It failed to find her. And she still failed to return. The growing search for Hesselschwerdt dragged on for a week. No one on the ground or in the air or working with tracking dogs uncovered anything resembling a solid clue.

Nearly two months later, on September 3, two fishermen discovered Hesselschwerdt's decomposed body. It had wedged in a narrow canyon portion of Bridalveil Creek just upstream of Bridalveil Fall. The river had stripped off her clothing except for her socks, one Eastern Mountain Sports boot, and two rings on her fingers. She had become jammed in midstream three air miles from where she was last seen. How and why she had gotten there, how she died, where she died, and what she might have been trying to do at the time remain unknown.

Again, at least 23 deaths to drowning (20 men and 3 women) went unwitnessed and remain as mysterious as Jeanne Hesselschwerdt's demise. This 14 percent of the total drownings cannot really tell us much about specific fatal errors. Yet it does reveal the biggest single take-home lesson for survival while traveling in an area with streams: Hiking solo increases one's odds of drowning. At least twenty-four Yosemite drowning victims were alone when they made their fatal mistake. Although most of these were hikers, a few were fishermen.

Fishing is a pursuit that might seem relatively less hazardous than scrambling cross-country. After all, one can fish from the safety of the bank. The reality is that fishermen do not just stay on the bank. Instead they enter the water for a variety of reasons: to net their catch, to free snagged tackle, to detour around obstacles, to get closer to better holes, to cross the stream, or simply because they slipped on the wet, mossy smooth rocks along shore and fell in by accident.

This happened on August 20, 1968, while 20-year-old Bruce Lupfer from Santa Ana, California, was fishing with two companions along the Merced River near Steamboat Bay about two miles upstream of the Park's Arch Rock Entrance Station. Adjusting his position, the young man slipped on the polished granite and fell in. Mishaps such as this have probably happened thousands of times to fishermen in Yosemite, but Lupfer experienced a freakish landing. As he struggled to regain his feet in the relatively deep water he became tightly wedged between two large boulders. He instantly became part of a small waterfall, held fast by the strong current funneling between the rocks.

Most often, if a person becomes entrapped by swift water moving around obstacles, such as a jammed log, the victim has a foot or a whole leg wedged. Nightmarishly, Lupfer ended up nearly chin deep and facing downstream. The Merced soon rushed over his head. Fortunately, he found, as long as he fought to stand up, his head created a small "hole" that allowed him to breathe. His predicament remained that he was stuck where he had to battle the current. He could fight only for so long before becoming exhausted—and the water, even now during August, was cold enough to strip away his body heat and cause creeping hypothermia that would further drain his strength.

Lupfer's two companions jumped in to assist. They soon discovered they could help him stay upright and breathe. This seemed promising. But even with all three men working together they could not yank him free of the boulders.

After struggling against the current unsuccessfully, one of Lupfer's buddies ran for help while the other fought in the chilly river to hold up Lupfer. Within minutes Park Rangers arrived. They found Lupfer still alive thanks only to the exertions of his now exhausted companion.

The rangers entered the river and tried "extreme efforts" to extract the man from that insidious crevice between the boulders. The pressure of the water slamming against the trapped fisherman still proved too great. Soon rescuers in wetsuits stood in the current and held his head out of the water. Plan "A" became plan "B," then "C" then "D." The SAR team used ropes and tried several mechanical-advantage techniques to haul Lupfer even a few inches upstream and free him. To everyone's growing dismay, nothing worked.

Hours passed. Despite now having air supplied to him from a SCUBA tank, Lupfer slowly succumbed to hypothermia. Finally the powerful current won, dragging Bruce Lupfer underwater, now dead from the prolonged effects of the heat-draining water.

Even now rescuers *still* could not extricate him. Somehow at least one of his feet had become perfectly entrapped.

Ultimately, removing his body required using dynamite to build a small coffer dam upstream to divert the Merced away from the dead man's position.

Again, thirteen victims—all men—were fishing when they died. This tally accounts for 9 percent of drownings in Yosemite.

On July 5, 1991, a similar entrapment happened. As with nearly every one of these episodes, this one too started out innocently. During a short family outing 13-year-old Steven J. Kilts waded into the shallow pond below The Cascades (falls) with his father Harold. The younger Kilts decided to "venture downstream" to where the creek sped up and funneled through a small field of boulders as it poured toward the next pool. Here the boy slipped. The current instantly nudged him into the cleavage between two rocks. And it jammed him there.

Luckily he was able, as Lupfer above had been, to hold his head above the surface. Kilts' father waded downstream to help support his son to breathe. Meanwhile the teenager braced himself such that the stream did not force him even deeper into the crack. Harold Kilts tried with all of his strength to pull his son from the crevice, but the boy was stuck tighter than a cork in a bottle. Seeing Harold Kilts fail at this, Steven's mother Judy drove to the Arch Rock Entrance Station for help.

While she was gone, the cold water sapped both father and son. Their fatigue accelerated as their body temperatures dropped. After about fifteen minutes of futile struggling—during which the boy sank ever deeper—both father and son hit their limit. Abruptly the current forced Steven farther into the crevice.

To his father's horror, the teenager sank quickly beneath the rushing water. Then he vanished altogether as the current forced the boy into some hidden passage between and beneath the two boulders.

Harold Kilts frantically groped underwater to locate his now missing son. He found nothing but water polished granite and dangerous current. His fears soared to new heights.

Gripped by this helpless panic he heard his younger son James yelling to him. Steven, the boy now yelled, had emerged downstream.

The creek had squirted young Kilts out the far end of the submerged tunnel into which he had vanished and sent him tumbling into the shallow pool below. Harold

Kilts hustled down to where the youngster now sat stunned and shaking his head in agonizing relief in the shallow water. Harold hauled his numbed, disbelieving son to shore just in time to meet the arriving dozen rescuers. Almost miraculously, Steven Kilts suffered only minor injuries.

Beyond all of the causes for drowning discussed thus far, yet another has become a cliché for disaster. This is a person's perceived need to record "being there" with a snapshot. All too often the "perfect" camera shot demands that the photographer compose the scene in one's viewfinder to be the most dramatic possible. As we saw in Chapter 1, people posing for, or taking, photos have shot off Yosemite's world-famous waterfalls in their quest to bag a snapshot literally "to die for." The same thing has happened to at least five other people (3.5 percent of the total drownings) along the Park's rivers and streams.

Illustrating this on May 22, 2003, 22-year-old Marcario Muniz, Jr. hiked to Vernal Fall with Daniel Voll, Rudy Santos, and Lucas Larkin, all of Riverside, California. Santos and Larkin joined Voll on a large polished boulder sticking out of the water near the footbridge. To document the moment Muniz also scrambled off the trail to work "his way out to the lower end of the boulder nearer the Merced River," noted the incident report, "so he could photograph his friends with Vernal Fall behind them. As Muniz positioned to take the photo, he slipped off the rock and into the river."

The month was late May. The river was flowing cold, high, and powerfully at thousands of cubic feet per second. Several witnesses who watched Muniz slip and fall said he was only visible for a moment in an eddy before he vanished down the cataract below.

That day a dozen searchers failed. A dog handler on the SAR team finally spotted Muniz's body the next day a mere 400 yards downriver, wrapped over a log and jammed against the current.

Flirting with powerful Yosemite snowmelt can be bad enough when one is of sound mind and body. Tragedy becomes far more surefire if one adds drugs and/or alcohol into the mix. Thankfully, only about a half-dozen Yosemite drownings (4 percent) can be attributed with certainty to the diminished mental abilities fostered by chemicals.

On June 21, 1969, 21-year-old Alice Grier Ranson, from Burlingame, California, had backpacked with her new boyfriend, Robert E. Snodgrass, over a five-day span to "Cascade Falls" on Triple Peak Fork of the Merced River. The scene was idyllic: The stream was crystal clear; the falls upstream were roaring; the granite was clean, polished and sculpted into smooth, organic curves; the grass and wildflowers were as lush as if drawn by a Disney artist.

Here, on day five the couple experienced "it" next to the stream. After bathing in the refreshingly cool water, Snodgrass suggested they make a short hike upriver to the waterfalls. They walked to where the mist from the falls created a rainbow. Enchanted, the young man started climbing the cliffs adjacent to the falls.

Ranson, wearing only an unbuttoned long-sleeve blue shirt, tried to follow her boyfriend. She made fair progress at first but eventually became stalled. To her dismay, she was unable to ascend higher but also felt too afraid to descend. She yelled up to Snodgrass that she was stuck and needed help.

As he downclimbed to assist her, she fell off the cliff, hit rock as she plummeted, and splashed into a pool. The current soon swept her into rapids.

Snodgrass searched downriver to find Ranson, but he never saw her again. He eventually returned to camp. Still panicked, he threw into the river her birth control pills, some pain pills from a dental prescription, and a small bit of unsmoked hashish. NPS rangers were able to recover the young woman's body more than a week later, on June 29. She had lodged in the current two miles downstream of her fall.

A variation on this pattern occurred July 26, 1980, when 22-year-old Lawrence S. Barash, from Los Angeles, and 23-year-old Gordon E. Van Zak, from Culver City, hiked with two other friends to the Emerald Pool on the Merced River above Vernal Fall. While their two companions—Jeffrey Sloane and Mark Frydman—continued onward, Barash and Van Zak sat down with two kids (aged 8 and 13) who were smoking marijuana. Whether or not Van Zak and Barash also smoked is unknown but they later caught up with Sloane and Frydman. They all ate lunch. Van Zak then announced his intention to slide down the river's polished bedrock above Emerald Pool on what is known as the Silver Apron.

Sloane told Van Zak that the Merced's high water made the slide far too dangerous. Barash and Frydman agreed and also tried to convince Van Zak not to do it. They reminded him that the posted NPS warning signs nearby said the same thing.

Unheeding, Van Zak walked over to the top of the Silver Apron, sat down on it, and shoved off hard into fast water. As if with a "poof," he vanished from the view of his three friends. They immediately hiked down to Emerald Pool to make sure that Van Zak had made the slide okay. To their relief they spotted him floating in calm water and looking "relaxed." Another nearby witness, however, would later describe him instead as appearing "dazed."

Van Zak's buddies soon realized too that he was not so much relaxed as he was mentally confused. As they were changing their minds, he drifted downriver across the Emerald Pool heedless of everything around him. He sank, then rose, then sank and rose again, all the while drifting like a discarded melon toward the "boils" downstream.

As Van Zak sank yet again while drifting ever closer to more dangerous water, Sloane and Barash jumped into the Merced to rescue him. Immediately all three men were in trouble. The water was cold, the current powerful, and mere seconds separated the trio from cascading over the foot of the pool into deadly whitewater. Sloane quickly realized he had to save someone alright, but that someone was himself. He turned and swam as hard as he could, angling horizontally out of the current. He fought his way back to the riverbank with scant seconds to spare.

Meanwhile, would-be rescuer Barash remained vertical in the current, stunned perhaps by the cold. Then he sank. Both he and Van Zak drowned.

This tragedy brings us to an unfortunate reality in Yosemite waters. This is the phenomenon of Good Samaritans cashing in their last chips by trying to save a swimmer in trouble. While helpful people have safely saved many lives, yet in the water they have all too often sacrificed themselves without having affected a rescue. During ten independent episodes in the Park's streams nine men and one woman have died this way (this tally does not include the three other similar events above waterfalls described in Chapter 1). These ten would-be rescuers died (accounting for another 7 percent of the drowning total) by manifesting a truly selfless impulse spurred by what is most noble in the human spirit. But these ten deaths combined racked up only one rescue. When we add in the three additional episodes involving one man and two more women as would-be rescuers above waterfalls, the total number of martyrs reaches thirteen. Again, only that same one victim was saved.

Of course possible drownings *have* been prevented by selfless rescuers. On July 7, 1970, 21-year-old Bernard R. Lamuth, from Concord, California, went swimming with his wife in the Merced River about a half mile east of El Capitan Bridge. First in and thirty feet out, she started to sink. Seeing this, he instantly felt alarmed. He dived in and caught her.

So far, so good. Lamuth now held her on the surface and tried to tread water for both of them. But the river was so cold the two soon succumbed to hypothermia. Both husband and wife now sank together to the bottom.

Fortuitously, three visitors—Andy Westerhoff, Nick Van Dyken, and Alex Baskin—happened along and saw the couple lying motionless down there. Disbelieving at first what they were actually seeing, the trio entered the river anyway and yanked Mrs. Lamuth to the surface. They got her to shore. There Baskin revived her with CPR. The other two Good Samaritans returned immediately into the deep water for Mr. Lamuth. Then they hauled him to the shore. Unfortunately CPR failed to revive him. Sadly, this martyred original would-be rescuer failed to save his drowning wife. Pure luck had saved her but had sacrificed him.

Please do not misinterpret these comments to mean you should never consider rescuing a person (or other living creature) in the water. What it does mean is that a dozen people who have attempted this in Yosemite have died for their efforts *along with the original victim*. Instead what we are saying is: Drowning people are notorious for assassinating their rescuers. If you are entering dangerous water you need to understand your risk and how to minimize and survive it. Virtually every course in lifesaving admonishes would-be rescuers to use every conceivable on-shore technique *first* before entering the water. The rule is: *Reach—Throw—Row—Go.* And if it should come down to "Go" (getting into the water) it is further advised to *never* close within touching distance of the person in trouble. Instead, even then, it is recommended to toss the victim something rope-like and tow them with it to a safer situation.

Rescuers face not only dangerous water but hazardous terrain. On September 21, 1972, 18-year-old Rhonda Jo Skifstrom, a Yosemite Park and Curry Company worker from Yorba Linda, California, went hiking with Jean Ann Cromie. The pair scrambled off the trail down to the creek at the base of Upper Yosemite Fall to go swimming. Although illegal, they had brought along a dog. Somehow the animal slipped into the water and the current quickly swept it downstream. Try as this pet might, the two women saw, it could not escape.

Both women sprang into action. They ran and rock-hopped along the broken and polished shoreline trying to guess where the animal might drift close enough to grab. A misstep here would be all too easy. Perversely, it seemed, the stream continued to sweep the dog beyond their reach.

In her bid to save the pet, Skifstrom slipped on the wet granite. Falling, she bashed her head on a boulder. Unconscious, she rolled face down into a pool.

Cromie pulled her from the water and heard her groan. Cromie propped up the injured girl then ran for help. Sadly, when she and the Park Rangers arrived, Rhonda Skifstrom had already died.

Another episode involving man's best friend unfolded on April 12, 1996, near Happy Isles. Jonathan Patrick Dainow, age 31, of Castaic, California was hiking with his wife and dog. The three started to cross over the Merced via a fallen tree. Partway across, the leashed dog fell off the log on its upstream side.

The tethered dog instantly became entrapped by the current against the natural bridge. The leash of course prevented it from passing under the log. Maybe the leash was irrelevant because the dog had become ensnared by branches underwater.

Either way, the man now tried to rescue his pet. But as Dainow struggled to haul it up against the current and back to the surface, he too fell off the log—also on its upstream side. Instantly the flow sucked him underwater and plastered him against the submerged portion of the log. The current here had proved far more powerful than it had looked.

Dainow, his wife now saw, was fighting for his life but still could not get himself to the surface. Terrified, Mrs. Dainow reached into the river and tugged on him for all she was worth.

Despite her best efforts, she could not budge him. Dainow seemed snagged somehow, maybe by his clothing or his daypack on one of the sunken limbs. Try again as she might, she could not pull her husband back up to air.

At least five minutes later a passerby arrived. By using the dog's leash as a tow rope the two worked together to finally haul Dainow free of the log and out of the river. He emerged glassy eyed and not breathing. Unfortunately, Jonathan Dainow had been underwater too long. CPR proved unsuccessful. What happened to the dog? Unfortunately, we could not find out.

A far more unusual incident unfolded on June 28, 1977, in Tenaya Creek above Mirror Lake. A wife and husband—24-year-old Byrna Rae Rackusin and 25-year-old Jeffrey L. Rackusin—from Van Nuys, California had been swimming at Hidden Falls. When the weather turned threatening the two doctoral candidates from the University of California at Berkeley decided to leave by hiking down a faint "social" trail adjacent to the creek.

Upstream of the pair a massive and unusual thunderstorm was pounding down, most intensely on nearby Half Dome. Soon marble-sized hail began pelting the Rackusins hard enough to force them to seek shelter by Tenaya Creek under nearby trees and rocks.

The hail soon diminished. Relieved, the couple started walking again. Perversely, it seemed, the storm almost instantly redoubled itself, again driving them scurrying for shelter. This time they hid under an overhanging cliff.

Within view of the Rackusins and also hiding under a ledge, visitor David Mahvi heard a "rumbling" and "whooshing" from up-canyon. Peering upstream he saw a "large amount of mud and debris coming down the canyon towards him." He yelled to the Rackusins, "Watch out!" Then he jumped and clambered higher for safety.

When Mahvi looked back over his shoulder, he saw Byrna Rackusin already caught standing in the flood. Jeffrey, he also saw, had turned around and was scrambling downslope toward her. The muddy flow quickly knocked Byrna Rackusin off her feet and started to shove her willy-nilly downstream. Almost immediately, however, she jerked to a halt as her foot became wedged between a boulder and a log.

She struggled in vain against the rushing mass of water and debris as it pounded and washed over her. Trapped as she was, she could not survive long.

Jeffrey waded in to save his wife. Three other good Samaritans—Robert Rogers, Bob Dubuison, and Clark Hine—appeared and rushed to the swollen creek to aid the Rackusins, both of whom were now engulfed by the rising flood. The trio went to work, entering the spate to do so. But even with four men working together, attempt after attempt to extricate Byrna failed. Rogers, Dubuison, and Hine continued struggling for an astounding twenty minutes in the frigid muddy flow and worked with Jeffrey Rackusin trying to free Byrna, still pinned by the log.

Nothing worked. Her leg seemed manacled to an anvil set in concrete.

Next, as if the woman's predicament were not bad enough, her situation bloomed into a full nightmare.

A second, higher flash flood wave came "gushing down Tenaya Creek from above." It slammed Byrna so hard it knocked her loose and swept her away. This new wall of water also carried off Jeffrey Rackusin and one of his helpers, Bob Dubuison.

Dubuison, despite already being hypothermic from his prolonged efforts at rescue, managed to swim, clamber, and grapple his way to shore. He barely escaped death. Both Rackusins proved less lucky. The spate swept them downstream where they drowned.

Because of the dramatic, localized nature of the storm atop Half Dome, the magnitude of the tragedy was confusing. At first, rescuers in the Valley believed only two people had been caught by the flood. But as word kept coming in—but with slightly different locations and details—rangers feared others too were in peril. They geared up in anticipation of multiple rescues. It took several hours before they sorted out the real situation.

After the flood subsided, Ranger Mike Power found Byrna's body a mere 100 yards downcanyon from her point of entrapment. She lay face down in a small pool. Jeffrey's body was not discovered until eleven days later. It had lodged a half mile farther downstream. As high as the potential had been for many victims to have been taken in this way over the years, only three people are known to have drowned due to flashfloods in Yosemite.

As we intimated earlier, not every attempt at river rescue has failed. A fortunate exception occurred on October 18, 1997, at Emerald Pool above Vernal Fall—the same spot in which Van Zak and his would-be rescuer Barash had drowned seventeen years before. On this later occasion, Arjuna D. N. Babapulle, a 29 year-old from Santa Clara, California, had just hiked to Vernal Fall with his 22-year-old wife, Juanita Babapulle, and a friend named Lejeune Pascal. As the trio walked the shoreline in search of a lunch spot, Juanita, walking last, started screaming.

Arjuna spun around and saw that Juanita had slipped and fallen. She had screamed but in reality her situation had not yet turned critical. She had managed to stop herself and was now standing in current lapping at the tops of her legs. Even so, she was afraid she could not make it back to shore against this current on her own without risking slipping and being swept deeper.

Arjuna stepped into the river to assist his nonswimmer wife. As he edged closer he too stumbled on the submerged rocks. Unable to swim himself, Arjuna somehow managed to recover his footing and, undaunted, continued to wade out to his wife. When he reached her he moved around to the midriver side of her. From there he shoved her back toward the shore. In so doing, however, in accordance with Sir Isaac Newton's maxim that every action produces an opposite but equal reaction, Arjuna had pushed himself farther out into deep water.

As this rescue attempt had unfolded, four bystanders had rushed over to assist. One of these men had a rope. He tossed it to Juanita. She caught it. The men quickly but carefully hauled her to shore.

The newcomers then tried to throw the same line to Arjuna. Unfortunately by this time, he not only had drifted out too far into Emerald Pool, not having learned to swim or even tread water, he also had sunk. This presented a new set of challenges, with time itself being the essence. The only way Arjuna Babapulle could be rescued would be by someone leaping into the Merced, swimming out into the lower end of Emerald Pool, diving under its flow, finding and recovering Arjuna, then hauling him to the surface, and next swimming while towing him back to shore—and accomplishing all of this before the current carried both victim and rescuer into the lethal whitewater downstream. Maybe if the rescuer were to try this while also carrying one end of the rope?

This was the scenario (but without the rope option) that had killed 22-year-old Lawrence Barash when he had tried to rescue his buddy Gordon Van Zak in 1980.

No one now risked that dive. Rescuers did pull him out of the river only ten minutes later. But the retrieval came too late even with CPR. Arjuna Babapulle was posthumously awarded the Carnegie Hero Award. We believe he remains the only river-rescuer in Yosemite history whose ultimate sacrifice actually helped save someone else's life.

Accidents happen. This statement may sound simpleminded. The point here is that nearly all of us draw a line of culpability separating an event such as Juanita's slip from shore (about fourteen people, or 10 percent of drowning victims, simply fell before they drowned) versus someone who ended up in the drink due to recklessness such as Gordon Van Zak did by sliding down the Silver Apron against all of his friends' warnings. We generally feel sympathy for the former but shake our heads over the latter. Ultimately such distinctions may not matter except in how we each may rise to the challenge *proactively* by warning those around us to be responsible and informed enough to not willfully place themselves in harm's way—and next perhaps drag us along with them.

Better education is vital. Clearly there existed in the minds of the vast majority of Yosemite's drowning victims a serious lack of understanding of the power of moving water and a dismal underestimation of the enervating heat-suck of cold water. Why? Does a profile exist that identifies those who so seriously misjudge the hazards of streams and lakes? Yes.

Of Yosemite's 144 non-motor-vehicle drowning victims up through the year 2006, nearly one hundred of them have been young males under 30 years old. In this same age class only twenty-one females have drowned. This ratio of young males drowned to young females is five to one. Clearly, when it comes to fatal errors in nature, young males commit most of them, including those connected with water. The average age of all Yosemite drowning victims was about 23 years old. And while about a dozen of these victims (8 percent of the total) were under ten; they drowned because they were poorly supervised. The rest were simply young people who fatally misunderstood the risks they were taking. At least eight of Yosemite's drowning victims worked for the Park's primary concessionaire. Meanwhile only two were NPS employees. Of course no guarantee exists that better education and training about the extreme dangers of fast cold water will eliminate drownings in the future, but it cannot hurt.

A prime example of underestimating—if not completely misunderstanding—the danger of fast-moving, cold water occurred on June 8, 1991, a time of very high and cold flows from spring melt-off. Twenty-nine-year-old Alessandro Mazzucato of Padova, Italy visited the Park with five friends from Stanford University. After hiking a mere 250 yards up Wawona's Chilnualna Falls Trail, the six decided to veer thirty feet off-trail to view the waterfalls along Chilnualna Creek. Mazzucato who, his companions explained, possessed a "positive zest for life," doffed his shoes and daypack, separated from his buddies, and walked farther out onto a slickrock ledge above the pool created by the first waterfall.

His friends stared at him in amazement. What was he *doing* there on the edge—and with bare feet? Amazed and alarmed, one of them now yelled to him to be careful. Seemingly unhearing, Mazzucato turned to walk back up the bank. Instantly both his bare feet slipped.

Startled, Mazzucato slammed down onto his stomach. His toes dipped into the creek. He desperately groped for a fingerhold to save himself from sliding in but failed to find anything. As he frantically clawed, he slowly slid backwards on his belly along the wet polished granite into the roiling pool.

Mazzucato's now horrified companions helplessly watched him sink into rushing water barely warmer than forty degrees. But maybe a chance still existed to save him…

He resurfaced for a blink then plummeted over the downstream edge of the pool with his feet first and his head up—exactly as if he were swimming a Class-III rapid while wearing a life jacket. Unfortunately, the Stanford student was not floating easy water. The descent immediately ahead consisted of forty-five feet of high-angle cascades studded with granite monoliths. Worse, he had no life jacket. Worse yet, chilly Chilnualna Creek now roared at close to 1,200 cubic feet per second—a respectable volume for an entire river.

Rangers recovered his body the next day.

Mazzucato's underestimating the danger of the wet and polished shoreline and of the implacable power of moving water pales compared to the fatuous error made during the next episode. On August 21, 1978, 16-year-old Chol Han from Kyoto Fu, Japan was visiting Yosemite with a Japanese school group. That day some of its members participating in the four-week tour sponsored by the International High School Extension and Pacific American Institute of San Francisco hiked up to the Vernal Fall's footbridge. Here some of the boys frolicked and showed off for one another by rock-hopping immediately upstream of the bridge.

Upping the ante, three teenagers jumped onto a boulder surrounded by rushing whitewater. Han, a sometime leader of this clique of boys, tried the same leap. He missed and plunged into the chilly water downstream of the big rock.

Han swam across the current and made it to shore. Here in slower water, he grabbed a log sticking out from the bank.

But instead of trying to climb out of the Merced at this point, Han simply stood in the current and held onto the wet snag. Witnesses watching him said his demeanor and lack of action implied to them he did not feel himself to be in any trouble. Indeed, nearly every one of them said they believed their friend was "just playing."

Abruptly Han lost his grip on the log and quickly washed under the bridge, immediately above a nightmare jumble of truck-sized boulders.

James Sumpter of San Diego had watched this boy's situation with growing concern. The 21-year-old man had seen Han slip and flop into the stream and then swim to shore. Now Sumpter also watched Han be swept downriver under the bridge. Sumpter and several other Good Samaritans speedily boulder-hopped downstream to rescue the teenager.

To his credit, Sumpter managed to get a hold on Han. In fact, he did so twice. The second time he used a "rope" of belts buckled together and hastily rigged by other helpers. Weirdly, though, even when Sumpter "had" Han gripping the makeshift lifeline only five feet from the shore, and even as the kid was thanking Sumpter, Han let go of the rescue belt.

Why Han might have done this proved to be a critical question. Was the teenager hypothermic, exhausted, or injured? Investigating rangers talked to several witnesses as they searched for the young man who had vanished downstream after relinquishing his lifeline on an apparent whim. Many witnesses suspected that Han's actions—right up to the moment of his being towed to safety—were capricious "show-off" behavior. During his swimming episode he had been getting a lot of attention from his peers and other onlookers. Was it possible the boy simply wanted yet more attention and felt he could get it safely by prolonging his "rescue?" Or was Han even thinking he could "save face" by sliding downriver farther where he then would reveal that he could extricate himself on his own with no help? Or instead had Han simply been too exhausted to hold onto that belt for five more feet?

In any event, when Han let go of the belt-rope a second time, the current sped him away. Indeed, Sumpter had ventured so far out into the river to help Han that he too was swept downstream in Han's wake. Two unidentified rock climbers who happened along the shoreline at this moment now rushed forward into the river to save Sumpter. By the time they hauled him out of the water, he had suffered cuts and bruises and head injuries. This helpful pair of climbers-now-rescuers then quickly turned their attention to yet another Japanese student, Uchi Urano. Also 16 years old, Urano too had jumped into the Merced to help rescue Han, and he too had been swept down the whitewater for his troubles. Luckily, the two mystery climbers managed to snag Urano too. In short, had it not been for the timely advent of these two climbers, Han's episode may very likely have resulted in the deaths of Sumpter and Urano—his two would-be rescuers.

Within two hours searchers found Chol Han's body 250 yards downstream.

His death led to $5 million in lawsuits by his parents. They dropped the one against the National Park Service after two years.

One quirk of nature emerges salient here. Han was one of eleven drownings in Yosemite during 1978. In contrast, during 1976 and 1977 California suffered a notable drought. During 1976 Sierra rivers carried barely a quarter their normal flows. How many people drowned in Yosemite that year? Only one. The victim was one-year-old Deanna Lee Bumgarner who died not in a river or creek but in a kitchen sink where she was being bathed in the Yosemite Park and Curry Company's Tenaya Apartments. What happened during the subsequent drought year of 1977? Four people drowned. Two of them were the Rackusins (described earlier) who were swept away by that freak flashflood in June. Of the other two, one died in a quiet pool and the other in the cataracts of the Merced. In general the pattern of drownings over the years suggests the bigger the snowpack, the higher, faster, and colder the flows, and the greater the number of accidents. In 1978 the Sierra snowpack piled well above normal. The following year, 1979, produced a lower snowpack. Two drowned in the Park that year.

The very last person to drown during the record 1978 raised more questions. On August 31st a school group of "mentally or emotionally disturbed" teenagers from Oakland's Fred Finch Youth Center made a visit to Yosemite. Counselor Jeffrey Hylton gave six of these students a safety talk and escorted them to the Vernal Fall's footbridge. Once there he told them to continue hiking to the waterfall, now in sight, on their own. Hylton then returned to camp.

After the counselor departed, some of the boys decided to drink from the river. Fifteen-year-old Jack Lee Smith of Oakland squatted down on a big rock and drank from his cupped hands. Upon standing and turning away, his foot slipped and he fell backwards into the water.

Two witnesses saw this happen. They agreed the young man had a "shocked look on his face" and that he never even tried to swim back to safety. Instead Smith simply submerged as the current swept him away.

Admittedly, more than one thing had gone wrong here, but why might Smith have acted as he did when he fell? Another counselor, Monica Ann Jackson, later explained that Smith was "slow, uncoordinated, had poor eyesight, and was an epileptic." He was so challenged even among these students that she had singled him out for an individual safety talk.

Despite customized verbal attention, Smith vanished in the maze of sewer-like tunnels beneath the jumble of water-worn boulders. Had he suffered an epileptic seizure brought on by the shock of the cold water? Rangers soon stretched ropes across the twenty-foot-wide gorge. They lowered Ranger Peter Fitzmaurice right down on to the top of the churning, water-filled holes. Dangling there, he poked and probed for the missing boy with a ten-foot long pole. After hours of finding nothing, the frustrated SAR team feared that Smith's body might never emerge. The crew next tried using SCUBA where possible. But again the rangers came up with zero.

Months passed. The location of the disabled youth's body remained a mystery. Nearly a year (352 days) went by before even a part of poor Smith turned up. When it did, the SAR people were amazed to find these remains a mere 100 yards downstream of where he had innocently taken a drink then slipped into the water.

One lesson highlighted by this tragedy is that one need not take much of a misstep to then die from it. As Table 10 clearly demonstrates, it is all too easy for most of us to underestimate, or fail to recognize, this real danger in nature.

Even a ribbon-like flow of creek can become a problem in worst case circumstances. On September 14, 1996, 74-year-old Ruth C. McIntosh and her husband Donald and their friend Jimmy Fields were visiting the upper reaches of Piute Creek in south Slide Canyon in the northeast Yosemite Wilderness about 16 miles from the trailhead. Ruth, an Alzheimer's disease victim, told Donald she needed to go off by herself for a moment. As time passed and she failed to reappear, he became worried. So he and Jimmy Fields began searching. They hunted the rest of that day but found no sign of her.

Stymied, they spent the next day hiking out then driving out via the road. At the end of that second day, the two men were able to notify the Mono County Sheriff's Office in nearby Bridgeport. Next they notified the NPS.

Ruth McIntosh had disappeared two days before the SAR team was informed to help in the search. Even so, it quickly found her. She was lying face down in a shallow pool. This section of Piute Creek flowed as a mere trickle. Trickle or not, Ruth had drowned in it. More puzzling yet, she also had managed somehow to clamber a mile and a half downstream of where Donald had last seen her. This descent could not have been easy. For her to have covered this distance required her to scramble down along a narrow gorge choked with huge polished boulders through which this thread of a creek now flowed. Bizarrely, searchers found no clue as to how Ruth McIntosh had traveled to her final resting point. No footprints, scuff marks, or other telltale signs revealed her passage. This lack of signs of course failed to obviate the fact that she was indeed there, lying face down, unmarred by traumatic wounds—except for a single head injury. Evidently she had fallen, hit her head on a rock, and then landed face down in that small pool and drowned.

Moving water—streams, rivers, and waterfalls—is always dangerous. Little rapids and even smooth flowing current cause hydraulics which are magnified by rocks, trees, and bends in the shoreline. These are always stronger than any human being, including those who consider themselves excellent swimmers.

The whiter the water, the more air in it, the less buoyancy it offers. This means a swimmer will find far less out there to hold him up.

Rocks and bigger boulders along the water's edge and out there in the stream can be truly treacherous. Green algae you can see is of course slippery. More deadly is the covering on the granite that you cannot see. This invisible coating of slime has fatally ambushed scores of otherwise intelligent people. When wet from dew, sweat, rain, a splash, damp boot soles, or bare feet, such granite becomes so unbelievably slippery that, in addition to causing drownings, it has led to uncountable incidents wherein rangers have been called to assist people who have slipped and broken an arm, a leg, or split their skull.

The lesson from all of this? Caution is always mandatory near—or in—moving water.

TABLE 10. DROWNINGS IN YOSEMITE. (Incidents discussed in text are noted.)

Name, age	Date	Location	Circumstances
John Morgan Bennett, "boy"	June, 1870	Merced River, Yosemite Valley	*Bennett was riding a mule across the river in the Valley but somehow drowned. He is reportedly the first person ever to be buried in the Yosemite Cemetery.*
John Carlon, 43(?)	August 30, 1870	Merced River, Yosemite Valley	*Carlon, an Irish immigrant to "Savage's Diggins" (a.k.a. Groveland), went camping in Yosemite with his wife Katherine and their 8 children but drowned in the river.*
John Filk, 40	July 1, 1895	Grouse Creek, below old Wawona Road	*Filk of Fresno Flats was a teamster on the Yosemite-Wawona Road. He went* ***swimming*** *to cool off but as he tried to get out the current swept him over 30 feet of cascades. Nearly 4 months later Indians found his body upstream of Ward Ranch.*
Sadie Schaeffer, 28	July 7, 1901	Merced River, El Capitan Meadow	*Schaeffer of Packwaukee, Wisconsin was a waitress at the Sentinel Hotel. She went* ***boating*** *with Sadie Young and Johnny Van Campen in his canvas boat, which flipped. Van Campen made shore, Schaeffer did not.* (in text)
Mary Garrigan, 17 John L. Yates, 20 (would-be **rescuer**)	August 2, 1905	Yosemite Creek, Yosemite Valley	*On a family trip from Los Angeles, Garrigan was "****playing****" next to the creek and fell in. Two nearby soldiers stationed in Yosemite tried to rescue her. Corporal Potts had to return to shore. Yates refused to give up and "proved himself a hero" by drowning while unsuccessfully trying to* ***rescue*** *Garrigan.*
Mrs. Pennington, adult	July 18, 1907	Merced River, Happy Isles	*Pennington of San Francisco slipped off a log into the river.*
L. Rehfuess, 24	June 13, 1911	Merced River, upstream of the Powerhouse	*Rehfuess of Richmond, California was* ***scramble-hiking*** *when he slipped off a log into the river. He was found on August 18, 75 yards downriver.*

Fred Joseph Beale, 7

May 11, 1914 — Indian Creek, Yosemite Village
Beale of Yosemite "stumbled, striking his forehead on the timbers" of the Indian Creek footbridge, then fell in.

M. Lee, 33

August 30, 1917 — Merced River, below Pohono Bridge
Off-duty NPS power plant worker Lee of Poteau, Oklahoma was ***scrambling*** *when he slipped in. He was found 14 days later.*

Emma French, 49

August 14, 1919 — Merced River, Camp #17, Yosemite Valley
French of Los Angeles ***bathed*** *in the river as Mr. French set up camp. She suffered instant cramps and sank. Despite a heroic rescue by M. J. Mertens, Jr., she drowned. (Camp #17 existed near the southwest corner of Ahwahnee Meadow.)*

Gertrude Kistler, 12
Herbert J. Pink, 26
(would-be **rescuer**)

July 7, 1920 — Merced River, above Happy Isles
Kistler of Lock Haven, Pennsylvania drowned ***trying to cross*** *the river above Happy Isles. Pink of Los Angeles slipped as he tried to* ***rescue*** *Kistler. He fractured his skull on a rock, dying "instantly" on the shore.* (Technically Pink was a fall-fatality not a drowning.)

Arley Kellam, 50

May 3, 1921 — Tuolumne River, O'Shaughnessy Dam
Utah Construction Co. employee Kellam "drowned accidentally" on the job below the dam. He was found 15 days later.

Robert G. Ray, 45

June 20, 1921 — Merced River, below Powerhouse Dam (now dismantled)
Ray of San Francisco went ***fishing*** *and slipped into the river.*

Dale Talbot, 23

August 22, 1921 — Merced River, Yosemite Village
Talbot of Santa Ana, California stepped into a deep "hole" while ***bathing****.*

Allen C. Morrison, 20

July 7, 1922 — Merced River, Yosemite Valley
Curry Co. employee Morrison of San Francisco went ***swimming.***

Leonardo Ramiero, 20

July 16, 1922 — Tuolumne River, Hetch Hetchy area
Off-duty Utah Construction Co. employee Ramiero of Italy drowned while ***swimming****.*

Mary E. Jones, 16

August 6, 1922 — Merced River, below Vernal Fall
Jones of Princeton, New Jersey visited Yosemite with her father. ***Posing for a photo*** *near "Register Rock," she slipped in. He tried to rescue her but ended up barely able to save himself.*

Bernice C. Leonard, 4

August 4, 1923 — Wawona
Leonard drowned, no details available.

Frederick W. Ott, Jr., 1½

October 3, 1923 — power ditch, Wawona
Ott, a toddler and son of a local teacher from Wawona, drowned in a power ditch while ***playing****.*

Edith Bronson, 38 — May 27, 1925 — Merced River, Camp 8, Yosemite Valley
Dr. Bronson of San Francisco ***sleepwalked*** *out of her campsite and into the Merced where she drowned.* (Camp 8 existed in the site of the current Ahwahnee Hotel.)

Frank J. O'Shea, 34 (would-be **rescuer**) — July 6, 1925 — unspecified location on Merced River
O'Shea of San Francisco drowned trying to ***rescue*** *Anne Horton, who survived without help.*

Donald C. Netz, 19 — August 13, 1925 — Merced River, Camp 14, Yosemite Valley
Netz of Alhambra, California was ***swimming*** *with 2 friends and caught "in a whirlpool."* (Camp 14 is Upper Pines Campground.)

John Morall, age? — April 4, 1927 — Lake Eleanor
Morall drowned while rowing a boat on Lake Eleanor.

Waldo E. Beard, 33 — September 18, 1928 — Merced River, Camp 6, Yosemite Valley
Beard of Oakland went ***swimming*** *"in an unusually deep hole due to dredging..."* (Camp 6 was where today's parking lot is between Sentinel Bridge and the Village Store.)

Phil W. Webber, 49 — July 7, 1930 — Tuolumne River below Glen Aulin
Dr. Webber of Oakland was ***fishing*** *when he slipped on a rock.*

Marie G. Rompelman, 29 — July 28, 1933 — Merced River, Camp 6, Yosemite Valley
Rompelman of Oakland was ***swimming*** *and drowned despite the Red Cross lifeguard.*

Florence Hendra, 35 — July 30, 1934 — Benson Lake
Hendra of San Francisco was on a backpacking trip with a Sierra Club group and fell while ***scramble-hiking****. She struck her head on a rock then drowned in Benson Lake.*

Hugh McFadden, 59 — December 24, 1935 — South Fork of Merced River, Wawona
McFadden of Wawona had imbibed alcohol heavily on Christmas Eve and was clowning around. He fell ***drunk*** *into the Merced.*

William Johnson, 47 — July 15, 1936 — Merced River, Camp 16, Yosemite Valley
Johnson of Vallejo, California, ***swam*** *in the "swimming hole." Fast water overcame him.* (Camp 16 was Housekeeping Camp.)

Thomas F. Healy, 19 — July 21, 1936 — Merced River, Camp 16, Yosemite Valley
Healy of San Francisco was ***swimming*** *at the Camp 16 "swimming hole" when fast water overcame him, too. A pulmotor was used by rescuers, but to no avail.*

Savino Lazzaro, 23 — September 6, 1936 — Bridalveil Creek, above Bridalveil Fall
Lazzaro of San Francisco was ***fishing*** *and slipped into a deep hole 1/4 mile above the waterfall. A rescue attempt by his partner failed.*

John Federoff, 15 — July 3, 1937 — Merced River, Camp 19, Yosemite Valley
Federoff of Los Angeles was ***swimming*** *in the river and lost control.* (Camp 19 was 400 yards upstream of Sentinel Bridge.)

unidentified male, 45-50 (?) | July 1(?), 1937 | South Fork of the Merced River, 4 miles below Wawona
A body was discovered on July 29, after 3-4 weeks in the water. No identification but the victim likely had been hiking or fishing.

Edward K. Davis, 35 | June 19, 1938 | Hetch Hetchy Reservoir
*Davis of Sonora, California went **fishing** and disappeared. His drowned body was discovered on July 22 in the lake.*

Fred Britten, 24 | July 31, 1938 | Merced River, Camp 16, Yosemite Valley
*Britten of Oakland tried to **swim** across the Camp 16 "swimming hole" but was overcome by cramps and sank.*

Richard M. Spurgeon, 24 | June 30, 1940 | Merced River between Camps 7 & 16
*Spurgeon of Wilmington, Ohio drowned while **swimming**.*

Henry A. Sanford, 21 | August 19, 1940 | Merced River, Camp 16, Yosemite Valley
*Sanford of Arroyo Grande, California was **swimming** and drowned in the deep Camp 16 "swimming hole."*

Samuel Carter Simpson, 18 | August 23, 1942 | near Mirror Lake, Yosemite Valley
*Simpson of Dayton, Ohio went **swimming** in a deep pool just downstream of Mirror Lake, experienced severe cramps, and sank.*

Edison Dale Bonar, 16 | July 8, 1943 | Merced River, above Nevada Fall
*Curry Co. employee Bonar of Merced was **fishing** a mile above Nevada Fall and slipped into the river. His body was recovered almost 2 months later by a professional hardhat diver.*

Whitney Williams, 18 | July 5, 1945 | Merced River, Yosemite Valley
*Williams, a patient in the Navy hospital (the Ahwahnee Hotel), drowned while **swimming**. His body was recovered a week later.*

Robert J. Fouche, 22 | July 5, 1946 | Tuolumne River, O'Shaughnessy Dam
*Fouche of Oakland was **fishing** and slipped into fast water.*

William Beckett, 12 | July 30, 1946 | Merced River, Camp 7, Yosemite Valley
*Beckett of Keyes, California was **swimming** and lost control.* (Camp 7 was where Lower River Campground was before a flood destroyed it.)

Charles L. Reuther, 31 | July 31, 1946 | Merced Lake
*Reuther of Inglewood, California was **hiking solo** at Merced Lake and either slipped into it or went swimming and drowned.*

Gary Page Knappen, 10 | August 11, 1946 | Mirror Lake, Yosemite Valley
*Knappen of Los Angeles was **playing solo** on a log in the small lake but sank to the bottom.*

Warren Deverl Montague, 10 | August 20, 1948 | Merced River, near The Cascades
*Montague of Redwood City, California was a nonswimmer. His father left him by the river to go fishing. Likely while **playing solo**, Montague slipped in. Late artificial respiration failed.*

Gladys Noble, 49	August 20, 1949	Merced River near the "Annex" *Yosemite Concession worker Noble drowned while* ***swimming****.*
Stanley Francis Guimond, Jr., 21	March 19, 1950	The Cascades, Cascade Creek *Guimond of Coalinga, California was* ***scrambling*** *to help a companion climb ledges* at the base of the falls. *He slipped on a wet rock, hit his head, and fell into the creek.*
Thomas Art Boese, 4	June 4, 1952	Merced River, Camp 7, Yosemite Valley *Boese of Fresno went* ***swimming*** *and was found 1 month later.*
Virginia Jane Willis, 15	July 27, 1952	Merced River, Arch Rock Entrance Station *With 4 companions, Willis of Stockton,* ***waded*** *barefoot in the Merced. She climbed wet rocks, slipped, and fell into swift current.*
Benjamin Day Anderson, 6	July 30, 1952	Lyell Fork of the Tuolumne River ***Hiking,*** *Anderson of San Diego* ***fell*** *off the logs of the trail* ***crossing*** *the Lyell Fork.*
Ray D. Beebe, 19 James Hemsley, 19	August 7, 1952	Merced River, Coulterville Road/Hwy140 *Beebe and Hemsley of Venice, California went* ***swimming*** *in the deep pool but drowned unwitnessed in the rapids below. Beebe's body was recovered the next day; Hemsley's 2 weeks later, in pieces.*
Harry Johnson, 62	February 4, 1953	Merced River, Yosemite Village *Off-duty Park laborer Johnson drowned* ***unwitnessed****.*
Lindsay B. Wilkinson, 39	August 4, 1953	Merced River, Coulterville Road / Hwy 140 *Wilkinson of Long Beach was* ***fishing*** *with his family when he slipped off a rock into the river.*
Mary Jo Knickerbocker, 5	June 22, 1956	Merced River, Camp 14, Yosemite Valley *Knickerbocker of Sacramento was* ***playing unattended*** *along the bank. She fell unwitnessed into the river.*
Thomas Sheridan Mathew, 17	July 23, 1957	Merced River, Vernal Fall footbridge *Non-swimmer Mathew of Los Angeles tried to "follow" a buddy who had jumped off a steep bank into a shallow section of a pool to then* ***cross*** *the river. He reluctantly* ***scrambled*** *down to enter the pool from a different angle. He sank in the deep water.*
Merigo D. Francesconi, 17	July 2, 1961	Merced River, below Pohono Bridge *Francesconi of Selma, California* ***scrambled*** *along the river but* ***dropped his shoe*** *in the water. Trying to retrieve it, he slipped in.*
Steven R. Cochran, 10	June 24, 1962	Merced River, El Portal Administrative Site *Cochran of Merced was sitting and* ***playing*** *on some midstream rocks with an adult while his father was fishing. He slipped and fell into swift water flowing under the El Portal Bridge. The adult did not attempt a rescue. The body was found 5 days later.*

Wayne W. Staton, 32

September 29, 1962 Sentinel Bridge, Yosemite Valley
*Staton of Visalia, California was **riding in a car** with a soon-to-be-cited felony DUI driver who lost control and drove off the road into the Merced River.* (also listed in Chapter 8. Wheels)

Robert A. Crenshaw, 13

July 28, 1965 Merced Lake
*Crenshaw of Fremont, California went **fishing** and disappeared. His body was found 27 days later.*

Gilbert Reid, 23

June 7, 1966 Merced River, Steamboat Bay
*Reid of Newberry Park, California was **fishing** when he slipped into the river.*

Daniel G. Yee, 14

June 19, 1966 Merced River, Yosemite Valley
*Yee of Honolulu was **wading** near the Rocky Point Picnic Area and was pulled into faster water over his head.*

John Ignatius Buckley, Jr., 28

July 25, 1966 Tenaya Lake
*Curry Co. employee Buckley of San Francisco had jumped from a log raft to retrieve an air mattress. He **swam** a few strokes then sank in 35 feet of cold water. He was recovered by SCUBA.*

James Albert Randolph, 18

August 4, 1966 Merced River, Camp 6, Yosemite Valley
*Randolph of Walnut Creek, California went **swimming**.*

Donald A. Minter, 15

July 3, 1967 Illilouette Creek, Mono Meadows Trail
*Minter of Palos Verdes, California **hiked** with his father in a large group. Four miles upstream of Illilouette Fall he tried to **cross** the creek (running very high due to a record snowpack) by going across a log and using a rope "hand rail." He fell in. His father and others tried to rescue Donald as he still clung to the rope but they failed. Fishermen found his body 33 days later.*

Esther Lee Grace, 17

July 13, 1967 Merced River, Steamboat Bay
*With a Bible group at Steamboat Bay above Arch Rock, Grace of Montclair, California went **swimming** and was swept downriver with 2 teenagers. One got out. The other clung to a midstream snag and was rescued by being lassoed by Ranger Lee Shackelton while standing on the skid of a hovering helicopter that had descended through the tree canopy. Grace meanwhile vanished in whitewater. Fishermen found her 76 days later, 3 miles downstream.*

John Charles Gunn, 19

July 28, 1967 Yosemite Creek, above Lower Yosemite Fall
*Curry Co. service station employee Gunn of Richmond, California **hiked** with Kenneth Klein. The inexperienced hikers headed to Upper Yosemite Fall and Eagle Peak but failed to return. Gunn was found 5 weeks later on September 4, **mysteriously** drowned with a broken neck (from having slipped into the stream?) in a deep pool in the gorge above Lower Yosemite Fall. Klein remains missing.* (in text)

John E. Clifton, 42

September 17, 1967 Merced River, Yosemite Valley
On August 9, Curry Co. employee Clifton of Sanger, California

__dived off a log, hit his head__ on a rock, then almost drowned. He was rescued by a visitor and evacuated to a Fresno hospital where he died.

Sergei N. Ulitin, 21 — June 29, 1968 — Merced River, Vernal Fall footbridge
Ulitin of Burlingame, California __hopped from rock to rock in the river,__ trying to access/climb the bridge "by way of a large boulder in the center of the river. He lost his grip and fell back into the river." His body was found 250 yards downstream on July 9.

Meredith K. Mencer, Jr., 26 — July 27, 1968 — Merced River, Stoneman Bridge,
Mencer of Ferriday, Louisiana __dived off__ Stoneman Bridge and hit his head on the midriver table rock about 2 feet underwater and sank. Other visitors diving off this same bridge—despite posted signs warning against diving—have resulted in several spinal cord injuries and "tons" of lacerations. Park X-ray tech Chris Becker notes that one visitor from Los Angeles suffered 3 head lacerations due to 3 separate dives here during 3 annual visits.

Bruce R. Lupfer, 20 — August 20, 1968 — Merced River, Steamboat Bay
Lupfer of Santa Ana, California was __fishing__ with 2 buddies. He slipped off a rock and became wedged between boulders funneling strong current into a short waterfall. Despite extreme efforts over many hours to extract him he succumbed to hypothermia. (in text)

Douglas J. Brownlee, 3 — August 29, 1968 — Merced River, El Capitan Beach
Brownlee of Pleasanton, California wandered away __unnoticed__ from a family picnic in the evening (to __play?__). His body was found in the water 90 minutes later.

Nelson Henry Paisley, 5 — May 31, 1969 — Merced River, ½ mile east of The Cascades
Paisley of Folsom, California was __playing__ along the Merced, slipped in, and vanished forever. (see Chapter 12. Lost)

Hugh Potter Baker, 25 — June 10(?), 1969 — South Fork of the Merced River, Wawona Backcountry
On June 7 Baker left Long Beach, California on his Honda 450 cc motorcycle to go __solo backpacking__, likely to Gravelly Ford, where he and his motorcycle vanished. So did his gear. On September 11, 93 days later, a pack train found Baker's body ½ mile east of Iron Creek 6 miles from the South Entrance. On May 10, 1971, Baker was identified by X-rays of the few teeth in his cranium. What went wrong remains a __mystery__. (Foul play cannot be ruled out.)

Alice Grier Ranson, 21 — June 21, 1969 — Cascade Falls, Triple Peak Fork of the Merced River
Ranson of Burlingame, California backpacked with her boyfriend and tried to follow him __off-trail__ as he __scramble-climbed__ the face next to Cascade Falls. She got "stuck" then fell into the river. On June 29, rangers recovered her body 2 miles downstream. (in text)

Johan M. van Zanten, 17 — July 21, 1969 — Merced River, Clark Bridge, Yosemite Valley
*Van Zanten, a Dutch immigrant from Bakersfield, and James Schmier built a **raft** of 2 logs and floated it **without life jackets** from Happy Isles to Clark Bridge. Their raft hit a log jam. Both teenagers fell off. Van Zanten became entrapped between the craft and the logs. Schmier helped free him and both swam toward shore. Schmier reached it, turned around, and saw his buddy floating face down. Rangers retrieved his body ½ mile downriver.*

Guy Rosberg, 13 — June 17, 1970 — Merced River, Cascades Picnic Area
*Rosberg of Mills, Wyoming was camped with his family and wandered away at mid-morning to **solo scramble**. Two visitors found his drowned and battered body.*

Jerome R. Oldiges, 20 — June 20, 1970 — Merced River, junction of Hwy 120/140
*Oldiges of Covington, Kentucky **sat on a rock** next to the river but slipped off and vanished forever.* (In Chapter 12. Lost)

Bernard Richard Lamuth, 22 (would-be **rescuer**) — July 7, 1970 — Merced River, ½ mile E of El Capitan Bridge
*Lamuth of Concord, California went in **to rescue** his wife, who had swum out 30 feet and sank. Hypothermic, he sank too. Passersby soon discovered husband and wife and retrieved and revived her with CPR. But CPR failed to revive him.* (in text)

James Dante Bacigalupi, 13 — July 19, 1970 — Falls Creek, near Vernon Lake
***Hiking** with a full **backpack** and with 2 adults (and with other kids from the Learning Place School of San Francisco), Bacigalupi fell 8 feet off a rock into the creek.*

Randall Allen Fong, 16 — July 25, 1970 — Merced River, above Vernal Fall
*While fishing, Fong of Sacramento stopped to **fill his canteen** in the river. He slipped and fell in. Despite being described as a "strong swimmer," he could not hold himself afloat in the 10-foot deep pool into which he was swept. A rescue attempt failed.*

unidentified white adult male — June 9, 1971 — Merced River, Steamboat Bay
A body found remains unidentified. (see Chapter 12. Lost)

Craig Jairl Gardiner, 18 — July 4, 1971 — Merced River, above Happy Isles Bridge
*On July 19, a body was found snagged in the river 50 yards from the Happy Isles Trail Center. It was Craig Gardiner of Palo Alto, who seemingly had been **solo hiking**. Why/how Gardiner drowned is **a mystery**.*

Victor Michael Saucedo, 19 — May 28, 1972 — Merced River, east of Pohono Bridge
*Saucedo, of Chatsworth, California and his brother Robert went **rafting without life jackets** a mile east of the Pohono Bridge ½ mile through several rapids. Their boat capsized. Robert grabbed a rock and was rescued by rope. Victor drowned and drifted into a quiet deep pool above the Pohono Bridge.*

Sarah (Sally) B. Henderson, 25 — June 5, 1972 — Tuolumne River, east of Pate Valley Bridge
Henderson of San Francisco and Matthew Joseph Bard hiked toward Ten Lakes for 8 miles then lost the trail in deep snow. They

		*detoured **cross-country**, bivouacked twice w/o gear then reached the Tuolumne. They **tried to swim across** its high, cold flow. Bard made it. A trail crew found Henderson's body in a "strainer" 200 yards downstream of the bridge.* (in text)
Robert J. Dicks, 17	July 27, 1972	Smedberg Lake, Tuolumne Backcountry *Dicks of Carson, California had been **camping** and mysteriously drowned in the lake. Drugs may have been involved.*
Rhonda Jo Skifstrom, 18 (would-be ***rescuer***)	September 21, 1972	below Upper Yosemite Fall *Curry Co. worker Skifstrom of Yorba Linda, California hiked **off-trail** with Jean Ann Cromie to the creek to **swim**. Their dog (illegal) slipped into the water. Both women tried to **rescue it**. Skifstrom slipped on the wet rock, **bashed her head,** then slid face-down in a pool. Cromie pulled her out then ran for help. When rangers arrived Skifstrom was dead due to a fracture.* (in text—technically not a drowning)
Larry Ross Cathey, 29	May 19, 1973	Yosemite Creek, above Upper Yosemite Fall *Cathey of Redwood City, California was backpacking with 2 friends but vanished **mysteriously during a solo hike** to the top of Upper Yosemite Fall. The large SAR effort failed. His body was found a week later in the creek, still above the fall.*
James Walt Kanaley, 23	May 28, 1973	Merced River, near Sugar Pine Bridge *Kanaley of Long Beach, California and a buddy **rafted without life jackets**. Their craft hit a tree. Kanaley fell out. His body was recovered 20 minutes later at Stoneman Bridge.*
Peter Dike Williamson, 29	May 29, 1973	Bridalveil Creek, above Bridalveil Fall *To return from a climb of Leaning Tower, Richard Jack tried to help Williamson of Boulder, Colorado **cross** Bridalveil Creek (running fast, high, and cold) by acting as **"safety" by tethering him with a climbing rope**. The current swept Williamson away then underwater. It took Jack 10-15 minutes to "reel in" Williamson. CPR failed.* (in text)
Lois Ann Saunders, 49	June 23, 1974	Merced River, Camp 6, Yosemite Valley *Saunders of Los Angeles went **inner tubing** with **no life jacket**. She lost her tube and went under. Off-duty Ranger Everett "Dutch" Ackart pulled her from the water and initiated CPR, which failed.*
Deanna Lee Bumgarner, 1	February 5, 1976	Tenaya Apartments, Yosemite Village *Bumgarner, an infant daughter of Yosemite residents and Curry Co. employees, momentarily left alone while **being bathed** in the kitchen sink, drowned in it.*
Miguel Angel Soto, 20	May 29, 1977	Merced River, near The Cascades *Soto of Los Angeles was **swimming** with friends when he was swept into the rapids. Rangers recovered his body 40 days later on July 7, nearly 1/3 mile downstream.*

Byrna Rae Rackusin, 24
Jeffrey L. Rackusin, 25
(would-be **rescuer**)

June 28, 1977 Tenaya Creek, above Mirror Lake
The Rackusins of Van Nuys, California hiked downstream when the weather turned bad. A "large amount of mud and debris coming down the canyon" knocked Byrna Rackusin into the flood. Her ***foot became wedged between a boulder and a log****. A second* ***flash flood*** *swept both Rackusins downriver.* (in text)

Harvey P. Levy, 40

September 4, 1977 Merced River, Housekeeping Camp
Levy of Oakland was ***swimming*** *in one of the few deep holes remaining during the late season of this severe drought year. He became ill and sank.*

Mark Bradley Mentzer, 17
(would-be **rescuer**)

May 2, 1978 Merced River, Vernal Fall footbridge
Mentzer of Simi Valley, California visited the Park with friends on a Yosemite Institute trip. While sitting on a slab under the bridge, Sandra Botica, age 17, dropped her diary into the river, reached for it, slipped, and fell into the water. Mentzer ran and reached for Botica but he too ***slipped*** *off a 45-degree slab and was swept through cascades. Two hikers saved Botica. Mentzer's body was found 41 days later just above Happy Isles.*

Susan Joan Schantin, 26

May 14, 1978 Wildcat Creek
Schantin of Alameda, California was hiking with husband Michael on the Old Big Oak Flat Road. As she forded narrow Wildcat Creek her ***foot got entrapped between a boulder and log****. Her husband said he tried to save her but the flood swept her away. Her body was never found.* (in Chapter 12. Lost)

Amy Maris Drucker, 2½

May 21, 1978 Big Crane Creek, near Foresta Bridge
Drucker of San Anselmo, California was ***playing unattended*** *as her parents cleaned up a picnic. They saw Amy fall into the creek but could not get to her in time. Hikers spotted her a week later.*

Timothy Ward Ingles, 20

May 27, 1978 Merced River, Southside Drive
Ingles of Hayward, California was ***riding*** *with 3 others* ***in a convertible car*** *which struck a tree in the dark then skidded into the Merced and overturned. Ingles probably was trapped beneath the car before floating downriver.* (also listed in Chapter 8. Wheels)

Eric Steven Hansen, 15

June 10, 1978 Merced River, below El Capitan Bridge
Hansen of San Jose went ***rafting without a life jacket*** *from Yosemite Village with David Davis. They passed under El Capitan Bridge, ignored signs warning of dangerous water ahead, hit a midriver snag, and swamped. Hansen was knocked out. He made no effort to save himself even as Davis yelled instructions. A fisherman found Hansen on August 15th in Steamboat Bay.*

Glenn Aldi Mitchell, 30

June 17, 1978 Merced River, Valley Campground area
Friends reported that Mitchell of San Pablo, California had disappeared (while ***swimming?****). A week later his body was found between Upper Pine and Lower River Campgrounds.*

Douglas Gene Crawford, 18 June 23, 1978 Tenaya Creek, above Mirror Lake
Crawford's body was discovered ***mysteriously*** *in the creek.*

Stefan Becker, 19 August 8, 1978 Yosemite Creek, between Upper and Lower Yosemite Falls
Becker of Kastel, Germany started to ascend Sunnyside Bench with Georges Kock and Stefan Honstein. After leaving the west bank of Yosemite Creek barefooted, Becker decided to return ***solo*** *for footwear. He slipped* ***unwitnessed*** *on wet rocks and fell into the creek. His body was spotted from a navy helicopter the next day, face down at the bottom of a 4-foot-deep pool.*

Efrain Loza, 14 August 15, 1978 Merced River, Vernal Fall footbridge
As his parents visited the nearby restroom, Loza of South San Francisco ***scrambled off-trail unwitnessed*** *and slipped into the river. His body was found 27 days later, 100 feet downstream.*

Chol Han, 16 August 21, 1978 Merced River, Vernal Fall footbridge
With a Japanese school group on a 4-week tour out of San Francisco, Han of Kyoto Fu, Japan drowned while apparently "showing off." His body was recovered 250 yards below. (in text)

Jack Lee Smith, 15 August 31, 1978 Merced River, Vernal Fall footbridge
With a school group of "mentally or emotionally disturbed" teenagers, Smith of Oakland took a drink, slipped, and fell back into the river. Allegedly "slow, uncoordinated, had poor eyesight, and was an epileptic," he vanished for 352 days and was found only 100 yards downstream of the bridge. His was the 11th and last drowning in Yosemite during the record year 1978. (in text)

Victor James Robert Cox, 15 March 31, 1979 above Chilnualna Falls, Wawona
Cox of Pacoima, California ***hiked*** *the Chilnualna Creek Trail with 2 relatives. A mile out Cox went* ***off-trail*** *to look at a cascade, lost his footing on slick boulders, and fell 15 feet into a 10-foot deep, swirling pool. He grabbed a midstream log and tried to get to shore "several times" but failed. Rescuers tied a jacket to a pole to tow him. After 12 minutes in the swirling ice melt Cox, who did pull off one of his boots, became hypothermic and sank.*

Brian Michael Susla, 16 August 29, 1979 Merced River, footbridge above Vernal Fall
Susla of Redding, California hiked with his uncle Raymond Lemoine, age 27, and stopped on the bridge for a ***photo****. Through the viewfinder Lemoine saw Brian in the river! He had* ***slipped in while stepping backward****. Lemoine yanked his belt but couldn't reach the boy swirling in the pool. Lemoine entered it but the current was so swift he had to be rescued by others using belts.*

Lorinda A. Kimball, 20 April 21, 1980 Merced River, El Portal Administrative Site
Curry Co. employee Kimball ***crashed her VW bug upside down into the Merced River.*** *As her car was towed toward shore, 30 feet from it she was sucked free and carried downstream. Her body was recovered the next day.* (also in Chapter 8. Wheels)

Richard Martin Hansler, 21	July 17, 1980 Merced River, El Portal Administrative Site *Hansler of Merced* ***tried to cross*** *the river by going hand-over-hand on a cable suspended near El Portal, rather than use the Foresta Bridge. Halfway across, he lost his grip and fell. He surfaced once. A child downriver found his body shortly afterward.*
Gordon E. Van Zak, 23 Lawrence Seth Barash, 22 (would-be **rescuer**)	July 26, 1980 Merced River, Emerald Pool *Barash of Los Angeles and Van Zak of Culver City hiked with 2 buddies. Van Zak caught up, ate lunch, and said he was intent on* ***sliding down the "Silver Apron"*** *above Emerald Pool. His buddies told him it was too dangerous. Unheeding, Van Zak shoved off into fast water. Sloane and Barash jumped in to rescue him. Immediately all 3 were in trouble. Sloane escaped.* ***Would-be rescuer*** *Barash sank, drowning with Van Zak.* (in text)
Russell Michael Freitas, 14 Philip Eugene Borders, Jr., 21 (would-be **rescuer**)	September 1, 1980 Merced River, The Cascades *Freitas, a "retarded," nonswimmer from Santa Clara, California was* ***fishing*** *and fell into the river. Freitas' sister and her husband Borders jumped in to* ***rescue*** *him. Borders reached Freitas, who grappled with, then clung to Borders in a powerful death grip that sank them both.*
Glynn Willie Whitaker, 14	July 28, 1981 Merced River, Housekeeping Camp *Whitaker of Simi Valley, California tried at 10 p.m. to* ***swim solo across*** *the Merced to the Lower Rivers Campground while wearing long pants, shirt, and tennis shoes. Partway across he turned and cried "Help!" Then he sank 10-12 feet deep. Bystanders Kevin Shephard and Pat Yoshihiro stripped and swam out but could not find Whitaker in the dark. They too yelled for help. Ranger Tim Mestaz arrived and in a small raft located Whitaker with a flashlight within 5 minutes. In full uniform he dived into the hole, retrieved him, and began CPR, which failed.*
Kevin Patrick Taylor, 17	August 25, 1981 Merced River, Devils Elbow *Taylor of Los Angeles wore long pants and* ***waded*** *in the river. Standing on a submerged log, he lost his footing and was snagged by the leg cuff of his pants. The current held him underwater. CPR by untrained bystanders and his 3 friends within 3 minutes failed.*
Vincent Andrew L'Heureux, 23	July 3, 1982 Falls Creek, 1.5 miles above Vernon Lake *While* ***backpacking****, L'Heureux of Belmont, California tried to rock-hop* ***across*** *the cascades of Falls Creek during high water. Following buddy Tim O'Brien, he made a final leap and landed on all fours near the bank. The current swept him off and into "violent rapids." O'Brien searched for 3 hours then returned for help. Rangers located L'Heureux's body* $\frac{1}{4}$ *mile away 2 days later.*
Donna Louise Skinner, 40	April 6, 1984 Merced River, $\frac{1}{4}$ mile from Happy Isles Bridge *On August 12, 1983, Skinner and her husband of San Marcus, California flipped their small raft on a boulder. Rangers Peter J. Dalton, Gary Colliver, and Dan Dellinges found her trapped underwater by a log. They executed a daring, quick, award-winning rescue. But after 20+ minutes of submersion, hypoxia had plunged*

the woman into an irreversible coma, dying 8 months later in San Marcus. (in text)

Sung Bin Kang, 20

August 11, 1984 Merced River, Devils Elbow
Kang of Oakland went ***swimming solo and unwitnessed*** *by his friend and sank for unknown reasons. He was rescued by bystanders who began CPR, but unsuccessfully.*

Hector Manuel Aranda, 20

August 24, 1984 South Fork, Tuolumne River, Carlon Falls
Aranda of Los Angeles ***dived*** *into the river head-first and hit a submerged rock. Friends found him 10-15 minutes later and performed CPR (untrained) but unsuccessfully.*

David Dennis Decot, 40

May 19, 1985 Merced River, El Portal Administrative Site
Decot of Pacifica, California was ***kayaking****, details are unclear.*

Oscar Rolando Hernandez, 24

July 5, 1986 Merced River, El Portal Administrative Site
Hernandez of Los Angeles was found dead in the river. His demise remains a ***mystery****.*

John Shannon Frank, Jr., 24

October 14, 1986 manhole, Wawona
Frank of Summit City, California was ***working*** *with a contract maintenance crew on an open ditch 100 feet from a 2-foot wide manhole for sewage lines at the junction of Chilnualna and Yosemite Avenues. Fellow workers found him 3 feet underwater at the bottom of the 15-foot deep manhole (****unwitnessed****). CPR failed.*

Salvador Villareal Ruiz, 18

May 13, 1991 Merced River, above Pohono Bridge
Rafting without life jackets, *Ruiz and his brother Juan of East Los Angeles passed signs warning of river dangers ahead. Their boat capsized in class-III whitewater. Juan Martin got out. Salvador remained with their overturned raft then lost his grip.*

Mario Ernest Thomas, 3
Lance Brian Thomas, 5
Elaine Carol Watson, 44
(would-be **rescuer**)

May 25, 1991 Merced River, ½ mile east of Pohono Bridge
Watson ***dozed off at the wheel*** *of her Toyota and crashed into the river. The Thomas brothers of Compton mistakenly jumped into the current when their older sister did so (she was pulled to shore by a rope). They were swept away. Watson, the boys' aunt, jumped in to rescue them but drowned.* (also listed in Chapter 8. Wheels)

Charles Thomas Martz, 29

June 8, 1991 South Fork of the Merced River, Wawona
Martz left Oakland for a bachelor party of 8 friends in Yosemite. As fellow partiers Jim Hobbs (who had just met Martz) and George McKale explained, Martz, who was a good swimmer, had ***smoked 2 bowls of marijuana and drank 4 beers*** *over 2 hours then had gone* ***swimming****. He dived into a pool but never surfaced. His body was found well downstream, 10 feet deep.*

Alessandro Mazzucato, 29

June 8, 1991 Chilnualna Creek, Wawona
Mazzucato of Padova, Italy visited Yosemite with 5 friends from Stanford. 250 yards up the Chilnualna Falls Trail, they veered 30 feet ***off-trail*** *to view waterfalls. Mazzucato* ***doffed his shoes*** *and* ***walked*** *onto a slickrock ledge, slipped into the pool, and washed over*

the brink in the 45-degree water flowing about 1,200 cubic feet per second over a 45-foot cascade. (in text, arguably might be categorized in Chapter 1. Waterfalls)

Michelle Ann Boettcher, 23

July 5, 1991 Merced River, ½ mile east of Arch Rock
Boettcher of Huntington Beach, California ***scrambled*** *on slick granite to* ***pose for a photo****. She slipped and fell. Rangers recovered her body 24 days later. The final photo shows her slipping in.*

Adam James Guida, 18

April 11, 1992 Merced River, Vernal Fall footbridge
Guida of Redwood City, California ***hiked*** *with 3 friends to the bridge. Guida climbed over the railing at center onto an upstream boulder. As his girlfriend Robin L. Williams followed to* ***pose for a photo****, Guida moved aside and fell off. He grabbed the rock but the river swept him into "heavy whitewater" which sent him 100 yards downstream and pinned him against a boulder.*

Matthew Scott Waters, 17

September 5, 1993 Chilnualna Creek, Wawona
Camping with friends, Waters of Arvada, Colorado went on a short ***solo hike.*** *He apparently slipped and fell 20 feet, hit his head, and fell into the creek.*

Gregory Sholders, 19

March 29, 1994 Merced River, Vernal Fall footbridge
With 5 friends from Point Loma Nazarene College on spring break, Sholders of Greeley, Colorado hiked to the bridge then ***rock-hopped the shoreline****. He slipped and fell and was swept under the bridge 100 yards and pinned submerged against a boulder.*

Jeffrey Lynn Ubelhart, 36

May 29, 1995 Merced River, El Portal Administrative Site
Ubelhart of Willits, California ***rafted*** *with 3 fellow guides from American River Recreation. They capsized above the bridge. Ubelhart, despite wearing a wetsuit, life jacket, helmet, and being considered a "strong swimmer," was found drowned the next day.*

James David Baker, 35

July 4, 1995 Merced River, below Pohono Bridge
Baker of Modesto ***crashed his motorcycle*** *and was thrown into the river.* (also listed in Chapter 8. Wheels)

Jeanne Hesselschwerdt, 37

July 9, 1995 Bridalveil Creek, above Bridalveil Fall
Hesselschwerdt of Arlington, Massachusetts started a "short" ***solo hike*** *near Badger Pass and failed to return. On September 3, 2 fishermen found her decomposed body wedged upstream of Bridalveil Fall, 3 air miles from where she had vanished.* (in text)

Jonathan Dainow, 31
(would-be **rescuer**)

April 12, 1996 Merced River, Happy Isles
With his wife and dog, Dainow of Castaic, California started to ***cross*** *the river via a fallen tree. The leashed dog fell off. Dainow tried to rescue it but fell off too on the upstream side and became* ***entrapped*** *underwater. At least 5 minutes later bystanders hauled Dainow to shore via his dog's leash.* (in text)

Sam Meier, 24

July 5, 1996 Tenaya Creek, Hidden Falls
*Curry Co. employee Meier was training David Scott Mitten in **rappelling**. Mitten acted as safety. Meier rappelled to the base of the falls into what he may have assumed was a shallow pool but trapped himself on his rope in the falls.* (see Chapter 9. Climbing)

Ruth C. McIntosh, 74

September 14, 1996 Piute Creek, south Slide Canyon
*Alzheimer's victim McIntosh of Gardnerville, Nevada separated during a **hike (solo)** from her husband Donald and friend Jimmy Fields. Both searched for her then hiked out and nearly 2 days after her disappearance, notified Mono County and the Park. Ruth was found face down in a shallow pool 1.5 miles downstream.* (in text)

Chang-Jye Lin, 27
Wen-Chin Chang, 26

December 26, 1996 Merced River, El Portal Administrative Site
*Lin from Santa Clara and Chang from Troy, New York were traveling in **a motor vehicle** and drove it into the Merced.* (also listed in Chapter 8. Wheels)

Chuen Park, 34

December 29, 1996 Merced River, El Portal Administrative Site
*Park of San Jose was riding in **a motor vehicle** which slid on diesel oil leaked from a tour bus. He crashed into the river.* (also listed in Chapter 8. Wheels)

Richard Dean Eldredge, 46

June 24, 1997 Merced River, near The Cascades
*Eldredge of Merced evidently **drank alcohol** then went **swimming** in "rough water" a mile upstream of the Arch Rock Entrance Station. 32 searchers combed the river unsuccessfully. A week later rangers discovered him wedged between rocks.*

Arjuna D. N. Babapulle, 29
(**rescuer**)

October 18, 1997 Merced River, Emerald Pool
*Nonswimmer Babapulle of Santa Clara, California hiked to Vernal Fall with his wife Juanita, age 22. Juanita slipped and fell in. Arjuna waded out and pushed her back toward shore but shoved himself into deep water. A bystander pulled her to shore then threw the same rope to Arjuna but he had drifted out and sank. Rescuers got him 10 minutes later. Too late. He was posthumously awarded the Carnegie Hero Medal for **rescuing** his wife.* (in text)

Richard Azar "Ory"
Benabou, 23

August 9, 1998 base of Upper Yosemite Fall
*Benabou of Oakland hiked with friends who split into small groups going **off-trail** to cool off in the creek. **Solo**, Benabou tried to **scramble** away from the stream on a water-polished granite slope. He slipped over the edge of a cliff into 25-foot-high cascades that trapped him underwater for 3 hours.*

Frank Peter Gambalie III, 29

June 9, 1999 Merced River, El Capitan Meadow
*Gambalie of Zephyr Cove, Nevada made an illegal **BASE jump** off El Capitan onto the west end of the meadow. To escape, Gambalie—who had made a pact with himself to never be arrested—ran for hundreds of yards then dived into the Merced to swim **across**. He drowned within seconds. On July 7, his body was recovered 300 yards downstream.* (see Chapter 3. BASE Jumping)

Sergio (Shaje) Marcovich, 12 — August 3, 1999 — Merced River, junction of Hwy 120/140
About 0.3 miles east of the junction, Marcovich of Mexico City ***swam*** *with 6 other children in flat water below Table Rock. All drifted into 40 yards of cascades. Three swam these successfully; 2 lodged on rocks and had to be rescued by adults using tree branches; Marcovich was entrapped underwater by boulders. It took 50 people using plywood to divert the river to recover his body.*

James Verli Toumine, 25 — August 13, 1999 — Polly Dome Lakes
Toumine of Livermore, California camped at Polly Dome Lakes with his father and Robie Chelman, age 13. As his father ***videotaped****, Toumine and Chelman entered a lake to* ***swim****. 30 feet off shore Toumine sank. Minutes later Leo Alan Chelman and another camper hauled him out pulseless and initiated CPR.*

Tomoko Wantabe, 34 — June 19, 2000 — Merced River, Emerald Pool
Despite warning signs*, Wantabe of Toyota, Japan* ***hiked off-trail*** *but slipped on the wet sloping granite into the Silver Apron flowing into Emerald Pool. She recirculated, surfaced briefly then sank to the bottom. Extracted 90 minutes later by rescue personnel, she did not respond to CPR.*

Mark Gressman, 21 — May 28, 2002 — Merced River, El Portal Administrative Site
Gressman of Moorpark, California ***lost control of his pickup truck*** *and drove it in the river.* (also listed in Chapter 8. Wheels)

Marcario Muniz, Jr., 22 — May 22, 2003 — Merced River, below Vernal Fall footbridge
Muniz hiked to Vernal Fall with Daniel Voll, Rudy Santos, and Lucas Larkin, all of Riverside, California. Santos and Larkin joined Voll on a boulder in the high-flowing Merced. Muniz ***scrambled*** *to work "his way out to the lower end of the boulder nearer the river to* ***photograph*** *them with Vernal Fall behind." He slipped off and vanished down the cataract. The next day a SAR dog handler spotted his body wrapped over a log 400 yards downriver.* (in text)

Melvin L. Paballa, 20 — August 4, 2003 — Merced River, Emerald Pool
Paballa of Milpitas, California hiked with 21 other people up the Mist Trail. Ignoring posted warning signs, he tried to join the others ahead of him by ***swimming across*** *Emerald Pool. Paballa struggled at mid-crossing then sank. His friends rescued him after 2 minutes underwater. Five minutes later yet, with bystander help, they initiated CPR.*

Andrew Scott McVey, 26 — May 5, 2004 — Tenaya Creek, below Mirror Lake
A third of a mile east of the bike trail intersection with the Mirror Lake Road, McVey of Maryland Heights, Missouri ***rock-hopped in*** *the high flow of Tenaya Creek with David A. Marler* ***while being videotaped*** *by Virginia S. Burrill. He slipped. 125 feet downstream the current pinned him underwater against a boulder. Neither Marler nor bystanders nor SAR rangers could extract McVey. A mechanical pulley system worked the next day.*

Steve Klausen, 41 — December 2, 2004 — Merced River, upstream of Arch Rock
Klausen of Torrance, California argued with then strangled and struck his girlfriend Carolyn Zepeda in her Mazda pickup on the

road. He then walked N carrying his Shih Tzu dog "Ricky." About 10 minutes later Zepeda searched for him—despite his attempted homicide and prior history of domestic violence. She waited 4 days to report his disappearance. Rangers issued 2 assault warrants for him. Nine months later, on August 27, 2005, Klausen's decomposed remains appeared in midriver 1 mile E of Arch Rock. ***Why there is a mystery****. About 2 weeks after the drowning, Ricky showed up half-starved on the road by Grouse Creek.*

Rachael Neil, 22 — August 19, 2005 — Merced River ¼ mile above Nevada Fall

During a pool-swimming junket, Neil of Mesa, Arizona tried to scramble ahead of Josh Twelmeyer by going ***barefoot across the Merced above a short waterfall*** *in the narrow canyon. She slipped and fell. No one saw her surface. Searchers found her the next day but were unable to recover her body until low water on September 10. The current had pinned her deep and between boulders. Her recovery required building a diversion dam.*

Kiran Srinivasa Yellajyosula, 27 — May 19, 2007 — Merced River, Vernal Fall footbridge

Yellajyosula of Santa Clara, California and India hiked with friends to the bridge, walked solo ten yards to the river's edge, and slipped into the raging current. Immediate searches failed. On May 29, Yellajyosula's body led to a 3.5-hour recovery effort.

Katrin Lehmann, 29 — May 18, 2009 — Merced River near Mist Trail W of Vernal F

Lehmann of San Diego, California was walking with when she slipped off trail and slid downslope into the river, running at peak. The 6-foot, 150-lb Lehmann vanished downstream. Her body was found on July 14 wedged 150 yards downstream.

Keith Michael Robinson, 62 — August 18, 2009 — Merced River near Windy Point pullout

Robinson of Mariposa, California went fishing and failed to return home. His wife alerted SAR which located the 5' 10", 240-lb Robinson 100 yards downstream from his Toyota, in a boulder field in the river. This ***unwitnessed*** *event seemed a fall followed by positional asphyxiation in the river.*

Kent S. Butler, 60 — May 13, 2011 — Merced River 100 yards upstream of Vernal Fall Footbridge

Butler of Austin, Texas was hiking down the Mist Trail when he stepped aside (too far) toward the edge to let Thomas Schultz pass on his way up. He ***lost his footing*** *and* ***fell****. Schultz grabbed for Butler but missed by inches. Butler slid headfirst down a steep slab and toppled face first into the big whitewater of the Merced. He sped downstream 100 yards in seconds then "catapulted" onto a large boulder where he became entrapped or pinned with his head submerged and showing no sign of life. His drowning likely was mitigated by severe heart disease and cardiac arrest.*

Richard Allen Fox, 53
Gregory Wayne Meyer, 53 — June 29, 2011 — bridge over Wapama Falls feeding Hetch Hetchy Reservoir

Ending a 3-night ***backpacking*** *trip, Fox of Hacienda Heights and Greg and Paula Meyer of Whittier, California, plus Dave Samuelson and Harold Sintov (all 5 were E.R. personnel), stood*

poised to cross the bridge to their car. 2.5 inches of rainfall had just swelled the creek to flood a 10-foot span of the bridge and now CCC Trail Supervisor Mark Allee had arrived to close it due to its dangerous flooding. Allee gesticulated 30 feet from the hikers not to use the bridge. Fox and Meyer ***tried to cross*** *anyway. Paula followed. Samuelson assessed it as impassible and stayed put. Fox quickly was knocked to his knees. Meyer reached down to help Fox. Meyer also lost his footing. The current pinned both men against the railing then slowly shoved and oozed them under the guard rail and into Falls Creek flowing at >1,000 cfs. Both suffered blunt-force trauma. Meanwhile Allee had heroically climbed the upper railing across to assist the Meyers, ultimately rescuing Paula, also pinned. She soon confirmed that Greg Meyer had understood Allee's "clear" warnings not to cross but said Meyer had called Allee "some schmo" and thought he could cross regardless. 2 weeks later a bear found his body.*

Francisco Javier Garcia, 41 — July 16, 2011 — South Fork of the Merced River near Wawona Campground

While camping with his family, Garcia of South Gate, California went for a ***swim*** *in the river and for reasons unwitnessed, drowned.*

Russell Robert Wright, 57 — August 1, 2012 — The "Cosmic Hole" on the Merced River 1 mile W of Arch Rock Entrance Station

Camping with his 20-year-old daughter Monica, R. R. Wright of San Mateo, California had a years-long goal "to swim in as many rivers in America" as they could. After smoking ***marijuana****, the Wrights* ***swam*** *the Cosmic Hole downstream with* ***no life jackets****. While stopping above a small rapid pinching the Merced between "school bus-sized boulders" preparatory to walking around it, he entrapped his left foot. The current pinned him fully underwater in the rapid. Monica tried to pull him out but quit after she felt him die. Crew 7 rescuers used mechanical advantage to free him.*

Jacob Michael Adams, 6
Andres Andy Adams, 10 — August 15, 2012 — Merced River, Vernal Fall Footbridge

During mid-afternoon, 15 members of the Adams family of Yorba Linda, California paused from a ***day hike*** *to* ***cool off*** *20 feet upstream of the footbridge. Four* ***entered the Merced*** *and were swept downstream into boulders the sizes of cars and houses laced with snags. Two managed to self-extricate. Andy was found within minutes, lifeless, 150 yards below the bridge. 30 minutes of CPR failed. Jacob was found a week later 50 yards downriver from the bridge. The brothers were the 11th & 12th victims to drown here.*

Walter Gonzalez, Jr., 17 — March 23, 2014 — Merced River, Devil's Elbow

After his mother lost control while ***swimming*** *then his father tried to rescue her but needed* ***rescue****, too, Gonzalez of Simi Valley, California tried to rescue both parents. Both survived. Bystanders pulled Walter, Jr. from the river but could not revive him.*

Ernest Hager, 60 — June 6, 2016 — Sentinel Beach, Merced River

In a large group, Hagen of Oakhurst, California was ***rafting with no life jacket*** *(required) on a small inflatable raft that deflated. Hagen said he did not need help, then vanished and drowned.*

Yongrui Li, 55	June 11, 2016	Merced River, below Happy Isles Footbridge *His wife and daughter nearby but not witnessing, Li of Lusqang, China* ***scrambled*** *along shoreline boulders trying to take* ***photos*** *but fell into the Merced, hitting his head. He tried to swim, but the current soon trapped him face down between large boulders and logs 400 yards downstream. Rangers Hoeflich and Bonner extricated Li and performed CPR for about 50 minutes while transporting him to an air ambulance.*
Keith Canavan, 21	July 5, 2016	South Fork of Merced River, Wawona *Seventh Day Adventists Camp Wawona employee Canavan of Watsonville, California went swimming in Medicine Pool with several others. He vanished* ***unwitnessed****. The next day he was found* ***mysteriously*** *drowned.*
Kevin P.U. Nelson, 50	June 5, 2017	Merced River off Vernal Fall Trail *Hiker Nelson of Yosemite, California veered off the Mist Trail near the Vernal Fall Footbridge* ***unwitnessed*** *and drowned.*
Douglas Schlittner, 68	June 22, 2017	Wapama Fall footbridge, Hetch Hetchy area *Schlittner of Huntington Beach, California was crossing the bridge during a Wapama Fall* ***flashflood****, was swept off it, and carried to the confluence with the reservoir.*
Ghaocui "Tree" Wang, 27	July 29(?), 2017	Rancheria Creek, Kerrick Canyon *Last seen on July 17, 2017, Wang of Shanghai, China had quit her job to fulfill her dream of* ***backpacking*** *the 2,600-mile Pacific Crest Trail (PCT)* ***solo****. Possibly while trying to cross Rancheria Creek,* ***flowing above seasonal high****, she was swept off her feet and drowned. She was found on July 29 half a mile downstream of the standard trail crossing. (In a similar crossing tragedy, on July 23 other PCT hikers in Kings Canyon National Park found the swept body of* ***solo backpacker*** *Rika "Strawberry" Morita of Japan submerged in the South Fork of the Kings River.)*
Christopher M. Mangan, 53	June 5, 2019	Wapama Fall footbridge, Hetch Hetchy area *While* ***crossing the footbridge*** *(one of three) at 1,400-foot Wapama Fall, Los Gatos, California resident Mangan's hiking partner turned away to take a photo. Mangan then vanished* ***unwitnessed*** *among large boulders and explosive,* ***powerful waters****. Despite searches, his body was not found until June 25.*
Matteo Piero Porcedda, 29	October 6, 2021	Merced River, Little Yosemite Valley area *Former star high school athlete Porcedda of San Mateo, California was hiking in Ahwahnee Meadows and miscalculated somehow by entering the Merced.*
Hayden T. Klemenok, 24	July 2, 2023	Chilnualna Creek near Upper Chilnualna Fall *Backpacking with a group, Klemenok of Petaluma, California knelt on hands and knees to wet his face but slipped into the unusually swollen creek. A search located his body a week later on July 9.*

Chapter Eleven

FAUNA & FLORA

DEER

As Nurse Sandy Coberly and I (Farabee) drove the Park's primary ambulance back into Yosemite Valley, unbeknownst to us a unique drama began just a few miles away. It was November 6, 1977, and we had just reentered the Park after transferring an injured young climber to a Fresno ambulance. He had fallen and suffered a basilar skull fracture—an injury serious enough to warrant prompt transport. But as it would soon turn out, "prompt transport" was about to take on a whole new meaning for Sandy and me.

As we approached Wawona we overheard faint bits and pieces of a radio transmission. A voice asked, "Do you want the EMT kit?"

Because the person asking this question (we would later learn it was Ranger Fred Elchlepp) was transmitting on "local" and not routing through a radio repeater, we could not hear both sides of the conversation. So we did not know what was happening. Even so, emergencies were so common in Yosemite that Fred's question seemed pretty routine. Or so we thought.

I hit the transmit button on our radio and broadcasted in the blind that I was riding in the Park's main ambulance with a nurse from LMH (we always referred to Lewis Memorial Hospital in Yosemite Valley as "LMH") aboard and we were only a mile or so away. I closed with "Can we help?"

Wawona District Ranger J. T. Reynolds responded, "Ten-four, come to the RO (Ranger Office)."

We arrived a few minutes later. Sandy and I found J. T., Fred, and several others administering to a tiny figure on the floor. Nearby, the small boy's parents hovered anxiously. The victim at our feet was Colin Neu. And right now all that we newcomers could see was he was bleeding from his right armpit. Someone had placed a large compress into it, partially stemming what had been a copious flow of blood.

The little 5 year-old was experiencing so much pain that he was trying to thrash around despite the medical team's effort to hold him still. Colin was only semi-coherent, but he still seemed to respond appropriately to instructions by his parents and the rangers.

Sandy quickly assessed the boy's condition. Then she phoned LMH and consulted with Head Nurse Kathy Loux. Loux relayed the specifics on Colin to the doctor on duty. A critical question surfaced: In which direction should we take the injured boy? LMH was forty-five minutes away. True, the twenty-bed hospital was an excellent facility run by a highly skilled staff. On the other hand, its capabilities were limited; it was not really set up for surgical operations beyond emergency stabilization and first response. Our other option was the ninety-minute drive to Fresno's Children's Hospital. It possessed Level One Trauma capabilities and a full complement of surgical staff and related specialties.

As we waited for the decision from the other end of the line I glanced again at the bloody clothes and then at the small boy who had lost all that blood. He did not seem big enough to have much more of that stuff still in him. Unless Colin Neu received advanced medical care quickly, I realized, the question of which place to take him might soon become moot.

After a few tense moments Kathy instructed us to head toward Fresno, she would have an ambulance meet us on the way.

I drove onto Highway 41. Nurse Coberly positioned herself in the back to monitor Colin. His father Larry rode with them, ready to help if needed. Speed was critical here, but I knew patches of ice glazed the pavement in the shade of the many curves in front of us. To do any good here I had to keep the machine on the road.

Having many times ridden in the rear of a speeding ambulance myself, I also knew it was all too easy for those in the back to get car sick. So, in addition to making good time and while keeping the ambulance from sliding off the road I wanted to avoid nauseating Sandy—and Colin. If the little boy vomited while strapped down on his back, he could aspirate and choke.

Luckily, traffic proved light. I was running with emergency lights only. Each time I saw another vehicle I turned on the siren to move them over. I had to use our siren sparingly because the wailing made it impossible for Sandy to monitor the boy's faint heartbeat and feeble breathing sounds.

For probably twenty minutes all of us seemed to be doing okay. Sandy periodically yelled from the rear to tell me Colin appeared to be holding his own—although his bleeding had not totally stopped and his breathing was slowly becoming more labored. We exited the Park and passed through the little hamlet of Fish Camp. We were making such good progress that I now began looking for the approaching ambulance from Oakhurst.

Unfortunately, our sense of everything being under control was about to evaporate.

As we sped downhill on a section that was even more curvy and narrow than usual, I heard Sandy yell: "Butch, you better pull over; I can't get a pulse!"

Maybe I should bring you up to speed on why 5-year-old Colin Robert Neu was bleeding. He and his family from Clovis, California had been picnicking in the old Wawona schoolyard. Ironically, while entering the Park earlier that day, Colin's parents had seen a visitor feeding a deer. His father had commented that it was not a smart thing to do.

This was an important point. They also saw the posted NPS sign warning: "ALL PARK ANIMALS ARE WILD—FOR YOUR SAFETY DO NOT FEED OR TOUCH THEM." They knew the sign was there for good reason. Through the years people had been feeding some of the not-so-wild deer here.

Ever since this terrible accident, I had believed Colin was doing exactly what his parents had warned him not to do—feed the deer. Today, Yosemite rangers tell Colin's tragic story in an effort to keep unthinking visitors from giving animals food and, most importantly, to prevent similar incidents.

Yet in August of 2008 and "out of the blue," Colin's younger sister Kerrian contacted us. She had been three and a half years old at the time. She now told us that the story being repeated in the Park was wrong and she wanted to correct the record. "There are two days that I can remember everything," she told us, "the day my brother died and the day my mom died."

"We had tuna fish sandwiches with chips that came in two smaller bags. My brother was a quick eater, so my parents let him take a bag of chips and play in the dirt not too far away. He was trying to keep the deer away from the food. It happened so fast, and all of a sudden my big brother was hurt." The animal spooked. It yanked its head upward and caught Colin in the side of his chest, almost in his right arm pit, stabbing him with a five inch antler.

Larry Neu heard his son yell in pain and leaped toward the cries. He scooped up Colin and drove to the nearby Ranger Station where he placed him on the floor in front of Ranger J. T. Reynolds. What none of us knew at the time was why Colin's condition was deteriorating so steadily. A vital artery near his heart, we would later learn, had been nicked by the antler tip. Colin was slowly bleeding out while fluid collected in the space between his lung and chest wall. Even not knowing this, LMH had made the right call. This sort of injury was beyond the local staff's capability to repair. Colin definitely needed advanced pediatric surgery.

As luck would have it, just as Sandy yelled she could not find Colin's pulse I saw a wide spot on the road. I pulled over and ran to the back of the ambulance. I threw open its double doors. She yelled, "We have to start CPR now!"

Sandy and Mr. Neu lifted Colin so I could slide a wooden backboard under him. Sandy next ventilated Colin mouth-to-mouth and I began pressing on his tiny chest in the fifteen compressions-to-two breaths ratio. She and I had co-taught several CPR classes over the previous year, so we were already a good team. Even so, I felt extraordinarily conscious of the boy's fragile frame as I pressed on his thin ribs.

Seconds after we started CPR, the Neu's family sedan skidded into the turnout right behind us. Colin's mother sat in the front passenger seat. An adult male unknown to me sat behind the wheel.

He now rushed up to our open rear doors and asked, "Can I help?" Again, I didn't know this man, but after only a split-second assessment of the situation I said as calmly as I could, "Get in the front and drive—but don't kill us!"

Colin's tenuous future began to dominate me. My son Lincoln was not yet three at this time. These little guys are so delicate. Colin's life now lying under my hands triggered my parental instincts in a major way. To say that I did not want to lose Colin would be a vast understatement.

The scene in our now swerving ambulance started seeming to me almost movie-like. Sandy and I are giving cardiopulmonary resuscitation to a frail, dying little boy. Colin's father is crouching next to the nurse and watching us work on his fading son. Up front behind the wheel of our large, expensive, government ambulance some guy I don't even know is now in control of our destinies. He is racing us all down one of the most curvy and dangerous roads in all of California with red lights flashing and sirens blaring. The boy's shaken mother is driving the family car right behind us, speeding beyond the legal limits, while being all too aware that her 5 year-old is in dire jeopardy. Our race must have appeared ludicrous but our circumstances were truly life or death.

After what seemed like an eternity but was probably only ten minutes, the ambulance out of nearby Oakhurst appeared. We pulled over and swiftly transferred Colin and his dad. This new rig held only a driver and one other volunteer. Because these two Oakhurst EMTs were shorthanded and also because I suspected Colin would die (if he was not already dead), I elected to stay with the boy and help. Meanwhile Sandy drove the Park's ambulance back into the Valley.

Off down the road we screamed yet again—with Colin's father still keeping vigil on our actions. Mrs. Neu and our unknown former ambulance driver (I never did learn his name), now back at the wheel of the family car, followed. They kept up with us, even though we were barreling down the highway Code-3 (with lights flashing and driving at the fastest safe speed).

The lady EMT ventilated and I compressed for an hour, all the way into Fresno. As we neared the hospital I began talking with Larry Neu. As gently as I could, I started preparing the father for what I sensed was inevitable: His son might not make it. He slowly nodded, understanding.

The Emergency Room staff met us at the door. We now placed Colin's fate in their hands.

An hour later, after the little boy had been operated on, I spoke with Colin's thoracic surgeon. He told me even had they been "on scene" when the lad had been gored, survival would not have been guaranteed. We now had surgical confirmation that the deer had nicked the boy's pulmonary artery—and as I had pushed on his tiny chest during CPR, I may have exacerbated his "bleeding out." But because Colin had been quietly "coding" with cardiac arrest, Sandy and I had faced no choice other than to begin CPR. It had been the boy's only hope in our race to save his life. And we had lost that race.

Despite continually reminding myself that these realities had been unavoidable, I cried some nights for weeks over Colin's needless death. Ranger J. T. Reynolds and I anonymously sent flowers "on behalf of the Park's ranger staff" to Colin's Memorial Service. Maybe because of my deep love for my own two sons, 5-year-old Colin Neu is the one death in Yosemite that still bothers me most, even to this day.

Perhaps because of Walt Disney's 1942 movie *Bambi*, few of us believe deer pose a serious menace. Even so, in Yosemite they have inflicted injuries on numerous people, mostly children, over the years. Conversely, no one will be particularly surprised to learn just how badly deer in the region have suffered at the hand of man. As mentioned in the chapter on Hetch Hetchy, when the Park's boundary was reduced in the early 1900s much of the area's prime wintering range lost its protection from hunters. These market hunters decimated the local herd. By 1920 deer were rare in the Valley. But just because they were scarce did not mean semi-tame ones did not still pose a risk for poorly supervised children.

As early as 1927, the *Superintendent's Monthly Report* for July noted:

> There have been no less than five or six cases brought to our attention where children and even grown people have been suddenly attacked by does and, in a few cases, they have suffered quite severe lacerations. A small boy was attacked...and knocked down and jumped upon by a doe. Had not an older person been close to frighten the deer away, no doubt the child would have been killed.

Why were these attacks by otherwise "harmless" deer taking place? Just like today, many Park visitors in the 1920s proved unable to stop themselves from feeding deer by hand. This repeated handing out of the goodies had converted many of these shy animals into bold, dominating beggars.

Meanwhile, ironically, government hunters were being paid to wipe out tens of thousands of deer. In the mid-1920s hoof and mouth disease hit parts of California with an apparent vengeance. At least sixteen counties, many of which encompassed the foothills and high country of the Sierra Nevada, were affected. Deer carried the disease and spread it as they migrated or otherwise moved about. The *Superintendent's Monthly Reports* for 1924 and 1925 devoted large sections to the disease and its control, specifically as it related to the Park. So serious was the concern that Mariposa and Merced Counties proposed enacting ordinances prohibiting travel into the counties from outside—which quickly were deemed illegal. As noted by the June 1924 *Superintendent's Monthly Report*:

> A fumigation and disinfection station was operated just east of the

> Tioga Pass and at the Nevada State line near Bridgeport and Lake Tahoe. At these stations motorists with camping outfits were obliged to undress completely and be fumigated for a full hour. Their clothes and camping outfits were likewise fumigated, and certain foodstuffs were not allowed to pass. Automobiles were thoroughly sprayed inside and out with disinfectant. Tourists who were obviously not campers, traveling with hard baggage only, were required to have their cars and shoes fumigated and disinfected. As a result of this there was very little eastbound travel beyond Tuolumne Meadows.

On December 1, 1925, the state and federal governments discontinued control and eradication efforts. Up to 220 men working at one time during these two years destroyed 22,000 deer throughout the area. No surprise, this created a lasting effect on the deer population here for years into the future.

We will never really know to what degree the competition between wildlife and the welfare of livestock resulted in the deer disappearing locally. What we do know is that these hunters succeeded so well they nearly destroyed the deer population—and that of its predators—within the region. Even the Park's bighorn sheep had vanished completely from the high country due to these human pressures and to falling prey to diseases imported by grazing domestic sheep.

In an attempt to partially remedy this ecological mess in 1930, Ranger Bill Reymann became a "Pied Piper." Reymann, reported one local newspaper, had been hand feeding Yosemite Valley's wild deer so often that when he "rustles the oats and calls 'Hey, Nanny!' the trusting creatures follow him eagerly—into the corral!" This report may sound silly or self-indulgent at first, but Reymann was on a mission.

One hundred of his "pets," that he tricked into an enclosure fenced with barbed wire, were transplanted fifty miles to Miguel Meadows, north of Hetch Hetchy to repopulate the slaughtered herd that once ranged there. The ranger's plan worked. The deer slowly repopulated much of their former habitat. Fortunately too, they also regained their fear of humans.

By 1931, mule deer in the Valley had rebounded in numbers to the point of raiding trash cans. Begging deer would also often stand for hours right outside kitchen doors waiting to be fed. Many of Yosemite's human residents complained that deer had become pests "just like the bears."

In the Valley, the conflict between fearless deer and naïve visitors offering them goodies episodically erupted into unfortunate incidents. One occurred on August 21, 1941, when a little girl followed a doe, stalking her with a camera too far into the animal's defensive radius. The girl, the doe apparently decided, was too close to her hidden fawn. She attacked her and knocked her facedown on the ground. Using its front hooves, the doe shredded the girl's clothing into ragged strips and lacerated her. Other kids, such as Bobby Lynch six years later, suffered similarly. On July 26, 1947, a deer trampled over the 6-year-old boy at Camp Curry, cutting and bruising him.

As simpleminded as it might seem, the solution that would prevent these sorts of incidents lies in treating all wildlife as if it were indeed wild, in educating all visitors, and in parents supervising their children responsibly, and in *never feeding wildlife.*

THE BEAR FACTS

On a warm August night in 1966, 17-year-old Susan Dowell, a high school senior from Visalia, California, slid into her tent pitched in her Yosemite camping spot then zipped it up. Not long after the teenager fell asleep, she awoke to what some consider the quintessential woodland nightmare: An aggressive mother bear was breaking into her tent. The bear, a specimen of *Ursus americanus*, also called the American or "black" bear, ripped through the material easily. Susan screamed. The sow clawed Dowell's face and shoulders. The girl's cries brought other campers at a run with flashlights. Together they scared off the strangely aggressive mother bear.

Rangers soon shot the sow. Next they shot both of her young cubs. These, they said, would not otherwise survive the coming winter. The girl, now shocky, required forty-two sutures. Susan was lucky she was not killed.

But what odds of being killed had she *really* faced? Or, to ask this question differently, exactly how many people have been killed by bears in Yosemite during its 150+ years of visitation by whites?

Yosemite's bears have all too frequently been persona non grata in their own habitat. During the Park's early days nearly everyone—with the exceptions of some pioneers such as Galen Clark, John Muir, and their ilk—considered Yosemite valuable almost solely for its scenic majesty, far less so for its wildlife. Things were so bad for Park fauna a century ago that, in 1906, Acting Superintendent Major H. C. Benson noted that even after the Valley was ceded back to the United States and became part of the national park:

> The Yosemite Valley itself has, during recent years, been a death trap to all game that was unfortunate enough to enter it. Practically every person living in the valley kept a rifle, shotgun, and revolver, and any animal or bird...was immediately pursued by the entire contingent, and either captured or killed....A bear pen [log trap] constructed about three years ago was found by me within 400 yards of the Sentinel Hotel.

In September of that year at least two bears ventured back into the Valley. Superintendent Benson was chagrined that nearly every person in the Village seemed to think "these bears should at once be pursued and driven out." Benson was unusual in his sympathy toward wildlife, especially inside the Park. To protect these wild animals he recommended the U.S. Army be permanently stationed in Yosemite, not merely during the summer season. Soldiers were needed all year because "immediately upon withdrawal of the troops from the park it is overrun...

these same men often remain throughout the entire winter, killing and trapping all the game in their vicinity."

Even after Benson had made his reports, done his work, espoused the firm protection of all wildlife, and set new policy while he was in charge, however, his words and actions may as well have been sucked into a black hole. On November 11, 1910, Benson's successor, Major William W. Forsyth, received a report from an early civilian park ranger Gabriel Sovulewski "if possible, some action should be taken to rid the valley of [the bears'] presence….If the bears remain here, camping in Yosemite will be a very serious proposition." Several tourists agreed with Sovulewski. Forsyth somewhat reluctantly sided with the tourists. He requested legal authority "to hunt the bears out of the Valley using shotguns loaded with very small shot."

How well did Major Forsyth's semi-humane dispossession of these four-legged nuisances work? Within two years one ranger, Jack Gaylor, assigned to stinging the bears with birdshot, instead admitted he had killed "perhaps eight or ten bears" in self-defense.

Fifteen years later (in September 1927) the Yosemite Park and Curry Company complained they had to close early in the fall because many guests were too fearful of these animals to remain in the Valley. Despite everything the Park Service did about and to bears, the Company and many tourists would continue to voice an anti-bear sentiment for more than half a century. Some advocated utter extermination of *Ursus americanus* in the Valley.

If things were bad for black bears, other large predators fared even worse. Yosemite's grizzly bears among them—ironic in that the Miwok word "Yosemite" has been thought for more than a hundred years to mean grizzly bear. Mountain lions fared only a little better. Again in 1927, in the Wawona area, California's official lion hunter Jay Bruce killed ten mountain lions. He also removed another thirty-three in Yosemite for a total of forty-three mountain lions in that year alone. Bruce "has killed close to 400 lions," noted Acting Superintendent Ernest P. Leavitt, "since he has been engaged in this work."

Concerned about this level of slaughter, notable Vertebrate Zoologist Joseph Grinnell of U.C., Berkeley wrote to Leavitt, "I wish to repeat my belief that it is wrong to kill mountain lions within Yosemite, or within any other of our National Parks of large area. They *belong* there, as part of the perfectly normal, native fauna, to the presence of which the population of other native animals such as the deer is adjusted."

How much good did Professor Grinnell engender for Yosemite's natural predators? For a scary (for Park wildlife) glimpse inside the mind of Leavitt's successor, Superintendent Charles Goff Thomson, consider how he worded an April 1929 report: A mountain lion, he wrote, was "very active around Alder Creek, a liver-pancreas-eating savage that is making a nine or ten day circuit with almost daily kills."

In short, Grinnell's ecological perspective of America's national parks as wildlife sanctuaries—as opposed to mere geographical collections of scenery in which human visitors might frolic—was far ahead of its time.

Luckily for pumas, at least, they neither raided the food stores of campers nor ate the campers themselves. Otherwise they would have suffered the same fate as its grizzly bears (the last known Yosemite grizzly was killed around 1895). Superintendent Thomson was a bit more lenient with black bears than with the lions because, he admitted, it was less their fault: Visitors had "spoiled" them. Still, he added, the Park could not allow "the bears to go unchecked." As Alfred Runte notes in his *Yosemite the Embattled Wilderness*, to control the visitors and the bears the Park would feed them separately—on opposite sides of the Merced—at the "bear show." "On the night of July 16, 1929," notes Runte, "nearly two thousand visitors in 336 private cars and 4 large buses had filled the viewing stands for the evening demonstration."

That same year, eighty-one people did seek aid at the local hospital for injuries inflicted by these animals. During 1932, 16,400 people gaped and guffawed as "trained" Yosemite bears ate garbage. Meanwhile, for the rest of the decade, Park rangers killed up to fourteen bears per year.

Accustomed to people, a bear in El Capitan Meadow in September of 1930 bit a man twice, both times in the same leg. Even so, no visit to Lewis Memorial Hospital was needed for the victim (or for the bear). The man had a wooden leg.

For many Americans, wildlife was simply a source of amusement. The Park often felt compelled to play to this latter crowd. In 1918 three orphaned mountain lion cubs (their mother had been killed by the government hunter) were placed on display. Soon a bear cub joined them. Other creatures followed. The Park housed this growing menagerie in a small assortment of metal cages in the Valley. There exists no shortage of photographs of government employees hand-feeding these wild animals from the 1920s to the early 1930s. Visitors were enthralled by these minor spectacles. They were impressed with the cute, seemingly tame wildlife. Many people took their cues from these exhibitions as well as from charming stories told by other tourists. In short, the Park's "do-as-I-say-not-as-I-do" approach to visitor education left something to be desired.

Things had to change. To begin this process, in 1925 Superintendent "Dusty" (Fred) Lewis banned all trapping of mammals in the Park. Congress had passed the National Park Organic Act in 1916 creating the National Park Service to promote and regulate America's national parks "to conserve the scenery and the natural and historic objects and the wildlife therein and to promote for the enjoyment of the same in such manner and by such means as will leave them unimpaired for the enjoyment of future generations." Under Section 3, however, predators did not enjoy inviolate protection. The "loophole" of sorts was spelled out: "He [the Secretary of the Interior] may also provide at his discretion for the destruction of such animals and such plant life as may be detrimental to the use of any of said parks, monuments, or reservations." Balancing the interests of visitors versus the welfare of natural predators in Yosemite proved to be an uphill drag.

The NPS long ago determined that native animals should be kept well stewarded in the parks. The National Park Service policy on predatory mammals was spelled out in 1931 and signed by Director Horace M. Albright. It reads in Section 1. "Predatory animals are to be considered an integral part of the wild life protected within national parks and no widespread campaigns of destruction are to be countenanced. The only control practiced is that of shooting a coyote or other predators when they are actually found making serious inroads upon herds of game or other mammals needing special protection." Despite this enlightened perspective on paper, there still existed at this time a concept of "good" animals versus "bad" animals. The good ones were the ones the public wanted to see: deer, elk, buffalo, moose, antelope, and their ilk. The bad ones were wolves, coyotes, mountain lions, and other predators that ate the good ones.

Coyotes, too often characterized as mere "cowardly scavengers," have suffered extremely bad press in the West for more than a century. No less an authority than Edward A. Goldman, Senior Biologist in the Department of Interior's Fish and Wildlife Service (in the 1940s) identified coyotes as "the archpredator of our times," ones deserving no quarter. Thus labeled as undeserving of any bona fide place in nature, coyotes have been vilified as the lowlife hyenas of North America. Literally millions of these little "prairie wolves" have been killed by government hunters, trappers, and setters of poisoned baits, then controlled further via bounties paid to citizen trappers, so called "sportsmen." What about in Yosemite? Over the years some visitors have been bitten by coyotes. Some were bit while sleeping in campgrounds, others while feeding the predators (such feeding not only instills the familiarity that leads to their biting humans it also increases the animals' dependence on humans for food). In a recent season, notes Ranger Dave Lattimore, in 1997, nine people were bit by coyotes during one month in the Crane Flat Campground alone. These sorts of dynamics have led to intermittent attempts to control problem animals. During one year in the Glacier Point area, for example, forty such coyotes were trapped. One turned out rabid.

Back to earlier days, in 1932, Yosemite finally abolished the zoo of caged animals and the hand-feeding by rangers. Sadly, NPS Director Albright gave his approval to killing the last three mountain lions held captive in it. Why? First, so that Jay Bruce, the state lion hunter, could skin them and collect the bounties, and secondly because these lions were not expected to be able to readapt to life in the wild after years of captivity.

Finally, on November 12, 1934, eighteen years after passage of the National Park Service Organic Act and three years after National Park policy spelled out that predators may only be killed to protect struggling populations of prey mammals, Director of the National Park Service Arno B. Cammerer, announced yet again the killing of natural predators in parks was to be terminated.

Also positive, in the fall of 1940 Yosemite complied with the policy by abolishing shows featuring the feeding of bears (at garbage pits and elsewhere). Despite this prohibition, Park Superintendent Frank A. Kittredge tried to revive the feeding of bears for tourists in 1943. As Alfred Runte notes, Western Regional Director Owen

A. Tomlinson wrote firmly to Kittredge: "the bear feeding ground and all appurtenances of the 'bear show' were to be obliterated."

Even so, where bears were concerned this era of minimal-rights-for-wildlife proved not to be a passing one. "People-first, bears-second" had been nearly a century-long standard operating procedure. Indeed this conflict got so bad for bears that in 1973 mountaineer and photographer Galen Rowell investigated the clash. His probe revealed that between 1960 and 1972 the Park had eliminated more than 200 of these animals—some intentionally and some accidentally.

Many of them were then disposed of over a cliff along the Big Oak Flat Road. Investigators from the *San Francisco Chronicle* climbed down this steep bank to take photos. They found "bloody carcasses wedged in trees or collapsed on rocks." A few of these bears had been skinned for rugs after they had been disposed of. In its defense, the Park labeled the dead animals as "garbage bears" or "nuisance bears." During the summer months when the Park was full, at least in the early 1970s, it was a regular, nightly occurrence for rangers patrolling in the Valley to spot at least ten or more bears making an almost clocklike swing through each campground looking for what had become easy pickings.

How bad had those Yosemite bears been in reality? Of Yosemite's 2.1 million visitors in 1973, sixteen suffered some sort of injury from a conflict with a bear. A few of these injuries were serious, requiring multiple sutures, including one lady who needed at least forty-four in her face alone and also lost an eye. Rowell also added up the property damage by bears that year during 268 incidents and computed the average cost—or average loss—per visitor. His total? In Rowell's expose' article "The Yosemite Solution to *Ursus americanus*" published in the February 1974 *Sierra Club Bulletin* he provided the answer: About one penny per visitor (of $29,192 total property damage for the year). Admittedly, had those 200 "problem" bears remained free instead of being killed, damages could have been higher. Especially noteworthy here, Rowell added, the Park had issued *no* citations or written warnings to visitors involved in any of those 268 incidents.

An excellent photographer but untrained as a biologist, Galen Rowell analyzed what was going on in the interplay between visitors and bears. He soon saw that within Yosemite there existed no clear cut policy on how to deal with troublesome animals. These decisions, he noted, seemed to rest on the philosophies of individual superintendents and more importantly, each supervisory ranger.

Rowell was further intrigued to find that even during the *same* span of time different administrative areas of Yosemite contrasted dramatically with regard to whether "problem" bears survived or not. Between 1972 and 1973, in Yosemite Valley where damage was less (173 property disturbances), twenty-one bears were killed. In the far larger Mather District, where bear incidents were more (272 of them) during that same time, none were killed. Why the difference? "Because the ranger in charge of the Mather District," wrote Rowell, "believes bears should not be killed except in extreme circumstances."

It turns out that Rowell's comparison is not as easily made as he would like. In fairness, this difference "between rangers" can be traced to other variables besides individual supervisory philosophy. These include numbers of officials in each area available and trained to respond to incidents, the fact that locating troublesome—but habituated—bears was far easier in the small confines of the Valley rather than in the far flung campgrounds of the Mather District (one of which, the Tuolumne Meadows Campground, was the biggest in the entire National Park System). Moreover, the more closely grouped campers in the Valley were not as "easy pickings" as those campers in more isolated sites. The reality is that rangers and wildlife technicians never took the killing of a bear lightly, whether in the Valley or in either of the two other Ranger Districts.

The bottom line, notes Galen Rowell, became: "In situations involving humans and bears, rangers have found it more convenient to pick on bears. No one has to advise them of their rights or worry about due process of law."

Rowell's conclusion, valid or otherwise, could not simply be shrugged off. Nor was Yosemite the only national park locked into seesaw battles with "problem" bears.

During the twentieth century in Yellowstone, notes Lee H. Whittlesey in his *Death in Yellowstone Accidents and Foolhardiness in the First National Park*, five people were killed by grizzlies. In 1912, a grizzly apparently killed a 63-year-old bear trapper named John Graham on Crevice Mountain under conditions which remain murky but likely self-imposed. In 1916, an old grizzly boar grabbed 61-year-old government teamster Frank Welch as he slept under a wagon. Welch's companions twice diverted the bear away with food. But each time the bear abandoned Welch, instead of playing possum he got up and tried to climb into the wagon for safety. Playing possum—remaining perfectly still as if one is dead—has proved an excellent survival tactic during most times when humans are attacked by grizzlies, who are highly defensive territorial animals; yet it is a very bad tactic against black bears, which attack more often with the intent to eat a person. Tactics aside, this grizzly finally killed Welch—almost, one suspects, to get him to quit moving. In 1942, at the Old Faithful Cabin Camp, 45-year-old Martha Hansen left her cabin to go to the ladies room and bumped into a grizzly. She turned and ran. The bear caught and killed her. The fourth grizzly-caused fatality—noted by Whittlesey and also by Mike Cramond in his *Killer Bears* and by Stephen Herrero in *Bear Attacks Their Causes and Avoidance*—could be a poster incident for what not to do in bear country.

Just after midnight on June 26, 1972, 25-year-old hitchhiker Harry Eugene Walker and his buddy Phillip Bradberry returned in the dark from a local party and walked into their isolated and illegal camp a half mile from Old Faithful. Here they met a 20-year-old female grizzly coming at them from only "five feet away." Both men ran. The 232-pound sow (who had a history as a "garbage bear") caught Walker, crushed his trachea, and ate about a quarter of him.

Ranger Michael Weinblatt investigated Walker's and Bradberry's camp. He found it "the dirtiest I have ever seen." A pot of putrid-smelling rice stew perched five feet from the ground in a tree a mere eleven feet from the tent. In the (illegal) fire pit right in front of the (illegal) tent sat half-burned food. The two campers had literally surrounded their tent with yet more food items and dirty cooking utensils. In short, they had created a garbage bear magnet. Rangers trapped and killed the grizzly, whose stomach contained Walker's hair.

A dozen years later, notes Whittlesey, in late 1984, Grizzly #59 killed and ate victim #5, photographer William J. Tesinsky, who had been hiking solo and apparently trying to photograph the bear. Rangers caught grizzly #59 eating Tesinsky and shot it on the spot. Why had the bear attacked him? His camera might offer a clue. Rangers found it close by. Tesinsky, they saw, had chosen his short range lens for this occasion. It was focused for twelve feet.

Although most media attention seems to be paid to grizzlies killing people in Yellowstone National Park, in fact, bears in Montana's Glacier National Park have proven more dangerous. Between 1910 and May 17, 1998—when "Chocolate Legs" and her two cubs killed and ate Craig Dahl—ten people in Glacier died in attacks by grizzly bears in circumstances similar to those in Yellowstone and also in different ones. Rangers in both Yellowstone and Glacier deliberate hard over "problem" grizzlies. After satisfying a strict set of protocols on when, why, and how to deal with them, rangers may still end up putting them down, despite these majestic animals being listed as an endangered species.

At any rate, Galen Rowell's allegation that rangers in Yosemite preferentially picked on bears instead of citing irresponsible people—because the former were more helpless and lacked lawyers—stung the Park. While Rowell's summation often had been true during much of the twentieth century, by no means had it always been true in the National Park System.

Illustrating this, in 1947, Carl P. Russell, who had been Yosemite Park's naturalist in the predator-slaughtering era of the late 1920s, became its superintendent. Russell was unusual in that he held both a Masters and Doctorate Degrees in ecology and would run the Park until 1952. "Almost alone," Russell had lamented to his longtime colleague Professor Joseph Grinnell, "I've stood for no molestation of bears." After having spent decades in Yosemite, Russell was in a good position to state that the "bear problem" was more accurately an issue of visitor irresponsibility. Furthermore, more often than not, injuries were due to people insisting upon feeding bears—even sows with cubs—by hand despite rules against this since 1902. The answer, Superintendent Russell said, lay in visitor responsibility, in educating visitors, in enforcement of infractions, and in the intelligent management of bear-proof food storage and garbage handling.

All of these insights had been spelled out well before Russell was in a position to supervise Yosemite. As early as 1933, George Wright, Joseph Dixon, and Ben Thompson, all three of whom had experience with Yosemite and all now were working at a policy level in Washington, D.C., had written the ground-breaking book: *Fauna of the National Parks.* In it they had outlined specific infrastructural strategies, including "bear safes" for food and garbage to eliminate the clash between animals and visitors.

But sadly it took the scandal of the early 1970s instead of the science revealed by Russell, Grinnell, and Wright and his colleagues to light the fire of revision of Park policies in the field. For the remainder of the decade (and continuing into today), Yosemite National Park worked aggressively to prevent problem encounters between visitors and bears.

The Park issued a comprehensive "Human-Bear Management Plan" in 1975 which placed emphasis on managing the behavior of people rather than that of bears. The plan required participation from all levels of the various Park divisions: Interpreters to inform visitors, protection to enforce regulations, maintenance to ensure a bear-proof garbage system, concessions to work with visitors at the lodges and restaurants, wildlife management to manage the animals themselves, and the Superintendent's Office to coordinate all of these departments.

The Park now placed bear-proof trash dumpsters throughout the Village and Yosemite's outlying areas. Technicians also installed cables from which hikers could safely hang their food in the more popular backcountry camping sites. Bear-proof lockers now stud Valley Campgrounds. At the entrance stations, the Park began aggressively distributing literature to inform visitors about bears and about visitor responsibilities. When rangers found campers improperly storing food these rangers warned and occasionally cited them. Over time, rangers have become ever more prone to issue tickets for improper food storage and related infractions. Meanwhile, though, the Park's budgets intended to support measures aimed at rescuing bears from becoming "problems" continued to shrink. Between 1998 and 2008, bear incidents and property damage decreased 79 percent.

Instead of bears being shot, they now were routinely relocated to more distant areas. While this technique did constitute an improvement, it did not prove to be a surefire cure. Some bears began plodding a "treadmill of relocation," repeatedly finding their way back to the land of plunder to earn yet another tranquilizing dart and then yet another free ride into the backcountry.

In 2006, Park Biologist Steve Thompson told us that, in the late 1990s:

> I decided to back off on the intensive management of bears and spend more time on long-term solutions. We were able to get bear-proof food lockers for all of Yosemite's campsites and all of its major trailheads. We worked closely with Maintenance personnel to reduce the overflow of trash cans and dumpsters by increasing the number of receptacles and/or increasing the frequency of their emptying.
>
> By 1998, however, we had accumulated a large number of bears conditioned to human food, and incidents (over 1,500) and property damage ($665,000) peaked, primarily from bears breaking into cars that contained food. Most of this occurred in parking lots of conces-

> sion lodging facilities. We implemented new regulations that required people to remove all food and other bear attractants from their cars. This included people staying in tent cabins, which requires us to provide food lockers for these visitors, as well. It should be noted that this problem was not reduced by the killing of bears, which did not increase, even in this year of rampant problems.

This record number of human-bear conflicts in 1998 caught the media's attention and ultimately that of Congress. With the support of Congressman Henry Waxman, Yosemite was granted a $500,000 base funding increase to be used exclusively on reducing clashes between bears and people. To manage these funds and address persistent or new problems, noted Thompson, the Yosemite Bear Council was formed of representatives from all Park divisions, the concessionaire, and other interested partners.

Despite all these positive revisions that saved the lives of bears, the inertia of visitor naïveté has proven the slowest factor to upgrade in the equation of bears-plus-humans. Education, nearly every Park official laments, is the toughest and most endless job they ever face. However true this might be, it also remains among their most important. The Park's new program of aggressively educating visitors and making nightly patrols, Thompson points out, "has been a resounding success, with incidents and property damage reduced over 80 percent from the peak levels of 1998."

What about the question posed earlier of how many people in Yosemite have been killed by bears? It has taken us several pages to get around to providing the answer: None. No one has been killed by any bear—black or grizzly—in Yosemite since written records began in 1851.

This is not to say that Yosemite bears have been, or are, "harmless." Chris Becker, a long-time X-ray technician at the Park's hospital, saw several people after they had experienced run-ins with bears. Much like the old television cartoons featuring Yogi Bear, whose obsession for stealing picnic baskets in Jellystone National Park provided an endless theme, Yosemite bears too are interested in people solely for the sake of raiding their food. Chris remembers once having to X-ray a camper who had been safely ensconced in his tent in Little Yosemite Valley. The man had been lying there and feeling confident that his food cache was safe. Abruptly he heard rummaging outside.

He emerged from his nylon haven to peer through the darkness. Neglecting to use a flashlight at this moment would soon become an error he would regret.

Irritatingly, in the dim starlight, this camper saw another person rifling at his food cache. "That son of a—" The outraged camper now rushed forward and took a roundhouse swing at the lowlife jerk trying to steal his precious food. His punch connected solidly. Surprisingly, the "jerk" seemed unfazed by this punch. And instead of reeling from it, the would-be thief took a swing back at the camper. Luckily, this return punch connected with its forearm instead of its claws. Even so, with one swipe the bear in the dark knocked the camper flying into a ten-foot ravine.

When, in the middle of the night, Becker was called out of bed to X-ray this vision-impaired camper, he found the impact in the gully had broken three of the guy's lumbar vertebra.

Sometimes the bear does not even have to be present to injure someone. Chris Becker also examined an injured camper who had sustained a bad laceration to his head. He had been in Hetch Hetchy with two buddies. Worried that animals would rifle their food cache, they wisely decided to suspend it high from a limb.

The campers found a sizable rock and tied their rope to it. One of them heaved this geological specimen over a high branch preparatory to hauling their cache up. The weak link in this procedure was their knot. When the rock cleared the limb and swung back toward them, the knot failed. The rock flew loose. Then it bashed the thrower in the face.

He howled in pain. Both his buddies raced for their little first aid kits then went to work to staunch the man's bleeding. Meanwhile, two bears entered their camp and walked off with the bags of food that the men had been about to hang.

What is the upshot of the endless arms race between human visitors and natural predators in Yosemite? Not only has no visitor been killed by a bear in Yosemite, neither has anyone died because of a puma, coyote, or any other mammalian predator—except, ironically, other humans.

HORSES & MULES

The most dangerous non-human animal in Yosemite has proven to be neither a predator nor even a large wild herbivore. Instead, the menace turns out to be man's second best friend. The earliest of the dozen (also see Chapter 8. Wheels) or so known fatalities involving a horse occurred on July 13, 1867 when 55-year-old John C. Anderson was plodding along a Valley trail. Anderson, who had left Illinois for the Gold Rush of 1849, had worked in Yosemite for more than ten years, mostly as a builder. He was a carpenter on the Lower Hotel. Anderson was performing some task now lost to history (possibly, notes historian Hank Johnston, breaking a young horse). What we do know is that, in so doing, a horse or maybe a mule kicked him in the head fatally. His friends buried him at the foot of what was to become the Four-Mile Trail.

Later his body was moved to the Valley cemetery, which was established around 1870. Yosemite lore has it that some well-intended mourner jammed Anderson's locust wood switch into the soft earth of his original grave to serve as a personal marker. This staff took root, grew, bloomed, and may have become the progenitor of every locust tree now in the Valley (although historian Jim Snyder also notes that other people brought locust wood into the Valley because it provided a strong material for tool handles).

Almost thirty years passed before another such episode. This one happened on

September 14, 1896, when Private George Rochette, age 26, of K Troop, 4th U.S. Cavalry, was thrown from his horse at Wawona where he was stationed. He sustained head injuries when he hit the ground and died the next day.

A few years later, in August of 1902, two women from Stent, California went riding in their horse-drawn rig in Yosemite Valley. They stopped for a stretch and for a view of the scenery. One of the women disembarked from the wagon. The other was about to step to the ground when their horse was spooked by the woman's sun bonnet. The animal abruptly flew into a gallop. The second woman fell from the speeding wagon. "She was cut dreadfully about the head and one of her ears was torn off," noted the *Mariposa Gazette*. "They say she cannot live." Unfortunately the *Gazette* included neither woman's name. In light of no followup stories on the demise of this unidentified unfortunate, the possibility exists that she survived.

On October 10, 1910, 38-year-old Henry "Harry" Eddy experienced his own unpleasant equine episode. Eddy, a Yosemite resident who had been employed as a laborer by the government for three months, was working with a horse on a now unknown task when it kicked him in the chest. The note on his obituary mentioned him having a "weakened heart." According to the official State of California Death Certificate, the horse's kick had ruptured his pulmonary artery. Eddy next had staggered to his tent in the laborers' camp and died.

On May 9, 1916, May Pewing of Los Angeles was riding a horse in Yosemite Valley. It threw her from the saddle. The 28-year-old woman died when she hit the ground.

More than sixty years passed before another horse-related fatality occurred. During much of this time dudes could hire a horse and ride trails in the Valley as well as in parts of the backcountry. Another way of putting this is that thousands of people rode many hundreds of horses in Yosemite in varied terrain for more than sixty years with no rider killed. On July 29, 1980, however, this period ended when 31-year-old Karen V. Hardage of Milpitas, California was riding the bridle path west of Tenaya Creek Bridge near Yosemite Village in the company of about two dozen other equestrians on a guided trip. As the group rode within about 500 yards east of the stables, a gap of more than a hundred feet opened between the first fifteen horses and the final eight or ten animals in the line. One of these latter mounts served as Hardage's.

Meanwhile a wrangler rode alongside this slower group to urge the animals forward. The horses in this last bunch began to trot, probably to close up the space, or else, being "barn sour," they simply knew they were nearing home. Hardage, in this last group, either fell off or was thrown off her mount. Abruptly several horses spooked and ran in multiple directions. Riders started screaming. Two other girls also fell from their mounts. The horse following Karen Hardage fatally struck her in the head with an iron-shod hoof.

Several more years passed before another like incident. This time the victim was barely a toddler. On July 17, 1992, 2-year-old Garren Reid Walbridge sat on a rented "walk and lead" pony being led by his mother Elizabeth. Near the concessionaire stables in Yosemite Valley the animal threw Garren, who somehow became entrapped in the tack. Then the spooked horse dragged the toddler along the ground. His mother tried to stop the pony but she sustained injuries in her attempts and tragically failed to stop it. Finally rescued, the seriously injured boy was evacuated to a hospital in Modesto. Two days later medical personnel took Garren Walbridge off life support.

SMALL, "SNEAKY" CRITTERS

There exist very few of us these days who have not seen some unlucky cowboy (usually one who "deserved" it) get nailed by a rattlesnake in a Hollywood Western movie and then die an agonizing (but fake) death. This evil icon of the West is so pervasive and durable that it still gives tourists the willies today and sends many of them scurrying for the impermeable security of their tents when the summer sun sets—because it is during the evening, the Nature Channel tells us, that rattlers become active.

Just how bad are these snakes? When Dr. Thomas Myers and Ghiglieri tried to answer this question in Grand Canyon National Park—a rattlesnake paradise located in the state with the greatest number of varieties, seventeen of them—try as we might we could not find any record of a person who had died from the bite of a rattlesnake or coral snake in the Park. Ironically, the only human death connected with a snake in Grand Canyon dated from 1933. A pair of prospectors had begun their descent on foot toward Kanab Canyon, on the North Rim. A rattlesnake struck at one of the two men but missed. The man, terrified of snakes, died of a heart attack despite never having been touched by its fangs.

Almost the same level of reptilian lethality can be said of Yosemite. Almost.

On June 28, 1919, William Gann was working as a government lineman on the El Portal phone line. He stepped into some brush without looking before he leaped. A rattlesnake nailed him. A buddy on the crew helped Gann up to the road. Next he flagged down a passing car. The driver took the poor man to the hospital. Three weeks later William had made a full recovery.

On October 4, 1935, Frank Kahl was cutting brush at Hetch Hetchy. He felt a sting in his hand, but thought he had merely hit a thistle. Very soon he found the angry snake. He killed it and went on hacking away at the dead snake's habitat. Within minutes he felt bad. Then worse. Kahl's co-workers took him across "the lake" where, an hour after his bite, the doctor "made incisions and drew considerable blood" then injected him with serum. He too recovered, though his hand was never the same.

In June of 1959, 15-year-old Richard Rodriguez picked up a rattlesnake along the roadside near Mirror Lake to have his way with it. It bit him. Richard's buddy killed it. Unlike the poor serpent, however, Rodriguez survived.

Overall, notes naturalist and editor Roger Tory Peterson in Steven Foster's and Roger Caras' *Venomous Animals & Poisonous Plants*, about ten people per year in the United States die from rattlesnake bites. "This makes your chance," notes Peterson, "of dying from snakebite about one in 25 million." Peterson goes on to explain how almost every victim of snakebite became a victim by encroaching upon or invading the snake's immediate habitat—or worse, as with Rodriguez above, by picking up the snake to play with it. Indeed the profile of "victims" of rattlesnakes is so crisp that it has its own tongue-in-cheek nickname, "the five Ts" (Testosterone, Tequila, Tattoos, Teeth missing, T-shirt). A lesson or two resides in Peterson's assessment. Longtime Yosemite Physician Jim Wurgler estimates that the average number of people who get bit by a rattlesnake per year in Yosemite is about two or three. Who gets bit most often? Rock climbers.

An incident occurred on July 11, 1931, that proved harder to understand—and harder to prove. Forty-one-year-old Louise R. Barnes of Hermosa Beach, California was hiking with her husband Alonzo in Tenaya Canyon. As she walked she felt something hit her leg. Thinking that it was merely a stick that scratched her, she trekked three or four more miles. At this point, she felt faint and collapsed. Two days later she died. What remained unclear about this episode was that not only did neither Barnes nor her husband ever see or hear a rattlesnake, the medical examiner was not certain either that he had found incontrovertible fang punctures on the woman's leg. Even so, at 2:45 the next morning, Dr. Dewey in Yosemite signed the standard certificate of death "accidental—Rattlesnake bite." To date, this is the only known human fatality to snakebite in Yosemite. An interesting sidebar here, in reaction to this 1931 death, Park Superintendent Charles Goff Thomson proposed introducing hogs into Yosemite as a public service because they would eat the rattlesnakes. Luckily, it never happened.

This next episode of venomous critters occurred to 26-year-old Alice R. Brewer on July 25, 1915, but it remains a mystery. Brewer, a school teacher of seven years in the Dunlop School District in nearby Fresno County was in the Valley vacationing. While she was here she was bitten on the face by an unspecified—or unknown—"poisonous insect" or arachnid. Abruptly ill, she left the Park and sought medical care in the Burnett Sanitarium in Fresno for her severe pain. She languished there during several days of "mysterious illness." Then she lapsed into a coma and died a few hours later. Perhaps the culprit had been a black widow spider. Or possibly she had been allergic to something normally less lethal. Either way, some very small and mysterious critter had killed her.

TREEFALLS

"Here indeed is the tree-lover's paradise;" John Muir penned in *The Yosemite*, "the woods, dry and wholesome, letting in the light in shimmering masses of half sunshine, half shade; the night air as well as the day air indescribably spicy and exhilarating; plushy fir boughs for campers' beds, and cascades to sing us to sleep."

For the Yosemite Indians, the Valley was profligate with tree growth. For centuries the Valley's broad, open meadows—the ones which existed at the time of the 1849 Gold Rush—had been biologically sculpted by these Indians. The Miwoks (a.k.a. the Yosemites) regularly burned the Valley floor to protect the black oaks and their valuable acorn crops by preventing conifers from taking hold and then shading out the smaller trees. Burning also fostered grasses in the meadows for their edible seed crops and for the grazing mammals that these open areas attracted. Once white Americans dispossessed the local Indians (see Chapter 14. Homicide), the Valley's floral community soon entered into an ecological succession of conifers.

As noted by Robert Gibbens and Harold Heady in their 1964 article "The influence of modern man on the vegetation of Yosemite Valley" (*California Agricultural Extension Service Manual 26*) the upsurge and growth of new trees in the Valley had already occurred within a decade or so after the departure of the Yosemite Indians.

Those young pines and cedars grew fast. And they grew together. In competition with one another for light, they grew ever taller, each "seeking" tallness above all else to harness sunlight at the expense of thickness and strength to protect against wind. Because they now also grew so close to each other, they accidentally, through sheer numbers, protected one another from the periodic strong winds that swept the Valley. Thus they could survive their thinness. Ultimately, however, this race for tallness at the expense of stoutness would prove fatal.

The first known victim of a treefall was not only a Native American, but a 14-year-old mother encamped during a trek across the Sierra Nevada to visit the Mono Lake area. On August 7, 1902, May Tom had camped with a party of Paiutes at the head of Upper Yosemite Fall. A tree fell that night and crushed her. She was one of only two women in the group and she soon died from her injuries. A huge funeral was held which nearly everyone in the Valley attended. The girl's tiny baby was taken by the other woman among the party, whose leg and collar bone had been broken by the same tree. It was uncertain at the time when this story appeared in the local *Mariposa Gazette* (August 9, 1902) whether or not this second woman or May's baby would survive the treefall.

More than half a century would pass after May Tom's untimely demise before another lethal encounter would take place between John Muir's dry and wholesome woods and a Park visitor. And when it finally did happen, it happened in spades. On October 15, 1960, dozens of trees began snapping off during one of the worst recorded windstorms in Yosemite Valley. Forty-one-year-old Margaret Gnall of New Jersey was in bed in a rented double cottage at the Lodge when the "Mono gale" knocked a 160-foot ponderosa, twenty-two-inches in diameter, through her roof. It killed her instantly.

Meanwhile, a half mile away, 19-year-old Kenneth C. Miner, a Curry Company kitchen helper from Council Bluffs, Iowa, was also asleep in his employee tent in Camp 6. Twenty minutes after the gust that killed Gnall, another burst funneled through the Valley and sheared off yet another pine at fifty feet above the ground and sent it through his flimsy shelter. It crushed him to death. This same tree knocked down three other big trees that smashed eight adjoining tents in which several more people had been getting ready for work only minutes earlier. Luckily, all of them had left for work just before the gust hit. Gnall's relatives sued the Park for $100,000 but later settled for a lesser amount.

For millennia Yosemite has been swept by what are now called "Mono Winds" or simply "Monos." One of the earliest recorded blasts is from a March, 1882 *Mariposa Gazette* which reported "cyclone swept down nearly every tree for a breadth of 300 yards." Monos usually appear as sudden, near-explosive microbursts sometimes touching only parts of the Valley. They may exist for only a few minutes or they may last for hours. Those who experience them, generally while standing beneath tall pines whipping and roaring like an approaching freight train, will tell you they are absolutely terrifying. The forest sways back and forth. Large limbs cascade down. Thankfully, only a few dangerous Mono Winds occur per decade. Predicting them, unfortunately, remains an imperfect science. We do know they generate due to strong pressure gradients when Great Basin areas to the east are subjected to high atmospheric pressures which move west and funnel down Sierra Nevada canyons toward the lower pressures in California. Other infamous winds arising in this way include the Santa Anas and the Chinooks.

Monos are bad enough on their own, but when they rumble through after a heavy rain or snow has softened the soil, things become even more dangerous. On January 26, 1969, for instance, 23-year-old Iris P. Pope of Downey, California was asleep in Cabin #136 of the Yosemite Lodge. More than three inches of rain had fallen during the previous twenty-four hours in Yosemite. At 4 a.m., when nearly everyone was asleep, a sudden gust hit the area and knocked down many trees. Blowing at nearly fifty miles per hour, it toppled a thirty-four-inch-thick incense cedar that had been loosened in the wet earth. The falling giant flattened Iris Pope's cabin.

Ron Mackie, the ranger on call and the first to arrive, found the woman. She was still alive. But only barely. Hundreds of pounds of shattered lumber held by the tons of tree now pinned her down. Ron contacted the Park's Forestry Crew, a highly skilled team experienced in removing hazardous trees in various inconvenient places. Led by Jay Johnson this team worked feverishly to remove the fallen cedar that now pinned Pope to her crushed bed. After what seemed like hours of work but was actually only minutes, the trapped woman died of suffocation before the final weight could be removed. Johnson was a local Yosemite Indian who possessed an intimate knowledge of the winds, having lived in the Valley most of his life and grown up with them. But on this night neither his Native American knowledge nor his skill proved a match for the gale.

Exactly fifteen years later another Mono wind blew no good. Just like Iris Pope, John Douglas Callaway was also 23 years old. The ex-Marine from San Jose, California was now a Curry Company employee. He had chosen against residing in a solid wood structure to instead remain quartered in employee Tent #87 in Camp 6 with his high school buddy, 23-year-old Greg Tardieu. At about 5:30 on the morning of January 26, 1984, the weather in the Valley abruptly shifted from calm to breezy. In the next two hours the wind built up to increasingly worse gusts, threatening to reach legendary Mono Wind speeds that can blast at nearly ninety miles per hour.

Knowing he had to get to work, Callaway awoke, dressed, and left. Eight minutes later, his roommate Tardieu heard a tree smash the ground at the end of the tent. It sounded gigantic. Alarmed, Greg got up and checked the damage. He found their kitchen smashed. The fallen giant now blocked the tent's single exit.

Tardieu radioed for help. Several minutes later, he began wondering where Callaway was. He had heard his friend leave. He must have gone to work. But now he began to worry. He tried to radio Callaway. Receiving no response, Tardieu radioed his concerns to Ranger Harry Steed.

Because of multiple and continuing treefalls, Steed had already decided to evacuate the already mostly empty Camp 6 and was now methodically trying to get everyone from their tents ASAP. Very soon Steed and Ranger Mike Quick discovered Callaway buried under the thick foliage of an uprooted, 193-foot tall ponderosa forty inches in diameter. The two rangers cleared away the heavy limbs to find that Callaway had died due to head trauma and hemorrhage from a severed foot. This giant tree had nearly crushed Tardieu's tent #87 but, again, had clipped only the small kitchen area. It was sheer bad luck that Callaway, awake and mobile, had been in the exact wrong place at that instant. At 8:18 a.m., Dr. James Wurgler arrived and pronounced John Callaway dead.

This episode—and the winds—continued to grow ever scarier. Within two minutes, rangers used heavy equipment and chainsaws to extricate Callaway's body. Minutes later, yet another large ponderosa, this one 190 feet tall, blew down (among a total of thirty pines and cedars that would topple in Camp 6), hitting three tents and two vehicles.

As the wind continued to roar like a volcano, Search and Rescue Ranger Mike Durr stood next to the ambulance into which he and others had just loaded Callaway. Durr now asked himself what might be his best course of action should yet another big tree topple in his direction. He looked at the vehicle. The best close place, he figured, should be adjacent to the rear wheel. Mere seconds later, Durr heard the unmistakable cracking of yet another big tree. He dived for his cover and flattened himself up against that rear wheel and axle. This falling tree now crushed the ambulance. But it did not smash deeply enough to slam Durr with it. His imaginative forethought and quick reactions had just saved his life.

Overall, this Mono Wind knocked over 150 big trees in Yosemite. It had killed Callaway and created other havoc—including closing the main roads.

Six months later, on a hot July 28, 1984, a sad but miniature version of this accident happened to a miniature person near Wawona Campground in Yosemite

Valley. Rhiannon Serrano, age 5, had been camping with her family when they decided to take a dunk in the Merced River. Rhiannon went swimming. In a very freak accident, a dead tree merely four inches thick fell onto the girl while she was swimming only six feet from her mother. She died instantly of skull fractures caused when the small tree hit her. CPR by responding rangers within fifteen minutes proved futile.

Not much more than a year later, on September 19, 1985, another unexpected treefall took its toll—and in an unexpected way. Twenty-two-year-old Greta Breedlove Ross and her 26-year-old husband Robert Wiley Ross of Pleasanton, California, had decided to ride in an open air tram near Yosemite Lodge. This was one of the Curry Company's high-capacity "Green Dragon" Valley Tour open-air vehicles. As the guide onboard waxed eloquent over some attribute of the Park the vehicle drove under a huge old oak tree at the intersection between the Lodge and the Lower Yosemite Falls' Parking Lot.

As the large vehicle passed under the tree, it lost a massive branch two feet in diameter. The 6,000-pound limb fell thirty feet onto the Green Dragon, injuring many people aboard and killing Greta and Robert Ross.

The Park's medical response proved quick and massive. Shift Supervisor J. R. Tomasovic immediately implemented the Incident Command System to manage the tragedy and triage the twenty other injured riders. Otherwise unbeknownst to everyone, including possibly the now deceased Greta Ross, an autopsy indicated that she was pregnant. Her father filed a lawsuit on behalf of the unborn child. He won because the Park could not show conclusive evidence that the offending tree had ever been individually inspected. Likely this suit was won even more for emotional reasons pivoting on a natural sympathy over the death of a pregnant woman.

Litigation over responsibility for this freak accident prompted Chief of Law Enforcement Lee Shackelton to query arborist experts from the University of California for some explanation for why the oak might have "behaved" as it had. The tree, the university expert now explained, had undergone a phenomenon called "Summer Oak Limb Fall." This process occurs when prolonged dry heat dehydrates oak fibers. When this drying is followed by thunderstorms or summer showers which provide so much water that the dry wood over absorbs, its internal pressure grows. In one of those "luck of the draw" events on September 19th, the vibration of the passing Green Dragon possibly triggered this phenomenon. The limb did not so much "fall" off the tree as explode outward from it horizontally. Summer oak limb fall is far more common than people might guess. The phenomenon is all too well known because livestock frequently seeks shade under such trees throughout much of California, resulting in cattle and horses becoming regular casualties.

The 1980s proved to be a bad decade for Yosemite Valley treefalls. On February 18, 1988, Mono Winds struck again. Indeed the winds proved so fierce that the Park evacuated the cabin area west of the Yosemite Park Lodge. They cordoned it off with yellow tape reading, "Closed Area." The concessionaire placed security officers to patrol the perimeter now taped. Inside, the lodge announced the closure of the cabin area and the reason for it. Everyone would be safe in the lodge, but for the immediate future the cabins would remain closed and off limits.

Inside the lounge sat 9-year-old Jasmine Shyanne Bitts and her mother Nancy Lee Earle, age 31, of Garden Grove, California. With them was Earle's 36-year-old boyfriend Charles Ross of Carpentaria, California. Witnesses overheard Ross saying that he was going to go back into their cabin anyway.

Indeed, when one of the company's security guards left the perimeter for a toilet break, Ross, Earle, and Bitts slipped under the yellow tape and made their way back to Cabin #151. Meanwhile the gale built up force and soon hit fifty to sixty miles per hour. At about 8:15 p.m., Nancy Earle lay awake and staring out the cabin window. The roaring noise of the wind through the trees made her uneasy.

Through the window in the near dark she now saw an unbelievable sight. A truly gigantic tree was falling directly onto their cabin. The mother rolled out of bed and "ran to her daughter and was knocked to the floor by the falling roof."

She had not quite reached her daughter. As she now tried to wriggle nearer to Jasmine she heard the girl whimpering.

An upper beam slammed across the frantic mother's neck. Stunned and blocked from moving any closer to Jasmine, Nancy Earle and Ross changed direction and crawled out of the collapsed cabin to go for help. The two adults now stared at the collapsed cabin trapping her daughter. The tree—a monster close to five feet in diameter—had toppled and crashed though its roof as if it had been constructed of paper.

In five minutes Park personnel arrived on scene with chainsaws. One ranger crawled inside the crushed structure. The massive tree, he now found, had stopped only a few inches from the floor. He continued crawling and shining his flashlight beam through the wreckage.

He found Jasmine. He called to her. She made no response. Not even a whimper or a groan. Dismayed, he struggled through the tightly pinned debris to get closer. Finally he was able to check her pulse. Nothing.

The tree, he now saw, had trapped and quickly killed young Jasmine Bitts. Yet it had inflicted relatively minor injuries on the two adults in the same cabin.

This Park crew removed the tree. Meanwhile other workers evacuated more than 400 Park visitors to elsewhere in the Yosemite Lodge and up the road in the Ahwahnee Hotel.

The Park sought to charge the two surviving adults from Cabin #151 with reckless child endangerment but the Assistant U.S. Attorney decided not to prosecute. In a bizarre turnabout, the mother, Earle, sued in a civil venue. Almost no one in the Park correctly guessed the suit's outcome. Due to the sentiments felt by the jury over the poor little girl being crushed to death and for the bereavement of her distraught mother, they decided in favor of Earle.

TABLE 11 . FATALITES CONNECTED WITH ANIMALS AND TREEFALLS IN YOSEMITE. (All incidents are discussed in the text unless noted.)

Name, age	Date	Location	*Circumstances*
Animals:			
John C. Anderson, 55	July 13, 1867	Yosemite Valley	*Anderson left Illinois for the 1849 Gold Rush and worked in Yosemite for a decade. A horse or mule kicked him in the head, killing him instantly.*
George Rochette, 26	September 14, 1896	Wawona	*Private Rochette of Manchester, New Hampshire and K Troop, 4th U.S. Cavalry, was thrown from his horse. He lived through one intensely painful night, and died of head injuries the next morning.*
Henry "Harry" Eddy, 38	October 10, 1910	Yosemite Village	*Eddy, a Yosemite resident and government laborer, was working with a horse that kicked him in the chest.*
Alice R. Brewer, 26	July 25, 1915	Yosemite Valley	*Brewer, a school teacher of 7 years in Fresno County, was bitten on the face by an unknown "poisonous insect" or arachnid. She died in the Burnett Sanitarium in Fresno.*
May Pewing, 23	May 9, 1916	Yosemite Valley	*Pewing of Los Angeles was riding a horse that threw her. She died upon impact.*
Louise R. Barnes, 41	July 12, 1931	Tenaya Canyon, above Mirror Lake	*On July 11, Barnes of Hermosa Beach, California was hiking with her husband and felt something hit her leg. Thinking a stick had scratched her, she continued 3 or 4 miles. She died at 2:45 the next morning. Her legs did not show obvious rattlesnake fang marks.*
Colin Robert Neu, 5	November 6, 1977	Old Wawona School yard	*While picnicking with his parents, Neu of Clovis, California fed a spike mule deer potato chips. The deer spooked, jerked upward and gouged the right side of the boy's chest with a 5-inch antler that punctured his lung and nicked a pulmonary artery.*
Karen Valann Hardage, 31	July 29, 1980	bridle path west of Tenaya Creek Bridge, Yosemite Village	*Hardage of Milpitas, California was riding a horse among many equestrians. Hardage fell or was thrown off. Abruptly several horses spooked and scattered. The horse following Hardage struck her in the head with a hoof.*
Garren Reid Walbridge, 2	July 17, 1992	near concessionaire stables, Yosemite Valley	*Garren of Simi Valley, California was sitting on a rented "walk and lead" pony led by his mother. The pony threw then dragged him. He survived only 2 days on life support.*

unnamed female — July 2012 — Signature Tents in Curry Village
unnamed male, 37 — July 31, 2012
unnamed male, 45 — August 12, 2012

Three semi-known victims (from Los Angeles and Alameda County, California, and from Pennsylvania) died of ***hantavirus pulmonary syndrome*** *out of at least 10 known tourists (aged 12-58) who contracted the* sin nombre *strain of hantavirus allegedly while staying in one of the 91 new (built in 2009) "Signature" luxury cabins at Curry Village. This virus is spread in the feces and urine of deer mice* (Peromyscus maniculatus), *of which 18% in Yosemite test positive. The mice tend to survive and reproduce better after mild winters, such as that during 2011-2012, and in warm places to nest, such as in the well-insulated foam walls of the new tent cabins. Human survival of hantavirus pulmonary syndrome is only 36 percent among 587 documented cases since 1993 when the syndrome was identified. All Yosemite victims remain anonymous as per CDC protocols, so details remain murky. Additional victims may exist in France. On December 10, 2012 dismantling of the 91 new, double-walled "Signature Tent" cabins began. (not in text)*

Robert D. Judd, 71 — July 23, 2016 — Wawona

Judd of Yosemite West fell off a ***horse*** *while on the Meadow Loop in Wawona and died in the hospital. (not in text)*

Treefalls:

May Tom, 14 — August 7, 1902 — head of Yosemite Fall

Tom was camped with a party of Paiutes atop Yosemite Fall en route across the Sierra to Mono Lake. A tree fell that night and crushed her. She was buried in the Yosemite Cemetery with a significant, well-attended ceremony.

Margaret Gnall, 41 — October 15, 1960 — Yosemite Lodge

Gnall of Roselle Park, New Jersey was in bed when a "Mono Gale" knocked a 160-foot ponderosa 22 inches in diameter through her roof. It killed her instantly.

Kenneth C. Miner, 19 — October 15, 1960 — Camp 6, Yosemite Village

Twenty minutes after Gnall was killed, Curry Co. kitchen helper Miner of Council Bluffs, Iowa was asleep in his tent when another gust of wind sheared off a pine about 50 feet up and sent it through his quarters, crushing him.

Iris P. Pope, 23 — January 26, 1969 — Yosemite Lodge

After 3½ inches of rain fell during 24 hours, Pope of Downey, California was asleep in Cabin #136. At 4 a.m., a 50-mph wind toppled a 34-inch thick incense cedar through it, crushing her.

John Douglas Callaway, 23 — January 26, 1984 — Camp 6, Yosemite Village

Curry Co. housing employee Callaway of San Jose was exiting his tent #87 when a "Mono Wind" blew a 40-inch thick, 193-foot tall ponderosa on top of him.

Rhiannon Serrano, 5

July 28, 1984 near Wawona Campground
A small dead tree with a 4-inch trunk diameter fell onto Serrano of Pasadena, California while she swam. Multiple skull fractures killed her instantly.

Greta Breedlove Ross, 22
Robert Wiley Ross, 26
"unborn fetus"

September 19, 1985 near Lower Yosemite Fall's Shuttle Bus stop
The couple from Pleasanton, California was riding in an open-air tram with 34 aboard. A branch 2 feet in diameter and weighing 6,000 pounds fell 30 feet from a huge oak. It killed the Rosses and injured 20 others. Mrs. Ross was pregnant. Her father sued the NPS, alleging inadequate hazard tree removal.

Jasmine Shyanne Bitts, 9

February 18, 1988 Yosemite Lodge
Bitts and her mother Nancy Lee Earle of Garden Grove, California with boyfriend Charles Ross of Carpentaria, California were in their beds during winds reaching 60 mph—despite their cabin having been closed and cordoned off as too hazardous for occupancy. At about 8:15 p.m. a tree nearly 5 feet thick crashed through the roof of Cabin #151, killing Jasmine.

Ryan Hiller, 27

January 21, 2012 Tent Cabin #12, Delaware North Concession Stables
Hiller, a concession employee and seasonal ranger from Chapel Hill, North Carolina was asleep around 6:30 a.m. when a major winter thunderstorm with heavy winds toppled 7 large trees. One, a 3-foot diameter, 181-foot tall ponderosa, slammed across his tent cabin and his torso. (not in text)

Dragon Kim, 14
Justin Lee, 14

August, 14, 2015 Upper Pines Campground, Yosemite Valley
Kim of Tustin, California and Lee of Irvine, California were in their tent early in the morning when a black oak above them lost a large limb which crushed their tent and them in it. (not in text)

Destiny Rose Teixeira Borges, 20

March 5, 2017 Concession Village, Yosemite Valley
Borges of Ceres, California & Yosemite Village was asleep when high wind and snowfall toppled a tree onto her tent cabin.

Harry Partington, 22

October 8, 2024 Union Point on the Four-Mile Trail
As Partington of Perth, Australia hiked near Union Point at 6,300 feet elevation on the temporarily closed, steep switchbacking trail, gusts of wind knocked a tree down upon him fatally. Coincidentally, a nearby but unrelated woman also was seriously injured.

Angela Lin, 29

July 19, 2025 Tuolumne Grove
As Lin of Mountain View, California hiked with 3 friends during afternoon along the paved, main trail about 1 mile from the parking lot, a large limb from a giant sequoia (Sequoia gigantea) *fell on her causing death due to head trauma.*

Chapter Twelve

LOST

On a hot July 15 in 1978, 25-year-old David Cunningham of Santa Barbara shouldered his heavy backpack, kissed his wife goodbye and headed up the Illilouette Trail east into the high Sierra. Susan Cunningham, only three weeks short of their first child's due date, did not accompany him. Instead she stayed in a tent cabin in Curry Village and waited patiently for his return. Maybe, she hoped, that new fishing license would at least keep him company.

David Cunningham was scheduled to return from his hike on July 19. But when that Wednesday came, he did not. A day later Susan was worried enough about the missing father of her unborn child to report him as overdue. She broke down in tears as she explained to rangers how David really did not have all that much hiking experience. Her imagination painted mishap after potential mishap that may have left her husband stranded somewhere off-trail and injured, perhaps trapped, and now desperately in need of rescue.

On the positive side of the scale, David Cunningham had been a YMCA Indian Guide. He was not entirely devoid of outdoor skills. And searchers should not have too hard a time recognizing him. He was thin and good looking, she said, even though his brown hair was receding. He had been wearing old canvas work trousers with a tan corduroy patch on the left knee. He also wore size 10½ Lowa Scout boots. These had a common sole pattern, although the five stars molded into the middle of their soles would leave distinctive prints.

As Susan wrote all of this down for the searchers, she also felt compelled to add onto page five of the Park's "Lost Person's Questionnaire" that David was "looking forward to fatherhood—taking Lamaze classes."

But when asked about her husband's specific hiking plans, Susan became vague.

She did not really know. She accompanied Ranger Butch Farabee to the trailhead near Glacier Point where she had last kissed David goodbye. He had walked "that way," she said, pointing. With her gesture, she indicated hundreds of square miles of rough terrain stretching southeasterly into the middle of Yosemite. Her gesture encompassed a lot of territory.

Thus began a long week of intense work. Fifty searchers from five California mountain rescue teams donated their time and risked their necks to scour the most awkward chunks of the Park. As few to no signs of the missing husband became evident, every searcher soon found him- or herself second guessing in what hidden nook this soon-to-be father might have broken his neck. Searchers compared their hypotheses about what-the-heck kind of mistake this guy had made to vanish like this. Despite their imaginative theorizing, however, none of them guessed the truth.

YOSAR's John Dill stationed radio relay teams atop several peaks to enable all searchers to be kept informed of one another's findings—or, in this case, their lack of them. Horse patrolmen swept the trails. Groups on foot focused on the quadrant of the Park that included areas south and east of Glacier Point, between Ottoway and Washburn Lakes, to the crests of the Red Peak Pass area. Volunteers climbed from 7,000 feet elevation to 10,500 feet, 700 feet above the snow line. Helicopters crisscrossed the densely wooded ravines and white granite benches. Searchers, including David's father, peered from the helicopter into the deep, shady gorge of the Merced River and wondered: Had his lost son somehow drowned down there in *that*?

Despite this immense investment of person power, no one on this SAR mission discovered even a single boot print or any other sign of Cunningham.

As the efforts of so many well-trained search and rescue personnel continued to come up clueless, Dill soon resorted to using the Park's Backcountry Permit forms so he could question everyone else who had been hiking this same area during the same week as the missing man. Dill patiently dialed hundreds of phone numbers to contact these other hikers.

"A tall, slender guy wearing baggy work pants with a tan corduroy patch on the left knee?" Each voice on the other end of the line would ask to be sure of what they were supposed to remember. "No, sorry; I never saw anyone like that."

But, as it turned out, a few hikers *had* seen David Cunningham. As Dill added up these few positive sightings, something weird became clear: Every sighting had occurred within a short distance of the trailhead. Yes, the missing hiker had departed exactly as his wife had reported, but apparently he had not gotten far at all. Indeed, his sojourn into the Yosemite backcountry seemed to have lasted for only minutes. The searchers now wondered anew: What on earth had happened to him?

After a week had passed, the effort for Cunningham wound down frustratingly unsuccessful. This mission had consumed 1,715 man-hours, dozens of helicopter hours, and it had cost $21,379. Most of the people involved were working without pay and risking their necks to do so. This sort of sacrifice is rarely begrudged. The reward to volunteers is saving a life. Sure, sometimes a victim is found too late. Worse, sometimes the lost person is not found at all. Then, maybe years later, a hiker or climber wandering off the beaten track in some out-of-the-way pocket of the Park stumbles onto a skeleton with an ID still faintly legible in its faded, rodent-chewed pocket. Then closure.

In short, when a SAR mission begins for someone lost it is folly to anticipate only one specific outcome. Sometimes bad things do happen to relatively decent people.

Finally, on August 1, a bit more than two weeks after David's disappearance—and only a few days before the birth of his first child—a big clue surfaced. More than just a clue, in fact, it was more like a flashing neon light. A friend of David's received an unsigned postcard from Bangor, Maine. The card was written in the missing man's handwriting.

This friend immediately contacted Susan. She felt relieved, infuriated, and immensely saddened. The same friend now also contacted the Park.

When finally confronted by frustrated (a mild term considering their actual condition) Park investigators, David cavalierly announced that the prospect of fatherhood had terrified him and he had wanted out. So he had executed, he explained, a planned about-face after his wife had driven beyond view. He had doubled back to the pavement then exited the Park. Once out, he fled as far away from her as he could get yet still be in the United States.

For his selfish and dangerous (to searchers) act, David Cunningham was cited into court for "creating a hazardous or offensive condition." This was a Disorderly Conduct violation of the Code of Federal Regulations. The U.S. Magistrate fined David the maximum allowable penalty—$500.

Yes, it does seem a bit mild.

Cunningham's plan to vanish off the face of the Earth via Yosemite's backcountry to escape a spouse or the duties of fatherhood by "dying" and to then begin a new life elsewhere was neither an original thought nor even an original plan of action. Back in 1915, Thomas J. Brown concocted a similar gambit. Brown, a married man, had left home in the summer of 1914 to work in Yosemite as an engineer. During the spring of the following year he entered the Park's high country in the company of one other person, a Mexican whose name has now been lost to history. During this trek both men vanished.

A search uncovered nothing definitive. Several locals in the Park concluded that some accident had befallen the two, but as time passed people began to suspect something more sinister. Had this Mexican murdered Thomas Brown, hidden his body, and then fled with his money?

Apparently this is precisely what Brown hoped people would suspect and then ultimately come to believe. But Brown now sabotaged his nearly perfect transition from his old life to a new one by committing a tiny oversight. The clue that now obviated his carefully orchestrated "death" resided in a letter written by one of the young bookkeepers in the Valley.

She had already left her job and had written to her boss an explanation for why she was quitting. But, she added, her sister was also an excellent bookkeeper and would he please strongly consider hiring her as a replacement? This letter—lacking a return address—failed to wave a red flag until its very end. The young woman had not signed her own name, the one under which she had been employed. Instead she had signed it "Mrs. Thomas J. Brown."

Apparently the new Mrs. Brown remained unaware that there already existed a Mrs. Thomas J. Brown, one currently grieving for her poor husband who had been killed in Yosemite. An investigation soon revealed that during the previous summer the second wife, the bookkeeper, indeed had been swept off her feet by the engineer who, witnesses concurred, was also enamored of her. "It now seems certain," noted the *Mariposa Gazette* for April 3, 1915, "that the man is still alive and living somewhere in California while a faithful wife who mourned his death now bears a great sorrow for his living."

Indeed.

It remains unclear what happened to Brown's Mexican associate.

Of course most hikers who go missing have not faked their disappearance. On October 14, 1986, 30-year-old Michael Kalantarian took two days off work to hike Mount Clark. This 11,522-foot peak, barely ten miles east-southeast of the Valley, is composed of whiter than usual granite such that it stands out brightly among the surrounding Sierra peaks. More enticing, Mount Clark offers an incredible view of the Park's backcountry. Kalantarian wanted so badly to bag his first summit and to behold the panorama that he pushed the guidelines of safe mountaineering beyond their limits.

Fellow Curry Company employee Margaret Colvin dropped him off at the Mono Meadows Trail. She left without learning his return route or hiking plan. Michael Kalantarian immediately hiked toward his goal then camped. The next day he found himself part way up Mount Clark but behind schedule for a safe, ropeless scramble up its steep knife-edged arêtes. Even so, he remained unwilling to turn back.

Already tempting fate by climbing here alone, with not even a companion waiting back in camp, Kalantarian had pushed his luck even harder by deciding to trek incognito. He had not registered his hike with the Park. No one in the Backcountry Office would know when, or even if, he was overdue to return. Nor did anyone working for Curry Company know exactly where he was, schedule or not. Only Colvin possessed an idea of his goals, and her information remained unavoidably vague. As fate would have it, none of these risky elements of rugged individuality now tempered Kalantarian's decision to continue climbing alone despite finding himself behind schedule and in a race against the clock during a short-daylight month.

Kalantarian now made yet another pivotal decision. To enhance his ability to travel light and fast—scrambling, using just his hands and feet—he had left his camping gear a mile and a half behind in a bivouac spot. More ominous, along with his pack he had also dumped his survival gear.

Pushing harder to make up time, Kalantarian abruptly halted. Ahead a steep slab of new ice dropped by an early fall storm now paved his route up. This ice was disappointing. Irritating actually. With so little daylight left it would be a challenge to locate, scout out, and ascend a good secondary route. Despite the dismal feel of now being forced to find another way up, he wisely admitted to himself this ice constituted a recipe for disaster. With virtually no technical climbing experience or even a pair of crampons, he would not even try to ascend it.

Kalantarian had been "here" before during an earlier attempt on Mount Clark. Back then, however, he had begun feeling sick and had turned back. This time he was determined to reach the top. He was using as his guide Steve Roper's *The Climber's Guide to the High Sierra*. Roper referred to this route as the Northwest Arête and described it as a Class 4 ascent—to be done prudently only with a rope. Regardless of what elements of psychology now ruled Kalantarian's decision making, instead of taking this lethal sheet of ice and the late hour as signs to turn back, he now backtracked a bit then located another steep but ice-free route up. Despite his being ropeless, as Kalantarian sized up his new potential route it did not look too ridiculous.

But it was.

Kalantarian slipped while free-soloing his "new" 5.7-rated route. He fell a whopping seventy feet. He awoke an hour later draped in the boughs of a low, brushy pine tree. He had shattered one ankle, broken a wrist, and had sustained a miscellany of lesser injuries from his impacts, including a battered head. He stood up. It hurt. He found he was unable to walk even one step, although with pain he could stand up to try to get his bearings.

His hat was gone. His sunglasses too. So was his water bottle. Search as he might, given his now limited ability, he never did find any of these. Because of the late hour, he could not afford to waste time looking for anything. He had to get back to his gear before the cold of the night got him. And to a lower elevation. He began crawling downslope.

The terrain proved tortuous. Each foot of ground he covered exacted a price in pain. Excruciating pain. Worse, this being mid-October at 11,000 feet, as soon as the sun set the landscape became cold. Really cold. The mercury would soon drop to about fifteen degrees.

Despite his polypropylene underwear, bunting jacket and cotton shirt, the cold numbed some of Kalantarian's pain from his shattered ankle and broken wrist. Next it numbed the rest of him.

He pried off and discarded the boot from his swelling ankle. Now, without either a hat or a boot, the risk of frostbite and hypothermia increased. All he possessed to fight the cold during this long, freezing high Sierra night were the moderate clothes he wore. Wisely, he wrapped his shirt around his head to retain some heat (about 25 percent of one's body heat escapes via one's head and neck).

The night proved at least as miserable as he had anticipated. At dawn Kalantarian continued crawling in the direction he reckoned led to his camp. He had a map but he was not carrying a compass. To complicate things even more, crippled as he was, he could not manage to scramble down the same steep Class 4 terrain he had ascended earlier to get to this point, so he detoured to the west and down along somewhat easier topography. West would not take him back to his pack and to the supplies inside it that he desperately needed to survive. These lay to the northwest. Despite this discrepancy, his backpack did remain his prime goal even while he crawled steadfastly in a direction that would not take him to it.

Even on this "easier" route to the west his progress was snail-like and painful. If he could swing back soon in the correct direction, he would be facing only a mile and a half crawl back to camp. He knew he had to somehow manage to accomplish this. If he were to survive this mess, it would be up to him. No one else was around, and no one else knew about his plight.

During the day Kalantarian tried to stick to crawling ridgelines that offered better visibility. Ridgelines also offered more direct sun. The sun felt incredibly good. No wonder people worship it. Besides, he reckoned, he could use the sun as a replacement for his nonexistent compass to orient himself and to choose his route. He continued crawling then resting, alternately, all day. At dusk he looked for water to drink from ice melt. Reviewing his long agonizing day was not exactly a cause for celebration but, again, he felt at least that he was closer to his camp, closer to the supplies he needed to curb hypothermia and closer to the vital tools he could use to light a fire to warm himself and to send a distress signal. Even if no one saw the fire, at least it would keep him from freezing to death.

By the time Michael Kalantarian had missed two days of work his boss alerted the Park of his absence. At first no one had any idea of where to look. But by telephone interviewing many backcountry hikers of the past few days and then by talking with his friend Margaret Colvin, the SAR coordinator narrowed the search zone to the western drainages of Mount Clark.

Meanwhile Kalantarian's second night on all fours had turned out bad, a nightmare of cold. So had his next day. And so too would his next, next night. And ditto for his next, next day. And so on. His nights felt unbelievably miserable. His feet and fingers seemed to literally freeze each night. As if trapped in some endless nightmarish hell of cold for condemned solo hikers, Kalantarian continued creeping painfully downslope. Despite never actually arriving at his camp and despite starving and literally freezing at night as he lay on the hard ground next to whatever water source he found, with each painful foot he gained during the day he consoled himself with the thought that he knew where he was going. Shivering, he stared up at the stars arcing across the sky and oriented himself by their movement. He then would convince himself he had been crawling all that previous day in the correct direction.

What Kalantarian did not know—despite his map and his ridgelines and his sun and his stars—was that he was not crawling on a heading that would return him to his camp. Neither was he going in the right direction to creep back to the route he originally had used to get here. His misdirection was also despite lights now being visible at night in the distance at the Clark Range Viewpoint on the Glacier Point Road. This "lights and siren" set up was part of the massive search for him—one combing a fifty-mile circumference of territory—and it was intended to give *him* some basis for orientation. Sadly, Kalantarian did in fact see the lights but he assumed they were merely shining from vehicles driving the Glacier Point Road. In short, Kalantarian was lost. He had been lost for days. But he did not know it.

The SAR effort led by John Dill enlisted 150 searchers, six helicopters, and six dog teams. These volunteers hailed from at least eighteen different agencies, only one of which was the Park itself. Margaret Colvin led rescuers directly to the place where she had dropped off Kalantarian days earlier. There his boot tracks still lay clear in the soil. Dill now sent climbers to the top of Mount Clark as well as to other summits nearby. Maybe Kalantarian had been really ambitious—or really lost. Frustratingly, none of these mountaineers hit pay dirt.

This multi-source team tried just about every trick in the SAR book. One question kept surfacing: Had Colvin remembered *everything* she had heard and seen regarding Kalantarian's plans? John Dill resorted to asking her to be hypnotized by an expert examiner. Maybe she would recall an additional critical detail this way that Kalantarian might have divulged to her about his specific route plans. Colvin agreed. This session worked. She now remembered far more about his pack and other gear—but nothing more about his plans.

Helicopters shuttled searchers hither and thither. One broke down. Another one flew low and slow right over Kalantarian. He painfully waved his shirt at them. He was certain they must have seen it. But they had not (despite popular thought, a helicopter search team is often the *least* likely type of searcher to locate a missing person). Coordinator Dill scrambled to keep the effort's intensity at a peak. Still no one found a trace. This missing 30 year-old seemed to have vanished.

Finally, on October 20, on the seventh day after Margaret Colvin had dropped off Kalantarian, searchers found boot prints matching his. They followed these, heading up Mount Clark along his ascent route. Next they found a cap with a "Yosemite" logo at the base of the steepest section of the route. A recent photograph of the missing man earlier taken as evidence revealed him wearing this same hat. The team sent this hat and hair samples from Kalantarian's tent housing in the Valley to a forensics lab in Fresno for identification. This process would not yield what anyone might term "timely" data that would guarantee discovering the missing man, but the team still needed to confirm the found items as his.

By noon the next day a "discarded" leather boot on a lower, forested slope caught someone's eye. Its sole pattern and size matched the lost man's tracks. How, these searchers wondered, had he lost his boot? About fifteen minutes later a nearby dog team discovered Kalantarian's pack 1¼ miles north of the boot. The backpack sat on the northwest ridge leading to the top. This was a logical place to leave one's gear during a summit bid. But the location of the boot revealed that the missing hiker had been somewhat off route if he was attempting to return to his pack.

An hour after finding the boot someone spotted drag marks trailing down slope through the woods. By this time almost a week had passed since the lost man had fallen those seventy feet into that tree.

Through skill and diligence, the searchers were able to stick with the often faint drag marks. In fact the team who found the first such marks immediately alerted other people downhill of them about these signs and the direction they were leading. Others now leap-frogged ahead, looking for fresher clues and hopefully the lost man himself.

This strategy worked. Within twenty-six minutes of finding the first drag marks searchers lower on the slope found the lost man. $115,704.76 worth of effort had finally located Kalantarian in the drainage 1¾ miles west of Mount Clark.

Amazingly, after crawling for five and a half days he was still alive. On top of this he had actually crept more than far enough to have reached his pack. But, again, he was so far off course that when informed of where he was versus his equipment, he was dumbfounded.

Given the mystery of his disappearance and the long delay before an alarm was rung, this effort was an incredible success—but for one sad detail; due to hypothermia, to nightly repeated freezing, and to consequent gangrene, both of Michael Kalantarian's feet had to be amputated. He also lost several fingers to frostbite.

Over twenty years earlier, another employee of the Curry Company had started out alone to scale the same 11,522-foot Mount Clark. On Tuesday, August 8, 1967, 21-year-old Tom Opperman of Fresno, working as a porter at the Tuolumne Meadows Lodge, left from Tuolumne Meadows (rather than from the Mono Meadows Trailhead, as Michael Kalantarian would). The college student and state-winning Fresno High School athlete (cross-country and wrestling) was hiking by way of Merced Lake. He planned to trek up a ridge on its eastern slope. This route was hard enough on its own, but Opperman also planned on retreating through Red Peak Pass and then hightailing it all the way to Glacier Point where he hoped to hitch a ride back to work. Moreover, he intended on doing all of this during just his two days off. Although his route was doable, pulling it off in two days would demand a Herculean effort by anyone's standards, even for a 21-year-old athlete.

On Tuesday, Opperman hiked to Merced Lake. He did well and moved fast. He soon met with Clyde Deal, Manager of the High Sierra Camp. Deal gave him instructions on a safe route up Mount Clark. Deal was familiar enough with the region to also be concerned with how hard the trip would be for the young man to accomplish in such a short time. As he watched Opperman vanish he wondered how much more this kid was biting off than he could chew.

On August 11, a day after Tom Opperman was to be back at work, his parents, staying at the Tuolumne Meadows Lodge, reported him overdue from his trek.

"Approximately 7,000 acres were searched by ground crews," Yosemite Superintendent John M. Davis would note in a memorandum to the NPS Regional Director on November 9, 1967. "[Another] 8,000 acres [were] intensively searched by helicopter, [and] 27,000 acres [were] generally covered by helicopter."

Sixteen Marines from the Mountain Warfare Center near Bridgeport, California joined this search and worked for three days with Park rangers on this mission. The searchers checked the summit register on Mount Clark as well as on several other peaks in the area. Opperman had signed none of them. No substantial clues appeared to suggest which way to go that might lead them to the lost man. So, on August 25, after two weeks of looking, the Park terminated this search.

Tom Opperman was never seen again.

But he was not the first person known to have vanished forever into the thin air of Yosemite. A 37-year-old jeweler from San Francisco who recently had emigrated from England was the first person known to have totally vanished in the Park. The missing man, F. P. Shepherd, was last seen on the afternoon of June 17, 1909, in the company of two female companions as he left the Glacier Point Hotel. Their goal was Sentinel Dome, only one mile away.

Soon a thick fog quickly rolled in and obscured visibility ahead. Shepherd kept trekking on, even though his two hiking companions wisely turned around. When he failed to return from his hike, the question of whether or not the British jeweler had made it up Sentinel Dome in the fog soon took a backseat to where he was at all.

Alerted about his disappearance, a detail of U.S. Cavalry spent the next four days "with rope ladders and grappling irons…descending the sheer cliffs which look down on the Illilouette falls and the rapids in the upper Merced Canyon." The dangers faced by these Army searchers—as well as to Shepherd himself—were not lost on the *San Francisco Chronicle* (on June 22, 1909 and on June 18, 1909, respectively):

> One slip on the part of the soldiers would send them to a terrible death thousands of feet to the rocks below.
>
> [and also] It is feared now that he may have been attacked by wild beasts or that in trying to find his way in the thick fog at night he may have fallen over some cliff and been dashed to death. If he is still alive he will be in a deplorable condition, as he is without food and blankets…chilling rain which has fallen in and around the valley will leave him in a badly weakened physical state.

Those working in the Park considered Shepherd's disappearance a "thoroughly needless accident." Reconstructing the lost hiker's actions, searchers decided that he "became excited when he found himself lost at nightfall, and that instead of building a fire and waiting until dawn he frantically dashed through the brush, fighting his way in the fog and darkness, and before he knew it he was dashed to pieces."

On June 21, the Army terminated its hunt for this hiker. "Shepherd is now considered to be beyond human aid, and the only object in continuing the hunt would be to save the unfortunate man's body from being left in the wilderness, a prey to birds and wild beasts."

How had Shepherd's mere one-mile hike gone so wrong? "[H]ad Shepherd remained on the trails which are all safe for pedestrians or saddle animals," noted Major W. W. Forsyth, the Park's Acting Superintendent, "he would be alive and safe today."

No sign of F. P. Shepherd was ever found.

Much has been written by authors determined to provide hikers, hunters, fishermen, campers, and other wilderness devotees with failsafe guidelines for how to avoid getting lost. Despite all their rhetoric, probably the first four "Cardinal Sins" committed by people who get so seriously lost that they cannot be found by searchers are simply: 1. not telling someone where they are going, 2. not leaving word on when they will be back, 3. hiking alone, and 4. detouring off-trail onto a hoped for shortcut. Shepherd had committed only error #3, then maybe error #4.

These days many hikers in the backcountry rely upon Global Positioning System (GPS) devices to tell them where they are. These operate by receiving radio transmissions from three or more (more is better) of twenty-four satellites (with two more up there as spares) placed in orbit 12,000 miles above Earth by the U.S. Military as its "NAVSTAR" program designed to provide nearly pinpoint accuracy on the planet's surface for navigation—and for targeting. For several recent years this system has been available with no financial charge for precise use by civilians. Indeed, GPS devices now costing less than $100 are so nifty that they have seduced many thousands of people in the outback into a false sense of security. Why false?

For several reasons. First, GPS units are mere mechanical electronic devices that can fail when damaged or when their batteries run low. Second, when the unit is forgotten and left hours behind on a log upon which one was sitting during a break, or lost otherwise, the user is instantly weaned into the confusion of real world terrain. Third, in thick forests or narrow canyons GPS units cannot attain a fix on enough satellites to provide accurate data. Worse—and this is true all of the time—GPS units can tell the user where he or she is and then plot a course to where the user wants to go, but the route plotted will not take into account intervening terrain which is hazardous—or impossible. In short, one must know how to navigate without a GPS unit to be safe using one. Indeed the prime rule for GPS use (articulated by Arizona's Coconino County Sheriff's Department SAR trainer

Art Pundt) is one that all too many outdoors enthusiasts have broken to their ultimate dismay: *"You should never substitute GPS use for sound map and compass skills. Be sure you have competent map and compass skills and cross check your GPS with these skills as you navigate."*

But why should anyone need navigation skills while following an NPS trail? Weren't these trails built to make it simple and easy? Arguably, under ideal circumstances, one does not need a high level of skill (if one can read the trail signs…). On the other hand, when snow, fog, washouts, nightfall, vandalism or some other factor has concealed trail markers, or when one has inadvertently wandered off-trail and cannot relocate it, possessing the skills to know where one is can be very useful. No skill with electronics can safely replace that of being able to read an appropriately scaled and drawn topographic map. Or of using a quality compass. Or, better yet, of being able to use a topo map in combination with a compass. Or, best yet, using every natural orientation feature out there, terrestrial or celestial.

Most people agree that prevention is preferable to seeking a cure. The same holds for avoiding becoming lost instead of panicking after the fact. The primary preventative measure is to continually pay attention to where one is. By regularly asking oneself "where am I right now?" (then answering that question), one can never become hopelessly lost. Looking behind oneself to learn and memorize what the terrain looks like on your return route is also vital. Beyond these habits and the dedicated use of map and compass (and a GPS unit) there exist tricks to help prevent getting lost.

Many of these tricks—using an "attack point," a "catch feature," a "handrail," "check points," "funnel features" and "aiming off"—apply to situations where one is forced to navigate off-trail. An *attack point* is simply a very recognizable point of intersection between two major features—a trail and a river, a road and a power line—as the *origin* point to begin one's off-trail hike. A *catch feature* refers to a planned "collision" of one's route against something with a wide horizontal presence—a stream, trail, ridgeline, road, or power line. A *handrail* refers to planning part of one's route to parallel a terrain feature with wide horizontal presence closely enough to use it visually as a guide. *Check points* refer to knowing in advance a series of recognizable landmarks one should encounter en route to one's destination. Using *funnel features* means planning part of one's route between two nonparallel handrail-like features and toward their intersection. *Aiming off* applies to situations where one is shooting for a pinpoint location such as a parked vehicle. A direct aim that misses it imposes the need to either turn right or left. But which way? Each direction offers a 50 percent chance of success—or of missing it and then hiking a long distance away (then turning around to hike back but maybe not far enough and then end up freaking out). If instead one deliberately aims too far right or too far left of one's pinpoint destination then hits the road or trail, one merely turns onto the road in the known compensatory direction and hoofs it confidently to the point of interest.

Okay, what if one gets lost despite all of these measures?

Because panic and impulsive action when lost are proven killers many times over, nearly every expert agrees that **the ultimate key to survive being lost resides solely in keeping one's head, in assuming full responsibility for one's actions, emotions, and situation, and in possessing (or adopting) a positive mental attitude and a powerful will to survive.** This self-responsibility then allows a lost person to STOP! This acronym translates to *Stop* where you are, calmly *Think* hard and unhurriedly about your precise situation and your resources (map, compass, GPS, cell phone, whistle, field glasses, signal mirror, survival gear), *Observe* your surroundings carefully to identify its clues, resources, and dangers, then *Plan* (including a plan "A" and a plan "B") for your return hike or your rescue and extrication. Your plan of action may dictate staying where you are—but this should also be in an open area where you are discoverable. Or instead it might involve careful backtracking to the last place where you *knew* exactly where you were. One's plan should not involve shortcutting. Nor should any part of any plan *ever* be subservient to salvaging one's personal pride. Survival is the goal, not a good score card.

Despite all these lifesaving guidelines the bottom line remains: *Nothing replaces intelligent prior planning and doing one's homework to avoid altogether the possibility of getting lost.*

Getting—and staying—lost often requires having made more than one error. Indeed it usually requires a chain of mistakes. For one of the weirdest examples of this, and even more than this, consider this next one from another national park. It unfolded in August of 1999 when two buddies—David Coughlin and Raffi Kodikian—arrived in New Mexico's Carlsbad Caverns National Park during a cross-country road trip from Massachusetts. Coughlin was about to enter a graduate program in the Donald Bren School of Environmental Science and Management connected to the University of California at Santa Barbara. Kodikian, his closest buddy for years, was a journalism graduate accompanying him on this last hurrah together before they went their separate ways in life. On August 4, the pair signed up for their overnight permit. Coughlin next bought a topo map at the local bookstore while Kodikian purchased three pints of water and a quart of Gatorade at the gift store (instead of hauling the two gallons of water recommended by the Park). Next the pair drove five miles and parked Coughlin's car at the trailhead into Rattlesnake Canyon. From here they backpacked more than a mile and camped at sunset.

As Jason Kersten notes in his provocative *Journal of the Dead: a Story of Friendship and Murder in the New Mexico Desert*, no one had ever vanished in Carlsbad's 47,000 acres during its entire sixty-nine-year history as a park. But on August 8, after noting that a car had been parked for multiple days on the road at the trailhead, Ranger Lance Mattson decided to hike down and see if something was amiss. About half an hour later the ranger found Raffi Kodikian bivouacked 275 feet from the trail leading out of Rattlesnake Canyon to the paved road and also still within view of the cairns marking that trail.

Mattson gave the 25-year-old man a water bottle. Next he asked: "Where's your buddy?"

"Over there," Kodikian answered, pointing toward a long pile of rocks about thirty feet away.

As Mattson stared toward the stones but still failed to see a person near them, Kodikian added an explanation, "I killed him."

A moment later the young man added, "He begged me to do it."

Mattson's mind shifted into high gear as he stared at the macabre scene. The camp was a mess of scattered food wrappers and gear. Sitting under a semi-shredded tent, Kodikian, black-mustached and dressed only in shorts, bore superficial-appearing injuries to his forearms. Only thirty feet away, David Coughlin apparently lay buried under a heap of boulders, some of them weighing more than fifty pounds each.

Kodikian added that he had stabbed Coughlin through the heart only six hours earlier.

Mattson wondered: What the hell had gone wrong here?

The short version is, after camping that first night the two buddies could not relocate the trail to their car. They also felt that hiking cross-country out of the canyon via its sloping sides was impossible. As Jason Kersten notes further in his *Journal of the Dead*, in an attempt to find their way out they hiked up the side of Rattlesnake Canyon opposite from that which they had entered. The pair had rimmed out 700 feet above their bivouac site. Although they now found themselves in equally arid surroundings, they could see water towers and buildings off in the distance. Here, the two were about eight miles from the main highway. Kodikian said he did not feel that he had the energy to make that long a hike. Further complicating things, neither man was able to understand (or read) the topographic map Coughlin had bought. So the two men had scrambled back down to their makeshift camp. There they had stalled out and simply waited for Park Rangers to rescue them (their expectation of this was based on their being overdue as per the dates on their camping permit). To help this happen they built a small "SOS" from rocks on the canyon floor. Barring rescue, they would die where they were.

As their thirst grew ever worse, Kodikian said, and vultures circled overhead, the friends finally forged a suicide pact as the ultimate escape from their dehydration-incited misery. Coughlin's pain, he added, seemed to exceed his own.

As responding Chief Ranger Mark Maciha, a veteran of several very hot, dry national parks, would note (to Ghiglieri), Kodikian's behavior during his first hour of rescue seemed incongruous. The self-admitted killer appeared far from incapacitated. Instead he seemed almost chipper. He chided the rangers and wisecracked "My grandmother can fly a Blackhawk faster than those Army boys can."

(Ranger Mattson had called for this SAR response from Fort Bliss). Maciha admitted that some of the details of that day still fail to quit flopping like beached fish. For one thing, Kodikian felt the need to urinate in the emergency room after his rescue ("how dehydrated could he have been?"). For another, the rocks Kodikian had used to bury his murdered buddy weighed at least fifty pounds each: "If he had the strength to lift these rocks, why didn't they walk out?" Another strange fact was that Kodikian had been carrying in Coughlin's car a textbook on criminal justice, yet Kodikian had majored in journalism. Moreover, on the day of his rescue, Kodikian hired the most famous and successful murder defense attorney in New Mexico. Even more contributory to Ranger Maciha's chagrin, he never saw Kodikian exhibit remorse.

Kersten reports that Kodikian went before the court for a hearing on second degree murder. He decided to plea bargain and to plead no contest, thus avoiding a jury trial.

An autopsy later revealed Coughlin to have been about 12 percent ("moderately") dehydrated, well short of a fatal level. His kidneys had still been functioning. Possibly exacerbating his discomfort, however, Coughlin had been eating prickly pear fruits, a few of which were likely unripe. When not ripe, these *tunas* tend to spur painful stomach cramps. Medical Investigator Dr. Dennis Klein concluded that had Coughlin not been stabbed, he would have lived quite a while longer.

The serrated edge of the stout, lock-blade knife found on scene, the investigation would reveal, was *still* sharp. It had been sharp enough to slice through Coughlin's chest and fatally sever his heart with two strokes—and it had remained sharp enough to sever Kodikian's wrists. The killer's failure to carry out his end of the suicide pact by slitting his own wrists, claimed the prosecutor, had not been through dullness of the blade but instead through Kodikian's lack of commitment to commit suicide.

Chief District Judge Jay Forbes, notes Kersten, found Kodikian guilty of voluntary manslaughter and sentenced him to fifteen years in prison. Forbes then suspended thirteen of these. Kodikian ultimately served sixteen months in New Mexico State Prison near Santa Rosa before being released for good behavior.

According to Kersten's research, Kodikian's "mercy homicide" of David Coughlin is the only known case of one lost person killing another with dehydration as the putative primary ailment of the victim. Of course even this oddity begs the question of how two otherwise capable and intelligent young men could feel compelled to bivouac in the Chihuahuan Desert in summer and remain lost for days in a short, five-mile-long canyon that ended a couple of miles downcanyon by trail at Rattlesnake Springs and how they also decided to park themselves to die a mere 275 feet from the one-mile trail leading to their car and about eighty feet from the marker for that trail. For a deeper look at this classic example of being lost in an American national park, we refer the interested reader to Kersten's book. At least one lesson here is: Take responsibility for *knowing and understanding* your route exactly—before you leave the pavement.

A macabre postscript now exists to Kersten's unsuccessful quest to find some other example of a suicide pact spurred by dehydration while lost in the desert. During a BORSTAR (U.S. Border Patrol Search, Trauma and Rescue) field course on tracking Ghiglieri learned from Agent David Hagee of a unique rescue that took place on August 4, 2006. The BORSTAR team had responded to two Hispanics, one 26 years old and the other 21. They had been traveling across the hot desert west of Organ Pipe National Monument with a group of illegals immigrating north. The group had abandoned the two and moved on. After three days lost with neither food nor water and in temperatures exceeding 110 degrees the two men had decided their torture exceeded even the power of their early inculcation by the dictates of Catholicism. They formed a suicide-murder pact to escape the final throes of agony to dehydration.

One man prepared himself by carving into his own chest the words in Spanish: "Forgive me, Mother, for what I'm about to do." He then stabbed the other in the inner thigh, attempting to sever his partner's femoral artery. The stabbed partner then reciprocated by stabbing the branded one in the neck, aiming to sever his carotid artery or jugular vein.

Both men thrusted deeply and in full expectation of mercy killing the other. Both, however, missed the critical blood vessels. One was now unable to turn his head due to his neck wound, the other barely able to walk due to his punctured leg. But neither bled much. Realizing they had failed, the pair next decided to leap off a cliff. As they hobbled toward a likely one, they saw a dirt road below. Dust rose as a U.S. Border Patrol vehicle drove by. Suddenly infused with a renewed desire to live, the two injured, dehydrated men hurried, reeling downslope to the road. When they reached it the vehicle had already passed. Stoically, the two near wraiths of the desert waited in the sand. An hour later the vehicle returned. The Patrol radioed BORSTAR, who evacuated them by helicopter to a hospital.

So, yes, a mercy killing based on dehydration *can* happen.

Back in Yosemite the legacy of Frank J. Koenman offers another example of the ease of vanishing. On May 31, 1925, he checked into Tent #156 of Camp Curry. In that era it was customary for strangers to share a tent. Despite this economizing by Curry Company, its desk clerk did not add a roommate to Tent #156 for ten days. On that tenth day, June 9, Walter Hancock took up residence in the same quarters but he stayed for only a single night.

On June 18, Koenman's employer in San Francisco called Camp Curry on "the long distance telephone" and inquired about him. He had failed to report back to work as planned during the previous week.

Curry Company's desk clerks checked Tent #156. After a few false starts they found that Koenman still had his suitcase, a camera case, and a large hat in the tent when Mr. Hancock had checked out. They incorrectly assumed at first this property belonged to Hancock because they found a tag in the two men's shared tent with

Hancock's name on it. Now, upon opening the abandoned suitcase, they found its contents to be the property of Koenman. Realizing finally that one of their guests had become a missing person, Curry Company turned over Koenman's goods to Park rangers, who began investigating.

In the meantime, Walter Hancock had taken a job as a clerk at the local ice cream parlor and had taken up living in the public campground. When the rangers finally found him he told them he had last seen his one-night roommate on June 10. On that date Koenman had told Hancock he planned to hike to Inspiration Point. Further investigation found another person who had seen Koenman "leaving the camp on the morning of June 11 or 12, he could not remember which, at which time he had his camera on his back and was headed in the direction of Yosemite Falls."

This destination being on the opposite side and end of the Valley from Inspiration Point, searchers now faced a wider search area. Too wide, apparently. The *Superintendent's Monthly Report* for June of 1925 summarized:

> Every possible clue has been followed and the rangers have made a number of trips around the rim of the valley looking for places where a person might fall, but nothing has been found. It is feared that Mr. Koenman, who is quite a photographer, climbed to some point or cliff to take a picture and fell to his death, but there has been nothing to indicate this except his continued absence.

The lessons? Had Koenman hiked with a companion, left word as to his destination, and said when he would return, he might have lived. Instead, he violated all three simple cardinal rules. And what's left of him is still out there somewhere.

In the summer of 1954 two major searches for missing young men in Yosemite emerged notorious—so notorious that they are still occasionally referred to today. Despite having vanished nearly three months apart the two missing people shared uncanny similarities. Both were young men; both were graduate students from the University of California at Berkeley; and both felt drawn to the Yosemite backcountry on solo hikes. These commonalities plus what emerged in the Park's searches for them have firmly planted them in the Park's collective "SAR memory."

The first of these notables was 26-year-old Walter A. Gordon. He was a Phi Beta Kappa research fellow in history who worked as a summer desk clerk at Curry Village. At 1 p.m. on Tuesday, July 20, he packed a light lunch and told fellow clerk Jerry Johnson that he was going to hike alone up the Ledge Trail. He also said he would be back by 5 p.m.

Gordon failed to return on time. Because he was considered extremely punctual and well organized—and an able hiker—his buddies immediately reported him as missing. Rangers began looking that night.

The searchers questioned employees at the Glacier Point Hotel at the upper end of the very steep Ledge Trail, 3,000 feet above Curry Village. No one had seen Gordon. Rangers looked for signs of him along the road at the top. They found none. At this point Chief Ranger Oscar Sedegren, a veteran of many Yosemite searches, decided to wait until the mid-morning before ringing the panic bell. He imagined that darkness itself comprised the main reason why their overdue hiker was slow in returning. If Gordon was even only half as smart as the rangers had been led to believe, then he would have just hunkered down and sat tight and waited until daylight made it safe to move.

Walter Gordon, however, did not appear with the sun. Now the Chief Ranger shifted into a higher gear. The *San Francisco Chronicle* (on July 25, 1954) monitored the story. "The search by rangers afoot, on horseback or hanging from ropes down the precipitous walls of rough granite," it informed its readers, "began Wednesday." For the first several days, searchers thoroughly checked trails in and out of the Valley. They also scoured the bases of the cliffs in the immediate area. Far above, a team of four rangers rappelled down the walls near the Ledge Trail. They inspected ledges and ravines as they went. Volunteer crews drawn from Gordon's coworkers searched nearby along the Merced River—maybe the summer heat had spurred the Phi Beta Kappa scholar to take an ill-fated swim instead of continuing to hike.

On day five, the escalating search added air recon to its tool kit. An open-cockpit, two-person crop-dusting helicopter out of Fresno flew three hours "low and slow" over the few passable routes Gordon might have followed in the Glacier Point area. The aerial searchers spotted no sign of the missing man. The pilot parked in a meadow just in case he was needed to fly Gordon out should he be found injured. This marked the second time in Yosemite SAR history that a helicopter was used. How had the aerial search missed him? "Gordon may have fallen beneath a concealing boulder," explained the Park, "or may have been injured and crawled from the trail to shelter."

Chief Ranger Sedegren used the news-hungry media to send a message of prevention to the public. "This is why we emphasize the three rules that Sierra hikers should always follow. Never start out without telling someone where you're going, never go alone, and never leave the beaten trail."

On day six the searchers conscripted three bloodhounds owned by Deputy Sheriff Norman Wilson of San Jose. These dogs had proved their abilities elsewhere in California. Within an hour after arriving, the team sniffed a piece of Gordon's clothing taken from his tent then lunged up the start of the Ledge Trail. The hounds quickly alerted to a scent trail. They seemed to stay with the scent all the way up to Glacier Point. But they did not sniff out the missing Gordon.

Over the next two days, these dogs twice ascended the Ledge Trail and circled back down the Four-Mile Trail. Both times and in both directions, the bloodhounds signaled a positive response. The dogs were insisting that Gordon had made this hike along this route. Why then, the rangers wondered in frustration, could the canines not find their man?

"Gordon May Be Out Of The Park" read the July 28 *Fresno Bee* headline. Experts now suggested amnesia as a possible culprit. This led to investigating a variety of outside leads. They all led nowhere.

Had Gordon purposely vanished—as father-to-be David Cunningham would do in 1978? Gordon's friends and family said they did not believe so. He was too responsible for that sort of antic.

Ten days of searching exhausted every lead and resource. At this point (although later Yosemite searches would prove successful even after twelve days), the Park terminated its search for the 26-year-old scholar. Half a century later we still have no clue as to what happened. Maybe one will emerge someday—from under a rock ledge or instead from an obscure, small-town obituary—to explain what happened to Walter Gordon.

Only eighty days after Walter Gordon vanished in spite of the massive search for him, so did Orvar F. von Laass. This 30-year-old Ph.D. candidate in economics at U.C., Berkeley registered at the Ahwahnee Hotel with his wife and parents. Von Laass had been in America for four years, but he had done some mountaineering in his native Sweden before coming here. At 2 p.m. on October 9, 1954, he borrowed a pair of field glasses and expressed an interest in "reaching an eminence from where he could see various falls and peaks." He told his wife he would be back in two hours and would meet them all for supper. Next he started off on his short, but vaguely described hike across the Sugar Pine Bridge. From there he headed up canyon.

He never came back.

The search for von Laass began at daybreak. It too fell under the command of Chief Ranger Oscar Sedegren. Comments by the missing man's wife convinced Sedegren that the overdue husband had probably headed directly for the base of the Royal Arches, an imposing, overhanging granite wall that rises 1,800 feet directly above where the von Laass family was staying. First climbed in 1936, the technical Royal Arches route remained the only feasible way up the cliff to that spectacular view von Laass had been seeking. By 1954, it had become popular among rock climbers. Sedegren focused here.

Veteran Park Ranger John Henneberger and newly appointed Seasonal Ranger Jack Morehead (who recently had served in the Army's famed Tenth Mountain Division and later would become Chief Ranger then Superintendent of Yosemite) searched the base of this trendy climb. Other rangers worked both ways along the cliff for about a mile. Searchers sectioned off the amazingly jumbled talus slope above the Ahwahnee Hotel with string then thoroughly searched every grid. The scatter of talus here includes many house-sized boulders behind or under which the would-be economist could have been lying hurt or dead. Rangers methodically searched under each one.

On day two, climbers from the Sierra Club's newly formed Mountain Rescue

Service joined the rangers by nosing into nooks and crannies on the arching cliff above the Valley. Five men scrambled over its lower ledges and gullies. Meanwhile a second team of three, including Henneberger and Morehead, walked in from the Tioga Road above and spent the day rappelling down the 1,800-foot high smooth granite wall, searching as they went.

Sheriff's Deputy Norm Wilson again brought in his bloodhounds from San Jose. And, just as they had done with Walter Gordon, the dogs quickly alerted. Repeatedly, the hounds kept returning to the bottom of Royal Arches, leading everyone to rule out the idea that Orvar von Laass had gone anywhere else. But as the days continued to pass and searching revealed absolutely no trace of von Laass, speculation intensified that he no longer was even in the Park.

The eerie nature of the utter and complete disappearance of von Laass and of Gordon led to relatives of both men jointly suggesting the Berkeley students may have been victims of foul play. "The trails of the two ended near roads," Gordon's brother-in-law, Jack Delson, pointed out in the October 23 *Los Angeles Times*. "They could not have been injured in falls or swept away by rivers...it makes me wonder whether they didn't fall victims to foul play, maybe even murder."

In early November, after about a month, the Park finally ended its efforts to find von Laass. But during the many dark months of the ensuing winter, rangers in Yosemite openly shook their heads in befuddlement over the dual mysteries of Gordon and von Laass.

Today, more than a half century later, what fate befell either young man will probably never be known. Their unsolved disappearances continue to tantalize us.

Six years before von Laass crossed the Sugar Pine Bridge on his one way trip to oblivion and before Walter Gordon vanished on his trek to Glacier Point, another young man started the same trip to Glacier Point and probably ended up the same way. Maybe even in the same spot. The man was Malcolm McClintock, an 18-year-old student from Glendale, California who was visiting the Park with his family. The teenager was last seen on August 8, 1948, leaving Camp 7. "Exhaustive searches have been made and all clues followed," noted the *Superintendent's Monthly Report,* "but to date no tangible evidence of his whereabouts or what may have happened to him have been gained."

Malcolm McClintock too was never found.

Sometimes, people disappear under such benign circumstances that one has to wonder how it was even possible. On July 18, 1943, 62-year-old Emerson Holt from Southern California had almost completed a fairly routine group hike to Merced Lake. Needing a break from his long sweaty trek, he paused along the well-defined trail a mile short of their destination. His fishing companions bid him adieu and said they would see him at the lake. They went ahead without him. Holt was never heard from again nor was any clue to his disappearance ever found by searchers. What happened to him still remains an utter mystery.

Getting lost is a lot more common than one might imagine. Illustrating this, on July 5, 1952, the *Mariposa Gazette* ran an article titled "Rangers advise 'watch your child,'" noting that already in that year *twenty-six children had been lost in Yosemite*—one of these kids had vanished for more than thirty hours. How easily these incidents can happen is illustrated by one five years later, on August 10, 1957. On that day young Terry Dunbar of Portland, Oregon was hiking with a large family group. When it split into slow and fast factions on the Yosemite Falls Trail, he managed to become separated. Each group thought Terry was safely hiking with the other one. When the group reunited and found that Terry was gone, his parents quickly reported him as missing.

Rangers cruised up and down the trail. This was not the sort of terrain where wandering off the path routinely leads to pleasant meanderings. Instead, nearly every detour could lead to tragedy. So after the SAR team searched all day and into the night and then *all through the night* and still discovered no sign, each searcher felt in his heart that little Terry Dunbar would never be found alive.

The next morning the SAR team enlisted bloodhounds. As Ranger Jack Morehead, assisted by Rangers Frank Doig and Dick Pack, recalls to us half a century later:

> I was with the dogs and their trainer when we started searching in the morning. The dogs stopped and looked off the trail at one spot. The trainer told me it was very unusual, and it probably needed to be looked into. I rigged a rappel and went down 50 to 70 feet, calling Terry's name as I went.
>
> I got a reply. I pendulumed over to the near vertical crack where he had spent the night. He was right above a cliff below the trail. If he had slipped another couple of feet he would have fallen all the way.
>
> After we were hauled up I asked him why he stayed in one place after he had wandered off the trail and slipped/fallen to where he had spent the night. He said he had heard snakes and was afraid to move around anymore. Good snakes! (or ground squirrels, more likely).

That this mission had proven a success is unquestioned. But you might still be wondering: Just how old was this Terry Dunbar, who had perched in his T-shirt and shorts all night (fifteen hours in total) in his high-anxiety location a mere one step from a cliff dropping hundreds of feet down?

Terry was six.

In June of 1932, as 4-year-old Carrie Lou Lenz's parents set up their tent at Camp 14 in Happy Isles, she wandered off alone barefooted and in her bathing suit to meander along the Merced. She never returned.

A quick search by her parents produced nothing but rising panic. Soon every available ranger, assisted by campers, combed the area (they thought). No one found any sign of her. Very early in this search the question arose: Had Carrie Lou fallen into the Merced and drowned?

Late the next morning Ranger Scott found Carrie Lou more than half a mile away sitting on a rock "east of Happy Isles" and quietly crying. Aside from a few scratches, she was in perfect condition. Carrie Lou Lenz's overnight adventure illustrates one of the differences between lost children and lost adults. Young children who realize they are lost usually (though not universally) do not go far, do not go into ridiculous places (as Terry Dunbar did), frequently do hunker down into a protected spot, and often even hide from the "strangers" who are searching for them—even when those adults are calling out the child's own name. In contrast, adults usually do plod onward in meandering routes, sometimes to places far from where they got lost; adults frequently trap themselves in ridiculous places; and when many adults finally do hunker down, they do so in less protected spots than most 4 year-olds would choose.

In Yosemite *many* adults have gotten themselves lost. And again, in contrast to children, instead of staying put and going to sleep in some protected place, many adults keep going like the Energizer Bunny, getting more lost and even harder to find. In July of 1959, 38-year-old Maria Lip of Merced walked off by herself, wearing shorts and tennis shoes, to visit the big trees of the Mariposa Grove. Then she vanished. She was a native of Holland but had been living in America for six years during which she had visited Yosemite as an "experienced" hiker.

Her disappearance led to a 114-hour search by seventy-five men (including volunteers from the Seventh Day Adventist Church Camp and from Castle Air Force Base near her home town of Merced) aided by bloodhounds and airplanes. Four days of this did not uncover her whereabouts. After nearly five days, Clyde Barber, caretaker of the church camp near Wawona and a veteran of several SAR missions, finally found the missing woman holed up scratched and exhausted in a box canyon tributary of the Merced.

"We are proud of the rescue of a woman lost for five days," noted Superintendent John C. Preston. "But it took a lot of shoe leather and we nearly exhausted all of our resources."

What did Lip have to say about her experience? "I just got lost—I don't know how, but I did."

What did Superintendent Preston offer for advice to future hikers? "Never get off the trail and don't hike alone."

If Lip's experience sounds naïve, remember, even rangers get lost. As reported by the *Mariposa Gazette* on June 28, 1934, Ranger William J. Corless of Kansas City set off on a solo "training" hike from Tenaya Lake to the Valley. He was supposed to simply follow the standard route, not invent a cross-country one. After he failed to appear, it took forty rangers assisted by "Indian trackers" three days to find him. Corless, the searchers learned after an epic of bushwhacking, had left the trail and ended up trapped in Tenaya Canyon. Luckily it was June, a warm month. This made the lost man's problems fairly minor. He merely felt very hungry and exhausted and likely humiliated.

No, Ranger Corless probably did not get a passing grade on his training hike. But he did get assigned to go back on duty right away.

Whenever any high-profile search takes place in Yosemite to the point where one feels prompted to ask "how big was the search?" the answer is not as straightforward as one might hope. The magnitude of a SAR mission can be defined several different ways. These include: manpower used, financial cost, days spent, area covered, complexity of the region requiring searches, and variety of modes of searching (aircraft, SCUBA, rock-climbing, et cetera). The magnitudes of each of the largest searches in Yosemite National Park over history must be measured by "all of the above."

One we have not talked about yet illustrates this. Stacey Anne Arras was a bright 14 year-old from Saratoga, near San Francisco. On July 17, 1981, the teenager was doing a four-day saddle "loop trip" of the Park's famed High Sierra Camps with her father George. Their tour—ten people and a wrangler—left the concession stables at Tuolumne Meadows. They stopped for lunch at Upper Cathedral Lake and then climbed back in the saddle. At 3 p.m., after an exhilarating but relatively easy Friday's ride, the girl and her dad arrived at their first overnight stop, Sunrise High Sierra Camp.

Established in 1961, this camp sits just below the tree line of mixed conifers at 9,600 feet. It is about nine miles from the Tioga Road by way of the John Muir Trail and four airline miles southeast of Tenaya Lake. The setting is glorious. It looks over the western edge of a broad meadow dotted with small lakes and ponds, glaciated domes, cliffs, and rocky granite ridges.

The energetic girl unpacked, took a quick shower, and settled into their rustic tent cabin. But she also needed to work out new kinks from her day in the saddle and wanted to stretch her legs. So she started off with 70-year-old Gerald Stuart—who had also ridden in that day—on an easy, mile-and-a-half hike west to Sunrise Lakes. Along the way they hoped to enjoy the grand views overlooking the vast backcountry. Several trails existed here. Enough to be confusing. They soon asked directions from a camp employee, then from backpackers, and finally from wrangler Chris Grimes.

Finally on the trail, it took mere moments for Stuart to become winded at this elevation. He stopped to rest. The teenage girl continued onward. On the trail only fifty yards above the corral, Stacey Arras stood on a rock and gazed into the distance. Wrangler Grimes saw her up there as he worked in the corral below. His casual glimpse of her would soon become important. Grimes was about to become the last person on Earth known to have seen her.

Despite an extensive, nine-day search that included 8,004 man-hours and fifty-seven hours of helicopter time by four different agencies, no clue as to what happened to her was ever found. The search effort cost $99,845. Up to that time, the hunt for Stacey Arras was probably the largest ever by most measurements (although this total would be overshadowed before the end of the 1980s).

Unfortunately, young Arras would not be the last person to vanish in Yosemite. At 9 a.m. on Tuesday, July 5, 1988, friends dropped off 24-year-old Timothy John Barnes from Cucamonga, California at the Murphy Creek Trailhead. Barnes intended on making a day hike from here at the northwest end of Tenaya Lake to Polly Dome Lakes then back. His route first followed the trail then veered up the drainage. His roundtrip should total less than eight miles. Barnes now told his friends he would be back at their site in the Tenaya Lake Walk-in Campground by 3:30 p.m. Then he started hiking.

Into, it would seem, infinity.

Barnes, his buddies later told investigators, was tall and lanky and in at least average condition. They also said he was a solid hiker with several years of experience. Moreover, he was a moderately experienced (5.3 to 5.6) climber. So far so good. The plot thickened when people who knew him began to describe his emotional life.

Barnes, it would turn out, was on probation for a prior arrest. One friend insisted that Barnes "loves his 17-month-old son and wife." Some of the interviewees, though, intimated that he might have problems because he had married early and felt shackled by child obligations, because he lacked the freedom to go climbing every weekend and felt jealous of the freedom of his unmarried friends to do so, and because he was working a dead-end job. Possibly significant too was that he had mentioned three times in the past month his wanting to go hike alone.

Investigators searched for Barnes and for clues of Barnes. They thought they found five. Four turned out negative. The fifth was merely a footprint at the nearby Tenaya Lake Campground. Searchers thought—with 75-percent certainty—the print was his. This dearth of signs and clues fertilized the nagging suspicion among some that Barnes was not lost at all; instead he had intentionally absconded from Yosemite to start a new life as had David Cunningham who made his great escape at the beginning of this chapter. Unlike Cunningham, however, Barnes was never heard from again.

Whatever had happened to Timothy John Barnes in reality, the process of finding no significant trace of him had cost $178,501. More man-hours—11,912 of them—were dedicated to this 1988 mission than to any other search in the entire history of Yosemite SAR. Ever.

Until 2005.

More than $452,000 was spent in 2005 trying to find Michael Ficery. The 51 year-old from Santa Barbara, California had gone hiking alone in the Tiltill Valley area northeast of Hetch Hetchy on June 21st then never returned. A lot of late spring snow still blanketed the backcountry. Once the SAR mission for him began, logistics and safety considerations dictated transporting searchers over swollen creeks and around difficult snowfields by helicopter to "spot place" them.

The effort to locate Ficery unfolded in two phases. The first lasted more than a week in June and yielded absolutely no results. The second probe took place in early October when it was suggested that he might be possibly in a different drainage than originally believed. Now, because the creeks were dry and the snowfields had melted, it was easier to transport searchers into these rugged areas. Easier or not, as of the end of 2006, still no one has turned up any sign of Ficery.

Because Ficery disappeared recently, there may remain a chance that someone yet will find a clue—clothing, bones, camping gear—of his fate in some obscure pocket of the Park. This sort of unexpected discovery long after a victim has been lost seemingly forever has happened in the past.

Early on the morning of September 14, 1972, I (Farabee) was called into the office by the Park Chief Law Enforcement Officer Lee Shackelton. My assignment, Lee explained, was to take a shovel, lots of drinking water, and accompany "John Jones" back up Tenaya Canyon. "Mr. Jones"—whose name has been changed here for reasons soon to become clear—had found a human knuckle bone two days earlier. Because of the location of Jones' little find, Lee and Chief Ranger Jack Morehead were now nursing a mutual hunch that the digit belonged to Quin Charles Frizzell.

How would anyone be able to tell this much simply from staring at one little bone? Lee had been on the original, unsuccessful search for Frizzell and knew all too much about him (with the exception of exactly what had happened to him in the end). I, on the other hand, had never heard of this guy.

Even so, when Frizzell had gone missing on June 4, 1966, he had created a stir that sent ripples all the way to Washington, D.C. Frizzell was a 31-year-old scientist working at the Lawrence Livermore National Laboratory about thirty miles east of San Francisco. He had vanished while hiking to the Valley from Tenaya Lake. The week-long, intensive search for the man had revealed no clue whatsoever. He seemed to have vanished into thin air.

Due to Frizzell's professional focus on nuclear science within the nation's premier weapons lab, suspicions immediately bubbled during this, the height of America's Cold War paranoia, that he had defected to the Russians. In fact, the original SAR mission to find the missing scientist had been subjected to such intense pressure that it became the impetus for the formation of the now well-respected Bay Area Mountain Rescue Unit.

Again the Park's search effort in 1966 had turned up nothing on Frizzell. Almost five years later, on April 8, 1971, a clue finally emerged. A hiker found a human skull and credit cards on a stairway of obscure cliffs at the base of Mount Watkins, up Tenaya Canyon from Mirror Lake. The Park investigated this site intensively but uncovered no other remains or clues—until the next year, 1972, when Chief Shackelton called me in to his office.

Scrambling well off the beaten path, Mr. Jones had stumbled across the exact obscure spot where the ill-fated Frizzell had crashed to a halt six years earlier. Now, after a hot scramble up to this obscure place, Jones and I stared at the hard evidence.

A pair of weathered boots lay side by side on the ground. I picked one up. A wreck of a ragged sock remained inside it. I felt lumps inside this rag. Naked foot bones rattled around in the tattered sock. Nearby a shredded, faded backpack hung from a tree limb.

Jones and I spent a major part of that sweltering Thursday poking under rocks, looking in crevices, and trying to guess where scavenging animals might have dragged the still missing remains of the lost nuclear scientist. We eventually located more than a hundred of his bones. I took photos. Lots of them. To document the scene.

But I had other instructions beyond the normal protocols of recording the scene of a fatal accident. After the discovery of the skull the year before, Frizzell's widow had asked the Park to discreetly inter, in place, whatever might be found of the man. Having never buried a person before and ignorant of the niceties involved, I dug a shallow, two-foot-square "grave" then placed all the once scattered bones into it. I then filled the hole with dirt. Probably due to having watched far too many old cowboy movies, I decided it was only proper to then lay a cross of rocks on top of what was left of Quin Charles Frizzell.

Jones and I had not been merely on a bone hunt. Again, I was also conducting an investigation of a fatal episode. I tried to analyze the scene as we searched then dug. It appeared to me that Frizzell had fallen and tumbled at least 100 feet. But, from the way his pack seemed intentionally placed, the lost hiker may have been conscious for at least a short time after hitting bottom—long enough to set his pack up in that tree as a distress signal. We will never know for sure what happened. One can only hope he did not suffer long.

Jones and I then headed down to Tenaya Creek and to some very welcome shade. The cool water proved refreshing beyond words. As we sat, and after I had thanked him for his gracious assistance, he quietly pulled a softball-sized baggy of "grass" out of his backpack and nonchalantly asked if he could toke up—

This was 1972 and the middle of Yosemite's hippie era. As it was in much of California, use of marijuana now in the Park was often blatant. Most young people in the Valley seemed to partake. That Jones wanted to light up after gathering up and burying a lost nuclear scientist did not particularly surprise me. But as a ranger with law enforcement responsibilities, he now had me over a moral barrel.

On the other hand, Jones had been very much a Good Samaritan. He had spent his entire day—a blisteringly hot one at that—up there on hard granite helping me locate every little bit of what was left of Frizzell and then helped give those remains a "proper" burial. "Okay, go ahead and light up." I finally told him as I unwrapped my much anticipated Velveeta cheese sandwich, "But if I see you tomorrow, you're going to jail!"

Despite my promise of dire consequences in the future, he savored his joint.

As noted earlier, the strange case of Quin Charles Frizzell was not unique. While hiking in Little Yosemite Valley on July 17, 1997, Park visitor Stacy Denney found a human mandible with a few teeth still rattling in their sockets. This gruesome little find was located 400 yards upstream from the campground and only ten feet from the edge of the Merced River. Despite further searching over the next several days, investigators found nothing else.

Park investigators did remember that almost four years earlier, on July 27, 1993, a wet passport belonging to a Yoshitake Osawa of Japan had been found. The finder had turned it in at the Yosemite Post Office. Exactly who the lost-and-found angel was who had done this went unrecorded. Inconveniently, *where* the passport had been found also had gone unrecorded.

Even so, when rangers followed up on this passport then, they learned that 25-year-old Osawa, residing in Teaneck, New Jersey, had been missing since at least late December of 1992. They ultimately obtained a Missing Person Report from the Teaneck Police Department. Osawa's roommate in Teaneck said that Osawa had been traveling to San Francisco on a Greyhound Thirty-Day Bus Pass. This was about all the rangers could find on the owner of the passport. Even thorough questioning of his parents by the Japanese Consulate revealed little more. None of the information gained indicated that Osawa had planned to visit Yosemite.

At that point in 1993, investigators had no leads to follow. That is, until four years later when a hiker stumbled across that eight-inch long mandible while hiking in Little Yosemite Valley.

Almost five years after Osawa's solitary disappearance, on October 20, 1997, Dr. Alan S. Benov, a Forensic Dentist in Fresno, compared records obtained from Osawa's family in Japan against the errant mandible. He then wrote "an opinion that the found human mandible containing teeth were consistent with dental records (X-rays) reportedly those of missing person Yoshitake Osawa." Under what circumstances—drowning, a fall into the river, foul play—the young traveler had died will probably never be known.

Admittedly, a huge element of mere chance played pivotal roles in such revealing discoveries as Osawa's mandible or Frizzell's knuckle. Another such serendipitous discovery happened on June 19, 2001, when Yosemite Trail Crew Foreman Erin Anders found a weathered wallet in Cold Canyon, north of Tuolumne Meadows. The wallet belonged to Michael Eric Randall, last seen two years earlier on July 6, 1999. This deteriorating little packet of identification soon flopped onto the desk of Daniel Horner, one of the Park's Special Agents. He now faced the unenviable task of phoning and asking the parents of the missing 26 year-old in Palos Verdes, California for their son's dental records. Doing this sort of thing tactfully in the face of parental grief was never easy.

Who *was* the missing man? Randall had been an Eagle Scout and an experienced backpacker who had loved nature. He had strongly embraced religion as a teenager. His close friends described him as "a great thinker…very intuitive, very compassionate…[and] almost thought too much." Randall's mother believed, "He was kind of a Thoreau throwback." Sadly, young adulthood brought Randall bouts of severe depression and other manifestations of mental illness including paranoia and delusions. In 1998, while working for a concession in Yosemite, he "suffered what his father describes as a psychotic breakdown." After this breakdown Randall had returned home.

On July 4, 1999, Michael Randall had accompanied his father back to the Park to, among other things, "see the sunset." This was the first time the troubled young man had been back to Yosemite since his psychotic episode a year earlier. While being here now may have been cathartic or otherwise renewing, however, this visit also sealed his fate.

Almost immediately upon returning home, Randall borrowed his sister's 1985 white Honda Accord. He needed it, he said, to go see his psychiatrist in San Jose. Michael Eric Randall never made it to that appointment. His family suspected that he had instead returned once more to Yosemite.

No one ever saw him again. Indeed, more than a month passed (until August 10) before anyone even located Randall's sister's car. It sat parked in the lot in Tuolumne Meadows.

For the next nineteen days the Park conducted a limited search. Investigators interviewed the missing man's friends and family. "Ground pounders," dogs, and helicopters prowled the region around Tuolumne Meadows. Hampering the effectiveness of all this effort was the reality that Incident Commander Maura Longden and her SAR team had no clue where to focus. Eventually, on August 29, the Park scaled back the mission. Technically, such searches are never officially terminated, but their "open" aspect equates mostly as unclosed paperwork—unless a new clue turns up.

That weathered wallet was just such a clue. So, on June 28, 2001, Special Agent Horner flew by Park helicopter to the region where Randall's wallet had been found ten days earlier. While trying to identify with something like Randall's mindset Horner soon discovered a campfire ring. Nearby it sat a weathered gym bag, a pair of shoes, a pair of shredded pants, an empty medicine bottle with its label now unreadable, and a set of car keys. While all of this provided a "hot" lead, none of it boded well.

Horner now widened his search radius from the fire ring. Not far away he discovered a human femur and skull.

Within five days, Dr. Von Goodin, a dentist in Merced charted the teeth in the weathered skull and compared them to the X-ray records provided by the Randalls' dentist. On July 4, 2001, two years to the day after Michael Randall and his father had taken their final journey together to Yosemite, the Park informed the Randalls of this positive match.

Agent Horner found no evidence of foul play. Nor did the Park's investigation identify anyone with motive to cause Randall harm. Forensics offered no clue. The overall gestalt of Michael Eric Randall's death does fit the profile for young male suicides. "[U]ntil the cause of death can be determined or evidence to indicate the cause of death," notes the Park Coroner's Report, "this investigation will remain open."

Unlike Osawa, Frizzell, Randall, and others who disappeared and were reported missing but eluded searchers only to be found years later through sheer luck, other people have been lost and died in Yosemite then found by accident only to remain unidentified. At least eleven people have met such ends here but remain complete mysteries. All of them had real lives before they entered the Park. Somewhere in the world there exist—or at least, once did exist—parents, siblings, children, and/or friends who will never know what happened to these lost souls. This frustrating lack of closure must create recurrent torment.

An early episode of this transpired on July 29, 1937, when local fisherman Frank Williams found the remains of a middle-aged white man "mutilated by bears and other wild animals" on the bank of the South Fork of the Merced River about four miles below Wawona (Wawona had been brought into the Park in 1932—with the exception of the private holdings of Section 35). Mariposa County officials, rangers, and a team of nine young men from the nearby Civilian Conservation Corps camp hauled out these remains. County Coroner Walter D. McNally investigated them. He believed the 45 to 50 year-old had been immersed in a deep hole in the river but finally had been "dragged from the water and eaten on by the bears." The victim appeared to have been dead about three to four weeks. Other than what little the mauled and decomposed body itself could tell investigators, only a pair of shoes and socks remained present to add a clue. And they failed to add enough. "No one has been reported missing in that section of the county," Coroner McNally noted on the front page of the *Mariposa Gazette* on August 5, 1937, "and no clues have been offered that would lead to the identity of the man."

The State of California Certificate of Death in the Mariposa County Hall of Records lists the mauled dead man as "John Doe #8." The document guesses that the cause of death "probably or may have been drowning accidental or suicide or homicide." In short, he remains a total mystery. But, as we will see, not a lonely one.

Two off-duty police sergeants from San Jose, California—Gary Leonard and Bruce Morton—and their buddy Charles Manley were enjoying the feel of the Sierra granite as they climbed Tenaya Peak, sitting above and south of Tenaya Lake. It was Sunday, September 8, 1968. The three ascended while roped together. They had made it to about 400 feet below the 10,300-foot peak. This climb was looking pretty darned good. Indeed, life itself was good…

As the trio moved up the cracks of the North Face Arête, they abruptly came upon the nude body of a man wedged into a diagonal crack like a human jammed into a huge taco shell.

For reasons now lost, the Search and Rescue Report dubbed the nude body "LeRoy." The naked 18- to 25-year-old white male was "sun-blackened and putrid" and had been there in his fissure "probably two to four weeks." Fairly or not, his long hair and beard branded him as a "hippie" type. But this offered little help in narrowing down the man's identity—Park rangers of that era would tell you that half the people then in Yosemite seemed "hippie" types.

Who was he and what had he been doing and why did he die? The climb here is "easy" Class 5. It would be doable by someone without a rope if they were daring and, let's face it, also foolish.

The autopsy revealed a broken right ankle and a crushed chest. These strongly suggested the victim had taken a fall. It seems he then had worked his way into a partially upright position on his left side on the bare rock where he was sheltered from the August sun within this crevice. From his small ledge he could look out over Tenaya Lake. How long he lay there before succumbing to exposure or his chest injury can only be conjectured. Even so, what he had been doing when he got hurt, may be easier to figure out.

Several weeks before his discovery other hikers had found a shirt and a sleeping bag stashed among boulders less than a mile from the summit. These same hikers next found a second shirt on the peak itself. Weeks later, when the climbing policemen reached the top, they found a pair of cutoff tan corduroys—waist size thirty-three—left there as a "sort of flag" on a five-foot-long stick. Of course no one could determine whether or not the trousers, shirt, or other found items definitely belonged to "LeRoy." Rangers Steve Hickman, Bob Dunnagan, Bob Pederson, and Joe McKeown climbed to the body and removed it by helicopter. FBI investigators severed his fingers and sent them to a forensic lab. All to no avail. Nothing helped to identify him. Who LeRoy was remains a mystery today. That psychoactive drugs might have influenced his decision-making about leaving his shorts as a flag (or about making the climb at all), however, endures as a possible factor leading to his ultimately fatal injury.

Of the eleven mystery people "found but never identified" seven were discovered simply by someone scrambling in some obscure spot in the Park and stumbling across their bleached bones. The first record of this sort was made at the base of Washington Column in late May of 1938 by the Sierra Club Hiking Club. Amongst the few scattered bones the hikers also found a pair of weathered hiking boots with the foot bones still inside. A camera and a spectacle case also sat nearby. "Chief Ranger Forest Townsley and assistant Rangers have been endeavoring to find clues which would lead to the identity of the remains," noted a short article in the *Mariposa Gazette* on June 2, 1938. "It is believed the body had been there six or seven years." Today the exact location of this find has been lost. Indeed, so too has every other detail about who this person may have been and what might have happened to him. These remains do vaguely hint at the final demise of the otherwise unsolved disappearance of photographer Frank J. Koenman on June 11, 1925, from Tent #156 of Camp Curry (discussed earlier) but the vital specific details of both men (type of camera, dental features, et cetera) have been lost to time.

Two sets of mysterious human remains were found below Half Dome. The first of these was stumbled upon on June 7, 1975, as climbers William Tuttle, Harrison Ross, Bryan Lamoreau, and David Zimmerman were in their second day of a retreat from the base of the Northwest Face of Half Dome. On one of their numerous rappels—they still had nine more to go before reaching Mirror Lake—as Zimmerman scouted a way down the confusing cliffs he spotted two femurs sticking out of the sand of a small watercourse. This location stood approximately 1,000 vertical feet above the Valley floor. The climbers now scanned for additional remains in this tiny seasonal creek at the base of a small waterfall. Thirty minutes yielded parts of a skull, ribs, a pelvis, vertebrae, a clavicle, a tibia and fibula, and a mandible lacking teeth. A few of these bones still had flesh on them, but none of them revealed a definitive cause of death.

The next day a team of rangers climbed to the site—midway between the base of Half Dome and the Valley floor—but it uncovered no additional clues. What had happened here? Even considering the potential for water to flush a body down from above, this place was still probably too low for the victim to have jumped or fallen off the top of Half Dome. Who this was and how he or she ended up here remain unknown.

The second set of Half Dome mystery bones was also found by climbers, this time on July 26, 1987. Volker Krugel from West Germany was looking for water when he stumbled across a human skull, mandible, and a maxilla. Shredded cloth sat nearby, along with a "greenish colored, ankle high, leather boot and a white shirt." A few minutes more of hurried searching yielded two femurs and a pelvic girdle. Now racing the fading daylight in his ascent, Volker built a rock cairn to mark the spot and returned to his four companions. The team put the bones in a pack and over the next three days proceeded to successfully climb Half Dome, *with* the bones.

Back in the Valley on July 30, the climbers turned in their find to the Park. Three days later, Rangers Bob Wilson and Dan Dellinges and two climbers, Dan McDevitt and Walt Shipley, from the Camp 4 Rescue Site, spent two hours working their way up to where Krugel had found the skull. Here they recovered "the majority of the bones with the exception of the hands, feet, and spine."

Local dentist Dr. Chuck Woessner analyzed the jaw bones and interpolated them as from a male between 18 and 25 years old. Forensic investigators decided the remains could have been exposed on the slope from two to fifteen years. The "victim was hiking either up or down and slipped on water, ice, or snow…crossing the top of a steep slab," interpreted Ranger Wilson. "There were some fractures in the frontal region of the skull above the eye sockets which indicates facial and head trauma from a fall…" This cranial trauma did not seem drastic enough, however, for this person to have fallen 1,800 feet from the summit of Half Dome. On the other hand, the type of boot found was not something any climber would wear while on a cliff.

The Park placed this information into the National Criminal Information Center Missing/Unidentified Person System. Today, nearly twenty years later, no hits have been recorded. There probably never will be.

The last mystery bones found thus far (more such finds are inevitable) were discovered on July 13, 2005. Several hikers from Southern California stumbled across a human skull cap while following the Old Tioga Roadbed a few hundred yards east of the Yosemite Creek Campground and west of the current Tioga Road. A forensic anthropologist from Fresno, Dr. Roger LaJeunesse (Chair of the Department of Anthropology at Fresno State University), confirmed it was from a woman between 45 and 50 years old. To scour the region for additional clues about forty-five Explorer Search and Rescue (ESAR) Scouts from Marin County abetted by a local team from Mariposa County SAR conducted an intensive grid search. They found several more bones, enough that investigators are now pursuing leads. DNA analysis so far had produced no known match.

Although one may glean many lessons from the episodes listed in this chapter, perhaps the most salient one is: Virtually every lost hiker in it who ended up a statistic was hiking alone when they made their fatal error.

TABLE 12 . VICTIMS OF GETTING LOST FATALLY IN YOSEMITE. (Incidents discussed in text are noted.)

Name, age	Date	Location	*Circumstances*
Lost and Found:			
Quin Charles Frizzell, 31	June 4, 1966	Tenaya Canyon	*Frizzell, a nuclear scientist at the Lawrence Livermore National Laboratory, vanished during a* ***solo hike*** *to the Valley from Tenaya Lake. On April 8, 1971, a hiker found a human skull and Frizzell's credit cards on cliffs below Mount Watkins; further searching revealed nothing. On September 14, 1972, another hiker found more bones in the same general area. Next his boots, backpack, and more bones were found, the latter interred in place.* (in text)
David Wade Huckins, 21	January 30, 1986	Curry Village	*At his Curry Village housing Ahwahnee Hotel employee Huckins of San Jose, California told his father he planned to jog westerly. He never returned. A huge search for him failed. On July 6, a decomposing human arm was found near Lower River Campground. The next day other remains were found a mile above the Happy Isles footbridge. On October 11, the scapula and distal humerus turned up nearby. If these remains are Huckins, his cause of death remains a* ***mystery****.*
Yoshitake Osawa, 25	before December 1992	Little Yosemite Valley	*On July 27, 1993, the wet passport of Osawa, residing in Teaneck, New Jersey, was found and turned in anonymously. On July 17, 1997, Stacy Denney in Little Yosemite Valley found a mandible with a few teeth 400 yards upstream of the campground and 10*

feet from the Merced. Dental records from Japan matched the mandible. Osawa had been missing since December, 1992, while traveling ***solo*** *to San Francisco on a Greyhound Bus Pass.* (in text)

Keita Chijiwa, 21

March 6, 1994 below Sentinel Rock, off the Four-Mile Trail

Chijiwa of Tokyo, Japan left the Sunnyside Campground during early March. When he did not return, he was listed as missing. Because his destination was unknown, no concentrated search area could be determined. "Missing Person" flyers were circulated throughout the Park for weeks. Climbers found his body on March 24. The postmortem suggested hypothermia had killed him during a ***solo hike****; otherwise his death remains a* ***mystery****.*

Michael Eric Randall, 26

last seen July 6, 1999 Cold Canyon, north of Tuolumne Meadows

Randall of Palos Verdes, California suffered from severe depression, paranoia, and delusions. He took his sister's Honda on July 6, 1999, drove to Tuolumne Meadows then vanished. A 19-day search failed. On June 19, 2001, Randall's weathered wallet turned up in Cold Canyon, then a human femur and a skull matching Randall's dental X-rays. Randall was a likely suicide. (in text)

Fred Clausen, 46

last seen July 31, 2003 Whorl Mountain

Clausen of Livermore, California vanished on a 4-day ***solo backpacking trek*** *from Twin Lakes into northeast Yosemite, which included Burro Pass and Matterhorn Peak. A joint search by 142 people from the NPS, Mono County, California Highway Patrol, Inyo and Stanislaus National Forests, and the California Air National Guard until August 10 did not find him. He was finally found on September 3, 2010 on Whorl Mountain.*

Ottorrina "Terrina" Bonaventura, 80

July 30, 2007 4 miles from Vogelsang High Sierra Camp

Bonaventura of Schererville, Indiana was experiencing bouts of memory loss. She started a hike with 4 women to Evelyn Lake but returned to camp to retrieve her peaches. She then left ***solo*** *to catch up with them but headed in the wrong direction—toward Emerick Lake. A massive search failed. Her body, dead due to* ***hypothermia/exposure****, was found on August 13 about 4 miles cross-country (rough terrain) from her point last seen. Bonaventura was a European survivor of WW II and was in the habit of always carrying money and a passport. When found she had $2,600 in cash and a passport copy pinned inside her underwear.*

Joshua Blundell, 35

February 23 (?), 2014 Yosemite Creek Campground Road

Last seen ***solo*** *on February 23 carrying his bicycle up the Snow Creek Falls Trail, Blundell of San Jose, California soon disappeared. Days earlier he'd been denied a Wilderness Permit due to lacking sufficient equipment for his planned hike. His unusual "preparation" led to a welfare BOLO, "Be On the Look Out," for him. Later, on April 18, 2014, while opening the Yosemite Creek Campground Road, maintenance crewmen found Blundell's bicycle along the road, then a bivouac beside a large downed tree. His ID was found along with bits of clothing and personal items. On August 3, 2014,* *firefighters found his skull nearby. Animals, probably an American black bear, had eaten Joshua, scattering his remains. Death likely due to* ***exposure****(?)*

Alexander Joseph Sevier, 24 — May 1, 2017 — below Vernal Fall
Last seen in Yosemite Valley on May 1, the on-leave active-duty serviceman at the Navy Medical Center in Portsmouth, Virginia, Sevier, originally from Jacksonville, Florida, made ***solo day hikes*** *from Housekeeping Camp. He vanished during a period of extreme high runoff in the Merced River. At the end of August, remains were found 500 feet downstream of the Vernal Fall Footbridge near the river (now flowing lower). DNA testing confirmed his identity but not cause of death. Had Sevier* ***drowned?***

Richard Allan Judd, 69 — July 25, 2021 — Lower Merced Pass Lake
Judd (5', 11" & 150 pounds) of Berkeley, California started on a 3.5 mile day hike with a buddy from camp on Lower Merced Lake (elevation 8,800 feet) uphill to Red Peak Pass (elevation >11,000 feet) but became separated short of Lower Ottoway Lake then vanished. Judd's scattered remains were found on August 11, 2022 by a fire-fighting crew in the original search zone.

Lost but Never Found:

F. P. Shepherd, 37 — last seen June 17, 1909 — leaving Glacier Point Hotel for Sentinel Dome
Shepherd of San Francisco headed for Sentinel Dome on a ***solo hike*** *during heavy fog. A 4-day search found no clue.* (in text)

Frank J. Koenman, adult — last seen June 11 or 12, 1925 — Camp Curry
Photographer Koenman of San Francisco was a guest at Camp Curry. His supervisor reported him missing on June 18. Rangers had no specific place to look so they conducted a minimal search for the apparent ***solo hiker****.* (in text)

Godfrey Wondrosek, 26 — last seen April 26, 1933 — leaving Camp 7 for Half Dome
Wondrosek of Chicago had camped with his sister who reported he planned to ***solo hike*** *to Half Dome. "A large party of rangers and Indian trackers were immediately sent out to the area...and worked feverishly to locate some traces of the missing man. Day after day the searching parties have worked over this area and have battled wind, rain and snow almost continuously and have tramped through underbrush and made descents over slippery granite surfaces in their efforts to find Wondrosek, but without success."*

Norris Parent, 60 — last seen July 9, 1941 — possibly hiking north from Tioga Pass
Our sole source—the Mariposa Gazette, *July 31, 1941—found on Parent of Oakland suggests no one knew where he had* ***solo hiked.*** *His 2 sons believed they followed his tracks into the "Shepherd's Crest country" about 7 miles north of Tioga Pass to a dead fire. Rangers Carl Danner and Jules Eichorn concluded "the remains of the fire are at least a year old." Mrs. Parent was to hire Sierra mountaineer Norman Clyde to head a final searching party, "although the family has virtually abandoned hope of finding him alive."*

Emerson Holt, 62	last seen July 17, 1943	1 mile west of Merced Lake *Holt of Riverside, California stopped to rest and became a **solo hiker** during a group trek when his companions went ahead. Neither Holt nor any clue of him was ever found.* (in text)
William Henry Dickenson, adult	car found May 27, 1945	1 mile below Arch Rock *Pasadena Junior College student Dickenson of Roswell, New Mexico vanished in late March. On May 27, the wheel of his car turned up in the Merced River. Searching revealed his Model A Ford. Only 3 gaps existed in the guard wall through which the "crippled" young man could have driven.* (also listed in Chapter 8. Wheels)
Malcolm McClintock, 18	last seen August 8, 1948	Glacier Point (?) *McClintock of Glendale, California visited the Park with his family and decided to **hike solo** to Glacier Point. The* Superintendent's Monthly Report *stated: "Exhaustive searches have been made and all clues followed but to date no tangible evidence of his whereabouts or what may have happened to him have been gained."*
Louis Miller, 73	last seen September 3, 1950	between Dana Meadows and Mono Pass *Miller of Modesto was last seen on a **fishing trip** by his son near their car on a spur road south of Tioga Pass. Rangers, volunteers, and family members searched for several days in vain.*
Walter A. Gordon, 26	last seen July 20, 1954	leaving for the Ledge Trail *Curry Co. summer clerk Gordon, and a Phi Beta Kappa researcher at U.C., Berkeley, left at 1 p.m. with a lunch to **solo hike** the Ledge Trail. He failed to return. This massive search for him made the second ever SAR use of a helicopter in the Park.* (in text)
Orvar von Laass, 30	last seen October 9, 1954	leaving the Ahwahnee Hotel *Von Laass, a Ph.D. candidate in economics from U.C., Berkeley and registered at the Ahwahnee Hotel, told his wife he was going to **solo hike** but be back in 2 hours. Bloodhounds "alerted" twice, both times heading toward the base of the Royal Arches. Searchers both climbed and rappelled the cliff face without luck. The search ended mid-November.* (in text)
Kenneth Klein, 23	July 28, 1967	Upper Yosemite Fall, Eagle Peak *Curry Co. service station employees Klein of San Antonio, Texas and John Charles Gunn, age 19, of Richmond, California went on an apparent loop hike from Camp 4 to Upper Yosemite Fall and Eagle Peak. Inexperienced, they did not carry bivouac or climbing gear. Gunn was found with a broken neck and mysteriously drowned in a pool above Lower Yosemite Fall. Klein never surfaced at all; no death certificate exists for him in the Mariposa County Hall of Records.* (discussed in Chapter 10. Drowning)
Tom Opperman, 21	last seen August 8, 1967	leaving Merced Lake *Tuolumne Meadows Lodge porter Opperman of Fresno intended to **solo climb** Mount Clark and return on August 10. An intense SAR effort lasted until August 25 but did not find him.* (in text)

Nelson Henry Paisley, 5	last seen May 31, 1969 Merced River east of The Cascades *While* ***wading in the Merced*** *½ mile east of the picnic area, high water swept Paisley of Folsom, California from his mother, 10 feet away. Two SCUBA divers searched beneath the banks for 200 feet.* (in Chapter 10. Drowning)
Christine Fuentes, 9	last seen June 18, 1970 Vernal Fall *Fuentes of Los Angeles went over.* (in Chapter 1. Waterfalls)
Jerome R. Oldiges, 20	last seen June 20, 1970 Merced River, junction of Hwy 120/140 *Oldiges of Covington, Kentucky was sitting on a rock next to the river and slipped off, disappearing in the high flow. (in Chapter 10. Drowning)*
"Vartkess"(?)	disappeared in 1972 Location uncertain *Remains found November 14, 2016 NPS #-2017-00162. More information pending.*
Dikran Knadjian, 20	last seen July 24, 1972 Curry Village *Cambridge University medical student Knadjian of Ethiopia checked into Curry Village on July 24. When he had not checked out by July 31, his belongings were found in his Cabin #486 with the bed undisturbed. MISSING flyers were released. With no single place to look, no searchers entered the field. Park investigators found no hint at what may have happened to Knadjian.*
Linden Moore, 24	November 4 (?), 1973 Glacier Point *On October 26, after failing to secure a full-time teaching position and after a "severe disagreement" the previous day with a teacher for whom she aided, former Curry Co. employee Moore, who had quit because she could not make any friends, drove from home in Fremont, California. She left suicide notes with her minister and her analyst. She parked at Glacier Point, left another suicide note inside her car and a list of phone numbers. Did she jump from Glacier Point? She never was found.* (also listed as a probable in Chapter 13. Suicide)
Jeff Estes, 25	last seen May 24, 1976 junction, May Lake and Tioga Roads *Curry Co. bus dispatcher Estes said he planned to spend the night at May Lake then* ***hike solo*** *down the Snow Creek Trail to the Valley. He expected to return no later than the morning of May 26. He never showed. An intensive 4-day search found nothing.*
Susan Schantin, 26	last seen May 14, 1978 crossing Wildcat Creek *Schantin of Alameda, California was hiking with her husband Michael, down the Old Big Oak Flat Road. While* ***fording Wildcat Creek*** *flowing high with snowmelt, she allegedly slipped and was carried downstream into a narrow, boulder- and log-choked stretch where a body would quickly hang up. Unexpectedly, an intensive search did not find her.* (in Chapter 10. Drowning)
Stacey Anne Arras, 14	last seen July 17, 1981 leaving Sunrise High Sierra Camp *Arras of Saratoga, California and her father were on the 4-day saddle "loop trip" of the High Sierra Camps. On Day #1, she* ***solo***

	***day hiked** 1¼ miles to an overlook and was never found despite 8,004 man-hours of searching that cost $99,845.* (in text)
unknown	September 8, 1985 near Upper Yosemite Fall *John M. Pohlman said he "observed a person jump off the cliff, 100 yards east of the Yosemite Point overlook, ¼ mile east of the top of Yosemite Falls." An extensive focused helicopter and ground search over rough terrain along the "fall line" and below found no victim. Park Investigator Bob Wilson concludes his Case Incident Report (#85-16468) by saying: "At this point I...believe his* [Pohlman's] *sighting is creditable."*
Timothy John Barnes, 24	last seen July 5, 1988 northwest end of Tenaya Lake *Barnes of Cucamonga, California told friends at Murphy Creek Trailhead he would **solo hike** to Polly Dome Lakes and return by 4:30 p.m. An intensive air and ground search covered 50+ square miles. He was declared legally dead on July 19, 1990. In man-hours* (11,912) *this was the largest search in Yosemite history up to this time. It cost $178,501, second to that for Michael Ficery, who would disappear on June 15, 2005.* (in text)
Donald W. Buchanan, 86	last seen November 10, 1988 trail below Half Dome *Buchanan of Mariposa, California was dying of cancer. He had hiked in the Park for 50 years (in the 1920s and 1930s as a seasonal employee) when he **solo hiked** into infinity. A 3-day effort by 100 searchers found only a campfire and his false teeth. A year later his wallet turned up. He is a suspected suicide.* (also in Chapter 13. Suicide)
David Paul Morrison, 28	last seen May 25, 1998 trail in Little Yosemite Valley *Morrison of San Francisco intended a **solo day hike** to Half Dome and back. He was described as a determined and experienced hiker, but unprepared for bad weather. Nearly 250 people, 15 dog teams, and 4 helicopters searched for 5 days unsuccessfully.*
Kieran Burke, 45	last seen April 5, 2000 Curry Village *Burke of Dublin, Ireland likely went for a **solo day hike** but never returned. With no exact location of focus, 25 people and a helicopter searched Vernal, Nevada, and Yosemite Falls plus other likely spots in the Valley until April 17. Rangers phoned hundreds of people who had been in the Park at that time. This yielded no clues.*
Ruthanne Rupert, 49	last seen August 15, 2000 Eagle Peak area *Rupert of South Daytona, Florida planned to join an organized 7-day NPS group backpacking trip on August 13 but the leader turned her back due to an infection in her artificial eye. She told him that, after taking care of her eye, she might or might not rejoin the group. On September 11, relatives reported her missing. Investigators concluded that she may have **solo day hiked** to the top of Eagle Peak.*

Walter H. Reinhard, 66

last seen about September 20, 2002 White Wolf area

Described as a fast and strong hiker in excellent shape from Oro Valley, Arizona, Reinhard likely ***solo day hiked*** *from White Wolf. His vehicle was found at the trailhead on September 30. 21 days passed before he was reported overdue. The Park searched for 5 hard days. A week later, a new search was ordered. Reinhard had been a Force Recon Marine. Convinced his skills would have sustained him, the Force Recon Association put pressure on the Marine Corps via the Dept. of Defense and ultimately the White House. This second search went 4 more days and used marines from the Mountain Warfare Training Center in Bridgeport, but it—and spending $119,550—found no clue of Reinhard.*

Michael Ficery, 51

last seen June 15, 2005 Tiltill Valley area

Ficery of Santa Barbara, California vanished while ***solo backpacking*** *north of Hetch Hetchy. Drifts of deep, late spring snow made route-finding difficult. High runoff also necessitated helicopters to place searchers on spot. Despite this becoming the most expensive SAR effort in Yosemite history at $451,930 and 8,632 man-hours, Ficery remained lost.* (in text)

George Penca, Jr, 30

June 20, 2011 Upper Yosemite Fall Trail

Penca of Hawthorne, California had ***day hiked*** *to the top of the upper fall, although he had not wanted to hike at all, with 13 relatives and members of the Apostolic Church of the Nazarene. As his brother Anthony Penca had filled water bottles at 3:00 p.m., he saw George for the last time* ***solo*** *sight-seeing, standing near the creek upstream of Upper Yosemite Falls and south of the footbridge. At 5:45 p.m. group members noted him as missing (now for nearly 3 hours). Despite potential witnesses, "out of shape and portly (240 pounds)" Penca had* ***vanished unwitnessed****. Whether he ended up in the creek then the falls or instead vanished via trails has not been discovered despite a massive search effort.*

Peter Fancher Jackson, 74

September 17, 2016 ~7 (?) miles west of White Wolf camp

In excellent physical condition and commonly making 5-mile day hikes, Jackson (5' 10" & 150 pounds) began a ***solo day hike*** *from his campsite at White Wolf Campground but never returned. His vehicle remained at White Wolf Campground at site #58, paid until 9/21/16. In 2019 a fisherman found Jackson's pack on the bank of the Middle Fork of the Tuolumne River about 7.5 miles west of White Wolf as the crow flies. Where and how Jackson died remain* ***mysteries. Drowning*** *is one possibility.*

Sandra Lyn Johnsen-Hughes, 54

July 4 (?) 2020 Johnson Meadows or Chiquito Pass Trailhead

Weeks after moving from Maui, Johnsen-Hughes (5', 4"& 150 pounds)) planned a ***solo backpacking*** *hike into Yosemite. But she crashed her silver Saab 9-5 into a tree. It rolled into a ravine. She unloaded it "carelessly." She was witnessed with a facial bruise walking barefoot but refused assistance. Her gear and IDs were found in her campsite near Portuguese Overlook 5 miles south of*

		her car. Her sleeping bag was found in Yosemite NP. On August 9, a pair of hunters saw a woman matching her description leaning against a tree on Forest Road 5S01, 5 miles from her campsite, but they did not realize she was "missing." A renewed search failed. May or may not be in the Park.
Joel Thomazin, 31	September 6 (?), 2021 between Hetch Hetchy & Lake Eleanor(?)	*Thomazin (5', 10") of Denair, California planned a **solo** 3-day **backpacking/fishing** trip starting at Hetch Hetchy, upstream possibly to the Grand Canyon of the Tuolumne River. He carried a small inflatable kayak and other appropriate gear but **no life jacket**. He vanished. Repeated extensive searches did not find him or his gear.*

<u>Found but Neither Identified Nor Known To Be Lost:</u>

"John Doe," adult male	found June 2, 1918 Merced River, Little Yosemite Valley	*On June 2, 21-year-old Curry Co. employee William Myers found a man's body in the river and "dragged him out dead." Details came to light only in 2006 and remain sketchy; they exist in the personal diary Myers wrote at the time. Myers' boss "Mother Curry" had asked him to look for a man (who likely had been staying at Camp Curry) who had gone missing in late May after climbing the snowy Mount Starr King (9,092 feet). Other searches had failed. In late May the Merced had risen with spring melt and offered only a hazardous crossing back into the Valley. As of this writing, the deceased man's identity is unknown.*
"John Doe #8," male	found July 29, 1937 South Fork of the Merced River	*A fisherman found a long-immersed, gray-haired man in his 40s weighing 150 pounds and wearing only shoes and socks 4 miles downstream of Wawona. His cause of death and identity remain mysteries.* (in text)
human bones, ?	found May 28, 1938 base of Washington Column	*The Sierra Club Hiking Club found parts of a human skeleton in rocks near the base of Washington Column. "It is believed the body had been there six or seven years." Age, sex, identity, and cause of death all remain mysteries.* (in text)
"LeRoy," male	found September 8, 1968 North Face, Tenaya Peak	*While climbing Tenaya Peak, 2 off-duty police from San Jose and a buddy found the nude body of an 18- to 25-year-old, bearded white male dead 2-4 weeks and wedged into a large diagonal crack 400 feet below the summit. An autopsy revealed a broken right ankle and crushed chest suggesting the victim fell then died of exposure. Despite FBI efforts, no ID was made.* (in text)
"John Doe," male	found June 9, 1971 Merced River, Steamboat Bay	*A bicyclist spotted a white male 18 to 30 years old and wearing only Levi cutoffs floating face down in "Steamboat Bay." It had been immersed about 2 weeks and carried no identifying marks. The fingers were removed for fingerprinting but could not be identified. The body bore no signs of trauma.* (see Chapter 10. Drowning)

human bones, ?	found June 7, 1975 midway between Half Dome and Mirror Lake *Climbers discovered human bones in a small creek about 1,000 vertical feet above the Valley. A ranger team located nothing more. The who, why, and how of this corpse remain unknown.* (in text)
human bones, ?	found September 23, 1975 Illilouette Creek above Happy Isles *Two Curry Co. employees hiking the drainage 20 minutes above Happy Isles found a mandible partially buried in sand and rocks. They accompanied Ranger Jim Lee and California State Park Exchange Ranger Dave Bartlett to search for more but found only one additional piece of human bone and a green nylon swim suit.*
human bones, ?	found November 25, 1977 cliffs near North Dome Gully *A cross-country scrambler stumbled across a human skull hundreds of feet above the Valley floor near North Dome Gully. Rangers Henry, McKeeman and Farabee spent hours combing for more clues and turned up additional bones, mostly in a watercourse. Despite forensic specialists, identification proved inconclusive.*
human bones, male	found July 26, 1987 below Northwest Face of Half Dome *While looking for water, a climber found a human skull, mandible, and maxilla. He left a cairn. He and 3 buddies put the bones in a pack and climbed Half Dome. The bones belonged to a male hiker 18 to 25 years old whose body had been in place 2-15 years. Frontal skull fractures suggest a fall.* (in text)
human bones, ?	found September 14, 1990 100 feet east of Lower Yosemite Fall, base of Sunnyside Bench *A human jaw bone was found and anonymously set atop a rock next to the trail. Ranger Mike Mayer was led to the site and collected the mandible. Both the identity and fate of its former owner remain mysteries.* (not in text).
human bones, female	found July 13, 2005 Old Tioga Road, the Yosemite Creek Campground area *The human skull cap found on the Old Tioga Road east of the campground and west of Tioga Road was of a 45-50-year-old female whose identity remains unknown.* (in text)

Chapter Thirteen

SUICIDE

On August 26, 1925, two young men—Leonard L. Casey and John B. Peak—hiked about 2,500 feet up to the top of Upper Yosemite Fall to experience the stupendous view. Looking around the polished granite near the lip of the waterfall they found a discarded coat. As almost anyone might do, they probed its pockets. There they found two letters, dated June 3rd and 4th. Both had been written on Yosemite Lodge stationary by 55-year-old Count Theodore James Jackowski. More ominous, these two pieces of stationary proved to be a suicide letter and a will.

Upon their return to the Valley the boys turned in the coat and papers to the Park.

As the Park's investigation proceeded, the strange story of Count Jackowski began to shape up as high drama—then as pure melodrama. Jackowski, it turned out, was indeed a Polish nobleman. He was also a former resident of San Francisco. As if in the hackneyed plot of some cheap novel, he had been contacted a few years prior by relatives. They had instructed him to return to his homeland if he wanted to inherit a "huge" fortune ($250,000 then, which equates to nearly $4 million today) from other relatives of Jackowski residing in South America.

Of course the count had traveled to Poland for his impressive inheritance. Next Jackowski sailed for South America to visit those other family members. Finally he returned to the United States. Tellingly, during all of his travels Count Jackowski had lavished on himself every luxury to which a person of his position and his new fortune might aspire.

This is understandable. He indeed now possessed a fortune. Why not live it up a little? Well, the nouveau riche count did not just live it up a little. He lived it up a lot. So much so, amazingly, that he proceeded in just a few years to squander his entire fortune.

Depressed by his own stupidity and now humiliated by being virtually penniless, on June 7, Jackowski made the long, weary trudge to the top of Upper Yosemite Fall. There he doffed his coat in the summer heat and made sure his scribbled out letter and will remained safely sequestered in his coat pocket. Then he laid his coat down on the bare rock. Next he threw himself 1,430 feet off the cliff.

His letter contained (among other items): "Last night [I] saw wonderful fire-fall. Now see me fall. Don't get shocked. I am at end of trail. Please plant some redwood on me."

Beyond Jackowski's fabulous windfall and luxurious living, it turns out that more recently yet he had been arrested in San Francisco (likely for being indigent). In his will he left a twenty-dollar traveler's check to the city's Sheriff Finn with instructions for Finn to pay five dollars each to the two policemen who had arrested him and then another ten dollars to the jail trustee who had been good to him while behind bars. Jackowski also left another five dollars to the local Mariposa sheriff to pay for a redwood to be planted on his grave.

Once these letters came to light, the Park launched a search below the waterfall. There they found human bone fragments (now about seventy days old) believed to be the remains of the spendthrift count. Whether or not these fragments ever nourished a young redwood tree, though, is unknown.

Unlike nearly every other type of mishap in Yosemite, suicide, which might be classified as a serious emotional mishap but almost always can be defined as a permanent solution to a temporary problem, drags everyone involved into an entire new realm of thinking—and into a new realm of response. Suicide devastates friends and relatives with sadness and sometimes guilt. Suicide also often poses a real test of self-control for first responders. Some suicide events are so screwy they truly challenge anyone trying to report them. To fully convey the "Twilight Zone" quality of some of these episodes is not easy. In this light, we decided to offer a simple example of what can happen in Yosemite but written in the passive bureaucratic style of the *Yosemite NPS Morning Report* in 2000:

> 00-357- Yosemite NP (CA) – Rescue: Attempted Suicide
>
> Park dispatch received a 911 call from nearby residents early on the morning of June 28th, reporting that a man was yelling for help from Ahwahnee Meadow in Yosemite Valley. Responding rangers found a man from Modesto, California, bleeding from severe lacerations on his neck and wrists. He told rangers and special agents that he had attempted suicide because he "wanted to see what was on the

> other side of death." Modesto police were asked to make a welfare check on his wife and were told that she had also attempted suicide in the same manner that same morning at their home in that city. The man was flown by helicopter ambulance to a trauma center in Modesto, where he was operated on for his wounds and committed for psychiatric evaluation. Investigation indicates that the injuries both husband and wife suffered were self-inflicted.

Some cases are so murky they have to be pieced together like the jigsaw puzzle of a mystery story. On December 27, 1972, William St. Jean and Jeff Mathis were searching for mushrooms near the Indian Caves, not far from the Upper Pines Campground. Instead of fungi they discovered a human body that appeared to have been eaten by bears. Near the remains lay a .38 Super Colt automatic pistol among the frozen pine needles. The two mushroom hunters made a beeline to Ranger Dan R. Sholly. An investigation ensued.

Based on the condition of the victim's feet—protected in a pair of size 11 boots—the coroner estimated the man had died three to eight days earlier. Other clues helped, but they failed to spell out the dead man's strange story. Near the widely scattered skeletal parts lay a pair of wire-rimmed glasses, an Omega watch, a padded, zip-up wallet for a pistol (not a holster), and the .38. It lay cocked, with its safety off, and ready to fire with a bullet in the chamber—exactly as if it had been discharged then dropped. In the magazine there remained two more live rounds. On the ground eight feet from the rusting weapon lay a single spent cartridge; about the right distance for it to have been automatically ejected if the gun had been fired from where it had been found. A few feet away lay yet another cartridge, this one unfired. It apparently had been left there as if whoever had loaded the pistol had abruptly decided four rounds in the magazine (one was fired, a second automatically entered the chamber upon firing the first, and the last two remained in the magazine) would be plenty—or else he ejected it while checking whether the gun was truly loaded.

So far the scenario seems clear-cut: Someone had committed suicide. Of course an alternate possibility was someone had been murdered and the scene then doctored to cover the crime. Which was accurate? And who was the victim?

This is where the investigation got rough. The clothing on this half-eaten carcass consisted of male apparel suitable for winter. Inside the left rear pocket of the trousers was a wallet. It contained ten dollars and a few receipts, but no identification cards. The plastic window of the wallet intended for a driver's license was empty. Helpfully, the plastic did reveal an ink stain from the ID once enclosed there. It spelled out a partial signature, "Richard La..." then it became indecipherable. Again, all IDs had been removed from the wallet.

For a while this six-foot tall dead blond man went unidentified. But investigation soon revealed that a Richard Lawrence had spent the night around December

21 in a local lodge. He had listed his home address in Santa Barbara. This proved unhelpful because Lawrence had already moved out from this address. Rangers did learn from former neighbors, however, that Richard Lawrence had been a "loner" who kept to himself.

Meanwhile a trace of the .38 Colt revealed it had been bought twice before until finally being sold in Chicago by a licensed gun dealer on April 9, 1971, to Richard Lawrence. The Chicago Police Department informed the Park that Richard Lawrence was actually Richard Lawrence Fudge.

The Park next sent in the skull for dental chart comparisons. These confirmed the victim to have been the 38-year-old Fudge.

Fudge was a 1957 graduate of Carnegie Tech Architectural School in Pittsburgh, Pennsylvania. Over the years since, he had grown to consider his surname to be a handicap and had dropped its usage, unbeknownst to his parents. Fudge had successfully held a pair of architectural jobs in Chicago, one with a private firm and the next with the planning commission. These jobs totaled about eight years.

Apparently Fudge quit his good job, sold his condo and his furniture, and left Chicago to explore the American West. Before leaving town he had mailed his father, Herman Fudge, a check for $500 to repay an old debt (one which his father said he did not feel that he was owed) along with a letter thanking his parents for their support over the years but also explaining that he "had gotten into a rut and wanted to make a change."

Richard Lawrence (minus the "Fudge") had then driven his 1966 blue Corvette convertible out of Chicago on old Route 66. He ended up in Santa Barbara, a place he liked and had known from a previous visit. He deposited a large sum of money into a local Home Savings and Loan branch ($24,000 still remained in this account during the investigation). A check on Richard Lawrence's phone account revealed that he had stopped his service on December 11.

Ranger Sholly next learned the California Highway Patrol had impounded the dead man's Corvette in Merced, but the CHP had experienced problems in identifying its owner because the license plates and registration were missing. Fudge, it appeared, had driven from Santa Barbara to Merced. There, strangely, he had either abandoned or lost his Corvette (and likely obliterated his "embarrassing" name from it) and then caught a public bus to Yosemite.

Before ever leaving the Pacific coast, it seems, he had become friends with a man named James R. Cowan. Once Cowan learned of the death he wrote to Fudge's parents to tell them that "Richard Lawrence" had been telling him his job prospects were not working out and he would probably be "moving on" once he returned from Yosemite. Cowan also said he had asked Lawrence to "drop him a card" upon landing elsewhere. Cowan mentioned too that Lawrence had recently spoke of a woman he knew "who always looked at the world through rose-colored glasses" but that Richard himself had added he "felt just the opposite."

Upon analyzing the various clues and information and after weighing the contents of Cowan's letter regarding the victim's depression, investigators filed Fudge's December 22 (?), 1972 death as likely suicidal.

A similar and equally puzzling case occurred twenty-five years later. In late 1997, a Forest Service maintenance man glanced into a dumpster near Groveland and felt puzzled at what he saw. The metal box was loaded with what appeared to be someone's worldly possessions. Among these were journal-like notebooks expressing militia philosophy as well as names of survivalist and militia personalities. These writings—and everything else in the dumpster—prompted the Forest Service office to contact the FBI. Investigators studied the notes and other possessions and quickly connected them to 42-year-old Clark Wilbur Rowland.

By following up each lead, the FBI learned that Rowland was homeless and living in a van, earning his meager expenses by sweeping chimneys in Mariposa and neighboring towns in the foothills. He periodically placed fliers at homes to advertise his services. Occasionally, when he had enough money, Rowland stayed in one specific Motel 6 where he found the proprietor to be friendly. Rowland's writings suggested he was a rugged individualist who believed in taking care of himself, the government be damned.

With nothing but this sketchy bio, the FBI had no lead as to why the man's life belongings had ended up in that dumpster. But such a find was a strong signal that something had gone amiss in Rowland's life. Unhelpfully, investigators found no one who had recently seen the man or his vehicle or who could offer any clue otherwise as to his well being or location. In fact, based only on the evidence in hand, it was possible that nothing at all had happened to Rowland. Maybe this guy was alive and well and living in Idaho.

The following spring rangers found a van abandoned at Curry Village. They contracted its removal to Ponderosa Towing. A trace of the vehicle revealed it to be Rowland's. A follow-up with the FBI quickly yielded the still unanswered question as to why the man's worldly effects were seen in a dumpster and now why his van had been discovered abandoned in Yosemite.

Coincidentally, on May 12, 1998, not long after the van had been traced to Rowland, hikers found a human skeleton scattered about half a mile west of Mirror Lake and a mile from where the van had been noticed. Near it were a meager campsite, scattered clothes, a liquor bottle, beer cans, and a .22 revolver, fully loaded with no expended cartridge. Park Special Agent Dan Horner could not help but conclude that all of this had to add up: Rowland's possessions in that dumpster, his van in Curry Village, and now this skeleton here with a deadly weapon lying beside it—but, try as they might, investigators could not find the skull anywhere. Maybe a bear had dragged it off. Or some person had collected it as a souvenir. It would not be the first time. Either way, without that skull, identification was a problem. Were the bones Rowland's?

Horner then decided other bones might do the job just as well as the skull. After all, DNA could be extracted and compared to that of Rowland's sister. They tried just this. It matched. The skeleton near Tenaya Creek was Clark Wilbur Rowland.

But what, exactly, had happened? Admittedly, it would be almost impossible in this late stage of the game to know the details with certainty. All of his stuff being thrown into a dumpster, as in symbolically trashing a life that no longer seemed worth living but had instead may have begun to feel like a burden, was typical of suicidal depression. Driving his now empty van to beautiful Yosemite Valley and walking to an attractive spot near the creek to end his life were also classic goodbye-cruel-world elements.

But, if so, why had his revolver not been fired? Had he brought it along while still undecided as to his mechanism of suicide? Had he also been prepared to end his life in other ways, say with pills? Now it was impossible to tell. Once scavengers had completed their "processing" of Rowland, they had virtually eaten the evidence needed to answer these questions.

A murder of Rowland seemed a far less likely scenario. Murder would have been inconsistent with the gun not having been fired but instead left apparently abandoned. Indeed the weapon being present and fully loaded and unused was a very strong indication that only Rowland had been at the scene at the critical moment. A suicidal moment. It would also appear that a probable cause of the depression that fostered Rowland's suicide—as it had done with Fudge—was loneliness.

Yet another episode started to unfold on August 7, 1996, when a Park maintenance employee spotted gear abandoned at the railing atop Glacier Point. Poking out from the top of a partially unzipped duffel bag were two notes. The first read: "Guess WHA-A-t?!" and "At the bottom of this hill lies a big, big man—Big John."

Again, Special Agent Horner arrived to examine the abandoned pile. It included a dirty pillow, a couple of shopping bags, clothing, and a box of Kleenex. Dan found more notes, some in addressed envelopes; others were just writings. Much of the eighty-seven pages of writings piled inside the duffel were semi-religious and characterized by mixed pieces of quotes and confused, incomplete thoughts. One page offered a short dedication to the writer's "eternal flame, Angelica Carol Huston Haler." This conveyed a partial insight into the missing man's thinking.

Horner, a two-time Department of Interior Valor Award winner, peered over the edge. No body was visible from above. A search from the Park's helicopter did spot the lower half of a body on the second ledge system, 1,200 feet below. Special Agent Greg Jablonski and Rangers Cameron Sholly and Jason Torlano managed the recovery of the jumper (part of the upper body had continued falling to a ledge 250 feet lower yet) and the documentation of the scene. No surprise, no portion of the divided body carried an ID.

As if in postmortem complicity with this deliberate mystery, the victim's teeth and jaws had been ejected and lost upon impact. The rangers tried identification via a single right thumbprint. Fortunately the California Department of Motor Vehicles made a match. That thumb belonged to 42-year-old John Parker Dack of Fresno. Dack had been separated from his wife. Further research revealed that he had jumped off Glacier Point on August 6.

Not every episode of this sort comes on untelegraphed. Indeed most suicides are broadcast in advance, often repeatedly, sometimes in Technicolor. On Christmas Day of 1998, for example, Park Dispatch received a request for a "welfare check" from a local Yosemite resident who had just returned from "out of town" to discover his son acting suicidal. Ranger Keith Lober responded first. He found the boy in the bathroom with a large butcher knife. He had already slashed furniture and scattered it around the house, "destroying" the place and had now positioned himself to compromise Lober in his movements. The young man immediately threatened the ranger and yelled, "Shoot me; shoot me now!"

Lober called for backup as he tried to reason with the boy. Ranger Gordon Gilbert arrived next. He too found the teenager brandishing the weapon in close quarters. Both men understood that this distraught kid intended to provoke at least one of them into shooting him. Gilbert calmly maneuvered into a position that allowed him to distract the boy and offer Lober a means of escape without harming the young man.

Ranger David Hajdik next arrived and also tried to negotiate with the boy. He had brought capsicum spray as a non-lethal tool to disarm him. The teenager now begged the three rangers to shoot him and thus facilitate his "suicide by police."

This sort of situation was so unusual that the Park had no standard protocols for dealing with it. The rangers now called for a crisis negotiator and for additional personnel to set up a perimeter around the house. They suspected that if this disturbed teenager's plan "A" failed, he would go to plan "B," which could quickly prove lethal to him and/or to someone else.

Meanwhile the boy advanced on the rangers three times. He continued to physically and verbally taunt them. He slashed at his own wrists (causing minor wounds) to emphasize how serious he was.

The disturbed boy next went to his back door. By now Ranger Jim Tucker and Special Agent Scott Hinson had also arrived. Tucker knew the local boy and now tried to talk him into relinquishing the knife. This failed. The teenager retreated inside the house. Tucker followed, continuing to negotiate and reason with him.

Finally Hinson directed the tactical containment, the use of tear gas, and the Park's entry into the dwelling. Hajdik entered the tear-gassed house without a mask (none were available). His presence—and the irritating gas—drove the boy to try to escape out the bathroom window. By now nine other personnel, including rangers, firefighters, and civilians, were aiding at the perimeter. Ranger Tucker intercepted the disturbed boy at the bathroom window and, with the boy's recently arrived father, convinced him to drop the knife. Tucker apprehended and immobilized the hysterical teenager for a "medical hold." After this he was committed to a long-term mental health facility.

In a ceremony in Washington, D.C., Rangers Loren Fazio, Gilbert, Hajdik, Lober, Tucker, and Special Agent Hinson were granted Department of Interior Valor Awards in 2000 for their careful work in this incident.

It is highly unfortunate that no one was present (as they had been for this boy) to stop the next bizarre episode. At about 6:30 a.m. on August 17, 2001, three Spanish mountain climbers on the northwest face of Half Dome heard a whoosh from above. They looked up to see an outstretched figure coming toward them at high speed. The falling man had adopted a flat stable position with arms spread, as if skydiving. The surprised trio heard no scream or vocal distress. In the brief moment they had to assess what was happening, it seemed to them that the falling man was willingly dropping, and positioned as if flying, 1,800 feet down the face of Half Dome.

If this guy was BASE jumping, then he was long past the point of popping his pilot chute. But no canopy appeared, even too late. As the skydiver neared the ground, he slowly oriented to headfirst. Two seconds later he slammed into the granite a mere 250 feet from the three witnesses. Stunned, they soon reported their bizarre observations to the Park.

Special Agent Dan Horner investigated the scene. The mystery jumper's head was now mostly gone. Who was he? He was not dressed as a climber or a BASE jumper or even as a typical hiker. He was clad in western wear and jewelry. He also was still wearing a small backpack. Nowhere on the man's destroyed body or in his pack could the agent find any type of identification.

Horner next went to the top of Half Dome. This too proved fruitless. He could find nothing atop the monolith that might be tied to the falling man or would prove otherwise useful in figuring out what had gone wrong here. The investigator would have to rely on fingerprints. Luckily the corpse still had them.

Four days later the California Department of Justice computer system made a match. The jumper was 24-year-old Vladimir Boutkovski. He was a Russian national who had immigrated to the USA about nineteen months earlier. He worked for a technology company in the San Francisco Bay Area and lived in Santa Clara with his parents, his brother, and his long-time buddy, Andrew Smirnov.

Because Boutkovski had arrived in the Park late on August 16, Horner concluded he had hiked up to the top of Half Dome at least partially in the dark. This revealed a very serious dedication to execute a dawn jump. Why, Horner now wondered, was a young, recent immigrant with a good job and a family and friends suicidal?

The eerie answer was: He was not.

Boutkovski (nicknamed "Bobbin") had borrowed his friend Smirnov's car to drive to Yosemite that previous day. He had left a note to his friend saying:

> Hi dude! I'm going to undertake an endeavor of possibly utmost conceivable stupidity, though it is this irrationalism in the full sense that controversially attracts me. Let me just say that if this is the only thing you see from me, then look for your car at the Yosemite Park, on the parking near the shop. The key is going to be in the exhaust pipe. /Bobbin

After initially evading questions and withholding critical information from investigators, Smirnov finally came clean with details vital to understanding Boutkovski's bizarre death leap. He explained these to Horner. The agent's summary letter to the Fresno U.S. Attorney's Office interprets these insights gained from Smirnov:

> Boutkovski's purpose for jumping from the top of Half Dome was not to commit suicide, but to release his spirit. Smirnov said that Boutkovski followed the teachings of Carlos Casteneda and believed in magic and mysticism. He said that Boutkovski believed that jumping from something would free him from the bounds of earth, and that he would find some greater spirituality. Smirnov said that Boutkovski had discussed this type of jump for about the past five years.

On October 15, 2004, yet another weird suicide incident unraveled in Yosemite. That morning the Yosemite Helitack had responded to a 100-acre fire north of Hetch Hetchy behind Kolana Dome. The crew spotted two backpackers—Mike Ulawski and Gilbert Sauceda, Jr.—below in the Rancheria Creek area. And due to rapidly expanding fires, the rangers evacuated them.

The two hikers quickly reported a strange story. They had seen several fires spring up as if being lit by an arsonist. So they had investigated. They soon met the bad guy (later identified as 33-year-old Richard N. Celebrini). The heavily muscled man had been dressed only in black and was hand carrying a propane bottle. When the two hikers "had words with him" about his idiocy in igniting forest fires on purpose, Celebrini threatened them with a pistol. Despite this bellicosity, the beefy arsonist next told them, "You better run for the water; I don't want to kill you, too."

As the two hightailed it away from this insane encounter, they heard Celebrini ignite a dozen more fires. This bozo's wanton destructiveness had infuriated them, they now told rangers, but what could they do?

No one seriously doubted the story these two hikers told. On the other hand, it *was* pretty damned bizarre. Even if these two had exaggerated a bit, this mission should be prepared to encounter armed resistance.

The helicopter crew now spotted a white male below in the Tiltill Valley. And, yes, he was lighting more fires. The crew flew off with the intention of returning in force to arrest the criminal. Unfortunately, once they returned to search for him later that day, the multiple law enforcement agencies cooperating to arrest Celebrini were foiled by the thickening smoke roiling up from his fires. These crackled and burned over an area that now exceeded 1,300 acres (two square miles). And no one could clearly see anything on the smoking ground below.

But when rangers returned the next morning they did locate Celebrini, still dressed in black, from the air. He appeared dead. But was he? They landed and cautiously approached the armed but inert pyromaniac dressed as a ninja.

He did not move. They edged closer. Closer yet, they could see that he had shot himself.

The Park's ensuing investigation uncovered Celebrini's history of violence. The unemployed man just had been questioned twice for recent domestic violence assaults. But the police had not gone much beyond those interviews. Far more strange, when he was younger and after a relationship of his had not worked out, he had actually jumped off the San Mateo Bridge over San Francisco Bay with weights attached to him to commit suicide. He had hit the bay, sank, but then had changed his mind and fought to successfully survive his own foolproof suicide attempt. Clearly the man was unstable mentally. Also obvious, he was violent. Indeed, in October of 2004, the level of his violence would shock even investigators inured to the darkest side of the human psyche.

Worse than surviving his own suicide, Park investigators now found, Celebrini, who had been living off his mother's credit card, had recently left his home in Brentwood, California to burn down Yosemite. But before leaving home that morning, Celebrini had committed several brutal acts. He shot to death his wife Michelle. He also shot and killed his two stepdaughters Jessica and Samantha Fouch (but he had not shot his own biological daughter, Nina).

Celebrini, it turns out, emerged from a family with a history of suicide. His grandmother and great grandmother had both killed themselves. Neither of them, though, had first committed mass murder. This was something new that Richard N. Celebrini added as a legacy.

What is the upshot of suicide in Yosemite? Do people really travel to the Park—as has been reputed—just to do themselves in? Does Yosemite host an inordinate number of suicides? Or, more inexplicably, does simply being there make some people want to kill themselves?

While fully understanding the underlying processes of early life trauma, later depression and pathological self-absorption that lead to suicide is not easy, the answers to most of the questions above are. In Yosemite's 170+ years since its post-Gold Rush discovery, there have been at least 90 suicides—by at least 76 men and at least 14 women. Roughly a half dozen more deaths here are likely but not confirmed suicides. These ninety account for more than 7 percent of traumatic deaths in Yosemite. These numbers are similar to the overall record within Grand Canyon National Park, where suicides account for about 11–12 percent of traumatic deaths below the rim and far more above it. This is despite the human population within 200 miles of Grand Canyon being only about one tenth of that within an equal distance of Yosemite. In even more remote Yellowstone National Park suicides have accounted for about 6 percent of its 300 or so traumatic deaths. Thus Yosemite does not appear to attract more than an infinitesimally small fraction of California's tens of thousands who have committed suicide.

Moreover, about half of Yosemite suicides did not occur in a location one might describe as "scenic" or "Yosemite-like." Instead most were in parked cars, tents, cabins, or secluded little humdrum spots. When one thinks of Yosemite and suicide, the normal connection seems to be jumping off one of those famed cliffs. Indeed, twenty-three people—about a quarter of Yosemite's known suicides—have made such a leap.

It is impossible to poll these victims to learn how important the role of scenery might have played in their choice of locations. Several probably would have rated it as low. For jumpers, it was the quality of the jump, we suspect that many would answer, not the view that mattered most. Indeed a similar number of people killed themselves with a firearm (at least twenty, but possibly a few more, more than another quarter of the total) in Yosemite as have jumped. Regardless, only thirteen *non-jumper* suicides occurred in a "scenic" location—and most of these were shootings. Again, one interpretation from this brief analysis might be: Even suicidal people seldom travel to Yosemite for reasons having to do with it being their choice of places to kill themselves.

Why then these suicides in Yosemite? Unfortunately, more than half the suiciders gave no reason for their actions. Of the twenty or so who did, only four were women. The most common reason for men who did was they could not bear having lost their wife or girlfriend (at least six men). Another three men were simply lonely. Five more were in deep financial trouble, and another four men and one woman were terminally ill. At least three men were insane. Others yet were highly disturbed.

Gender differences were also noticeable in the method of death. Only one man and only one woman drove off the road to kill themselves. Otherwise, differences were glaring. Eight of the twelve women took overdoses of pills. Only one male took pills. Eight men hung themselves, three used poison, four slit their wrists, one man even dynamited himself. One woman hung herself. Twenty-one men jumped off a cliff, only two women did. At least nineteen men used a firearm; one woman did this. And so on. Sixteen men left some kind of note behind, only five women did (similar proportions).

Hence, the question of Yosemite and suicide may be the reverse of: Why do people go to the Park to commit suicide? A more appropriate question might be:

Why don't *more* people go to Yosemite to commit suicide? Psychotherapist Susan Ash-Ghiglieri notes that most suiciders are not merely ending their lives, they are making a statement. But if one jumps off a cliff and explodes into unidentifiable pieces upon impact in the talus, or if one goes into the dense woods and shoots oneself and remains undiscovered except by scavenging bears, that statement becomes silent; nothing concrete and shocking gets communicated to the ones whom the suicider had decided must be "informed." Consequently most suiciders opt for more obvious locations closer to home. Compare these numbers, for example, with the high number of people who have suicided by jumping off San Francisco's Golden Gate Bridge since it was built in 1937. How many? More than 1,600 people.

An interesting element of Yosemite's seventy or so known suicides is that thirteen of them—one-sixth—were committed by concession employees of the Yosemite Park and Curry Company or its successors. Meanwhile no NPS employee in Yosemite has committed suicide in the Park. This seems a notable difference, though one we hesitate to try to explain.

The final anomaly in Yosemite suicides is their timing. Unlike in Grand Canyon where suicidal deaths were disproportionately packed into the off-season winter months, in Yosemite only five suicides occurred during December, two in January, and none at all in February. But in August, fifteen people killed themselves; this includes nearly 20 percent of all of the Park's confirmed suicides packed into that specific month. This August tally is twice as high as the next highest month of November, during which eight occurred. Only two of those fourteen suicides in August had been by concession employees in the Park, so it was not the dismal prospect of ending a summer job that had prompted most of these final acts in summer. Why so many in August then? We have no idea.

Above all the other "noise" of this tragic sample it is clear that Yosemite suicides are most likely to happen among younger people. Two-thirds of these victims were between the ages of 19 and 39 years old; twenty-five of them (more than a third) were in their twenties, and most of these were committed by young men.

Perhaps these now more obvious trends will help someone out there prevent some of these ill-made decisions formulated in a state of severe emotional depression and made to end temporary problems (most of which can be fixed relatively easily) with *permanent* solutions that prove tragic for all concerned.

TABLE 13. SUICIDES IN YOSEMITE. (Incidents discussed in text are noted.)

Name, age	Date	Location	*Circumstances*
Jay Bruce Cook, 42	December 25, 1910	Sentinel Hotel, Yosemite Village	*Sentinel Hotel manager Cook shot himself in the chest in his office on Christmas afternoon. He had been plagued by "years of severe stomach problems," had just lost his job as Valley Postmaster, and was expecting "an impending investigation by the federal government into irregularities in his Yosemite business affairs."*
J. E. Mack, 35	April 22, 1914	trail to Chilnualna Falls, Wawona	*Mack of Brisbane, Australia shot himself with a .45 caliber revolver. He left a note but had destroyed all identification of himself; so "Mack" may not be his real name.*
George Fiske, 85	October 20, 1918	Fiske's house/studio, Yosemite Village	*At age 85 Fiske was the oldest resident of Yosemite, where he had lived as a photographer for 40+ years. He had been brooding over the loss of his wife 9 months earlier. He also suffered "unbearable headaches." He reclined on his couch and shot himself with a pistol. He left behind carefully written letters and instructions, dated months earlier, as to the disposal of his property.*
Peter Arioli, 40	March 17, 1919	Arch Rock Construction Camp for El Portal Road	*Italian immigrant Arioli awoke after midnight, left his bed, and walked up the road in the dark to the locked box of construction dynamite. He broke it open then exploded the half-box of 40 percent dynamite, blowing himself into small bits. His motive was unknown.*
Fred McDonald, 34	May 24, 1920	Wawona	*McDonald, likely of New Bloomfield, Missouri, was a local hunting and fishing guide in poor health. He had been despondent for months when he shot himself with a .32 caliber Winchester.*
Count Theodore James Jackowski, 55	June 7, 1925	Upper Yosemite Fall	*On August 26, 1925, 2 young men found a discarded coat containing a suicide letter and a will dated June 3 and 4, 1925, written and signed by Jackowski. He had inherited $250,000 then squandered it. Depressed, he jumped 1,430 feet off the cliff.* (in text)
Charles W. Howard, 36	May 29, 1926	Yosemite Valley	*Howard of San Francisco was depressed about his wife's death the day before. He swallowed sodium cyanide.*
John Hill, 32	October 19, 1927	Hetch Hetchy dam site	*Utah Construction Co. worker Hill from Finland "went to…a somewhat secluded spot…drew the keen edge of his razor through the greater part of his throat."*
Vincent E. Herkomer, 23	September 21, 1930	Half Dome	*U. C., Berkeley biochemistry honors student Herkomer had been accepted into Annapolis. He took the train to Yosemite from the Bay*

Area, climbed to the base of Half Dome, and swallowed the contents of a small bottle of poison. His scattered bones and personal effects were found nearly 4 years later in March, 1934, by workers monitoring bark beetle infestations. Herkomer's father could only attribute his son's motive to recent illness and over studying.

Frank Castello, 39 — August 28, 1932 — Yosemite Village
Castello, employed by contractors Goerig and Dalberg, returned to the job after a protracted drinking spree. He made statements of self-disgust and later, in the middle of the night, hanged himself from a beam in the camp bunkhouse.

Paul Otis Shoe, 30 — July 4, 1934 — Glacier Point Road, near Bridalveil Creek
"Popular and well-liked" Curry Co executive assistant Shoe was found dead in his car. A hose led from his exhaust pipe to the car's interior. He left a pair of notes of undisclosed contents.

Frank Albert Kraback, 22 — September 5-15 (?), 1937 — near Merced Lake
Kraback of Oakland went missing in September, 1937. On September 9, 1938, Park employees rounding up stray horses near Merced Lake found his skull with a bullet hole in the right temple. In August, 1939, investigators found nearby an Oakland Tribune *dated September 5, 1937, and a Harrington & Richards .32 caliber pistol with one expended round. His motive was unknown.*

Henry B. Menke, 30 — March 4, 1938 — top of Cascade Falls
U.S. Army deserter Menke of Boston slit his wrists, legs, and throat.

James John Stergar, 30 — August 25, 1956 — Half Dome summit
Stergar of Pomona, California leapt 2,000 feet off Half Dome. He left behind a pack and note expressing his intent to jump and his feeling despondent over being lonely. In his car he left several letters, one to the Park Superintendent apologizing for jumping but requesting his bones remain where they fell (they were removed).

Marian E. Campbell, 43 — December 19, 1958 — Lewis Memorial Hospital
Curry Co. employee Campbell swallowed an overdose of prescription medications.

Ernest Lee Medecke, 34 — August 4, 1963 — Tamarack Flat Campground
Medecke, a service station attendant at Banning, California, shot himself.

Arthur Ellson, 59 — August 17, 1963 — Camp Curry
Ellson of the Bronx, New York hung himself from a beam in his tent cabin.

Harold A. Dittmore, 65 — August 8, 1966 — Yosemite Village
Dittmore of San Francisco was conducting a management survey of Curry Co.'s operations. In the afternoon, he was found in the bathroom of his hotel room with severe lacerations to his right arm from which he had bled to death. Dittmore left no note. Interestingly, neither did he leave behind any instrument or weapon by which he could have slashed himself. (Possible homicide?)

Helen Joy Rennels, 52	September 13, 1966 El Portal Administrative Site *Rennels of El Portal took an overdose of prescription medications.*
Donald C. Campbell, 42	August 21, 1967 Wawona *Campbell of Norwalk, California swallowed an overdose of prescription medications.*
Bruce Douglas Norris, 24	December 1, 1972 Upper Yosemite Fall *Norris of Fair Oaks, California committed a murder-suicide by shooting his girlfriend Lorraine J. Sutton and throwing her over the waterfall and then following her off.* (detailed in Chapter 14. Homicide)
Richard Lawrence Fudge, 38	December 22 (?), 1972 near Indian Caves, Upper Yosemite Valley *On December 27, 1972, 2 men searching for mushrooms near Indian Caves discovered a human body eaten by bears but dead due to self-imposed gunshot.* (in text)
Leah Oliver Good, 49	April 30, 1973 Vernal Fall *Wife of the Park's assistant superintendent Good left a note for her husband that she was* ***solo*** *hiking the Mist Trail near Vernal Fall. She also was reportedly terminally ill with cancer. She never returned. Hikers spotted her body in a rapid below Vernal Fall. She had not drowned. The coroner's report indicated a possible suicide by jumping.* (also listed in Chapter 1. Waterfalls)
Roger Alan White, 28	November 2 (?), 1973 off-trail near Nevada Fall *On November 2, Roger White reported his son Roger Alan of Long Beach missing, suicidal, and attracted to Nevada Fall. A search failed to find him. On November 18, 8 hikers saw a bear feeding on a human carcass 30 feet above the trail to the fall. Using a metal detector in the deep snow, rangers found White's* cocked *revolver. Death was due to a self-inflicted gunshot wound.*
Linden Moore, 24	November 4 (?), 1973 Glacier Point *On October 26, after failing to secure a full-time teaching position and also having a "severe disagreement" the previous day with a teacher for whom she aided, former Curry Co. employee Moore (she had quit because she could not make any friends) drove from her home in Fremont, California. She left suicide notes with her minister and her analyst. She parked at Glacier Point, left yet another suicide note in her car and on her windshield the phone numbers of her father, minister, and analyst. Her body was not found. Had she jumped?* (also listed in Chapter 12. Lost)
Cynthia Louise Burton, 22	October 12(?), 1976 Glacier Point *Burton of Arcadia, California leapt off Glacier Point 1,500 feet onto Glacier Point Apron. She left a suicide note on her vehicle which tipped off Ranger Dean Paschall. After a 2-hour search 3 days later, a Lemoore helicopter lowered John Dill and Joe Abell on October 15 to recover her destroyed body.*

Bisera G. Filipova, 33	April 19(?), 1977	between Ahwahnee Hotel and Indian Caves *On April 24, 3 teenage girls reported finding a person asleep on the ground in a sleeping bag but with flies on her face. It was Curry Co. housekeeper Filipova of Bulgaria in rigor mortis—she had somehow committed suicide. The Park employed a little known section from 16 United States Code 17(e), permitting it to pay for her indigent remains to be buried in Mariposa.*
Timothy John Clark, 22	June 20, 1977	Bunnell Switchbacks, Merced Lake Trail *Clark of Dearborn Heights, Michigan was found near the trail dead from a 250-foot fall. His death was a suspected suicide.* (also listed in Chapter 6. Falls while Scrambling & Hiking)
Mohammed Ardakan Faeghi, 36	August 17(?), 1977	upstream of Happy Isles *On October 13, 1977, a visitor found a decomposing "John Doe" in secluded woods 400 yards south of the Happy Isles Nature Center. Nearby lay a bloody sleeping bag, an empty pint of vodka, empty beers, a jacket containing a suicide note written in a foreign language, a package of double-edged razor blades (one had been used), and a Safeway receipt dated August 17. The victim was Faeghi from Iran and now recently divorced from his American wife. It appears he had slit his wrists in Happy Isles 2 months earlier.*
Grace Ann Runcie, 55	November 14, 1977	Yosemite Lodge *Runcie of San Jose, California checked into Room #824 and asked not to be disturbed. She swallowed an overdose of prescription medications then penned an increasingly sloppy suicide note.*
James John Walton, 23	August 8(?), 1978	Sunnyside Bench *Walton left his home and job in Buffalo, New York and arrived in the Park on August 8. Ten days later, boys scrambling above the Lost Arrow residential area found a body 60 feet below a small ledge holding his backpack and neatly folded clothes. "Investigators believe Walton took his own life by consuming a container of [Black Flag] insecticide which was found near his decomposed body."*
Jimmie D. Marsh, 29	May 8(?), 1983	Wawona Campground *Marsh, a Marine from El Toro Marine Corps Base, stayed in the campground for a few days with new, cheap gear and little real food. He hung himself from a tree near his campsite.*
Andrew Julius Koller, 65	November 22, 1983	El Portal Administrative Site *Koller of El Portal shot himself.*
Francis J. Matranga, 22	March 1, 1985	Yosemite Lodge *Curry Co. employee Matranga hung himself in concession housing.*
Richard Russell Mughir, 29	August 17, 1985	Glacier Point *At 7:45 a.m., Sean O' Neill, camped with 2 friends, saw Mughir leap off Glacier Point after having murdered Sonia Janet Goldstein in a "suicide pact."* (detailed in Chapter 14. Homicide)
Thorne Wesly Hayden, 23	August 19, 1985	Camp 6, Yosemite Valley *Curry Co. employee Hayden of Atwood, Kansas was apparently*

obsessed with death. He hung himself from the poles of Tent #86 in what today is a parking lot.

unknown, ?

September 8, 1985 Upper Yosemite Fall
At about 11:30 a.m. visitor John Pohlman made a report deemed creditable of seeing a person jump off the cliff ¼ mile east of the top of Upper Yosemite Fall. "After two days of searching the area [by ground and air personnel]," noted Incident Report #85-16468, "the search activities were suspended. No physical evidence of the incident was discovered." (not included in suicide statistics)

Patrick Charles Allen, 26

October 20, 1985 Vernal Fall
Allen of Capitola, California "surfed" as an apparent suicide over Vernal Fall into the pool at its base, dying instantly.

Betty Jo Jordan, 57

April 21-27, 1987 Chinquapin area, Bishop Creek
Jordan of Fresno drove her 1981 Malibu off the road ¼ mile south of Bishop Creek, leaving no skid marks. The car flew 88 feet down an embankment to slam into a pair of oaks. Jordan's body landed 140 feet away, 100 feet below a cliff. The car contained 2 suicide notes, indicated Incident Report #87-853.

Donald W. Buchanan, 86

November 11, 1988 Half Dome
Former Park seasonal worker Buchanan of Mariposa had hiked in Yosemite for 50+ years since the 1920s. He solo backpacked to Half Dome on November 9 then failed to return from his 3-day hike. Nearly 100 searchers failed during increasing snow. Buchanan had terminal cancer and was believed to have purposely gone out on his final hike.

Jung Hoon Suh, 21

early June 1990 Ledge Trail
Suh of Hawthorne, California left a note expressing thoughts of suicide and entered the Park on May 30 then vanished. A 3-day search failed. Hikers found his skeletal remains a year later, on June 9, 1991, on the old Ledge Trail route below a fall below Glacier Point.

Elizabeth A. Roberts, 14

July 18, 1991 Lyell Canyon, 6 miles south of Tuolumne Meadows
Roberts of Long Beach, California had a 4-year history of hospitalization for depression but had recently improved. She shared a tent on July 17 with her sister, Tricia, with whom she had emotional issues over "competition." Elizabeth, unseen, took a deliberate overdose (89 tablets of 50 mg.) of the antidepressant Norpramin. She exhibited breathing problems at 2:30 a.m., noticed but unreported by Tricia. At 6 a.m. Tricia awoke to find Elizabeth dead.

Luis Antonio Moncada Margain, 24

October 9, 1991 Bridalveil Meadow, Yosemite Valley
When the high school bus broke down, 2 wandering students spotted Margain of Tijuana, Mexico wedged between boulders on the south shore of the Merced near "20-mph curve." Investigators Horner and Sullivan found a bullet hole to his right temple and beneath him a .38 caliber S&W revolver with one expended round under the hammer. Margain left 5 suicide notes.

Donald L. Nieto, 47 — October 16(?), 1991 — Glacier Point

Nieto of San Francisco parked his 1974 Mercury Capri at Glacier Point, drank a Budweiser, smoked a few cigarettes, left his keys in the ignition, then jumped off. A search of his residence located a suicide note in a room set up and decorated as a "shrine" to Yosemite. On November 30, a helicopter spotted his body on a ledge 1,200 feet below. Recovery and identification both proved difficult.

Joe C. Felipe, 38 — June 3, 1993 — near top of Nevada Falls

Depressed and asthmatic, Felipe of Napa, California parked his Honda sedan in the Village Store parking lot then vanished. Searches failed. On April 30, 1994, visitors found human remains off the John Muir Trail near the top of Nevada Fall. Investigators found clothing scattered under a cave-like ledge with a gym bag and medicine with Felipe *on the prescription label. His bones lay strewn, mostly intact.* (suspected suicide, not included in analysis)

Gordon D. Gasvoda, 33 — May 21, 1994 — Ribbon Fall

Gasvoda of Concord, California hiked to the top of Ribbon Fall. He then solo scramble-climbed to its brink. What happened next is unknown but he fell 1,612 feet to the base. He exploded on impact—along with a Bible he had been carrying. (suspected suicide, not included in analysis)

Albert Charles, 20 — June 1, 1994 — Curry Village

Concession housekeeper Charles, a Native American of Ganado, Arizona, first tried to suicide by self-inflicting knife wounds to his stomach. Next he hung himself from the center roof beam in "Boystown" tent #48. He told a friend of his intent. He left a note that read, "Good bye, Albert."

Brian Robert Hilliard, 24 — June 22, 1994 — Camp 6, Yosemite Valley

Concession employee Hilliard, suffering from depression due to problems with a girlfriend and recent troubles with the law, hung himself in his tent cabin #69. He left no note. He died 2 days later.

Linda Darlene Waller, 26 — June 28, 1996 — Sentinel Dome parking lot, Glacier Point

Her family knew Waller of Fresno was thinking suicidally. She was found in the driver's seat of her car with a gunshot wound to the head. In her hand was a .45 caliber pistol.

John Parker Dack, 42 — August 6, 1996 — Glacier Point

On August 7, a Park maintenance employee found equipment at the railing atop Glacier Point and 2 "notes" in a duffel bag. NPS Special Agent Dan Horner and the Park helicopter spotted the lower half of a body 1,200 feet below. Dack of Fresno, had been separated from his wife. (in text)

Ross William Blue, 51 — September 13, 1996 — Taft Point, Valley Rim

Two Germans—Klaus Ritter and Manfred Ganser—witnessed a white male wearing a blue track suit yell "It's over now," then run and dive off the Point. Ranger Michael Brindero investigated. A van parked at the top contained an ID of Ross Blue of Hayward, California. Rangers found his remains 1,200 feet below.

David Azvedo, 37	December 28, 1996	El Portal Administrative Site
	Three days after Christmas, Azvedo, who had been drinking alcohol, stabbed himself in the chest superficially with scissors in his house trailer then fled outside in the rain in his underwear and jumped into the Merced. He drowned. (not in Chapter 10. Drowning)	
Joachim Peter Tolksdorff, 29	July 5, 1997	Northwest Face, Half Dome
	On July 9, a pair of Japanese climbers on the Tis-sa-ack Route found a brain-avulsed body 80 feet above the base of Half Dome. Tolksdorff of Herrenberg, Germany was a recent recipient of a liver transplant and was in very poor health and facing future repeat hospitalization. He had left a note stating "key [to the rental car] on body or in the clothes."	
Clark Wilbur Rowland, 42	September 1997	½ mile west of Mirror Lake
	Chimney sweep Rowland lived in his van. It turned up abandoned in Curry Village. On May 12, 1998, hikers found much of his skeleton nearby. Special Agent Dan Horner found a campsite and bones but no skull. The ID was made via DNA. (in text)	
Rex Wayne Redding, 48	April 16(?), 1998	Liberty Cap Moraine, Little Yosemite Valley
	Redding was an insurance salesman of 24 years for the same company but had been recently unemployed for 4 months and also separated from his new, second wife. Now in "extreme" debt, he was reported missing on April 15 from Pleasant Hill, California. On May 24, hiker Bill Manieri found a jawbone with a gold crown plus vertebra and a Gucci watch among oaks and boulders. The last person Redding had spoken to was his estranged wife (who had given him the Gucci), telling her he wanted her to be "the beneficiary of all his stuff." He died due to a gunshot to the head.	
Dana Brian Farnsworth, 48	January 30, 1999	Hodgdon Meadows Campground
	Fugitive Farnsworth of Moreno Valley, California sat in the driver's seat of his stolen Saturn sedan (from Florida) parked at Site #64 and shot himself in the chest with a .243 caliber Winchester rifle.	
Michael Eric Randall, 26	July 6(?), 1999	Cold Canyon, north of Tuolumne Meadows
	Former concession employee Randall of San Jose was reported missing in July 1999 by his family. In June 2001, a trail crew member hiking cross-country found Randall's wallet in Cold Canyon. NPS Agent Dan Horner found Randall's skeleton. Cause of death remains unknown but is suspected suicide. (in text of Chapter 12. Lost)	
Anke B. Hocker-Smith, 28	November 27, 1999	Taft Toe area, Southside Drive
	Hocker-Smith of Fresno abused prescription medications and had suicidal tendencies. On November 30, her red Mustang was found near Taft Toe. The next day, 0.17 mile SE, searchers found her, dead due to acute Amitriptyline ingestion (fraudulently obtained).	

David V. Promessi, 53 — August 8, 2000 — Tuolumne Meadows
For 3 years Promessi of Concord, California had been diagnosed with chronic major depressive disorder with suicidal thoughts and prior attempts. On August 8, he left a suicide call on his therapist's answering machine. Alerted, rangers found him near the Tuolumne Lodge sitting with his back against a tree facing the river with a small pistol in his hand. "...while Ranger Longden attempted to handcuff him it became apparent that he was deceased."

Vladimir Boutkovski, 24 — August 17, 2001 — Northwest Face, Half Dome
Three climbers on Half Dome heard a whoosh and saw Boutkovski falling past in a skydiving position. The immigrant, following the teachings of Carlos Casteneda and believing in mysticism, had jumped to free his spirit from the bounds of earth. (in text)

Joseph P. Breen, 57 — September, 2003 — Tuolumne Meadows
Breen of Menlo Park, California sent a suicide letter to his sister from Tuolumne Meadows Post Office in September 2003 then vanished, leaving a journal detailing his suicide plans. On May 31, 2004, hikers found a human maxilla SW of Parson's Lodge. Agents Jeff Sullivan and Steve Yu found a .32 Colt at the scenic site plus bones chewed on by bears, and possessions of Breen. He had shot himself.

Eric Eugene Frolkey, 33 — November 28, 2003 — Curry Village
Frolkey of Sacramento was having relationship problems with his girlfriend. He hung himself from a ceiling beam of his rented tent.

Richard N. Celebrini, 33 — October 15, 2004 — behind Kolana Dome, Hetch Hetchy area
Park fire crews spotted a man lighting fires. After the smoke cleared, rangers found Celebrini had shot himself. (in text)

Steven R. Tucker, 47 — November 10, 2005 — Wawona Tunnel parking lot
Tucker of Northridge, California drove his vehicle at high speed through the retaining wall at Discovery View then over the edge. His vehicle flew 132 vertical feet, hit, then cartwheeled another 150 feet. He left his wife a 6-page suicide note.

Stiles A. Cummings, 26 — September 29, 2006 — base of The Cascades
After witnesses saw Cummings of Iowa City, Iowa wandering away from the Tamarack Campground barefooted, a major SAR ensued. 13 days later searchers found his body in a pool in Cascades Creek. Suspected suicide.

Bonita Christine McDonald, 40 — February 7, 2007 — South Fork Merced River, Wawona
While taking a water sample, NPS employee Ben Cunningham found the body of McDonald of Santa Paula, California in the South Fork. Her blood toxicology revealed a higher-than-toxic level of ***Sertraline****. She had left suicide notes and emails.*

Zachariah D. Gleason, 36 — June 12, 2008 — North American Wall, El Capitan
Using pebbles atop El Capitan, Gleason wrote "Zack" and added an arrow pointing to the wall. Then he jumped 2,500 feet.

Levi Chitwood, 27
July 29, 2008 Half Dome
Chitwood of Dublin, California jumped 2,000 feet, "doing a half gainer." Rangers collected "the majority of the deceased."

David Zerbe, 37
March 9, 2009 Upper Yosemite Fall
Zerbe of Waterbury, Connecticut left suicide notes with his family and in his rental car. He climbed to Upper Y Fall and phoned 911, threatening to suicide. A ranger team tried to talk him down for 5 hours. Zerbe, who had gulped a load of drugs, slipped into Yosemite Creek. He was swept over the fall and dismembered. A month earlier he had been fired for falsifying his law school credits and faced a felony conviction for impersonating a federal officer.

Stephen William Anderson, 32
August 19, 2009 Half Dome
Anderson wrote suicide letters in Bend, Oregon then rode his motorcycle to Yosemite, climbed Half Dome, and shot himself with a Glock .40. He recently had separated from his wife and lost his job.

Anthony C. Green, Jr., 40
November 6, 2009 California Wilderness parking lot
Green of Modesto, California committed suicide via an undetermined method and was found 9 months later on July 14, 2010.

Estila Velasquez, 49
November 12, 2010 Wawona
Concession employee Velasquez hung herself. Days earlier she had falsely claimed a car-jacking after stealing money from her family.

Sonny Lawhon, 72
January 20, 2012 El Portal Administrative Site
Lawhon, a retired NPS maint./trail crew specialist, shot himself.

Holly Mauro, 32
April 6, 2012 El Portal residence
Mauro, of New Paltz, New York had been a difficult child and as an adult was plagued by worsening undiagnosed mental illness for which she refused to seek help. Extremely driven and successful, she had quit a career in real estate after making a "fortune" to indulge her passion for rock climbing. On March 27, after leaving suicide notes and planning the disposition of her estate, she drank a lethal cocktail of Pentobarbital and Coca-Cola, walked to the house of her ex-boyfriend, texted him: "body on your drivew…," and collapsed. He found her and performed extended CPR. She died 11 days later in Doctor's Medical Center in Modesto.

Scott Leyton Rials, 21
May 28, 2012 Glacier Point
Terminated concession employee Rials of Louisiana approached a Canadian tourist and asked that he dial a phone number to explain what came next. Then Rials jumped off the retaining wall 600 feet. Rials had not shared his thoughts with friends but was depressed. He left many suicide notes and discarded drafts indicating unrequited love and having given up.

Scott Caleb Brickman, 35
July 4, 2013 El Capitan
Witnesses reported seeing a person with no BASE jump parachute deployed falling to the ground near the base of the North American Wall. Brickman of Cedar Park, Texas had e-mailed Park HQ his intention to suicide jump on July 4 before doing so.

Nathan C. Shemwell, 23 — September 1, 2013 — Ostrander Trail area
Owl researchers discovered Shemwell's remains in a remote wooded area near the Ostrander Trail. Death by self-inflicted gunshot wound at an unknown date with a .357.

Jeffrey Moore, 36 — April 11, 2014 — The Rostrum
Moore of Mariposa, California parked his vehicle near the Highway 41 Tunnel, in a pullout often used to access the top of The Rostrum, then jumped 1,000 feet.

Gerardo Cruz Hernandez, 18 — November 22, 2017 — Glacier Point
Hernandez of Santa Barbara, California was suffering from depression. He left three suicide notes with family and girlfriend then jumped 1,200 feet.

Maximillian Lee Schweitzer, 41 — January 1-4(?), 2018 — Lower Yosemite Fall
On July 12, 2018 Park visitors found the remains of Schweitzer of San Francisco, California among west-side boulders above Lower Yosemite Fall Footbridge. Schweitzer had a criminal record, a history of mental illness with suicidal feelings, and had been arrested by the CHP protection detail of California's Lieutenant Governor for threats to his wife, Mrs. Jennifer Siebel Newsom (later First Lady of California). Schweitzer was released after being found mentally incompetent to stand trial. He jumped (?) unwitnessed above Lower Yosemite Fall.

Scott Andre Tenczar, 48 — July 25, 2018 — Suicide Ridge, Eastern Yosemite
After the Park was notified of an overdue and despondent hiker, on August 18, 2018 two hikers discovered the decomposing, bear-gnawed body of experienced backpacker and Afghanistan veteran Scott Tenczar of Manteca, California. On July 25 Tenczar had departed from the Bridgeport Ranger Station east of Yosemite on Highway 395 during a 40-mile solo backpacking hike planned from Robinson Creek to Crown Lake, Matterhorn Canyon, Smedberg Lake, Seavey Pass and Peeler Lake. Death by self-inflicted gunshot wound.

John Blevins Cogdell III, 55 — August 15, 2018 — Yosemite Slabs, Half Dome area
Last seen at midday on August 15 at the Upper Pines Campground in Yosemite Valley, off-work NPS employee Cogdell disappeared solo then was discovered several days later dead due to a self-inflicted gunshot wound.

Brian Alan Rathke, 37 — June 12, 2019 — Taft Point
Rathke of LaCrosse, Wisconsin was suffering from depression and jumped.

Joseph DiTore, 65 — July 31 or August 4, 2019 — Glacier Point
DiTore of Long Beach, California jumped.

Raul S. Soans, 21 — October 21-23, 2019 — Hodgdon Campground
Cal Poly Pamona student Soans of Texas died of a self-inflicted gunshot wound.

Neil Keung, 37	June 24, 2020	Bernice Lakes *Keung hung himself.*
"Alice" Yu Xie, 41	January 15, 2021	Upper Yosemite Fall (1,430 feet) *Yu Xie, a Chinese National, embarked on a solo day hike from the Valley to above the Upper Yosemite Fall then vanished. Searchers found her body at the base of the fall. (Suicide?)*
Gavin William Harrell, 52	February 27, 2021	Tuolumne Grove *Harrell of Mariposa, California shot himself in a restroom.*
Ralph M. Elliot, 52	April 22, 2021	Eagle Peak near Half Dome (?) *Elliot, known to be suicidal, possibly headed to Eagle Creek then vanished. On August 13, 2021, his remains were found in the treacherous Inner Gorge.*
Suzanne Lorene Dobbs, 66	July 22, 2023	Vernal Fall *Dobbs of Granite Bay, California jumped unwitnessed into the waterfall.*
Mason James Kirk, 35	July 28, 2023	Glacier Point *Kirk of Los Angeles, California jumped witnessed.*
Jesus Andre Soto, 25	February 9, 2024	Huff Cabin #209 *Soto of Fresno, California died by apparent self-strangulation.*
Kevin Diaz Ramirez, 30	August 25, 2024	Taft Point *Ramirez of Santa Ana (Los Angeles), California jumped.*
Steven Mathew Oda, 40	November 1, 2024	Hodgdon Meadows Campground *Oda of Newport Beach, California died of a self-inflicted gunshot wound.*
Patrick Michael Donahue, 27	September 8, 2025	Taft Point *Donahue, a Yosemite concession employee of the Firefall Lodge and originally from Burr Ridge, Illinois, left a suicide note then jumped off the cliff unwitnessed.*

Chapter Fourteen

HOMICIDE

"James Wilson Marshall's discovery of gold at Coloma," notes historian H. W. Brands in his *Age of Gold*, "turned out to be a seminal event in history, one of those rare moments that divide human existence into before and after....As the golden news spread beyond California to the outside world, it triggered the most astonishing mass movement of peoples since the Crusades." From the perspective of pure economy and politics, it might be argued that California, which by the year 2000 had developed the world's fourth largest "national" economy, actually "benefited" from this 1849 Gold Rush. But from the point of view of most living plants and animals and Native Americans in California at the time of Marshall's discovery of gold, it was the kiss of death.

The California grizzly, the symbol on the state's flag, numbered about 10,000 bears when James Marshall stood and puzzled over that now infamous dense yellow nugget in his hand. As Tracy I. Storer and Lloyd P. Tevis, Jr., point out in *California Grizzly* that the state's very last known grizzly, a female, would be shot dead outside Sequoia National Park by Jesse B. Agnew at Horse Corral Meadow in Fresno County in 1922. Paradoxically, the "last" California grizzly is that one on the state flag. The bear depicted had been a real one, a 1,500-pound giant trapped alive in the region of Yosemite in late 1854 and named Samson then placed on exhibit in San Francisco by James Capen "Grizzly" Adams (1807-1860). In 1857, artist Charles Nahl carefully drew Samson true to life. His drawings were used later to pattern California's flag. Samson still waves up there on those flagpoles, reminding us all about the pioneers' pogrom against his subspecies.

Meanwhile in Gold Rush California, vast herds of Tule elk (*Cervus nannodes*) exclusive to California were being shot down to a pitiful few dozen. Even these would ultimately prove homeless and dwindle further as their lowland habitat in the immense San Joaquin Valley was usurped by farmers. In 1921, to rescue the species from extinction, the last dozen animals were shipped to Yosemite Valley. Here rangers raised them in captivity and highlighted them as if in a zoo. In 1933, California Fish and Game personnel transported the now larger herd of elk and resettled it in the Owens Valley, east of the Sierra. Today several small, scattered herds exist in the state.

Before the Gold Rush, the state's immense Central Valley was home to some of the world's richest wetlands (where those Tule elk had lived), one hosting unbelievably abundant waterfowl in many millions that literally turned day to night when they took wing. Over the next century 95 percent of these wetlands would be drained and destroyed—as if Attila the Hun had become a farmer there. Beyond this, the Army Corps of Engineers would build more than 1,200 dams on California's rivers, destroying the once huge salmon spawning runs (among many other things). Giant redwoods (of two species), the largest and among the oldest living things on the planet, would mostly be felled. Their ignoble fate would be as structural lumber and non-rotting picnic furniture.

Even a brief history of the post-Gold Rush destruction of California's natural resources would fill a fat book. More to our subject here, among these living creatures consigned to the fate of persona non grata were the Native Americans.

Two-thirds of California's 300,000 Native Americans had already died due to European diseases and homicide (noted by Edward D. Castillo in the Smithsonian's *Handbook of North American Indians, Volume 8, California*) due to the Spanish missionaries having invaded in 1769 then forcibly gathered the Indians around their twenty-one missions via their "reduction" policy. There the padres converted them into Catholic peons via their *encomienda* system. Here so many people were subjected to "new" diseases to which they possessed no natural immunity that they died in staggering numbers. At Mission San Jose, for example, survivors buried 6,000 Ohlone Indians dead from an epidemic in one mass grave. One ray of light here, the Spanish padres and dons enslaved the indigenous populations in the lowlands, but luckily the Spaniards held little interest in the nearby mountain ranges. It was here California's last free Native Americans made their ultimate stands. As bad as the proselytizing Spanish were, the discovery of gold made things far worse. Emigrant whites assumed a carte blanche to exterminate whole groups of Indians on the pretext that just a few of them had balked at their lands being taken.

California's version of a Native American "Shangri-la" was Yosemite Valley. It remained unvisited by the outside world until after the Gold Rush. By some accounts its isolation and natural fortifications supposedly beguiled even the West's most accomplished explorer and guide Joseph Rutherford Walker from discovering the place. On October 20, 1833 the 35-year-old Walker led forty-four fur trappers from the Rocky Mountains across the Sierra. They soon broke trail through an early, deep snow. At about 10,000 feet elevation they slogged west along what has been interpreted as the main ridge separating tributaries of the Merced and Tuolumne rivers. Footsore and having butchered two dozen of their starved horses for food, however, Walker's pioneering party did stare down into Yosemite Valley. The men decided descending into it was impossible. But, revealingly, before Walker died on October 27, 1876 he instructed that his tombstone be inscribed "Camped at Yosemite—Nov 3, 1833."

Fortunately for the Miwok-speaking "Yosemites," the Valley would remain uninvaded for another eighteen years.

This was despite its "re-discovery" in October of 1849, when a carpenter-millwright by the name of William Penn Abrams and his companion U. N. Reamer out of Savage's Trading Post on the South Fork of the Merced tracked a grizzly. They ended up at what is now known as Old Inspiration Point. The elusive bear led to Abrams penning the first known description of Yosemite Valley:

> While at Savage's Reamer and I saw grizzly bear tracks and went out to hunt him down, getting lost in the mountains and not returning until the following evening. Found our way to camp over an Indian trail that led past a valley enclosed by stupendous cliffs rising perhaps 3,000 feet from their base and which gave us cause for wonder. Not far off a waterfall dropped from a cliff below three jagged peaks into the valley, while farther beyond, a rounded mountain stood, the valley side of which looked as though it had been sliced with a knife as one would slice a loaf of bread, and which Reamer and I called the Rock of Ages.

Abrams had just described what we recognize as El Capitan, Bridalveil Fall, Cathedral Rocks, and Half Dome. But the two would-be hunters continued no farther from their cliff into the Valley. Nor did anyone learn of Abrams' diary until it came to light almost a century later in 1947.

The beginning of the end of Yosemite's isolation occurred in 1850, when Indians raided a trading post on the Fresno River owned by James D. Savage near present Coarsegold. Although not tall and weighing less than 140 pounds, Savage seemed to have been a larger-than-life figure with blue eyes and long blond ringlets. Savage had lost his wife and child during the journey to California from Illinois in 1846. He soon served with brevet-Captain John C. Fremont's California Battalion in Fremont's successful bid to seize California from Mexico during the Mexican-American War. Afterward he had worked for John A. Sutter, Marshall's employer.

After Marshall's discovery of gold in the tailrace of Sutter's lumber mill, Savage became a prospector. He soon found pay dirt on a small tributary of the Tuolumne. He parlayed his gold into entrepreneurial enterprises. Near Jamestown he staked claims and taught hundreds of local Indians how to placer mine, trading them cloth and beads for their gold dust. He stocked his trading post with essentials for miners, who by 1850 numbered 100,000 in California.

Unusual for these times, Savage had repeatedly gone out of his way to maintain good relations with the local Miwoks and Yokuts. He adopted several of their customs and actually protected many of them from whites who considered them fair game. Perhaps less surprising, Savage also reportedly had taken numerous Indian wives (some say five, others up to thirty-three) ranging in age from 12 to 22 years old. "Savage is a blaspheming fellow," wrote Yosemite's "discoverer" William Penn Abrams, "who has five squaws for wives for which he takes his authority from the Scriptures."

Savage expanded his enterprises to setting up additional trading posts, as many as five, though not all operated at the same time. One of these was southwest on the Fresno River at Coarse Gold Gulch. Business for this charismatic, impulsive, and notoriously generous entrepreneur was more than good.

At least it *was*, until Indians had pin-cushioned with arrows three of the men who ran his store on the Fresno River. Indeed, this raid was no isolated incident. The combination of this raid and many others finally prompted John McDougal, governor of California and an alleged Indian-hater, to explain to the state legislature that "extermination of the Indians is inevitable." McDougal then authorized the formation of the Mariposa Battalion. This was an all-volunteer militia of 204 men whose mission was to pacify the local Indians and prevent their further raids. Predictably perhaps, Savage was elected its major and commanding officer. Even at this point, however, the militia lacked a green light to proceed against the Indians. As noted by Hank Johnston in his *The Yosemite Grant, 1864-1906 A Pictorial History,* in March of 1851:

> Before any formal action could be taken, three United States Indian Commissioners arrived, escorted by more than a hundred U.S. Army troops, and halted proceedings while they attempted to persuade the Indians to accept treaties and move to reservations being set up along the base of the foothills. Many of the tribes accepted the offer [eighteen treaties were signed, including 25,000 Indians], but several of the wilder bands, including the Yosemites, refused to consider leaving their mountain homelands. The state legislature, confident that Congress would later reimburse California for the cost of the campaign, then authorized the governor to send the Mariposa Battalion against the holdouts.

That spring, Savage learned that a group of "renegade" Sierra Miwoks who refused to be resettled were instead living north in a secret valley secure from discovery. This valley was allegedly protected by witchcraft and could be defended by rolling rocks down upon invaders. Savage led two companies of the Mariposa Battalion toward this unknown valley. The troops largely followed the route of what would become the original Wawona Road. Along the way, Savage was met by Chief Tenieya. (This spelling is from Lafayette H. Bunnell of the 1851 Mariposa Battalion. Although now often spelled Tenaya, Tenieya, we think, is more accurate.) The chief insisted that he wanted no part of a relocation that would place his people among tribes in the lowlands who were enemies. Upon Savage's threat, Tenieya allegedly said that his people would surrender and sign a treaty. Savage warned that if they failed to do so the consequences would be unpleasant.

After waiting three days for these "renegade Yosemetos" (through the early years, Yosemite was spelled about ten different ways) to show up, he experienced only a "no-show." Savage, with young Indians as his guide, now marched north yet again toward this mysterious renegade stronghold.

Savage's men soon met seventy-two Yosemites, mostly women and children, struggling toward them through the snow. The major sent these Indians to a temporary camp near the mouth of Bishop Creek.

On March 27, the Mariposa militia first saw the Valley. The grandeur of the view struck 27-year-old Private Lafayette Houghton Bunnell. He soon suggested they name the valley "Yo-sem-i-ty." The inhabitants of this secret valley, including Chief Tenieya, already called it Ahwahnee, "Place of Gaping Mouth." The word "*Oo-ham-i-te*" or "*uzumati*" ("Yosemite") was originally translated as Miwok for grizzly bear.

As far as the Yosemites were concerned, this first entry of whites—and of Savage—into their valley was equivalent to the serpent entering Eden. Things went to hell fast.

Major Savage pushed into the Valley and set up camp near Bridalveil Meadow. Meanwhile the rest of the Indians had escaped up the route near Nevada Fall; all except for one woman "over a hundred years old" squatting in a cave. She told the major she was "too old to climb the rocks." But she was not too old to keep a secret. The woman refused to tell him where her people had gone. Her recalcitrance plus orders from the governor prompted the now petulant Savage to order his militia to burn all the Yosemites' houses and their large acorn storage cysts. Savage's goal was to starve the Indians out of the Sierra.

This failed. By one account, some of Tenieya's people circled through the mountains to Mariposa and liberated the women and children Savage had taken prisoner by helping them sneak out while the major's guards slept. Meanwhile Savage retreated south from Yosemite.

Beginning on May 5, 1851, Captain John Boling led a punitive expedition of thirty-four men into Yosemite Valley with orders from Savage to "surprise the Indians and whip them well, or induce them to surrender." Four days later, Boling's troopers camped near present Sentinel Bridge. These men surprised and captured five Yosemites, three of whom were sons of Chief Tenieya, which prompted Bunnell to subsequently name the capture location "The Three Brothers." Boling ordered Tenieya's son-in-law and one of his three sons to be released to convey a message to Tenieya to surrender.

Meanwhile the troopers became entranced watching one of the three remaining prisoners in a demonstration of his archery prowess. The amazed troopers moved the target ever more distant. Soon the boy's errant arrows became difficult to recover. As the young archer searched farther than ever for a missing arrow he suddenly broke into a run. Neither militiaman had a rifle with him. The boy escaped toward the spire which, according to Bunnell in his book *Discovery of the Yosemite, and the Indian War of 1851, Which Led to That Event,* one of Boling's Indian scouts wryly christened "Lost Arrow."

Now Boling ordered the last two boys tied back to back against a tree and guarded by two militiamen. Despite these prisoners being so personally important to him, Tenieya still refused to surrender. A bit later, on May 10, the men on guard duty noticed that the boys had untied their bonds. Instead of calling for backup or simply grabbing the boys, the troopers simply watched them jump up and run. At this point they shot at them, "wantonly" killing Tenieya's youngest son. The other young captive escaped under heavy fire, slightly wounded.

Next a militiaman captured Tenieya. As John Muir notes in *The Yosemite,* Tenieya, furious, blasted Boling and his soldiers in a combination of Miwok and Spanish (here Muir was quoting Lafayette H. Bunnell):

> Kill me, Sir Captain. Yes, kill me, as you killed my son, as you will kill my people if they should come to you! Yes, Sir America, you can tell your warriors to kill the old chief. You have made my life dark with sorrow. You have killed the child of my heart, why not kill the father?—But wait a little, when I am dead I will call to my people to come and they shall hear me in their sleep and come to avenge the death of their chief and his son. Yes, Sir America, my spirit will make trouble for you and your people, as you have made trouble to me and my people. With the wizards I will follow the white people and make them fear me. You may kill me, Sir Captain, but you shall not live in peace. I will follow in your foot steps; I will not leave my home, but be with the spirits among the rocks, the waterfalls, in the rivers and in the winds; wherever you go I will be with you. You will not see me but you will fear the spirit of the old chief and grow cold. The Great Spirit has spoken. I am done.

Boling knew he could not harm Tenieya. He still needed him to inveigle his people to surrender. He waited for a supply train, then shoving Tenieya forward with a pistol in his back, tromped up Tenaya Canyon. His red-clad militiamen grunted with the effort. One of Boling's Indian scouts found a trail through deep snow up Snow Creek. His troops surprised Tenieya's band of thirty-five starving Indians camped on the shore of what is now Tenaya Lake (the Yosemites called it "py-we-ack," which translates to "sparkling water").

The Yosemites surrendered. Boling marched them—and Tenieya—for several days. The soldiers asked their captives endless questions about where the rest of their band was. But Savage's men found the Native Americans' elusive answers irritating. For the Yosemites, who were innocent of wrongdoing and were the victims of an unwarranted invasion and murder, this entire ordeal was a waking nightmare as well as a prime episode of violated rights.

The soldiers herded the Yosemites many miles to Fort Miller along the San Joaquin River, also the headquarters for the Mariposa Battalion. From there the Indians were driven onward to a common "reservation" on the Fresno River and forced to mingle with their more numerous enemies. Within several weeks Chief Tenieya convinced the sympathetic agent-in-charge to allow him to return to the Sierra to conduct a funeral "cry" for his slain son. Chief Tenieya's followers soon slipped away and joined him in Yosemite again.

Meanwhile the Mariposa Battalion had been disbanded. No one now chased Tenieya's followers. In fact things went okay back in Ahwahnee until approximately May 28 of 1852. Then, possibly in retaliation for Tenieya's youngest son having been killed by Boling's militiaman, the Yosemites night-ambushed a party of eight miners from Coarse Gold Gulch who had traveled thirty-five miles north to enter Yosemite Valley on a prospecting trip. Two of these men, named Rose and Shurborn, had been separated from the others near Bridalveil Fall and were killed. Of the six survivors, three were injured. Despite their powder being wet due to rain, all six managed to defend themselves and escape from a "horde of wild Indians." Over several days the prospectors struggled back to Coarse Gold Gulch to tell their tales.

A punitive party of close to thirty miners then set out for Yosemite to retaliate. They failed to find the Indians but they did bury both of their peers.

Now Lieutenant Tredwell Moore (an 1847 graduate of West Point) at Fort Miller was ordered to punish the Yosemites for killing those two prospectors. On July 4, the soldiers crossed the "main ridge of the Sierra" a few miles from Tenaya Lake. The troopers surprised and captured fifteen Yosemite women and children plus six men. The whites found some of the captive men wearing clothing from Rose and Shurborn. When questioned, one of the six admitted to seeing the killing of the two whites. Others of the men denied involvement in the deaths. Despite these mixed testimonies, on July 5, 1852, Moore ordered all six adult male Yosemites immediately executed by a firing squad. No one at the time, it seems, bothered to record the names of these six murdered men.

On July 1, Lieutenant Moore had ordered Lieutenant Nathaniel H. McLean and ten soldiers to destroy a large store of the Indians' acorns. This destruction took more than a week, during which a sentry named Riley (to date no historian has found his first name) received two arrows to his neck on July 4. The life of Riley expired on July 7, 1852.

Chief Tenieya and the rest of the Yosemites had escaped over the Sierra to live adjacent to the Monos, a Shoshonean tribe. Ties between the two groups were close; Tenieya's mother in fact was a Mono. But in 1853, many of the Yosemites returned yet again to the Valley to build new bark lodges and resettle.

Meanwhile, the charismatic Major Savage remained a "friend," or at least a self-interested patron, of the local Indians. But his proprietary attitude soon would seal his fate. Allegedly, in August of 1852, well beyond Yosemite, he angrily took to task a Major Harvey over the latter's killing of several Indian women and children earlier that summer. The killings, Savage insisted, had been wanton and uncalled for. The two fought. Bystanders grabbed Savage, who was pummeling Harvey. Harvey pulled Savage's gun and shot him through the heart. A local court ruled Harvey's action as justifiable self-defense despite Harvey using Savage's gun.

This next part of the story is also a bit murky. Apparently, in the late summer of 1853, a year after Tenieya's Yosemites joined the Monos, some sort of dispute arose between them. By some accounts its source was the Yosemites having stolen several of the Mono's horses; by other accounts no horses were involved. Even more complicated, perhaps the dispute revolved around an unresolved gambling disagreement. Either way, this dispute would prove deadly. To return home from the Mono's territory, the Yosemite Indians took a roundabout route intended to trick the Monos. Not tricked, they caught up with Tenieya and his band, apparently somewhere in what now is Yosemite National Park, and launched a surprise attack. The Mono warriors stoned the chief to death and killed "many of his followers" (notes Hank Johnston). They also took as hostages the Yosemite women and children to be absorbed into their tribe at Mono Lake. During this melee, eight warriors somehow escaped this ambush.

No matter what the exact circumstances of Chief Tenieya's demise, his death spelled the end of this tragic and unnecessary "Indian War" prosecuted by whites in the central Sierra. It also disbanded what was left of the Yosemites. As we will see, other homicides would be committed in Yosemite, and Indians would be involved in some of them, but no longer in self-defense of Ahwahnee.

More than twenty years later, on the night of August 12, 1875, a 21-year-old Indian "renegade" named Paiute George was seen with a six-gun jammed in his waistband while standing in the doorway of the road toll booth near present-day Cascades and talking to its proprietor 51-year-old George Ezra Boston. Hours later the building was found burned to the ground and, as historian Hank Johnston notes, inside the charred structure lay Boston "horribly burned and crisped." Paiute George resisted his arrest in Yosemite Valley by deputies. It took several revolver shots to the upper body and a shotgun blast to the lower back to subdue him. Amazingly, he survived this fusillade and stood trial.

Three other Indians—"Zip," "Tom," and "Lame George"—were suspected of aiding Paiute George to rob and kill Boston. They were arrested separately over the next several months and incarcerated in the Mariposa Jail. All three pled not guilty. After several delays, a trial began on April 22, 1876, before an overflow crowd of Indians and whites. Paiute George was found guilty. The next day, Lame George, who had demanded a separate trial, was acquitted. Zip and Tom eventually gained release as well due to lack of evidence. Paiute George, however, was sentenced to life in San Quentin Prison. He died there years later.

A similar event took place around July 17, 1887, when Lame George again made the news. He allegedly robbed Eleven Mile Station on the Wawona-Yosemite Turnpike. As the story in the *Mariposa Gazette* (on July 30, 1887) goes, intent on stealing the proceeds from the road, Lame George and Fly-Blow Jim entered the station after its proprietor West Wood had stepped out for a moment. When Wood returned he saw the money was gone. When he accused the Indian, the latter went for his gun. Wood quickly retreated to find his own. Meanwhile the thief mounted his horse and made a run for it. Wood fired at him but thought his bullet had missed.

A second shot rang out from an unknown source. Lame George's horse appeared later without its rider. A search located Lame George with a hole in the back of the head. Whether Wood or Fly-Blow Jim had killed him remained uncertain. Nor is it clear whether the corpse still had the stolen toll money on him. Meanwhile, Fly-Blow Jim had made his escape and was not seen again.

Far clearer was the witchcraft assassination of "Old Bullock" in Wawona. He was reputed to be a medicine man. On June 19, 1890, four other Indians led by "Indian Wilson" accosted the old man and shot him four times. Why? The assassins considered their act to be one of self-defense. Old Bullock was believed by many local Native Americans to have possessed not only the power to cause the death of others without even being near them but also to have used that power to cause virtually every recent death of an Indian. This assassination was merely a preventative measure to stop the deaths of yet others through Old Bullock's sorcery. Despite this seemingly cogent explanation, the sheriff arrested these four plus one white who had been involved. A jury eventually convicted all five. According to the May 16, 1914 *Mariposa Gazette*, "Several Indians and one white man were sent to the California State Prison."

As the events above suggest, the Yosemite region went through a prolonged Wild West phase. Just part of this was colored by its nearby "houses of ill repute." One near Wawona bore the name The Tipperary Resort. It stood a third of a mile inside what is now the current Park boundary on the Chowchilla-Wawona Road—although this piece of illicit real estate was not yet within Yosemite National Park until 1932. For years before then it remained one of several notorious local saloons and houses of prostitution. Its heyday soared during the era when the Madera Sugar Pine Company had hired several hundred laborers to cut major sections of nearby forest.

Mixing alcohol, gambling, and prostitutes with lumberjacks carrying firearms will yield a surefire recipe for, well, mayhem. On Sunday, July 7, 1918, Tiburcio Minez, a "Mexican" employed by the lumber company, had been dallying and enjoying the Tipperary's pleasures. Late that morning he paid dearly for his fun during a brawl when Gene Whitener, the head logger for the company, shot him twice with a .38-Special Smith and Wesson revolver.

Whitener proved none too fastidious about who stood between him and his target. One of the head logger's two rounds "passed through the body of a Mexican called Joe and struck another man named Louis in the breast." Whitener's second round killed Minez instantly. The *Mariposa Gazette* (on July 18, 1918) tried to make sense of this gunplay.

> It is reported that jealousy over the women inmates was the cause that led to the shooting. That a hard fight took place is evidenced by the reported condition of the house. The place was strewn with broken bottles, rocks, etc., and everything about the house was wrecked. It is said that all were intoxicated at the time. This notorious resort, "Tipperary," has been allowed to remain open in defiance of all law for several years and has been the scene of much trouble in the past. The officers [of the sheriff] have paid but little, if any, attention to this state of affairs and the life of one man, with possibly two more, is the result of the failure of these officers to perform a sworn duty.

The *Mariposa Gazette* also said "two other men are believed to be fatally wounded." Both were taken to the company's hospital. But the absence of a follow-up article in any of the local papers keeps us in the dark over whether "Joe" or "Louis" also died from their bullet wounds.

The *Gazette's* scathing condemnation of the sheriff's department apparently prompted little change in the modus operandi of the Tipperary. About nine weeks later, on Monday evening of September 16, 1918, 29-year-old Taylor Teaford was there pushing his luck in the pursuit of pleasure. Fortunately, he exited the place none the worse for his choice of entertainments.

During his short drive back to Wawona, fate seems to have caught up with him. Teaford offered a ride to two young men. Both later admitted to the County Coroner that they had deserted from the Army. At any rate, after one of these two hitchhikers, Cathenas E. Runyon, plopped into Teaford's backseat, he began examining the man's rifle.

He asked Teaford if the weapon was loaded. The gregarious driver said it was not. Runyon now worked the rifle's lever and pulled the trigger. The gun fired a bullet that entered Teaford's left shoulder and emerged a few inches above his heart. The shocked hitchhikers quickly drove their benefactor to Wawona. He died there of his bullet wound two hours later.

It seems that America's first park went another thirty-five years without hosting an intentional homicide. When murders resumed, instead of men killing men—as had occurred during the Gold Rush and ensuing pioneer era—the patterns had changed. On January 27, 1952, Helen Telles, a local Native American living in Yosemite Valley, hit her Portuguese husband, 31-year-old John Telles, Jr., over the head fatally with a beer bottle. The judge must have considered fairly convincing Helen's story—whatever it might have been—justifying why her husband deserved a beer bottle over the head. The magistrate sentenced her to a mere three years of probation.

In a strangely connected tragedy, on November 1, 1963, a woman hiker found 19-year-old June Joslin Leonard of Yosemite dead near Camp 4 in Yosemite Valley. Ranger Lee Shackelton was one of the first to arrive at the scene. He found June Leonard lying in the open and "naked from the waist down with her legs still spread from the rape. The suspect's knee impressions were still visible in the ground between them." The victim also had been badly beaten then strangled one week before. A physical examination confirmed she indeed had been raped.

The last person seen with Mrs. Leonard was David Lee Telles, a 23-year-old U.S. Army private stationed at Fort Devens, Massachusetts. Interestingly, David Telles is the Portuguese/American Indian son of Helen Telles who was convicted of killing David's father by hitting him with that bottle eleven years prior. David now claimed he had been riding with Mrs. Leonard in her car when they had an argument. It had gotten physical and she had swerved off the road and hit a tree. After that, he had simply left and claimed not to know what happened to her next.

A Federal Grand Jury found enough evidence to indict Telles. He and Leonard, it found, both had been in Mariposa. Because she was returning home to her husband and son in Yosemite, she had offered Telles a ride back to the Indian Village near Camp 4 where he was visiting his relatives. While driving into the Valley, Leonard had badly handled a turn. Her vehicle hit a tree. The impact left her slightly dazed.

It was at this point that Telles had made sexual advances on her. She resisted. Telles had become angry and had beaten her up. He forced her to, then beyond, the side of the road then raped her and finally strangled her to death.

Once the Grand Jury indicted David Lee Telles for murder and rape, he was denied bail and sent to the Sacramento County Jail. On June 14, 1965, still behind bars, David Lee Telles committed suicide. Nineteen-year-old June Joslin Leonard was survived by her husband, Clarence Leonard, Jr., a local woodcutter, and by their 8-month-old son.

The strange case of 24-year-old Evelyn Consuela Rosemann still defies any ironclad interpretation. On October 19, 1968, a woman and two men were hiking and found a badly battered body about 200 feet from the base of Nevada Fall, east of and close to the Merced River. It was that of a young woman. Her only garments consisted of a badly torn pair of trousers and a sweater. No underwear.

But her clothes were not as they should have been, even after a 600-foot fall. Her tan corduroy pants had been yanked down to gather at her ankles. Her bright, tri-colored sweater had been pulled up and over her shoulders and head. A second, black sweater was laying on the rock a foot from her feet. It appeared the young woman had fallen—or had been thrown—from the top of Nevada Fall 594 feet above. Furthermore, after her fall she had been man-handled.

An autopsy revealed Rosemann had died the day before being discovered and had sustained "severe and tremendous traumatic injuries of the type ordinarily seen only in mountain climbing accidents or in train vs. auto collisions. The cause of death appears to be a massive head injury with avulsion of the brain."

This part of the woman's death seems more or less clear. Additional facts, however, muddy the picture. For starters, other hikers later found the victim's purse hanging by its shoulder strap on the bridge atop Nevada Fall. Rosemann, the investigating rangers now found, was currently employed as a massage parlor masseuse in San Francisco and formerly had been a topless waitress. Receipts in her purse and lodge records revealed she had arrived in Yosemite two days earlier and had spent one day in the Valley. On her third day here she hiked to Nevada Fall. Once there, she somehow had launched off the top of it.

As we saw in Chapter 1, more than four dozen people have gone over high waterfalls in the Park, a dozen shot off Nevada Fall. Some of these victims had been dunking or even swimming to cool off, others were trying to get a drink, a few were posing for snapshots, and others yet were trying to take photos.

But this was late October at about 5,000 feet elevation. The days were no longer hot. Further, no one goes swimming recreationally while wearing a wool sweater and corduroy trousers. Moreover, the Merced was flowing quite low at this time of year, low enough to allow a chance of self-rescue if one fell in. Indeed, of *all* of the accidental fatalities off *any* of Yosemite's waterfalls during more than a century of records only three or four had occurred during the combined seven months from September to March. Moreover, only five of *all* known victims, no matter what month they died, had been adult women. Therefore it seems extremely unlikely that Rosemann could have slipped into the stream for any reason and then not have been able to walk right back out again.

Beyond the very slim chance that she had been trying to get a drink or dunk and then slipped irreversibly, she was probably alone. So it is improbable she was posing for a photo. Nor was a camera found that might suggest she had been trying to take a picture. In short, the facts imply that her death was no accident.

So how did Rosemann end up where she did?

Weirdly, when discovered by the three hikers, her body already had been moved for a significant distance from its point of impact. Investigators found traces of the corduroy material at least halfway to the base of the fall. Additionally, they discovered parts of her brain on a rock in the middle of the stream, fifty feet away. That Rosemann's clothes had been yanked almost off was also hard to explain. Yes, it could have happened in the river (had she been in the river). Or it could have been done by human hands. Far more bizarre, the pathologist's autopsy report noted that sexual intercourse had occurred either shortly before or, more likely *after*, her death—as hinted at by bloodless lacerations of her vagina. The latter strongly suggests someone had raped her mutilated corpse after her fall.

Hence the questions remain: Was she attacked prior to going over, maybe by a stalker and former client from the Bay Area? Had the attacker been rebuffed and then pushed her off the cliff and afterward raped her corpse? Or instead, after her fall—accidental or otherwise—had someone simply happened upon her corpse and then had sex with it?

Whether Rosemann's death was due to a very rare sort of accident, or to a suicide (which seems very unlikely after a three-day, hiking visit to Yosemite and with no known predisposing personal situation), or whether she was murdered by being pushed into the river and/or off the cliff was never determined. Nor is it certain whether she had been raped pre- or postmortem, although, again, evidence suggests the latter as far more likely. All tolled, the facts suggest but do not confirm homicide. In any case it remains an unsolved mystery.

During most winters, the falling spray from 1,430-foot Upper Yosemite Fall creates a frozen white pyramid up to a hundred feet high at its base. This giant, upside-down "frazil-ice cone" can last for months. It coats every nearby boulder as well as the bedrock itself. On December 2, 1972, hikers arriving at the top of this waterfall a third of a vertical mile above this cone were surprised and perplexed to find two piles of clothing. One pile was topped by high lace-up boots stacked neatly just beyond the guardrail—on its dangerous side.

A bit later that day, and 1,400 feet lower, two other hikers spied a nude body on a flat ledge on the far side of the gorge about 100 yards from the foot of the waterfall. Ice from the spray made the pinkish corpse glisten. The couple stared at this anomaly then worked closer over treacherous terrain to be sure of what they were seeing. Yes, it was a dead, frozen, nude body. Looking around more curiously now, the two then noticed another pink "thing" also partially frozen into the white ice, halfway up that inverted cone and much closer to the bottom of Upper Yosemite Fall.

The two hikers bushwhacked back to the trail. Here they encountered the party who had earlier discovered the clothing piled neatly atop the waterfall. The parties now compared notes on their gruesome finds then promptly returned to the Valley and reported them by 5:30 p.m.

But because the victim—or victims—were definitely dead and no real urgency existed, the rangers decided to do the dangerous recoveries during daylight. They assembled a platoon of twelve and before dawn lit the Valley the next day, they approached the giant ice cone.

Here they split into squads. Two rangers climbed higher by trail to retrieve the clothing and to investigate the crime scene. One clipped himself into a rope up there to dangle from the lip and study its foot far below with binoculars.

The spray obscured everything down there, including Rangers Pete Thompson, Jim Brady, Tony Andersen, and Chief Ranger Jack Morehead as they donned black neoprene wet suits and orange helmets to retrieve the bodies. Armed with ice axes and crampons and roped up with safety lines, three of them climbed across the cone and down to that first-seen body on the far side of the fast-flowing creek.

Meanwhile Brady worked his way up toward the second grayish-pink blob on the cone above. Almost immediately after heading onto this cone under the spray from the waterfall, the sun heated up the cliff. Sheets of ice the size of refrigerators exfoliated from above and sailed down. One slab fell, then another, and yet another. These unpredictable ice falls proved not only disconcerting but so dangerous that the team quickly reassessed its game plan. It would be stupid, the rescuers decided, to get killed or maimed here while trying to recover a dead person. Even so, they still had to retrieve the mystery corpse.

But these chunks of ice from the cliff above were proving to be a bit much. A century earlier, John Muir had tried exploring this cone just for the heck of it when it was about 250 feet high. He was initially knocked right off its face by "blinding, suffocating blasts of wind and water." Muir had then retreated and waited for the perfect day when the wind was just right. Then he managed to summit the cone just as a multi-ton mass of frozen spray from above calved off and struck close to him. Almost immediately the wind shifted and the shower hit Muir again, forcing him off the cone.

Today's plummeting ice was not as much fun to the rangers as the old one apparently had been to Muir. They decided to assign one of their number—Everett "Dutch" Ackart—the sole responsibility of monitoring the flaking ice and radioing warnings of moving slabs before they brained somebody.

The climbers now managed to cross safely to the opposite side of the gorge and retrieve the body of the nude man frozen on the ledge. In the meantime, Jim Brady was also able to recover the other body frozen up the ice cone. Only this second corpse turned out to be merely a leg.

The ensuing investigation found that this leg's former owner was very likely (though not certainly) 21-year-old Lorraine J. Sutton of Forest Ranch (near Chico, California). On December 1, 1972, she had apparently hiked up the four miles to the top of the fall with 26-year-old Bruce D. Norris, whose nude body NPS Rangers had chopped intact out of the ice on the other side of the stream. (In addition to other forms of identification, the morgue photo was eventually verified by Norris' mother.)

NPS investigators learned further that Norris had earned an M.S. in physics from U.C., Berkeley and currently was a student in physics at Sacramento State. Sutton, a very pretty girl, had been his girlfriend for several months. Once atop the waterfall, the best interpretation goes, Norris had either sweet-talked her into ending their lives together by becoming one with this world famous waterfall or he instead had somehow tricked Sutton into a position where he could murder her then shove her off before committing suicide himself.

Based on circumstantial evidence, the Park Coroner's report for this Incident #72-2790 concluded Norris had probably murdered Sutton. The most likely scenario had been that he killed her, stripped off her clothes, then folded and piled them up with his own. Norris, it concluded, had slid Sutton off the fall's viewpoint and into the current immediately above the fall. He soon followed her by jumping off the cliff adjacent to the waterfall.

Why would Norris have murdered Sutton?

Inside his wallet was the business card of a Logan, Utah psychiatrist named Dr. C. Jess Groesbeck. Norris, it turns out, recently had been a patient in the mental hospital run by the Yolo County (California) Mental Health Service. More complicated yet, he was also already married to Ann Marie Pierce Norris, who recently had separated from him. Indeed, when his estranged wife had, in March of 1972, returned to their cabin to retrieve her belongings he had ranted to her, "Everything stays." For emphasis he fired a .20 gauge shotgun into the ground at her feet. Next he fired yet more shots, emptying his gun.

At this point she and her brother managed to wrest the weapon away from Norris. They also immobilized him by tying him up. Butte County Sheriff's Deputy Smith had next arrived in response to their phone call, "Gun brandishing and man gone berserk."

Smith arrested Norris, who "had a very strange look on his face" and took him to the county mental hospital on a seventy-two-hour hold.

Nine months later, shortly after Norris' apparent murder-suicide, Park investigators examined his vehicle. They found a box of fifty, .22 caliber rounds. Seven were missing. Also gone was his .22 pistol. This highly suggests but of course does not prove that he may have shot Sutton then tossed the murder weapon into space (the pistol was never recovered). And then he tried to toss her. The fact that her leg was found so far up the ice cone, coupled with the fact that the only other body parts searchers ever found were her other leg and a partial scalp cape, suggests *she had not jumped aggressively outward* but instead had dropped directly off the edge of the waterfall to collide at high speed with the cliff face and then cascade directly onto the ice cone where she broke apart. In contrast, Norris' body was found in one piece much farther out from the base of the waterfall, suggesting a voluntary jump which allowed him to clear the ledges below.

Also in Norris' car investigators found strange, confused, depressed, and sadomasochistic writings in which, over several pages, he expressed feelings of doubt, the desire to end his life, and to be the "Christian Killer." Underneath much of these cryptic entries ran the theme that he actually knew he was seriously losing control of himself. His writings clearly reveal that he was worried about making it as a graduate student, that he felt lost, depressed, suicidal, and very definitely sexually frustrated, and significantly, that he also felt himself to be a danger to others.

Reputedly Sutton's parents—she had lived in a tree house on a commune in Butte County run by her father—considered Norris to be an inappropriate companion/boyfriend for her. If true, they were very sadly proven correct.

This would not be the only relationship between young people to go badly wrong in Yosemite. During midmorning of October 14, 1974, 23-year-old Dana Lynn Laudenslayer of Redwood City, California was hiking with his fiancée Marsha Ann Savko (also from Redwood City) on the Ostrander Lake Fire Road. The two were returning from having camped overnight near the lake.

About three hours later, Rangers Scott Connelly, Chris Andress, and Lyle Rogers arrived at the Bridalveil Creek Campground in response to a report of a young man with a gunshot wound. Here at the campground they questioned two people, Vincent Lico and Marsha Savko, both sitting on a log next to a yellow Volkswagen.

Connelly said, "I understand that there has been a shooting."

Savko, who seemed anxious, nervous, and frightened, responded with "Yes, it is in my car and I shot him."

As Connelly then frisked Lico for weapons, he clarified by telling Connelly again: "The gun is in the car."

Andress retrieved a .22 caliber revolver. Scott then asked Savko for permission to further search the VW. He also asked her to waive her rights so she could answer questions.

She signed the waiver and said, "It was an accident; I have nothing to hide."

She explained further that she and Laudenslayer had been hiking down to the Bridalveil Campground that morning and had stopped for water. Laudenslayer had taken off his pack and walked over to the creek. Savko had opened his pack looking for his canteen and instead found the revolver. She pulled it out, she said, gripping it by the butt with her finger on the trigger. As her boyfriend of nearly five years had walked toward her, she had pointed the handgun toward him, unconsciously, she added—and it had fired.

When Laudenslayer fell to the ground wounded, Savko said, she started screaming for help. No one had responded. So she fired the gun in the air several times to attract wider attention. This did not work either. She said she tried to reload the firearm, but it was jammed. When still no help appeared, she screamed "FIRE!" Again no one appeared.

She next said that Laudenslayer, still alive and conscious and with his wound almost bloodless, told her to please go and get help. She had hesitated, telling him again that she was sorry. When he fell unconscious, she explained, she finally did leave.

Then, she added, she promptly got lost.

At about 10:00 or 10:30 a.m., Michael E. Keller and Nancy J. Fruedenfeld also happened to be hiking back from Ostrander Lake to the Bridalveil Campground. The pair found the wounded man lying perpendicular to the trail about two miles short of the road. "His skin was yellow, eyes glassy, and his lips were blue." Both hikers saw a bullet hole in his chest, but virtually no blood. Keller now remembered having heard what he thought were gunshots the previous evening while camping at Ostrander Lake.

Both Fruedenfeld and Keller now thought Laudenslayer looked dead. Next to him were two blue packs with some of their contents strewn out. These included an open box of .22 caliber long rifle shells with several missing. Nearby lay a pamphlet titled "Spiritualism, Sorcery, and Witchcraft." (Also in the pack investigators would later find a small stash of marijuana plus several items and tools that were government property stolen from the Ostrander Ski Hut.)

Keller now tried talking to the supine man. He did not answer. Keller felt for a heartbeat. Neither he nor Fruedenfeld could firmly detect anything. But just in case they were wrong, the two built a quick sunshade using a jacket and sticks above the man's head. Noting that two packs were present and then finding a woman's driver's license in the pocket of the small one, the pair concluded that Laudenslayer had been hiking with a companion and she must have already gone for help. So they both decided to stay with Laudenslayer and do for him whatever they could. They got his army sleeping bag out and covered him with it.

After fifteen more minutes passed the two hikers reevaluated all this and decided that at least one of them should go for help—just in case Laudenslayer's companion had failed.

Keller now hurried down the trail. He then drove his friend's car to a phone and called in the wounded man's position. Meanwhile Fruedenfeld watched over Laudenslayer, not touching him except "to keep bugs off his face."

It was about 11 a.m. by the time Savko found people—hikers Vincent Lico, Bob Martin and Tim McGarry—to help her. To them she appeared hysterical, crying, still carrying the pistol, and saying, "I shot my man."

Martin and McGarry would later report that they were hiking about three miles above the trail junction leading to Ostrander Lake when they spotted the woman "stumbling" toward them with a gun in her hand. Upon seeing the trio she collapsed to the ground and dropped the revolver.

Savko admitted to them that she was lost. McGarry reckoned from her tale she had been running around for nearly an hour. As she spewed her story, Lico figured the wounded Laudenslayer must be roughly two and half miles up the trail, but the Ostrander Lake Trail, not the Chilnualna Lakes Trail along which they currently were hiking.

The three soon understood this to be an emergency. So Bob Martin ran back for his truck to get to a phone. He reached it by 11:50 a.m. and tried to make the emergency call on the pay phone. It would not work. As he started to drive to search for another phone he encountered a camper who told him the shooting already had been called in (by Keller).

Meanwhile, back up the trail, Lico had picked up Savko's dropped revolver and carried it as they escorted her toward the campground. He too remembered there having been a phone there. As they walked, Savko kept asking if a bullet to the stomach would kill a person. Lico answered that if it did not hit a vital organ, it would not. Soon after the three started walking she told the two men she had not done any first aid but had just left Laudenslayer leaning up against a rock or tree (actually the road embankment). Lico and McGarry decided that McGarry should hurry the opposite direction on the trail to render Laudenslayer some sort of assistance.

After McGarry left, Savko continued chattering hysterically to Lico that it had been an accident and that she had reached in the pack just to get a cup or canteen and had found the gun and thought it had a safety and it just went off when she pointed it at him. To get Savko to walk, Lico later said, he had to take her hand. "If I hadn't found help," Savko added to Lico, "I would have shot myself…"

Meanwhile McGarry jogged along the trail to find Laudenslayer. He knew from Savko's description of his gunshot wound there was little he would be able to do when he found him. Still he knew he had to try. About two miles along the trail, McGarry found Nancy Fruedenfeld sitting with Laudenslayer. She told McGarry that she and Keller had found him at least an hour earlier.

Laudenslayer, McGarry now saw, was still sitting propped half up. He looked dead; his eyes partially open and glazed. McGarry sought a pulse. He found none. He felt the victim's forehead. It was cold. He could detect no breathing motions. Not even the faintest movement. Even so, McGarry decided if even a spark of life remained in Laudenslayer that he should be lying supine, with his head less propped up. So he and Fruedenfeld repositioned him. Then they waited for rangers to arrive. An hour and a half later Keller arrived escorting Ranger Bill Eastman and Dr. Peter Hackett, who had been helicoptered into the closest possible landing site.

Meanwhile, finally arriving at the campground with Savko, Lico dropped a quarter in the phone slot. This telephone (again) was out of order. So Lico asked for her keys and drove her Volkswagen to find the next closest phone. Instead of a phone, at the nearby entrance gate, he found Lyle Rogers and the other two rangers.

The three followed Lico back to the campground. Here Lico sat with Savko on the log next to her car. She now asked Ranger Rogers, "Will he live? Oh, I hope so."

Rogers answered, "If a vital organ was not damaged. Where was he shot?"

"In the center of the stomach….Oh, I'm sorry; I'm sorry; I'm sorry."

At almost this exact moment, at 1:25 p.m., two miles back up the trail, Dr. Hackett pronounced Dana Laudenslayer dead. The autopsy would conclude he had been shot fatally in the "area of the heart" with a copper-jacketed .22 long rifle bullet.

This would seem like the end of Incident #74-3073.

But it wasn't.

No matter how the investigating rangers cut it, Savko's story seemed fishy to them. Why would anyone pull a pistol from someone else's pack, aim that gun pointblank at him, and then pull the trigger and shoot him through the middle of the chest—except by intent?

Investigators found that, due to his prior arrests, Laudenslayer was legally prohibited from purchasing the .22 caliber revolver that killed him. Who did buy it? Savko. In light of this, one might wonder how conceivable it is for a woman to go into a gun shop and fill out all the legally required forms and then purchase a handgun but never actually look at it. Well, yes, it is conceivable. Subsequently, this same woman then travels with the man for whom she bought the pistol and observes him plinking with it, carrying it, loading it, and generally handling it. Is it credible she never noticed it was a simple pull-the-trigger model? Just how likely is it that she *never* looked at the thing at all to see and therefore understand how it worked? Not very, but neither is it impossible. For these reasons, investigators now experienced such a hard time believing that Savko could do what she had done accidentally that they arrested her for murder. Despite any suspicions by law enforcement, though, when Savko went to court, *she* remained the only witness to the homicide. Hence the prosecutor sought a charge of mere involuntary manslaughter.

Yosemite's Chief Law Enforcement Officer Ranger Lee Shackelton entered the courtroom of Savko's trial as required. There he spotted the defendant's "spiritual guide," a woman who much earlier had advised Savko that Laudenslayer was not religious enough for her to marry. When the spiritualist saw Shackelton, she stood up and walked toward him in her long flowing robe. She stopped a few feet away, extended both of her arms and aimed her claw-crooked fingers and piercing eyes at him. Poised histrionically tense as if energy were flowing through her—like the Sith Emperor of *Star Wars* shooting fatal bolts of electricity from the Dark Side of the Force—she placed a curse on the ranger.

After his retirement Shackelton ruminated over this hex: "I guess it worked," he admitted to us ruefully, "I never did get promoted after that."

After the jury delivered its guilty verdict of involuntary manslaughter for Marsha Ann Savko, the U.S. District Attorney who prosecuted the case polled the jury as to their thoughts on the case. Their response, Shackelton said, was the following: If he, the prosecutor, had instead asked them for a conviction for first degree murder, they unanimously would have voted yes.

Far less mysterious, on New Year's Day of 1975, 51-year-old Robert Aal, a worker for the Yosemite Park and Curry Company, met Kerry S. "Corky" Lougee, a 24-year-old Company coworker, as the latter exited the drivers' lounge of the Company Garage. Aal belligerently questioned the younger employee's right to be there. Lougee, a relative "bantam rooster" of a man with the reputation of liking to drink a lot and also liking to fight, responded by striking Aal and knocked him onto the concrete where he hit his head.

After that single punch, Lougee quickly exhibited a sudden fit of concern for his victim. Small as Lougee was, he physically picked Aal up and carried him in his arms while jogging two blocks to Lewis Memorial Hospital. To no avail. Aal's head injury proved fatal.

FBI investigators looked at Lougee for a charge of manslaughter but ended up releasing him, pending further information. Ultimately this episode was chalked up as more of an accidental homicide than as a purposeful action.

As has become probably apparent thus far in this book—as exemplified by the brief episode immediately above—concession employees in the Park, who outnumber NPS employees by a factor of three or more, are seemingly inordinately represented in almost every category of fatal mishap. Take, for another example, 19-year-old Barbara Lynn Bentley of Fremont, California. Bentley worked as a waitress at the Company's hamburger stand in Curry Village next to the Mountaineering Shop. The five-foot, four-inch, 110-pound teenager loved hiking and riding horses.

She made a decision to go out on a date on April 26, 1976, with a new guy, Bruce Alan Curtis, age 24, of nearby Groveland, California. He had been employed at Curry's climbing store for only a week.

The pair went out for dinner at the Four Seasons Restaurant and then had cocktails at the Mountain Room Bar. Later that evening, at around 11 p.m., witnesses saw the two walking together near the Camp 6 intersection, about 200 yards from the Tecoya "D" Dormitory, where Curtis lived in room #3.

The next day Curry Company Supervisor Bill Germany was walking his dog on a leash along the Ahwahnee Meadow. He was in for a shock. He found Bentley dead 300 yards from "D" Dorm. She was fully dressed but braless. Strangely, her panties had been pulled up only as high as her pubis—as if someone else had hurriedly dressed her. Likewise her slacks were on and buttoned but not zipped up, seemingly again as if someone else had done the job too rapidly. Her face showed bruises from forceful blows. She had been strangled by hand—the marks on her throat were consistent with fingers gouging into her neck. The young woman's back was scraped from having been dragged across the ground for quite a distance. Her autopsy revealed a blood alcohol level of 0.12 percent, plus 0.1 milligram of Valium—enough to have impaired her judgment. The autopsy also revealed she had experienced sexual intercourse within seventy-two hours prior to her death, but she did not show any vaginal lesions attendant to rape.

Curtis became an instant prime suspect. He admitted to investigators that, at about 11 p.m., she had been lying on his bed and he had been lying on top of her when she pushed him away and then scratched him on the face with her fingernails and told him that she did "not want to go any further." She then got up and left his room, he said, slamming the door behind her. He added that the two had not had sexual intercourse and they both had been fully dressed while on his bed and that he had not seen her again after that door slammed.

During this interview, NPS Investigator Scott Connelly observed a maroon, wool-like blanket on Curtis' bed. An examination of the dead girl's body had revealed maroon-colored fibers wedged between her buttocks, in her groin, and on the backs of her thighs. A search warrant allowed confiscation of that blanket. The fibers proved a match.

Curtis also told investigators that Bentley had a leather-strapped purse with her. Despite searches, this was never found.

Rangers arrested Curtis the next day (April 27). This was not the first time the Park had had to delve into the man's unsavory side. A year earlier they had arrested him for impersonating an NPS Ranger by wearing a park ranger uniform, badge, and hat, and by claiming to be a ranger with the apparent—but unproven—intent of molesting a 10-year-old girl. The U.S. Magistrate convicted Curtis and expelled him from the Park for one year. Somehow, after that year expired, he had oozed back in on a thin thread when the prime screener for "new" concession employees had been out of her office when his file was okayed. Had she been in that day, she emphasized, she would have blocked his reentry and rehiring.

Park investigators now interviewed Curtis' one known friend, Joseph Donahue. He told them that he already had asked Curtis point-blank: "I heard you killed (or they say you killed) some girl and were picked up and put in jail?" Donahue further reported that Curtis avoided answering this question. He did tell Donahue that he had "been with a girl and they got in a fight," further stating, "She was a bitch."

Donahue told investigators that as Curtis spoke, he (Donahue) "was thinking that a girl would not have a chance with Curtis if he lost his temper—some men would not have a chance either." Curtis, Donahue stated, had a violent temper. He had personally seen him "super killing mad" four or five times. Donahue characterized his friend as "super strong" but "immature," and suggested he needed a doctor to treat him for anger management. In fact, Curtis had earlier deserted from the U.S. Marine Corps upon receiving orders for Viet Nam. He had also run out on his marriage, deserting his wife. A recent roommate of Curtis later added: "There was not one day that passed that Curtis did not talk about ladies and fighting."

On April 29, 1976, Park Chief Law Enforcement Officer Lee Shackelton happened to pass Curtis' cell in the Yosemite Jail. Curtis called him over. As he and the Ranger talked, Shackelton asked point-blank if he had murdered Bentley.

"I don't remember doing it," Curtis said. "Maybe I need a doctor."

"You mean a psychiatrist?" asked Shackelton.

"You guys have got all this evidence against me; so maybe I did it. So maybe I need a doctor or something."

"Let me check on that."

More than six months later, on November 11, 1976, a federal court in Fresno convicted Bruce Alan Curtis of first degree murder based on significant circumstantial evidence. Curtis never testified during the four-day jury trial. Two weeks later he was sentenced to life in prison.

More than three years later another young female Curry Company employee met tragedy. On September 11,1979, Daepaula Byers reported that 19-year-old Carol Laughlin of Fairfax, California had not shown up for work at the Village Gift Shop for the past two days. Ranger Jim Reilly investigated her tent in Camp 6 for clues. No one around Tent #51, it turned out, had seen Laughlin for two days. One of them added that Laughlin was a responsible person. She took her job seriously and would not miss work unless something was really wrong.

Something indeed was wrong. Weeks passed and the young woman never showed up.

As a concerned and progressive supervisor, Chief Law Enforcement Officer Lee Shackelton, author of the forthcoming book *High Ground: A Ranger's Tale of Adventure,* continued to espouse to his rangers that they use every available resource needed to get the job done right. Puzzled by everyone's inability to solve Laughlin's mysterious disappearance, Shackelton now decided he too had to walk the walk. Reluctantly he engaged the last possible tool that occurred to him, Bay Area psychic Kathleen Rhea. Rhea had volunteered her services several times before to the Park, but because most law enforcement types are skeptics, she never had been offered an opportunity to perform here.

Rhea now focused on Laughlin.

She ultimately decided the missing teenager was now located beneath a large steel grating of some sort. In that Yosemite had very few structures that even remotely met that description, Lee went ahead and asked the Park's plumbing crew to open up every grate in the Valley and inspect below them. These personnel did so but turned up no lead. Lee now sighed in resignation and settled with knowing that he had at least tried everything.

The following year, on April 28, 1980, hikers Pat Timson and Russell Erickson arrived at the Park Visitor Center. On the counter they placed a paper sack. In it was a human skull. They had found a skeleton, they explained, above The Cookie Cliff. The rest of the remains, including clothes, still lay there on the granite slope.

These two climbers took Rangers Dick Martin and Norm Hinson to the site. It lay about a quarter mile above the cliff, 500 yards up the Old Coulterville Road from where it intersects Highway 140. The very secluded spot is 400 feet below the longest tunnel on the Big Oak Flat Road. More specifically, it lies directly beneath the air vent in the middle of the tunnel. The rangers found the bones scattered here amid empty beer cans and other trash that drivers parked at the side shaft had tossed out of it. Every bone the rangers found remained within a fifteen-foot radius.

Dental records revealed that 19-year-old Carol Laughlin had finally been located.

Why was she beneath this air vent?

This location is not as bizarre as it might seem at first. The tunnel is long enough to need more fresh air than its two entries allow. But the side shaft is seventy-five feet long, perpendicular to the highway in its own seven-foot-high tunnel. And it is horizontal. Anyone inside the road tunnel could easily walk into this smaller corridor or even ride a bike or a motorcycle along it to its opening overlooking the Merced River Canyon below. Indeed, the air vent itself and the view from its mouth are both so attractive that it had become a minor hangout, a place to drink beers, enjoy the view, and maybe smoke something.

In 1979 that opening remained wide open and unprotected by a grate. In April of 1980 a grate did cover the opening.

But how would Laughlin have ended up down there?

Laughlin had had a roommate who had a boyfriend named William. William was an itinerant biker from Pinole, California. He was in his late 20s and alleged to be a hard drinker. Nor was William a model citizen in other respects. Even before the teenager vanished, Rangers had to arrest him for assaulting Laughlin's roommate. They later released him.

Laughlin had a weakness for motorcycles. She loved them but did not own one. She normally walked back to her tent from her work at the gift shop. Park investigators now wondered: On that fateful afternoon of September 9th had she been offered a motorcycle ride after work by William? Maybe the two of them then zoomed up Highway 120 to the airshaft for a short walk and a long view? And what sort of terrible accident—or worse—had taken place at the mouth of the airshaft that sent the young woman flying 400 feet into the beer cans below?

Investigators looked into William's recent history. He had returned to the Bay Area shortly after Laughlin's disappearance. Was he truly connected with her death?

When interviewed, William denied having anything to do with Laughlin. And with no other known witnesses and an ice-cold trail nearly eight months old (which equals no evidence) and little to no motive besides, rangers were stopped.

Despite this, they, Lee Shackelton included, did conclude that the pretty young woman was a homicide victim, not a suicide or accidental death. Even today her case remains unsolved.

The mysterious case of Carol Laughlin continues to be frustrating, but compared with the next one, hers seems clear-cut. During late spring of 1982 a visitor at the Summit Meadow turnout (south side of the Glacier Point Road) stumbled across a decomposing hand emerging from the melting snow. It looked like a bear paw. Was it?

No. It was not a bear's paw. It was a human hand. But the strangeness of this find did not stop there. The hand had been chopped off.

This macabre find led to an investigation of the area. This uncovered yet a second hand. It too had been chopped off. Decomposition of the tissues rendered fingerprint identification impossible for both finds. Evidently these hands had been tossed here before the previous winter had set in. Further searches within a radius of few hundred yards uncovered nothing else. The investigation stopped with the uneasy knowledge that something evil had happened here—but that something now seemed to lack a trail.

More than a year later, on June 28, 1983, a family stopped to picnic at Summit Meadow. One of smallest of the family, let's call him "Junior," wandered off to play by himself. When he reappeared he was dragging a stick in the dirt. No, wait, that's not a stick. One of Junior's parents stared in alarm. The boy was dragging a bone, a long one, on the ground. The parent peered even closer. Junior was dragging a human thigh bone.

Park investigators collected what they could of the rest of the skeleton and processed the scene. They did not have much to go on. The mystery body seemed to have been there for a couple of years. How did this person die? The scattered, weathered remains revealed no clue. In fact, other than a few parts of the skeleton itself, the Park's search of the area yielded no leads whatsoever. Facial reconstruction of the skull—found and collected nearly a year later and several hundred yards from the thigh bone—by forensic anthropologist Roger M. LaJeunesse of Fresno State University did reveal the victim had been a young woman in her early twenties at the oldest. And she had probably been of Hispanic or Native American descent. Other than that, the Park had zilch. Not even the coldest of trails.

Several months later Lee Shackelton sat watching the evening news on TV. He perked up. The anchorman was saying something about serial killer Henry Lee Lucas, now in custody in Texas. He had just "invited" law enforcement officials plagued by unsolved homicides to speak with him candidly.

Lucas had been recently indicted with multiple counts of serial killings. At this point in his unbelievably homicidal career he had nothing to lose by coming clean on other murders and, paradoxically, a lot to gain. This was because every new investigation that centered on him created a reason to keep him alive—for the secret information on missing persons he might divulge. And to keep his vocal chords "greased," Lucas knew the law would house him far from death row and in a location convenient for interviewers.

He was correct on both counts. He ended up in a personal prison cell equipped with amenities such as a color TV. He could dine on just about any food he asked for. And officials kept him supplied with an endless flow of his favorite two drug sources: coffee and cigarettes.

As different law officers drove Lucas to various crime scenes to which he had admitted complicity, on each trip he weighed more. Lucas grew from being an underfed highway predator to looking like a chubby but sinister little Santa Claus.

Shackelton got the ball rolling from Yosemite. He orchestrated a trip in which investigating rangers Kim Tucker and Don Coelho flew to Georgetown, Texas to interview Lucas. They later drove to Sacramento to reinterview him. In the backs of their minds each time was the dominating awareness that Lucas was not just a slippery suspect; he was an outright and sometimes outrageous liar. And he was deviously clever from having assiduously read crime files while doing prison time during his early years. His ability to trick interviewers into first giving *him* the critical crime scene details to thus enable him to then give them back as if he had been there was becoming infamous. Tucker and Coelho had promised themselves that the convicted serial killer would pull no such nonsense on them.

Even so, interviewing Henry Lee Lucas was no picnic. He was living proof that truth is one hell of a lot stranger than fiction, albeit far more challenging to ascertain. Born in 1936, Henry Lee was the son—and also ninth and last child—of an aging prostitute named Viola Lucas who literally refused to provide care for *any* of her brood. Many of them (though not Henry Lee) ended up under the care of someone else. Those she could not farm out she put to work guarding the family moonshine still, hauling water to their dirt-floored cabin, et cetera. For reasons not understood, she was particularly cruel and abusive—both physically and mentally and with an apparent vengeance—to her stunted mess of a son, Henry Lee. She once brained him as a kid with a chunk of firewood. He laid unconscious for more than a day.

That he managed to survive at all is probably due to Viola's "live-in" mate, a crippled reprobate named "Uncle Bernie." Uncle Bernie, for whatever his reasons, kept Henry Lee alive. Uncle Bernie also taught him—and repeated his lessons often—how to torture, rape, and kill animals and then sometimes have sex yet again with their corpses. Young Henry Lee became so obsessed with sex, and with the torture, killing, and dismembering of his victims he metamorphosed into a fledgling human monster.

In 1951, before Lucas had reached age 15, he made his first attempt to have sex with a human. He kidnapped a teenaged Laura Burnley near Lynchburg. When she resisted his attack, Henry Lee strangled her, raped her corpse then buried her body near Harrisburg, Virginia. Burnley's disappearance remained an unsolved murder for more than thirty years—until 1983 when Lucas finally confessed.

Lucas landed in jail at age 18 for burglaries. He escaped twice, was recaptured, and finally released in 1959—after having studied many criminals' case files to learn how they had made the mistakes that had got them caught. His now 74-year-old mother soon turned up on his doorstep in Tecumseh. They argued incessantly. She wanted him to come home and live with her and take care of her. He wanted no part of her ever again.

After hours of arguing Viola Lucas hit Henry Lee over the head with a broom, snapping the handle in half. The one-eyed Lucas (he had lost an eye as a child during a mishap while playing with a knife) instantly responded by slugging her in the neck. In his hand happened to be his knife. She slowly bled to death. Lucas later bragged that he raped her corpse, though later he recanted on the rape part of his story. For killing his mother, he went back to jail until 1970, spending much of that time in Ionia State Hospital for the Criminally Insane in Michigan (Lucas never expressed remorse for his murders). Almost immediately after his release he was charged with molesting two teenaged girls. Back to jail for another five years.

In late 1976 Lucas met 29-year-old Ottis Elwood Toole in a soup kitchen in Florida. Toole was an even more creepy piece of work than Lucas—if such a thing is possible. He was a six-foot-tall bisexual transvestite into voyeurism, arson, murder, and cannibalism ("with barbecue sauce," Toole once noted, "tastes like real meat"). On July 27, 1981, Toole kidnapped and decapitated six-year-old Adam Walsh, leading Adam's father John to create and host the TV show "America's Most Wanted." Twenty-seven years would pass before Reve and John Walsh would learn their son's horrible fate. Toole and Lucas swapped bloody and cruel stories of foul heinous acts and discovered they were soul mates. The two began living together in Springfield, Florida. Next they traveled the highway together, murdering together, raping victims, hitting convenience stores and occasionally gratuitously killing the clerks. Often, it seems, these occasional lovers murdered on mere whim, spur of the moment, hitting hitchhikers standing along the road for the fun of watching their surprised faces, and sometimes committing multiple homicides in one day. Lucas said he considered women along the road whose car had broken down "free lunch" (a.k.a. easy murders). When Ottis Toole dressed as a woman and Lucas drove, almost any hitchhiker would, disarmed by Toole's camouflage, hop into their car. Often fatally.

In 1981, Lucas and Toole added Ottis' nephew Frank Powell and niece Becky (a.k.a. Frieda) Powell to their road trips. As a mentally impaired pre-teenager, Becky had fallen hard for Lucas when they lived together in Florida. In 1981, the two kids' natural mother had just committed suicide. Poor young Frank would soon witness so many despicable murders and necrophilia episodes by Lucas and/or Toole that in 1983 he ended up in a mental institution.

Becky fared even worse. Lucas considered her his wife even though he was about thirty years older. In 1983, after they had "lived" together for about two years and were in Texas, Becky wanted to return to Jacksonville. Lucas did not want to go to Florida due to an outstanding warrant for him there. They argued. Off the highway where they had been hitchhiking they continued arguing. She got so irritated she hit Lucas "upside the head." He immediately stabbed her in the chest. "She just sorta sat there for a little bit and then dropped over, ya know. I cut her up into little teeny pieces and stuffed her into three pillows....I stuffed all of her in there except her legs." Two weeks later he returned and buried Becky's body parts. Police later exhumed these, confirming his story, one which for the only time in Lucas' life, he told with remorse—although he also admitted having sex with her corpse before chopping it up.

How Lucas finally got caught was by being arrested for illegal weapons' possession that year. In his cell, he eventually admitted to several murders, including Becky's. He was convicted and sentenced to life in prison. Afterward, he started spilling confessions like a slot machine dumping coins during a jackpot of how he and Ottis had murdered other women. Dozens of them. Then hundreds. Ultimately, investigators from nineteen states questioned Lucas regarding roughly 600 homicides. As many as a hundred or more of these turned out to seem genuine and more or less corroboratory. Most of the 600, though, seemed spurious.

Upon careful analysis, Lucas remains firmly a serial/sexual killer whose profile not only makes him a poster boy for such monsters, but whose heinous murders remain supported by a huge body of conclusive evidence from multiple sources. Moreover, Ottis Toole corroborated many of Lucas' murders. In short, Lucas, unfortunately, was the real thing.

Rangers Tucker and Coelho met with the twisted little killer. Again, the two knew he had everything to gain by stringing them along with fabricated and elaborate tales and nothing to lose. To establish an index of veracity, they had to nudge Lucas into divulging—without them feeding him—highly specific details about the scene unknowable except to the real killer.

This process proved easier than the two rangers had expected.

Lucas said that he and Ottis—with Frank and Becky Powell along—had driven through Coarsegold on Highway 41 and had picked up a teenage girl. Passing through the Park gate, they stopped to buy a picnic lunch at the Wawona General Store. Then they drove on to Summit Meadow. They soon parked then walked into the woods near a log and sat down to eat. After they ate their fried chicken wrapped in aluminum foil and drank their beers, Lucas and Ottis looked at each other meaningfully. It was "time," they said to one another silently, to kill their new friend.

Lucas said he then walked up behind the unsuspecting girl and strangled her. They murdered her for fun, as if it were a satisfying dessert at the end of lunch.

But dessert was not over. Lucas admitted far more heinous details to Coelho. For starters, Lucas said he then had sex with the dead woman's corpse. Afterward, to make her body unidentifiable via fingerprints, he chopped off both her hands. He tossed these, hundreds of yards away on the other side of the road, near that turnout.

The two rangers worked to conceal their revulsion for Lucas. One problem at this point remained that his story was still general enough he could have been making up most of it. It contained few specifics to prove he had murdered their mystery girl.

So, among their many questions, they also asked Lucas: "Was there anything unusual about the location where all of this happened?"

Lucas answered, "I noticed a part of a license plate nailed about twenty feet up in a tree right where we were eating. It seemed odd to me that someone would do that. What's the point of going to all the trouble to nail something like that so far up in a tree?"

Both rangers knew that what had been nailed up in the tree was not a license plate per se; it was a yellow metal trail marker, which from even a short distance might have looked like a license plate. It had been tacked high enough that even a deep snowpack would not bury and conceal it and thus get cross-country skiers lost. Eerily, they remembered there indeed had been one of these markers at the scene where "Junior" had found the thigh bone of this unfortunate young woman.

"What else can you tell us about the scene? Can you tell us something specific, something to prove *you* were actually there?"

Lucas puzzled a bit then said, "Well, we had all this trash left over from lunch. We thought about just leaving it there, but it was an eyesore. It might call attention to the girl's body....So we gathered it all up and jammed it under one of the logs we'd been sitting on. Jammed it in good so as none of it would get seen."

"Which log?"

Lucas then detailed which log.

When the two rangers returned to Yosemite they drove up to Summit Meadow. They found Lucas' homicidal picnic spot close to where the bones had been scattered. They saw the "license plate" nailed up in the tree. Then they found the log, a good one to sit on. They probed underneath it. Yes, someone had actually jammed some trash under there. It was hidden so well, in fact, that it was missed by investigators the first time. They extracted it. Beer cans and aluminum foil wrapping...

Tucker and Coelho now knew it was extremely likely their mystery girl had been killed by Henry L. Lucas in 1981 exactly as he had admitted to them. Maybe if they pressed Lucas harder, he might reveal clues about who the girl was. After all, she likely had a family somewhere. Somebody would care what had happened to her. Somebody would want closure.

At this juncture it turned out that, instead of green-lighting additional interviews, the Assistant United States Attorney decided against prosecuting Lucas and Toole for their Summit Meadow murder partly because the feds lacked an identity for the victim. This would have made the case difficult. The second reason for not prosecuting was several other legal jurisdictions were already preparing capital cases against these two psychopaths. After all, the murderers could only be executed once.

In retrospect, Lucas' orgy of confessions, many of which turned out spurious, was brilliant on his part. Those murders which he did not commit cast a shadow of doubt over crimes for which he was guilty. Indeed, based on his confession, Texas convicted him of killing a woman named "Orange Socks" (due to a lack of any other possible identification) and sentenced him to death. Later evidence, however, seemed to contradict the basis for this conviction. For this "miscarriage of justice" on June 26, 1998, Governor George W. Bush commuted the death sentence of Henry Lee Lucas to life in prison without the possibility of parole. Meanwhile Ottis Toole died in prison of cirrhosis of the liver on September 15, 1996. Lucas, however, lived long enough to "help" with those 600 otherwise unsolved murders. Eventually, after years of sitting at a sewing machine and tailoring trousers for correctional officers, the chubby little monster finally died of heart failure on March 13, 2001, while snoozing in his bed in the Ellis 1 prison unit in Huntsville, Texas. By at least one account, he had been serving time there for nine murder convictions.

One sad upshot here is the girl in Summit Meadow remained unidentified and mysteriously missing to friends and family for several decades. In 2021, however, Special Agent of the Investigative Service Branch Cullen Tucker, son of original investigator Kim Tucker, resurrected this mystery by seeking a DNA analysis of Lucas's Summit Meadow victim. Amazingly, via a complicated pathway, the DNA sequencing provided an identification: Pat Marie Hicks-Dahlstrom of Spokane, Washington, who was 29 years old when she accepted the wrong-est of wrong rides.

Gratuitous murders like those committed by Lucas and Toole may work well for horror films, but in real life they constitute the most unfathomable, most unjust, and most heinous of interpersonal crimes. Consider the tragic case of 18-year-old Helle Olsbro. On March 16, 1985, Olsbro was an exchange student from Gentofte, Denmark and also the daughter of a Scandinavian diplomat. She had been in Yosemite only two hours when she walked alone east along the tree-lined scenic trail from the Ahwahnee Hotel toward Indian Caves beneath Washington Column in the land that John Muir wrote as having "the most songful streams in the world and noblest forests."

Olsbro's sudden screams were heard by a couple hiking more than a hundred yards behind her. They were so bloodcurdling they froze the man and woman in fear and indecision.

Finally after two, maybe three minutes passed, the pair rushed toward her. They found Olsbro collapsed and bleeding heavily, literally gasping for her last breath. She'd been stabbed a shocking forty-seven times. Unfortunately, these responders were not only too late to have prevented young Olsbro's attacker from killing her, they were even too late to have seen the perpetrator escaping through the woods.

"We have no idea how the attacker got away without being seen," noted Ranger Mallory Smith in a *San Jose Mercury News* article on March 28, 1985, "That leads us to wonder if it was someone who knew the park really well."

Rangers arriving ten minutes later found the teenager already dead. They sealed the exits to Yosemite within half an hour. But largely due to the ground cover of pine needles they found no tracks to follow or identify. The Park's investigation included more than 150 interviews but none revealed motives among the 1,000 residents of the Park and the thousands of tourists. Rangers with SCUBA plumbed the nearby waters in search of a discarded weapon but found nothing. Olsbro's hideous murder seemed a truly random killing.

But why and by whom?

The Park did soon identify a possible suspect, a concessionaire rooms' keeper. The man had a history of having stalked a blond student at Stanford University. When questioned, he provided an alibi. Upon scrutiny the alibi only held firm beginning forty-five minutes after the attack, more than enough time for a person to have murdered Olsbro and then to return, change clothes, and make himself conspicuously present to other employees. Even so, Rangers could not rely on the mere fact of opportunity for an arrest. Without a motive, a weapon, or a witness and without any other specific forensic evidence, they just did not have a case. In short, the investigation came up stone cold.

Unfortunately the next murder was only months away. At 7:45 a.m., on the warm Saturday morning of August 17, 1985, Sean O' Neill, David Gunning, and Perry Harrison sat on the tailgate of their pickup truck parked in the campground. Sean stared up at the 7,214-foot-high Glacier Point and contemplated having a better breakfast than the junk food he had just eaten. Still, at least the view here was pretty amazing. As he now stared at the monolith of granite, something black and white plummeted down its face. Was it, he wondered, a black and white dog? How would a dog fall off? No. He now could see it was a person wearing black and white. Probably a BASE jumper.

O'Neill yelled a heads up to his buddies and continued to stare at the falling figure. He waited to see the canopy pop open and to watch it gently spiral toward the meadow below.

No chute opened.

Instead the body slammed at high speed down the cliff face for more than a thousand feet then vanished below the field of view of the shocked trio.

"Whoa! What was *that*?" the three young men asked each other. One of them grabbed his binoculars. They now peered upward to the viewpoint atop Glacier Point.

"Hey, look; there's a guy standing up there." The three reluctantly shared the glasses to see what appeared to be a stocky man dressed in orange and posing with his arms spread-eagled in a "Sermon on the Mount" posture about 3,000 feet above the Valley floor on the Glacier Point Overlook.

"Yeah, he's just standing there—like he's gonna fly or something." Several seconds passed, then several more passed, and still the Christ-posing figure in orange continued to stand on the brink like a dramatic statue. Then he moved…

At 200 pounds and five feet and eleven inches tall, 29-year-old Richard Russell Mughir looked uncannily like a hybrid between Charles Manson and an overfed, red-bearded Viking. This mentally unstable, flaming-maned resident of Silver Springs, Maryland now stood poised to complete an odyssey whose insane basis defies belief.

While it was Mughir's journey, he had brought along a sidekick, a 33-year-old woman named Sonia Janet Goldstein. Mughir and Goldstein had been living together in a terminally dysfunctional relationship.

Goldstein lived off her father's support. Mughir lived off his mother's. This parental funding made possible the couple's renting a house and paying their bills even while holding no jobs. Not only jobless, these two troubled people also were dedicatedly isolated from the rest of the world, including from their families—except for those checks. Even so, their life together remained punctuated by domestic squabbles. Frequently these quarrels squirted out the front door of their house where they disturbed their neighbors. The commonest pattern of these fights consisted of Mughir yelling loudly and abusively at Goldstein and slapping her around. Then he would storm off, leaving her standing drooped in front of their little blue house on Laredo Road in Silver Spring (where they had lived for the past three and a half years). She, often physically injured from his assaults, would then beg in a small voice, "Don't leave me. Please come back..."

Neighbors considered Mughir to be "nasty, rude, violent, scary, weird, and crazy" with "nasty" the most frequent epithet. When one neighbor tried to intervene to rescue Goldstein, Mughir threatened him with, "I'll murder her and kill myself if you and other people don't quit interfering with our disputes—it's no one's business!"

Sometimes, in a milder vein, Mughir would simply yell at the top of his booming voice: "I'm the most intelligent person here!" Then he might blast out some lines from Shakespeare to prove his point.

Despite Mughir's threats, when a neighbor witnessed the two dysfunctional lovebirds spill out onto their front porch where Mughir punched and kicked Sonia, he called the Montgomery County (Maryland) Police. They arrived and tried to intercede. Mughir confronted the officers as if they were infinitely inferior beings and no more than an inconvenience. Perhaps it would be helpful here to point out that Mughir had told Goldstein that he was a very high-level super spy with a number of aliases. He may well have believed this himself. Indeed, he had also told certain people that when government agents descended upon him he would kill Goldstein and then himself.

One of the police now tried to separate Mughir from Goldstein, whom he was holding in a controlling grip and trying to steer back into the house away from all of these petty Earthlings. The cop instructed him to let go of her. He told the policeman to mind his own business. The officer then tried to step between the two quarrelers. Mughir turned away as if he could not see the man then suddenly slammed the cop in the midsection with a powerful, martial arts-like elbow to the gut. Other officers swarmed over Mughir.

What seemed at first like a free trip to jail escalated into a court order for Richard Russell Mughir to be placed in Eugene Leland Memorial Hospital, under the care of psychologist Dr. Cyril G. Hardy. Meanwhile Sonia Goldstein was admitted—at the behest of her sister, Susan Urban—to Washington Adventist Hospital in Takoma Park.

Hospitalized during June of 1985, Mughir, in his obsessive way, began two projects. One was a letter writing campaign to Goldstein to soften her up and exert remote control over her. He wrote in one letter:

> You must not say [anything] about me hitting you. Have you? You must deny it in some way—Say you provoked me and hit me first.

> You must somehow deny suicide pact idea. Say you were mistaken, over-tired, overwrought, etc.

Mughir's second project proved more weird and ominous. He launched a personal research quest for "the perfect high." This is not what it sounds like. His scattered papers included a long section under the title "Project Notes" in which page after page, then ten pages after ten more pages, listed reference sources to be consulted. Sometimes Mughir stalled out and simply filled a page with nothing except all the numerals from 1 to 100, apparently just to keep busy. His *hundreds* of pages of "project notes" open a window into a deranged mind.

In an organized way, Mughir listed what to him seemed the critical questions pertinent to identifying the perfect high. Question #6, for example, spelled out his quest.

> What distance from peak would I have to extend an object in order for it to fall perfectly vertical to the ground at base of mountain? Therefore, from this analytical perspective, what is Best Mountain: Best Peak For Maximum Vertical Range from top & minimum Angle of sloping thereafter [?].

Mughir perused thick books of topography. He narrowed his list of possibilities. No surprise, he looked first at Grand Canyon, noting its notorious high points—Cape Royal, Toroweap, Point Imperial—but for some reason he rejected them all. Mughir got stuck for a while on Dead Horse Point, a Utah State Park near Moab. Dead Horse, he noted, allowed a 2,000- to 3,000-foot vertical drop. Although not common knowledge, Dead Horse Point would later become the location for the now infamous final scene in *Thelma and Louise* where Hollywood would film the movie's two heroines committing suicide by driving their car off the rim of what the audience was to believe was Grand Canyon. Either way, his research also revealed that during the summer monsoon one might need a four-wheel drive vehicle to get to the overlook. Dead Horse Point was out.

Then he discovered Glacier Point. A paved road led to its summit. Under "Glacier Point" in Mughir's Project Notes he wrote: "most accessible maximum vertical-like drop from rock monolith, mtn. in the United States."

Now Mughir furiously focused on Yosemite. He wrote down a swarm of phone numbers for everything from renting sleeping bags, hiring mules, plane reservations, getting hiking information, to booking local lodging. Below the additional pages that he scrawled during this frenetic clerical fit he added a poem:

> I believe that when death closes our eyes
> We shall awaken to a light, of which our sunlight
> is but the shadow.

Dr. Hardy noted that Mughir had a whopping case of denial, never discussed any of his emotions, and he would instead only intellectualize. His "thought processes are distorted with some grandiose and unrealistic ideas about being a corporate executive and having a fortune in jewelry and ancient books," Hardy wrote. "The patient is unable to function (He has not worked in seven years).... He shows very poor judgment." Harding's final diagnosis was: "schizophrenic disorder, paranoid type, with mixed personality disorder."

Mughir told Hardy he was going to start a rock and roll band once he was free and then record his own music. So he might as well be released now so he could get going on this. Significantly, Mughir's 60-year-old mother, who, again, was his sole financial support, told Dr. Hardy, "No!" to releasing Mughir. This apparently was the first time she had told her son a firm "no" to anything.

Goldstein, for her part, had been an off-and-on psychiatric patient for fifteen years suffering acute, undifferentiated schizophrenia, experiencing hallucinations and wishes to kill her parents (even though her father was still supporting her). Moreover, she frequently obsessed on suicide. Just before Mughir had been arrested, she had even tried to buy a handgun for him, telling her sister that it was of "life or death importance" and was to be used when the federal agents descended upon him.

To make a complicated story less so, both Mughir and Goldstein eventually were released from their respective mental institutions. On August 5, Mughir shepherded the compliant Goldstein onto a commercial flight to California.

The pair spent nearly two weeks in or near Yosemite to scope out the location for his perfect high. This odd couple stayed in motels. But as the various managers would later testify, Mughir found multiple things wrong with every room. The TV did not work right, the sheets, towels, or the bathroom was not clean enough, the room was too noisy, and the crackers in the store were not crispy enough. Mughir, for his own paranoid reasons, also used multiple aliases. This proved ludicrous when he gave a false name to a clerk then cashed his traveler's checks made out in his real name which he then countersigned with his real name and then handed to the same clerk to whom he had just given his alias.

As he proceeded to irritate virtually everyone with whom he interacted, Goldstein followed Mughir as docile as a whipped dog. Indeed many Yosemite area concession providers were impressed not only with how subdued and yielding she was but also with how rude and nasty he acted toward her, yelling into her face to do things. Bafflingly, others noticed that she frequently acted solicitous of the pudgy Mughir, especially when he was out of breath from walking uphill.

Local resident Mark Clemons (who, less than two years later in 1987, would doze off behind the wheel fatally while driving home from work in Yosemite) collected a fee of seventy dollars from the pair to drive them to Glacier Point. During this ride, Clemons recalled, Mughir bragged a lot about being a professional photographer and also a parachutist (neither was true). This was a scout run for

Mughir. After they arrived at the world-class overlook he expressed disappointment that Glacier Point was not nearly as vertical as his research had led him to expect. Instead he now admired Half Dome, a vertical phenomenon of global significance. But, Clemons remembered, Mughir bemoaned how getting to the top of Half Dome was too difficult. Mark informed Mughir two different hiking trails fed the one to the summit and added that many climbers had actually scaled the face.

"No, that's impossible," Mughir replied authoritatively. "No one could climb that." Evidently Mughir's obsessive research—as well as his vaunted intelligence—failed him here.

Campers O' Neill, Gunning, and Harrison still sat on the tailgate of their pickup and watched the Christ-like poser atop Glacier Point. "What is this guy doing?" one of them asked.

Abruptly Richard Russell Mughir dropped off the face of Glacier Point. The trio of witnesses below agreed that he was in the air barely more than one second before he collided with the cliff face. For all of Mughir's hundreds of pages of research into the perfect vertical drop, he had picked a place to commit suicide where he had slammed into the granite less than fifty feet down a 3,000-foot decline. It must have hurt.

Mughir continued to tumble and bounce down the face of Glacier Point. He disappeared near where his companion's body had vanished minutes earlier.

The three amazed witnesses reported their observations to the Park.

Ranger Don Coelho and others combed the scene atop Glacier Point. Blood had splattered the normal unfortunate scatter of cigarette butts and beer cans. Lots of blood. The retaining walls were spotted with it. The soil was soaked. This mess was not some mishap with a Swiss Army knife. Someone had been butchered here.

The investigators found a black fake-leather briefcase nearby with identification cards for both Richard Russell Mughir and Sonia Janet Goldstein. What is now clear from analysis of the evidence and from the recovery of the scattered body parts of Goldstein and Mughir—as well as from those hundreds of pages of Mughir's writings which he had cast into space from the top of Glacier Point—is that he had murdered an apparently willing Goldstein and then shoved her body into the air. He then had jumped to experience that "light, of which our sunlight is but the shadow."

We doubt that it worked out exactly as either of them had expected it to.

When Investigator Coelho contacted Dr. Cyril G. Hardy for Mughir's clinical background, Hardy quickly interrupted the ranger and said, "Don't tell me; Richard killed Sonia, then killed himself, right?"

Right.

Although Mughir gleaned no financial profit from having murdered Sonia Goldstein, men have decided to murder their female partners for this reason alone. More than two years after Mughir's last stand, at 5:45 p.m. on December 5, 1987, 22-year-old Stevie Allen Gray drove to the ice rink in Yosemite Valley and told an employee there he needed to report a missing person. Gray had just come from the Discovery View parking area—although why he had not used the phone there at the east end of the Wawona Tunnel to make his report went unexplained. At any rate, the ice rink employee helped him.

Gray told the rangers he and his 24-year-old wife, Dolores Contreras Gray, had arrived in Yosemite in her Camaro. That afternoon they stopped at the view point and had picnicked and drunk champagne. He had drunk too much, he added, and decided to nap in the car. Meanwhile his wife had taken a walk. When he awoke it was already dark. He had looked for her, he said, but had no luck. So he drove into the Valley to report her as missing.

Ranger Grady Bryant accompanied Gray back to Discovery View (also called Tunnel View). He reiterated that, as he had been asleep, he had no idea where Dolores might have gone. Since a search in that area was nearly impossible in the dark, the two returned to Yosemite Valley. Once there, Gray told rangers he could not spend the night because he had to return to Lemoore Naval Air Station. Au contraire, insisted Ranger Randy August to Stevie Gray, he could indeed stay over.

The next morning a SAR mission began using a helicopter and ground personnel. Gray accompanied the officials back to that parking area where he had last seen her.

Dolores' stepfather, Joe A. Martinez, who had raised her from age 4, had been alerted by rangers. So he had driven up from nearby Clovis. The feeling in the pit of his stomach now that he was on the scene was telling him that something had gone very wrong. He testified later that he had observed Stevie Gray at 1 p.m., right after searchers had found Dolores' battered body 350 feet below the cliff at Discovery View. "Stevie showed no emotion," reported Martinez. "He did not cry, nor did he appear sad."

During his many years of being Dolores' father, Martinez had grown very close to her. He had taken her and the whole family on numerous camping trips in the nearby Sierra Nevada. He added that not only had he taught the family survival rules, but that she in particular had been, and still was, afraid of heights. In the past when she approached a vertical drop, she would stop and say, "Too close!" Her stepfather added that she had always been an especially careful hiker, particularly near heights or in the mountains. To get her near an overlook at all she had to be carefully coaxed. How she could have gone so close as to accidentally fall here baffled him.

These were not the only aspects of the Dolores Contreras Gray fatality that smelled fishy. Indeed Ranger Kim Tucker happened to be in the maintenance area where the helicopter and ground personnel were situated immediately after Dolores' body had been found. Tucker had just heard that Dolores had just been recovered so she asked a coworker where the woman's poor husband was. Someone pointed him out for her.

Tucker stared in surprise. The man identified was sitting playing cards with several crew members from Lemoore. He was wearing a flight jump suit—just as the helicopter crew wore—and otherwise was not distinguishable from them in demeanor. Tucker's take on Stevie Allen Gray, so shortly after learning his wife had died in a horrible fall, was that he was exhibiting apparent mild boredom and equally mild interest in the card game. And nothing more.

A ranger near Tucker expressed bewilderment and wonder about how or why Dolores Gray might have accidentally fallen 350 feet. Tucker looked at the ranger pointedly and said something like, "There's why," pointing to Stevie Allen Gray sitting playing cards as if nothing had happened.

The other ranger rounded on her and said, "Do you *know* what you just said! You should be ashamed. Think about what you just said!"

Tucker did not think her intuition, intelligence, law enforcement training, and considerable field experience could all be so wrong but, either way, it would play no role here; she was not assigned to this case. More to the point, she did not in the least feel "ashamed" of suspecting Stevie Allen Gray of foul play.

The day (December 7) after Dolores was discovered, Gray contacted his wife's employer and asked about claiming her life insurance. This amounted to $66,000 from a policy that Dolores had signed up for at the IRS office where she worked. This may sound like a hefty sum to insure such a young woman, but this one policy was only the tip of the iceberg.

Stevie Gray, a high school dropout, was currently on active service in the U.S. Navy. But the performance of the five-foot, seven-inch, 135-pound seaman proved to be no better than bilge water. His official personnel records show he consistently was in trouble. The navy had recently charged him with "forgery of documents and numerous unauthorized absences." Moreover, he was the subject of "numerous disciplinary actions" for "impulsive, disruptive behavior." Convicting him on charges of malingering would have proved easy. Off base he was implicated in vehicle theft. And he was labeled a liar and con man.

The Navy psychiatrist who examined Gray (in April of 1987, a few weeks before he would meet Dolores) characterized him as manifesting a "mixed personality disorder with antisocial, narcissistic, and borderline features." The upshot? "It is predicted that he will be a continuing drain on command resources." This navy shrink recommended that Stevie Allen Gray be given a general discharge, and not allowed to serve out his hitch for an honorable discharge. As it turned out, however, Stevie *would* complete his four-year hitch in 1988, not many months after Dolores' death.

Stevie and Dolores had met in Fresno in May of 1987 and soon began dating six months before her fatal visit to Yosemite. Things had gone fast. After three months, on August 29, they were married. Things, in fact, went more than fast. Nine days *prior* to their wedding, Gray had requested a life insurance application for Dolores from a national life insurance company, the Uniformed Services Benefit Association (USBA). Dolores, remember, was already insured for $66,000 by the government.

Very soon after getting married, he went to sea for a few weeks. On October 2, USBA received an application apparently signed by Dolores for an additional $292,000 in coverage for herself—with her husband named as the primary beneficiary. When he went to sea again—aboard the U.S.S. Enterprise—he sent in yet another insurance application to USBA to insure himself for $292,000. Interestingly, this second policy also would pay him $145,000 if his wife were to die first. In total, Stevie had insured Dolores for $437,000. Adding in her IRS policy, she became worth $503,000 to him if she died. Stevie Allen Gray had been making premium payments on both of these additional policies with money orders from the aging aircraft carrier.

On December 11, Dolores was buried. On that same day, he contacted USBA with a "death claim statement" for the $292,000 for which he had originally insured her. Tellingly, Stevie failed to pay the $3,000 in funeral bills for Dolores (her mother, Ramona, and her mother's husband, Joe Martinez, had to pay these). A month later, on January 19, 1988, Gray contacted the insurance company yet again with a second signed statement claiming the remaining $145,000 under that second policy he had taken out on himself.

Yet even before making this final claim, Stevie Gray's behavior was so suspicious that the Park requested a polygraph test. The examiner asked him if he had pushed his wife off a cliff in Yosemite. Gray said, "No." The examiner next asked him if he had planned her death in order to collect life insurance. He again answered no. The examiner reported that in both cases that Stevie Gray's responses were "indicative of deception."

Interestingly, when Park Investigators acting jointly with the FBI had previously interviewed Gray he had told them that he had no life insurance policies on Dolores. Officials now informed Stevie for the first time that at roughly 4 p.m., two hikers had been walking directly above where her car had been parked. They heard about five "desperate" female screams.

Stevie now instantly changed his story from having been asleep in her Camaro to he and Dolores having been standing outside the vehicle drinking champagne. Dolores, he said, had told him she would be right back then had walked down a trail. A moment later he heard her scream. He ran down the trail to look for her, he said, but was unable to find her. He admitted that he had not told this story originally because he feared her family would seek reprisals against him. At this point a ranger asked Stevie point-blank whether he had killed Dolores. Stevie Gray got angry and denied it. This outbreak terminated the interview. He then went free.

Stevie Allen Gray, it turned out, had been having sex with other women even during his brief marriage to Dolores. Indeed, he had been wooing at least one of his girlfriends during this time as if he were single. Now he lost no time in chasing more women.

Meanwhile the Park and FBI investigation continued—albeit at a slower pace.

A year and a half later, on June 21, 1989, police arrested Gray in Hanford, California and charged him with battery (the abuse had gone on all night) on his live-in girlfriend of the past two months—Mickie Jordan, now bruised, bleeding, and clad in torn clothes. Stevie skated on this charge with mere probation. On July 3, police arrested him again, this time for "willful cruelty to children." Stevie had forced Jordan's 7 year-old and 9 year-old to stay awake all night by beating them with his belt and/or whipped them on their hands and buttocks if they nodded off. The court sentenced him again to three years probation, to 365 days in jail—a sentence which, inexplicably, the court immediately suspended—and to 160 hours of community service. The court also instructed Stevie to go to counseling sessions.

These soon proved moot. On October 20, 1989, the FBI finally arrested Gray under the charge of having violated 18 United States Code 1111—more specifically: "During the evening hours of December 5, 1987, the defendant, Stevie Allen Gray, committed premeditated murder by pushing his wife, Dolores Contreras Gray, off a cliff in Yosemite National Park. Mrs. Gray fell 350 feet to her death."

On July 6, 1990, after a twelve-day trial based on circumstantial evidence, the jury found Stevie Allen Gray guilty of murder in the first degree. The court sentenced him on September 10 to life in prison.

Even as the FBI investigation on Stevie Allen Gray was still in progress, another fatal tableau unfolded. In late December of 1987, 35-year-old Roderick Eugene Daniels, a Curry Company employee, had invited Mustafa Hassan El-Amin over to his Cabin #224 in Curry Village to watch TV. Well past midnight, El-Amin told Daniels he had to leave to get some sleep. The 220-pound Daniels followed El-Amin to the "Rock Bathroom" then grabbed him and yanked him into a stall of the restroom. He forced the 135-pound young man down to his knees and commanded him to commit fellatio. At this point another person entered the restroom. El-Amin pulled loose from the much larger Daniels and escaped.

Daniels now followed him back to his room and said, "Come on, let's get into the shower; do you have any Vaseline?" El-Amin resisted Daniels, fled then told his roommate about the assault. Later, when El-Amin heard that Daniels was sexually harassing women at the Ahwahnee Hotel, he finally decided he should report this earlier incident. Thereafter, El-Amin tried to avoid Daniels.

El-Amin succeeded for several weeks. But Daniels had been stalking him for an opportunity. On the evening of February 21, 1988, El-Amin was walking in Curry Village near the public restroom by the Terrace. Out of the dark Daniels grabbed El-Amin, placed an opened lock-blade knife to his throat, and forced him into a cabin.

Once released from the chokehold, El-Amin looked quickly toward the door.

Daniels smirked at him then dragged a dresser over against the door, blocking it.

Daniels held his knife menacingly and approached him again. "You might as well get started."

El-Amin felt no desire to provide oral sex for Daniels. He had to come up with a plan to escape. But the man weighed twice what he did and was a brutal bastard.

"Okay," El-Amin said, looking cowed…feeling cowed.

Daniels grinned and dropped his pants. Then he lay back on the bed with his knife still in his left hand. Ready. He glanced at El-Amin meaningfully.

El-Amin dropped to his knees.

As he settled in between Daniels' legs, Daniels let the knife loose from his hand and closed his eyes.

The frightened El-Amin saw the weapon roll an inch or so from Daniels' left hand. He realized he now had a chance. A slim one, but still…

He placed one hand gently in Daniels' crotch and simultaneously grabbed the knife off the bed with his other. He quickly put the weapon between his own thighs. Suddenly Daniels moved, squirming to the right.

El-Amin's heart nearly stopped. He tried to shuffle with him and still keep the knife between his legs. As El-Amin moved, the knife dropped onto the floor.

It sounded to him as if the roof had caved in. He tensed, expecting Daniels to rise up off the bed, grab the knife, and slit his throat.

El-Amin could not believe it. Daniels apparently had not heard the knife drop.

El-Amin quickly snatched the weapon off the floor and, gripping its hilt in both hands, stabbed Daniels in the center of the chest, pounding the blade in as hard as he could—as if trying to nail Daniels to the bed with a single thrust. Then, leaving the knife rammed home, El-Amin jumped to his feet and raced toward the dresser. He grabbed it and shoved it away from the door.

Behind him, Daniels rose from the bed with the knife still stuck in the middle of his chest. He reached for his pants and pulled them up.

El-Amin raced out the door. Never had the fresh air of Yosemite ever smelled this good. If he could get to the telephone near the restroom fast enough, he could dial 911 before Daniels caught up to him. El-Amin now sprinted.

Meanwhile, Daniels also ran out of the cabin, staggering but still powered by adrenaline. As he pursued El-Amin, the knife fell out of his chest onto the ground.

Only seconds ahead, El-Amin stopped himself by grabbing the side of the phone. He yanked the receiver off its cradle and glanced back toward the cabin. Shit! Daniels was still on his feet and still coming. Abruptly, as El-Amin dialed, Daniels, in an uncoordinated run, collapsed dead, stabbed through the heart.

Park Rangers responded to El-Amin's 911 call in minutes. They arrived to find Daniels dead (although the Park Paramedic started advanced life support on him anyway). El-Amin was not indicted. Given the evidence plus background on Daniels' nasty history, the Federal Grand Jury had no trouble in concluding justifiable homicide.

More than a decade would pass before Yosemite National Park experienced its next (and by 2007, still its last) homicide. This one would receive front page coverage coast to coast.

On February 12, 1999, 42-year-old real estate agent Carole Sund left Eureka,

California, with her 15-year-old daughter Juli and their friend, 16-year-old Silvina Pelosso from Cordoba, Argentina. Their plans were to stop in San Francisco then in Stockton and finally drive on to Yosemite—their main destination. On February 14, Carole and the girls checked into room #509 at Cedar Lodge in El Portal, a few miles outside Yosemite National Park on Highway 140. The three spent their next day, February 15, in the Valley. They returned to Cedar Lodge and had dinner in the coffee shop. Within minutes after returning to room #509, Carole and the two teenage girls vanished into a black hole of terror.

The three failed on February 16 to meet Carole's husband Jens Sund in San Francisco at the airport where they had planned to catch a flight together. Instead of sounding an alarm over this, Jens decided that his wife must have decided to drive from Yosemite to Grand Canyon, Arizona for their planned family rendezvous there. But after making a few calls and never being able to contact her, Jens did soon report Carole, Juli, and Silvina as missing. Maybe the four *had* driven on to visit Grand Canyon. Jens now flew to the Canyon to look for them. Once there he hit a frustratingly blank wall.

Shortly thereafter, the FBI began their investigation of the three missing persons. The Sacramento Office of the FBI assigned Special Agent Jeffrey L. Rinek as lead agent for the case. This assignment was no plum.

This is because some Bureau higher-ups suspected this case would eventually resolve itself into a simple one-vehicle auto accident in which Carole Sund had simply slid off an icy road into some recondite canyon. Someday her rented Pontiac would turn up crumpled and the case would be closed. Meanwhile FBI resources likely would be wasted. Hence Jeffrey L. Rinek.

Newspaper reporters later would characterize 47-year-old Agent Rinek as a bit of a maverick in the FBI office. He tended to be outspoken and direct (to some, overly and crudely direct), occasionally insubordinate, and he was ruled by a rare core value of wanting to be a good cop—politics be damned. So he sometimes failed to score points with other agents who were playing it safe and looking for that one sexy case that might make their career.

As Rinek considered the few details of this case he began to harbor doubts about it being an auto accident. Ultimately, the irony of what little the FBI did with Agent Rinek versus what major breakthroughs Agent Rinek did for the FBI (and for the public) would assume mythic proportions.

The Bureau was so certain initially that Rinek's belief the women had been kidnapped was wrong that his boss yanked him off the case. Rinek not only felt humiliated over this, it also shook his faith in the organization to which he had dedicated twenty years of his life. Off and on for years his wedding anniversary or his sons' birthdays had taken backseats to overtime on cases he thought vital. Sometimes he even instructed suspects to phone his wife Lori and personally apologize to her for their having kept Rinek away during such special occasions. This sort of thing failed to positively impress his bosses.

On February 19, a high school student found Carole Sund's wallet insert at the intersection of Briggsmore Avenue and Tully Road in Modesto. How it got there remained a mystery for months (one that Rinek, against the odds, would solve). The next day the Sund family offered a $250,000 reward for information leading to the three women's safe return. For two weeks, despite extensive interviews and a forensic processing of room #509, no breakthrough emerged.

At any rate, Rinek's supervisor figured if there indeed were bad guys, they would be notable scumbags. Agents also questioned 37-year-old Cary Anthony Stayner, a handyman working at the Cedar Lodge. He assisted slightly the FBI in its processing of the ill-fated room, but they failed to tie him to the missing women. Meanwhile parole agents and sheriff's deputies engaged in standoffs with, and arrests of, fugitives in the region west of Yosemite near Modesto. The FBI added eleven arrestees—a varied lot with scatterings of sex, violence, and weapons violations, drug dealing and abuse, robbery, theft, fraud, and parole violations—to the list of "people of interest" in the disappearance of Carole and Juli Sund and Silvina Pelosso. A few of these suspects were released soon for lack of any evidence, but several were held in custody.

Searchers brought in dog teams on March 11 to aid the hunt for the missing women around El Portal, but these too failed. The FBI now finally announced they feared the women were dead. A total of nine agencies poured resources into the search. Despite this manpower, nothing turned up.

A week later, a target shooter found Carole Sund's rental car well off Highway 108 in nearby Tuolumne County. Her 1999 red Pontiac Grand Prix was 100 yards north of the highway and had been driven down a brushy slope opposite Wheeler Road. The now burned rental car was invisible from both roads, implying an intent to conceal it. Based in Sacramento, FBI Special Agent-In-Charge James M. Maddock stated, "This is not an area someone would have just stumbled across."

On the contrary, the site of the torched Pontiac would eventually prove to have been exactly that.

Again, it had been burned. In the trunk the killer had stashed the naked and now burned bodies of Carole Sund and Silvina Pelosso. The ensuing hunt for clues—and for Juli Sund—would focus on the surrounding forest land for a one-mile radius in all directions. The small army of searchers included more than one hundred personnel from the FBI, the California Office of Emergency Services, the U.S. Forest Service, the California Highway Patrol, and the Tuolumne County Sheriff's Office. Highway 108 between Lyons Dam Road and Long Barn was closed on March 19 to protect the scene. Despite all of this, nothing new came to light.

A week later the FBI received in the mail an anonymous, somewhat taunting letter torn from a spiral notebook. It provided directions to where Juli Sund's body had been hidden near Don Pedro Reservoir (on the Tuolumne River). Agents soon found her dead as described. The investigation now expanded to questioning the Bureau's lowlife suspects still in custody. The Sacramento Office of the FBI's belief that one or more of these incarcerated men were culpable continued to dictate the direction of their investigation.

Four months passed. Still no one whom the FBI task force of fifteen agents plus other local law enforcement detectives had arrested and been questioning repeatedly in the San Joaquin Valley had proven to be a cinch suspect. Bogging things down, one drug dealer/methamphetamine abuser made a spurious, taunting "confession" of sorts about the kidnapping—then he waffled on it. Why, the FBI asked rhetorically (notes the *Los Angeles Times* on July 30, 1999), would some of these scumbags have stood off the police with gunfire unless they had something very serious to hide—as in the murders of the Sunds and Pelosso? *The Fresno Bee* noted in late April that FBI Special Agent-in-Charge James M. Maddock had publicly stated the key players in the sightseer slayings had been arrested and were in jail on unrelated charges. The implication here was that the public was therefore safe from a repeat of the Sund-Pelosso crime by its perpetrator(s). Anyone's assumption of safety from this, however, would prove premature.

Five months after the Sunds and Pelosso were murdered, on July 21, 1999, Jennifer "Joie" Ruth Armstrong, a natural history teacher employed by the Yosemite Institute (a non-profit environmental educational institution mostly for school kids), was planning to drive to the San Francisco Bay Area from her semi-isolated residence, the "Green House," in Foresta. The 26 year-old intended to visit friends from Chico State who worked at the Headlands Institute at Golden Gate. She also wanted to visit her grandmother. Then she would go backpacking with six female friends near Lake Tahoe. Before she was to leave, she also needed to deliver some files at about 6:30 p.m. to Sonny Montague, the wife of Joie's supervisor, Pete Devine. Joie in fact had called Sonny just before 6:30 and told her she was coming over. Montague later noted to investigators that Joie's plan was to make the five-minute walk across the wooded margin of the creek to their house to deliver the files.

Joie Armstrong failed to show up at the home of her boss. She also never made it to her friends' place near San Francisco. Nor did she arrive at her grandmother's house. Nor did she show up anywhere else.

When Joie was an hour late in delivering the files, Montague walked over to Joie's house. She found Joie's car there. She also found the front door of the house open and the stereo playing. But despite a quick search, she did not find Joie Armstrong. Puzzled and worried, she returned home. She wondered if there was something she should do about this.

Very early on July 22, at 3 a.m., Park Dispatch received a missing person report from the Sausalito Police Department—made by Joie's San Francisco friends. The area of Foresta, west and north of the Yosemite Valley, was originally platted out as a Mariposa County Township in the 1920s. Since then the National Park Service has strived to acquire land in Foresta and to obtain titles to as many as possible pre-existing lots and improvements. By now the Park's several legislative and criminal jurisdictional boundary adjustments have absorbed about eighty-five privately owned lots there, thus making them subject to Exclusive Jurisdiction of the United States. Only about twenty-five private in-holdings remain. But even these are subject to the Park's Exclusive Jurisdiction such that the Park's rangers and special investigators perform all investigations and coroner functions for fatal events in Foresta for the Mariposa County Sheriff's Office. Now, with Joie Armstrong reported missing in Foresta, the Park was responsible for investigating why.

NPS Patrol Ranger Mark D. Harvey started his search at Armstrong's residence. He too found the truck belonging to the pretty five-foot, five-inch, freckled, strawberry blonde parked there and, oddly, only half-packed for her trip. More ominous, Mark also noted the house's front and rear doors standing wide open.

Harvey looked around. He found no one. He did find a pair of sunglasses, folded and possibly bent, lying on the right corner of the top step. The ranger quickly realized that this was a crime scene. So he backed off, got on his radio, and requested NPS Investigator Dan Horner and a SAR team.

Rangers cordoned off the house and began their investigation. Horner examined the scene. Harvey called in Ranger Mark Fincher, a tracking expert. Horner also notified the FBI of a potential kidnapping. The FBI then responded that Agent Mardee J. Robinson would arrive from Fresno.

Fortunately, Ranger Fincher found soil and weather conditions to be textbook perfect for good tracks to form and also to remain. He first had to mentally sift out the footprints and tire tracks left by Ranger Harvey. Employing the five elements of visual perception—edge, shape, value, color and texture—the tracker also had to untangle those made by several neighbors. By eliminating these other prints, Fincher was now able to visualize the footprints of two other people. The first set was of Joie Armstrong. The next prints were bigger and revealed that their maker had stood for a long time where he had parked his vehicle.

These tracks told a story, one of an intense struggle. Ominously, the big prints leading away from the Green House were "too close" to Joie's prints. They strongly suggested that someone was forcibly holding and leading her as they both moved toward a parked vehicle. The Park tracker also found nine-inch-wide tire tracks made by two types of tires, one set in front and the other in the rear of the vehicle used by the person who had made the second, larger set of footprints.

Fincher soon walked FBI Agent Robinson through the story these tracks told. This ranger's uncommon skill at tracking would prove pivotal both in understanding what had been done to Joie Armstrong and in pinpointing who had been responsible for having done it.

By early afternoon, at about 1:20 p.m., after only five minutes of searching, an NPS team led by Tom Woods found Joie several hundred feet east of her house. Her body had been semi-concealed in a creek. Someone had pushed it under a grassy bank in the two- to three-foot-deep stream. The perpetrator, searchers quickly saw to their horror, had also decapitated Armstrong. FBI Special Agent

Chris Hopkins would later note the beheading had been "a fairly clean and forceful cut, probably from a relatively sharp instrument."

Even after the Park and the FBI expanded their hunt, Joie Armstrong's head was still missing. Two search dogs, Tasman and Euro, handled by Rangers Rich Baerwald and Maura Longden, now aided in the search.

Ranger Harvey set up a command post and handled logistics (later, Assistant Chief Ranger Don Coelho would be assigned the Incident Commander position, with Jeff Sullivan as NPS supervisory agent for this case #99-1900). Harvey interviewed Anne Matteson, one of Joie's friends who also lived in Foresta. She told him that Joie had recently said she was very afraid of a man who worked at the Ahwahnee Hotel whom she had also known at Chico State but who, she thought, was currently laying low to evade prosecution for computer fraud.

Sadly, investigators also learned during an interview with Joie's father Frank Armstrong that he had recently told Joie that he was worried about her safety due to the unsolved Sund-Pelosso murders, but Joie had responded to him, "The FBI said that the murderers are in jail."

A vital lead in the Armstrong case came the same day from NPS Helitack Foreman Jeff Power, a long-time local resident of the Park. Power told Horner that while driving home from the Crane Flat Helibase on the night of July 21 at about 7:30 p.m. he had seen a distinctively unfamiliar vehicle—a white-over-light-blue International Scout—parked at the Big Oak Flat Road junction with Foresta Road. Power added that he again had seen the same vehicle the next morning parked in front of the El Portal Yosemite Institute Office (where Joie Armstrong worked). He added that a man was working on one of the tires when Power first saw it.

The Park now broadcast a BOLO (Be On the Look Out) for that vehicle.

NPS employee Don Ramsey next told investigators he had stopped and picked up a hitchhiker on Highway 140 outside the Park on that same night, just before 10 p.m. He had driven the man to Cedar Lodge where he lived. During the ride, the man had told Ramsey that his vehicle, an International Scout, had broken down. The hitchhiker had been in the Park, he added, because he wanted to get some "decent food."

Investigators also interviewed Darlene Schuetz, bartender at the Mountain Room Bar in the Valley. She immediately said, "You probably want to know about the 'creepy guy' I saw last night." Schuetz, it would turn out, had also spotted this same hitchhiker—but had done so before Ramsey had happened along—on the side of the road beside an International Scout. The man had waved her down. She stopped for him and asked, "What's up?"

The hitchhiker said his wheel studs were bad and he needed a ride to Cedar Lodge. Schuetz added that as he was asking her for a ride he kept smiling—and that his smile "seemed evil." He seemed so sinister to her that she denied him a ride and drove on alone.

The next day at 4:30 in the afternoon, Park Dispatch sent Rangers Bonnie

Schwartz and Ruth Middlecamp, in company with Mariposa Sheriff's Office Detective Cathi Sarno, to investigate a sighting of a 1979 white-over-blue International Scout outside Yosemite and parked on Highway 140. The three found the Scout near "25-mph Beach" as reported. They walked down to the river to find its owner.

There they found 37-year-old Cary Anthony Stayner, six feet and one inch tall and weighing 200 pounds, lying nude and hairy in the sand. While not wearing clothes, he did possess marijuana. Nearby was a green Jansport pack. The trio of female officers asked Stayner for permission to search it. They also advised him he was within his rights to refuse them permission.

Stayner, the maintenance man for the Cedar Lodge in El Portal—the place where the Yosemite Institute (for whom Joie Armstrong worked) held its conferences—refused to allow the search. The trio next asked for permission to look through his Scout. He agreed to that, but remained adamant about his pack. At least one of the women present now wondered if it contained Joie Armstrong's head.

Detective Sarno informed Stayner they would secure his pack anyway and arrange for a search warrant to look inside it later. Next they searched his vehicle but found nothing. Earlier, during the trio's initial approach, and unbeknownst to them, Stayner had surreptitiously removed from his Jansport his pistol, knife, and gloves. He had stashed the gloves under a log and then had secreted the two weapons under a nearby rock underwater at the river's edge.

When the rangers and Detective Sarno confiscated the Jansport most of the evidence once in it was now missing. But not all of it. The pack still contained a paperback copy of John Saul's horror novel *Black Lightning* allegedly about a crazed serial killer, a bottle of Corona beer, a camera, a harmonica, and a bag of sunflower seeds. Unexpectedly, the latter would provide clinching evidence.

Stayner now agreed to the search of his pack. Despite this belated permission, the officers now declined to look inside because his previous refusal might be used in court to disallow the contents as possible evidence. Instead they wanted a valid search warrant before looking in that thing. Stayner handed over his Jansport. Again, it would turn out that despite Stayner's quick purge, it still contained evidence.

Later that Thursday (July 22), as NPS Special Agent Jeff Sullivan and FBI Special Agent Jeff Kearl questioned Stayner about his whereabouts the day before, rangers were photographing the tires of his Scout. He denied having been in Foresta that day. Instead, he said, he had only been in the Valley and had never driven up Highway 120, the only main road into Foresta. He had been swimming in the Park, Stayner said, then had driven back to his room at Cedar Lodge. There he had showered, changed, and next drove himself back into the Valley to dine. Ranger Schwartz and others immediately thought this story strange because Highway 140 was under construction and subject to long delays during the day. Why would anyone elect to endure driving it four times, twice in each direction (even if it *was* open), just for a better than average meal?

Earlier that day, at about 5:30 p.m. and more than four hours after searchers had found Joie Armstrong's body, one of the two search dogs, Tasman, prowled the creek flowing past the murdered woman's isolated Green House. Alerted by a blood trail, Tasman abruptly dropped down the steep embankment to the creek about forty feet from where her body had been found. "It seemed," reported Tasman's handler Rich Baerwald, "that she was interested in a deep pool of water adjacent to the creek."

From twenty feet away Baerwald saw nothing there. Even so, the dog continued to sniff at the pool and paw at the water. She pawed so persistently that she dislodged something from under the embankment and freed it to drift farther out in the calm pool. Curious as to what Tasman was so excited about, Baerwald approached, stood next to Tasman, and stared down.

From within the murky water he glimpsed "a flash of color." He saw the thing was a human head. The dog handler now not only had to control his dog but also his gut. Baerwald now alerted the FBI agents on scene.

As suspicious as all this was, at this point the law officers still did not believe they had enough solid evidence to arrest Stayner. His marijuana possession might have been good for a detainment, but then again maybe not. Very soon, however, everyone involved would regret not arresting Stayner at their first opportunity. It remained a moot point. They had let Stayner go.

And go is exactly what he did.

Friday morning, July 23, Ranger-Tracker Mark Fincher examined the Polaroid prints of the tires of Stayner's Scout that had been photographed the evening prior. The vehicle had two different types of tires mounted on it front and rear. Fincher compared these photos to the tire tracks he had observed and sketched at the victim's residence and also near her body. They were a match.

Despite Fincher's ten years of tracking experience, he next showed this evidence to Dave Givens, a certified "man-tracker" on the Mariposa County Search and Rescue Team. Givens studied it and agreed the tire photos and tire tracks were a perfect match.

The match clinched this investigation.

Now, on the morning of July 23, Sullivan and Kearl tried to relocate and detain Stayner. Their attempts failed.

Cary Stayner was gone. He had been renting employee room #4 above the Cedar Lodge Restaurant for two years. It now sat abandoned. Moreover, Stayner had failed to show up this morning for his handyman job—one he considered vital—without reason for the first time ever. His International Scout too was gone. Stayner had worked this job for the past two years, the investigators were now told. He had been laid off for a couple of months during early 1999 due to lack of business but on March 20, several weeks after Carole and Juli Sund and Silvina Pelosso had vanished, the Lodge had rehired him. His not showing up for work today, after having been interviewed the previous evening by a small platoon of investigators, sent up a red flag. When his coworkers also reported he had just sold his $700 TV for $300 and also said he had given away his VCR with it last night in a "panic," that red flag waved.

People who knew Stayner seemed divided into two camps. Most people thought highly of him. Ironically, when older ladies felt unsafe walking from the dining room back to their vehicles at night, they asked the polite young—but big—Cary Stayner to accompany them. In contrast, the young women who knew him feared him and/or felt repulsed by him. This seemed unanimous for those at Cedar Lodge. One referred to him as "a pervert" and "an asshole, arrogant and selfish." She said of women and Stayner, "Once they get to know him, they get away."

As the investigation into Cary Anthony Stayner progressed, notes the *San Francisco Chronicle* on July 30, 1999, other women interviewed from Stayner's home town revealed that the fugitive had been surreptitiously sexually molesting and exposing himself nude to girls as young as age 14 when he was 16 years old.

Later on July 23, Jana Bacerre, a friend of Cary Stayner, told investigating FBI and NPS agents that he had visited her at one o'clock that same morning at her home near Mariposa. She said this was an unusual thing for him. He was driving his Scout and had now complained to her that it was not running right and that he might need a tow truck. Bacerre, the mother of two pretty daughters aged 8 and 11, got the impression that Stayner was hinting that he wanted to come inside her house. On this night she happened to have a boyfriend present. So Stayner left within five minutes, not mentioning where he might be going. She watched him get into his car, start it, then drive away. His Scout started up instantly, she added, and seemed to have no mechanical problem.

Stayner's whereabouts remained a mystery for only a day. A woman at Laguna Del Sol Nudist Park in Wilton, about twenty miles southeast of Sacramento, recognized him from his "wanted" picture televised on a news report. She called in her sighting on July 24. The FBI responded instantly by sending to Laguna Del Sol Special Agent Jeffrey L. Rinek, assisted by agent John Boles in a second car.

Rinek drove to the nudist camp and rendezvoused with his coworker and two Sacramento County Sheriff's deputies. At 9 a.m., they spotted Stayner wearing shorts and a T-shirt as he sat eating breakfast in the restaurant. Rinek had not been completely briefed on Stayner and now only knew that he was an important witness in the sensational case of murdered Joie Armstrong. Bizarrely, the veteran agent—as did nearly every other long-term Central Valley resident—knew far more about Stayner's famous younger brother (described below) who had been kidnapped and held as a sex slave. And, because Rinek's specialty was in rescuing children, he hoped to create the opportunity to talk to Cary Stayner about his younger brother's experience.

As the two agents entered the nudist colony's restaurant, Stayner stood up and raised his hands in surrender. Rinek, who was there to interview Stayner, not arrest him, inwardly blinked in surprise but projected a casual façade. "They want us to interview you," he explained. He next told Stayner they were seizing his vehicle as evidence, pending a search warrant.

As Boles handcuffed Stayner, Rinek could hear the unmistakable sound of opportunity knocking. The game had begun. He immediately began his "good cop" routine of softening Stayner.

"Hey, you ever see that movie *Billy Jack*?" Rinek now asked Stayner. "You look just like him."

Stayner mumbled that he had never seen the movie.

"No kidding," Rinek said. "I don't know why we're here. They want us to interview you. Would you be willing to be interviewed here or back at the office?"

"Back at the office."

Stayner slid onto the seat in Rinek's government Ford. It was glaringly clear to the agent that Stayner was much more than a mere witness. For a moment the two heavyweights (Rinek too was built like a wrestler) sat together in silence. Rinek knew he had to ensure that whatever transpired next remained legally bulletproof.

"I'm going to read you your rights now ('pursuant to Miranda')."

Stayner waived his rights verbally then signed them away in writing. Next he talked. As Boles followed the two in another vehicle for the anticipated forty-minute drive, Rinek and Stayner continued talking. Delays due to road construction would soon stretch their ride to an hour and a half.

"Tell me about your brother," Rinek coaxed.

Eerily, twenty-seven years earlier, in 1972, Cary Stayner's 7-year-old brother Steven had been kidnapped off a Merced street while walking home from Charles Wright Elementary School by Kenneth Parnell, a convicted child molester who posed as a church minister. The little boy had been held prisoner and abused for more than seven nightmarish *years* of sexual slavery. Parnell had held the boy captive in several small communities (the first was Catheys Valley forty miles away from Merced). In each place Steven's captor, with the help of accomplice Ervin Edward Murphy, had passed him off during the day as his son, Dennis. Then, at night, he had used him for sex. Interestingly, one of these places of captivity was a Curry Company employee dorm in Yosemite Valley.

In 1980, Steven's captor kidnapped yet another boy, a 5 year-old named Timmy White. Now after a horrific seven years of abuse and torture, Steven Stayner decided to rescue Timmy White before he was subjected to the same fate.

Steven took Timmy and escaped. He then hitchhiked his way from Manchester in Mendocino County to Ukiah, California. Young Stayner had been held captive and brainwashed for so long that he could no longer remember his own last name. When asked by the police who he was, he answered, "I know my first name is Steven."

The surprised police searched for the boy's identity. They found it and finally reunited Steven in Modesto with his family, including Cary, who was four years older. Instantly Cary, who had missed Steven very much, took a permanent and somewhat frustrating backseat to that of his traumatized little brother. Steven's abduction and ordeal was dramatized in a 1991 book by Mike Echols and earlier yet as a May 22, 1989, television miniseries titled *I Know My First Name is Steven*. Sadly, on September 16, 1989, when Steven Stayner was only 24 years old, a hit-and-run drunk driver killed him while he was riding his motorcycle. Meanwhile (and perhaps shockingly), Kenneth Parnell, the abuser who had kidnapped Steven, was again released from prison. (In January of 2003, police arrested Parnell yet again at his Berkeley home after he tried to purchase a young boy.)

Now during the drive to the Sacramento FBI office Stayner talked about Steven. He expressed anger that his brother's kidnapper had been let off so easily, with a mere seven-year sentence. He then expressed more anger at his brother's death. Rinek saw tears in his passenger's eyes and he actually felt sorry for him. Even so, he began to pry open Cary Stayner's hideous heart.

Surprisingly, the handcuffed man—who allegedly also had been sexually abused at age 11 by a distant relative—soon admitted to murdering Joie Armstrong. As you will see below, Stayner supplied details known only to law enforcement, thus instantly supporting his confession. On a roll, Stayner also admitted to murdering Carole and Juli Sund and Silvina Pelosso. He added yet more specific details about these murders that again corroborated him as the killer. Just one of these details was his description of the contents of that letter torn from a spiral notebook and tauntingly mailed to the Modesto Office of the FBI. With some pleasure, Stayner even explained how and where he got another person's saliva to seal the envelope and thus avoid DNA identification.

Jeffrey Rinek's and John Boles' astonishing FBI interview with Cary Stayner on that July 24th in Sacramento took place over pizza and sodas. It lasted for hours and contained 214 pages of transcription, some of which went like this (grammatical errors included):

> Rinek: "Do you realize that I don't think you're a bad person and even after all that stuff you told me, I don't feel any differently about you?"
>
> Stayner: "Thank you."
>
> Rinek: "You know what is really gonna happen when we're done? You're gonna feel a lot of relief."
>
> Stayner: "I already do feel something. I—I feel a chest pain right now."
>
> Rinek: "You're gonna feel good. Not good, but you're gonna feel peaceful, probably a feeling you haven't had in a long time."
>
> Stayner: "It means I can die with a clear conscience now, whenever that day comes."
>
> Rinek: "Well, you know you have a choice in life, anyone can give

up and wanna die, or end it, or do all that stuff."

Stayner: "I'm not into suicide, believe me."

Rinek: "No, I'm not saying you are, but what I'm saying is, when this is over, what we're doing here today is the beginning of the rest of your life, and you have a choice in the rest of your life, you can use your experience to prevent this from happening."

Stayner: "I know they're gonna give me the death penalty. Even if I confess, they're gonna give me death."

Rinek: "I don't know. I'm not a prosecutor. I think…"

Stayner: "You know it. At least that's ten, fifteen years down the road the way things work."

Rinek: "I'll be there for you as long as it goes, as far as it goes, because I believe in you. I'd like you to stop for a moment, Cary, and think about the fact that you're giving life; you're giving life back, and you appear to me to be a person that cares about that. You're gonna restore life that's been taken."

Stayner: "Well it's so weird 'cause I love life so much, I can breathe, I can wake up and see the sun, I like my friends. There's just don't—I—I can't tell you why this is happening."

Rinek: "Well…"

Stayner: "I don't know myself, but I know one minute I'm thinking great thoughts and world peace and all of this, and the next minute it's like I could kill every person on the face of the earth. It's…"

Rinek: "Do you think you're the only person in the world that's like that?"

Stayner: "No, but—oh, God, it just mentally tortures you, constantly back and forth, it's like a tennis match. Hope inside and then it's over the bad side."

Rinek: "But this is over now, you have taken control, you have taken control today. Today is the beginning of the rest of your life…"

Stayner now tells Rinek that he wants the $50,000 reward for discovering the Sunds and Pelosso ($250,000 if found alive) as a condition of his confession.

Rinek: "Okay, I, you know, the reward that's out for the Sund/Pelosso case is a reward that's offered by the Sund/Pelosso family."

Stayner: "Right. You have to talk to them, I guess…"

Rinek: "The conditions under which that award is granted is going to depend on, you know, them. Now, I can tell you now sitting here that you stated one condition, if you're going to enter other conditions into it, and then we have to keep going back to these people and asking them more—for more authority—they're gonna get very

> angry at me and John, and they're gonna get angry at you."
>
> Stayner: "Well, that's the deal on the table right now then."
>
> Rinek: "Let's get all the conditions out right now so we can deal with what we can deal with, and not deal with what we can't deal with, and then you have to make your decision…"

Stayner now also reminds Rinek that, as part of his deal he wants "a good-sized stack of child pornography, preferably with a video." (Providing Stayner with these items of course would have been illegal.) After several minutes of "bonding" and of jockeying over Stayner's confession deal, Rinek convinces Stayner to talk about Joie Armstrong.

> Stayner: "Aah, I was driving up to Foresta and went down to a bridge that was washed out and closed down, and I went down the river in the creek and I was walking around just checking it out 'cause I'd seen Big Foot in the area, several years ago, back in the early eighties. And since then there's a barn that they'd rebuilt."
>
> Rinek: "Uh-huh."
>
> Stayner: "I saw Big Foot in the barn, and there was this house on the edge of the, aah, meadow, I guess that's where she lived."
>
> Rinek: "What—did the house look like?"
>
> Stayner: "It's a little box-style house. Been there for probably a hundred years or so or close to it."
>
> Rinek: "Uh-huh."
>
> Stayner: "There was a little pickup truck out in front of the house with the, aah, camper shell lid open in the back. And she was loading things into it."
>
> Rinek: "Uh-huh."
>
> Stayner: "And I just noticed her, there she is, you know, fairly attractive girl."
>
> Rinek: "Uh-huh."
>
> Stayner: "And I—I didn't go down there with any intent [of] doing anything."
>
> Rinek: "Uh-huh."
>
> Stayner: "She was going in and out of the house, loading things into her vehicle, and I was just over there throwing rocks in the creek and just happened to notice her walk out again and again. It seemed like she was alone."
>
> Rinek: "Uh-huh."
>
> Stayner: "I had a small green backpack [the Jansport]. And in the backpack I, aah, had a .22 revolver."
>
> Rinek: "Is that the one you told me about in the car?"

Stayner: (Nods yes) "and a large knife."
Rinek: "Uhm."
Stayner: "And duct tape."
Rinek: "Okay."
Stayner: "I went by the house once and went down to the barn, just walking around it. I walked back by the house and she was out in front, and we started talking."
Rinek: "What did she tell you? Did she tell you her name?"
Stayner: "No. Just started talking about, uhm, talk—actually talked about Big Foot that I had seen there."
Rinek: "Uh-huh."
Stayner: "Some years ago. And I asked her if she'd ever seen or heard anything, and she said no, but maybe my roommates had. I said, oh, is any of them around right now? Then go ask them, she said well, they're not here. And I started talking about the little house, how I told her I, you know, I'd come here for so many years and I'd really never seen anybody living in the house, and I walked up to the front of it, and just—just kinda glancing at it, commenting on how well it was fixed up and they'd done some rock work out in front."
Rinek: "Uh-huh."
Stayner: "And she stepped up on the porch and was talking to me, and then she turned around, that's when I pulled out the gun and put it to her head. She turned around and freaked out. I told her to go inside. I took her into the back corner of the—the house, two bedrooms, where I duct taped her. Okay."
Rinek: "Uh-huh. You're doing fine. This is hard. You're being good, brave. Go ahead."
Stayner: "She resisted quite a bit."
Rinek: "Uh-huh."
Stayner: "I didn't hit her or anything, I just used threats and a gun to subdue her. As I was trying to duct tape her hands behind her back she kept fighting me. I finally got her duct taped and I gagged her with the duct tape."
Rinek: "Uh-huh."
Stayner: "Before that, though, I'd—I'd done it saying that I just needed money."
Rinek: "Okay."
Stayner: "Yeah, she was okay, I wasn't going to hurt her. I just needed her to cooperate."
Rinek: "Okay."
Stayner: "After I duct taped her I led her out of the house. I held her by the arm and I went by her truck. I took the keys out of her

truck that were in the back of the hatch and the camper shell and closed the door. My truck was parked down by the bridge, I took her down to my truck and put her in the back seat, and she was fighting all the way."

Rinek: "Could she talk? Was she expressing herself?"

Stayner: "She couldn't talk. She was making noise but she didn't talk. I proceeded to turn around and drive down 'cause I was gonna drive up through the residential area and back side of the hill around where there's a little more privacy. I didn't duct tape her feet. She started kicking and fighting. She was very strong, very wired girl. And as I was driving she started going crazy, just jumping all over the place in the back of the truck, and I couldn't really control her. And she fell out through the window onto the—on the road right in front of the barn."

Rinek: "Uh-huh. So she fell—fell out of the camper?"

Stayner: "No, out of my truck."

Rinek: "Oh, okay. Out the passenger window."

Stayner: "Out the passenger window."

Rinek: "Did she force herself out the window?"

Stayner: "She forced herself out."

Rinek: "Oh, I see. She was trying to get away from you."

Stayner: "She did a very good job of it. She was out very quickly. Surprised me. I slammed my truck into park and jumped out and she'd got up off the ground and started running. This was on the dirt road we were on. She started running for the asphalt road. I caught her in time before she got there, and there was quite a few cabins that, you know, could easily if someone was looking out a window or sitting on a deck they could have seen what was going on. I kinda freaked out. And aah, I had my knife in my back pocket, I tried to subdue her but she was fighting very hard, even being tied up."

Rinek: "Uh-huh."

Stayner: "Surprised me. She was tough. And it was—the area that we were in was in plain view, so I tried to drag her off into the side of the hill."

Rinek: "Uh-huh."

Stayner: "She kept fighting me."

Rinek: "What did you do next?"

Stayner: "Took the knife from my back pocket and I slit her throat. And she didn't die right away."

Rinek: "How long did it take her to die?"

Stayner: "It took her—drug her another ten, fifteen feet to an area where I thought she was more [less?] visible, I finished the job."

Rinek: "So you cut her again after the first cut? How many more times did you cut her after the first cut?"

Stayner: "Well, after I cut her she was obviously dead."

Rinek: "Uh-huh."

Stayner: "I drug her down to the little canal by some bushes, I left her there, and I went up to my truck 'cause it was parked in the middle of the road with the engine running. I parked my truck in a parking area next to an asphalt road."

Rinek: "Uh-huh."

Stayner: "And I went back to the little canal."

Rinek: "You okay? You alright? Go ahead."

Stayner: "And I cut her head off."

About ten minutes after focusing on this and other details of July 21st, Rinek asks Stayner again about what he did with Joie Armstrong's body and why he cut off her head. Stayner explains that he was primarily curious about how much arterial spurt might result but was disappointed at the lack thereof. After this, for several minutes more, Rinek again covers other questioning.

Rinek: "You knew it was wrong when you were doing it?"

Stayner: "Most definitely."

For several minutes again Rinek covers other questioning.

Rinek: "Okay. Just like you did the first time [referring to Stayner's testimony on Joie Armstrong], why don't you just walk us through what happened [with the Sunds and Pelosso] and we'll go back and do it again. Go ahead."

Stayner: "It was the day after Valentine's. I'd been gone most of the day off the property. I was at a girlfriend's house, and, aah, I guess it's this girlfriend [Jana Bacerre] and her two daughters were my original intended victims."

Rinek: "I'm sorry, say that again. I—I misunderstood you."

Stayner: "The girl I was seeing and her daughters were my original intended victims. But I couldn't do it [because a man was present at Bacerre's house]. I got back to the motel late. I went to soak in the hot tub to try and calm down. And the hot tub was dirty. I didn't work—I wasn't working at the time. Whoever was taking care of it didn't take care of it so I was a little annoyed. So I went to the front office and got the maintenance man's keys and I went and serviced the pool and spa but it's too late for me to sit in it so I took a walk around the property. And it was the night before, I was in the pool and there was a four or five girls that were in there, all very young. They were uhm, parked down in the certain building, I think they were in room 177 but there was a man in there with them. Otherwise they would have been my victims. As I walked, there was a red car in the 500 Building all by itself. The window was open, the curtain was open, and I can see inside that there was two young women and the mother and no man. I went back to my room and got my backpack, and (inaudible), first I stopped off at the office and faked like I turned the keys back in, I didn't. Turned out I didn't need them anyway."

Rinek: "Why ?"

Stayner: "They let me in the room. I knocked on the door, said I was maintenance, had a leak in the room upstairs. They let me in. I went to the bathroom and checked out the fan where I told them the problem would be. When I came out of the bathroom, I pulled my gun out, and I told them I wanted the money and the keys to the car. The two girls were on the bed closest to the front door. The girls turned around, the mother got up to get the money out of her purse, and I told her to get back on the bed, I'd get it. So they all got on the beds and put their hands behind their backs, I tied them all up. I led the two girls into the bathroom, set them both down on the bathroom floor, and I strangled the mother, appeared dead, with a piece of rope. I put her in the trunk of the car.

"I went back into the room and took both girls out of the bathroom back into the main room, and I stripped their clothes off of them—cut their clothes off of them. And the Pelosso girl couldn't speak very good English, was crying a lot and Juli was calm. I [raped] Juli. And the Pelosso girl…said she was on her monthly cycle so it's a turn off. I took her into the bathroom, put her in the bathtub and I strangled her.

"Went back into the main room and continued with Juli, sexually assaulting her….Seeing afterwards that she wanted to go into the bathroom, I couldn't take her into the bathroom with her—her friend dead in the tub, so I took her next door into room 510. I made her shave herself….While she was doing that, I went and removed the body from the shower, put it in the trunk. [Elipses denote simple "Uh-huh" prompts from Rinek.]

"It was getting pretty late, probably five or so in the morning. I told Juli we had someplace to go and I wouldn't harm her. So I put her in the car, her hands were duct-taped in front of her. I wrapped a pink blanket around her and just drove….I'd driven to Mariposa and I hit Highway 49. I drove and I drove. I didn't know what I was gonna do or how I was gonna do it or anything. I just kept driving and uh, see-

> ing I was in Tuolumne County…and I saw I was at Vista Point, with the parking lot off the main road so I pulled in there [at dawn]….I took Juli out of the car and I carried her in the pathway. I laid out the blanket and she performed oral sex on me.
>
> "I guess I knew what I was gonna do because I had the knife with me. And I turned around, I believe I told her the gun was never loaded because it wasn't at the time, and I slit her throat. I covered her body with some brush. I picked up the towel and the blanket and I left and I threw the blanket on top of the hill. And I left in the car. Before I left, you know, I opened up the trunk of the car and I removed all the clothes off the bodies and the duct tape, and I put it in the bag, in the pillowcase.
>
> "I drove towards Sonora and I went through Sonora. At one time, I was surrounded by CHP officers at an intersection in Sonora. I drove to New Melones Lake and I was gonna drive the car off into the lake, but there was someone down there fishing. So I got out and threw the pillowcase with all that debris with sheets, clothes and duct tape into a dumpster. And I drove back to Sonora. I hit Highway 108, looking for a place to ditch the car, couldn't find anything under the snow. All the dirt roads off the side were impassible for that little car. So I head back down till I got to…a gated community off the side of the road and I noticed there was a dirt road across the road from them. I drove down the road and this, there wasn't a whole lot of snow so I was able to get there, and there was a depression in the road. I went down into a wooded area, I backed the car up as far as I could get.
>
> "I left the car there and I aah, walked to Sierra Village and I just missed the bus. I was gonna take the bus into Sonora. Bought a book and I called a cab. The cab driver took me to Yosemite Valley. There I caught the bus back down to Cedar Lodge. Two days later, then drove my Scout back up there, [got] some gasoline, and I torched the vehicle. And I took the wallet and drove to Modesto and threw it in the intersection. Then several weeks later, a month or so, I'm not sure how long it was, I wrote a letter [to the FBI office in Merced]."
>
> Rinek: "What did the letter say?"
>
> Stayner: "We had fun with this one. I drew a map to where Juli's body was at."

Again, this interview went for 214 pages. It covered ground, recovered the same ground, and clarified by coaxing and testing Stayner with false information which he then had to counter with accurate information. Rinek was the father confessor. Stayner the sinner. Together they made the previous FBI investigation of the Sund-Pelosso case look botched.

Special Agent-in-Charge James M. Maddock of the Sacramento FBI Division and his assistant who had prematurely assured the public that the Sund-Pelosso killer(s)—the FBI had code-named this case "Tournap"—were behind bars were reassigned (a.k.a. "dumped" according to newspaper accounts) in January 2001.

The confession that Agent Rinek extracted from Stayner led to his being charged with first degree murder within the territorial jurisdiction of the United States, a capital offense. Stayner pleaded guilty, which in federal first degree murder cases allows the defendant to plea bargain a life sentence and avoid the death penalty.

As Rinek's interview progressed with Stayner, it became clear he had "researched" several women whom he had planned as potential victims. Joie Armstrong was just one of these. Stayner had also targeted Jana Bacerre and her two daughters for rape and murder, but it was too risky on the night of February 11, 1999, because of the presence of a male caretaker for the property on which the three lived, so Stayner impulsively replaced them with the unprotected Sunds and Silvina Pelosso.

Although Stayner claimed the Sunds and Silvina Pelosso were his first victims, they may not have been at all. In May of 1997, a woman named Vanessa Smith vanished off a street corner forever only a few blocks from where Cary Stayner lived with his parents in Winton. (Indeed, it was only his parents' insistence at this time that he, now nearing his mid-thirties, needed to go out into the world and try to make it on his own when Cary began to become independent.) No evidence surfaced to firmly link Stayner to Smith's disappearance—or to any of the other unsolved but suspected killings of young women by him.

The weird case of Cary Stayner (who admitted to one 17-year-old girl whom he was hitting on, "I've only woke up with a woman about twelve times in my life") gets even weirder. A couple of months after he murdered the Sunds and Silvina Pelosso (but before Rinek arrested him) he was chatting with Elvia Delatorre, the new desk clerk at Cedar Lodge. She recalls him casually mentioning how he did not believe in God. He also told her that the night before his uncle Jesse "Jerry" Stayner was murdered on December 26, 1990, Stayner had a dream (on Christmas) in which his uncle was murdered by his own gun. Suspiciously, while Jerry Stayner was being shot in the chest that day and then in the back of the head execution-style—with his own shotgun—Cary was actually living with Jerry as his roommate. But Cary told police that he was having lunch with his boss at the time of the shooting. The shooter then stole his victim's truck. This killer was never found. Police, in fact, reopened the case once Cary Stayner confessed to having murdered the four women. So far, however, nothing has emerged.

Four years before Stayner's killing spree, in 1995, notes the *San Francisco Chronicle* on July 30, 1999, he worked for the Merced Glass and Mirror Company. One day a friend there, Mike Marchese, found Stayner outside the office pounding his hand against a piece of plywood. "Stayner," Marchese related, "said he felt like getting in his truck, driving it into the office and killing the boss and everyone else in there, and torching the place." Marchese told their boss about this. The boss then drove Stayner to a Merced psychiatric center. Soon thereafter Stayner returned, picked up his final paycheck, then left never to be seen by those people again.

He found his next job at Cedar Lodge.

Some psychologists have linked Cary Stayner's sexual murder proclivities to his obsessive-compulsive (hair-pulling) tendencies, to his brother's bizarre kidnapping, and to he himself having been sexually molested when he was 11 years old. Certainly both latter events must have been traumatic. Flying in the face of this interpretation, Stayner, the oldest of five siblings all raised as strict Mormons, admitted to TV reporter Ted Rowlands his first having contemplated the prospect of killing women long before all of this, when he was 7 years old. At this age, while sitting in the car and peering through a grocery store window at the clerks inside it as they rang up purchases, he visualized himself murdering them. He continued to imagine repeated secret fantasies of trapping women and killing them for the next thirty years. Rowlands, shocked, noted that Stayner seemed proud of himself for having waited so long before actually murdering women.

Feeling "remorse" for the murders he committed was for Cary Stayner a meaningless concept. Remorse was not an emotion he felt in connection with his victims. In September of 1999, while awaiting trial, Cary Stayner phoned a talk show—the "Leeza Show"—to ask the producers to interview him in the Fresno County Jail and then air his interview. He told the television producer he did not want to die. The cast and producers of the show were immensely impressed with Stayner's patently "self-serving" attitude.

"What surprised us," noted Leeza Gibbons, "was how cavalier he was about these gruesome murders. He says he has a basic desire to live, which was just sickening to all of us."

No surprise, Cary Stayner also wanted a book and a "movie of the week" done on his life and on his murders, just as had been written and filmed on his younger brother's short life—but his should be done better. He said he would give his proceeds to the families of his victims as restitution for his damage to them.

Wasn't Stayner worried, one might wonder, about his self-promoting publicity campaign implicating himself adversely prior to his trial? "Stayner has confessed," Leeza Gibbons said, "and confessed again, and obviously has an ego as big as Yosemite."

In November of 2000, Stayner pled guilty to the murder of Joie Armstrong. A federal court found him guilty but due to his voluntary plea, he was sentenced to life in prison without parole. Had he pled not guilty it is extremely likely that the overall evidence would have convicted him for a death sentence.

A damning amount of forensic evidence had been collected. Much of this we have already mentioned, but it also included the knife Stayner used to decapitate Joie and his sunglasses on the steps of the Green House in Foresta. Indeed, so much evidence was collected that some of it was not even used. For example, remember that green Jansport pack containing his abduction kit? Inside it were some innocuous items such as an empty Corona beer bottle, a harmonica, suntan oil, a camera, and a small, open bag of sunflower seeds. The bag of sunflower seeds had its corner torn off. Investigators found that missing corner of the bag—a microscopically perfect match—inside Joie's house.

Cary Anthony Stayner next pled not guilty to the murders of Carole and Juliana Sund and Silvina Pelosso. In September of 2002, a jury convicted him of first degree murder in all three cases. This jury also determined that he was sane. On December 15, the court sentenced him to three death sentences in San Quentin Prison.

He appealed this trial on the basis that three of his jurors were childhood victims of sexual abuse and had not disclosed it. One juror, however, noted that this issue never surfaced during deliberations. Juliana Sund's father, Jens Sund, commented on Stayner: "I know he's got no trouble killing little girls in the middle of the night. He should step forward and take his punishment like Timothy McVeigh did."

In August of 2003, the Sund family received a wrongful death settlement of $1 million from Cedar Lodge. The Sunds' specific complaints were the lodge having placed the three women in an isolated wing with no other guests around and also in not checking on the employment history of their handyman, Stayner—who in fact did have a violent employment history.

Stayner later informed investigators that the act of killing his four admitted women victims did not live up to his expectations; Stayner described having murdered them as "anti-climatic."

And Joie Armstrong, whose intense will to live drove her to muster such fierce resistance to her overwhelming attacker that she almost escaped him? Many people still grieve for her. "Joie was a bright light to all who knew her," explained Mike Lee, Executive Director of the Yosemite Institute, "She was an amazing woman who touched so many lives."

Only a few days before Cary Anthony Stayner destroyed the life of Joie Armstrong, she had emailed a friend in delight: "You should come see this place. I wonder if you will. I love my garden and living in Yosemite—one of the most beautiful places in the whole wide world."

In view of the crimes committed by Stayner, Lucas, Curtis, and the other murderers, what is the upshot of homicide in Yosemite? Overall, the Park has experienced a relatively few killings given its more than 150 years of recorded history. While few, though, every one was a tragedy. Nearly half of the victims—both Native American and white—were killed during conflicts long ago by whites to control, if not eliminate the Yosemites from the area in the early 1850s.

During the next 150 years another two dozen or so other people were murdered. More than a dozen of these later homicides were committed over the thirty-six years between 1963 and 1999. These fit into a far different category than the earliest killings. Most of these later victims (eleven out of a total of fourteen, or 79 percent) were unusual among homicides in America in that the victims were predominately young women, aged 16 to 33 with an average age of 21, who had been gratuitously murdered by scumbag men. Nationwide in America this ratio is reversed. About 80 percent of murder victims in the USA for several decades have been men, not women, although close to 90 percent of all killers in America are also men—as was at least the case in Yosemite.

Lifesaving lessons can be gleaned from these murders. Certainly the old lesson our parents taught us still holds: When in doubt at all, do not trust *anyone* who has not earned your trust. But one of the most salient lessons emerges from Pauline Bart's and Patricia O'Brien's investigation in their *Stopping Rape: Successful Survival Strategies*. These two investigators found that women who were compliant when faced with an assailant because they were worried most about not being hurt or killed in fact became rape victims *twice* as frequently as women whose main concern was in *not* being raped. These latter women fought back using every strategy that occurred to them against male assailants, and their doing so correlated with being victimized half as often as their more compliant sisters. Fighting back also correlated with a far lower injury rate to themselves.

The big lesson from this, notes Bart and O'Brien, is: When threatened, resist to your utmost. This advice could have been useful on February 5, 1999, and during many other incidents.

Despite the disproportionate number of women victims in Yosemite, the actual number of homicides per se compares closely with those committed in Grand Canyon and in Yellowstone National Parks. All three parks, it turns out, are far less dangerous than any sizeable city in America. Indeed, the most recent twenty years of history *within* Yosemite National Park includes only two murders. Frankly, this low number makes it one of the safest places in America. Even so, let us all hope that its history gets even better in the future.

TABLE 14 . HOMICIDES IN YOSEMITE. (Incidents discussed in text are noted.)

Name, age	Date	Location	*Circumstances*
youngest son of Chief Tenieya, ?	May 10, 1851	Sentinel Bridge area, Yosemite Valley	*On May 5, Captain John Boling led a punitive expedition against Chief Tenieya and captured 5 Yosemites. One of Boling's troopers* ***"wantonly" shot*** *Tenieya's youngest son.* (in text)
(?) Rose, adult (?) Shurborn, adult	May 27 or 28, 1852	Bridalveil Meadow, Yosemite Valley	*At night the Yosemites* ***ambushed*** *8 prospectors from Coarse Gold Gulch and killed Rose and Shurborn, separated near Bridalveil Fall. The 6 survivors, 3 injured, escaped.* (in text)

six unnamed male Yosemite Indians	July 5, 1852	"within a few miles of Tenaya Lake"	*Lieutenant Tredwell Moore was ordered to punish the Indians for killing Shurborn and Rose. Moore's militia captured 21 Yosemites. Some captive men wore the miners' clothing. Despite mixed testimonies, Moore ordered* ***6 men executed by firing squad****.* (in text)
(?) Riley, adult	July 7, 1852	Yosemite Valley	*Lieutenant Moore ordered destruction of a large store of the Yosemite Indians' acorns. On July 4, a sentry named Riley* ***received 2 arrows in his neck****.* (in text)
Chief Tenieya, elderly "many" (6?) unnamed male Yosemite Indians	late summer, 1853	Yosemite Valley?	*Chief Tenieya and other Yosemites escaped east to join the Mono Indians. By one account, a year later some of them stole several "Mono" horses and herded them back to Yosemite via a roundabout route. The Monos caught up with and attacked Tenieya's band. The accounts say the Monos* ***stoned Tenieya, and killed "many" of his followers****—although 8 men escaped.* (in text)
Joseph or Jesse Starkey, adult	1853	Yosemite Valley	*After having entered the Valley, Starkey* was ***shot by Indians****; details are unclear. Almost no detail exists on this note from the* Mariposa Gazette *(date lost).*
John Gould, adult	November, 1862	Empire Meadow	*The Mariposa County Coroner's Office ruled Gould killed by Indians. His body was found in August, 1864 in the Wawona backcountry.*
George Ezra Boston, 51	August 12, 1875	Cascades Road Toll Booth	*A 21-year-old Indian "renegade" named Paiute George was seen with a six-gun and standing in the toll booth talking to Boston. Hours later the station was found burned to the ground with Boston dead in it. The Mariposa District Court found Paiute George* ***guilty of murder*** *and sentenced him to life in San Quentin Prison. He died there years later.* (in text)
Pomposo Merino, 26-ish	July 24, 1883	sheep camp 10 miles above Little Yosemite	*As Mexican sheepherder Merino was demonstrating to fellow shepherd Henry Montijo how a person who had been in a shooting brawl and had been caught with a pistol pointed at his head but had struck the pistol away, Merino's demonstration pistol fired,* ***accidentally killing himself****.*
Leonidas G. Whorton, 50	April 4, 1887	near The Cascades, lower Yosemite Valley	*Whorton was a Yosemite local from 1865 or 1866. Abel Mann had "run off" with and married the 15-year-old daughter of Whorton's cousin. Upon their return Whorton had offered Mann a job. A deep animosity prompted Whorton to go after Mann,* ***who shot him in self-defense****. Mann rode into Mariposa and turned himself in to the sheriff. Mann was tried and acquitted.*

"Lame George," 35	July 17, 1887	Wawona-Yosemite Turnpike, near Eleven Mile Station	*Intent on theft, Lame George, with Fly-Blow Jim, entered the station after its proprietor West Wood stepped out. Wood fired at the Indian then heard another shot. A search located lame George,* ***shot through the back of the head****. Fly-Blow Jim had vanished.* (in text)
"Indian Sam," adult	February 18, 1888	Wawona	*Indian Sam was* ***shot accidentally*** *by another Indian.*
Granville Lafayette Ward, 16	September 8, 1888	Monroe Meadows, Glacier Point Road	*Ward of Mariposa was handling his very first six-gun but possessed no prior experience with firearms. He* ***accidentally shot himself*** *in the head.*
Thomas "Bushyhead" Hainbridge, adult	June 13, 1889	Wawona	*Hainbridge, a Miwok Indian and "the Terror of Wawoona," had been convicted of thrashing his wife (who divorced him), resisting arrest, and stabbing a man 9 times. Later, while carrying a string of fish to sell at the hotel, Hainbridge was shot in cold blood by "squaw man" James Lawrence, a "good-for-nothing loafer" who had been threatened by Hainbridge earlier when Lawrence tried to stop Hainbridge from having sex with Lawrence's daughter. The Coroner's jury voted "justifiable homicide."*
"Old Bullock," adult	June 19, 1890	Wawona	*Many local Indians believed medicine man "Old Bullock" possessed the power to cause death to others without being near them and had caused every recent Indian death. Four Indians led by "Indian Wilson"* ***assassinated*** *Old Bullock with 4 bullets to prevent the deaths of yet other Indians via witchcraft.* (in text)
"Indian Rueb" Austin, 17	July 28, 1905	Yosemite Valley	*Austin of Bull Creek, California "met his death by a pistol in the hands of a [20-year-old] half breed by the name of Charlie Hart." Hart immediately "skipped out" despite witness Joe Rueb claiming the* ***shooting was an accident****. "As far as could be learned, no trouble existed between the Indians, and all were sober at the time of the shooting." Hart was captured but no subsequent* Mariposa Gazette *article indicated the outcome of this arrest.*
Tiburcio Minez, adult	July 7, 1918	Wawona, Tipperary Resort	*Gene Whitener, head logger for the lumber company,* ***deliberately shot*** *Madera Sugar Pine Co. worker Minez and "Joe" and "Luis." Jealousy over prostitutes seemed their dispute. Whether "Joe" or "Luis" died from Whitener's bullets remains unknown.* (in text)
Taylor Teaford, 29	September 16, 1918	Wawona	*Teaford of nearby Crane Valley offered a ride back to Wawona to 2 admitted U.S. Army deserters. One, Cathenas E. Runyon, examined Teaford's rifle in the backseat and asked if it was loaded. Teaford said it was not. Runyon worked the lever and pulled the trigger,* ***accidentally firing a fatal bullet*** *into Teaford.* (in text)

Antonio Bena, 51

September 16, 1933 unknown canyon, possibly but not certainly in Park

Bena of Richmond, California went missing during a **solo hike** *while hunting. Searchers from the Forest Service, Park, and local residents found Bena's body after, the* Superintendent's Monthly Report *noted, a "very tiresome and difficult" 5-day search in "rugged and brushy" terrain. Evidently Bena had* ***accidentally shot himself.***

John Telles, Jr., 31

January 27, 1952 Yosemite Valley

Helen Telles, a local Native American, ***hit*** *her Portuguese husband John Telles,* ***over the head fatally with a beer bottle****. She was sentenced to 3 years probation.* (in text)

June Joslin Leonard, 19

October 25, 1963 Camp 4, Yosemite Valley

Leonard of Yosemite, was found dead near Camp 4. She had given a ride to 23-year-old David Lee Telles, the son of Helen Telles, above. He beat Leonard, ***raped her, strangled her,*** *and left her on the ground. A Grand Jury indicted him. On June 14, 1965, in jail, he committed suicide* (in text).

Evelyn Consuela Rosemann, 24

October 18, 1968 Nevada Fall

After 3 days in Yosemite, Rosemann of San Francisco was found on October 19, 200 feet from the base of Nevada Fall. Her autopsy revealed "severe and tremendous traumatic injuries." Someone had moved her from her impact point. ***Whether her death was due to an accident, suicide, or murder-rape was never determined****. Nor is it clear whether she had been raped pre- or post-mortem.* (in text and also listed in Chapter 1. Waterfalls)

Lorraine J. Sutton, 20

December 1, 1972 Upper Yosemite Fall

Physics student Bruce D. Norris, a recent psychiatric patient, and his girlfriend, 20-year-old Lorraine Sutton of Forrest Ranch (near Chico, California), were found below the falls. The coroner concluded ***Norris had murdered Sutton*** *then committed suicide.* (in text, also listed in Chapter 13. Suicide)

Dana Lynn Laudenslayer, 23

October 14, 1974 Ostrander Lake Fire Road

Laudenslayer of Redwood City, California was hiking with his fiancé Marsha Ann Savko (of Redwood City). Laudenslayer dropped his pack and walked to the creek for water. She opened his pack "looking for his canteen" but instead pulled out his .22 revolver, pointed it at him, and pulled the trigger (accidentally, she said) killing him. A jury found her ***guilty of involuntary manslaughter****.* (in text)

Robert B. Aal, 51

January 1, 1975 Curry Co. Drivers' Lounge, Yosemite Village

Curry Co. employee Aal encountered Kerry S. Lougee, age 24, also a Curry employee, as he exited the drivers' lounge. Aal questioned Lougee's right to be there. Lougee struck Aal and knocked him to the concrete where he hit his head fatally. An FBI investigation of ***manslaughter*** *released him.* (in text)

Barbara Lynn Bentley, 19 — April 26, 1976 — Ahwahnee Meadow

Curry Co. employee Bentley of Fremont, California went out with Bruce Alan Curtis, age 24, of Groveland, also employed by Curry Co. The next day she was found beaten and strangled. Curtis, a U.S. Marine Corps deserter and wife deserter with a serious anger management problem, claimed he was innocent. On November 11, 1976, a jury convicted him of ***first degree murder****.* (in text)

Carol Laughlin, 19 — September 9, 1979 — below tunnel airshaft, Big Oak Flat Road

By September 11, Curry Co. clerk Laughlin of Fairfax, California did not show up to work at the Village Gift Shop for 2 days. Searching failed. On April 28, 1980, hikers found her skeleton ***mysteriously*** *400 feet below the air vent in the longest tunnel on "Highway 120." A lack of witnesses, a cold trail 8 months old, and no motive stymied investigators.* (in text)

Patricia Marie Hicks-Dahlstrom, 29 — summer, 1981 — Summit Meadow, Glacier Point Road

On June 28, 1983, human bones were found at Summit Meadow. Facial reconstruction suggested the victim as a young woman of Hispanic or Native American descent. DNA sequencing in 2021 revealed the woman to have been Pat Marie Hicks from Spokane, Washington. Serial killer Henry Lee Lucas confessed that he and Ottis Toole in 1981 had picked up a "teenage" girl near Coarsegold, ate a picnic lunch at Summit Meadow, then ***strangled*** *her for fun. (in text)*

Helle Olsbro, 18 — March 16, 1985 — trail between Indian Caves and Ahwahnee Hotel

Exchange student Olsbro of Denmark had been in Yosemite only 2 hours when she hiked alone east below Washington Column then screamed. Responders found her stabbed 47 times. Olsbro's unsolved death seemed a ***random, gratuitous murder****.* (in text)

Sonia Janet Goldstein, 33 — August 17, 1985 — Glacier Point

At 7:45 a.m., witnesses saw Goldstein plummeting down Glacier Point. Richard Russell Mughir age 29, of Silver Springs, Maryland then jumped off the face. He apparently convinced her to join him in a suicide pact in which he ***stabbed Goldstein and tossed her off****. He followed.* (in text)

Dolores Contreras Gray, 24 — December 5, 1987 — Discovery View, Wawona Tunnel

At 5:45 p.m., 22-year-old Stevie Allen Gray reported his wife, Dolores, had vanished. She was found 350 feet below. Gray had taken out several life insurance policies on Dolores totaling $503,000. On July 6, 1990, a jury found him guilty of ***murder in the first degree****. He was sentenced to life in prison.* (in text)

Roderick Eugene Daniels, 35 — February 21, 1988 — Curry Village

Curry Co. employee Daniels had stalked Mustafa Hassan El-Amin and sexually harassed the smaller man for weeks. El-Amin stabbed Daniels in self-defense. A Federal Grand Jury concluded ***justifiable homicide****.* (in text)

Carole Sund, 42	February 15, 1999	Cedar Lodge, El Portal (outside Yosemite)
Silvina Pelosso, 16	February 15, 1999	Cedar Lodge, El Portal (outside Yosemite)
Juliana Sund, 15	February 16, 1999	Don Pedro Reservoir (outside Yosemite)
Jennifer "Joie" Ruth Armstrong, 26	July 21, 1999	Foresta
	On February 15, 1999, Carole Sund and her daughter Juli of Eureka, California and Silvina Pelosso of Argentina vanished from Cedar Lodge on Highway 140. All searches failed. On March 18, Carole's burned-out rental car was found with her and Pelosso's bodies in the trunk. A week later Juli was found, her throat slit. On July 21, 1999, Joie Armstrong was found decapitated near her house in Foresta. Evidence led to 37-year-old Cary Anthony Stayner, who ***confessed to all 4 murders****. Stayner received a life sentence for murdering Armstrong and 3 death sentences for killing the Sunds and Pelosso.* (In text, only Armstrong is counted in statistics.)	
Roland Goldberg, 31	April 21, 2021	Yosemite West (non-Park enclave)
	Goldberg of Lebanon, Missouri was shot by girlfriend Elisabeth Shauck age 22, of Salinas, California using a Glock 17. She then committed suicide. (not in Yosemite statistics)	
woman, name not released, 34	March 20, 2025	location undisclosed
	A Yosemite concession employee was found in a facility barely alive with multiple suspicious, serious injuries due to an assault. She was hospitalized in Fresno but died the following day. An investigation was begun by NPS Investigative Services Branch, the Fresno County Sheriff-Coroner's Office, and the FBI.	

WHAT CAN WE LEARN FROM ALL OF THIS?

Paradoxically, the desire to experience something like what Webster's dictionary defines as "adventure" (in the sense of facing real hazard during an activity) in America has increased neck-in-neck with our growing preoccupation over "safety." Indeed adventure has emerged as such a highly desired commodity since the mid-twentieth century that it has become marketable in almost every form. Potentially lethal trips up Mount Everest titillate some of us so much that we shell out $65,000 to go there and get frostbite, breathe from an oxygen mask, and generally experience misery to inject into our lives some meaning, some definition, some adventure. True, some people in this Everest category are also seeking special status, the ability to boast, however subtly, "Oh yeah, I've done the toughest thing there is." Others of us feel stimulated enough just by reading about it or by watching the IMAX film. We set our sights on experiences of a more survivable—and affordable—form.

It can be argued that despite our recent yen for "adventure," in America's generations-long quest for security we have mentally domesticated ourselves. We train and hire specialists to do nearly everything for us to avoid the risk of doing it ourselves. We hire police to protect us from sociopaths, contractors to build our houses, farmers to grow or raise our food, programmers to make our computers run faster (and to be more fun), Ralph Nader to keep our cars safe, guidebooks to keep us on the safe routes, and Hollywood to flash vicarious dangers to jack up our adrenaline so we don't have to face the risks of getting trapped by the real thing. If Hollywood pales, we still have organized sports with lots of rules for safety and referees to enforce them. We have laced our social lives into a network wherein rights and wrongs are defined by hundreds of thousands of laws enforced in various ways by millions of professionals. And we have airbags and parachutes and orthopedic surgeons and seat belts and life vests and helmets to protect us when something does go wrong. If all of these fail, we can call one of those lawyers we see on daytime TV and sue somebody. In short, we have become what would be referred to in biology as a domesticated species. We are no longer *Homo sapiens*, the "wise" or "knowing" being. Instead, psychologically, many of us have inched across the line to become sheep.

Baaa…

As sheep—or *Homo sapiens "domesticus"*—many of us now make the habitual and unquestioned assumption that somebody else is supposed to be watching out for us. We blindly follow the rest of the flock and assume that the sheepherder, wherever he or she might be, is keeping his eye peeled for the wolves.

This sort of lack of self-responsibility by so many visitors to national parks is all too obvious and all too often lethal.

As Lee Whittlesey concludes in his book *Death in Yellowstone*, the primary lesson for all of us once we get off the pavement is: "**Nature demands that we pay attention**." Even so, every day, Whittlesey adds, someone enters a wilderness area unprepared.

As we have seen, the same might be said for Yosemite—but resulting in a far more spectacular number of tragic mishaps. See Table 15 on the next page.

With about 900 accidental deaths, the need to pay attention is certainly genuine in Yosemite (as it is in Grand Canyon, Yellowstone, and literally everywhere). But what can we do to fix this situation? A lawyer friend, an ex-Marine, river guide, and wilderness addict named Daniel D. James, revealed that he was appalled to encounter law students who firmly believe that every possible location in the American West where someone might die accidentally should be labeled with warning signs. *Every* location. The problem with this idea is even after posting the tens of millions of signs, these places would still be dangerous to people who fail to think—or to even read the sign or who cannot even read it because they don't speak the sign's language. Should we then pave, sanitize, declaw, and defang the last patches of remaining American wild lands so that those who hold no respect for reality will not be able to hurt themselves in their blissful ignorance and arrogance? At the onset of the twenty-first century, a time during which money-chasing lawyers and "feel-good" jurors have nearly abolished the legitimacy of the concept of self-responsibility for the consequences of one's own actions, this question is a complicated one. Indeed, making natural terrain so "safe" that mentally and/or physically unprepared people are guaranteed to survive in it unscathed is a tort lawyer's dream come true.

"In my experience with over twenty years as Yosemite's Tort Claims Officer," reflects now-retired Chief Law Enforcement Officer Lee Shackelton, "I believe that a common misperception in Wrongful Death Civil Suits, especially in those made by East Coast plaintiffs, was their idea about the word 'Park.' They saw negligence in that Yosemite is not manicured, lighted, fenced, and paved like New York's Central Park."

TABLE 15. SUMMARY OF TRAUMATIC DEATHS IN YOSEMITE, 1851 into 2025
(No victim has been counted in more than one category.)

Type of Mishap	Male Victims	Female Victims	Total
Waterfalls	47	10	57
Snow	8	0	8
BASE Jumping	6	2	8
Park Builders	30	0	30
Aircraft Down	37	8	45
Hiking & Scrambling Falls	141	17	158
Freak Accidents:			
Lightning	5	0	5
Rockfall/Icefall	10	5	15
Logging/Wildfire	13	2	15
Freak/Miscellaneous Errors	18	6	24
Wheeled Vehicle Accidents (excluding crash drownings)	130	41	171
Bicycle Crashes	4	1	5
Big Wall Climbing Falls	127	10	137
Drowning (non-MVA)	140	28	168
Vehicle Crash Drownings	10	2	12
Fauna & Flora:			
Horses**	5	2	7
Other Critters	1	2	3
Natural Treefalls	7	8	16*
Hantavirus	2	1	3
Lost:			
Lost & Found	9	1	10
Lost & Not Found	28	5	33
Found but Unidentified	5	1	11*
Totals, accidental deaths	783 (84%)	152 (16%)	941* (100%)
Suicide	77	17	95*
Homicide	35***	10	45
Grand total all non-natural	895	179	1,081*
Grand total natural causes			916*
Grand total ALL CAUSES			1,997*

* Grand Total also includes 6 additional victims in all categories of unknown sex.

** Horse-related deaths also include 4 men & 2 women in wagon wrecks, counted only in "Wheeled Vehicle Accidents."

*** Total includes a "guess-timated" 13 Yosemites killed during 1852–1853.

This perceived lack of safeguards in Yosemite exists because making the world perfectly safe (as human-constructed "parks" are intended to be but actually are not) cannot be done. This is because human foolishness is unlimited, while wild areas themselves offer an infinite number of opportunities for someone to carelessly hurt him or herself. So if a mandate did exist to attempt to make the wilds safe, America's one million lawyers (70 percent of all lawyers on Earth) would be assured of litigation income forever. Therefore, the strategic and logical means to combat this sort of legal nightmare is simply to bar all human entry by land, water, or air into our wilderness.

Crazy? Maybe. But the question of the degree to which government should be required to *change* anything in wilderness involves complicated issues of legality, practicality, fiscal reality, morality, and value. The 1916 National Park Service Organic Act dictates that the NPS must leave national parks in their natural state, unchanged and unencumbered for future enjoyment. Thus no one is allowed to "fix" wilderness to make it safe. Instead, park systems are legally required only not to be *negligent* in safeguarding visitors. Mainly this consists of forewarning people of local dangers in a systematic, easily understandable way through pamphlets, signs, local radio broadcasts, and so on. Unfortunately, warnings that 999,999 people out of a million agree are quite clear and useful fail to make sense to number 1,000,000, who does not bother to read or understand or heed and, in his ignorance, kills himself.

Each "frivolous" suit (and there are many) nudges government to install more warning signs, erect more railings, pave more trails, forbid any step off the path, continually lower and restrict visitor access, and in general treat most people as something less intelligent than a blind cow. Many of us find this increasing trend to be a negative one when it comes to *enjoying* a visit to a national park or other natural area. And because protecting the ignorant or foolish from their own mistakes is an endlessly spiraling arms race between administrators' efforts and some visitors' lack of common sense, restrictions on us will only increase in the never-ending war to protect people who are too lazy or naïve to protect themselves.

Nor can the NPS bring more resources to bear on this war. In other words, making designated wilderness safe is not only illegal and impractical, it is also unaffordable (to put it mildly) even if vastly greater funds were available—which they are not. During the last twenty years of the twentieth century the agency budget decreased 40 percent in real dollars while visitation increased by 48 percent. The backlog in maintenance, resource management, construction, and land acquisitions for the national parks alone was estimated in 2005 at more than $8 billion. This leaves the NPS with no choice but to employ the cheapest possible weapons in this war against visitor irresponsibility. Unfortunately, the cheapest possible weapon is simply restricting the places a visitor can visit.

Beyond the questions of legality, practicality, and affordability are perhaps even more important issues of morality and value. As has become increasingly clear, the human population on this planet is exploding. Humanity is not an endangered species (yet). Meanwhile, wilderness—and merely pleasant and quiet scenery—is shrinking as people co-opt every scrap of unprotected landscape for economic use. Our shriveling natural areas contain and are vital to the survival of uncounted species. Indeed, wilderness itself is an endangered environment. We recognize here that Yosemite is not purely "wilderness" under the strict definition. It contains numerous areas of surpassing beauty, many of which could safely be termed unique. Clearly many of these pose hazards: vertical cliffs, wild animals, swift rivers, dangerous waterfalls, falling trees and rocks, narrow winding roads, unseasonable snows or cloudbursts, and more. Therefore sanitizing and "human-proofing" Yosemite is impractical, unaffordable, often illegal, and ultimately impossible. Morally, some might add, it is also unconscionable in the sense of destroying the very qualities that led to its becoming a park to begin with.

So where does that leave us? Morality and practicality both dictate that when it comes to the question of man versus these protected natural areas, the onus devolves on people to take on the personal responsibility to prepare for the challenges this terrain poses. If a prospective visitor to Yosemite is unwilling to show these scenic wild areas and his fellow humans this respect, he instead should rent the video and stay home.

Most of the nearly four million people each year who drive or fly out of their way to visit Yosemite do so not because they have been assured that it has been made as safe as (or safer than) their local neighborhood park. Instead, they come to experience an inspirational and unique chunk of *wild* scenery, or to climb, to hike, to camp, to work for a living, to cross the Sierra, or you name it. We do know that some people come here specifically to push their own limits and to test themselves—to go up to "the edge." Although a few visitors may want to see the Park completely "danger-proofed," most of us know it is instead our job to safeguard ourselves by respecting its hazards.

Most of us also know Yosemite reciprocates neither our fascination nor our love for it. If we fail to respect its dangers, we realize, not only might those dangers hurt us, as we have seen, they may kill us—or an innocent child who is depending on us.

The take-home lesson here, one obvious in the first dozen chapters of this book, is that the people who die traumatically in Yosemite die mainly—almost universally—due to their own poor judgment. It is impossible for the rest of us to protect them fully from these personal failings. It is up to the personal and individual responsibility of each of us to avoid killing ourselves. We hope this book fully forewarns each of us of the dangers Yosemite poses. This done and thus armed, perhaps we and Yosemite National Park will both survive.

THE REST OF THE STORY

As you now have read, *Off the Wall* chronicles the ways in which people have met traumatic, untimely ends in Yosemite National Park. As of January 1, 2025, the data base for *all* deaths contained more than 1,900 entries, with 1,076 (56 percent) of them dying while hiking, climbing, swimming, parachuting, jumping off a cliff, sightseeing, constructing a dam, riding in a car, feeding a deer, trying to escape a lightning bolt by hiding under a ledge, suicide, homicide, or in some dozen other ways. Twenty-two (1 percent) died from unknown causes.

We would be remiss, we believe, if we did not at least touch upon the "rest of the story." Beginning with William Cowan who succumbed on September 4, 1859, the Park has seen at least 739 (42 percent of the total) deaths from "natural" causes. Of this total, 390 died from cardiac problems. Galen Alonzo Clark, the 26-year-old son of Park Guardian Galen Clark, was the first victim recorded to die of a "heart attack," on April 19, 1873.

This is not to suggest that most natural deaths occurred simply when a person's "time was up" after having lived a long and healthy life. The parents of 2-year-old Letitia Farnsworth and her 4-year-old sister Daisy, both of whom died in Wawona of scarlet fever on successive days in 1898, would vehemently disagree. Twenty years later, 4-year-old Park resident Mary Higgins died on a Tuesday in November of 1918. On Wednesday her 26-year-old father Perry immediately followed her into eternity. These two seem to be the only people to die in Yosemite from the Spanish Flu pandemic which took the lives of approximately half a million in the United States and twenty million worldwide. In 1931, twin girls Clarice and Nadine Jobe died of whooping cough in Yosemite five days apart. They were only a few months old. To refer to these tragedies as "natural" begs the question: Is it traumatic to be killed by a rattlesnake or a horse but merely natural to be done in by a flu virus?

Our data base tallies many other natural causes for demises. Viewed through time, this list reveals a schematic but important insight into the evolution of the art and science of medicine. Listed below is a partial inventory of causes of these deaths between 1859 and 1950. It reflects how officials and doctors understood the problem through time. Remember, some of these terms are now obsolete

pneumonia
hemorrhage of lungs
apoplectic fit
stroke of apoplexy
consumption
neuralgia of the heart
scarlet fever
typhoid fever
stomach trouble
tuberculosis
diabetes
Spanish Flu
cerebral hemorrhage
paralysis
kidney failure
alcohol poisoning
prostatic hypertrophy
muscular atrophy
epticemia
diphtheria
hemorrhage of brain
dislocation of vertebrae
premature birth
intestinal obstruction
whooping cough
influenza
Bright's Disease
cancer of uterus
stomach cancer
heat stroke
paralytic stroke
tonsillitis
hydrocephalic stillborn
childbirth
meningitis
pulmonary edema
bowel obstruction
appendicitis
old age

("consumption," for example, is tuberculosis) and do not reflect today's science.

We should point out that at least fifty-five people have died natural deaths while hiking in the Park, most but not all on trails out of the Valley. The two youngest were a 9-year-old boy who in 1960 was hiking near the Lower Lyell Base Camp and "died of unknown natural causes" and then, in 1966, a 13-year-old Girl Scout who died similarly in Little Yosemite Valley while hiking. Forty-three of these natural deaths have been due to "heart attacks." The youngest (35 years old) and the oldest (83 years old) were both women and account for two of the five females to die of heart failure while hiking. Twenty-four of these people were sixty years old or younger. Did stress and exertion bring on their premature ends? Of course, we will never know. All trails out of the Valley lead up. Gains in altitude—especially while carrying backpacks—on paths that are often steep and rocky, may kill you if you are not conditioned and/or acclimated.

Essentially the same can be said for skiing. Six people, the youngest 23 years old, have died while downhill skiing. Two, suffering heart attacks, died while cross-country skiing.

As of January 1, 2011, there have been 1,292 males (78 percent) die of all causes in the Park, 524 succumbing nontraumatically, and 10 more meeting their ends in an unknown manner. At least 360 females (22 percent) have died, with 193 by natural causes, and 2 in an unknown manner. We do not know the sex of six of the victims. The first death of a female recorded in Yosemite was 2-year-old Agnes Armour Leidig, who ate spoiled peaches. Sadly, she died just before Christmas on December 21, 1868.

Not surprisingly, the vast majority of *all* of the people who have died in Yosemite were Californians, 1,274 (77 percent). The next four states represented are New York (24 victims), Illinois (17), Ohio (16) and Nevada (14). People from forty states and the District of Columbia have met their ends here. Eleven states are not represented: Alabama, Alaska, Arkansas, Maine, Mississippi, North Carolina, North Dakota, South Carolina and South Dakota. The only three people to ever die in the Park from the state of Minnesota were all tragically killed on the same day while hanging off the same bolt, 1,000 feet up the face of El Capitan on May 14, 1978. The homes of fifty-one of the deceased remain unknown. Interestingly, the first person to die in Yosemite from other than California was a man from clear across the continent, Rhode Island, who expired of natural causes in 1888.

At least eighty-three people from twenty-nine other countries are represented in the data base with the most traveling from Germany (16 people), Great Britain (9) and Japan (11). No one died from Japan until 1978, and all of them since then have ended traumatically. We have records of sixty-one Native Americans, all but one local, who died in the Park. Twenty-nine expired due to natural causes, nineteen due to homicide, and two others from unknown situations. Gaps exist in our information on Native Americans, and almost certainly we will learn of more on those occurring since 1851.

Not everyone died out in the woods somewhere. An early, possibly even the first, death in a "Park Hospital," was Luce Beebe Butters on June 20, 1909. Pneumonia claimed this 65-year-old "wife of a millionaire miner" of Piedmont, California. This was in the Army's six-bed hospital located near what is now Yosemite Lodge. In 1912, the military built a more substantial medical center which served the Army until they left the Valley two years later.

This Army clinic, along with the rest of the departing military's buildings, was given to the Park. On May 1, 1915, the Park Hospital opened. "These physicians were allowed to sell drugs" noted the *Superintendent's Annual Report for 1915* and "were aided by a trained nurse." The doctors even made house calls. It served as the area's medical facility until it was replaced by Lewis Memorial Hospital (named after Park Superintendent Washington B. "Dusty" Lewis who managed Yosemite from March, 1916 to July, 1928). Located west of the Ahwahnee Hotel, LMH, now known as the Park Clinic, was formally opened on February 19, 1930. Within weeks, the first births took place there, triplets. The first death at LMH seems to be Ross M. Boggs, a 44-year-old tourist from Los Angeles who, after being "kept alive with artificial respiration for 32 hours," died on April 18, 1930. Sadly, within a three week period in 1936, LMH saw three infants live less than a day after birth.

In July of 1943, the U.S. Navy converted the Ahwahnee Hotel into a convalescent hospital staffed by sixty to serve an initial fifty patients. In July of 1945 the navy renamed it the U.S. Naval Special Hospital. For about ten months that year navy doctors also served other Yosemite residents. On December 15 the navy decommissioned this facility and turned over remaining supplies to the Park. During the hospital's two and a half years, 7,762 patients convalesced in it, 1,000 of them at the same time.

Some notable natural deaths occurred in Yosemite. George Anderson, the first person to climb Half Dome in 1875 died here at age 47 in 1884 of pneumonia. Professor Joseph LeConte, an 1892 charter member of the Sierra Club, died at age 78 of a heart attack in Camp Curry on July 6, 1901. The LeConte Memorial Lodge west of Camp Curry was dedicated in his honor on July 3, 1904 and became the summer home of the Sierra Club (and entered the National Register in 1977). Jennie Foster Curry, the founding matriarch of the Curry Company and long known as "Mother Curry," died in the Valley in 1948 at age 86. At 3:50 a.m. on October 29, 1970, Mary Curry Tresidder, the "First Lady of Yosemite" and the President of the Curry Company, died in her sleep in her Ahwahnee Hotel apartment. She was 76. James Johnston, the Pole Vault Gold Medalist in the 1906 Olympic Games (a.k.a. the Intercalated Games) in Athens and longtime resident of the Park, died at age 87 in his Foresta home on October 21, 1975.

Effective since at least the mid-1920s Yosemite is one of at least three areas within the National Park System that has staff which act as coroners; the others are Yellowstone and Hawaii Volcanoes National Parks. As of 2006, fifteen special agents and rangers within Yosemite serve as a Mariposa County Deputy Sheriff/Coroner, and eight are similarly designated for Tuolumne County. Several are deputized for both counties. With so few deaths in the Park's small portion of Madera County, a Deputy Sheriff from that county will be called if the need arises.

Three cemeteries exist within Yosemite National Park. Around 1870, the Yosemite Cemetery was established immediately west of the Valley's Visitor Center. It contains at least forty-five marked graves and a fair number of unmarked ones in which Native Americans were interred. The *Guide to the Yosemite Cemetery*, by Hank Johnston and Martha Lee, is an excellent source of information for this site. Per Johnston and Lee, "From at least 1910 on, special permission was required from the Department of the Interior for a new burial.... The last interment took place here in 1956." The second graveyard, Pioneer Cemetery, sits on a hill several hundred yards north of the Pioneer Yosemite History Center in Wawona and consists of two plots with a brown fence around it. As many as ten people are reportedly buried here and was used from about 1878 to 1905. The third and smallest cemetery in the Park is on the east side of the road into Foresta, not far from Big Meadow. It contains five marked graves of men who died between 1884 and 1918. This small site had been largely forgotten until 1957.

According to the *Guide to the Yosemite Cemetery*, "The last known cremation in Yosemite Valley occurred in 1873 when the remains of Miwok leader Captain Dick's nephew, killed in a hunting accident, were burned." In doing this research, I (Farabee) happened upon one death certificate in the Mariposa County Hall of Records for a stillborn to a Park family by the name of Stork on May 21, 1925. Over the years, there have been a number of stillborns in Yosemite, including my own son in 1973. What makes Stork's so unusual, however, is that the death certificate signed by Chief Ranger Forest Townsley says the baby was cremated at the Park Hospital (at that time, near the present-day Yosemite Lodge). Although there may be other instances of intentional cremation in post-European times, Farabee has not found them.

Who was the oldest person to die in Yosemite? Louisa Tom (her Paiute name was *Pa-Ma-Nie*) was born in Yosemite Valley. According to the *Guide to the Yosemite Cemetery*, she died at age 108. Lancisco Wilson, born northwest of Yosemite, was a Miwok-Paiute. "He was very old at the time of his [1885] death, one source recorded his age as 115."

So now... you have the rest of the story.

TABLE 16. YEARLY TOTALS FOR ALL KNOWN DEATHS IN YOSEMITE. (T = trauma, NT = non-trauma, Unk = unknown)

Year	Total	T	NT	Unk
1851	1	1	—	—
1852	9	9	—	—
1853	7	7	—	—
1859	1	—	1	—
1860	1	1	—	—
1862	1	1	—	—
1867	1	1	—	—
1868	1	1	—	—
1870	2	2	—	—
1871	1	1	—	—
1872	1	—	1	—
1873	1	—	—	1
1874	1	1	—	—
1875	3	1	2	—
1879	1	—	—	—
1881	6	2	3	1
1882	1	—	1	—
1883	2	1	1	—
1884	3	—	2	1
1885	2	—	2	—
1886	2	2	—	—
1887	3	2	1	—
1888	4	3	1	—
1889	2	1	1	—
1890	2	1	—	1
1892	1	—	1	—
1894	1	—	1	—
1895	3	1	1	1
1896	1	1	—	—
1897	3	—	3	—
1898	2	—	2	—
1899	2	—	1	1
1900	1	—	—	1
1901	4	1	2	1
1902	3	2	1	—
1903	2	—	2	—
1904	1	—	1	—
1905	5	1	4	—
1906	2	1	1	—
1907	3	1	2	—
1909	4	1	2	1
1910	4	3	1	—
1911	5	4	1	—
1912	2	1	1	—
1913	2	1	1	—
1914	6	3	3	—
1915	6	4	2	—
1916	5	4	1	—
1917	4	1	3	—
1918	12	5	7	—
1919	6	3	3	—
1920	9	6	3	—
1921	11	9	2	—
1922	5	5	—	—
1923	11	9	2	—
1924	8	4	3	—
1925	10	4	5	1
1926	17	11	6	—
1927	20	8	11	1
1928	12	3	8	1
1929	9	1	8	—
1930	14	5	9	—
1931	13	10	3	—
1932	10	3	7	—
1933	14	9	4	1
1934	22	9	13	—
1935	12	5	7	—
1936	23	8	15	—
1937	25	9	14	2
1938	19	13	5	1
1939	15	10	5	—
1940	18	14	4	—
1941	12	5	6	1
1942	5	2	2	1
1943	8	1	6	1
1944	19	7	7	—
1945	12	3	8	1
1946	20	7	13	—

Year	Total	T	NT	Unk	Year	Total	T	NT	Unk
1947	22	7	15	—	1987	23	16	6	1
1948	22	8	13	1	1988	16	10	5	1
1949	22	4	18	—	1989	13	7	6	—
1950	16	1	13	2	1990	9	3	5	1
1951	14	1	13	—	1991	22	15	7	—
1952	17	9	8	—	1992	13	9	4	—
1953	15	3	12	—	1993	22	15	6	1
1954	22	4	16	2	1994	13	11	2	—
1955	17	3	14	—	1995	18	8	9	1
1956	12	5	7	—	1996	24	18	6	—
1957	18	3	15	—	1997	12	10	1	1
1958	23	5	18	—	1998	15	8	6	1
1959	21	6	15	—	1999	13	9	3	1
1960	17	4	13	—	2000	14	7	5	2
1961	12	3	9	—	2001	6	5	1	—
1962	19	9	10	—	2002	8	5	2	1
1963	18	9	9	—	2003	12	7	4	1
1964	18	4	14	—	2004	14	10	4	—
1965	14	6	8	—	2005	16	7	7	2
1966	28	12	16	—	2006	10	8	2	—
1967	25	12	11	2	2007	10	7	3	—
1968	23	18	4	1	2008	9	4	5	—
1969	21	11	10	—	2009	16	11	4	1
1970	34	23	11	—	2010	13	5	8	—
1971	19	14	5	—	2011	21	14	6	1
1972	24	18	5	1	2012	21	13	8	—
1973	32	17	15	—	2013	16	8	8	—
1974	12	8	4	—	2014	15	8	7	—
1975	32	20	9	3	2015	19	8	11	—
1976	15	12	2	1	2016	15	7	8	—
1977	28	22	5	1	2017	19	13	6	—
1978**	**39**	**30**	**9**	—	2018	16	12	4	—
1979	26	21	5	—	2019	14	8	6	—
1980	26	21	5	—	2020	6	2	3	1
1981	18	9	8	1	2021	11	10	0	1
1982	13	8	5	—	2022	12	7	5	—
1983	18	12	6	—	2023	12	8	5	—
1984	26	20	6	—	2024	16	9	6	—
1985	23	16	7	—					
1986	22	15	6	1					

**1978 had the most total deaths (39) as well as most traumatic (30) deaths. 1973 and 1975 were second in total deaths with 34 each year.

Michael P. Ghiglieri grew up at Lake Tahoe, Nevada as the great grandson of a Forty-niner, served as a US Army platoon sergeant during the Viet Nam era, then earned his Ph.D. in Ecology in 1979 from the University of California at Davis for his pioneering research on wild chimpanzees in Kibale Forest, Uganda. In addition to teaching university courses in primate behavior and ecology and in human evolution and ecology, he has directed several semesters-overseas centers focusing on sustainable resource management (in Kenya, the Turks & Caicos, Palau, Far North Queensland, and Vancouver Island) and has worked as a wilderness river guide and EMT. Since 1974, he has run more than 700 commercial whitewater trips and also treks in Ethiopia, Java, Kenya, Papua New Guinea, Peru, Rwanda, Sumatra, Tanzania, Turkey, and the USA. These include 174, 2-week rowing or paddling trips through Grand Canyon and more than 52,000 miles of river overall, a few in the Canyon as an NPS ranger, plus several Kilimanjaro ascents. Ghiglieri lives in Flagstaff, Arizona, is happily married, has three children, and has authored documentary screenplays and seven other books (two on wild chimpanzees) and, with his wife Susan, is a volunteer for the Coconino County Sheriff Department's Search and Rescue Team. His books include ***East of the Mountains of the Moon, Canyon, The Dark Side of Man: Tracing the Origins of Male Violence, Over the Edge: Death in Grand Canyon*** and ***First Through Grand Canyon***.

Charles R. "Butch" Farabee Jr. went on his first SAR mission in 1958 as an Eagle Scout. In 1999, he retired with 34 years in the National Park Service. Working in ten parks, he rose through the ranks to Superintendent. As a field ranger in Glen Canyon, Death Valley, and Lake Mead, and then in Yosemite and Grand Canyon for seven years as the SAR Ranger, he participated in 1,000 SARs and acted as medic on hundreds of other medical emergencies (EMS). He assisted on over 150 fatal incidents and, while in Yosemite, served as a Deputy Coroner for two counties. In Washington, D.C., he was the agency's first Emergency Services Coordinator, responsible for SAR, EMS, diving, and aviation. He instructed on search and rescue to over 1,000 students and is the author of ***Death, Daring and Disaster: Search and Rescue in the National Parks, National Park Ranger: an American Icon*** and ***Big Walls, Swift Waters: Epic Stories from Yosemite's Search and Rescue***. He was honored with the Harry Yount Lifetime Achievement Award, as well as a Lifetime Honorary Member from the Mountain Rescue Association, a State Award from the National Association for Search and Rescue, and he received two Unit Awards for SAR from the National Park Service. He earned an M.S. in Public Administration, served as a Tucson Policeman, and graduated from the FBI Academy. A caver, climber, horseman, diver, kayaker, skydiver, pilot and a mountaineer on four continents, he says he is still trying to recover from all of these. "To me, however, the best thing I ever did was raise two fine sons as a single father."

YOSAR Ranger Butch Farabee in wetsuit hooking up a tow cable on March 8,1974 while sprawled atop the trunk of a classic 1957 Chevy "parked" via very bad driving in the Merced River near El Portal. The solo driver was en route to the Valley when he lost control but self-extricated successfully.

Index